Welcome to

Social Welfare: Politics and Public Policy, Sixth Edition,

with Research Navigator™

This updated version of *Social Welfare: Politics and Public Policy* contains additional material to help students succeed in this course. There are 64 pages of new front matter material that includes updates in social welfare policy since November 2004, along with critical thinking exercises for each chapter. Also included is an access code for Research Navigator™ that will aid students with the research process and writing research papers.

To gain access to Research Navigator™, go to **www.researchnavigator.com** and log in using the passcode you'll find on the left inside front cover of your text.

Research Navigator™ includes three databases of dependable source material to get your research process started.

EBSCO's ContentSelect Academic Journal Database. EBSCO's ContentSelect Academic Journal Database contains scholarly, peer-reviewed journals. These published articles provide you with specialized knowledge and information about your research topic. Academic journal articles adhere to strict scientific guidelines for methodology and theoretical grounding. The information obtained in these individual articles is more scientific than information you would find in a popular magazine, in a newspaper article, or on a Web page.

The New York Times Search by Subject Archive. Newspapers are considered periodicals because they are issued in regular installments (i.e., daily, weekly, or monthly) and provide contemporary information. Information in periodicals—journals, magazines, and newspapers—may be useful, or even critical, for finding up-to-date material or information to support specific aspects of your topic. Research Navigator™ gives you access to a one-year, "search by subject" archive of articles from one of the world's leading newspapers—*The New York Times.*

"Best of the Web" Link Library. Link Library, the third database included on Research Navigator™, is a collection of Web links, organized by academic subject and key terms. Searching on your key terms will provide you with a list of five to seven editorially reviewed Web sites that offer educationally relevant and reliable content. The Web links in Link Library are monitored and updated each week, reducing your incidence of finding "dead" links.

In addition, Research Navigator™ includes extensive online content detailing the steps in the research process, including:

- Starting the Research Process
- Finding and Evaluating Sources
- Citing Sources
- Internet Research
- Using Your Library
- Starting to Write

For more information on how to use Research Navigator™ go to
www.ablongman.com/aboutrn

SOCIAL WELFARE

Politics and Public Policy

with Research Navigator

Sixth Edition

Diana M. DiNitto
The University of Texas at Austin

with Linda K. Cummins
Barry University

PEARSON

Boston ■ New York ■ San Francisco
Mexico City ■ Montreal ■ Toronto ■ London ■ Madrid ■ Munich ■ Paris
Hong Kong ■ Singapore ■ Tokyo ■ Cape Town ■ Sydney

For my family
and
for everyone who has known AIDS

Senior Series Editor: Patricia Quinlin
Editorial Assistant: Sara Holliday
Production Supervisor: Beth Houston
Marketing Manager: Laura Lee Manley
Composition and Prepress Buyer: Linda Cox
Manufacturing Buyer: JoAnne Sweeney
Cover Administrator: Kristina Mose-Libon
Electronic Composition: Omegatype Typography, Inc.

ISBN 0-205-50347-0

Printed in the United States of America

10 9 8 7 6 5   10 09 08

Contents

THREE   *Defining Poverty: Where to Begin*   *80*

FOUR   *Preventing Poverty: The Social Insurance Programs*   *124*

ELEVEN Addressing Civil Rights and Social Welfare: The Challenges of a Diverse Society   441

Foreword

Writing a book on social welfare policy presents particular challenges. One is that events and social policy responses can change rapidly. Since the original publication of the sixth edition of this book, many events with important consequences for social welfare policy have occurred. President George W. Bush was reelected to a second term in office. The president continues to promote compassionate conservatism and increased opportunities for faith-based organizations to participate in social welfare services. Hurricanes Katrina and Rita made Americans realize how poorly prepared some cities and states and federal agencies are to respond to disasters. The country continues to discuss how to improve emergency preparedness. Iraqis have participated in historic elections following the U.S.-led invasion of their country. But violence in Iraq continues, and it is unclear how long U.S. troops will remain there.

In addition to updating readers on recent, major changes in social welfare policy, this foreword contains activities and questions for thought and further research using a tool called Research Navigator (the access code is in the front of this book). These updates and research tools are intended to help readers relate recent events to the themes of this book—that social welfare policymaking is an inherently political process that pits the values of individuals and groups, often those with more money, power, and influence, against the values of other individuals and groups, often those with less money, power, and influence.

CHAPTER 1

Chapter 1 lays out the basic framework for our consideration of social welfare policy by comparing a rational model of policymaking with the political forces that impinge on it. This includes the ways in which issues make it to the political agenda and how the federal government as well as state and local governments hammer out social welfare policy in legislative, administrative, and judicial terms. Liberals believe that the art of political compromise has become more difficult because U.S. politics has become increasingly polarized as neoconservatives and the religious right have gained increased power within the Republican Party. But more than one political pundit has suggested that the Democratic Party has lost ground because it has failed to appeal to the growing conservative movement in the country. That states are now typed as red (those with a majority of votes for the Republican presidential candidate) or blue (states with a majority of votes for the Democratic presidential candidate) serves as a vivid display of the growing political divide in this country. House and Senate votes are often polarized by political party, as they were for Samuel Alito, whom the Senate confirmed as the newest U.S. Supreme Court

Special thanks to Professor Miguel Ferguson for his comments and assistance on this foreword.

Justice on January 2, 2006. In the Republican-controlled U.S. Senate, only four of the 44 Democrats voted to confirm Alito. The differing political viewpoints, especially of conservatives and liberals, Republicans and Democrats, are discussed throughout this book.

Campaign Finance, Congressional Redistricting, and the Case of Tom DeLay

Meaningful campaign finance reform is difficult to achieve because winning even local elections generally seems impossible without hefty campaign coffers. Chapter 1 discusses an attempt at election reform called the Bipartisan Campaign Reform Act (BCRA) of 2002, also known as McCain-Feingold after its Congressional sponsors. Has the BCRA accomplished its purpose of stopping the flow of "soft money" into federal elections (the unlimited contributions that in the past could be made to political party committees for purposes such as supporting Democratic and Republican party platforms, but not to support individual candidates)? Though some believe that the BCRA inhibits free speech, others believe the reform was at least one step in the direction of preventing the undue influence of wealthy interests on elections. Political scientist Michael Malbin likens discussions of BCRA's effects to the story of "Goldilocks and the Three Bears"—for some, the BCRA's effects were too much, and for others too little; however, no one thought it was just right.[1]

Though most Americans do not contribute to political candidates, a success of BCRA is that in 2004, the number of donors making small contributions (less than $200) to the presidential candidates and parties increased substantially. The Democratic and Republican parties' national committees raised more hard money than they had previously raised in hard and soft money combined to support their presidential candidates. (Of particular note is that for the first time in decades, the Democratic National Committee raised more than the Republican National Committee.[2]) However, the two House campaign committees did not raise quite enough hard money to make up for the soft money lost, and the two Senate campaign committees did worse.

According to researchers, concerns were partly founded that organizations called "527s" would become the new soft money. The 527s, named for the section of the U. S tax code that exempts them from taxes, can raise unlimited amounts of money but are supposed to be run independently of parties and candidates. Most previous soft money donors did not give to the new 527s, but some very large donors did, making up for much of the loss. Many people view 527s as vehicles for soft money that the Federal Election Commission refuses to regulate, and some members of Congress are trying to restrict the 527s' use of soft money.

The BCRA did not diminish political advertising. For example, analyses indicate that there was more television advertising for federal elections, though it was highly targeted to areas where the election outcome could not clearly be predicted. Malbin notes that all these effects "occurred during a polarized election in which national security issues commanded the voters' attention," and the next election cycle will reveal whether they were unique responses in a particularly contentious election year, or more permanent effects of the BCRA.[3]

We cannot close our update of this section without a discussion of the situation that Tom DeLay, a long-time Republican U.S. Representative from Texas, now finds himself in.[4] DeLay's nickname is "The Hammer," a moniker attributed to "his enforcement of party discipline in close votes and his reputation for exacting political retribution on opponents."[5] In January 2006, DeLay stepped down as House majority leader after he was indicted in the state of Texas on felony charges of campaign money laundering and conspiracy to launder money. In April 2006, he decided to retire from the House rather than continue to pursue reelection. Delay's case, which involves other individuals and corporations, alleges that Texans for a Republican Majority Political Action Committee (TRMPAC), founded by DeLay, raised money from corporations and then sent it to the Republican National Committee (RNC) for use by the Republican National State Elections Committee to help Republican candidates running for state offices in Texas in 2002. The case boils down to whether TRMPAC illegally funneled $190,000 of corporate money to the RNC to get specific Republican candidates elected or whether the funds given to the RNC were separate and non-corporate, constituting two different and legal transactions. DeLay has called the charges, brought by Travis County District Attorney Ronnie Earle, a Democrat, politically motivated and contends he has done nothing wrong. The case got more interesting when it was learned that Earle had presented the case to three grand juries, and he allowed filmmakers into his office to make a documentary about the investigation of the case.

There is also intense interest around the case because Delay was a key player in congressional redistricting in Texas. After years of Republican accusations of Democratic gerrymandering, TRMPAC was founded to help Republicans gain control of the Texas legislature, which occurred in 2002. With a strong Republican majority, the Texas legislature was able to redistrict the state in a way that would be more favorable to Republicans and also helped them gain a Republican majority in the Texas delegation to the U.S. Congress. This round of congressional redistricting in Texas was especially bitter. Democrats in the Texas House and Senate actually fled the state to avoid a vote (a story in itself). The U.S. Supreme Court is set to review the redistricting plan in March 2006 to determine its legality. According to news reports, the decision to hear the case followed a *Washington Post* article that U.S. Department of Justice lawyers questioned the redistricting plan but were overruled by Bush administration officials.

One other note in this discussion of money and politics is that in January 2006, Jack Abramoff, a powerful lobbyist, pleaded guilty to felony charges of conspiracy, corruption, and tax evasion. His case has far-reaching implications because of the amounts of money involved and because of his ties, contributions, and gifts to Republican Congress members. (Tom DeLay received gifts from Abramoff,[6] though DeLay is reportedly not a target in the investigation into Abramoff's wrongdoings.) Congress members who received contributions from Abramoff have been trying to distance themselves from him by donating the same amount to charities. Now it remains to be seen whether Congress will make meaningful reforms in the high-stakes lobbying arena as it promises to do, and how Republicans will fare in the next election cycle.

Media and Social Welfare

Chapter 1 discusses the role of the media in setting the social welfare agenda as well as reporting on it. If the media accurately reflect the current political scene, then with so much of their attention focused on Iraq, terrorism, national security operations, and political scandal, social welfare programs have taken a back seat. For example, compared to topics such as terrorism, newspapers have carried few stories focusing on Temporary Assistance to Needy Families (TANF) or other public assistance programs.

A spate of natural disasters in 2005, particularly hurricanes Katrina and Rita, did cause the nation to turn its head and respond to the displacement of hundreds of thousands of people and the deaths that occurred in New Orleans and other U.S. Gulf Coast communities. Media coverage of the devastation and deaths was extensive. But the media don't always get it right, and sometimes information gets "hyped." Rapes, sexual assaults, and other crimes reported to have been committed at the Superdome were apparently unsubstantiated or false.

Philanthropy and Natural Disasters

Governmental response to disasters is extremely important, and the update of Chapter 12 addresses governments' failures in responding to Hurricane Katrina in the fall of 2005. The role of private charity or philanthropy is also part of the debate about the public sector's role in providing for social welfare. The American Red Cross has a critical role in the U.S. Department of Homeland Security's National Response Plan for providing aid to victims following natural disasters and terrorist attacks. Even the Red Cross, which many Americans probably feel is above reproach, came in for criticism for what has been considered its less than stellar performance in the wake of Katrina.[7]

As Chapter 1 indicates, each year the American Association of Fundraising Counsel (AAFRC) reports extensively on who gives, how much they give, and the causes to which they give. Americans contributed $249 billion to charity in 2004,[8] $241 billion in 2003, and $234 billion in 2002 (AAFRC's adjusted estimate for that year).[9] These figures constitute about 2 percent of the nation's gross domestic product (GDP) each year. Local charities may be worried that donations to them will drop due to the outpouring of aid to other parts of the world in response to events such as the December 2004 Indian Ocean tsunami, and natural disasters at home like Hurricanes Katrina and Rita. The *Chronicle of Philanthropy* is encouraging optimism, saying that donations to the biggest U.S. charities (some with local offices) have increased. At the top of the list of fundraisers in 2004 were the 1,350 local organizations that compose the United Way of America with $3.9 billion in donations, followed by the Salvation Army with $1.5 billion. The Salvation Army was the top fundraising organization in 2003; its donations also increased from 2003 to 2004.[10] Nevertheless, as you will see in Chapter 1, private philanthropy hardly rivals the help that governments, especially the federal government, provide.

EXERCISES AND ACTIVITIES FOR CHAPTER 1

1. Enter the keywords "campaign finance" in Research Navigator and other Internet search engines to look at the long controversy in the U.S. over the ways that campaigns are financed. Also look at the ways that political parties are supported. Check the website of the Federal Election Commission (http://www.fec.gov/) for regulations governing federal elections, and study regulations governing elections in your state. What alternatives have been suggested to improve the ways campaigns are financed?

2. Enter the keywords "Tom DeLay" in Research Navigator to follow the case of retiring U.S. Representative Tom DeLay. What has happened to the money laundering charges brought against him? Do you think that the charges were politically motivated or justified?

3. Invite representatives (reporters, editors) from the local newspaper(s), TV stations, and other media in your community as well as journalism professors from your college or university to discuss what makes news and how news is reported with regard to domestic and foreign issues. What do they think about accusations that the media has a liberal bias? How do those you contacted feel social welfare issues are treated in the media?

4. How have local charities in your area fared since the Indian Ocean tsunami in December 2004 and Hurricanes Katrina, Wilma, and Rita in 2005? Enter keywords such as "Hurricane Katrina charity" in Research Navigator and read about charitable giving following this major disaster. Then interview or invite to class one or more representatives of major charitable organizations in your community such as the United Way, Salvation Army, and American Red Cross, and representatives of small, local charitable organizations to discuss the effects they think that such catastrophes have on community giving. Ask representatives from each organization to discuss their views of philanthropy, who gives to their organizations, and the strategies they use to encourage donations in good economic times and in bad.

CHAPTER 2

Chapter 2 discusses life-changing experiences for Americans, in particular the terrorist bombings of the World Trade Centers and the Pentagon on September 11, 2001, and military actions in Afghanistan and Iraq and ongoing U.S. efforts to help establish democracy in those countries. These events have important consequences for social welfare policy in the United States. The chapter also addresses the U.S. budget, tax policy, and recent presidential administrations.

U.S. Intervention in Iraq

Iraq's citizens have now cast votes in their own historic, democratic elections. As Shiites and Sunnis vied for office, an estimated 70 percent of registered Iraqi voters went to the polls in December 2005 to cast votes for a new four-year parliamentary government, an impressive turnout compared with most elections in the U.S.[11] These elections occurred as Saddam Hussein was being tried for the atrocities (murders) he allegedly committed as Iraq's former leader, and as more mass graves of Iraqis were discovered.

For all practical purposes, discussion of whether the U.S. should have invaded Iraq has become an academic exercise, but discussion of military and civilian lives being lost in Iraq and how long it will be before U.S. troops pull out of the country remains at a high pitch. As of February 24, 2006, 16,825 U.S. service members had been wounded since the Iraqi invasion began, and 2,289 military personnel had died in Iraq, with 1,793 of those combat deaths.[12] The number of civilian deaths is more difficult to determine. Estimates vary widely. The volunteer organization Iraq Body Count reports approximately 30,000 civilians (non-combatants) killed from the time the war and military occupation began in 2003 until February 19, 2006,[13] whereas researchers reporting in the British medical journal *The Lancet* estimate 100,000 deaths from the war's inception to September 2004.[14] While many Iraqis express gratitude for U.S. intervention, suicide bombings and other violent acts continue to erupt in protest of the U.S. occupation and intervention and military and civilian casualties continue to mount.

Two researchers have now estimated that depending on how long U.S. troops remain in Iraq, this war and its aftermath will cost the U.S. between $1 trillion and $2 trillion dollars.[15] These figures include factors such as health care and disability benefits for veterans and civilians who have been seriously injured, payments to families of military personnel killed in the war, replacing military equipment, military reenlistment bonuses, interest paid on money borrowed to finance the war, and higher oil prices that are partly the result of the instability in Iraq. The size of these expenditures will affect the U.S. budget deficit and expenditures on other government functions like social welfare for years to come.

Terrorism and Torture

Several military personnel have now been convicted of mistreating prisoners at Abu Ghraib prison in Iraq. Some feel that the low-level military personnel convicted were scapegoats for higher-ranking officials who also should have been held responsible. Americans are unlikely to forget the photographs of naked and hooded Abu Ghraib prisoners and of the military personnel in those photos, but media accounts make it clear that the public is divided over the standards that are permissible for interrogation and treatment of prisoners. In November 2005, 74 percent of adults in the U.S. believed that the "U.S. troops or government officials have . . . tortured prisoners in Iraq and other countries," while 38 percent said they were "willing to have the U.S. government torture suspected terrorists if they may know details about future terrorist attacks against the U.S."[16]

The United States continues to face accusations about its treatment of individuals being held at the U.S. prison located at the Guantanamo Naval Base in Cuba, and the extent to which it is engaged in mistreatment and even torture of suspected terrorists in other locations as well. The United Nations has called on the U.S. to shut down the Guantanamo prison and either bring to trial or release the approximately 500 detainees there, most of them captured during the war in Afghanistan.

In attempts to clarify U.S. policy on treatment of foreign prisoners, particularly those held in other countries, Secretary of State Condoleeza Rice stated that the United Nations Convention Against Torture applies regardless of where prisoners are held. U.S. Senator John McCain (Republican-Arizona), a former U.S. Navy pilot who was tortured while a prisoner of war for more than five years in Vietnam, offered an amendment to the Department of Defense appropriations bill. It affirms that the U.S. will not subject any individual in U.S. custody to "cruel, inhuman, or degrading treatment."[17] President Bush eventually affirmed that the U.S. does not condone torture anywhere despite reports of previous administration statements that "cruel, inhumane, and degrading" practices did not apply overseas.[18] But President Bush's statement in signing the bill was criticized for indicating that he could override it if necessary due to his powers as Commander-in-Chief.[19]

Average citizens (i.e., most of us) may be questioning just what we can or should believe about the U.S. government's treatment of prisoners of war and suspected terrorists and what tactics may legitimately be used to extract information from those who may have information critical to U.S. security. Neither the United Nations Convention on Torture, the Geneva Conventions, nor the McCain amendment may make the definition of torture explicit enough to help prevent it.[20] While practices like ripping out fingernails may be obvious to most people as torture, other practices may not, such as "water boarding" in which "the prisoner is bound to a board with feet raised and cellophane wrapped around his head. Water is poured onto this face and is said to produce a fear of drowning which leads to a rapid demand for the suffering to end."[21]

USA Patriot Act

Chapters 1 and 11 of this book address the Uniting and Strengthening America by Providing Appropriate Tools Required to Intercept and Obstruct Terrorism Act, generally referred to as the USA Patriot Act, or more simply, the Patriot Act. Despite its name, many people in both the Democratic and Republican parties think that at least some provisions of this act go beyond activities that Americans should sanction because these provisions ignore important civil liberties and civil rights protections and checks and balances, such as court approvals for wiretaps. Groups such as the American Civil Liberties Union (ACLU) have insisted that Congress put an end to some far-reaching provisions of the act, such as unprecedented authority to conduct wiretaps and obtain other communications such as individuals' Internet and library records. Some Patriot Act provisions were due to expire on December 31, 2005. Congress gave the president two brief extensions of the act. These extensions came amid controversy as President Bush admitted that he had approved domestic spying by the National Security Agency without court approval, insisting that his actions were both "legal and necessary." He also criticized those who leaked and reported the information, which again raised the issue of how far presidential powers extend and whether there is justification for not obtaining court orders since they help to safeguard civil liberties and prevent abuses of power.[22] Some considered the president's actions particularly ironic because these types of safeguards are what the Bush administration is trying to establish in Afghanistan and Iraq.

On March 2, 2006, the Senate passed a renewal of the Patriot Act, 89 votes to 10. On March 7, 2006, the House followed suit with 214 Republicans and 66 Democrats voting for it, and 13 Republicans, 124 Democrats, and one Independent voting against it. President Bush signed it into law on March 9, 2006. The renewal contains some additional safeguards, but not enough of them to quiet critics.

Public Opinion and Public Policy

Just as former Army private Lynndie England became the image of prisoner abuse at Abu Ghraib prison, Cindy Sheehan, mother of a soldier killed in Iraq, has become the image of those who believe that the U.S. should never have invaded Iraq and that U.S. military personnel should be brought home quickly. To protest the war, Sheehan spent much of the summer of 2005 camped near the Crawford, Texas, home of President George W. Bush. Sheehan re-energized the anti-war movement and was invited by a member of Congress to attend the 2006 State of the Union message. Shortly before the speech began, she was arrested in the House gallery for refusing to cover the anti-war T-shirt she was wearing, but the charge was later dropped.

Public support for the Iraq war does seem to be waning. In January of 2003, 53 percent of Americans thought "it was worth going to war in Iraq"; by November of 2005, only 38 percent thought it was worth doing so.[23] During this same time period, the percent that approved "of the way [President] George W. Bush is handling terrorism" dropped from 71 percent to 48 percent.[24] In December 2005, when a representative sample of Americans were asked about "the most important problem facing the country today," a CNN News/New York Times poll indicated that the economy and jobs topped the list, followed by the war in Iraq. An NBC News/Wall Street Journal poll conducted at that same time found that the war in Iraq trumped both health care and job creation/economic growth, which tied for second place as issues that "should be the federal government's top priority."[25] Both the war and economic issues are weighing on the minds of Americans, and the two are tightly connected.

What's Next for the U.S. Tax Code?

A good deal of Chapter 2 is devoted to the ways social welfare programs are financed, primarily the tax structures of the federal government and state and local governments. As the chapter demonstrates, attempts to change the U.S. tax system are ongoing activities in U.S. politics. In January 2005, in keeping with promises for his second term, President George W. Bush appointed the President's Advisory Panel on Federal Tax Reform to simplify tax laws. His Executive Order asked the panel to suggest an "appropriately progressive" tax structure that would "recognize the importance of home ownership and charity" (in other words, make sure there are still tax advantages for home ownership and charitable contributions), "promote long-run economic growth and job creation, and better encourage work effort, saving, and investment." As you will see in Chapter 2, some of this later terminology is very similar to that used by President Ronald Reagan in his successful efforts to cut taxes. President Bush also requested that the panel's plans be "revenue neutral," that is, generate the same tax revenues that the current system does.

The panel offered two major proposals.[26] The Simplified Income Tax (SIT) Plan reduces the number of tax brackets to four and the Growth and Investment Tax (GIT) Plan reduces them to three from the current six. Both plans are supposed to make it much easier to file income taxes each year. The SIT Plan removes targeted tax breaks that benefit relatively few, eliminates the Alternative Minimum Tax (which is not currently indexed to inflation so it produces a higher tax bill for many Americans and has been criticized for penalizing middle-income Americans in particular), retains tax benefits for home ownership (but changes the method for calculating them), charitable giving, and health care, and makes them available to all Americans, not just those who currently itemize on their tax returns. SIT is also intended to remove disincentives to save by allowing taxpayers to save more tax-free. It also intended to simplify small business tax calculations and to change the tax structure to help American corporations better compete in global markets. GIT builds on SIT and would further reduce or eliminate taxes on savings or investments. For example, it recommends one lower 15 percent tax rate for dividends, interest, and capital gains. Businesses would be able to write off their investments immediately rather than writing them off over time.

There have been many critiques of the proposals.[27] Among them is that they eliminate too many deductions for individuals and businesses. For example, the plans would eliminate the deductions taxpayers can currently take for state and local taxes on their federal tax returns. This would be especially bitter pill for those living in states with high taxes. The mortgage interest deduction would be converted to a tax credit with a cap, eliminating additional tax advantages for those who own more expensive homes. The panel proposes a tax credit capped at 15 percent of the interest paid on the mortgage of the average regional price of housing, currently ranging from about $227,000 to $412,000. This approach would better target tax benefits to lower-income homeowners. However, high-end homeowners and even middle-income homeowners who reside in areas where homes prices are high would likely oppose such a proposal. Those involved in the lucrative real estate industry (builders, real estate agents, mortgage and insurance companies) would also fight any attempts to reduce deductions for home ownership because they may prompt homeowners to consider buying lower-priced homes. There are many other details in the plans. For example, workers would have to pay incomes taxes on child care benefits and life insurance provided by their employers and on health benefits exceeding $5,000 a year for individuals and $11,500 for families. The panel contends that though there would be fewer deductions, most Americans' tax bills would not rise and the plans would be revenue neutral as President Bush requested.

As drastic as some of these suggested changes might sound, there are critics who contend that the panel's plans do not go far enough to simplify the tax code. They call for more radical transformation of the tax code via a "flat tax" or through a national sales tax, options that might even allow Americans to file their income taxes on a postcard. Greater simplification and ease of filing might encourage greater compliance with tax laws. And sales taxes, which are collected at the time purchases are made, are easier to collect and harder to avoid paying than income taxes, which rely not only on individuals filing at all, but also filing correctly. Under the current, complicated tax code, it is easy to make errors when filing. As noted in Chapter 3, the federal government loses billions of dollars in tax revenues each year due to errors and outright "avoidance," a euphemism for failing to pay taxes.

Options like a flat tax and national sales tax meet with opposition from those who argue that they are not sufficiently progressive because they fail to give lower-income earners sufficient tax breaks. These options have been presented before, often by Republicans or Libertarians, and are discussed in Chapter 2.

Former Federal Reserve Board Chairman Alan Greenspan has suggested a combination of an income tax and sales (consumption) tax system, though critics again contend that lower-income individuals are disadvantaged because they must spend a higher proportion of their income on goods necessary for survival, while higher income individuals have more choice in how they allot their income.[28] National sales tax plans can address this problem by providing tax rebates to low-income individuals and families or by making necessities like food and medicines tax exempt, and flat tax plans can address it by exempting low-income earners from paying taxes.

As 2005 came to a close, the U.S. House of Representatives made no major tax changes. Instead it passed a bill to extend until 2010 the capital gains tax cuts that President Bush has championed. Since capital gains taxes are paid on the sale of investments, something that those in lower income brackets are unlikely (or at least less likely) to have, wealthier individuals would again benefit disproportionately. It was no surprise that the House vote was divided mostly along party lines, with the Republicans for and the Democrats against. As you will see in Chapter 2, this extension continues a trend toward bigger tax cuts for the rich than for less affluent American taxpayers, and at a time when the federal debt has significantly increased. In the Senate there was not enough votes to support extension of the capital gains tax cuts, and negotiations will take place to try to hammer out differences. In the meantime, tax reforms like SIT or GIT are unlikely to become law anytime soon.

The Re-election of George W. Bush

In the 2004 presidential election, as expected, no Republican challenged the incumbent President George W. Bush's bid for a second term. The Democratic field was initially crowded. Among the strong Democratic contenders who emerged was Howard Dean, former governor of Vermont, freshman Senator John Edwards from North Carolina, and Senator John Kerry from Massachusetts. Two-time Green Party presidential candidate Ralph Nader ran as an Independent. Democrats were concerned that Nader would siphon off votes from the Democratic nominee, and that this would be especially problematic in a close race. Eventually John Kerry emerged as the Democrat's choice, and he chose John Edwards as his vice presidential running mate. Though polling problems in key states like Florida and Ohio again tarnished the election, in the final analysis, Republican President George W. Bush and his Vice President Dick Cheney prevailed over Kerry and Edwards. President Bush won with nearly 51 percent of the popular vote and 286 electoral college votes to Kerry's popular vote, which was just over 48 percent, and his 251 electoral college seats (one member of the electoral college gave his vote to Edwards; the remaining votes went to other presidential candidates). The media were much more cautious in reporting following the incorrect predictions of the winner in the 2000 presidential election. Once again, there were many reports of voting irregularities, including excessively long lines and waits to vote, ballot and voting machine shortages and malfunctions, inadequate numbers of volunteer staffers, and claims of discrimination and intimidation. Problems in the state of Ohio caused it to become the cliffhanger in the race. The day after the election, The Ohio vote went to President Bush. Kerry conceded to avoid any prolonged inquiry into who would be president. The vote made George W. Bush the first presidential candidate since 1988 when his father was elected president, to receive a majority of the popular vote. But in terms of percentages, it was the closest popular vote margin ever (2.5 percent) for an incumbent president. It was also the smallest popular vote margin (at approximately 3 million more than Kerry) since incumbent Harry Truman was reelected in 1948.[29]

Some called President Bush's winning a second term a mandate for conservatism, though with 51 percent of the vote, others felt that conservatism barely squeaked by. Following the 2004 elections, Republicans remained the majority party in both chambers of the U.S. Congress. As of January 26, 2006, serving in the second session of the 109th Congress in the House of Representatives are 231 Republicans, 201 Democrats, and one Independent, and there are two vacancies. In the Senate there are 55 Republicans, 44 Democrats, and one Independent. Both House and Senate Independents are from Vermont.[30]

Much has been written about why the Democrats failed in the presidential election. The Democrats generally portray the Republican Party as interested in the rich and out of touch with most working-class Americans, but some said that Kerry appeared too aloof or too intellectual to appeal to broader segments of the population. Others called Kerry a "flip flopper' who was too willing to change his mind on issues to please others, while George Bush was more decisive. Bush had shepherded the country following the September 11, 2001, terrorist attacks, had led the charge for the Iraq war, and stood firm on fighting terror. There were also ideas about the Democratic Party being too liberal and its failure to adopt a platform sufficiently strong to capture more votes.

President George W. Bush's priorities for his second term are much like they were for his first. On the domestic front, some of them are to extend tax cuts and now to simplify the tax code, allow workers to funnel a portion of Social Security taxes into private investment accounts, fight the war on terror, and encourage new energy production to make the U.S. less dependent on other countries for fuel. On the foreign scene, some of his major priorities are to finish the job in Iraq, use diplomacy to stop North Korea's nuclear weapon's program, and continue to moderate the tense Arab-Israeli political situation.[31]

There is already talk of who will emerge as contenders in the 2008 presidential election. On the Democratic ticket, will John Edwards's charisma as a presidential candidate or Howard Dean's enthusiasm and chairmanship of the Democratic National Committee help them emerge in the presidential race? Many believe that Hillary Clinton will throw her hat in the ring, or perhaps Barack Obama, a popular first-term senator from Illinois will take a cue from John Edwards and shift his gaze to the national political arena. On the Republican ticket, will Senator John McCain, Senate Majority Leader Bill Frist, or perhaps former New York Mayor Rudolph "Rudy" Giuliani be a contender?

The Federal Budget and Its Deficit

President Clinton entered office with a budget in deficit and left office with the budget in surplus. President George W. Bush has not been as lucky. The surplus he inherited is now a massive deficit. The nonpartisan Congressional Budget Office reports that the federal budget deficit for 2005 will be about $317 billion. This is actually $96 billion dollars less than the deficit for 2004 and less than expected for 2005 due to growth in federal revenues (taxes collected). But tax cuts are still a major contributor to the deficit. Projections for the next few years are worse, making it less likely that President Bush will be able to keep his pledge to halve the deficit by the end of his presidency. The U.S. government is projected to spend $2.6 trillion in 2006. As of December 31, 2005, the national debt (the accumulation of budget deficits) stood at nearly $8.2 trillion.[32]

Now, in addition to the war in Iraq, another major spending issue concerns help for residents of the Gulf Coast displaced by recent hurricanes, especially Hurricane Katrina. To help offset the costs of hurricane relief, the occupation of Iraq, and the effects of tax cuts, Congress will make substantial cuts in social welfare programs over the next five to ten years. These cuts come about largely as a result of the Deficit Reduction Act (DRA) of 2005. The DRA vote was very close and split largely along party lines, with the Republicans for and Democrats against. In the Senate, it passed 51–50 with Vice President Cheney casting the tie-breaking vote. In the House, the vote was 216 to 214. The biggest hit will be in student loans (nearly a $12 billion cut), followed by a Medicare cut of more than $6 billion, and nearly $5 billion from Medicaid. Medicare is the federal government's health care program for older Americans and Medicaid is a health care program for some low-income Americans. Whether these cuts are helpful or harmful may depend on one's point of view. For example, President Bush said:

> *The Deficit Reduction Act makes important improvements to federal student loan programs. The bill cuts excess government subsidies to lenders and makes other reforms that will help us reduce overall student loan costs by about $22 billion. With that money we will save taxpayers $12 billion—because we intend to increase student aid by 10 additional billion dollars. What I'm telling you is, students are getting the money, and we're making the program a lot more efficient for taxpayers.[33]*

Many, from *Rolling Stone* magazine to the Coalition on Human Needs, saw it differently. *Rolling Stone's* analysis was:

> *A full seventy percent of those [DRA] cuts, the largest in history, fall squarely on the back of students and their parents. Rather than slashing aid directly, Congress simply raised the interest on student loans, replacing a lower variable rate with a higher fixed rate. As a result, students leaving college with $17,500 in loans will have to cough up an additional $5,800 to pay off their debt. The change will increase the cost of higher education for American families by $8 billion—at a time when public universities have already raised their prices by forty percent.[34]*

More than one political pundit has commented that given other spending priorities and tax cuts mostly for the rich, the budget deficit won't be cut at all, and many Americans will be hurt as a result.

EXERCISES AND ACTIVITIES FOR CHAPTER 2

1. Have a class debate on whether the U.S. should have invaded Iraq. Begin by reading the sections on the Iraq war in Chapters 1 and 2 of this book. Then enter the keywords "Iraq war" in Research Navigator and other search engines and read more about the events leading up to the war, such as whether there was evidence that Saddam Hussein possessed weapons of mass destruction. You may also wish to interview individuals or invite speakers to class to discuss differing viewpoints on the Iraq war, including military personnel, individuals who have lost family members in the war, and peace activists. You can supplement this exercise by looking at levels of support for the Iraq war and the continued U.S. presence in Iraq since the war was initiated by entering the keywords "Iraq war opinion polls" in Research Navigator and by reviewing the results of public opinion polls at PollingReport.com (http://www.pollingreport.com).

2. Have a class discussion on renewal of the USA Patriot Act. Using Research Navigator, enter the keywords "Patriot Act" to learn more about the act and the debates surrounding it. Study the various provisions of the act and discuss which should or should not be included in the act. Also visit websites of the U.S. Attorney General (http://www.usdoj.gov/ag/) and of the American Civil Liberties Union (http://www.aclu.org/) to gain different perspectives on the issue.

3. Who is Jose Padilla and why is being held by the U.S. government? Using Research Navigator or other search engines enter the keyword "Jose Padilla" and find out more about the controversies concerning his case. Do you agree with the actions that have been taken in his case? If not, what action do you think should be taken?

4. Enter the keyword "torture" in Research Navigator and read more about the debate on the use of interrogation practices they may or may not constitute torture. Also use other Internet search engines to locate materials about the Geneva Conventions, the United Nations Convention on Torture, and Senator John McCain's views on the use of torture. What practices do you think constitute torture and what practices do you feel are acceptable in obtaining information critical to U.S. security?

5. Enter the keywords "tax plan " in Research Navigator and investigate the most recent ideas for reforming the U.S. Tax Code. Which make most sense to you? Is the idea of a flat tax, consumption (sales) tax, or a progressive tax system more appealing to you and why? Read more about the SIT and GIT plans described above. How do you think various segments of the population will react to the plans' features?

6. How important is the budget deficit? Enter the keywords "budget deficit" in Research Navigator and follow discussions of how important the size of the U.S. budget deficit is and the impact it has on the economic well being of Americans. Also check the Congressional Budget Office website (http://www.cbo.gov) and determine what current deficit projections are. Then enter the keywords "national debt" in Research Navigator and read about the national debt. Check the latest national debt figure at the web site called the U.S. National Debt Clock (http://www.brillig.com/debt_clock/). Since this foreword was written, how much has the national debt increased? Check the Census Bureau figures for the U.S. population. Divide the debt by the population. How much is now owed for every individual in the U.S.?

7. In the wake of recent U.S. hurricanes, particularly Hurricane Katrina, what should be done to help victims and who should pay the costs? Enter the keywords "Hurricane Katrina" in Research Navigator to determine what is currently being done and how displaced individuals are faring with help from the federal, state, and local governments, insurance companies, and private charities. Are you satisfied with the responses from each sector?

8. Problems at the polls were at the heart of the controversy in determining who won the 2000 presidential election. There were also concerns during the 2004 presidential election. Enter the keywords "2004 presidential election" in Research Navigator to identify problems at the polls during the 2004 election. Invite a local election official to class to discuss the procedures used in the local jurisdiction to conduct elections, the types of voting machines and equipment used, and any problems encountered and how they have been addressed. What does this official see as the next steps in protecting voting rights and encouraging greater voter participation in the jurisdiction?

9. Take a look at President Bush's approval ratings in the latest public opinion polls. In what direction is his approval rating moving? What events are influencing any changes?

10. Enter the keywords "Republican Party" and "Democratic party" in Research Navigator and go to the websites of the Republican National Committee (http://www.rnc.org) and the Democratic National Committee (http://www.dnc.org) to learn more about the parties. Hold a class discussion on what each party stands for, to whom it appeals, and how you view the strengths and weaknesses of each party. How did your local precinct, city or town, and state vote in the 2004 presidential election; was the vote primarily Republican, Democrat, or possibly for another party? You may wish to invite Democratic and Republican elected officials and party committee members to discuss their party's platform, as well as representatives of other parties that might be active in your area.

CHAPTER 3

Chapter 3 reviews the state of poverty in the U.S. and the many theories that try to "explain" poverty.

Rules for Avoiding Poverty

Theories of poverty generally vary between conservative treatments, which focus on the importance of individual decisions and personal initiative, and liberal treatments, which stress structural causes such as economic conditions and discrimination against groups like people of color and women. For example, conservative political columnist George Will cites "three rules for avoiding poverty": (1) "graduate from high school,"(2) "don't have a baby until you are married," (3) "don't marry while you are a teenager."[35] Self-discipline is an important theme among conservatives, so it is no surprise that conservatives suggest remedies like abstinence training, marriage counseling, school vouchers, and mentoring to avoid or escape poverty.

Liberals would likely agree with Will's three rules, but they would add others: don't be born to a family that is financially insecure, don't attend overcrowded and underfunded schools, don't develop serious or costly health problems (medical expenses cause half of personal bankruptcies in the U.S.[36]), don't lose your job to illness or disability or to recession or other economic factors, and don't work at jobs with low pay and few benefits. These causes of poverty are generally outside an individual's control. They prompt liberals to promote programs for quality education and health insurance for all, and reducing discrimination and other barriers to self-sufficiency through decent wages, childcare, transportation, or other tangible remedies.

Poverty and Income

There is widespread agreement that the method the federal government used to calculate the number of people living in poverty is outdated. But there is disagreement about how or even whether the method should be changed. Poverty thresholds, the federal government's official poverty measure, are increased each year to keep pace with inflation.[37] Using the summary or weighted average figures, the poverty threshold for one person was $9,645 in 2004, and for a family of four it was $19,307. Chapter 3 provides critiques of the poverty guidelines and discusses ways of considering what it actually takes to live in communities in the U.S.

As an update to the figures in Chapter 3, we find that:

♦ Poverty has increased every year since 2000. In 2004, 12.7 percent of the population or 37 million people were in poverty. (Poverty rates for children, women, and people of color are much higher.) In addition, in 2004, another 12.7 million people or 4.4 percent of the population lived within 125 percent of the poverty threshold.

♦ The *income deficit* is what it would take to bring a family in poverty up to the poverty threshold. Looking at all families in poverty, it would have taken an average of $7,775 to bring them to the poverty threshold in 2004. In 2002, it would have taken less—$7,205.

♦ Other income measures are also important in considering the state of the economy and the well being of Americans. Each year the Census Bureau reports median household income figures. Half of all households have income below this figure and half have income above it. After adjusting for inflation, in 2004, the median income for all U.S. households averaged $44,349 compared to $46,058 in 2000.

◆ The Gini index is a measure of income inequality with zero indicating perfect income equality (every individual or group has the same income) and 1 indicating perfect inequality (one person or group has all the income). The Gini index has risen from .45 in 1995 to .47 in 2004.

◆ The poorest one-fifth of U.S. families continues to take home less of the country's personal income. In 2004 that figure was just 4%. In comparison, the top one-fifth of earners took home 48 percent of the nation's income in 2004. Using this measure, income inequality has also grown.

With no new major poverty reduction initiatives in sight, one perspective is that Americans have grown complacent about poverty rates and income inequality.

Poverty in International Perspective

Poverty rates in the U.S. are higher than in most other developed nations, though material deprivation in the U.S. is far less than in other parts of the world. The United Nations (U.N.) reports that "over half the world's six billion people live lives of substantial deprivation," defined as subsisting on $2 a day or less.[38] The U.N. has called upon the world's richest countries to do more to help. In 1970, these nations pledged 0.7 percent of their gross national income to do so, but only five countries—Denmark, Luxembourg, the Netherlands, Norway, and Sweden—have met or exceeded their promise to help impoverished regions of the world.[39] Six other countries, all also in Europe, have promised to do so by 2015. Though the U.S. provides more than other countries in absolute figures, it continues to take a thrashing in the media for not doing more. President Bush is reportedly increasing the 0.15 percent of gross national income that the U.S. has been spending to help the United Nations meet its goals, such as cutting in half the number of people who live on $1 a day or less and achieving universal primary education. But there is very different viewpoint on international aid based on the principle of limited government: The U.S. Constitution does not give the president the power to provide such aid, criticisms directed at the U.S. for not providing "enough" are wrong, and giving money is an individual matter for those who own it to decide.[40]

"Ownership Society"

To the lexicon of American social welfare, President George W. Bush has added the term "ownership society."[41] In this vision, more Americans would be able to afford and chose private health care coverage, own a home, get tax relief, and have adequate retirement income. To help more Americans enjoy home ownership, the president points to programs such as the Department of Housing and Urban Development's (HUD's) American Dream Downpayment Initiative, which helps low-income individuals make a down payment and pay closing costs on a home, and the Self-help Homeownership Opportunities Program, which aids organizations like Habitat for Humanity International that help individuals who provide "sweat equity" (their own labor) build or rehabilitate a home. Bush also advocates simplifying the home buying process, providing a single-family affordable housing tax credit, and options for saving money tax free for a home (or for an education, a car for work, or retirement). Critics of this conception of an ownership society indicate that is ownership for those who already have and not for the "have nots."

Though home prices seem astronomical to many Americans, especially in some areas of the country, home ownership has steadily increased in the U.S. In the third quarter of 2005, the U.S. home ownership rate was 68.8 percent.[42] Home ownership among members of various socioeconomic and ethnic groups has also increased, but recent research provides some interesting analyses of what happens *after* low-income homebuyers purchase a home.[43] Data from the Panel Study of Income Dynamics (described in Chapter 3 of this book) reveal that only 64 percent of low-income home purchasers owned their homes two years later, dropping to 47 percent five years after purchase. In comparison, 77 percent of high-income purchasers still owned their home five years later. Since long-term home ownership stabilizes families and communities, programs are needed that help people maintain ownership, especially when financial emergencies occur.

Perhaps one problem in raising home ownership rates is that a scandal always seems to be brewing in the housing industry (see Chapter 3). The latest one is apparently major accounting problems at Fannie Mae and Freddie Mac, large mortgage financing companies. Fannie Mae is reportedly adjusting its earnings downward by nearly $11 billion![44] In response, the U.S. House of Representatives is considering a new oversight body for these mortgage companies, financed by assessments on the companies and on federal home loans.[45] The Senate is considering another approach—limiting the size of these mortgage companies portfolios. How best to regulate these mortgage companies is a complex issue and among those that await the new Federal Reserve Chairman Ben Bernanke.

Homelessness

Prior to Hurricanes Katrina and Rita in 2005, HUD made another extensive attempt to count the homeless population.[46] Results will not be official because difficulties in counting the homeless make the numbers suspect, but according to information obtained by *USA Today* from participating cities, the count of about 727,000 homeless is similar to past estimates of the homeless population.

In the fall of 2005, Hurricanes Katrina and Rita temporarily swelled the ranks of the homeless. Evacuees from the affected Gulf Coast communities were moved from emergency shelters to other types of housing, including cabins on cruise ships, hotel and motel rooms, travel trailers, and manufactured housing units. In February 2006, the Federal Emergency Management Agency (FEMA) reported that it had aided 770,000 families displaced by these two hurricanes with longer-term housing aid.[47] With the hotel and motel room assistance fast coming to an end, FEMA and other governmental and charitable organizations were trying to find more permanent housing alternatives for those still in these units and for those not eligible for federal housing assistance. In February 2006, FEMA was still taking criticism for the number of trailers that remained empty while homeless evacuees continued to wait for them. According to *USA Today,* the director of the White House Interagency Council on Homelessness estimated that in the fall of 2006, 23,000 Katrina evacuees would still be without a home.[48]

EXERCISES AND ACTIVITIES FOR CHAPTER 3

1. Enter the keyword "poverty" in Research Navigator and read about current issues in poverty. Then go to the U.S. Census Bureau website (http://www.censusbureau.gov) and find out what the poverty rate is for the city in which you live. How does is compare with the poverty rate for the state your city is in and with the national poverty rate? What factors contribute to differences in poverty rates in your area compared to those in other parts of the U.S.?

2. Devise a poverty threshold or poverty line for your community (consider how much it costs to rent an apartment, buy food, and cover other essential expenses) and then compare it with the federal government's poverty thresholds and figures for the Self-sufficiency Standard discussed on page 85 of this book, if one is available for your community. How do your own calculations compare with the federal government's thresholds, the Self-sufficiency Standard, and your own standard of living?

3. Using Research Navigator, enter the keywords "development aid" to read more about what developed countries give to poorer countries. Discuss the differences in what countries give and what you think the U.S. should contribute. How do you react to views that the U. S government has no authority to provide such aid, and that while giving is virtuous, it is a matter for individuals?

4. Go to the Census Bureau web site (http://www.census.gov/hhes/www/housing/hvs/annual04/ann04ind.html) and look up housing statistics, including home ownership rates for your area of the country. How do they compare with the rest of the country? Discuss factors that may contribute to differences in home ownership rates in your area compared to other areas of the country.

5. Using Research Navigator enter the keyword "housing" and read about current housing issues. Then invite to class representatives from local agencies that run home ownership programs for low-income and first-time homebuyers in your area, including organizations such as Habitat for Humanity International. Ask them to describe their programs and what the requirements are to get assistance. You might also invite representatives of conventional mortgage companies in your area and ask them what it takes to buy a home, including the paperwork and fees involved in the process. Also ask them about procedures used to qualify potential homebuyers. Do you own a home? If so, what are your comments on what it takes to qualify for and purchase a home? If you do not own a home, what will it take for you to own one?

6. Learn more about organizations like Habitat for Humanity International. You may even wish to spend some time volunteering. What are your impressions of these nonprofit programs? How do you see their role in relation to governments' role in helping people achieve home ownership?

7. Using Research Navigator and other search engines, enter the keyword "homeless" to see what the scholarly journals and national media are currently reporting about homelessness. Also check for updates regarding housing homeless individuals and families following Hurricanes Katrina and Rita. Then investigate how homelessness is addressed in your community. Does your community have a homeless shelter? What local laws are directed at the homeless population? Can people solicit money on the streets? Are there "camping bans" to prevent homeless people from sleeping in streets, parks, or other public places? How would you rate your community's response to homelessness?

CHAPTER 4

The subject of Chapter 4 is the social insurance programs. These programs are designed to prevent poverty. Workers and/or their employers contribute to these programs, and the benefits are there when workers retire, become disabled or unemployed, or in the case of their death, to aid family members.

What's the Fix for Social Security?

In 2005, about 48.4 million Americans received benefits from the world's largest social welfare program—Social Security (also called Old-Age, Survivors and Disability Insurance).[49] About 33.5 million were retired workers or their dependents, about 8.3 million were disabled former workers or their dependents, and about 6.7 million were survivors of deceased workers who had received or were eligible for Social Security payments. In 2004, cash benefits paid (not including administrative costs) totaled about $493.3 billion, about $415.1 billion for Old Age and Survivors Insurance benefits and about $78.2 billion for Disability Insurance benefits.[50]

Social Security's sheer size, particularly the rapidly growing number of retirees and escalating benefit payments, causes the program to loom large on the social welfare agenda. One debate is whether the Social Security program should be portrayed as a crisis requiring drastic measures or whether more modest modifications will do. Still controversial and still on the table is the idea of allowing workers to invest a portion of their Social Security withholding taxes in private investments.

Social security privatization in the country of Chile, and in the U.S. city of Galveston, Texas, is often hailed as examples of privatization's success. Detractors point out the downside of these systems, particularly increased risk, less program oversight, and loss of the longstanding *social* insurance, or collective mission, of Social Security. Privatization's success would ultimately depend on how well private investments do in the long run, how safe the investment instruments are that participants use or are allowed to use, and the extent to which workers participate or take out funds prior to retirement if permitted to do so.

Another idea being promoted to help the Social Security program is "progressive price indexing," credited to Robert Pozen, former vice chairman of Fidelity Investments and a member of President Bush's Social Security Commission. The plan is called progressive because workers with higher incomes get less of a return than those with lower incomes (even today Social Security replaces a higher portion of lower-income workers' wages than of higher-income workers). Under progressive price indexing, low-income workers, those currently earning about $20,000 or less annually, would be treated the same way as they are today by Social Security. Their benefits would continue to be indexed (adjusted) according to the average increase in wages, and their benefits would not be reduced. Higher-income earners (those earning $90,000 or more today) would get lower benefits. Their benefits would be indexed according to prices (increases in the costs of goods and services). The benefits of high-income earners would be lower because prices grow more slowly than wages.[51] The Social Security benefits of workers earning in between low- and high-income earners would be indexed using a combination of wage and price indexing.

An analysis of progressive price indexing by the Center on Budget and Policy Priorities (CBPP) makes the plan sound like a trip on the *Titanic*. Perhaps the plan's biggest drawback would be lower retirement benefits for many current workers. For example, an average-income earner who is 25 years old in 2005 and retires at age 65 in 2045 would realize a 16 percent cut in projected benefits compared to the current formula; average-income earners retiring in 2075 would see a 28 percent benefit reduction. Furthermore, despite differences in what workers would pay into the system, they would end up with about equal benefits at retirement.

Other concerns the CBPP notes with progressive price indexing include the perverse effect that larger benefit reductions would occur when economic and wage growth are strongest and Social Security coffers would benefit from increased payroll taxes. Conversely, benefit reductions grow smaller when the economy is performing poorly and Social Security coffers fare worse. Though the plan preserves payments for those who earned the lowest wages, it detracts from the social insurance aspect of the program and makes it look more like public assistance.

Not everyone agrees with these critiques of progressive price indexing. Some see it as a solid centrist solution to Social Security's problems because the costs would be borne by those best able to afford them, and the approach could keep costs in check while preserving the social insurance safety net.[52]

Progressive price indexing could also be combined with private investment accounts that President Bush supports. If so, the CBPP indicates that Social Security would produce tiny or no benefits for retirees who were high-income earners because the private accounts of those who opted for them would be financed by additional cuts in their Social Security benefits. Pozen himself has encouraged President Bush to abandon the idea of using four percentage points of Social Security taxes for private investment accounts since it would reduce tax revenues and Social Security benefits too much.[53] These cuts in benefits are likely to further erode broad support for the Social Security program. Though President Bush toured the country to drum up enthusiasm for privatization, there was been no groundswell of support.[54] Perhaps this is because it is difficult to make major changes to a program that affects so many people and has worked well for so many years. Workers who have been paying in want to make sure they get what they put in, and younger people may not know what to think about a retirement that is well down the road.

Other plans now being discussed, some of which are hardly new, are to raise the amount of income on which current workers would pay Social Security taxes, raise the tax rate on wages, impose a smaller tax on wages above the wages currently taxed, and/or impose a modest estate tax which would go to the Social Security fund. There is no shortage of proposals, just lack of agreement on how to proceed.

Unemployment, Sick and Injured Workers, and the Other Social Insurance Programs

How much unemployment has there been in recent years? During each month of 2002 and 2003, between 5.7 percent and 6.3 percent of workers were unemployed. In 2005, this picture improved. National unemployment hovered at around 5 percent each month, even though Hurricanes Katrina and Rita had a major impact in the Gulf Coast area.[55] As Chapter 4 describes, this low 5 percent unemployment rate belies the differences in rates among various ethnic groups. The Bureau of Labor Statistics, part of the U.S. Department of Labor, provides information at its website that may help people avoid future unemployment, such as occupations projected to have the largest growth in the next decade.

Unemployment compensation, also called unemployment insurance, is a social insurance program also discussed in Chapter 4 of this book. Most workers have this coverage and are able to use it if they are unemployed and cannot find work. But readers might be surprised at just how few unemployed workers are able to collect unemployment benefits at any given moment.

Workers' compensation programs for those who are injured or contract diseases on the job, another topic of Chapter 4, have long been a bone of contention in many states because of the number of workers seeking compensation, the litigation that often ensues among workers, employers, and insurance companies over who deserves benefits, and most of all, rapidly rising program costs. Chapter 4 discusses some ways states have addresses these problems. Other states continue to struggle with ways to make changes that are fair to all.

EXERCISES AND ACTIVITIES FOR CHAPTER 4

1. Using Research Navigator, enter the keywords "Social Security" to read about the latest discussions on the subject. Then study Robert Pozen's plan for progressive price indexing to reform the Social Security system and other plans discussed in Chapter 4 and elsewhere. Which would you select and why? You may also wish to interview current Social Security beneficiaries and prospective beneficiaries in different age groups. What are their beliefs about how the Social Security system works, the adequacy of the benefits, and how they think Social Security should be changed?

2. Using Research Navigator, enter the keywords "unemployment," "unemployment insurance," or "unemployment compensation" to find any new stories on these subjects. Then visit the U.S. Department of Labor's Bureau of Labor Statistics website (http://www.bls.gov). Investigate recent unemployment rates for various segments of the population—men and women, individuals of different ages and ethnic groups. How do unemployment rates for those with demographic characteristics similar to you compare with those of other segments of the population?

3. Using Research Navigator, enter the key words "workers' compensation" to locate any new information on these programs. Learn more about how the workers' compensation program operates in your state compared to other states and about the number, percentage, and characteristics of workers being assisted.

CHAPTER 5

The focus of Chapter 5 is disability and public policy. This section provides updates on the approaches the U.S. has chosen—including cash payments and civil rights legislation—to provide individuals with significant disabilities more opportunities to live in the community and participate in mainstream society.

SSDI

The number of individuals *applying* for Social Security Disability Insurance (SSDI) benefits has increased rapidly, from 1.3 million in 2000 to 2.1 million in 2005.[56] The percentage who are *approved* for disability payments has fluctuated over the years from highs of nearly 53 percent in 1967 and 52 percent in 1998 to lows of 29 percent in 1982 and 30 percent in 1981. In 2005, 39 percent of the 2.1 million applications were approved. There were 5.7 awards for every 1,000 insured workers. Providing disability benefits is a contentious issue because it raises questions about why disability claims have risen rapidly in an era of medical advancements that make it possible to prevent more disabilities and in an era of civil rights and technological improvements that should provide more opportunities for people with disabilities to work.

Like the SSDI program, the Supplemental Security Income program for individuals with disabilities discussed below has also experienced substantial growth. As you will see in Chapter 5, qualifying for disability payments is often not an easy process. Many people who believe they are disabled are not approved for payments and many hire attorneys or seek other advocates who can help them prove they are disabled.

SSI

Supplemental Security Income (SSI) is a public assistance program that provides cash benefits to individuals with little or no income if they are aged or disabled, with special provisions for those who are blind. An update of figures shows that the number receiving payments based on age continues to decline. In 2000, there were slightly more than 1.3 million aged recipients compared with about 1.25 million in 2004.[57] Over the years, much of the decline has been attributed to more people aged 65 and older receiving Social Security retirement and disability payments. The number receiving SSI payments due to blindness saw a small decline, from about 79,000 in 2000 to about 77,000 in 2004. With advances in blindness prevention and greater successes of individuals who are blind in securing employment, the size of this program component has remained relatively stable. The number receiving payments based on other disabilities has continued to grow, from 5.3 million in 2000 to 5.7 million in 2004. Among recipients with disabilities, about 30 percent received Social Security benefits but still had incomes low enough to receive SSI; 10 percent had other unearned income (income from sources other than work), and less than 5 percent had earnings from work.[58] A major concern of the SSI program is how to help more individuals receiving payments based on disability engage in meaningful employment.

Veteran's Administration and PTSD

Disability claims and cases are also a concern for the Department of Veterans Affairs (VA). The VA makes disability compensation payments to veterans with injuries or diseases acquired or aggravated during active military service. To receive SSDI or SSI payments, individuals must be so disabled as to not be able to perform any gainful employment in the economy; that is, they must be permanently and totally disabled. The VA system differs because it pays for cases in which there is partial disability. A problem of all the disability compensation (payment) programs is that they pay people who remain sick or disabled, with few incentives for them to get better, or to work despite their illnesses or disabilities. In the SSI and SSDI programs there may be trial work periods, but by and large, once a person is deemed to be capable of earning even a very modest amount, disability payments are terminated. The VA's disability compensation program also differs in important ways because its payment structure is more generous, and since it makes compensation payments for partial disability, payments may be reduced rather than terminated.

The VA drew criticism in 2005 when it announced that it would review the cases of veterans receiving disability compensation due to a diagnosis of posttraumatic stress disorder (PTSD). The American Psychiatric Association characterizes PTSD as persistent and intense fear, helplessness, or horror after being subjected to events such as serious injury or threatened death or witnessing traumatic events such as serious harm or death of others.[59] Military personnel may experience such events during combat or while being held as a prisoner of war. The concern over PTSD arose following a VA report that said:

> While the total number of all veterans receiving disability compensation grew by only 12.2 percent [from 1999–2004], the number of PTSD cases grew by 79.5 percent, from 120,265 cases in FY 1999 to 215,871 cases in FY 2004. During this same period, PTSD benefits payments increased 148.8 percent from $1.7 billion to $4.3 billion. Compensation for all other disability categories only increased by 41.7 percent. While veterans being compensated for PTSD represented only 8.7 percent of all compensation recipients, they received 20.5 percent of all compensation payments.[60]

The number of PTSD cases also varied by state. New Mexico had the highest percent; 12.6 percent of all its VA disability compensation cases were diagnosed with PTSD. Illinois had the lowest rate at 2.8 percent of all its cases. These differences raised questions about whether the diagnosis of PTSD was being applied consistently.

The announcement that PTSD cases would be reviewed was met with a barrage of criticism from veterans groups and from members of Congress. If timing is everything, then with so many military personnel deployed in Iraq, the VA's announcement was ill planned. Eventually the VA called off its review saying that after examining a sample of claims and finding a great deal of missing documentation, it would instead increase training in case assessment and provide more administrative oversight to insure diagnostic accuracy.[61]

Americans with Disabilities Act

Chapter 5 illustrates the courts' role in deciding important social welfare issues. The Americans with Disabilities Act (ADA) is a legislative centerpiece of the rights of individuals with disabilities, but there have been many legal challenges to federal disability law. As noted in Chapter 5, one issue at the heart of ADA debates is states' sovereign immunity, that is, whether the states should be protected from ADA lawsuits under the

11th Amendment to the U.S. Constitution. This amendment holds that states cannot be sued without their permission. Responding to continuing state claims of sovereign immunity, the Fifth Circuit Court of Appeals ruled in October 2005 that the states are *not* protected from lawsuits that individuals may file claiming that their ADA rights have been violated because the states accept federal funds to carry out disability laws.[62] Despite this ruling, many disability advocacy groups are concerned that individuals with disabilities continue to lose cases against employers and that ADA protections are too weak. Some disability rights advocates are also concerned that any effort to overhaul the ADA in the current conservative political climate might only further weaken the law.[63]

Individuals with Disabilities Education Act

Another subject discussed in each edition of this book is the education of children with disabilities. The current cornerstone legislation on this topic is the Individuals with Disabilities Education Act (IDEA). In an ideal world, parents and school personnel would work hand-in-hand to insure that each child receives the best education possible. In the real world, parents, teachers, and schools sometimes disagree on what children should receive. In a 6 to 2 decision in November 2005, retiring U.S. Supreme Court Justice Sandra Day O'Connor expressed the majority opinion that since IDEA is silent on the issue of burden of proof, the burden of showing that a school district's plan for assisting a child with disability is inadequate lies with the plaintiff or the party seeking relief, usually the child's parents. Justices Ruth Bader Ginsburg and Steven Beyer disagreed, noting that since the law requires school systems to provide a "free appropriate public education," the proof that they are doing so lies with the school system.[64]

EXERCISES AND ACTIVITIES FOR CHAPTER 5 ───────────

1. Read Chapter 5 and then enter the keyword "disability" in Research Navigator to learn more about current disability issues before proceeding with the activities below.

2. Using Research Navigator and other search engines, enter the keywords "Supplemental Security Income" or "SSI" and "Social Security Disability Insurance" or "SSDI" to determine if there are new developments or issues in these programs. Also visit the Social Security Administration website (http://www.ssa.gov) to learn more about these programs. You may wish to invite a speaker from the Social Security Administration or other office that conducts disability determinations to learn more about the process, the disabilities most often seen, and the issues that disability determination specialists encounter in their work. You may also wish to invite physical and occupational therapists, mental health professionals, such as social workers or psychologists, or other professionals from public agencies like Vocational Rehabilitation and nonprofit agencies like Easter Seals, Goodwill Industries, and independent living centers, that assist individuals who have disabilities. Ask them what their work entails, issues that may hamper their work, and the methods they use to help people achieve work goals and other goals such as independent living. How would they like to see public policy and programs changed?

3. Invite speakers who have physical and/or mental disabilities to your class to talk about the problems they have encountered in realizing their potential or goals and the policies and programs, individuals and organizations, that have helped them the most and why.

4. Interview or invite speakers from advocacy groups like American Disabled for Attendant Programs Today (ADAPT) to class to discuss their work, the issues they face, and what they expect to happen in the near future with regard to disability rights and services.

5. Compare U.S. policies related to individuals with disabilities with policies in other developed countries. Class members can each investigate a different country. What are the differences in policies? Which policies do you regard as most progressive? What suggestions do you have for improving disability policy in the U.S.?

6. Use Research Navigator and other search engines and enter the keywords "VA PTSD" to read more about the controversy the Department of Veterans Affairs created when it was going to review the cases of veterans receiving disability compensation for a diagnosis of posttraumatic stress disorder. You can also learn more about the diagnosis of PTSD and other mental disorders in the American Psychiatric Association's, *Diagnostic and Statistical Manual of Mental Disorders* (4th ed., text revision, 2000). Would you have encouraged the VA to pursue its review, use the training and oversight measures it decided to adopt, or do both?

CHAPTER 6

Chapter 6 is concerned with policies that help support families with minor children and two major and interrelated programs intended to accomplish that goal: Child Support Enforcement and Temporary Assistance for Needy Families.

Child Support Enforcement

The Child Support Enforcement (CSE) program that each state operates helps custodial parents collect the support due to children from noncustodial parents. CSE programs define a case as a mother, father, or putative father who is obligated or may in the future be obligated to pay child support. In 2004, there were 15.9 million CSE cases. Divorce is one reason that CSE programs are important in collecting child support, but the growing number of births to unmarried mothers is even more significant. More than one-third of U.S. births are to unmarried mothers. In 2004, 35.7 percent of births were to unmarried women, up from 34.6 percent in 2003.

The federal government's Office of Child Support Enforcement notes the following trends from 2000 to 2004 in this important topic. [65]

♦ Despite the increase in births to unmarried women, there have been small decreases in the size of child support caseloads.

♦ The number of paternities established has remained between 1.5 and 1.6 million per year.

♦ The percentage of cases with support orders established increased from 62 percent to 74 percent.

♦ Collection of payments that are currently due increased from about 54 percent to about 59 percent.

♦ The number of cases in which at least some arrears (past due) collections are paid remains at about 60 percent.

♦ CSE programs have become slightly more efficient. In 2000, $4.23 was collected for every dollar spent; by 2004, $4.38 was being collected for every dollar spent.

Chapter 6 also notes that in 2002, the average amount of child support due custodial mothers was $5,138, and the average amount received was $3,193. Taken together, these figures indicate that under current policies and programs, (1) child support orders can be difficult to establish, (2) child support payments are often not easy to collect, and (3) many orders are for amounts that are likely insufficient to meet children's needs. Particularly vexing is that more progress has not been made in collecting current and arrears payments. These problems may be made worse by the 2005 Deficit Reduction Act that cut federal support to states to help collect child support and could result in $24 billion less in payments being collected over the next 10 years.[66] Chapter 6 addresses some reasons that child support enforcement has not been more successful, such as the unemployment or low-wage employment of the noncustodial parents who are required to make payments and the rifts or lack of contact that often occur between the custodial and noncustodial parent. About 80 percent of custodial parents are mothers, but a growing number of fathers are assuming this role. Most single parents work hard at raising their offspring, but it is no secret that parenthood is a difficult task, especially for financially strapped, single-parent families. Collecting child support is important because it can allow children a better standard of living. It also reduces the burden on public assistance, in particular, the program known as Temporary Assistance for Needy Families.

TANF

As discussed in Chapter 6, in 1996, legislation called the Personal Responsibility and Work Opportunity Reconciliation Act (PRWORA) established the Temporary Assistance for Needy Families (TANF) program to replace the Aid to Families with Dependent Children (AFDC) program. AFDC and TANF are often simply referred to as "welfare." In an attempt to "end welfare as we knew it," the word "temporary" in the title of the new program means that limits have been imposed on the length of time many families can receive assistance. Under TANF, more families are also expected to work.

Following the change from AFDC to TANF, caseloads dropped dramatically, by about 50 percent nationally. These changes were attributed as much to a strong economy that boosted low-wage employment as they were to TANF rules. In the last few years, caseloads have continued to decline, though at a slower rate. In fiscal year 2002, TANF caseloads averaged about 5.1 million recipients a month; in 2003, the average was 5 million recipients, and in 2004, 4.7 million recipients.[67] In March of 2005, approximately 4.5 million recipients comprising 1.9 million families were receiving TANF. As you will see in Chapter 6, this does not mean that families that left TANF are doing better financially. Some are working at jobs that do not afford sufficient salary or benefits to adequately provide for their families. Others have been terminated from TANF because they have not followed program rules, and some have "timed out."

The PRWORA expired in 2002. Due to a stalemate on reauthorizing the act, a series of temporary extensions were passed until February 2006 when Congress reauthorized the program until 2010 as part of the 2005 Deficit Reduction Act (DRA). Much of the disagreement centered on the Republicans' desire to increase work participation for parents but not increase childcare funding. The Republicans' argued that increased work is necessary for families to raise themselves out of poverty and off welfare. The Democrats' position was that if more parents are expected to work or to work more hours, increased childcare funding is critical because most TANF recipients are young children who cannot be left unsupervised.

Beginning in October 2006, the DRA changes the way states must calculate whether they are meeting the requirement that 50 percent of all TANF families and 90 percent of two-parent TANF families are working. Prior to this time, required work participation rates were reduced if the state kept TANF caseloads below 1995 levels. When TANF was first enacted, caseloads fell rapidly, resulting in lower (or no) work participation rate requirements for states. Now, states must meet the full work participation requirements unless they get caseloads below 2005 levels. This is a much more difficult task (especially the 90 percent participation rate for two-parent families) since caseloads can no longer be expected to drop rapidly. To avoid substantial financial penalties imposed by the federal government, states unable to meet these goals would have to drop families from TANF or find much more creative ways to assist them. Still to be decided is exactly what in addition to paid employment will count as work activities (volunteering, attending school, etc.). The DRA does include $1 billion more for childcare through 2010, but much less than the $6 billion the Senate wanted.[68] DRA also provides $150 million to help the Bush administration carry out its controversial agenda to strengthen marriages, $50 million of which can go to programs that encourage responsible fatherhood.

EXERCISES AND ACTIVITIES FOR CHAPTER 6

1. Enter the keywords "child support" in Research Navigator and read about any recent development or issues in national or state child support efforts. You may wish to invite a speaker from the public child support enforcement program in your community to talk about the procedures used to establish paternity, establish child support orders, determine the amount of support, and methods used to collect when a parent is in arrears. The speaker may also wish to comment on how federal cuts in child support enforcement funding have affected the program. How does your state compare with other states in child support collections? To add to the discussion, you may also wish to invite a representative of a private child support collection office.

2. Enter the keyword "welfare" in Research Navigator. Check to see if there are any updates on how changes brought by the 2005 Deficit Reduction Act have affected the Temporary Assistance for Needy Families program. Then check to see if TANF caseloads are remaining constant, increasing, or decreasing in recent months for the nation and for your state at http://www.acf.hhs.gov/programs/ofa/tanfindex.htm. You may wish to invite a speaker from the TANF office in your community, perhaps an eligibility worker, to discuss how a family applies and how eligibility is determined, how often cases are reviewed, and how childcare arrangements are being handled. You may also want to invite staff involved in the work participation aspects of TANF to discuss what activities now count as work requirements and how

new TANF regulations have affected efforts to help people become employed. You may also wish to invite current or former TANF recipients to discuss their experiences with the program.

CHAPTER 7

Chapter 7's main considerations are nutrition assistance for low-income individuals and families and encouraging the general population to eat healthier. This update also considers some of the growing international issues surrounding the sale of agricultural products and food aid to other countries.

Health, Weight, and Exercise

The primary domestic concern in the area of nutrition continues to be curbing growing rates of overweight and obesity. Adding a serving of humor to the issue, a writer for *The Oregonian* newspaper noted that the secretaries of Agriculture and Health and Human Services "urged Americans to do something about a national obesity level that threatens to affect the rotation of the planet."[69] Much of the advice on curbing this problem and the growing health concerns it raises sounds very familiar—eat less, eat healthier foods, and exercise more. A Texas legislator offered another approach—putting children's Body Mass Index on their school report cards. A nutrition expert at the American Council on Science and Health quickly countered the idea by saying that this "might cause undue focus on body image, resulting in stress, anxiety and possibly even eating disorders."[70] The bill failed, but news reports indicate that Britain's Education Secretary wants to go further, recommending "that superintendents of any schools that continue to serve junk food to children after it has been banned could face criminal prosecution."[71] Starting with school children may be easier than starting with adults, but eating habits may be established well before the first grade. Obesity is a growing issue even in some countries with high rates of malnutrition like India, which "struggles to eliminate malnutrition among the rural poor" while its "wealthy urbanites are packing on extra pounds because of sedentary lifestyles and the growing abundance of sugary, high-fat foods."[72]

USDA's New Nutritional Advice

To help Americans adopt healthier lifestyles, in 2005, the United States Department of Agriculture (USDA) issued the sixth edition of its recommended dietary guidelines, which put more emphasis on reducing calories and increasing physical activity. As sectors of the food industry vie for a position in the guidelines, the Sugar Association was "disappointed that the Guidelines chose to continue the recommendation to limit added sugars, particularly since [then U.S. Department of Health and Human Services] Secretary [Tommy] Thompson applauded the scientific basis of the 2005 Guidelines." The Association said "we stand firm in our assertion that every major scientific review, including the Institute of Medicine's macronutrient report, has concluded that there is not a direct link between added sugar intake and any lifestyle disease, including obesity."[73]

The USDA has retained its well-recognized food pyramid to dispense nutritional advice, but rather than one pyramid, there are now 12 because the population has different nutritional needs based on age, gender, and activity levels. Other differences are the vertical rather than horizontal segments to represent the different food groups, the different segment widths indicating how much intake should come from each group, and making clearer what a serving size is. The USDA website allows people to select a pyramid appropriate for them and contains interactive tools to help people eat right in order to maintain their current weight or lose weight.

In response to health concerns and to insure its profits, the food industry continues to modify its practices. For example, the National Automatic Merchandising Association has launched a campaign called Balanced for Life that focuses on helping customers make healthier selections from vending machines and educating children to make better snack choices.[74]

Food Stamp Program

The federal government's largest nutrition program for low-income Americans is the Food Stamp Program (FSP). From 1994 to 2000, food stamp program participation dropped from an average of 27.5 to 17.2 million individuals per month.[75] Since then participation has increased substantially. In 2005, an average of 25.7 million individuals participated per month, and total annual benefits have increased from $15 billion in 2000 to $28.6 billion in 2005. When administration costs are added, the federal government spent a total of $31 billion on the FSP in 2005. In 2005, the FSP was spared cuts that would have eliminated 300,000 individuals from the program to help address the budget deficit. The school meal programs were also spared cuts that would have eliminated 40,000 children from the programs.

It could be said that the FSP saves the federal government money because many eligible individuals do not participate in the program. A Brookings Institution report demonstrates that some communities (and therefore the states in which they are located) are losing out on billions in food stamp allotments that could benefit their economies and help individual households.[76] This is because communities even in the same state may have widely different participation or "take up" rates (the number receiving food stamps compared to the number eligible to receive them). Some of these differences are related to population characteristics. For example, as discussed in Chapter 7, young families are more likely to participate than the elderly. The extent to which people in a community know about and use the program and barriers such as distance to the application sites may also effect take up rates.

Farm Subsidies

Questions remain as to how fair it is for the federal government to continue to pay large subsidies to members of a particular industry, especially to major corporations that increasingly dominate the agriculture industry. This form of agricultural "corporate welfare" is estimated at about $19 billion annually, not counting other benefits like low-cost water contracts.[77] President Bush's attempts to cut farm subsidies and his desire to end them altogether do not set well with people in the Midwest, who provided a strong base of support in his presidential elections. They also do not set well with others in the farming industry and their elected representatives.

Farm subsidies have international as well as domestic implications. The U.S. is facing increased international pressure to cut or eliminate farm subsidies because farmers in poorer countries that do not pay subsidies are disadvantaged compared to farmers that receive subsidies. The Bush administration position is that "dismantling trade barriers multilaterally holds immense potential for the United States," and the Doha Development Agenda [named after talks in Doha, Qatar, located in the Middle East] would "open markets, reduce poverty, and expand freedom through increased trade among all countries in the global trading system, developed and developing."[78] There is a long way to go before this goal is reached as countries battle with each over what they consider illegal or unfair trade practices. While President Bush tries to reduce farm subsidies, the World Trade Organization (WTO) ruled in a case brought by Brazil that the U.S. has exceeded subsidy limits on cotton. And in another case brought by Brazil, Australia, and Thailand, the WTO's ruling was that the European Union had exceeded subsidy limits on sugar.[79] The U.S. has also used the WTO process to challenge other countries' subsidies.

In addition to subsidies, tariffs on goods are also criticized as another "trade distorting" barrier. For example, tariffs keep sugar from other countries out of the U.S. and inflate sugar prices for Americans. Apparently, the price of sugar is causing candy makers to move elsewhere.[80] A case in point is the Lifesaver plant, which moved from Holland, Michigan to Canada. And in Niger, Africa, one of the least developed countries in the world, people are starving, in part because getting food into a country with bad roads and African civil wars is difficult. But even within sub-Saharan Africa, tariffs are as high as 33 percent, making it difficult for countries in the region that could help to provide food to countries in need. [81]

EXERCISES AND ACTIVITIES FOR CHAPTER 7

1. Study the U.S. Department of Agriculture's (USDA's) new dietary guidelines and food pyramids at http://www.fns.usda. Look at the pyramid for your gender, age, and activity level. Chart your food consumption and activity level for a few days. How close do they come to the USDA's recommendations? Do you think the guidelines will help Americans eat healthier and exercise more? If not, discuss what you think can be done to make Americans healthier.

2. Learn more about farm subsidies and how they work by visiting the websites of the U.S. Department of Agriculture, Word Trade Organization, organizations representing farm groups in the U.S., or other relevant organizations. Using Research Navigator, enter the keywords "farm subsidies" and find out if President Bush has been successful in cutting them. Also enter the keyword "tariffs." Discuss in class the effects that subsidies and tariffs have on the U.S. and other countries and what your thoughts are regarding the elimination of trade barriers throughout the world.

3. Using Research Navigator, enter the keywords "famine" or "starvation" and learn more about current food crises in the world. Visit the sites of organizations that address hunger worldwide like Oxfam or Feed the Children. Also visit sites of organizations such as the United Nations and World Health Organization. You may wish to invite representatives of anti-hunger

organizations in your community to discuss causes of hunger and long-term solutions to the problem. What steps should be taken to prevent hunger in the U.S. and across the globe? Investigate further what the U.S. and other developed countries give to help those in other parts of the world. Do you believe the U.S. and other countries should do more or are they meeting their obligations? Discuss the possible impacts of eradicating world hunger.

CHAPTER 8

Chapter 8 is dedicated to health care policy, including the rising rate of uninsured and increasing health care costs that leave Americans vulnerable when they need health care and cannot afford it.

More Uninsured as Health Care Costs Rise

In 2004, 45.8 million individuals in the U.S. (15.7 percent of the population) were uninsured,[82] up from 44.2 million (15.2% of the population) in 2002. These figures cover individuals with no health insurance at *any* time during the year and exclude those that were covered for part of the year. Those least likely to have health insurance were poor, young adults, and people of color, especially Hispanics. Texas remains the state with the highest rate of uninsured (25.1% of its population based on 3-year averages from 2002 to 2004), while Minnesota had the lowest uninsured rate (8.5 percent).

Government-sponsored health insurance programs continue to increase in importance. This is because the percentage of the population covered by employer-based health insurance has decreased (to just under 60 percent or 174 million individuals in 2004), while the percent covered by government programs has increased (to just over 27 percent or 79 million in 2004). This increase is largely due to those helped by Medicaid, the joint federal-state program for some segments of the poor and low-income population. As health care costs rise, more employers have dropped health insurance coverage for employees. Even if coverage is offered, employees may not participate because their share of the coverage for themselves or their family members is too costly. The Chapter 3 update noted that medical bills are the leading cause of bankruptcy in the U.S. Researchers at the Commonwealth Fund have also found that medical debt is a problem for the insured as well as the uninsured.[83] Some individuals with insurance have high deductibles, co-insurance payments, or other out-of-pocket costs.

In addition to an expanding Medicaid caseload, enrollment in Medicare also continues to rise as the older population in the U.S. grows rapidly. Medicare is the federal government's health care program for virtually all Americans aged 65 and older and some younger people with long-term disabilities or illnesses. The 2005 Deficit Reduction Act hit health care hard. Predictions are that by 2015, 65,000 individuals, mostly children, who would have received Medicaid will not be getting it, and 13 million more Medicaid recipients, already poor or low-income by definition, will be paying substantially higher costs out of their own pockets.[84] Costs for Medicare recipients will also increase.

At the same time that the uninsured population is growing, U.S. health expenditures continue to rise, not only in absolute terms, but also as a percent of the country's gross domestic product (GDP). In 2001, the U.S. spent 13.9 percent of its GDP on health care;

in 2003 that figure was 15 percent. Per capita health expenditures for these same years grew from $4,887 to $5,635.[85] These figures remain well above other developed nations as described in Chapter 8. When the uninsured are forced to use expensive emergency room care for routine health care needs like a bad cold or wait until their health problems are so severe that they require extensive treatment, the costs of health care rise needlessly. Yet the federal and state governments do not even offer basic well-care (routine or preventive) coverage for all Americans who cannot afford to pay for it themselves.

Medical Marijuana

A topic not previously discussed in this book is the use of marijuana for medical purposes. Despite contentions that marijuana has a legitimate use in treating some medical conditions, such as the nausea that often accompanies chemotherapy treatments, marijuana, or cannabis, is classified as a Schedule 1 drug under the U.S. Controlled Substances Act. Schedule 1 "is reserved for the most dangerous drugs that have no recognized medical use," and includes drugs like heroin and ecstasy (MDMA). [86] Though many college students might laugh at the thought of classifying cannabis with heroin, and think of it more as a recreational drug like alcohol, cannabis for medical use has gained public attention. The Bush administration's position is that there is no legitimate use of cannabis.

Eleven states now have laws that allow marijuana use for medical purposes. The question arises as to whether these state laws conflict with federal law, since federal law bans marijuana use for any purpose. The U.S. Supreme Court agreed to hear a case brought by two California residents that focused on growing marijuana at home for personal, medical use. Federal agents raided the home of one of the women where she grew marijuana, and federal lawyers argued that growing marijuana affects the supply of drugs, and therefore, drug trafficking and interstate commerce. The women's lawyers argued that marijuana grown for personal use does not result in interstate commerce and is therefore not subject to federal law. [87] In June 2005, the U.S. Supreme court affirmed that federal law supersedes state law and that the federal law is a legitimate exercise of power because the matter concerns interstate commerce. The justices' vote was surprising because some of the court's more liberal members took the position that federal law prevailed, while some of the more conservative members, including then Chief Justice William Rehnquist, were more amenable to limiting federal authority in this case. [88] The ruling said nothing about whether marijuana might be an effective medical treatment. The Marijuana Policy Project contends that the U.S. Supreme Court decision does nothing to change the legality of state laws.[89] But that point seems moot since federal authorities can arrest individuals for using marijuana, even for medical reasons.

Since federal law supersedes state law, the U.S. Congress could play an important role in medical marijuana use. Though some Congress members, such as Representative Barney Frank (Democrat-Massachusetts), have tried to raise the issue in Washington, Congress is highly unlikely to pass a law supporting medical marijuana use any time in the near future. For those who believe in the legitimacy of marijuana use for medical reasons, the interstate commerce clause may seem like a stretch as a point of argument. More important from the point of common sense is whether there are legitimate medical uses of marijuana. In 2001 the American Medical Association took the position that more study of marijuana for medical purposes is needed, but for the time being, marijuana should remain on Schedule 1 of the Controlled Substance Act.[90] An October 2002 CNN/Time poll indicated that 59 percent of adults in the U.S. opposed legalizing marijuana (down from more than 70 percent in the 1980s), but that 72 percent thought that those arrested for possessing small amounts should "just have to pay a fine without serving any jail time"; even more (80 percent) thought that "adults should be allowed to legally use marijuana for medical purposes if their doctor prescribes it."[91] The next medical marijuana case we might be discussing is one that the California Supreme Court is set to hear. It involves a man who was fired from his job for medical use of marijuana.

Medical Ethics

Concerns about medical ethics continue to mount as science advances at a rapid rate. This update contains information on two medical ethics issues: (1) the Terri Schindler-Schiavo right-to-life case and (2) physician-assisted suicide.

Terri Schindler-Schiavo developed a medical problem that resulted in her long-term incapacitation. Her case drew international media attention because her parents believed she was responsive (had some brain activity) and could be helped with treatment, while her husband contended she was in a persistent vegetative state and wanted to remove the feeding tube that was keeping her alive. The case is especially noteworthy because of the unprecedented intervention it received from Florida Governor Jeb Bush, the Florida legislature, the U.S. Congress, and President George W. Bush. The history of the case, including actions in Florida, is discussed in Chapter 8. To update, the U.S. Congress passed a law that allowed Schindler-Schiavo's parents to appeal to the federal courts to challenge her husband's directive to remove her feeding tube, and President Bush signed it. [92] These actions pitted those who felt that the federal government had no right to intervene in this personal family matter against those who felt that it was Congress's duty to assure Schindler-Schiavo equal protection under the law. A federal judge refused to order reinsertion of the feeding tube and an appeal to the 11th Circuit court failed. The U.S. Supreme Court also refused to intervene. Terri Schindler-Schiavo died on March 31, 2005. An autopsy revealed that the brain damage she suffered was irreversible, but the legal and ethical issues in this case continue to be debated.

Physician-Assisted Suicide

Since 1998, approximately 200 people have reportedly hastened their deaths under Oregon's Death with Dignity Act, which permits physician-assisted suicide. In January 2006, the U.S. Supreme Court issued a narrow decision regarding the act. The decision said that in 2001, then-Attorney General John Ashcroft overstepped his authority by threatening to prosecute doctors who prescribed lethal doses of drugs regulated under the federal Controlled Substances Act of 1970.[93] Ashcroft had issued an "interpretive rule" contending that the use of federally controlled substances to assist suicide is not a legitimate medical use of the substances. The Supreme Court's 2006 ruling does not, however, change its 1997 decision that there is no constitutional right to take one's own life.

Oregon remains the only state with a physician-assisted suicide law. Assisting suicide is a crime in 44 states and the District of Columbia. Though other states have not joined Oregon, the 2006 ruling will certainly invigorate advocates' efforts to press for such laws. Also at issue is whether the U.S. Congress will pass a law on the subject. If it does, it is likely to be a law that makes physician-assisted suicide illegal.

EXERCISES AND ACTIVITIES FOR CHAPTER 8

1. Check the publication Carmen De Navas-Walt, Bernadette D. Proctor, and Cheryl Hill Lee, *Income, Poverty, and Health Insurance Coverage in the United States: 2004,* Washington DC: U.S. Census Bureau, August 2005, to see where your state stands in the percent of uninsured individuals. Invite health policy experts to discuss factors that account for your state's ranking.

2. Using Research Navigator, enter the keywords "right to life," "right to die," and "physician-assisted suicide" to determine if there have been new events or decisions on these matters. Invite speakers such as medical ethicists, members of the organization End-of-Life Choices, clergy, and staff of organizations or agencies that serve people with severe disabilities to discuss their positions on the issue or hold a class debate on the topic. Think about the choices you would like to have if severely disabled or near the end of life.

3. Investigate living wills and advance medical directives. Discuss the opportunities that these documents provide to individuals to express their desires and allow others to carry out their wishes. Also consider problems or drawbacks they may pose. Do you or your loved ones have these directives? If not, do you see the need to have them? If so, as a personal exercise, think about the desires you would express.

4. Using Research Navigator, enter the keywords "medical marijuana" to determine if there has been any change on the subject. Also study the research on whether or not cannabis is an effective treatment for some conditions and whether or not it is more effective than other treatments. Does the research convince you one way or the other? Invite individuals representing agencies like the Drug Enforcement Administration or the Food and Drug Administration and organizations like the Drug Policy Alliance (http://www.drugpolicy.org/homepage.cfm) or Marijuana Policy Project (http://www.mpp.org), individuals who may be using marijuana for medical purposes, and physicians to discuss the issue, or hold a class debate on the topic.

CHAPTER 9

Chapter 9 addresses changing paradigms in the poverty wars and focuses on the policies and programs of the 1960s War on Poverty and the Great Society. Many programs that emerged during this period have grown in importance, including food stamps, Medicare, and Medicaid, discussed in other chapters of this book. Policies and programs discussed in Chapter 9 include Head Start, legal services, community action, education legislation, minimum wage legislation, job training, and enterprise and empowerment zones.

Recent waves of the poverty wars have been of a different genre than the 1960s War on Poverty. During the Clinton era, there was retrenchment of public assistance through the Temporary Assistance for Needy Families program and more emphasis on work requirements. This was called "ending welfare as we know it." During the George W. Bush administration, the emphasis has included using faith-based organizations and other private community organizations to address poverty. One might also say that today, no war to end poverty is being waged. Below are updates on two topics of Chapter 9, the No Child Left Behind Act and the minimum wage.

No Child Left Behind

The No Child Left Behind (NCLB) Act is the Bush administration's centerpiece educational legislation and the latest incarnation of the Elementary and Secondary School Act of 1965. NCLB, discussed at greater length in Chapter 9, has many states and school districts in an uproar, in part because it forces them to comply with educational mandates, primarily in reading and math, which the federal government does not fully fund, and imposes sanctions when schools do not perform well enough. Among other things, the act also contains prescriptive language about teaching techniques and gives parents options to move children out of schools that fail to meet goals. In 2005, a U.S. district judge granted the U.S. Department of Education's request to dismiss a lawsuit alleging that the federal government should not force the states to spend their own money to comply with NCLB. The judgment stated that the law only prohibits "federal officials and employees from imposing additional, unfunded requirements, beyond those provided for in the statute."[94]

NCLB is also controversial because education has largely been the purview of states and communities, which resent federal direction when they believe that goals are too prescriptive, unrealistic, or punitive. Battles over NCLB will continue to be fought. In February 2006, the *New York Times* reported that about 226,00 students (less than 12 percent of eligible students) were using tutoring services provided for by the act. Among the reasons given were that these services are new and not well funded, parents are not well informed about them, and signing up is complicated.[95]

Still No Raise for the Minimum Wage

Despite the continuing efforts of Senator Edward Kennedy (Democrat-Massachusetts) and the work of Republicans such as Senator Rick Santorum of Pennsylvania and Senator Michael Enzi of Wyoming, the federally established minimum wage has not been raised in nearly a decade. Unlike federal social welfare benefits such as Social Security, Supplemental Security Income, and food stamps, which Congress allows to increase automatically with inflation, the minimum wage must wait for Congress to act. Since the federal minimum wage was established in 1938, Congress has never gone this long without enacting an increase. Thus, the purchasing power of the minimum wage has plummeted.

We might have sympathy for a small business owner struggling to make ends meet and unable to pay more than the minimum wage. Minnesota has begun to address this issue by requiring businesses earning at least $625,000 a year to pay higher wages than those earning less. Approximately one-third of states have already enacted a minimum wage higher than the federal minimum, and Washington (which currently has the highest hourly minimum wage at $7.63) and Oregon index their minimum wage to inflation.

Nevada is considering requiring employers that do not provide health insurance to pay higher wages. [96]

As Chapter 9 notes, only 3 percent of U.S. workers aged 16 and older earn the federal minimum wage or less, but this amounts to more than 2 million individuals and does not include the millions who earn only slightly more. At $5.15 an hour, the current federal minimum wage barely puts a single full-time worker over the poverty threshold. If small business owners cannot afford to hire lobbyists to work against raising the minimum wage, then other richer and more powerful business interests must be doing so.[97] In light of Congressional inaction on the minimum wage, living wage campaigns such as Let Justice Roll are targeting states to establish higher minimum wages.

EXERCISES AND ACTIVITIES FOR CHAPTER 9

1. Enter the keywords "No Child Left Behind" in Research Navigator to find out if there have been any new developments in the No Child Left Behind Act. Invite local school personnel or representatives of teachers' unions and organizations to discuss the act and their views of whether it is helping or hurting students and schools.

2. Enter the keywords "minimum wage" in Research Navigator to find out if there has been any movement on federal or state minimum wage legislation. Determine if your state and/or community has minimum wage legislation. If so, how does it differ from the federal minimum wage and that of neighboring states' policies? Contact local employers to determine their starting wage. How do the federal minimum wage, state minimum wage (if any in your state), and prevailing wages in your community compare with what it takes to live in your community? Read more about the arguments for and against raising the federal minimum wage and discuss them in class.

CHAPTER 10

The topic of Chapter 10 is social services. It focuses on services to people who have a mental illness or alcohol or drug problems, youth who are served by the child welfare system and need protective services or adoption, and older Americans in need of social services, especially services that help them live more independently.

Mental Health Policy

In the mental health arena, results from a new study called the National Comorbidity Survey (NCS) Replication are now being published as a follow up to the original NCS discussed in Chapter 10. Like the original study, the replication found that nearly half (46 percent) of Americans will have a mental disorder at sometime in their life. [98] Most mental illnesses begin early in life—half of all cases occur by age 14 and three-quarters by age 24. The study also found that more individuals experiencing mental illness in the last 12 months are receiving some form of treatment, increasing from 19 percent in the 1980s, to 25 percent in the 1990s, and now 41 percent.[99] Those treated in the specialty mental health sector get more and better services than those treated in the general medical sector. Those most likely to have unmet treatment needs are older persons, people of color, low-income persons, those with no insurance, and rural residents. These findings confirm that many people still do not get treatment and that much more focus is needed on the mental health needs of youth, since problems often manifest early, and segments of the population that are underserved.

The work of President Bush's New Freedom Commission on Mental Health, appointed in 2002, is discussed at length in Chapter 10. As a follow up to the report, the federal government's Substance Abuse and Mental Health Services Administration has published an ambitious set of action steps to bring these ideas to fruition. The steps encompass everything from use of technology and websites to provide the public with information on mental illness, to developing new medications and use of evidenced-based mental health treatment practices. Also among the steps is establishment of a Federal Executive Steering Committee on Mental Health to "model the type of collaborative efforts required for system transformation at the state and local levels." [100] But providing mental health services is largely a state and local responsibility, and services are woefully underfunded in many areas. Improving the mental health of Americans, especially those with severe mental illnesses, is also going to take an ongoing infusion of cash to hire treatment providers and encourage service use among the various segments on the population.

Child Welfare

The 2005 Deficit Reduction Act (DRA) made some changes to child welfare legislation. In particular, it reverses the Rosales decision, which allowed children removed from their homes by child welfare authorities and living with other relatives to receive TANF based on these relatives' income. Prior to this decision, the child was eligible only if the home from which he or she was removed was eligible for TANF. The decision applies only to nine western states covered by the Ninth Circuit Court, but other states have filed appeals based on the decision. As a result of the DRA, children living with grandparents and other relatives may be penalized and the entire low-income family will have less to live on.

On a more positive note, the DRA provides some funds for improving courts' oversight of child welfare cases through performance measures, and to train state supreme court judges, attorneys, and other child welfare personnel in case proceedings. It also provides an additional $200 million for the Safe and Stable Families Act for family preservation, family reunification, and adoption services, but the Coalition on Human Needs says that the cuts in child welfare services "far outweigh" the increases. [101]

White House Conference on Aging

In the area of policy for older Americans, the fifth White House Conference on Aging met in December of 2005 with older individuals from the around the country serving as delegates. Delegates passed 50 resolutions. The top 10 are:

1. Reauthorize the Older Americans Act.

2. Develop a coordinated, comprehensive, long-term care strategy by supporting public and private sector initiatives that address financing, choice, quality, service delivery, and the paid and unpaid workforce.

3. Ensure transportation options to retain mobility and independence.

4. Improve the Medicaid program for older Americans.

5. Improve the Medicare program.

6. Support geriatric education for all healthcare professionals, paraprofessionals, health profession students, and direct care workers.

7. Promote innovative models of non-institutional long-term care.

8. Improve recognition, assessment, and treatment of mental illness and depression among older Americans.

9. Attain adequate numbers of healthcare personnel in all professions who are skilled, culturally competent, and specialized geriatrics.

10. Improve state and local based integrated delivery systems to meet 21st century needs of seniors.[102]

The recommendations remain lofty, but hopefully they will spur legislative and executive action to insure better treatment of older Americans. The rapidly graying baby boom generation will demand it.

EXERCISES AND ACTIVITIES FOR CHAPTER 10

1. Enter the keywords "mental health" or "mental illness" in Research Navigator to read about recent developments in mental health and mental illness policy and services. Invite representatives from your state's mental health and substance abuse authority and local mental health and alcohol and drug agencies to discuss how mental health and alcohol and drug services are funded and inquire about the numbers served, the gaps between the numbers served and the numbers in need, and policies that the speakers believe are especially helpful in delivering services. You may also wish to invite past or current clients or consumers of mental health and alcohol and drug services to determine what they feel are helpful mental health policies and which they feel are detrimental to clients.

2. Using Research Navigator, enter keywords such as "older Americans," "older adults," or "aging" to read about recent developments in the field of aging or gerontology. Interview older relatives and friends about services they have used or wish were available. Invite speakers to class from the state aging agency or organizations like the American Association of Retired Persons, the Area Aging on Aging, or the Meals on Wheels program to learn more about policies and social services for older people in your community. What seem to be the strong points of the services? What are the weaknesses or gaps?

CHAPTER 11

Chapter 11 discusses many civil rights issues and related concerns that affect people as a result of their gender, sexual orientation, color, or country of origin. Significant events continue to unfold in each of these areas.

Violence Against Women Act

In October 2005, Congress reauthorized the Violence Against Women Act (VAWA), originally passed in 1994 and first reauthorized in 2000. The new VAWA continues programs established under the act and adds new provisions. Changes include a new definition of stalking, new housing provisions, the first federal funding stream for sexual assault programs, and broader service provisions for children and teenagers. VAWA's reauthorization was hailed as a success by women's organizations and criticized by a number of men's organizations and some conservative groups. For example, an organization called Respecting Accuracy in Domestic Abuse Reporting (RADAR) claims VAWA "blatantly discriminates against men."[103] Among the opposition's criticisms of VAWA are that it fails to recognize that men are often victims of domestic violence, judges may issue restraining orders on the word of a woman without sufficient evidence that violence has occurred, and it unjustly promotes separation of men from their children. Among the counterarguments are that women are overwhelmingly the victims of domestic violence and that men who are victims of domestic violence can also seek assistance under VAWA.

Sexual Assault and the Military

Another recent development in the area of sexual assault is the policy changes made in response to the U.S. Congress's order to the Department of Defense to prevent and address the problem within the branches of the military. This order resulted from several sexual assault scandals in the military. The fiscal 2005 Defense authorization bill required the Pentagon to review the Uniform Code of Military Justice and the Manual for Courts-Martial to better assist sexual assault victims. Among the elements of the new policy are closer monitoring of cases and increased care and support for victims, including increased confidentiality protections.[104] Victims can obtain medical treatment or counseling without their commanders knowing, and they do not have to press charges against the assailant. The intent of this policy is to encourage victims to seek help without fear of triggering an investigation, as was previously the case. Commanders would receive information on cases but information that would identify the victim is supposed to be excluded except under certain circumstances, for example, if the victim's or others' future safety is in jeopardy.[105]

The military academies, where other well-publicized sexual assaults have occurred, are also attempting to take action. The Task Force on Sexual Harassment and Violence at the Military Service Academies noted that "the record of the two Academies [the United States Military Academy and the United States Naval Academy], much like the record of the Department of Defense, is one of sporadic and incomplete attempts to eliminate sexual harassment and assault."[106] It urged a sexual assault confidentiality procedure similar to that adopted by the Pentagon, increasing the number of female officers in key positions and the number of female cadets and midshipmen at the academies, and insuring victims that their federally mandated rights will be protected.

Abortion

The U.S. Supreme Court has not heard an abortion case in several years, but in January 2006, it issued a decision on a parental notification case. The ruling was unanimous but narrow. It said that a lower court erred in striking down New Hampshire's parental notification law. An appeals court must now reconsider the law. The Supreme Court did not rule on the major issues that parental notification raises, such as whether the law places undue burden on young women seeking an abortion. Most states have parental notification or consent laws. The court suggested that the New Hampshire law may be too stringent, and some of the justices indicated that allowing doctors to use a court order to forego parental notification in medical emergencies might solve the problem. [107] Abortion foes hailed the ruling as further evidence that parents have a right to be involved in critical medical decisions their daughters make. Pro-choice groups assailed it as another decision that chips away at abortion rights. The appeals court will now decide how the law might be amended and if it is unconstitutional.

The Supreme Court is now set to rule on the highly controversial procedure commonly referred to as "partial birth abortions," discussed in Chapter 11. A law passed by Congress in 2003 banned the procedure except to save the woman's life and did not include a provision to preserve a woman's health. The Supreme Court's decision to hear the case is unusual because three federal appeals courts concurred that it should be struck down.[108]

Emergency Contraception

Another reproductive rights issue that erupted in 2005 concerned the emergency contraception drug "Plan B," also called the "morning after pill." Plan B is not RU-486, the abortion pill. Plan B helps in preventing pregnancy, not terminating a pregnancy that has already occurred. According to its manufacturer, Plan B may be effective if used up to 72 hours after rape or other unprotected intercourse or contraception failure, but the sooner it is taken, the more effective it is. [109] One reason that Plan B became controversial is that some pharmacists have refused to fill prescriptions for the drug, causing the governor of Illinois to issue an emergency rule requiring that pharmacists fill prescriptions promptly.

Plan B is currently available only by prescription, but the drug also became controversial when the FDA failed to approve it for over-the-counter (without a prescription) sales despite scientific evidence of its safety and recommendations by the Food and Drug Administration's (FDA) joint advisory committee and FDA review staff to approve it. A Government Accountability Office (GAO) report also noted that the FDA did not use traditional practices in making its decision on Plan B.[110] The GAO reported that between 1994 and 2000, this was the only case in which a request to switch a drug from prescription to over-the-counter sales had been rejected after the advisory committees recommended it. Conservative pro-life groups applauded the FDA's decision and pro-choice groups lambasted it.

The FDA commissioner's explanation for the latest delay in making the drug available over-the-counter is that the drug should not be available over the counter for women younger than age 17 because of concerns that they may not use the drug properly. Susan Wood, then head of the FDA's Office of Women's Health, resigned in protest.

Supreme Court

Following the death of Supreme Court Chief Justice William Rehnquist, President Bush quickly nominated John Roberts to head the court, and his Senate confirmation hearings went as smoothly as might be expected in the current political climate. Roberts was confirmed with 78 votes for and 22 against. Historically, this is a narrow margin for a Supreme Court justice.[111] All the dissenters were Democrats.

Replacing retiring Justice Sandra Day O'Connor was far less smooth. Both Democrats and Republicans opposed President Bush's nomination of Harriet Miers, generally agreeing that she lacked the necessary judicial experience. Eventually she withdrew from consideration. The vacancies on the high court have led to debates about whether a priority should be placed on appointing a woman or person to color to fill these seats, but following Miers's withdrawal, President Bush nominated Samuel Alito, a white male, whom many conservatives and Republicans championed and many liberals and Democrats attacked.

In theory, justices are supposed to be selected for their knowledge of constitutional law and their willingness to decide cases based on constitutional principles rather than on personal views or a desire to legislate from the bench. Abortion is only one issue on the country's agenda, but it is a hot-button issue and garners a great deal of attention when it comes to filling vacancies on the nation's highest court. Pro-life and pro-choice forces try to discern just how a nominee will vote on the issue based on past comments or case decisions, though the justices rule on many other important matters that also deserve consideration.[112] Pro-choice groups stridently opposed Alito's confirmation. Democrats also raised concerns about whether Alito would provide a sufficient check on executive (presidential powers) and support of individual rights. After very contentious Senate hearings and threats of a filibuster, Alito was confirmed in a highly partisan 58 to 42 vote. Only four Democrats voted for his confirmation. In his first vote as a U.S. Supreme Court Justice, Alito took what some called the liberal position, refusing to overturn a lower court's decision to stay the execution of an inmate who argued that death by lethal inject constitutes cruel and unusual punishment. An appeals court will now determine whether the method used is cruel and unusual. Pro-life and pro-choice forces are also anxiously awaiting Alito's vote on the partial birth abortion case.

Gay Rights

There is no hotter issue on the gay rights agenda than that of marriage for gay men and lesbians. In January 2006, a Baltimore judge said Maryland's 33-year-old law banning gay marriage was unconstitutional, but Massachusetts remains the only state that issues marriage licenses to same-sex couples. Four states (New Jersey, New Mexico, New York, and Rhode Island) and the District of Columbia have no explicit provision prohibiting such marriages. Connecticut and Vermont sanction civil unions entitling same-sex couples to state-level spousal rights; Hawaii, Maine, and New Jersey provide some spousal-like rights to unmarried couples; and California has a domestic partnership law that provides nearly all state-level spousal rights to unmarried couples.[113] All other states have constitutional amendments or laws defining marriage as a union between a man and a woman and most assert that they will not recognize the marriage of same sex partners performed in another state.[114] In November 2005, Texas became the latest state to adopt a constitutional amendment to outlaw gay marriage. Worldwide, the Netherlands, Belgium, Canada, and Spain allow same sex marriages.

A July 2005 Pew Research Center poll found that 36 percent of Americans favored allowing gays and lesbians to marry; 53 percent were opposed, and 11 percent were unsure. More (53 percent) were favorable toward allowing legal agreements giving "many of the same rights as married couples," while 40 percent were opposed and 7 percent were unsure.[115] If public opinion polls are correct, they show more support for civil unions than marriage for gays, but considerable opposition to both apparently remains among voters.

Voting Rights

The Voting Rights Act (VRA) of 1965 has done a great deal to insure that all Americans have the same right to vote and to elect representatives of their choice. Section 2 of the act is permanent, pertains to all jurisdictions, and prohibits jurisdictions from using procedures that deny minorities the opportunity to elect officials of their choice. In bringing suit under the act, the burden of proof is on those claiming that practices are discriminatory. A University of Michigan project documented 323 lawsuits brought under Section 2 since 1982.[116]

Some VRA provisions are slated for reauthorization in 2007. To prepare for the renewal process, the Judiciary Committee of the U.S. House of Representatives has been holding hearings to determine what changes, if any, should be made. Many individuals' attention is focused on Section 5 of the act, which pertains only to "covered" jurisdictions.[117] On November 1, 1964, these jurisdiction had a "test or device" (e.g., literacy test) that restricted the opportunity to register and vote, and less than half of residents of voting age in the jurisdiction were registered to vote or less than half voted in the November 1964 presidential election. Later this date was extended to November 1968. Currently, covered jurisdictions include the entire states of Alabama, Alaska, Georgia, Louisiana, Mississippi, South Carolina, and Texas, most of Virginia, and some of California, Florida, Michigan, New Hampshire, New York, North Carolina, and South Dakota. Any changes in voting rules in these areas must be "precleared" (approved) by the U.S. Attorney General or following a lawsuit heard by the United States District Court for the District of Columbia.

The American Civil Liberties Union and other groups are urging Congress to restore Section 5 to its original meaning. They are reacting to the 2003 U.S. Supreme Court decision in *Georgia v. Ashcroft* which they believe weakened Section 5 by allowing approval of redistricting plans that limit minority communities' ability to elect candidates as long as " 'other factors' supposedly 'balance' the retrogressive impact of the changes."[118] The ACLU contends that as a result of this decision, minority voters may be able to effect election of White candidates but not minority candidates. Some people think that the need for Section 5 has passed because the direct voting barriers that prompted it no longer exist and because Section 2 provides the necessary protections to address problems today. Others believe that the problems that minorities have encountered in recent elections, including being more likely to have their votes discounted, show that Section 5 is still needed.

Congress has also been working on legislation that requires more proof of identity in voter registration. One viewpoint is that this would reduce voter fraud; another is that increasing the types of required identification could prove discriminatory. The need for a paper trail in electronic voting machines also continues to be an issue. Voting jurisdictions have a tough job in selecting from among the many choices that technology affords.

Immigration

President Bush has taken political heat from both Democrats and Republicans for push-ing immigration legislation that includes a guest worker program. The Bush plan would allow undocumented immigrants to apply for guest worker status that would permit them to remain in the U.S. for three years. Then they must be reapproved or return to their home country. Senator Jon Cornyn (Republican-Texas) has proposed an alternative that would require undocumented immigrants to return home after their allotted stay and then apply to return to the U.S. Both plans have drawbacks. The Bush plan might deter undocumented individuals from applying because they might be forced to return home after three years. The Cornyn plan would disrupt the lives of those in the U.S. with homes, families, and jobs with no guarantee that they would be permitted to return. This and other aspects of immigration reform continue to be major political issues.

EXERCISES AND ACTIVITIES FOR CHAPTER 11

1. Invite a representative from the local domestic violence coalition and/or sexual assault coali-tion or from the local domestic violence/battered women's shelter or sexual assault program to discuss the Violence Against Women's Act and its importance. You may also wish to invite representatives of men's groups to discuss their views (pro and con) on VAWA.

2. Using Research Navigator, enter the keywords "Plan B" and determine if there has been any movement on making the contraceptive drug Plan B available over-the-counter.

3. Using Research Navigator, enter the keyword "abortion" and track developments at the federal and state levels in abortion legislation and court decisions.

4. Using Research Navigator, enter the keyword "Supreme Court" and read about some recent U.S. Supreme Court decisions. Have a class discussion on whether you agree or disagree with the high court's decisions. What effects have the appointments of Chief Justice Roberts and Justice Alito had on the court?

5. Using Research Navigator, enter the keywords "gay marriage" and determine if other states have taken action for or against gay marriage.

6. Using Research Navigator, enter the keywords "immigration" and "guest worker" and deter-mine the current status of plans to modify immigration policy.

CHAPTER 12

The subjects of Chapter 12 are policy implementation and evaluation. Chapter 1 also notes the difficulties that ensue when large, segmented bureaucracies try to implement public policy. Two recent and noteworthy examples of the difficulties, and sometimes the debacles, of implementation are governments' response to Hurricane Katrina and the ini-tiation of the federal government's new prescription drug program for older and long-term disabled Americans.

Emergency Preparedness: The Buck Stops Where?

In the wake of Hurricane Katrina, Americans were stunned by the lives lost and damaged sustained, largely because the National Weather Service had forecasted that this would be one of the fiercest hurricanes in the nation's history. Criticism was directed at the city government of New Orleans, the state government of Louisiana, and the Federal Emergency Management Agency (FEMA), a part of the Department of Homeland Security (DHS). Since the size of the disaster clearly outstripped city and state resources, much of the blame was heaped on FEMA. Problems at FEMA, which predated Hurricane Katrina, were blamed on its being downgraded from a Cabinet-level agency, budget cuts, loss of staff, and staff with insufficient expertise to respond to problems of this magnitude. The inadequate response to Hurricane Katrina resulted in the resignation of FEMA's director.

Of particular concern was the treatment of those who lacked transportation or the funds to evacuate on their own. Pictures of people camped in the New Orleans Superdome and sitting on bridges without food or water, and coverage of the sick and disabled who died in hospitals and nursing homes, were heartbreaking. Thousands of residents were sent to other cities and some to states as far away as Utah and California to wait and hear when they would be allowed to return. Some families were separated in the process, unaware of the whereabouts of their loved ones.

The most stinging accusations were that people who were poor and African American had been forsaken. Knight-Rider News Service analyzed available, though incomplete, data on several hundred Katrina-related deaths and found that poor people and African Americans were not disproportionately represented among the dead.[119] Though of little consolation to their loved ones, deaths were proportionate to these groups' representation in the population. The analysis indicated that lack of transportation was not a factor for many of the dead because cars were found in their driveways. Consistent with news coverage of rescues, some people did not heed the belated warning to evacuate, perhaps because it was difficult to do so, or because nothing so bad had happened before. The group that did have higher deaths rates was older people. Nearly three-quarters of the dead were aged 60 or older, and nearly half were aged 75 or older. Many were at nursing homes and hospitals.

Communities such as Houston, Texas, welcomed tens of thousands of evacuees, but remuneration from the federal government fell short of expectations as state and community resources were stretched thin. The federal government has launched a massive initiative to house those displaced by Hurricane Katrina, rebuild New Orleans, and assist those in other communities in states affected not only by Hurricane Katrina but by Hurricanes Rita and Wilma as well. Criticisms of the rebuilding process are also mounting. The *New York Times* reported that low-income residents are having difficulty rebuilding because they are being turned down for loans due to low incomes or poor credit.[120] Dealing with insurance companies and what claims they will or will not pay may take years to resolve.

Statements, based on a preliminary study by the Comptroller General of the United States, sounded like an "I told you so." It emphasized that the Government Accountability Office (GAO) had long urged that a senior official in the White House be designated "to oversee federal preparedness for, and response to, major catastrophic disasters."[121] The report also sharply criticized the Secretary of the Department of Homeland Security for leadership failures. The GAO also found that the National Flood Insurance Program is not actuarially sound, that is, the premiums collected are insufficient to meet flood losses expected in the future.[122] Some of the Katrina-related deaths resulted because floodwaters poured over levees, but a greater number of deaths resulted in areas where floodwalls collapsed. Accusations were that the floodwalls were poorly designed, poorly engineered, or poorly maintained.[123]

In addition to leadership failures, a major theme that has emerged is the communications failures that occurred within DHS and FEMA and across agencies and units of government.[124] The many implementation failures before, during, and after Katrina continue to be investigated. In the future, residents will be spurred to evacuate sooner in the face of predictions of natural disasters, and government officials are realizing that they will be held to higher standards of accountability to prevent the loss of life and property.

Medicare Prescription Drug Coverage

Medicare Part D is the Medicare program's new prescription drug benefit, which became effective on January 1, 2006. Prior to this date, Medicare did not pay for prescription drugs under its Part B supplemental insurance program that covers outpatient medical care. Chapter 8 describes controversies surrounding Congressional approval of Part D, including serious underestimates of the program's total costs. In addition, a single national system in which the government could buy drugs at lower costs and operate using a uniform set of rules was rejected in favor of many private plans with varying coverage and different premiums. Many see Part D as more complicated than Medicare's hospital and outpatient medical care coverage and a major boondoggle for private pharmaceutical enterprises and insurance companies.[125]

Millions of Medicare beneficiaries were faced with the decision of whether to enroll immediately, later, or forego Part D. For those with no prescription drug coverage, the decision was probably easy. With modest premiums (some under $15 a month), substantial savings could result for Medicare beneficiaries who use prescription drugs. Even for those not currently taking prescription drugs, the need might arise and the Part D benefit could result in prescription drug savings. Many older Americans already had prescription coverage, some through former employers' retirement benefits. They were faced with deciding whether to keep what they had or enroll in Part D. But with so many plans from which to choose, the decision for everyone seemed overwhelming. The Social Security Administration website allowed individuals to enter some basic demographic information and the prescription drugs they were currently taking to compare plan premiums and other out-of-pocket costs. But many Medicare beneficiaries were not computer savvy and had to rely on family, friends, or social service workers to help them compare plans and make decisions. In February 2006, the Senate refused to extend the initial sign up deadline of May 15, 2006 to compensate for the program's slow and rocky start. Eligible individuals can still enroll later but at a higher cost.

For those who have enrolled, there have been many computer glitches (e.g., not showing up in the plan's computer system, being charged the wrong amounts for a prescription) and very long waits on the telephone to talk with someone who might help solve the problem. At least one plan's recorded phone message urged callers to call back on Saturday and even hung up on them without the choice of waiting on the line for assistance or leaving a message. This was not how people wanted to be treated by the plan they had chosen, especially if they badly needed a medication and a costly one.

Some of the most serious problems occurred for "dual eligibles," those Medicare beneficiaries who have incomes low enough that they also qualify for Medicaid. Many of them were randomly enrolled in the private Part D drug programs. The media reported stories of these individuals being denied coverage for their drugs or charged more than they should have been because of administrative problems. These dual eligibles will save the pharmaceutical industry billions of dollars because by switching them to Medicare Part D, the companies no longer have to pay rebates on drugs that the government previously purchased.[126] Some states are threatening to sue the federal government because they are being required to return some of their Medicaid savings now that they are not subsidizing the drug costs of dual eligibles through their Medicaid programs. The states could certainly use these savings to help individuals of all ages who might lose their Medicaid benefits under budget cuts the federal government passed as part of the Deficit Reduction Act of 2005.

Jonathan Chait of the *New Republic* called the passage of Part D and its implementation a "poison pill" for the Republican Party.[127] This remains to be seen. If the kinks are worked out, many Medicare beneficiaries, especially those with high prescription drug costs and no or limited previous prescription drug coverage, will benefit. If Part D becomes popular with the millions of Social Security beneficiaries, it will be difficult to change, regardless of the program's design flaws and costs to the federal government.

Exercises and Activities for Chapter 12

1. Think about what should have been done to avoid the tragedies that resulted from hurricane Katrina. Enter the keywords "hurricane Katrina" in Research Navigator to determine what the discussions are regarding communications, leadership, and other failures. What should be done to prevent similar tragedies from happening?

2. Go to the Social Security website (www.ssa.gov) and to the page that helps Social Security beneficiaries determine which prescription drug plan is best for them. Use a hypothetical case or the prescription drug list of someone you know. How many plans were available in the individual's geographical location? How easy was it to enter the information, including the drugs and their dosages? Ask some Social Security recipients you know if they enrolled in the new program, why they did or did not, and what their experience in enrolling and using the program has been.

3. Using Research Navigator, enter the keywords "Medicare Part D" or "Medicare prescription drug plan" to see if there are updates on the program. Discuss the way Part D is being implemented. Do you agree with way the way Part D is structured, including the way benefits are being administered? Do you think another method would have been wiser?

NOTES

1. This discussion of the BCRA relies on Michael J. Malbin (Ed.), *The Election After Reform: Money Politics, and the Bipartisan Campaign Reform Act,* Lanham, MD: Rowman & Littlefield, forthcoming. Retrieved January 16, 2005, from http://www.cfinst.org/studies/ElectionAfterReform/chapters.html.

2. "New Campaign Finance Law (BCRA) Pushed Parties, Candidates To Raise Dramatically More Money From Individuals in 2004," Press Releases, The Pew Charitable Trusts, February 14, 2004. Retrieved January 18, 2006, from http://www.pewtrusts.com.

3. Malbin, *The Election After Reform,* p. 13.

4. This paragraph relies on "Tom DeLay," *Wikipedia,* December 28, 2005 and April 9, 2006. Retrieved December 28, 2005, and April 9, 2006, from http://en.wikipedia.org/wiki/Tom_Delay; Laylan Copelin, "DeLay and his legacy are both on trial," *Austin American-Statesman,* December 18, 2005, pp. A1 & 14. Bill of Idictment, In the District Court of Travis County, Texas, 147th Judicial District, The State of Texas vs. John Dominick Colyandro, James Walter Ellis, & Thomas Dale Delay and Bill of Indictment, In the District Court of Travis County, Texas, 403rd Judicial District, The State of Texas vs. John Dominick Colyandro, James Walter Ellis, & Thomas Dale Delay. Retrieved April 9, 2006, from http://news.findlaw.com/hdocs/docs/delay/delay92805ind.html.

5. "Tom DeLay," *Wikipedia.*

6. Ibid.

7. See, for example, "Red Cross and Katrina: Too heavy a burden (*Philadelphia Inquirer*), *Austin American-Statesman,* January 17, 2005, p. A15.

8. American Association of Fundraising Counsel, "Charitable Giving Rises 5 Percent to Nearly $250 billion in 2004." Retrieved November 27, 2005, from http://www.aafrc.org.

9. American Association of Fundraising Counsel, "Americans Give $241 Billion to Charity in 2003." Retrieved November 27, 2005, from http://www.aafrc.org.

10. Debra Blum, Suzanne Perry, Elizabeth Schwinn, Holly Hall, Leah Kerkman, and Cassie J. Moore, "Giving Bounces Back," *Chronicle of Philanthropy,* October 27, 2005, Vol. 18, Issue 2. Retrieved December 28, 2005, from http://www.philanthropy.com.

11. Edward Wong, "Turnout in the Iraqi Election is Reported at 70 Percent," *The New York Times,* December 22, 2005. Retrieved December 28, 2005, from http://www.nytimes.com/2005/12/22/international/middleeast/22iraq.html.

12. Operation Iraqi Freedom (OIF), U.S. Casualty Status; Fatalities as of February 24, 2006, 10 a.m. EST. Retrieved February 26, 2006, from http://www.defenselink.mil/news/casualty.pdf.

13. Iraq Body Count, Civilians reported killed by military intervention in Iraq. Retrieved February 18, 2006, from http://www.iraqbodycount.org.

14. Les Roberts, Riyadh Lafta, Richard Garfield, Jamal Khudhairi, Gilbert Burnham, "Mortality before and after the 2003 invasion of Iraq: Cluster sample survey," *The Lancet,* October 29, 2004. Retrieved February 18, 2006, from http://www.thelancet.com.

15. Linda Bilmes and Joseph Stiglitz, "War's stunning price tag," *Los Angeles Times,* January 17, 2006. Retrieved January 21, 2006, from http://www.latimes.com.

16. "War on Terrorism," CNN/USA Today/Gallup Poll, PollingReport.com. Retrieved December 4, 2005, from http://www.pollingreport.com/terror.htm.

17. "McCain Amendment to 2006 Department of Defense Appropriations Bill." Retrieved February 4, 2006, from http://www.phrusa.org/research/torture/mccain_text.html.

18. "Rice moves to clarify U.S. interrogation methods," Associated Press, December 8, 2005. Retrieved December 28, 2005, from http://www.cnn.com/2005/WORLD/europe/12/07/rice.interrogations.ap/index.html/.

19. Charlie Savage, "Bush could bypass new torture ban," *Boston Globe,* January 4, 2006. Retrieved February 2, 2006, from http://www.boston.com.

20. Gary Thomas, "US Detainee Debate Complicated by Elusive Definition of Torture," *Voice of America,* December 16, 2005. Retrieved December 30, 2005, from http://www.voanews.com/english/2005-12-16-voa47.cfm.

21. Paul Reynolds, "Defining torture in a new world war," *BBC News,* December 8, 2005. Retrieved December 30, 2005, from http://news.bbc.co.uk/1/hi/world/americas/4499528.stm.

22. Ken Herman, "Bush: I approved domestic spying: Eavesdropping without warrants must continue, president says, *Austin American-Statesman,* December 18, 2005, pp. A1 & 12.

23. "Iraq," CNN/USA Today/Gallup Poll, PollingReport.com. Retrieved December 4, 2005, from http://www.pollingreport.com/iraq.htm.

24. "War on Terrorism," CNN/USA Today/Gallup Poll, PollingReport.com. Retrieved December 4, 2005, from http://www.pollingreport.com/terror.htm.

25. "Problems and Priorities," PollingReport.com, 2005. Retrieved December 29, 2005, from http://www.pollingreport.com/prioriti.htm.

26. President's Advisory Panel on Federal Tax Reform, *Simple, Fair, and Pro-Growth: Proposals to Fix America's Tax System,* Report of the President's Advisory Panel on Federal Tax Reform, November 2005. Retrieved December 11, 2005, from http://www.taxreformpanel.gov/index.shtml.

27. See, for example, Daniel Mitchell, "Grading the Tax Reform Panel's Recommendations," The Heritage Foundation, November 1, 2005. Retrieved December 30, 2005, from http://www.heritage.org/Research/Taxes/wm903.cfm; Marilyn Geewax, "Income tax overhaul pleases few," *Austin American-Statesman,* October 19, 2005, pp. D1 & 3.

28. Kevin G. Hall, "Greenspan floats 'hybrid' tax system," *Austin American-Statesman,* March 4, 2005, pp. C1 & 3.

29. "U.S. presidential election, 2004, *Wikipedia,* December 1, 2005. Retrieved December 4, 2005, from http://en.wikipedia.org/wiki/U.S._presidential_election_2004.

30. "109th United States Congress, *Wikipedia,* February 19, 2006. Retrieved February 26, 2006, from http://en.wikipedia.org/wiki/109th_Congress.

31. See Ron Hutcheson and Willima Douglas, "Next 4 years will be about finishing what he started," *Austin American-Statesman,* November 4, 2004, pp. A1 & 10.

32. You can check the latest national debt figure at a web site called the U.S. National Debt Clock at http://www.brillig.com/debt_clock/.

33. "President Signs S.1932, Deficit Reduction Act of 2005," The White House, February 8, 2006. Retrieved February 16, 2006, from http://www.whitehouse.gov/news/releases/2006/02/20060208-8.html.

34. Tim Dickinson, "The Deficit Lie," *Rolling Stone,* January 12, 2006. Retrieved February 16, 2005, from http://www.rollingstone.com/politics/story/9138154/the_deficit_lie.

35. George Will, "Liberalism's tired ideas of poverty," *Austin American-Statesman,* September 14, 2005, p. A17.

36. David U. Himmelstein, Elizabeth Warren, Deborah Thorne, and Steffie Woolhandler, "Illness and Injury As Contributors to Bankruptcy," *Health Affairs-Web Exclusive,* February 2, 2005. Retrieved April 9, 2005, from http://www.healthaffairs.org.

37. This section relies on Carmen De Navas-Walt, Bernadette D. Proctor, and Cheryl Hill Lee, *Income, Poverty, and Health Insurance Coverage in the United States: 2004.* Washington DC: U.S. Census Bureau, August 2005.

38. United Nations, "People and Poverty 2000: Globalization has yet to benefit the poor." Retrieved January 1, 2005, from http://www.un.org/events/poverty2000/backpp.htm.

39. See UN Millennium Project 2005, *Investing in Development: A Practical Plan to Achieve the Millennium Development Goals,* United Nations Development Program, 2005. Retrieved April 9, 2005, from http://www.un.org; Edith M. Lederer (Associated Press), "U.N. report: Rich nations have power to solve poverty crisis," *Austin American-Statesman,* January 18, 2005, p. A3.

40. Sheldon Richman, "Tsunami Aid: Not Theirs to Give," The Future of Freedom Foundation, January 7,

2005. Retrieved February 26, 2006, from http://www.fff.org/comment/com0501b.asp.

41. "Fact Sheet: America's Ownership Society: Expanding Opportunities," The White House, August 2004. Retrieved January 1, 2006, from http://www.whitehouse.gov/news/releases/2004/08/20040809-9.html.

42. U.S. Census Bureau, "Housing Vacancies and Home Ownership," Historical Tables, Table 14. Retrieved January 1, 2006, from http://www.census.gov/hhes/www/housing/hvs/historic/histt14.html.

43. Carolina Katz Reid, "Achieving the American Dream? A Longitudinal Analysis of the Homeownership Experiences of Low-Income Households," Department of Geography, University of Washington. Dissertation Discussion Paper, April 2004, © Carolina Katz Reid. Retrieved January 1, 2006, from http://www.google.com.

44. Annys Shin, Fannie Mae Finds More Errors, Names New CFO," *Washington Post,* November 11, 2005. Retrieved January 1, 2006, from http://www.washingtonpost.com/wp-dyn/content/article/2005/11/10/AR2005111000459.html.

45. The remainder of this paragraph relies on Stephen Labaton, "House Approves Overhaul at Fannie Mae and Freddie Mac," *The New York Times,* January 1, 2005, from http://www.researchnavigator.com/articles/article.asp?p=426276.

46. Martin Kasindorf, "Nation taking a new look at homelessness, solutions," *USA Today,* October 12, 2005. Retrieved February 13, 2006, from http://www.usatoday.com/news/nation/2005-10-11-homeless-cover_x.htm.

47. "FEMA Hotel/Motel Emergency Sheltering Transitions to Long-term Housing Assistance," FEMA News, February 11, 2006. Retrieved February 13, 2006, from http://www.fema.gov/news/newsrelease.fema?id=23539.

48. Kasindorf, "Nation taking a new look at homelessness, solutions."

49. These figures are from Social Security Administration, "Social Security Beneficiary Statistics, Number of beneficiaries receiving benefits on December 31, 1970-2005." Retrieved January 4, 2006, from http://www.ssa.gov/OACT/STATS/OASDIbenies.html.

50. Social Security Administration, Social Security and Medicare Benefits, Total annual benefits paid, by type of benefit and trust fund, 1937-2004. Retrieved January 4, 2006, from http://www.ssa.gov/OACT/STATS/table4a4.html.

51. This analysis is based primarily on Jason Furman, "An Analysis of Using 'Progressive Price Indexing' to Set Social Security Benefits," Washington, DC: Center for Budget and Policy Priorities, May 2, 2005. Retrieved December 15, 2005, from http://www.cbpp.org/3-21-05socsec.htm.

52. Ed Lorenzen, "Progressive Approaches to Benefit Changes in Social Security Reform," Centrists.Org, January 26, 2005. Retrieved February 15, 2006,

from http://www.centrists.org/pages/2005/01/26_lorenzen_wealth.html.

53. David E. Rosenbaum and Edmund L. Andrews (*New York Times*), "Social Security plan foundering," *Austin American-Statesman,* May 20, 2005, p. A13.

54. "Bush Extends Social Security Tour as Support in Polls Dwindles," Bloomberg.com, April 26, 2005. Retrieved February 15, 2006, from http://www.bloomberg.com/apps/news?pid = 10000103&sid = a3V6oM9quCfA&refer = us.

55. U.S. Department of Labor, Labor Force Statistics from the Current Population Survey, (Seasonal) Unemployment Rate, Unemployment rate, percent 16 years and over. Retrieved January 4, 2006, from http://data.bls.gov/PDQ/servlet/SurveyOutputServlet?data_tool = latest_numbers&series_id = LNS14000000.

56. Social Security Administration, Applications for Disability Benefits & Benefit Awards, Number of applications and awards, and awards per 1,000 insured workers, 1965–2005, updated April 15, 2005. Retrieved February 26, 2006, from http://www.ssa.gov/OACT/STATS/table6c7.html.

57. Most figures in the this paragraph rely on Social Security Administration, *Social Security Bulletin, Annual Statistical Supplement, 2005,* Tables 7.A3, 7.A4, and 7.A5. Retrieved December 4, 2005, from http://www.ssa.gov/policy/docs/statcomps/supplement/2005/index.html.

58. U.S. House of Representatives, "Section 3: Supplemental Security Income," *2004 Green Book.* Retrieved February 3, 2006, from http://waysandmeans.house.gov/Documents.asp?section = 813, pp. 3–44.

59. American Psychiatric Association, *Diagnostic and Statistical Manual of Mental Disorders,* 4th ed., text rev., Washington, DC: Author, 2000.

60. Office of the Inspector General, *Review of State Variances in VA Disability Compensation Payments,* Washington, DC: Department of Veterans Affairs, Report No. 05–00765–137, May 19, 2005. Quote from p. viii. Retrieved January 4, 2005, from http://www.va.gov/oig/53/reports/2005–2reports.htm.

61. Office of Public Affairs and Media Relations, "No Across-the-Board Review of PTSD Cases—Secretary Nicholson," Department of Veterans Affairs, November 10, 2005. Retrieved January 4, 2006, from http://www.houston.med.va.gov/HOUSTON/pressreleases/News_20051110a.asp.

62. See, for example, Lucinda G. Miller, "Elaine King-Miller versus Texas Tech University Health Sciences Center, et al." Retrieved November 27, 2005, from http://www.ca5.uscourts.gov/.

63. Andy Millison, "Some see peril in proposal to overhaul disabilities law," *Austin American-Statesman,* December 17, 2005, p. A32.

64. *Schaffer et ux, et al. v. Weast, Superintendent, Montgomery County Public Schools, et al.,* Decided November 14, 2005. Retrieved November 27, 2006, from http://www.supremecourtus.gov/.

65. Office of Child Support Enforcement, *Child Support Enforcement, FY2004, Preliminary Report,* June 2005. Retrieved January 4, 2005, from http://www.acf.hhs.gov/programs/cse/pubs/2005/reports/preliminary_report/index.html.

66. Robert Greenstein and Sharon Parrott, "Cuts in House Budget Bill Aimed at Low-income Families Reduced by Only 2%; Other 98% of Cuts Remain," Washington, DC: Center on Budget and Policy Priorities, December 5, 2005. Retrieved February 3, 2006, from http://www.cbpp.org/11–17–95bud2.htm.

67. Office of Family Assistance, Temporary Assistance for Needy Families, Separate State Program-Maintenance of Effort, Aid to Families with Dependent Children, Caseload Data. Retrieved January 4, 2006, from http://www.acf.dhhs.gov/programs/ofa/caseload/caseloadindex.htm#2005.

68. "Congress Reauthorizes TANF Program at FY 04 Levels," Thompson, February 2, 2006. Retrieved February 16, 2006, from http://www.thompson.com/grantsandfunding/newsbriefs/060202_grantmanage.html.

69. David Sarasohn (*The Oregonian),* Can diet rules slim our supersized nation?," *Austin American-Statesman,* January 20, 2005, p. A11.

70. Lynnea Mills, "Texas, don't use report cards to combat childhood obesity," *Austin American-Statesman,* February 7, 2005, p. A11.

71. Shelley Emling, "Britain aims to curb obesity among kids," *Austin American-Statesman,* November 30, 2005, p. A18.

72. Michael Morain (Associated Press), "In nation of malnourished, obesity a growing problem," *Austin American-Statesman,* December 19, 2004, p. A27.

73. Sugar Association, "Sugar Association Response to Dietary Guidelines," January 12, 2005. Retrieved November 22, 2005, from http://www.sugar.org/.

74. More information on the National Automatic Merchandising Association and its Balanced for Life Campaign can be found at http://www.vending.org/index.php.

75. United States Department of Agriculture, Food and Nutrition Service, "Food Stamp Program Particpation and Costs" (Data as of December 21, 2005). Retrieved January 27, 2005, from http://ww.fns.usda.gov/pd/fssummar.htm.

76. Matthew Fellowes and Alan Berube, "Leaving Money (and Food) on the Table: Food Stamp Participation in Major Metropolitan Areas and Counties," Washington, DC: The Brookings Institution, May 2005. Retrieved February 10, 2006, from http://www.brookings.edu/metro/pubs/20050517_foodstamps.htm.

77. "Slash farm subsidies—now," (Editorial, *The Sacramento Bee),* *Austin-American Statesman,* November 30, 2005, p. H3.

78. Statement of Ambassador Robert Portman, United States Trade Representative before the Commit-

tee on Agriculture, U.S. House of Representatives, Washington, DC, November 25, 2005.

79. "WTO Rules Against U.S. Cotton Subsidies & Export Dumping That Impoverish Millions Overseas," *Organic Consumers Association,* March 3, 2005. Retrieved February 13, 2005, from http://www.organicconsumers.org/clothes/wtocotton30405.cfm.

80. "Sugar tariff fails to yield sweet results for anyone," *The Daily Oakland Press,* April 19, 2005. Retrieved February 13, 2005, from http://www.theoaklandpress.com/stories/041905/opi_20050419004.shtml.

81. Todd Pitman (Associated Press), "In Africa, nations tip easily into food crisis," Austin American-Statesman, August 14, 2005, pp. H1 & 4.

82. Denavas-Walt et al., *Income, Poverty, and Health Insurance Coverage in the United States: 2004.*

83. Michelle M. Doty, Jennifer N. Edwards, and Alyssa L. Holmgren, "Seeing Red: Americans Driven into Debt by Medical Bills," New York: The Commonwealth Fund, August 25, 2005. Retrieved http://www.cmwf.org/publications/publications_show.htm?doc_id = 290074.

84. Congressional Budget Office, "Additional Information on CBO's Estimate for the Medicaid Provisions in the Conference Agreement for S.1932, the Deficit Reduction Act of 2005," January 27, 2006. Retrieved February 8, 2006, from http://www.cbo.gov/publications/collections/reconciliation.cfm.

85. Organization for Economic Cooperation and Development, *OECD in Figures,* 2005 edition. Statistics on the Member Countries, Paris: OECD, July 2005. Retrieved February 7, 2006, from http://www.oecdbookshop.org/oecd/display.asp?lang = EN&sf1 = identifiers&st1 = 012005061e1.

86. Drug Enforcement Administration, "Controlled Substances Act." Retrieved January 26, 2006, from http://www.usdoj.gov/dea/agency/csa.htm.

87. Marijuana Policy Project, "U.S. Supreme Court Rules on Medical Marijuana," Retireved December 16, 2005, from http://www.mpp.org/raich/.

88. See, for example, "Patients who use pot face legal rap," *Austin American-Statesman.* June 7, 2005, pp. A1 & 4.

89. "U.S. Supreme Court Rules on Medical Marijuana," Washington, DC: Marijuana Policy Project. Retrieved December 16, 2005, from http://www.mpp.org/raich/.

90. American Medical Association, "Featured Report: Medical Marijauna," updated August 10, 2005. Retrieved December 17, 2005, from http://www.ama-assn.org/ama/pub/category/13625.html.

91. PollingReport.com, "Illegal Drugs." Retrieved December 17, 2005, from http://www.pollingreport.com/drugs.htm.

92. See, for example, David Brown and Shailagh Murray, "Schiavo Autopsy Released, Brain Damage 'Was Irreversible,'" *Washington Post,* June 16, 2005, p. A1.

93. See, for example, Timothy Egan and Adam Liptak, "Fraught Issue, but Narrow Ruling in Oregon Suicide Case," *New York Times,* January 18, 2006. Retrieved January 18, 2006, from http://www.nytimes.com.

94. See, for example, National Education Association, "Plaintiffs In 'No Child Left Behind' Act Lawsuit Will Appeal Decision, November 23, 2005. Retrieved November 27, 2005, from http://www.nea.org/newsreleases/2005/nr051123.html.

95. Susan Saulny, "Tutor Program Offered by Law is Going Unused," *New York Times,* February 12, 2006. Retrieved February 12, 2006, from http://www.nytimes.com.

96. This paragraph relies on Kathleen Hunter, "States leads way on minimum wage hikes," Stateline.org, January 20, 2006. Retrieved February 15, 2006, from http://www.stateline.org/live/ViewPage.action?siteNodeId = 136&languageId = 1&contentId = 81956.

97. See, for example, Marilyn Geewax, "Wrangling over pay, How latest efforts to raise minimum wage were scuttled," *Austin American-Statesman,* December 11, 2005, pp. J1 & 3.

98. Ronald C. Kessler, Patricia Beglund, Olga Demler, Robert Jin, Kathleen R. Merikangas, and Ellen E. Walters, "Lifetime Prevalence and Age-of-Onset Distributions of *DSM-IV* Disorders in the National Comorbidity Survey Replication," *Archives of General Psychiatry, 62,* 593–602, 2005.

99. Philip S. Wang, Michael Lane, Mark Olfson, Harold A. Pincus, Kenneth B. Wells, and Ronald C. Kessler, "Twelve-Month Use of Mental Health Services in the United States," *Archives of General Psychiatry, 62,* 629–640, 2005.

100. Substance Abuse and Mental Health Services Administration, *Transforming Mental Health Care in America. Federal Action Agenda: First Steps.* DHHS Pub. No. SMA-05–4060. Rockville, MD: U.S. Department of Health and Human Services, 2005.

101. Coalition on Human Needs, "House Cuts $38.8 Billion from Budget; Slashes Health Care, Student Loans, Child Support and Help for People with Disabilities," *CHN Human Needs Report,* February 3, 2006. Retrieved February 15, 2006, from http://www.chn.org/humanneeds/060203a.html.

102. 2005 White House Conference on Aging, "Top 10 Resolutions Announced," December 14, 2005. Retrieved January 26, 2006, from http://www.whcoa.gov/.

103. Respecting Accuracy in Domestic Abuse Reporting (RADAR), "Analysis of the Violence Against Women Act," July 5, 2005. Retrieved February 5, 2006, from http://www.mediaradar.org/.

104. Department of Defense, "DoD Announces New Policy on Prevention and Response to Sexual Assault," News Release. January 4, 2005. Retrieved December 13,

2005, from http://www.defenselink.mil/releases/2005/nr20050104–1927.html.

105. Deputy Secretary of Defense, "Confidentiality Policy for Victims of Sexual Assault (JTF-SAPR-009)," March 16, 2005. Retrieved December 14, 2005, from http://www.defenselink.mil/news/Mar2005/d20050318dsd.pdf.

106. Defense Task Force on Sexual Harassment and Violence, *Report of the Defense Task Force on Sexual Harassment & Violence at the Military Service Academies,* Washington, DC: Pentagon, June 2005, p. ES-2. Retrieved December 14, 2005, from http://www.dtic.mil/dtfs/.

107. See Susan Jones, "Supreme Court Upholds Parental Notification Law," Cybercast News Service, January 18, 2006. Retrieved January 28, 2006, from http://www.cnsnews.com; Associated Press, "Supreme Court dodges major abortion ruling," January 18, 2006. Retrieved January 28, 2006, from http://www.msnbc.msn.com/id/10906861/.

108. Charles Lane, "Abortion Case to Test New Justices," Washingtonpost.com, February 22, 2006. Retrieved February 27, 2006, from http://www.washingtonpost.com/wp-dyn/content/article/2006/02/21/AR2006022100582.html.

109. Duramed Pharmaceuticals, "You Have a Second Chance," Plan B Consumer Home Page, Retrieved February 5, 2005, from http://www.go2planb.com/ForConsumers/Index.aspx.

110. U.S. Government Accountability Office, *Decision Process to Deny Initial Application for Over-the-Counter Marketing of the Emergency Contraceptive Drug Plan B Was Unusual,* GAO-06–109, Washington, DC: November 2005, Retrieved January 28, 2005, from http://www.gao.gov.

111. "John Roberts," *Wikipedia,* February 5, 2006. Retrieved February 5, 2005, from http://en.wikipedia.org/wiki/John_Roberts#Nomination_and_confirmation.

112. Michael Kinsley (*The Washington Post*), "How both sides distort the 'debate' on abortion," *Austin American Statesman,* November 21, 2005, p. A9.

113. Human Rights Campaign, "Relationship Recognition in the U.S.," April 2005. Retrieved November 27, 2005, from http://www.hrc.org.

114. Human Rights Campaign, "Statewide Marriage Laws," November 2005. Retrieved November 27, 2005, from http://www.hrc.org.

115. "Law and Civil Rights," PollingReport.com. Retrieved February 5, 2006, from http://www.pollingreport.com/civil.htm.

116. Ellen Katz et al., "Documenting Discrimination in Voting: Judicial Findings Under Section 2 of the Voting Rights Act Since 1982," Ann Arbor, Michigan: The University of Michigan Law School. Retrieved December 4, 2005, from http://www.voting report.org.

117. See, for example, U.S. Department of Justice, Civil Rights Division, Voting Section Home Page. Retrieved December 2, 2005, from http://www.usdoj.gov/crt/voting/sec_5/about.htm; "Racial discrimination lawsuits indicate Voting Rights Act still needed,"University of Michigan News Service, November 10, 2005. Retrieved December 2, 2005, from http://www.umich.edu/news/?Releases/2005/Nov05/r111005a.

118. "ACLU Calls on Congress to Correct Provision in Voting Rights Act: Court Decision on Redistricting Undermines Intent of Historic Civil Rights Law, " November 9, 2005. Retrieved December 3, 2005, from http://www.aclu.org/votingrights/gen/21266prs20051109.html.

119. John Simerman, Dwight Ott, and Ted Mellnik (Knight Ridder News Service), "Early data challenge assumptions about Katrina victims," *Austin-American Statesman,* December 30, 2005, pp. A1 & 8.

120. "The Poor Need Not Apply," *New York Times,* December 21, 2006. Retrieved January 30, 2006, from http://www.researchnavigator.com/articles/article.asp?p=437452.

121. "Statement by Comptroller General David M. Walker on GAO's Preliminary Observations Regarding Preparedness and Response to Hurricanes Katrina and Rita," GAO-06–365R, Washington, DC: U.S. Government Accountability Office, February 1, 2006, p. 3. Retrieved April 9, 2006, from http:// www.gao.gov/.

122. "Challenges for the National Flood Insurance Program," GAO-06–335T, U.S. General Accountability Office, January 25, 2006. Retrieved February 4, 2006, from http://www.gao.gov.

123. John Simerman, Dwight Ott, and Ted Mellnik (Knight Ridder News Service), "Canal breeches led to most New Orleans deaths," *Austin-American Statesman,* December 30, 2005, p. A8; also see John Simerman, Dwight Ott, and Ted Mellnik (Knight Ridder Newspapers), "Majority of New Orleans death tied to floodwalls' collapse," December 29, 2005. Retrieved January 30, 2006, from http://www.realcities.com/mld/krwashington/13509691.htm.

124. "U.S. Senate Homeland Security and Governmental Affairs Committee Hearing on DHS Preparation for and Response to Hurrican Katrina," February 15, 2006. Retrieved February 28, 2006, from http://www.washingtonpost.com/wp-dyn/content/article/2006/02/15/AR2006021501475.html.

125. Jonathan Chait (*The New Republic*), "The Republicans' poison pill," *Los Angeles Times,* January 22, 2006. Retrieved January 29, 2006, from http://www.latimes.com.

126. Larry Lipman, "Senate won't extend drug sign-up date," *Austin American-Statesman,* February 3, 2006, p. A7.

127. Chait, "The Republican's poison pill."

Preface

I can hardly believe that more than two decades have gone by since publication of the first edition of *Social Welfare: Politics and Public Policy.* Like previous editions, the sixth edition is intended to introduce students to the major social welfare policies and programs in the United States and to stimulate them to think about major conflicts in social welfare today. The book focuses on issues and emphasizes that social welfare in the United States involves a series of political questions about what should be done for those who are poor, near poor, and not poor, and for other individuals and groups—or whether anything should be done at all. This edition increasingly recognizes issues that international events and globalization pose for social welfare policy.

Social Welfare: Politics and Public Policy describes the major social welfare programs—their histories, trends, and current problems and prospects. But more importantly, it tackles the difficult conflicts and controversies that surround these programs. Social welfare policy is not presented as a series of solutions to social problems. Instead, social policy is portrayed as public conflict over the nature and causes of social welfare problems, over what, if anything, should be done about them, over who should do it, and over who should decide about it.

Some of the major policies and programs covered in this book are:

Social Security
Unemployment insurance
Workers' compensation
Supplemental Security Income
Vocational rehabilitation
The Americans with Disabilities Act
Child support enforcement
Temporary Assistance for Needy Families
General Assistance
Food Stamp Program
School lunch and breakfast programs
Special Supplemental Nutrition Program for Women, Infants, and Children
Community action programs
Job training
Minimum wage legislation
Mental health services
The Older Americans Act
Child welfare services
Medicare
Medicaid

Civil rights legislation
Affirmative action
Immigration legislation
Abortion policy
Gay rights legislation
Voting rights legislation

Although it is impossible to capture all the complexities of social welfare in a single volume, these policies and programs are described and analyzed, and alternative proposals and "reforms" are considered.

This book is designed for undergraduate and beginning graduate courses in social welfare policy. It does not require prior knowledge of social welfare, and it will hopefully spur further interest in social welfare policies and programs.

Many texts on social policy treat social insurance, public assistance, and social service programs descriptively; by so doing, they tend to obscure important conflicts and issues. Other books treat these programs prescriptively; by so doing, they imply that there is a "right" way to resolve social problems. *Social Welfare: Politics and Public Policy* views social policy as a continuing political struggle over the issues posed by poverty and other social welfare problems in society—different goals and objectives, competing definitions of problems, alternative approaches and strategies, multiple programs and policies, competing proposals for "reform," and different ideas about how decisions should be made in social welfare policy. A website (www.ablongman.com/dinitto) and other technology-assisted supplements are available to accompany the text.

I owe a special debt to Professor Thomas R. Dye. Although he no longer appears as a coauthor of the book, without him there would never have been a book at all. I am appreciative to Linda Cummins, who took on the task of helping with this edition. I wish to thank the reviewers who commented on previous editions, in particular Professor Robert B. Hudson of Boston University, who provided very helpful comments on the sixth edition as well. Thanks also to Stephen C. Anderson of New Mexico State University; Mark Hanna of California State University, Fresno; Beverly A. Stadum of St. Cloud State University; and Carole Upshur of the University of Massachusetts, Boston, all of whom reviewed this edition. Mary Margaret Just of Morehead State University assisted in many ways. As always, I thank my parents and Craig for their patience during the many hours it took to complete this project. My thanks to JongSerl Chun, Tricia Cody, Jill Henderson, Katie Gilley, Lorena Sanchez, Elissa Shaw-Fletcher, Anne Ogolla, and Ivan Rios for their assistance. My appreciation also goes to Dean Barbara White and the faculty and staff of The University of Texas at Austin School of Social Work for their support and encouragement. Linda Cummins wishes to thank Denny for his care and delicious suppers and Sonoya Powers for her able assistance.

Several users of the book, both faculty and students, have communicated with me about previous editions. I appreciate their interest and look forward to further contacts with readers.

D. M. D.

CHAPTER

Politics, Rationalism, and Social Welfare

POLITICS AND SOCIAL WELFARE POLICY

No one is happy with the nation's public assistance system—not the working tax-payers who must support it, not the social welfare professionals who must ad-minister it, and certainly not the poor who must live under it. Even the nation's social insurance system has become a source of controversy. Since the Social Security Act of 1935, the federal government has tried to develop a rational social welfare sys-tem for the entire nation. Today a wide variety of federal programs serve people who are aged, poor, disabled, sick, or have other social needs. **Income maintenance** (social insurance and public assistance) is now the largest single item in the federal budget, easily surpassing national defense. The Social Security Administration and the U.S. Department of Health and Human Services have the largest budgets of any federal agen-cies, and many additional social welfare programs are administered by other departments.

1

After seventy years of large-scale, direct federal involvement, social welfare policy remains a central issue in U.S. politics.

Social welfare policy involves a series of *political* issues about what should be done for the poor, the near-poor, the nonpoor, and other individuals and groups—or whether anything should be done at all. The real problems in social welfare are not problems of organization, administration, or service delivery. Rather, they involve political conflicts over the nature and causes of poverty and inequality, the role of government in society, the burdens to be carried by taxpayers, the appropriate strategies for coping with social problems, the issues posed by specific social insurance and public assistance programs, the relative reliance to be placed on providing cash rather than services to the poor, the need for reform, and the nature of the decision-making process itself. In short, social welfare policy is a continuing political struggle over the issues posed by poverty and inequality and by other social problems in society.

Policymaking is frequently portrayed as a *rational* process in which policymakers identify social problems, explore all the solutions to a problem, forecast all the benefits and costs of each solution, compare benefits to costs for each solution, and select the best ratio of benefits to costs. In examining social welfare policy, this book considers both the strengths and weaknesses of this rational model.

More important, it portrays social welfare policy as a *political* process—as conflict over the nature and causes of poverty and other social problems and over what, if anything, should be done about them. Social welfare policy is political because of disagreements about the nature of the problems confronting society, about what should be considered "benefits" and "costs," about how to estimate and compare benefits and costs, about the likely consequences of alternative policies, about the importance of one's own needs and aspirations in relation to those of others, and about the ability of government to do anything "rationally." As the chapters in this book indicate, the political barriers to rational policymaking are indeed very great.

What Constitutes Social Welfare Policy?

Social welfare policy is anything a government chooses to do, or not to do, that affects the quality of life of its people. Broadly conceived, social welfare policy includes nearly everything government does—from taxation, national defense, and energy conservation, to health care, housing, and public assistance. More elaborate definitions of social welfare policy are available.[1] Most of them refer to actions of government that have an "impact on the welfare of citizens by providing them with services or income."[2]

Some scholars have insisted that government activities must have "a goal, objective, or purpose," in order to be labeled a "policy."[3] This definition implies a difference between governmental actions in general and an overall plan of action toward a specific goal. The problem, however, in insisting that government actions must have goals in order to be labeled as "policy" is that we can never be sure what the goal of a particular government action is. We generally assume that if a government chooses to do something there must be a goal, objective, or purpose, but often we find that bureaucrats who helped write the law, lobbyists who pushed for its enactment, and members of Congress who voted for it all had different goals, objectives, and purposes in mind! Multiple goals are not necessarily a bad thing, especially when they mean that more people stand to benefit from a policy, but any of the intentions of a law (stated or not) may also be quite different from what government agencies actually do. All we can really observe is what governments choose to do or not do.

Political scientists Heinz Eulau and Kenneth Prewitt supply still another definition of public policy: "Policy is defined as a 'standing decision' characterized by behavioral consistency and repetitiveness on the part of those who make it and those who abide by it."[4] It might be a wonderful thing if government activities were characterized by "consistency and repetitiveness"—that they seem to have "rhyme and reason"—but it is doubtful that we would ever find a public policy in government if we insisted on these criteria. As you shall see, much of what government does is neither consistent nor repetitive.

Note that this book focuses not only on government action but also on government *in*action—that is, on what governments choose *not* to do. Government inaction can have just as important an impact on society as government action.

Lengthy discussions of the definition of social welfare policy are unnecessary, often futile, and even exasperating, since few people can agree on a single definition of social welfare policy. Moreover, these discussions divert attention away from the study of specific social welfare policies.

The boundaries of social welfare policy are indeed fuzzy. For practical purposes, much of the discussion presented in this book concerns government policies that directly affect the income, services, and opportunities available to people who are aged, poor, disabled, ill, or otherwise vulnerable. Specifically, the major government policies and programs addressed are:

Income maintenance
    Minimum wage legislation
    Earned income credit
    Social Security
    Unemployment insurance
    Workers' compensation
    Supplemental Security Income (SSI)
    Temporary Assistance for Needy Families (TANF)
    General Assistance

Nutrition
    Food stamps
    School lunches and breakfasts
    Special Supplemental Nutrition Program for Women, Infants, and Children (WIC)
    Child and Adult Care Food Program
    Elderly Nutrition Program

Health
   Medicaid
   Medicare
   Public health

Social services
   Child protective services
   Family preservation services
   Community mental health services
   Day care
   Independent living and long-term care services for people who are elderly or disabled

Employment
   Employment services
   Job training
   Vocational rehabilitation

Housing
   Public housing
   Housing vouchers
   Mortgage assistance

Education
   Preschool education
   No Child Left Behind Act

Some of these social welfare programs are called **public assistance** because people must be poor (according to legal standards) in order to receive benefits; benefits are paid out of general-revenue funds. Public assistance programs (what most people simply call "welfare") include TANF, food stamps, Medicaid, SSI, school lunches and breakfasts, and General Assistance. Other social welfare programs are called **social insurance** because they are designed to prevent poverty. Workers and their employers pay into these programs; then, upon retirement, disability, or unemployment, those who paid into the program are entitled to benefits, regardless of their wealth. Social insurance programs include Social Security, Medicare, unemployment insurance, and workers' compensation. Still other social welfare programs are labeled **social services** because they provide care, counseling, education, or other forms of assistance to children, elderly individuals, those with disabilities, and others with particular needs. Child protective services, day care, independent living services, and mental health care are all examples of social services. Other types of services are provided in areas like employment, housing, and education. Also considered are a number of social justice or rights issues that affect social welfare, such as civil rights legislation, the Americans with Disabilities Act, affirmative action, and other provisions that bear directly on the status of women, people of color, and the influx of immigrants to the United States.

This book seeks, first of all, to describe the country's major social welfare programs. But it is also concerned with the causes of social welfare policy—why policy is what it is. In order to understand contemporary social welfare policy, it is necessary to learn about some of the social, economic, and political forces that have shaped social welfare policy in America. This book is concerned with how social welfare policies have developed and changed over time. It is also concerned with the consequences of social welfare policies—their effects on target groups and on society in general. Furthermore, the chapters that follow consider alternative policies—possible changes, "reforms," improvements, or phaseouts. Finally, this book is concerned with political conflict over the nature and causes of poverty and other social problems—and conflict over how, or whether, they should be addressed at all.

Social Welfare Policy: A Rational Approach

Ideally, social welfare policy ought to be rational. A policy is rational if the ratio between the values it achieves and the values it sacrifices is positive and higher than any other policy alternative. Although this might be viewed as a strictly economic (cost–benefit) approach, we should not measure benefits and costs only in a narrow dollar-and-cents framework while ignoring basic social values. The idea of rationalism involves the calculation of *all* social, political, and economic values sacrificed or achieved by a public policy, not just those that can be measured in dollars.

Rationalism has been proposed as an "ideal" approach to both studying and making public policy.[5] Indeed, it has been argued that rationalism provides a single "model of choice" that can be applied to all kinds of problems, large and small, public and private.[6] Most government policies are far from being entirely rational. Even so, the model remains important because it helps identify barriers to rationality. It helps us pose the question "Why is policymaking not a more rational process?"

Let us examine the conditions for rational policymaking more closely:

1. Society must be able to identify and define social problems and agree there is a need to resolve these problems.

2. All the values of society must be known and weighed.

3. All possible alternative policies must be identified and considered.

4. The consequences of each alternative must be fully understood in terms of both costs and benefits, for the present and for the future, and for target groups and the rest of society.

5. Policymakers must calculate the ratio of benefits to costs for each alternative.

6. Policymakers must choose the policy that maximizes *net* values—the alternative that achieves the greatest benefit at the lowest cost.

Because this notion of rationality assumes that the values of society as a whole can be known and weighed, it is not enough to know the values of some groups and not others. There must be a common understanding of societal values. Rational policy-making also requires information about alternative policies and the predictive capacity to foresee accurately the consequences of each alternative. Rationality requires the intelligence to calculate correctly the ratio of costs to benefits for each policy alternative. This means calculating all present and future benefits and costs to both the target groups and nontarget groups in society. Finally, rationalism requires a policy-making system that facilitates rationality in policy formation.

Identifying **target groups** means defining the segment of the population for whom the policy is intended—those who are aged, poor, ill, disabled, or abused, or who have other needs. Then the desired effect of the program on the target groups must be determined. Is it to change their physical or economic condition—for example, to increase the cash income of poor people, to provide decent housing for inner-city residents, to reduce child maltreatment, or to improve the health of the elderly? Or is the program designed to change their knowledge, attitudes, or behavior—for example, to provide job skills, to improve literacy, or to increase awareness of legal rights? If several different effects are desired, what are the priorities among them? And what are the possible unintended or unanticipated consequences on target groups—for example, does public housing provide shelter for low-income individuals at the cost of increasing segregation between African Americans and whites? Do emergency shelters for homeless people risk forgoing the establishment of permanent housing units? Or do food stamps provide nutritional benefits while increasing stigma toward those who use them? What is the impact of a policy on the target group in proportion to that group's total need? A program that promises to meet a recognized national need—for example, to eradicate poverty or cover prescription drug costs—but actually meets only a small percentage of that need, may generate great praise at first but bitterness and frustration later when it becomes known how insufficient the impact really is.

Policies are likely to have different effects on various segments of the population. Identifying the effects of policy on important **nontarget groups** is crucial, but it can be difficult. For example, what is the impact of welfare reform proposals—such as a guaranteed annual income—on groups other than the poor (working families and government bureaucrats)? Rational policymaking also requires consideration of these **externalities** or **spillover effects.** These nontarget effects may be benefits as well as costs—for example, the benefits to the housing industry from public housing projects or the benefits to farmers, food manufacturers, and retailers from the Food Stamp Program.

When will the benefits or costs be felt? Is the policy designed for short-term emergency situations, or is it a long-term developmental effort? If it is short-term, what will prevent bureaucrats from turning it into a long-term program, even after immediate needs are met? Many studies have shown that new or innovative programs have positive effects initially—for example, model preschool programs and job training programs. However, the positive effects sometimes disappear as the novelty and enthusiasm of new programs wear off or as programs deviate from their original models. Other programs experience difficulties at first. For example, physicians and other healthcare providers were strongly opposed to the Medicare and Medicaid programs.

But these programs turned out to have "sleeper" effects. Today Medicare and Medicaid have achieved widespread acceptance and provide vast sums of money to the health care industry.

Rational policymakers must measure benefits and costs in terms of general social well-being. Government agencies have developed various forms of cost–benefits analysis to identify the direct costs and benefits (usually, but not always, in dollars) of providing aid and assistance to the *average* family, worker, or job trainee. The word "average," however, often doesn't fit many individuals or families. It is also difficult to identify and measure general units of social well-being in more than dollar terms. We need to know how to better measure health, job skills, employment opportunities, and other social values.

Comprehensive rationality in public policy not only fails to occur in the political environment, it may actually not be rational. Herbert A. Simon, a Nobel Prize winner for his studies of the decision-making process in large organizations, noted this apparent contradiction many years ago. It is so costly and time-consuming to learn about *all* the policy alternatives available to decision makers, to investigate *all* the possible consequences of each alternative, and to calculate the cost–benefit ratio of *every* alternative, that the improvement in the policy selected is not worth the extra effort required to make a comprehensive rational selection. Simon developed a theory of **bounded rationality,** which recognizes the practical limits to complete rationality. He wrote, "It is impossible for the behavior of a single, isolated individual to reach any high degree of rationality. The number of alternatives . . . [to be] explore[d] is so great, the information . . . to evaluate them so vast that even an approximation to objective rationality is hard to conceive."[7]

In contrast to completely rational decision making, Simon's notion of bounded rationality means that policymakers consider a limited number of alternatives, estimate these consequences using the best available means, and select the alternative that appears to achieve the most important values without incurring unacceptable costs. Instead of maximizing the ratio of benefits to costs, policymakers search for a "satisfying" choice—an alternative that is good enough to produce the desired benefits at a reasonable cost. Policymakers do not try to create the best of all possible worlds; rather they seek to get by, to come out all right, to avoid trouble, to compromise.

Rationalism, then, presents an ideal model of policymaking—in social welfare and in other policy fields. But policymaking in "the real world" is not usually a rational process. Policymaking occurs in a political context that places severe limits on rationality, especially in an increasingly partisan political environment.

Social Welfare Policy: A Political Approach

Social welfare policy is political because it arises out of conflict over the nature of the problems confronting society and what, if anything, should be done about them. Political scientist Harold Lasswell described politics as "who gets what, when, and how."[8] Politics is an activity through which people try to get more of whatever there is to get—money, jobs, prestige, prosperity, respect, and power itself. Conflict over the allocation of values in society is central to politics and policymaking. "Politics . . . consists of the activities—for example, reasonable discussion, impassioned oratory, balloting, and street fighting—by which conflict is carried on."[9]

Why do we expect conflict in society over who gets what? Why can't we agree on "a theory of justice" according to which everyone would agree on what is fair for all members of society, particularly those who are most vulnerable to social problems?[10] Why can't we have a harmonious, loving, caring, sharing society of equals? Philosophers have pondered these questions for centuries. James Madison, perhaps the first American to write seriously about politics, believed that the causes of "faction" (conflict) are found in human diversity—"a zeal for different opinions concerning religion, concerning government, and many other points . . . [and] an attachment to different leaders ambitiously contending for preeminence and power." More importantly, according to Madison, "the most common and durable source of faction has been the various and unequal distribution of property. Those who hold and those who are without property have ever formed distinct interests in society."[11] In short, class differences among people, particularly in the sources and amount of their wealth, are the root cause of social conflict.

A critical task of government is to regulate conflict. It does so by (1) establishing and enforcing general rules by which conflict is carried on, (2) arranging compromises and balancing interests in public policy, and (3) imposing settlements that the parties to a dispute must accept. Governments arrange settlements in the form of public policies that allocate values in such a way that they will be accepted by both "winners" and "losers," at least temporarily. Governments impose these settlements by enforcing public policy through the promise of rewards or threat of punishment.

From a political perspective, public policy is the outcome of conflicts in government over who gets what, and when and how they get it. A policy may be considered *politically rational* when it succeeds in winning enough support to be enacted into law, implemented by executive agencies, and enforced by the courts. Or it may be considered *politically rational* if it is supported by influential groups and believed to be popular among the voters. But this certainly differs from the type of rationality described earlier in the rational model.

The political approach raises serious questions about rationality in policymaking. It suggests that:

1. **Few social values are generally agreed on; more often there are only the values of specific groups and individuals, many of which are conflicting.** For example, even if everyone did agree that poor people need help in securing an adequate diet, whether they should receive food, food stamps or electronically distributed benefits, or cash is an ongoing political debate. On many issues, there is no fundamental agreement on the goal to be achieved. For example, there is little likelihood that antiabortion and prochoice forces will ever agree on the issue of access to abortion. More policymakers are coming to the table with strongly held philosophical positions that leave less and less room for compromise.

2. **Problems cannot be defined, because people do not agree on what the problems are. And what is a problem to one group may be a benefit to another group.** Consider discussion of what causes poverty. Explanations range from the willful behavior of those who prefer not to work, to discrimination and structural barriers to participation in gainful, economic activity. Remedies include low public assistance payments that provide a very meager standard of living for the poor, but save taxpayers' money, at least in the short run. Meager welfare payments may also force unemployed people to accept low-wage jobs benefitting industries that rely on this cheap labor pool. Or consider that saving the spotted owl would be viewed as a great benefit to some environmentalists but would represent a serious cost to those who rely on the logging industry for a living.

3. **Many conflicting costs and values cannot be compared or weighed.** For example, how can we compare the value of individual dignity with the cost of a general tax increase? Policymakers at all levels—local, state, and federal—face these challenges every day. A city or county government may choose to fund a residential program for people with developmental disabilities, rather than a drug detoxification program. Perhaps they view people with developmental disabilities as a more deserving clientele; perhaps they believe that program will be better administered. But they do not really know if their choice will achieve greater social values. In fact, many local governments appoint citizen advisory groups to recommend allocations of human service funding, because it takes the political pressure off elected officials in trying to distinguish one seemingly good cause from another.

4. **Policymakers, even with most advanced analytic techniques, cannot accurately forecast or predict the consequences of various policy alternatives or calculate their cost–benefit ratios when many diverse social, economic, and political values are involved.** Perhaps the best example of this concerns difficulties in economic forecasting. We may try to predict the effects of a general tax cut on consumer buying power, but other economic forces that cannot be foreseen well in advance—downturns in particular industrial sectors of the economy such as occurred in the auto and steel industries—may offset any beneficial effects on the country's overall economic well-being. Abrupt downturns in the stock market have altered many individuals' retirement plans. Many other events happen over which we have no control, such as earthquakes in California and floods in the Midwest. Even though governments try to respond rationally to these natural disasters, they may divert funds and attention from other activities already in place. Finally, there is fallout from events that perhaps could be predicted, but were ignored, such as events leading to city riots during the civil rights unrest of the 1960s, or the Los Angeles riots that erupted after the trial in the Rodney King police brutality case in 1992.

5. **The environment of policymakers, particularly the political system of power and influence, makes it virtually impossible to discern all social values, particularly those that do not have active or powerful proponents in or near government.** Those who are poor, ill, or do not speak English may have little access to governmental representation, even though their needs may be great. Children in the

United States face high rates of poverty, abuse, and neglect, yet they have no direct voice in the political arena.

6. **Policymakers are not necessarily motivated to make decisions on the basis of social values. Instead they often seek to maximize their own rewards—power, status, reelection, money, and so on.** Policymakers have their own needs, ambitions, and inadequacies, all of which can prevent them from performing in a highly rational manner. For instance, though the federal debt may place a severe strain on the country, members of Congress often do little about it, because any tax increase or budget cut may mean lost votes for some senator or representative anxious for reelection. Congressmembers also do their best to support pet projects in their districts to gain favor with constituents, whether or not these projects are good for the nation as a whole.

7. **Large, segmented government bureaucracies create barriers to coordinated policymaking.** It is difficult to bring all the interested individuals, groups, and experts together at the point of decision. Governmental decision making is so disjointed that it is a wonder how any legislation gets passed and any programs get implemented. Anyone who remembers the diagrams of "How a Bill Becomes a Law" from junior high civics classes knows that the maze of readings and calendars works to prevent most proposals from ever being seriously considered. Even when proposed legislation is considered, lawmakers use many tactics to pass or to defeat it, from filibusters to riders attached to other, sometimes unrelated, bills. Only a tiny fraction of legislation that is introduced to Congress and state legislatures ever makes it through the gauntlet (see Illustration 1.1, "Tips for the Legislative Process"). As described in this chapter and in Chapter 12, the process of implementing policy is no less daunting.

How can we bridge the differences between an ideal model of rational policymaking and the realization that policymaking is a political activity? Political scientist Charles E. Lindblom first presented an **incremental model** of policymaking as a critique of the rational model.[12] Lindblom observed that government policymakers do *not* annually review the entire range of existing and proposed policies, or identify all of society's goals, or research the benefits and costs of all alternative policies to achieve these goals. They, therefore, do not make their selections on the basis of *all* relevant information. Limits of time, knowledge, and costs pose innumerable obstacles in identifying the full range of policy alternatives and predicting their consequences. Political limitations prevent the establishment of clear-cut societal goals and the accurate calculation of cost–benefit ratios. The incremental model recognizes the impracticality of comprehensive rational policymaking and describes a more conservative process of public decision making.

Incremental policymaking considers existing policies, programs, and expenditures as a base. It concentrates attention on newly proposed policies and programs and on increases, decreases, or other modifications in existing programs. Incrementalism is conservative in that policymakers generally accept the legitimacy of established policies and programs. The focus of attention is on proposed changes in these policies and programs. This narrows the attention of policymakers to a limited number of new initiatives and increases or decreases in the budget.

ILLUSTRATION 1.1

Tips for the Legislative Process

Very few of the bills introduced in any body become law. In the U.S. Congress as well as most states, only about 10–15% of the bills introduced become law. A classic study by Ron Dear and Rino Patti of the bills introduced over several years in the Washington state legislature yielded seven tactics that were likely to improve a bill's chances of success. The bills that made it out of committee and onto the floor tended to share the following characteristics.

FACTORS THAT FOSTER SUCCESS

Early Introduction.   If your state allows bills to be prefiled before the session formally begins, that's a good time to get your bill introduced. It means there will be more time to consider it, hold hearings on it, build support for it, raise and answer questions about it.

Multiple Sponsors.   A bill that has several sponsors from the outset tends to look more like a winner. Bills with only one sponsor, by contrast, are sometimes assumed to be introduced just to please a constituent or do somebody a favor but not as a serious legislative proposal. Multiple sponsors increase credibility and also the number of advocates working for its success.

Bipartisan Sponsorship.   It is always essential to have sponsors from the party in the majority, but unless the legislature is overwhelmingly dominated by one party, it helps a bill's credibility and chances if its sponsors come from both parties. (On the national level, and anywhere that margins are close or party discipline is unreliable, bipartisan sponsorship is essential.)

Support of Governor and Relevant Executive Agency.   Since the executive branch will have to administer the resulting program (and in any case tends to have data, information, and expertise), legislators often are influenced by their support or opposition. If support is out of the question, the next best option is executive branch neutrality. The worst posture is outright opposition.

Influential Sponsors.   The job of getting a bill through hearings and out to the floor will be much easier if the chair or highest-ranking minority members of the subcommittees and committees are sponsors of the bill. If they, or highly respected senior members of the body, become sponsors and use their influence on its behalf, that's half the battle.

Open Hearings.   Hearings are a good opportunity to make a public record, bring an issue before the public, get questions and points of opposition out in the open and dealt with, and to give the advocacy groups a rallying point.

Amendments. Some advocates think their proposal has to be enacted exactly as they conceived it. That rarely happens. In fact, bills that are not amended tend to die. That's because everyone who amends a proposal has to be familiar with it and develops a bit of "ownership," a stake in its future if you will. Encourage amendments; they'll increase your bill's chances of success.

Ultimately, even these seven tactics are no guarantee of success. Bills are more likely to pass if they involve low costs, noncontroversial beneficiaries and purposes, and little

continued

significant change. Bills to create "National
Tuna Week," or name a building, have an easier time than bills to provide comprehensive
health or human services to low-income
families. Knowing the process won't ensure

victory, but not knowing it makes it hard to
even be a player.

Just keep reminding yourself: laws will be
passed with you or without you. The choice is
yours.

Source: Nancy Amidei, *So You Want to Make a Difference: A Key to Advocacy* (Washington, DC: OMB Watch, June 1991), pp. 19–20. Based on Ronald B. Dear and Rino J. Patti, "Legislative Advocacy: Seven Effective Tactics," *Social Work*, Vol. 26, No. 4, 1981, pp. 289–296. Copyright 1981, National Association of Social Workers, Inc.

There are important political advantages to incrementalism in policymaking. Conflict is reduced if the items in dispute are only increases or decreases in existing budgets or modifications of existing programs. Conflict is greater when policymaking focuses on major policy shifts involving great gains or losses for various groups in society or "all or nothing," "yes or no" policy decisions. To reconsider existing policies every year would generate a great deal of conflict; it is easier politically to continue previously accepted policies.

Policymakers may also continue existing policies because of uncertainty about the consequences of completely new or different policies. It is safer to stick with known programs when the consequences of new programs cannot be accurately predicted. Under conditions of uncertainty, policymakers continue past policies or programs whether they have proven effective or not. Only in a "crisis" do political decision makers begin to consider new and untried policies over existing ones. Thus, groups and individuals who seek more than incremental change in public policy usually try to generate a "crisis" atmosphere. A case in point is the view of some Americans that the country is facing a "health care crisis" necessitating a new program of national health insurance. A substantial number of people contend that either there is no crisis (most Americans have public or private health insurance, and there is a system of remedial care for others) or that the so-called crisis has been blown way out of proportion. Those who see a crisis advocate a major shift in health care delivery in the United States, while the remainder may prefer a more conservative course of action—trying some pilot or demonstration programs or using strategies that address only people who currently have no health care coverage.

Policymakers also realize that individuals and organizations—executive agencies, congressional committees, interest groups—accumulate commitments to existing policies and programs. For example, it is accepted wisdom in Washington that bureaucracies persist over time regardless of their utility, that they develop routines that are difficult to alter, and that individuals develop a personal stake in the continuation of organizations and programs. These commitments are serious obstacles to major change. It is politically easier for policymakers to seek alternatives that involve only a minimum of budgetary, organizational, or administrative change.

Finally, in the absence of generally agreed-on social goals or values, it is politically expedient for governments to pursue a variety of different programs and policies simultaneously, even if some of them are overlapping or even conflicting (and many are). In this way, a wider variety of individuals and groups in society are "satisfied." Comprehensive policy planning for specific social goals may maximize some people's values, but it may also generate extreme opposition from others. A government that pursues multiple policies may be politically more suitable to a pluralistic society comprised of people with varying values.

THE POLICYMAKING PROCESS

Policymaking involves a combination of processes. These processes are not always clear-cut and distinguishable, but we can identify them for purposes of analysis. They include the following:

♦ *Identifying policy problems.* Publicized demands for government action can lead to identification of policy problems.

♦ *Formulating policy proposals.* Policy proposals can be formulated through political channels by policy-planning organizations, interest groups, government bureaucracies, state legislatures, and the president and Congress.

♦ *Legitimizing public policy.* Policy is legitimized as a result of the public statements or actions of government officials, both elected and appointed—the president, Congress, state legislators, agency officials, and the courts. This includes executive orders, budgets, laws and appropriations, rules and regulations, and decisions and interpretations that have the effect of setting policy directions.

♦ *Implementing public policy.* Policy is implemented through the activities of public bureaucracies and the expenditure of public funds, often in conjunction with other organizations and agencies.

♦ *Evaluating public policy.* Policies are formally and informally evaluated by government agencies, by outside consultants, by interest groups, by the mass media, and by the public (and often these groups reach different conclusions about a policy or program's worth or utility).

This is a formal breakdown of the policymaking process used by many students of public policy.[13] What it says is that some groups succeed, usually through the help of the mass media, in capturing public attention for their own definition of a problem. Various government bureaucracies, private organizations, and influential individuals, then, propose solutions in terms of new laws or programs, new government agencies, or new public expenditures. These proposals twist their way through the labyrinths of government and eventually emerge (generally after many alterations and amendments) as laws and appropriations. Government bureaucracies are created to carry out these laws and spend these funds. Eventually, either through informal feedback or formal evaluation studies, the successes and failures of these laws, bureaucracies, and expenditures are examined.

All this activity involves both attempts at rational problem solving *and* political conflict. This is true whether we are describing Social Security or the Food Stamp Program, employment training or access to an abortion, fair housing, or immigration policy. Both rational and political considerations enter into each stage of the policymaking process, complicating everything from problem identification to policy evaluation (a focus of Chapter 12).

Agenda Setting

Deciding what is to be decided is the most important stage of the policymaking process. This stage can be called "agenda setting." Societal conditions not defined as problems never become policy issues and never get on the policymakers' agenda. Government does nothing, and conditions improve, remain the same, or worsen. But if conditions in society are defined as problems, then they become policy issues, and government is forced to decide what to do.

Think of all the conditions that existed for many years but were nonissues until they were broadly publicized. The "separate but equal" doctrine remained in place for decades until the civil rights movement swept the country, complete with marches, sit-ins, and even riots. Poverty has always been with us, but it first became a political issue in the 1960s with the help of television documentaries. Abortion and domestic violence would not have become part of the policy agenda without the rise of the women's movement. Policy issues do not just happen. Creating an issue, dramatizing it, calling attention to it, and pressuring government to do something about it are important political tactics. These tactics are employed by influential individuals, organized interest groups, policy-planning organizations, political candidates and officeholders, and perhaps most importantly, the mass media. These are the tactics of agenda setting.

Nondecisions

Preventing certain conditions in society from becoming policy issues is also an important political tactic. "Nondecision making" occurs when influential individuals or groups act to prevent the emergence of challenges to their own interests in society. According to political scientists Peter Bachrach and Morton Baratz,

> Non-decision making is a means by which demands for change in the existing allocation of benefits and privileges in the community can be suffocated before they are even voiced; or kept covert; or killed before they gain access to the relevant decision-making arena; or failing all these things, maimed or destroyed in the decision-implementing stage of the policy process.[14]

Nondecision making occurs when powerful individuals, groups, or organizations act to suppress an issue because they fear that if public attention is focused on it, something not in their best interest may be done. Nondecision making also occurs when political candidates, officeholders, or administrative officials anticipate that powerful individuals or groups will not favor a particular idea. They therefore do not pursue the idea because they do not want to rock the boat. Such was the case with publicly supported health insurance. Until the 1960s, powerful medical lobbies were successful in blocking serious consideration of these healthcare initiatives. They have successfully continued to block national health insurance legislation.

The Mass Media

The power of the mass media is their ability to set the agenda for decision making—to decide what problems will be given attention and what problems will be ignored.[15] Deciding what is "news" and who is "newsworthy" is a powerful political weapon. Television executives and producers and newspaper and magazine editors decide what people, organizations, and events will be given public attention. Without media coverage, the general public would not know about many of the conditions or government programs affecting poor people or other groups or about alternative policies or programs. Without media coverage, these topics would not likely become objects of political discussion, nor would they likely be considered important by government officials, even if they knew about them. Media attention creates issues and personalities. Media inattention can doom issues and personalities to obscurity.

The media, especially the major television networks, are often accused of having a liberal bias.[16] Even if this is true, today, countervailing opinions get their share of coverage from conservative television and radio commentators, talk show hosts, and newspaper columnists, and special television channels devoted to their opinions. With the advent of cable TV there are now many more networks from which to choose, but corporate mergers and the loss of local, independent radio stations and newspapers also have an effect. Many cities now have just one local, daily newspaper.

The media are key in directing attention to issues, though the consensus is that they do not change people's minds on issues as much as influence feelings about issues on which individuals had not yet formed an opinion.[17] Even when journalists' personal views are liberal, the media that employ them are owned by powerful business interests that exert a countervailing conservative influence, and they demand a focus on what produces the most profit.[18] Many important social issues receive little coverage, or little in-depth coverage, because the media are caught up in sensationalizing other events and especially personalities.

Perhaps the real danger today is that we are overwhelmed with the number of issues that have caught the media's attention. The media themselves are competing for attention to issues. Government inaction and public indifference may result when people feel that there are too many problems to consider or that problems continue to grow even when we try to intervene. The media work most effectively to bring light to a cause when there is some consensus about the problems to be addressed. But often, such consensus is elusive.

The Budget

The budget is the single most important policy statement of any government. The expenditure side of the budget tells us who gets what in public money, and the revenue side of the budget tells us who pays the cost. There are few government activities or programs that do not require an expenditure of funds, and no public funds may be spent without legislative authority. The budgetary process provides a mechanism for reviewing government programs, assessing their costs, relating them to financial resources, and making choices among expenditures. Budgets determine what programs and policies are to be increased, decreased, allowed to lapse, initiated, or renewed. The budget lies at the heart of all public policies.

In the federal government, the Office of Management and Budget (OMB), located in the Executive Office of the President, has the key responsibility for budget preparation. Presidential administrations are generally motivated to make optimistic projections to support their budget proposals. OMB begins preparing a budget more than a year before the beginning of the fiscal year for which it is intended (for example, work began in January 2003 on the budget for the fiscal year beginning October 1, 2004 and ending September 30, 2005). Budget materials and general instructions go out from OMB to departments and agencies, which are required to submit their budget requests for increases or decreases in existing programs and for new programs to OMB. With requests for spending from departments and agencies in hand, OMB begins its own budget review. Hearings are held for each agency. Top agency officials support their requests as convincingly as possible. On rare occasions, a dissatisfied department head may ask the OMB director to present the department's case directly to the president. As the following January approaches, the president and the OMB director devote a great deal of time to the budget document, which is nearing its final stages of assembly. Then, in January, the president sends his proposal—*The Budget of the United States Government*—to the Congress. After the budget is in Congress's hands, the president may recommend further amendments as needs dictate.

Congress has established separate House and Senate Budget Committees and a joint Congressional Budget Office (CBO) to review the president's budget after its submission to Congress. The CBO was created "to check OMB's growing power" in the budget process.[19] The House and Senate Budget Committees initially draft a concurrent resolution setting target totals to guide congressional actions on appropriations and revenue bills considered throughout the year. Thus, congressional committees considering specific budget appropriations have the president's recommendations to guide them and the guidelines of the budget committees. If an appropriations bill exceeds the target set by the earlier resolution, it is sent back to the budget committees for reconciliation.

Consideration of specific appropriations is a function of the Appropriations Committee in each house. Both of these important committees have about ten fairly independent subcommittees to review the budget requests of particular agencies or groups of related functions. These subcommittees hold hearings in which department and agency officials, interest groups, and other witnesses testify about new and existing programs and proposed increases or decreases in spending. The appropriations subcommittees are very important, because neither the full committees nor the Congress has the time or expertise to conduct in depth reviews of programs and funding. Although the work of the subcommittees is reviewed by the full committee, and the appropriations acts must be passed by the full Congress, in practice most subcommittee decisions are routinely accepted.

Even after all its work, Congress usually makes no more than small changes in the total budget figure recommended by the president. This is because so much of the federal budget is "uncontrollable." A great deal of the budget rests on "past policies of Congress and represents commitments in future federal budgets" like social insurance and some public assistance programs (people who meet legal definitions are "entitled" to receive benefits) and other items like interest on the national debt.[20] This is not to say that major struggles do not ensue over particular programs. On some social welfare spending issues (big ones like Medicare and smaller ones like the volunteer service program called AmeriCorps), budget battles have been especially acrimonious. Political partisanship is contributing to an increasingly contentious budget process, but there are so many appropriations that most are still determined by executive agencies interacting with the OMB. Congress usually makes only minor adjustments in them.

If this description of the federal government's budget process makes it sound as though it were the most rational aspect of policymaking, nothing could be further from the truth. The budget process is no less political than other aspects of policymaking. This is because government spending is very big business. The president's budget estimate for fiscal year 2005 is $2.4 trillion.[21] Methods such as "planning, programming, and budgeting systems," "zero-based budgeting," and performance-based budgeting have been introduced over the years to make budgeting more rational, but in the long run,

> if politics is regarded in part as conflict over whose preferences shall prevail in the determination of national policy, then the budget records the outcomes of this struggle. . . . The size and shape of the budget is a matter of serious contention in our political life. Presidents, political parties, administrators, congressmen, interest groups, and interested citizens vie with one another to have their preferences recorded in the budget. The victories and defeats, the compromises and the bargains, the realms of agreement and the spheres of conflict in regard to the role of the national government in our society all appear in the budget. In the most integral sense, budgeting—that is, attempts to allocate scarce financial resources through political processes in order to realize disparate visions of the good life—lies at the heart of the political process.[22]

Implementation

Policy implementation includes all the activities that result from the official adoption of a policy. Policy implementation is what happens after a law is passed. We should never assume that the passage of a law is the end of the policymaking process. Sometimes laws are passed and nothing happens! Sometimes laws are passed and executive agencies, presuming to act under these laws, do a great deal more than Congress ever intended. Political scientist Robert Lineberry writes,

> The implementation process is not the end of policy-making, but a continuation of policy-making by other means. When policy is pronounced, the implementation process begins. What happens in it may, over the long run, have more impact on the ultimate distribution of policy than the intentions of the policy's framers.[23]

Specifically, policy implementation involves:

1. The creation, organization, and staffing of new agencies to carry out the new policy, or the assignment of new responsibilities to existing agencies and staff.

2. The development of specific directives, rules, regulations, or guidelines to translate new policies into courses of action.

3. The direction and coordination of personnel and expenditures toward the achievement of policy objectives.

4. The monitoring of activities used to carry out the policy.

The best-laid plans of policymakers often do not work. Before a policy can have any impact, it must be implemented. And what governments say they are going to do is not always what they end up doing.

Traditionally, the implementation of public policy was the subject matter of public administration. And traditionally, administration was supposed to be free of politics. Indeed, the separation of "politics" from "administration" was once thought to be the cornerstone of a scientific approach to administration. But today it is clear that politics and administration cannot be separated. Opponents of policies do not end their opposition after a law is passed. They continue their opposition in the implementation phase of the policy process by opposing attempts to organize, fund, staff, regulate, direct, and coordinate the program. If opponents are unsuccessful in delaying or halting programs in implementation, they may seek to delay or halt them in endless court battles (school desegregation and abortion policy are certainly cases in point). In short, conflict is a continuing activity in policy implementation.

The federal bureaucracy makes major decisions about the implementation of public policy. There are about 2.2 million civilian employees of the federal government (not counting the nearly 700,000 civilian employees of the Department of Defense).[24] This huge bureaucracy has become a major base of power in America—independent of the Congress, the president, the courts, or the people. The bureaucracy does more than fill in the details of congressional policies, although this is one power of bureaucratic authority. Bureaucracies also make important policies on their own by (1) proposing legislation for Congress to pass; (2) writing rules, regulations, and guidelines to implement laws passed by Congress; and (3) deciding specific cases in the application of laws or rules.

In the course of implementing public policy, federal bureaucracies have decided such important questions as the extent to which women and members of particular ethnic groups will benefit from affirmative action programs in education and employment, whether opposition political parties or candidates will be allowed on television to challenge a presidential speech or press conference, whether welfare agencies will search Social Security Administration files to locate nonsupporting parents, and the foods available to WIC participants. The decisions of bureaucracies can be overturned by Congress or the courts if sufficient opposition develops. But most of these bureaucratic decisions go unchallenged, and there are analogous layers of bureaucracy at the state and local levels.

THE PUBLIC AND SOCIAL WELFARE

Public Opinion

Even in a democracy, public opinion may not determine public policy, but politicians are mindful of what their constituents—particularly their powerful constituents—think. Of course, the public, like politicians, frequently do not agree on public policy issues, and their own views are often inconsistent. For example, an analysis of public opinion surveys showed that although Americans tend to express resentment for "welfare" programs, they also say that they want to help people in need.[25] Historically, Americans, young and old, have voiced strong support for the nation's Social Security program.[26] There is less consensus on spending for public assistance. In the late 1980s, Americans voiced greater support for increased health, education, and nutrition spending than for defense spending,[27] but they were generally not disposed to pay much more in taxes to support programs for the poor.[28] By 1996, the year Congress passed a major overhaul of the country's public assistance programs, 53 percent were against cuts in social spending and 54 percent were against cutting defense spending.[29]

The Gallup Poll keeps its finger on the pulse of the country with continuous telephone surveys of scientifically selected samples of adult Americans. Since 1935 it has asked Americans what they think is the country's most important problem. From 1935 until the late 1980s, Americans were either most concerned about economic issues—unemployment, inflation, high living costs—or wars and related international matters, although racial problems and civil rights did appear at the top of the list a few times in the 1950s and 1960s.[30] Then in 1989, drugs topped the list for the first time and remained there through 1991, when the economy and unemployment again took precedence.[31] In 1994 these issues gave way to crime and later ethics and family values as the most important problem.

Following the September 11, 2001, terrorist attacks on the World Trade Center in New York City and the Pentagon in Washington, DC, terrorism and international issues topped the list, but as the economy faltered, it again took precedence. Given the war in Iraq, in late 2003, war and terrorism and the economy took equal place at the top of the list of most important problems.[32]

Public opinion polls also consider Americans' view on other policy issues. Taxes play an important role in the political environment because various segments of the population hold substantially different views of the appropriate tax burden that Americans should bear. A 2003 Harris Poll indicated that the public was more concerned about cutting the budget deficit and maintaining government services than cutting taxes, but there is considerable variation in the public's policy mandate for taxing and spending, as seen in Illustration 1.2. Given President George W. Bush's success in passing tax reductions, it also demonstrates that the public doesn't necessarily get what it says it wants. Of particular interest is the large number of respondents who think that maintaining Social Security and government-funded healthcare programs is more important than cutting taxes. Most Americans also want to prevent the federal budget deficit from growing. The poll also points to the irony that today more Democrats and liberals than Republicans and conservatives support a balanced federal budget. But the poll also shows Americans' divisions about whether to raise, cut, or keep taxes the same, and public opinion on this and most other subjects is subject to change.

America's Capacity for Giving

In addition to government expenditures for social welfare, we must consider private philanthropy and volunteerism as important sources of aid. Volunteers in the United States spend many hours helping those less fortunate than themselves—they visit elderly people in nursing homes, tutor children from disadvantaged environments, dish out meals in soup kitchens, assist people with AIDS, and perform many other services, all without much government help.

Independent Sector, an association of private, foundation, and voluntary organizations, reports that approximately 44 percent of all adults volunteer, and they spend an average of 15 hours a month doing so.[33] Slightly more women (46 percent) than men (41 percent) volunteer, and more individuals who belong to a religious organization (75 percent) volunteer than those who do not volunteer (58 percent), but there are no differences in number of hours volunteered with respect to age, gender, race or ethnicity, giving patterns, or religious attendance. The largest percent of the U.S. population that volunteers (19 percent) is involved in religious activities, followed by health-related activities (8 percent), and human services and youth development (7 percent each).

A number of Americans also dig into their pockets to help. According to the American Association of Fundraising Counsel (AAFRC) Trust for Philanthropy, in 2002 Americans gave nearly $241 billion.[34] Tougher economic times seem to have taken a toll. After adjusting for inflation, this was slightly less than in 2001, and a disappointment after banner fund-raising years in the late 1990s and the early part of the new millennium that were fueled by a strong economy and the September 11, 2001, terrorist attacks on the World Trade Center and the Pentagon.

Independent Sector also reports that, in 2000, 89 percent of households gave to charity; of all households that gave, the average contribution was $1,620 (3.1 percent

ILLUSTRATION 1.2

Little Support for a Big Tax Cut: Reducing Budget Deficit and Maintaining Government Services Seen as More Important to Americans Than Cutting Taxes

by Humphrey Taylor

There is relatively little public support for the kind of big tax cut proposed by the president and passed by the House of Representatives. Only 18% of the public believes that cutting taxes is more important than reducing the federal budget deficit. Only 15% thinks cutting taxes is more important than maintaining federal government services like Medicare, Social Security and Medicaid. And fully 84% believes that it will be a serious problem if the budget deficit gets bigger.

These are the results of *The Harris Poll*®, a nationwide survey of 2,179 adults polled online between April 17 and 23, 2003, using the same methods used by Harris Interactive® to forecast the 2000 elections with great accuracy.

Some of the main results of this research are:

♦ Almost half of all adults (46%) think that reducing the federal budget deficit and cutting taxes are equally important. Among the remainder, a 32% to 18% plurality thinks that reducing the federal budget deficit is more important than cutting taxes.

♦ There are substantial differences on this issue between Republicans and Democrats and between those with different political philosophies. Support for cutting taxes as the most important priority is higher among Republicans (28%) than among Democrats (10%) and higher among con-

servatives (31%) than among liberals (12%) and moderates (12%). (It is ironic that conservatives and Republicans, who for much of the 20th century were the strongest advocates of balancing the federal budget deficit, are now less committed to it than Democrats and liberals).

♦ An overwhelming majority of all adults (77%) think that it is more important to maintain federal government services like Medicare, Social Security and Medicaid than to cut taxes (15%). Majorities of Republicans, Democrats, independents, conservatives, liberals and moderates all think this way. However, larger minorities of Republicans (27%) and conservatives (31%) than of Democrats (4%) or liberals (4%) think that cutting taxes is more important.

♦ An overwhelming 84% majority of the public thinks that it is a serious problem if the federal budget deficit gets much bigger. Almost half the public (46%) thinks this would be a very serious problem.

While majorities of Republicans, Democrats and Independents, as well as of conservatives, moderates and liberals, agree that a larger budget is a serious problem, the proportions who think this way vary substantially. Majorities of Democrats (63%), of Independents (53%), of moderates (51%) and of liberals (62%) think that this is a very serious problem. Only 26%

continued

ILLUSTRATION 1.2 *(continued)*

of Republicans and 31% of conservatives agree with them. (Here again we see a reversal of traditional positions.)

♦ The public is split three ways as to whether the president's proposal for a large tax cut would, if passed, strengthen the economy (34%), damage the economy (36%), or who are unsure (30%).

♦ Historically we have almost always found more people trusting Republicans than Democrats to do the right thing on taxes and tax cuts. Now, presumably because of the reservations many people have about the benefits of a large tax cut, only 26% think that the Republicans can be trusted more, the same number who trust the Democrats. Fully 27% say that they cannot trust either party to do the right thing, and a further 12% are not sure.

Given all of these attitudes, what is the bottom line? What policy do most people support? The answer: there is no consensus. Almost a quarter of all adults (22%) favor "a big tax cut"—in other words, the president's proposal. A further quarter (27%) would favor a

smaller tax cut, making half of the public in favor of some kind of tax cut. One in five adults (21%) thinks that we should make no change to taxes, and a further 13% think that, far from cutting taxes, we ought to roll back recent tax cuts.

On this question also there are substantial differences between Republicans and Democrats, but nothing like a majority in either party favoring any one policy. Most Republicans favor either a big tax cut (36%) or a smaller tax cut (37%), but Democrats are much more likely to want to keep taxes as they are (24%) or to roll back recent tax cuts (24%).

THE BIG PICTURE

This Harris Poll shows that the public is very divided on many of these issues. What is clear, however, is that only about a quarter of the public—more on some questions and less on others—is supportive of the big tax cut which the president and many Republican leaders want. Furthermore, the president's push for a big tax cut has reduced or eliminated what is usually a substantial Republican advantage on tax issues.

Source: Harris Interactive.® The Harris Poll® #27, May 5, 2003
Humphrey Taylor is the chairman of the Harris Poll, Harris Interactive.

of their income).[35] AAFRC reports that in 2002 individual Americans remained the biggest givers, having contributed $184 billion of the $241 billion that went to charity. Although this is considerably less than the 10 percent that many churches encourage their members to tithe, it represents a substantial number of charitable donations. According to the *Chronicle of Philanthropy,* blacks give more of their income than whites (for example, in the $30,000 to $50,000 income bracket, blacks gave an average of $528, compared to $462 for whites).[36] Regardless of income, college graduates give at a rate two to three times higher than others. Religion affects giving in general, and particularly among blacks; 90 percent of their donations go to religious organizations, compared to 75 percent of the donations whites make. Those living in the West averaged the lowest amount of discretionary income but gave the highest percent of it (nearly 8 percent) to charity, compared to those living in the East, who had the highest amount of discretionary income on average but gave the smallest percent (about 4 percent) to charity. Utah County, Utah; Madison County, Idaho; and San Juan County, Utah, are among the nation's most generous counties, with church tithing thought to be a considerable influence in these areas. Religious giving is most prominent in the South and West and least prominent in the East. Foundations and corporations provided far less to charity than did individuals; in 2002 their contributions were $27 billion and $12 billion, respectively.[37]

As usual, religious organizations received the greatest share of all the funds donated ($84 billion), while education received $32 billion, health and human services each received $19 billion, and the arts received $12 billion.[38] The Salvation Army always tops the list of fundraisers, but in 2002 the Red Cross received the most ($1.7 billion) because donations following the September 11, 2001, attacks were counted in its 2002 fiscal year.[39] In 2002, the Salvation Army was second with $1.4 billion in donations. (In 2004 the Salvation Army's coffers got a boost in a single $1.5 billion gift from the estate of Joan B. Kroc, wife of the late Ray Kroc, the founder of McDonald's, which she designated for development of community centers around the country.) Next in line in the top ten were Gifts in Kind International, the American Cancer Society, Fidelity Investments Charitable Gift Fund (which invests donors' contributions and distributes grants to charities), Lutheran Services in America, YMCA of the USA, Nature Conservancy, University of Southern California (Los Angeles), and Feed the Children. Each of these organizations received more than $500 million in donations. Volunteerism and philanthropy allow Americans to channel their efforts and funds where they feel the needs are greatest.

Americans' tradition of voluntary service is also exemplified in federal organizations like the Peace Corps and the Corporation for National and Community Service. The Peace Corps supplies volunteers to other countries to assist with community development efforts. The Corporation for National and Community Service operates AmeriCorps, the Volunteers in Service to America (VISTA) program, the Retired and Senior Volunteer Program, and several other domestic volunteer programs.

Recent Republican and Democratic presidential administrations have spotlighted volunteer efforts. Saying that the government could not possibly meet all the country's social service needs, former President George H. W. Bush referred to the country's many volunteers as "1,000 points of light," and he supported the idea of a national service program for young people run by a foundation with substantial federal funding. Similar plans, many urging voluntary participation by youth in return for educational benefits to attend college or vocational schools, had been proposed for many years. Some people believe that such service should be required of all young people, similar to a military draft. President Clinton successfully encouraged Congress to enact Americorps, a national service program that allows Americans of any age to serve their country in exchange for help in obtaining a college education, and he convened the President's Summit for America's Future to promote volunteerism, with the support of all the surviving former presidents. President George W. Bush established the USA Freedom Corps to oversee Americans' volunteer efforts in the United States and abroad, and he established the President's Council on Service and Civic Participation to encourage more Americans to volunteer. He has focused on the efforts of faith- and community-based groups to aid Americans, particularly to reduce reliance on public assistance.

Everyone appreciates the efforts of those who are willing to give their time or money to help others. It is difficult for Americans to imagine a society where such assistance is not available. Citizen involvement is important to public, private, and church-affiliated social service agencies. Volunteers do much to aid their communities by helping these agencies provide more and better services. President Clinton once said, "Much of the work of America cannot be done by government."[40] It can also be said that much of the work of America cannot be done by volunteers alone. As Bishop John Ricard of the U.S. Catholic Conference commented on voluntary efforts to feed the hungry:

> Our efforts cannot and should not substitute for just public policies and effective pro-
> grams to meet the needs of the hungry. . . . [These efforts] should not be misread as a
> sign of success for volunteerism, but rather a desperate attempt to feed hungry people
> when others have abandoned their responsibility.[41]

And specifically in regard to help from corporations, Liz Krueger of the Community Food Resource Center in New York City said, "What I fear is the perception that these companies, or the public as a whole, can take the place of radically reduced government assistance."[42] Many people—those in need of job training or mental health care—need professional assistance. Volunteers alone cannot make up for gaps in social services when professional help is needed.

Though health and human services received a total of $38 billion in charitable giving in 2002, the costs of the Medicaid program alone are well over $200 billion annually.[43] As Julian Wolpert notes, the idea that charitable giving, even coupled with state and local government expenditures for welfare, can substitute for federal funding is highly implausible.[44] Many charitable organizations are locally based, and they spend their monies within their own communities, and many people give to churches, YMCAs, museums, and public television and radio—services that they use themselves, rather than those used by the needy. As figures on giving indicate, some communities are much more generous than others. Much of the aid that goes to help needy people comes from government. Wolpert also notes that communities and charities "lack the organization and resources needed for the much larger job of addressing serious inequality in income, education, health care, nutrition, and other areas for which we rely today on the federal government for assistance." One challenge of our social welfare system is to determine the best mix of public and private, professional and voluntary efforts to help those in need.

Political Ideology and Social Welfare

If Americans were pure in their political ideology, there would be clear differences in the conservative, liberal, and moderate agendas for the country. Just who fits each of these categories? According to the *New Political Dictionary,* a **conservative** is "a defender of the status quo"; "the more rigid conservative generally opposes virtually all government regulation of the economy, . . . favors local and state action over federal action, and emphasizes fiscal responsibility, most notably in the form of balanced budgets." But not all conservatives are this rigid. On the other hand, a **liberal** is "one who believes in more government action to meet individual need."[45] Liberals want the government to do much more to promote **distributive justice,** economic as well as social. Conservatives fear that the government has already done too much in this regard, destroying individual initiative and promoting economic and other social problems. Many Americans fall somewhere in between the extremes of liberal and conservative.

The Republican party platform has become highly conservative, especially on social issues such as abortion and gay rights. Many Republican members of Congress have also resisted initiatives like broad-scale healthcare reform, preferring a more incremental and narrowly targeted approach. Some Republicans think that their party has moved too far to the right.[46] Although they may favor the Republican ideology on spending and taxing matters, they are unhappy with the party's stance on abortion and gay rights. Meanwhile, many people who espouse the liberal agenda, which remains consistent in its prochoice and pro gay rights stances, have become more cautious about government spending. Although the term *liberal* (sometimes referred to as the "L" word) is most often associated with the Democratic party, not all Democrats are happy with the liberal agenda for the country. Some authors claim that liberalism is dead.[47] Democrats of more moderate or conservative persuasions may align themselves with the need for strengthening some social programs, but there are Democrats whose religious and moral convictions persuade them that access to abortion and gay rights are not issues they can support. Except for the most strident of ideologies, the lines between liberal and conservative, Democrat and Republican can be difficult to draw.

To the conservative rhetoric of the country we must now add the terms "family values" and "compassionate conservatism." The country has long debated the effects that out-of-wedlock births, divorce, and desertion have on its moral fiber. The Republican platform on traditional family matters sits quite well with the "religious right" of this country. No longer content to focus on matters of religion alone, this movement, the so-called *moral majority,* has taken a high profile on certain political issues, especially abortion. As one source described it, the religious right believes that "Government should enforce scriptural law," while "most mainstream religious people support the separation of church and state to ensure freedom of religion and speech for all."[48] Conservative jurist Robert Bork makes the counterclaim that "modern liberals try to frighten Americans by saying that religious conservatives 'want to impose their morality on others.' This is palpable foolishness. All participants in politics want to 'impose' on others as much of their morality as possible, and no group is more insistent on that than liberals."[49]

Though the religious right would like to see less government involvement in issues like education and public assistance, it would like more government intervention to outlaw abortion and restrict the behavior of gay men and lesbians. The ranks of the religious right feel that they hold the ideal for family values in the United States, even if public opinion polls show that most Americans favor access to abortion on some level.[50]

The presidency of William Jefferson Clinton provided its own study in political ideology. Clinton, a Southern Baptist, was well informed about scripture. During his first run for the presidency in 1992, Clinton called for a "new covenant" for social welfare. He wanted more job training and child care in return for greater responsibility on the part of public assistance recipients through stiffer work requirements, caps on the amounts given to those who have more children while receiving aid, and limits on the amount of time families can receive benefits—not what Americans think of as typical liberal rhetoric from a Democratic president. Those who espouse this combination of views have been called "New Democrats" or "centrists." This language of welfare reform was embodied in the Personal Responsibility and Work Opportunity Reconciliation Act of 1996 signed by President Clinton. The rhetoric also sounds much like that of President George W. Bush, who said, "I call my philosophy and approach 'compassionate conservatism.' . . . It is compassionate to aggressively fight poverty in America. It is conservative to encourage work and community spirit and responsibility and the values that often come from faith. And with this approach, we can change lives one soul at a time, and make a real difference in the lives of our citizens."[51]

The issue of religion and politics has taken on increased vigor during George W. Bush's administration. Bush established the White House Office of Faith-based and Community Initiatives, claiming that religious groups had been unfairly denied access to government funds to support their antipoverty and social welfare efforts. The president touched off a hailstorm of concern about the tenet of separation of church and state. Although federal money cannot be used to directly support religious activity, where religious activity begins and social services end may be difficult to monitor. Churches and religious or faith-based organizations have always helped the poor. Under certain circumstances these organizations were already entitled to pursue some government funding for their efforts, but whether and to what extent government should help them do so is a controversial matter. It raises questions as to which religious groups will be deemed worthy of receiving government funds, and there is virtually no solid evidence that religious groups are preferable to secular, nonprofit, and government agencies in delivering social services.

Special Interests and Social Welfare

The political model of policymaking provides a clear indication of the importance of influence in the political arena, but the poor and disadvantaged, who need help the most, are not represented in Washington in the same fashion as other groups in society.[52] They rarely write letters to members of Congress, and they do not make significant campaign contributions. They are rarely found on a representative's home state lecture circuit—service club lunches, civic meetings, and dedications. The poor cannot afford to come to Washington to visit their representatives' offices. Indeed, they do not turn out at the polls to vote as often as the nonpoor.

To the extent that the poor and disadvantaged are represented at all in Washington, they are represented by "proxies"—groups that are not poor or disadvantaged themselves but that claim to represent these groups. Among these proxy groups are the Children's Defense Fund, the National Low Income Housing Coalition, the Food Research and Action Center, and the National Association of Social Workers.

Lobbyists for the poor can be divided roughly into three categories: (1) churches, civil rights groups, and liberal organizations; (2) organized labor; and (3) welfare program administrators and lawyers. The churches (the United States Conference of Catholic Bishops, the National Council of Churches, B'nai Brith, and others) often support programs for the poor out of a sense of moral obligation. Likewise, liberal activist groups (Common Cause, Americans for Democratic Action, and others) often support social programs out of an ideological commitment. Civil rights organizations—the National Urban League, the National Association for the Advancement of Colored People (NAACP), the National Council of La Raza, and others—support programs for the poor and disadvantaged as a part of their general concern for the conditions affecting particular ethnic groups.

The success of lobbying efforts on behalf of the poor can also depend on the addition of organized labor's political power to the coalition of churches, civil rights groups, and liberal activists. Even though the clout of organized labor has waned in recent years with declining union membership, labor groups like the AFL-CIO do all the things that poor and disadvantaged members of society find difficult to do in politics: political organizing, campaign financing, letter writing, and personal lobbying. Historically, organized labor has tended to support programs for the poor, even though union pay scales have moved a great distance from the poverty line. Among those who comprise organized labor, labor leaders may be more likely to support social programs than the rank-and-file membership. Of course, the first concern of organized labor is labor legislation—labor relations, minimum wages, fair labor standards, and so on—but when labor leaders join other members of the welfare lobby in support of social programs, the result is a stronger political coalition.

Welfare program administrators and lawyers have a direct financial interest in supporting social welfare spending, and they may take the lead in organizing the others into coalitions that support particular programs. The welfare bureaucracy is said to create its own *poverty lobby*. Prominent among the organizations representing social program administrators is the American Federation of State, County, and Municipal Employees (AFSCME). Affiliated with the AFL-CIO, AFSCME is a labor union that includes many public workers whose jobs are directly affected by cutbacks in social programs. Another organization concerned about social welfare services is the Legal Service Corporation (LSC), whose attorneys provide legal assistance to poor and disadvantaged individuals. The LSC is chartered as an independent corporation, but much of its funding comes from the federal government. Conservative Congressmembers criticized the LSC for what they perceived as lobbying on its own behalf, and Congress limited the LSC's reach by prohibiting its involvement in activities such as class action suits. Of course, there are very few government bureaucracies—from the Defense Department, to the National Aeronautics and Space Administration, to the Department of Agriculture—that do not, directly or indirectly, lobby Congress for their own programs.

While the welfare lobby continues to go about its work, an anti-welfare lobby has grown increasingly vocal in this country. This sentiment has been fueled by the positions of authors such as Charles Murray who believe that public assistance programs are the cause, not the cure, of welfare dependency,[53] and conservative radio personalities like Rush Limbaugh who take a very dim view of liberals' positions. The religious right has also had success in promoting its social welfare agenda by getting anti-gay-rights measures on the ballots in several states, by influencing school board elections, and with its untiring efforts to erode reproductive freedoms.[54]

Lobbying for or against issues is a form of political activity that goes on every day with members of Congress and state legislatures. The Center for Responsive Politics reported that in 2000 businesses, unions, and other organizations spent more than $1.5 billion lobbying Washington.[55] An even more important form of political activity is support of individual candidates. Those interested in seeing specific types of legislation passed or defeated naturally support candidates who share their views. Support may come verbally through endorsements, and financially through campaign contributions at election time. Though a law passed in 1907 still makes it illegal for corporations to donate to federal candidates, and a 1947 law makes it illegal to use union dues to support candidates, one would hardly know it. Today, many candidates and special interests are supported through the use of **political action committees** (PACs). PACs are used by all types of interest groups. Virtually all forms of business and industry—real estate, agriculture, automobile, insurance, hospital—have PACs. The National Association of Social Workers, AFSCME, and other groups of social welfare service providers also operate some form of PAC. Although it does not identify itself as a PAC, the most prominent politically active group of the religious right is the Christian Coalition, founded by preacher Pat Robertson. There are approximately 4,000 PACs in the United States.[56] In the 1999–2000 election cycle, PACs raised $605 million.[57] In the Senate, $37 million in PAC funds went to Republicans and $24 million went to Democrats. PAC funds were more evenly divided in the House; $99 million went to Democrats and $96 million went to Republicans.

Many PACs have a vested interest in social welfare spending. The American Medical Association, long opposed to government intervention in the healthcare arena, now has a very large stake in the Medicare and Medicaid programs. The AMA closely monitors attempts to change the nature of healthcare delivery in the United States. So does the Health Insurance Association of America, which spent millions to influence the shape of health care when the Clinton administration tried to substantially alter the role of insurers in health delivery (see Chapter 8). Other groups that provide social welfare services also want to make sure that they are not adversely affected by new legislation, budget cuts, and government regulations, and they raise money to see that just the opposite happens.

A few politicians refuse to accept PAC money (in the 2000 presidential race, Al Gore did not accept PAC contributions; George W. Bush did). Though the number of politicians refusing PAC contributions may be growing, these contributions remain an important feature of election campaigns. In the 2001–2002 election cycle, the National Association of Realtors outpaced all other PACS, contributing more than $3.6 million to candidates. Other PACs that gave more than $2 million were the Laborers Union, Association of Trial Lawyers of America, National Auto Dealers Association, American Medical Association, AFSCME, Teamsters Union, United Auto Workers, International Brotherhood of Electrical Workers, Carpenters and Joiners Union, Machinists/ Aerospace Workers Union, and National Beer Wholesalers Association. Candidates generally prominently display the endorsements they receive from such organizations. The fear, of course, is that elected officials who are beholden to these special interests have a difficult time resolving public policy issues. For this reason, many individuals concerned about political ethics advocate campaign finance reform.

In 1974, Congress limited the amount of money that individuals and PACs could give to national party committees and candidates running for national offices. "Hard money" refers to the limited amounts that individuals can contribute directly to a candidate's campaign and that can be used for any legitimate campaign purpose. Republicans have been considerably more successful at raising hard money than Democrats, and they have raised considerably more than Democrats from relatively small donors using direct-mail solicitations.[58] To circumvent hard money limits, the concept of "soft money" developed. Soft money means "any contributions not regulated by federal election laws," and it used to refer to the unlimited contributions that individuals, groups, and organizations could give to party committees for general purposes at the state and local levels (e.g., voter education and "generic party-building activities such as TV ads supporting the Democratic and Republican platforms, but not naming specific candidates").[59] But the concern was that much of this soft money went to support federal elections in the form of items like administrative overhead and computer equipment, allowing more of the other contributions parties received to go directly to candidates.[60] The Federal Election Commission reported that national party committees collected $308 million in soft money from January 1, 2001, through June 30, 2002.[61] Both major parties have increasingly relied on soft money to finance campaigns, with the Democrats somewhat more reliant on it.[62] Table 1.1 lists the top ten soft money donors to the Democratic and Republican parties in the 2001–2002 election cycle.

In an attempt to reduce the influence of special interests, Congress passed the Bipartisan Campaign Reform Act (BCRA) of 2002, which amends the Federal Election Campaign Act of 1971. BCRA prohibits national party committees from raising or spending soft money. This legislation, championed by Republican Senator John Mc-Cain and Democratic Senator Russell Feingold, is the most sweeping federal campaign reform since Watergate era reforms were spurred by President Nixon's secret slush funds financed by business.[63] The U.S. Constitution gives Congress the power to regulate federal elections only, but the BCRA also has implications for state and local parties and elections.[64] For example, it prohibits "issue ads" that mention the name of a

TABLE 1.1

Top Ten Soft Money Donors 2001–2002 Election Cycle by Political Party

Democrats		Republicans	
Donor	*Amount*	*Donor*	*Amount*
1. Saban Entertainment, Inc.	$9,252,936	American Financial Group	$3,378,108
2. American Federation of State, County & Municipal Employees	7,483,500	Pharmaceutical Research & Manufacturers of America	3,249,087
3. Fred Eychaner; Owner, Newsweb Corp.	7,387,936	Texans for John Cornyn	3,100,000
4. Stephen L. Bing; Screenwriter and Producer	7,075,936	Phillip Morris Cos., Inc.	2,251,192
5. Service Employees International Union	4,872,618	Presidential Inaugural Committee	2,057,560
6. Communication Workers of America	4,028,150	Microsoft Corp	1,867,563
7. United Brotherhood of Carpenters & Joiners	3,926,209	AT&T	1,766,711
8. American Federation of Teachers	3,412,150	Governor Bush Committee	1,700,000
9. Stephen & Michelle Kirsch of the Kirsch Foundation	3,309,787	Freddie Mac[a]	1,605,615
10. Laborers' International Union of North America	2,334,500	Stanley E. Fulton; Owner Sunland Park Racetrack and Casino	1,250,000

Source: Common Cause. Available at http://www.commoncause.org/laundromat/stat/topdonors01.htm

[a]Freddie Mac is the Federal Home Loan Mortgage Corporation.

federal candidate within 60 days of an election. The law also raises the amount of hard money an individual can contribute to a federal candidate from $1,000 to $2,000 per election and contains limits of $25,000 each year to national party committees, $10,000 to state party committees, and $5,000 to each PAC. The soft money ban does not seem to be hurting the parties, because political polarization among Americans has apparently caused many more individuals to make at least small contributions to the party of their choice.[65]

Many groups, from the American Civil Liberties Union to the National Rifle Association, contend that the BCRA's restrictions, especially the ones on issue ads, violate the right to free speech. A 2003 Supreme Court decision upheld major provisions of the BCRA.

Given the soft money ban on national political parties, another phenomenon has occurred, the growth of tax-exempt 527 organizations that "may raise funds from unlimited sources in unlimited amounts,"[66] a new form of soft money. Though 527s are supposed to be independent of candidates and political parties, they have been characterized as "shadow parties."[67] Republicans were particularly concerned about the fund-raising success of liberal groups like America Coming Together, the Media Fund, and MoveOn.org, which has been very adept at raising funds on the Internet.

The Federal Election Commission (FEC), charged with enforcing federal election laws, has itself been criticized for allowing campaign finance loopholes. FEC rule making is having its own effects on how the BCRA is interpreted. In May 2004, the FEC failed to take action to close the 527 loophole. During the 2004 presidential campaign, the controversy over 527s intensified following ads by the Swift Boat Veterans for Truth, a 527 organization, claiming that presidential candidate John Kerry's heroic actions during the Vietnam War had been exaggerated.

Campaign finance laws are also issues in many states. Efforts to limit political expression continue to raise legal challenges. Given the amount it takes to get elected to federal, state, and even local offices, most politicians are unlikely to impose their own caps on what they spend on election campaigns, and individuals and groups will look for ways to circumvent the law.

Globalism, Terrorism, and Social Welfare Policy

Social welfare policy is usually considered **domestic policy,** but many U.S. policy decision have global implications. Americans are compelled to think globally and to act globally as well. For example, the economic well-being of the United States is affected by its ability to obtain from other countries resources like oil that the United States consumes in great quantities. Obtaining these resources is contingent not only on the United States's purchasing power but also on its relationship with other countries.

Perhaps more directly relevant to social welfare policy is that the fierce competition among United States manufacturers of products like athletic shoes, clothes, electronics, souvenirs, and many other products causes these companies to seek cheap labor in other countries. This has tremendous implications for working conditions, including wages, in those countries as well as job opportunities in the United States.

The number of individuals who wish to immigrate to the United States is strongly affected by their country's standard of living and political conditions (war, civil rights), which the United States often has a hand in shaping. Immigration policy is closely intertwined with social welfare policy. Congress not only determines the number of people who will be allowed to immigrate from various countries, it also determines how, or whether, social welfare policy and programs will be used to assist immigrants.

Another example of global interconnectedness and social welfare concerns Americans' seemingly insatiable appetite for illegal drugs that flow from poor countries. U.S. **foreign policy,** including humanitarian aid, influences the extent to which those in other countries engage in this very lucrative drug trafficking market and the extent of violence associated with it, both in supplying countries and the United States.

As people travel freely, health is another global issue, since some diseases can spread readily from one part of the world to another. Stopping the spread of HIV and AIDS though education and other prevention efforts and seeing that treatment is available regardless of location or wealth is a prime example. Illnesses like severe acute respiratory syndrome (SARS) also present global concerns.

Of course, the most compelling recent example of the need for concern about the global environment stems from the September 11, 2001, terrorist attacks on the World Trade Center in New York City and the Pentagon in Washington, DC. In the aftermath of this tragedy, Americans must consider the effects of recent legislation, like the USA PATRIOT Act, which gives the federal government far-reaching powers of surveillance and detention in the name of curbing terrorism. Some see the act as entirely appropriate to the situation, but many believe that it threatens civil liberties and efforts to prevent racial, ethnic, and religious discrimination.[68] Civil liberties are the core of democracy, and attempts to erode them shake the foundation of virtually every aspect of social policy. Although this book concentrates on social welfare policy in the United States, the implications of United States policy for other countries, and other countries' policies for the United States, must also be considered.

SUMMARY

Although there are elements of rationalism in policymaking, the policy process is largely political. Our abilities to develop policies rationally are limited because we cannot agree on what constitute social problems and on what, if anything, should be done to alleviate these problems. We usually hesitate to take bold, new directions in the social welfare system, because we fear making large, costly errors that may be difficult to reverse. Only occasionally do new directions like the welfare reform legislation of 1996 occur.

Many energetic lobbies and political action committees in the United States work to influence elected officials every day. The work of politicians is difficult because the values espoused by these competing interest groups can differ widely. When it comes to social welfare policy, Americans represent the political spectrum from conservatives to middle-of-the-road centrists to liberals. This diversity of opinion causes the country to pursue a pluralist approach to social welfare policymaking. Policymakers follow several lines of thinking and arrive at policies and programs that are often contradictory and overlapping because they try to see that there is something there for everyone.

Social welfare policy development and implementation are much more a political "art and craft"[69] than a rational science. It is not enough for human service professionals to know the needs of people and to want to pass policies and provide services to help them. Policy advocates for the disenfranchised must both understand the political process and be adept at working within it if they are to have a voice in shaping social policy.

NOTES

1. See, for example, David G. Gil, "A Systematic Approach to Social Policy Analysis," *Social Service Review*, Vol. 44, December 1970, pp. 411–426.

2. T. H. Marshall, *Social Policy* (London: Hutchison University Library, 1955), p. 7. Also see the discussion in Neil Gilbert and Paul Terrell, *Dimensions of*

Social Welfare Policy, 5th ed. (Boston: Allyn and Bacon, 2002), Chapter 1. The distinction between social policy and social welfare policy is discussed in George Rohrlich, "Social Policy and Income Distribution," in Robert Morris, ed., Encyclopedia of Social Work, 16th ed. (New York: National Association of Social Workers, 1971), pp. 1385–1386.

3. See Carl T. Friedrich, Man and His Government (New York: McGraw-Hill, 1963), p. 70; Harold Lasswell and Abraham Kaplan, Power and Society (New Haven, CT: Yale University Press, 1970), p. 71.

4. Heinz Eulau and Kenneth Prewitt, Labyrinths of Democracy (Indianapolis: Bobbs-Merrill, 1973), p. 465.

5. Other major theoretical approaches to the study of public policy include institutionalism, elite theory, group theory, systems theory, and incrementalism. For an introduction to these approaches, see Thomas R. Dye, Understanding Public Policy, 9th ed. (Upper Saddle River, NJ: Prentice Hall, 1998), especially Chapter 2.

6. Edith Stokey and Richard Zeckhauser, A Primer of Policy Analysis (New York: Norton, 1978).

7. Herbert A. Simon, Administrative Behavior (New York: Macmillan, 1945), p. 79. See also his Models of Man (New York: Wiley, 1957) and The Sciences of the Artificial (New York: Wiley, 1970). Simon was trained as a political scientist; he won the Nobel Prize in economics in 1978.

8. Harold Lasswell, Politics: Who Gets What, When, How (New York: Free Press, 1936).

9. Edward C. Banfield and James Q. Wilson, City Politics (Cambridge, MA: Harvard University Press, 1963), p. 7.

10. John Rawls, A Theory of Justice, rev. ed. (Cambridge, MA: Belknap Press of Harvard University Press, 1999).

11. James Madison, The Federalist, No. X, November 23, 1787, reprinted in The Federalist of the New Constitution (London: Dent, 1911), pp. 41–48.

12. Charles E. Lindblom, "The Science of 'Muddling Through,'" Public Administration Review, Vol. 19, Spring 1959, pp. 79–88.

13. See Charles O. Jones, An Introduction to the Study of Public Policy, 2nd ed. (North Scituate, MA: Duxbury Press, 1978); Dye, Understanding Public Policy, 9th ed.

14. Peter Bachrach and Morton S. Baratz, Power and Poverty (New York: Oxford University Press, 1979), p. 7.

15. Thomas R. Dye and Harmon Zeigler, American Politics in the Media Age, 3rd ed. (Monterey, CA: Brooks/Cole, 1989), especially Chapter 5.

16. Bernard Goldberg, Bias: A CBS Insider Exposes How the Media Distort the News (Washington, DC: Regnery Publishing, 2002); Christopher Hewitt, "Estimating the Number of Homeless: Media Misrepresentation of an Urban Problem," Journal of Urban Affairs, Vol. 18, No. 3, 1996, pp. 431–447; especially p. 440.

17. Dye, Understanding Public Policy, 9th ed; Morris P. Fiorina and Paul E. Peterson, The New American Democracy, alternate 2nd ed. (New York: Longman, 2002).

18. Fiorina and Peterson, The New American Democracy.

19. Ibid., p. 427.

20. Dye, Understanding Public Policy, 9th ed., pp. 225–226.

21. Executive Office of the President, Office of Management and Budget, Budget of the United States Government, Fiscal Year 2005 (Washington, DC: U.S. Government Printing Office, 2004).

22. Aaron Wildavsky, The New Politics of the Budgetary Process (Glenview, IL: Scott Foresman, 1988), p. 8; see also Kurt M. Thurmaier and Katherine G. Willoughby, Policy and Politics in State Budgeting (Armonk, NY: M. E. Sharpe, 2001).

23. Robert L. Lineberry, American Public Policy (New York: Harper & Row, 1977), p. 71.

24. U.S. Bureau of the Census, Statistical Abstract of the United States: 2002 (Washington, DC: U.S. Government Printing Office, 2002), Table No. 442, p. 296.

25. R. Kent Weaver, Robert Y. Shapiro, and Lawrence R. Jacobs, "Welfare (The Polls-Trends)," Public Opinion Quarterly, Vol. 59, No. 4, 1995, pp. 606–627.

26. Fay Lomax Cook, "Congress and the Public: Convergent and Divergent Opinions on Social Security," in Henry J. Aaron, ed., Social Security and the Budget: Proceedings of the First Conference of the National Academy of Social Insurance (New York: University Press of America, 1990), pp. 79–107.

27. The Gallup Report, Report No. 274, July 1988, pp. 4–9.

28. Jon Noble and Keith Melville, "The Public's Social Welfare Mandate," Public Opinion, January/February 1989, pp. 45–49, 59.

29. Lydia Saad, "Issues Referendum Reveals Populist Leanings," The Gallup Poll Monthly, May 1996, pp. 2–6.

30. Karen Branch, "An Eye on Drugs," Austin American-Statesman, August 29, 1989, retrieved from http://archives.statesman.com

31. "Most Important Problem," Public releases from Gallup Poll results, December 1997, retrieved from http://www.gallup.com/poll/data/problem.html

32. The Gallup Organization, "Economy, War/Terrorism Most Important Problems," November 12, 2003, retrieved February 2, 2004, from http://www.gallup.com

33. Independent Sector, *Giving and Volunteering in the United States 2001, Key Findings* (Washington, DC: Author, 2001), retrieved July 14, 2003, from http:// www.independentsector.org; U.S. Census Bureau, *Statistical Abstract of the United States: 2002* (Washington, DC: U.S. Government Printing Office, 2002), Table 558, p. 362.

34. AAFRC Trust for Philanthropy, *Giving USA 2003* (Indianapolis: Author, 2003), retrieved July 14, 2003, from http://www.aafrc.org

35. Independent Sector, *Giving and Volunteering in the United States 2001, Key Findings.*

36. The remainder of this paragraph relies on Michael Anft and Harvy Lipman, "How Americans Give," *Chronicle of Philanthropy,* May 1, 2003, retrieved July 17, 2004, from http://philanthropy.com/free/ articles/v15/i14/14000601.htm

37. AAFRC Trust for Philanthropy, *Giving USA 2003.*

38. *Ibid.*

39. Most of the remainder of this paragraph relies on Brad Wolverton, Stephen Greene, Marni D. Larose, Nicole Lewis, Elizabeth Schwinn, Nicole Wallace, and Ian Wilhelm, "Surviving Tough Times," *Chronicle of Philanthropy,* Vol. 16, No. 2, 2003, retrieved February 2, 2004, from http://philanthropy.com/stats/

40. Quoted in Scott Shepard, "Summit to Tap Volunteer Spirit," *Austin American Statesman,* April 27, 1997, pp. A1, 21.

41. Bishop John Ricard, cited in the *Los Angeles Times;* quote reprinted in *Hunger Action Forum,* Vol. 2, No. 3, March 1989, p. 20.

42. Quoted in George J. Church, "The Corporate Crusaders," *Time,* April 28, 1997, p. 56.

43. Committee on Ways and Means, U.S. House of Representatives, *2000 Green Book: Background Materials and Data on Programs within the Jurisdiction of the Committee on Ways and Means* (Washington, DC: U.S. Government Printing Office, 2000), pp. 912–913.

44. The remainder of this paragraph relies on Julian Wolpert, "We Can Take Care of Our Own . . . Or Can We?", *Washington Post,* June 29, 1995.

45. These definitions are from William Safire, *New Political Dictionary* (New York: Random House, 1993).

46. See, for example, Steve Goldstein (Knight Ridder Washington Bureau), "GOP Leaning Too Far to Right, Poll Finds," *Austin American-Statesman,* March 15, 1996, pp. A1 & 4.

47. H. W. Brands, *The Strange Death of American Liberalism* (New York: Yale University Press, 2001). For other views of liberalism, see John Rawls' *Political Liberalism* (New York: Columbia University Press, 1993).

48. "Unmasking Religious Right Extremism," *American Association of University Women Outlook,* Summer 1994, pp. 20–25.

49. Robert Bork, *Slouching toward Gomorrah: Modern Liberalism and American Decline* (New York: ReganBooks, 1996), p. 337. (For criticism of conservatives with a humorous tone, see books by Al Franken, Jim Hightower, Molly Ivins, and Michael Moore.)

50. "Public Opinion on Abortion Policies Making News," *Gallup Poll Tuesday Briefing,* July 24, 2002, pp. 105–108.

51. "President Promotes Compassionate Conservatism," speech by President George W. Bush to the Commonwealth Club and the Churchill Club, San Jose, CA, April 2002, retrieved February 3, 2004, from http://www.whitehouse.gov/news/releases/2002/ 04/20020430-5.html

52. This discussion of the "poverty lobby" relies on Bill Keller, "Special Treatment No Longer Given Advocates for the Poor," *Congressional Quarterly Weekly,* Vol. 39, No. 16, April 18, 1981, pp. 659–664.

53. Charles Murray, *Losing Ground: American Social Policy, 1950–1980* (New York: Basic Books, 1984).

54. See "Unmasking Religious Right Extremism"; also see materials of People for the American Way, Your Voice Against Intolerance, 2000 M Street, NW, Washington, DC.

55. The Center for Responsive Politics, *Lobbyists Database,* retrieved July 18, 2003, from http://www. opensecrets.org/lobbyists/index.asp

56. U.S. Census Bureau, *Statistical Abstract of the United States: 2002,* Table No. 399.

57. Federal Election Commission, *PAC Activity Increases in 2000 Election Cycle,* May 31, 2001, retrieved July 18, 2003, from http://www.fec.gov/press/ 053101pacfund.html

58. Center for Responsive Politics, *Soft Money's Impact at a Glance,* retrieved June 26, 2004, from http:// www.opensecrets.org/softmoney/softglance.asp

59. Center for Responsive Politics, "What Is Soft Money?", retrieved June 26, 2004, from http://www. opensecrets.org/pubs/glossary/softmoney.htm

60. *Ibid.*

61. Federal Election Commission, *Party Fundraising Growth Continues,* September 19, 2002, retrieved July 18, 2003, from http://www.fec.gov/press/20020919 partyfund/20020919partyfund.html

62. Center for Responsive Politics, *Soft Money's Impact at a Glance.*

63. Julia Malone, "Campaign Finance Laws Often Forgotten Thereafter," *Austin American-Statesman,* February 24, 2002, p. A9.

64. Lee E. Goodman, *Overview of the Bipartisan Campaign Reform Act of 2002* (Washington, DC: Wiley, Rein & Fielding LLP, 2002), retrieved July 14, 2003, from http://www.wrf.com/

65. Anthony Corrado, "National Fundraising Remains Strong, Despite Ban on Soft Money," Brookings Institution, May 19, 2004, retrieved June 22, 2004, from http://www.brook.edu/views/papers/20040519 corrado.htm; Norm Ornstien, "Soft Money to Parties 'Did Little to Strengthen Them,'" June 13, 2004, retrieved June 26, 2004, from http://www.startribune.com/stories/1519/4824538.html

66. Corrado, "National Fundraising Remains Strong, Despite Ban on Soft Money."

67. Lisa Lambert, "Soft Money, Hard Law," The Presidential Reporting Project, Graduate School of Journalism, University of California Berkeley, May 4, 2004, retrieved June 22, 2004, from http://journalism.berkeley.edu/projects/election2004/weblog/archives/002547.html

68. For various viewpoints on the Patriot Act, see, for example, information at the website of the American Civil Liberties Union (http://www.aclu.org) and editorials such as Jeff Jacoby *(Boston Globe),* "The Liberal's Unfounded Fury over Patriot Act," *Austin American-Statesman,* May 30, 2004, p. E3.

69. Aaron Wildavsky, *The Art and Craft of Policy Analysis* (Boston: Little, Brown, 1979).

CHAPTER

2

Government and Social Welfare

HISTORICAL PERSPECTIVES ON SOCIAL WELFARE

Social welfare policy as we know it dates back to the beginning of the seventeenth century in Elizabethan England. English colonists who settled in North America brought with them many English welfare traditions. In the colonies, as in England, the earliest sources of welfare aid for the destitute were families, friends, and churches.[1] Later, private charities emerged and local and state governments intervened as a last resort. As the twentieth century brought an increased number of social problems for Americans, the federal government was forced to enact its own social welfare legislation, known as the "New Deal" of the 1930s.

The Great Society programs of the 1960s were another large-scale attempt on the part of the federal government to alleviate poverty and suffering. But during the 1980s, a different response to hardship in America emerged. Concerned with growing costs and disillusioned with the perceived failure of many public assistance programs, the administration of President Ronald Reagan attempted to limit the federal government's role in social welfare and to increase reliance on state governments and the private sector in providing services. A major step toward achieving these goals was the passage of the Family Support Act (FSA) of 1988, which weakened the entitlement status of Aid to Families with Dependent Children (AFDC) and shifted the program toward a mandatory work and training program.[2] The George H. W. Bush administration followed a similar path. In 1993 Democrat Bill Clinton assumed the presidency with his own ideas about social welfare. After a long and often bitter debate, in 1996 Congress reached a bipartisan compromise on "welfare reform" which resulted in the passage of the Personal Responsibility and Work Opportunities Reconciliation Act (PRWORA). This legislation ended the entitlement status of public assistance, made work mandatory, and put time limits on receiving assistance.[3] As discussed in Chapter 1, President George W. Bush advocates a philosophy of "compassionate conservatism," addressing the needs of the poor with a proposal for reauthorizing the 1996 welfare reform that includes increased work requirements in exchange for aid.[4]

The following pages contain a brief review of the history of social welfare, a discussion of factors that have contributed to the growth of social welfare programs in the United States, and an overview of pressing social welfare concerns in the contexts of budgetary and social welfare policies, and within the context of global threats.

Elizabethan Poor Law

In Europe, the first source of welfare assistance was mutual aid. In time of need, the only recourse was reliance on one another. If a family's food crop failed or the breadwinner became ill and unable to work, brothers, sisters, or neighbors pitched in, knowing that they would receive the same assistance should they need it one day. Later, it became the duty of the church and of wealthy feudal lords to help the needy.[5] During much of the Middle Ages, the emphasis was on doing charitable works as a religious duty.[6] Attitudes toward the poor were benevolent. Those destitute through no fault of their own were treated with dignity and respect and were helped through the hard times.[7]

These early systems of aid were informal, but as the structure of society became more complex, so did the system of providing welfare assistance. The first laws designed to curb poverty were passed in England during the fourteenth and fifteenth centuries. In 1349 the Black Death (bubonic plague) drastically reduced the population of the country and caused profound social disorganization. King Edward III responded with the Statute of Laborers to discourage vagrancy and begging; all able-bodied people were ordered to work, and giving alms was forbidden.[8]

Changes in the structure of society eventually pushed the Elizabethan government to develop its own brand of social welfare. The first wave of industrialization in England occurred with a shift from an agrarian economy to an economy based on the wool industry. People left their home communities to seek industrial employment in the cities. The feudal system of life fell apart as this shift was completed. Government was becoming more centralized and played a stronger role in many aspects of society, including social welfare, while the role of the church in welfare was diminishing.[9]

The interplay of new social forces, the reduction of the labor force, the breakdown of the feudal system, and the move toward industrialization, brought about the Elizabethan Poor Law of 1601,[10] the first major event in the Elizabethan government's role in providing social welfare benefits. The law was passed mostly as a means of "controlling" those poor who were unable to locate employment and who might cause disruption.[11] Taxes were levied to finance the new welfare system. The demands placed on recipients were harsh. Children whose parents were unable to support them faced apprenticeship, and able-bodied men dared not consider remaining idle.

Distinguishing the "deserving" from the "nondeserving" poor was an important part of the Elizabethan Poor Law. More affluent individuals did not want to be burdened with assisting any but the most needy. The deserving poor were orphaned children and adults who were lame, blind, widowed, or unemployed through no fault of their own. The nondeserving poor were vagrants or drunkards—those considered lazy and unwilling to work. Outdoor relief was the term used to describe assistance provided to many deserving poor in their own homes. Indoor relief was also provided to those unable to care for themselves, but such relief was generally provided in institutions called almshouses. The nondeserving poor were sent to workhouses, where they were forced to do menial work in return for only the barest of life's necessities.[12]

All welfare recipients had to meet stringent residency requirements. Aid was administered by local units of government called parishes. Parishes were instructed to provide aid only to people from their own jurisdictions.

Early Relief in the United States

Many aspects of Elizabethan welfare were adopted by American colonists. For example, residency requirements were strictly enforced through the policies of warning out and passing on.[13] Warning out meant that newcomers were urged to move on to other towns if it appeared that they were not financially responsible. More often, passing on was used to escort the transient poor back to their home communities. These practices continued well into the nineteenth century. In one year alone, 1,800 people were transported from one New York community to another.

Life was austere for the colonists. The business of settling America was a tough job, and the colonists were by no means well off. "Many of them were paupers, vagrants, or convicts shipped out by the English government as indentured servants."[14]

Life in the colonies was preferred by many, but sickness or other misfortune could readily place a person in need.

The colonists used four methods to "assist" the needy. "Auctioning" the poor to families that were willing to care for them at the lowest cost was the least popular method. A second method was to place the poor and sick under the supervision of a couple who were willing to care for them at as little cost as possible. The third method, outdoor relief, was provided to most of the needy. The fourth method was almshouses. Many claimed that almshouses were the best method of aid because of the medical care they provided to the sick and elderly. Almshouses in the cities provided a higher level of care than rural almshouses, which were often in deplorable condition and little more than rundown houses operated by a farm family.

The 1800s brought more ideas about what could be accomplished for the poor.[15] The Society for the Prevention of Pauperism and successor groups emerged to help the poor overcome the personal shortcomings that had supposedly led to their condition. In this tradition, the private Charity Organization Societies (COS) that developed in the United States in the late 1870s offered a method called "scientific charity." They wanted to make relief giving a more scientific endeavor. To accomplish this goal, COS members studied problems in order to better understand the causes of poverty and methods to address these problems. They also worked with other community groups and agencies to provide services to the poor in a more coordinated fashion. COS workers became the forerunners of today's social workers, and their methods developed into today's casework services. The philosophies of Calvinism, the work ethic, and social Darwinism prevailed during this period. COS workers preferred to give advice and encourage people to work whenever possible rather than provide material aid. Politicians, welfare administrators, doctors, and charity workers seemed pleased with their progress in assisting the needy during the eighteenth and nineteenth centuries.

The Great Depression and the New Deal

From 1870 to 1920 the United States experienced a period of rapid industrialization and heavy immigration. Private groups such as the COS, settlement houses, and churches and big-city political "machines" and "bosses" provided much of the assistance to the needy. The settlement houses offered many services to those coming to the cities from rural areas and those immigrating from other countries, such as help in finding jobs, counseling, education, and child care. They also prepared people for their roles as citizens in their new communities, and they actively campaigned for social reforms. The political machines operated by trading baskets of food, bushels of coal, and favors for the votes of the poor. To finance this early welfare system, the machine offered city contracts, protection, and privileges to business interests, which in return paid off in cash. Aid was provided in a personal fashion without red tape or delays. Recipients did not feel embarrassed or ashamed, for, after all, "they were trading something valuable—their votes—for the assistance they received."[16]

As social problems mounted—increased crowding, unemployment, and poverty in the cities—local and state governments began to take a more active role in welfare. States adopted "mothers' aid" and "mothers' pension" laws to help children in families where the father was deceased or absent. Other state pension programs were established to assist poor people who were aged, blind, or disabled. This era was one of progressivism. Progressives went head to head with corrupt governments and businesses and industries that exploited workers and were successful in achieving many social welfare and labor reforms.[17] Many states adopted workers' compensation programs to assist those injured on the job. The federal Children's Bureau was established to investigate and improve the lives of children. Women won the right to vote, and additional laws were passed to better the working conditions of women and children. The Progressives were ahead of their time. They urged a program of social insurance rather than charity. Large-scale federal government involvement in social welfare was not far away.

The Great Depression, one of the bleakest periods in U.S. history, followed the stock market crash in October 1929. Prices dropped dramatically, and unemployment was rampant. By 1932 one of every four people had no job, and one of every six was on welfare. Americans who had always worked no longer had jobs, and they depleted their savings or lost them when banks folded. Many had to give up their homes and farms because they could no longer meet the mortgage payments. Economic catastrophe struck deep into the ranks of the middle classes. Many of the unemployed and homeless slept on steps and park benches because they had nowhere else to go.[18]

The Great Depression dramatically changed American thought about social welfare. The realization that poverty could strike so many forced Americans to consider large-scale economic reform. Movements formed on the left and right, including those that raised the specter of socialism or communism, and threatened the political establishment. As a response to the country's problems, President Franklin Delano Roosevelt began to elaborate the philosophy of the "New Deal" that would permit the federal government to devote more attention to the public welfare than did the philosophy of "rugged individualism" so popular in the earlier days of the country. The New Deal was not a consistent or unifying plan; instead, it was a series of improvisations that were often adopted suddenly, and some of them were even contradictory. Roosevelt believed that the government should act humanely and compassionately toward those suffering from the Depression. The objectives of the New Deal were "relief, recovery, and reform," and Roosevelt called for "full persistent experimentation. If it fails, admit it frankly and try something else. But above all try something. The millions who are in want will not stand by silently forever while the things to satisfy their needs are in easy reach."[19] Americans came to accept the principle that the entire community has a responsibility for welfare.

The New Deal contained many social welfare provisions. The most important was the Social Security Act of 1935, which remains the cornerstone of social welfare legislation today. The act included social insurance benefits for retired workers administered by the federal government and federal grant-in-aid programs to states to provide public assistance payments for dependent children as well as people who were elderly or blind. Job programs, established through projects such as the Works Progress Administration and the Civilian Conservation Corps, provided a living for many Americans. Other programs included unemployment compensation, employment services, child welfare, public housing, urban aid, and vocational education and rehabilitation. The Fair Labor Standards Act of 1938 established a minimum wage and overtime pay and restricted the work of children. Additional legislation protected workers' rights to organize and engage in collective bargaining.

The Great Society and the War on Poverty

Until the 1950s, there were few notable amendments to the Social Security Act. Dependents of retired workers and survivors of deceased workers did become eligible for social insurance benefits, eligibility requirements were loosened in some programs, and payments were increased, but there were few other changes in the system. Then, beginning in the 1950s, the number of workers covered under Social Security expanded substantially, disabled workers became eligible for social insurance benefits, and the states were able to obtain federal funds to provide public assistance payments to poor people with severe disabilities. Some medical care was also made available to public assistance recipients.

The 1950s and 1960s were unusual times for Americans. Although this was a period of increased prosperity for many, the dichotomy between the "haves" and "have nots" became more apparent. The relative affluence of the times was overshadowed by the nearly 40 million people, many of them members of ethnic minority groups, living in poverty as the decade of the 1960s began. Civil rights and the depressed economic condition of these individuals became the issues of the day. The writings of economist John Kenneth Galbraith directed attention to the existence of poverty in the midst of this affluent culture and influenced President John F. Kennedy to begin acting on the problem. Kennedy initiated a pilot food stamp program and aid to Appalachia and other severely depressed areas.

Following Kennedy's assassination in 1963, President Lyndon Baines Johnson took the lead of his predecessor by "declaring war on poverty" in the Economic Opportunity Act of 1964. The goals of the "war" were to allow ghetto and poor communities to develop their own programs to arrest poverty and to root out inequality in the lives of Americans. There was more than a little consternation among local officials when people took seriously a phrase in the law calling for "maximum feasible participation" of local residents. In some communities this meant organizing to fight city hall. Model cities programs, community action agencies, and other strategies, such as the Head Start preschool program, were tried as part of the Economic Opportunity Act. Although poverty declined to 25 million people by 1970, there was dissatisfaction with many of the more experimental strategies of the War on Poverty, which differed from community to community. Today, programs such as Head Start continue to enjoy strong support, but most enduring programs of the "Great Society" of the 1960s were enacted separately from the Economic Opportunity Act. They include the Food Stamp Program to improve the nutrition of low-income people; Medicaid, which provides health care to some poor people; and Medicare, which provides health care to almost all older Americans. A revolution in U.S. spending priorities was taking place (see Illustration 2.1 and Figure 2.1).

ILLUSTRATION 2.1

The Revolution No One Noticed

While Americans were preoccupied with the turmoil of the 1960s, the civil rights movement and the war in Vietnam—a revolution no one noticed was taking place.[a] For many years, the argument for increased attention to social welfare in America had followed clear lines: The United States was spending the largest portion of its budget for defense; programs for people who were poor, sick, or aged and for minorities were underfinanced. Social welfare proponents contended that in order to be more responsive to the needs of its citizens, the nation should "change its priorities" and spend more for social programs to reduce poverty and less on wars like that in Vietnam. The argument ended with a call for a change in national priorities.

In a single decade, America's national priorities were reversed. In 1965, national defense expenditures accounted for 43 percent of the federal government's budget; social welfare expenditures (social insurance, health, and public assistance) accounted for 24 percent. While the mass media focused on the war in Vietnam and Watergate, a revolution in national policy from "guns to butter" was occurring. By 1975, defense accounted for only 26 percent of the federal budget, and social welfare expenditures had grown to 42 percent of the budget. In fiscal year 2004 social welfare expenditures are expected to total 58 percent of the budget compared to 18 percent for defense. Health programs alone (primarily Medicaid and Medicare) will comprise about 20 percent of the total budget. Social welfare is clearly the major function and major expenditure of the federal government.[b]

Figure 2.1 shows the changing trends in spending for social welfare and defense. Note that defense spending jumped up at the beginnings of the Korean War (1950–1952) and the Vietnam War (1964–1968) and later in the military buildup begun under President Carter and continued under President Reagan. In contrast, social welfare spending rose slowly for many years and then "exploded" in the 1970s after the Great Society programs of the War on Poverty were in place. Social welfare and health spending remained at high levels despite a significant increase in defense spending. This reversal of national priorities occurred during both Democratic and Republican administrations and during the Vietnam war—the nation's longest war. "The mid to late 1960s were quite prosperous years. The unemployment rate fell under 4 percent, real income rose briskly. In the flush of affluence, new programs could be introduced with minimal fiscal strain, even as the Vietnam War expenditures were swelling."[c] In short, ideas that welfare expenditures are not likely to increase during Republican administrations or during times of war turned out to be wrong. America's commitment to social welfare was growing.

Not everyone was comfortable with this change in public spending priorities. There was fear that the nation was sacrificing national defense in order to spend money on social welfare programs that might not work. As the 1980s emerged, a more cautious attitude toward social welfare had developed. Far too many people remained poor in spite of increased welfare spending, and there were some successful attempts to curb these social programs.

Today, concerns about the poor and public assistance have largely disappeared from pub-

continued

ILLUSTRATION 2.1 *(continued)*

lic conversation, even when poverty levels rise.[d] Americans doubt that poverty can be ended even with increased federal spending.[e] The portion of the total federal budget devoted to social welfare continues to grow, largely due to the growing demands on the Social Security system, which will balloon in the coming years as the baby boomers begin to retire. The recent addition of prescription drug coverage for Medicare recipients will add another $530 billion over the next ten years to the social welfare budget.[f]

Through the 1990s the U.S. experienced reductions in military spending as a result of amazing political changes in various parts of the world—greater democratization in Russia and the other communist bloc countries, the fall of the Berlin Wall between East and West Germany, and the demise of the Cold War. The trend in military spending shifted upward slightly in 2000 and has continued to grow in response to terrorists' attacks on the World Trade Center and the Pentagon, and the subsequent ongoing wars in Afghanistan and Iraq.[g] Some contend that the nation has become increasingly unprepared militarily and that the country needs to beef up defense.

Social welfare problems at home continue to mount, from child poverty and child abuse to alcohol and drug abuse, unemployment, and the large proportion of the population with no health insurance. The U.S. population continues to live longer, necessitating even more and more varied social services. With the astronomical growth in the federal deficit during the early years of the new millennium, the growing social welfare demands of the U.S. population, the continued threat of terrorist attacks and the growth in the number of rogue states with nuclear capabilities, it will take even greater resolve in the years ahead to meet the country's social welfare needs.

NOTES

[a]See Aaron Wildavsky, *Speaking Truth to Power: The Art and Craft of Policy Analysis* (Boston: Little, Brown, 1979), especially pp. 86–89, for elaboration on this discussion of "the revolution no one noticed."

[b]Office of Management and Budget, *Budget of the United States Government,* Historical Tables, available at http://www.whitehouse.gov/omb/budget/fy2004/hist.html

[c]Robert D. Plotnick, "Social Welfare Expenditures: How Much Help for the Poor?" *Policy Analysis,* Vol. 5, No. 2, 1979, p. 278.

[d]Lynette Clemetson, "Census Shows Ranks of Poor Rose in 2002 by 1.3 Million," *New York Times,* September 3, 2003, retrieved from http://www.query.nytimes.com/gst/abstract.html

[e]"Poverty and Welfare: People's Chief Concerns" (Public Agenda), retrieved September 24, 2004, from http://www.publicagenda.org/issues/pcc_detail.cfm?issue_type = welfare&list = 3

[f]Press Briefing by Scott McClellan, Office of the Press Secretary, January 30, 2004, retrieved January 31, 2004, from http://www.whitehouse.gov/news/releases/2004/01/20040130-6.html; Robert Pear, "Bush's Aides Put Higher Price Tag on Medicare Law," *New York Times,* January 30, 2004, retrieved January 31, 2004, from http://www.nytimes.com/2004/01/30/politics/30DEFI.html?th

[g]Office of Management and Budget, *Budget of the United States Government,* Historical Tables, retrieved from http://www.whitehouse.gov/omb/budget/fy2004/hist.html

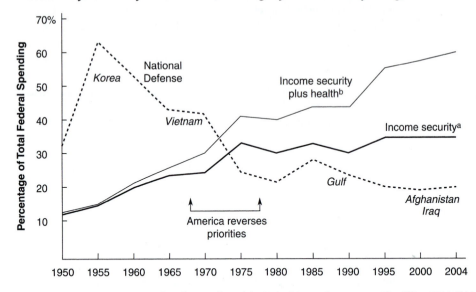

FIGURE 2.1

Social Welfare and Defense Priorities (Percentage of Total Federal Spending)

Source: Office of Management and Budget, *Budget of the United States Government, Fiscal Year 2004, Table 3.1—Outlays by Superfunction and Function.* Data for 2004 is an estimate.

[a]Income security values are sum of total Income Security and Social Security annual spending.

[b]Income security plus health values are sum of Income Security, Medicare, Medicaid, and Healthcare annual spending.

As the 1970s approached, the new presidential administration of Richard M. Nixon began dismantling the agencies of the War on Poverty. The "welfare rights movement" of the 1960s had raised the nation's consciousness about social welfare needs. Many more people were receiving public assistance. But with so many added to the rolls, a perception developed that the public assistance system now needed reform. President Nixon, determined to clean up the "welfare mess," proposed another type of reform in the early 1970s—a guaranteed annual income for all poor people. Parts of the plan were adopted, notably the Supplemental Security Income (SSI) program, which provides cash assistance to those who are aged, blind, or disabled and living in poverty. For the most part, however, Congress rejected the idea of a guaranteed annual income. Some thought it was too much welfare, and others were concerned that the guarantees were too low.

Meanwhile, another type of social welfare movement had arisen as social services designed to address problems in addition to poverty grew increasingly popular in the 1960s and 1970s. Consequently, new legislation was passed to assist abused children, to provide mental health services, and to develop social service programs for older Americans. During the twentieth century, the United States developed its own unique system of social welfare.[20]

THE EXPANSION OF SOCIAL WELFARE

Since the early 1900s, many factors have contributed to the increase in the number of social welfare programs, the number of people receiving assistance, and the amount spent on social welfare programs. Among these are (1) the rural-to-urban migration, (2) the elimination of residency requirements, (3) the welfare rights movement, (4) cost-of-living adjustments, (5) the aging of America, and (6) increasing numbers of single-parent families.

The Rural-to-Urban Migration

During the late 1800s and early 1900s, America experienced some of its sharpest growing pains as the Industrial Revolution reached its peak. The country changed from a rural, agrarian society to an urban, industrial society. People migrated from poor rural farming communities hoping to find jobs and brighter futures in the cities. People from other countries were also emigrating to American cities, seeking a better life. The dreams of many people were shattered. Those who found jobs were often forced to work long hours for low pay under poor working conditions. Housing was often crowded; sanitation and health problems were common. Those who had come to the cities to "make good" were often far from their families who could have provided financial and psychological support. Social welfare became a growing problem for governments. As the Great Depression unfolded, the cities and states were no longer able to cope with worsening social conditions. The federal government responded to this major economic crisis with emergency aid and temporary work programs, but its most enduring response was the Social Security Act of 1935. The act established the federal government's role in determining social welfare policy and programs.

Residency Requirements Eliminated

One method traditionally used to restrict the number of people eligible for public assistance was residency requirements. During Elizabethan and colonial times, the belief was that communities should be responsible for their own poor and needy residents. Financially dependent individuals were not welcome in new communities. As society became more mobile and people moved more frequently to seek jobs and other opportunities, the argument for residency requirements no longer seemed to hold up. Yet states and communities continued to impose these restrictions. Requiring that potential recipients had resided in the city or state for six months or a year, or even requiring that they intended to reside in the city or state, were ways to keep public assistance caseloads small. Following a number of court challenges, the U.S. Supreme Court in 1969 declared residency requirements in federally supported welfare programs unconstitutional.[21] As a result, it became easier to qualify for aid, and public assistance caseloads grew.

As public assistance costs continued to escalate through the 1980s and 1990s, some states with higher General Assistance payments tried to institute procedures to initially pay new arrivals no more than the amount offered to them in their previous state of residence. General Assistance programs provide help to low-income individuals and families. They rely on state or local funding and receive no federal funding (see Chapter 5) and are not encumbered by federal regulations. But these restrictions on welfare payments also failed to hold up under legal challenges. The Supreme Court said that such restrictions violated individuals' rights to equal protections under the law and also their right to travel.

Despite these legal precedents, the 1996 welfare reform law allowed states to impose a 12-month residency requirement before paying full TANF benefits, if their benefits were higher than in recipients' previous states. States quickly implemented the residency requirement, and welfare advocacy organizations, poverty law centers, and civil rights organizations filed lawsuits in protest. California's Supreme Court and other courts soon found these residency rules discriminatory and a violation of individuals' rights to travel and equal protections under the law.[22] In May 1999, the U.S. Supreme Court again agreed that such residency requirements are unconstitutional.

Welfare Rights

In the 1960s, poor Americans showed their discontent with the welfare system through the "welfare rights movement." It arose in the wake of the civil rights movements, as the poor expressed their dissatisfaction with a political system that had denied them the standard of living that many other Americans enjoyed. These movements were a stormy time in U.S. domestic history, especially from 1964 to 1968, when major cities were rocked by a series of riots. As the number of disturbances increased, so did the number of people applying for public assistance, many with the help of members of the newly formed National Welfare Rights Organization (NWRO).

The welfare rights movement helped people organize to demand the aid due them and better treatment of applicants and recipients. Among the strategies used were demonstrations, threats of legal action, legal action, and education about benefits. The movement brought changes in the behavior and attitudes of public aid recipients. Frances Fox Piven and Richard Cloward note, "The mood of applicants in welfare waiting rooms had changed. They were no longer as humble, as self-effacing, as pleading; they were more indignant, angrier, more demanding."[23] The mood of welfare administrators and caseworkers also changed. Many practices that had been part of lengthy background investigations ceased. The process of obtaining aid was speeded up, and welfare agencies were not so quick to terminate benefits when recipients did not comply with the rules. "For all practical purposes, welfare operating procedures collapsed; regulations were simply ignored in order to process the hundreds of thousands of families who jammed the welfare waiting rooms."[24]

By 1968 the NWRO had ceased operation. The welfare rights movement was coming to a close. Many goals of the movement had been accomplished. Applicants had been informed of their rights; they were being treated better; and a record number were being certified for benefits.

The idea that the poor have a right to public assistance took a serious blow with the 1996 welfare reform law. Time limits (generally five years) were imposed on TANF receipt. Food stamp benefits can be terminated more easily for able-bodied adults who do not meet work requirements. Alcoholics and addicts no longer qualify for Social Security disability payments or Supplemental Security Income (SSI), a public assistance program for individuals with disabilities (see Chapter 5). Nevertheless, the number of people receiving "welfare" is far larger than many people would like. Some contend this is because the public assistance system is too lenient and encourages dependency. Others contend that it is because the cards are staked against the poor. A low minimum wage, lack of health insurance, bad economic times, and discrimination keep people poor and in need of aid.

Cost-of-Living Adjustments

Much of the increase in federal social welfare spending since the 1970s has resulted from congressional approval of cost-of-living adjustments (COLAs), also known as indexing, designed to keep Social Security, SSI, and food stamp benefits in line with inflation. (TANF recipients do not receive automatic cost-of-living adjustments to their cash assistance checks.) COLAs were enacted in 1973 and became effective in 1975.[25] Prior to this, Congress had to approve any increase in Social Security payments and SSI payments. Political Scientist Aaron Wildavsky noted, "Such action was not intended to provide greater benefits to recipients, but only to automatically assure them of constant purchasing power."[26]

Since 1975, annual COLAS have ranged from a high of 14.3 percent in 1980 to a low of 1.3 percent in 1987 and 1999.[27] During the high-inflation years of the early 1980s, COLAs came under attack. Although social welfare payments were being adjusted for cost-of-living increases, the wages of many workers in the sluggish economy had not kept pace with inflation. Some modifications were made to control COLAs (see Chapter 4 on Social Security and Chapter 7 on the Food Stamp Program). To guard against overspending of the Social Security trust funds, in 1983 Congress decided that COLAs may be limited in Social Security retirement income benefits if the combined assets of the trust funds falls below 20 percent of annual expenditures. To date, trust funds have not fallen nearly this low.[28] COLAs continue to be an important component of social welfare programs. Welfare advocates and social welfare beneficiaries, especially those who are aged or disabled, would surely wage strong protests if these adjustments were eliminated.

The Graying of America

The growing number of older people places increased demands on the social welfare system. Today those over age 65 comprise 12.4 percent of the U.S. population, compared to 4 percent at the turn of the twentieth century. By the year 2030, this figure will approach 20 percent. The fastest growing segment of the 65-and-older population are those 90 and older.[29] Improved living conditions and advances in medicine have helped

Americans look forward to longer lives than ever before, but in advanced age people may become increasingly vulnerable and unable to meet all their own needs.

There is general agreement in the United States that older people deserve publicly supported care. The tripling of the proportion of the older population over the past century has meant the need for greater planning and more services to ensure that they receive proper treatment. The largest social welfare programs in the United States are Social Security and Medicare (see Chapters 4 and 8, respectively). The vast majority of recipients of these programs are older Americans, who are well represented at the polls, and who receive a higher level of social welfare support than any other segment of the population.

Increase in Single-Parent Families

The changing patterns of U.S. family life are among the most controversial factors explaining increased social welfare expenditures. The divorce rate has continued to gradually decline since it peaked in 1980, but family breakup is still common.[30] The number of children born to unmarried parents grew from 27 to 33 percent of all births between 1990 and 2000.[31] The increase in pregnancies among teenagers who are unmarried and ill equipped to care for children has slowed over the past decade but is still cause for alarm. These social and demographic trends mean that many families today are headed by single parents, primarily women. Since 1959, the number of female-headed households has more than tripled.[32] In 2002, 24 percent of all families had a single household head, most of them (74 percent) women.

Families headed by single women have an exceptionally high poverty rate. The poverty rate for female-headed households declined from about 35 percent in the early 1990s to lows of about 26 percent since 2000. This rate is more than double that of single male-headed families. Of all single-headed families living in poverty, 86 percent were headed by women. Poverty in married-couple families is substantially lower (5.3 percent in 2002). Public assistance programs (primarily TANF, Medicaid, and food stamps) and the earned income credit, a special tax credit for low-income workers, are crucial resources for making ends meet, especially for the large number of female-headed families living in poverty or laboring at low-wage jobs.

FINANCES IN THE WELFARE STATE

Prior to the Great Depression, local and state governments shouldered the major public responsibility for social welfare programs. Today the picture is different. Since 1935 there have been important changes in the way most social welfare programs are established and financed. Although federal, state, and local social welfare expenditures have all increased, the federal government is now the largest welfare spender. Today, more than 80 percent of social insurance expenditures come from the federal government.[33] Federal funds account for about 70 percent of public assistance benefits (cash aid, food, housing, medical, etc.).[34] Conversely, states and local governments pay for the majority of the cost (93 percent) of educating children.[35]

Types of Taxes

How does the federal government acquire the funds to pay for social welfare programs? The answer, of course, is through the taxes it collects. As shown in Figure 2.2, individual income taxes are the largest source of federal government revenues (budget receipts). Estimates for fiscal year 2005 indicate that individual income taxes will account for 43 percent of budget receipts—down from 50 percent in 2001.[36] This decrease is attributable to two events. First, the burst of the stock market bubble in 2001 (described later in this chapter) resulted in the loss of billions of dollars of highly taxed income, causing tax receipts to plummet in 2001 and 2002. Second, Congress passed tax cuts in 2001, 2002, and 2003 that accounted for a reduction in tax revenue, most dramatically among the top 1 percent of earners.[37] In 2002 federal revenues declined by 7 percent, the largest decline since 1946.

Income taxes are channeled to the federal government's general revenue fund, which is used for many purposes, among them, financing public assistance programs. The second major source of budget revenue is the Social Security tax. This special tax is levied against an individual's income and is used to finance the social insurance programs (also see Chapter 4). Social insurance receipts will account for an estimated 39 percent of the federal government's revenues in 2005, up from 32 percent in 2000. The federal government also collects revenues through corporate income taxes, excise taxes (taxes on products), and other sources. Corporate income taxes will account for an estimated 11 percent of government receipts; excise taxes, 4 percent; and other sources, 3 percent.[38] Clearly, individual Americans shoulder the major tax burden through the personal income taxes and Social Security taxes they pay (see Figure 2.2).

Although their overall financial role is smaller, the states are important players in social welfare, especially with respect to public assistance payments and social service programs. The states also collect taxes in several ways. Like the federal government, most states levy a personal income tax. Seven states (Alaska, Florida, Nevada, South Dakota, Texas, Washington, and Wyoming) have no state income tax, and two states (New Hampshire and Tennessee) levy income taxes against dividend and interest income only. State income tax rates are much lower than federal rates. Federal income taxes range from 10 to 35 percent of income; state income taxes range from less than 1 percent to 9.5 percent.[39] The sales tax is another major mechanism that states use to generate revenue. Some of these taxes are also used to provide social welfare services.

At the local level, the property tax, largely used to fund public school education, is the major source of revenue. Local governments (cities, counties, and municipalities) provide the smallest share of social welfare services. These governments are mainly concerned with providing other services, such as police and fire protection.

FIGURE 2.2

The Federal Government Dollar, Fiscal Year 2005 Estimates

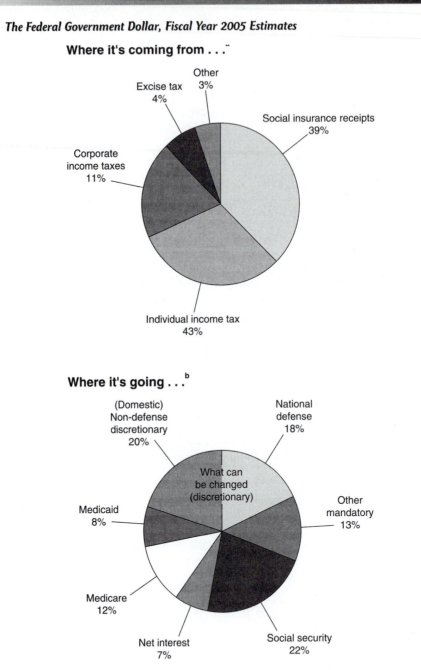

Where it's coming from . . .ᵃ

Other
3%

Excise tax
4%

Social insurance receipts
39%

Corporate
income taxes
11%

Individual income tax
43%

Where it's going . . .ᵇ

(Domestic)
Non-defense
discretionary
20%

National
defense
18%

What can
be changed
(discretionary)

Medicaid
8%

Other
mandatory
13%

Medicare
12%

Net interest
7%

Social security
22%

Source: Budget of the United States Government, Fiscal Year 2005, Summary Tables, retrieved from www.whitehouse.gov/omb/

ᵃTable S-10, Receipts by Source

ᵇSummary Table S-12, Budget Summary by Category

Who Pays? Who Benefits?

At each level of government, there is always concern about the types of taxes that should be used to generate revenues, who should pay those taxes and how much they should pay, and who should benefit from them. Some taxes are **progressive** (they tax the rich at higher rates than the poor), and others are **regressive** (they tax the poor at a higher rate than the rich). The Social Security tax and sales tax are regressive; poorer people use a higher percentage of their income to pay for them than richer people do. Federal and state income taxes are progressive, although they are less progressive than some people think they should be.

Many people believe that there are two distinct groups of citizens in the United States—those who pay taxes and those who receive welfare. But it can be said that "everyone is on welfare" because the government helps all people, some directly through social welfare programs, others through tax incentives.[40] Government-sponsored social welfare programs (public assistance and social insurance) comprise the bulk of help to the poorest citizens. Low-income workers may benefit from the **earned income credit** (EIC) (a special tax rebate paid to low-income workers through the Internal Revenue Service). President George W. Bush's tax cuts in 2001 and 2003 provided tax relief for families with children by increasing the child tax credit from $600 to $1000, with the intent of leaving more earnings in workers' pockets.[41] Tax credits are a popular way of helping those in need, especially during economically tough times, because they reward work, make use of the existing tax system, and impact a broader segment of the population than public assistance.

Compared to lower- and upper-income groups, those in the middle classes pay most of the federal income taxes in this country. Much of the social welfare assistance the middle classes receive comes in the form of fringe benefit programs (such as healthcare and pension plans) offered by employers. Most people don't use the word "welfare" to describe these benefits since they are not provided by government, but workers can also claim federal income tax deductions from their gross personal income for these fringe benefits. In fact, "fringe" is no longer a good word for them, because they comprise a substantial employment and tax benefit.

Workers also benefit from such provisions as the dependent care tax credit. The primary example is a deduction for working families who pay for child care. This credit is available to most workers, but it is used less frequently by those in low-income brackets, because the costs of child care may be beyond their reach. Some have called for eliminating this credit for upper-income workers in order to increase tax revenues and to concentrate more resources on poorer families. There have also been suggestions for expanding the dependent care credit to offer more incentives for families to care for their aged and disabled members, rather than rely on public assistance programs like Medicaid that cover the costs of custodial nursing home care for those who are poor.

The more well-to-do get much of their help directly from the tax system through various "loopholes," deductions, and credits known as tax expenditures. Some loopholes (such as certain deductions for real estate investment losses and business-related entertainment) have been narrowed or closed over the years, but others remain. According to the federal government, "tax expenditures are the equivalent of entitlement programs administered by the Internal Revenue Service."[42] Some of these deductions are for the mortgage interest paid on first and second homes and for property taxes and charitable contributions. These deductions are also very important for the middle class, although they generally have less to deduct.

Finally, while businesses pay corporate taxes, they also receive government assistance such as federal contracts, farm subsidies, and various tax deductions. This is called **corporate welfare.** Although some of this help goes to small-business owners who might be struggling to get by, much of it goes to more affluent business owners. Government tax deductions also help to offset the cost of fringe benefits that employers pay to workers. President George W. Bush's support of big business is reflected in corporate tax cuts in 2002 and 2003. Corporations also take advantage of offshore tax sheltering. Recent tax cuts for businesses are estimated to cost $177 billion in tax revenues from 2002 to 2005, and the cost of offshore corporate tax sheltering is estimated at $50 billion a year. The United States has the lowest corporate tax rate of industrialized nations. Microsoft Corporation received $12 billion in tax breaks over a five-year period, actually paying no taxes at all in 1999; and two companies that failed because of illegal business practices, Enron and Worldcom, paid no taxes in some recent years in spite of recorded profits in the billions of dollars.[43] Considered in this way, all groups benefit from government assistance. In fact, much of the redistribution of income that results from public policy favors the more rather than the less affluent.

There have been many calls to reform the nation's tax collection agency: the dreaded Internal Revenue Service (IRS). Congress has taken steps to ensure that taxpayers' rights are better protected. There have also been many calls to reform the tax system. Taxes were a major theme in the 1996 and 2000 presidential races. Staying true to campaign promises, Presidents Bill Clinton and George W. Bush pushed tax-cut legislation through Congress soon after election—Clinton in 1997 and Bush in 2001, 2002, and 2003.[44] There have been concerns about taxation since the country's beginning (remember the Boston Tea Party?). Today that tradition is continued by a number of citizen watchdog groups calling for tax reform.[45] While we complain a lot about paying taxes, Americans pay a lower rate of taxes than do residents of most industrialized nations (see Table 2.1).

Tax Reform

One popular tax reform strategy put forth by advocacy groups is the flat tax. In its purest form a flat tax means that everyone would be taxed at the same rate regardless of income level, removing the progressive tax structure used today. Some flat tax proposals do exempt people with low or even moderate incomes from paying any taxes. Under a flat tax, there would be no deductions as there are today for interest paid on home loans, high medical expenses, child care, or business entertainment. Flat tax proposals have historically been rejected for a number of reasons. For example, large deductions, such as mortgage interest payments, make buying a home affordable for

TABLE 2.1

Comparison of Highest International Income Tax Rates, 2002*

Compared to other industrialized nations, the U.S. income tax rate is low. The United States ranks 13th, with a highest personal income tax rate of 45.4%.

France, 60.4%	Netherlands, 52%	Norway, 47.5%
Denmark, 59.7%	Germany, 51.2%	Italy, 45.9%
Belgium, 56.2%	Austria and Japan, 50%	United States, 45.4%
Sweden, 55.5%	Australia, 48.5%	Canada, 43.4%
Finland, 53.8%	Spain, 48%	United Kingdom, 40%

Source: Tax Policy Center, Urban Institute and Brookings Institution joint venture. Available at http://www.taxpolicycenter.org/TaxFacts/TFDB/TFTemplate.cfm?Docid = 306&Topic2id = 95

*Tax rates take into account differences among countries' length of tax brackets, amount of tax relief, and rates of Social Security contributions. Highest rates of income tax include temporary special surcharges as well as rates of state and local income taxes as reported in the OECD Tax Database.

millions of people. In addition, this deduction supports the housing industry. Depending on the details of a flat tax, middle-income Americans may actually end up paying more taxes, thus some proposals have been widely criticized. The process of filing income taxes would, however, be simpler and could possibly result in less tax avoidance and evasion and fewer altercations with the IRS.

Another tax reform strategy is to replace the federal personal income tax with a national sales tax (like states' sales taxes, only higher). This is a tax on what one buys rather than on what one earns. Again, the proposal is criticized because it is not structured as a progressive tax. Depending on how it is done, food, prescription drugs, or other necessities could be exempt from the tax. Like the flat tax, a national sales tax might reduce tax avoidance and evasion. More dramatic is that it might do away with the IRS and the need to file tax returns altogether (cheery thoughts for many), saving the money now spent on running the IRS. Of course, some system would need to be put in place to monitor the national sales tax. Flat tax and national sales tax proposals have appeal despite their many problems, but there is little chance that Congress will do more than tweak the current system from time to time. The most pressing tax question before Congress today is whether to let the tax cuts enacted under George W. Bush's administration expire (as they are scheduled to begin to do in 2005), or to renew them.[46]

THE REAGAN AND BUSH YEARS

The number of people served by the various social welfare programs in the United States and the amount of money spent on these programs is impressive, but there has been considerable consternation with many aspects of the system, particularly public assistance. The most severe criticisms of the last few decades are that public assistance programs encourage dependency and are directly to blame for the large number of people who turn to governments for help.

During the 1980s concerns about welfare dependency resulted in more conservative social welfare policies and programs. Public assistance reform under the Reagan administration came in the Family Support Act (FSA) of 1988. The act was intended to (1) reduce spending on public assistance programs; (2) minimize the government's role in public assistance; (3) provide assistance only to the "truly needy"; and (4) provide assistance on a short-term basis only. FSA was the most sweeping reform to the public assistance system since the New Deal. Spending was cut in the Aid to Families with Dependent Children program and work and training mandates increased. In addition, eligibility requirements for other public assistance programs, such as the Food Stamp Program, were tightened. As a result, significant numbers of recipients were removed from the rolls. Homelessness became more evident in the context of these conservative welfare reforms.

The Supply Side

When Ronald Reagan entered office, the nation faced major economic problems: unemployment, inflation, low productivity, and low investment. Reagan saw this as an outcome of "big government." He believed, "The federal government through taxes, spending, regulatory, and monetary policies, [had] sacrificed long-term growth and price stability for ephemeral, short-term goals."[47] In addressing the economic troubles of the country, Reagan moved away from the more liberal Keynesian economic policies, and embraced conservative supply-side economics, dubbed "Reaganomics," during his tenure in office.

Keynesian economics is based on the notion that government can boost employment or cut inflation by manipulating the demand side of the economy—increasing government spending and expanding the money supply to boost employment, and doing just the opposite to hold down inflation. It also holds that unemployment and inflation should not occur together—unemployment should reduce income, which in turn would force down prices. But according to government figures, both unemployment and inflation remained high during the 1970s. Government efforts to reduce unemployment simply added to inflation; and government efforts to cut inflation simply added to unemployment. Reagan combined the unemployment rate with the inflation rate and called it the *misery index.*

To reduce the misery index and boost the economy, Reagan implemented a series of economic changes that concentrated on the supply side of the economy. These economic changes included: (1) cuts in the rate of growth in federal spending, (2) tax cuts for individuals and businesses, (3) deregulation of industry to reduce the cost of doing business, and (4) slowing the growth of the nation's money supply. During his first term, Reagan successfully encouraged Congress to cut personal income taxes by 25 percent, and to "index" tax rates to eliminate "bracket creep," which occurs when inflation carries taxpayers into higher brackets. Today, taxes are "adjusted" or indexed, so that taxpayers will not carry a heavier burden as inflation rises. Under Reagan's tax reform, the number of individual tax brackets was reduced from 15 to two primary categories—a 15 and a 28 percent bracket (actually, due to a complicated set of rules, some earners incurred a 33 percent rate). Corporate tax brackets were also reduced, and other reforms included increasing the personal income tax exemption; eliminating some real estate tax shelters used primarily by the wealthy; and taxing capital gains (taxes paid on profits from the sale of assets such as real estate and stocks) as ordinary income instead of using lower rates (a move that Reagan did not support). Reagan called it "the best anti-poverty bill, the best pro-family measure, and the best job-creation program ever to come out of the Congress."[48]

Reagan's policies were designed to encourage Americans to work, save, and invest. Taxes and regulations on businesses and affluent Americans were reduced in the hope that they would reinvest their profits and expand job opportunities for the poor and working classes. In other words, incentives were provided for the wealthy in the hope that benefits would "trickle down" to the poor in the form of new jobs.[49] These predictions did not hold true. The wealthy who had benefited most from deregulation and tax cuts did not reinvest their money in the economy and create more U.S. jobs. Corporations used their tax saving to buy other companies, and to take business abroad where labor was cheaper. This had the effect of diminishing the supply of high-paying industrial jobs and reducing government tax revenues.

As George H. W. Bush campaigned for the presidency and assumed the office after two very popular terms of the Reagan administration, his favorite phrase was "Read my lips—no new taxes." But a growing budget deficit and the inability to balance the federal budget caused him to eat his words. The budget battle that ensued resulted in a series of measures enacted in 1990 that raised taxes on alcohol, gasoline, and luxury items such as expensive cars and boats. The highest personal income tax rate was raised to 31 percent for individuals with annual taxable incomes of more than $125,000 and couples with incomes of more than $200,000 (the 33 percent rate incurred under the Reagan tax bill became 31 percent). The earned income credit was increased and new credits for healthcare and parents with newborn children were included. The payroll tax that supports Medicare was increased for higher-income earners. In exchange for his tax compromise, George H. W. Bush got new measures to strengthen spending ceilings to bring the budget into line. However, rescinding his promise of "no new taxes" was probably a major factor in President George H. W. Bush's defeat in the 1992 presidential race. By the end of the Reagan-Bush era, the federal budget deficit had grown to $290 billion.[50]

The New Federalism

President Reagan was anxious to restructure federal-state relations—specifically to turn over to the states many of the domestic programs of the national government. He believed that this would "end cumbersome administration" and make the programs "more responsive to both the people they are meant to help and the people who pay for them."[51] Critics contended that this would be a step backward in social welfare policy. Many social welfare functions were assumed by the federal government because the states failed to respond to the needs of the poor. Even when state governments are well motivated to care for their poor, differences in states' economic resources can result in unequal treatment from state to state. The devolution of social welfare was among the most criticized effects of the Reagan administration.

The Reagan administration instituted block grant funding as a means to cut federal spending, restructure state and federal relations, and establish a "new federalism."[52] Block grants are federal payments to state or local governments for general functions, such as health, welfare, education, law enforcement, and community development. The money must be spent for the general function of the block grant, but states and communities have a great deal of freedom to decide specific uses for the funds. Block grants were intended to reduce the power of "the Washington bureaucrats," to return decision making to state and local governments, and to make federal money available for various purposes with few "strings attached."

Block grants may have sounded like a good deal for the states, but they did not always work out that way. When Reagan consolidated many of the smaller social welfare programs into state block grants, the funds allocated were less than the sum previously spent on the individual social welfare programs. The block grants also shifted decision making about specific uses of federal social welfare dollars to state political arenas, where support for social welfare programs is not always as great as it is in Washington. As these changes occurred, much of the politicking and competition over funds also shifted from Washington to state and local levels.

The States as Laboratories

President George H. W. Bush also encouraged state responsibility for public assistance, but he called for a "kinder and gentler" America, perhaps to distance his administration from Reagan's harsh stance toward social welfare. George H. W. Bush referred to the "states as laboratories" and encouraged experimentation by providing federal funds to help support state demonstration projects and by granting waivers that allowed states to deviate from federal rules. State initiatives have been used to test ideas for program designs and service delivery that may have been too controversial to gain nationwide support. For example, Wisconsin's "Learnfare" program allowed the state to reduce a family's public assistance benefit if a teenage child dropped out of school. According to President George H. W. Bush, "some of these experiments are controversial, some may not work, others may prove to cost too much for the benefits produced. That is the nature of 'states as laboratories.' As any scientist knows, the road to success is marked by numerous laboratory failures."[53]

Privatizing Public Services

Another theme emphasized during the Reagan-Bush years was privatization of government services. Privatization means that federal, state, and local governments give nongovernmental organizations more responsibility for providing public services—from postal delivery and space exploration to mass transportation and even prisons, public assistance, and child protective services. "Generally, privatization can be defined as the transfer of government services, assets, and/or enterprises to private sector owners and suppliers, when [they] have the capability of providing better services at lower costs."[54] How often they provide better services at lower cost is a subject of debate.

Many social welfare services are already provided by the private sector (see also Chapter 10). For example, most childcare centers are owned by private for-profit and private nonprofit organizations. Most healthcare services come from private physicians and other private providers, private hospitals, and other privately owned facilities.

The line between the private and public sectors is no longer clear. Many so-called private enterprises rely heavily on government funds. The housing industry, for example, benefits from construction projects funded through the federal government's Department of Housing and Urban Development. Many of the country's community mental health centers (CMHCs) are actually nonprofit corporations originally established with federal funds along with help from state and local governments. Charter schools are private entities that receive public funds to educate children. Many organizations today are really quasi-public or semiprivate.[55] The United States is truly a public/private or "mixed economy," even in the social welfare domain.

The privatization of public services has raised an important question—does this practice result in federal, state, and local governments abrogating responsibility for social welfare services? Sometimes this abrogation has occurred through deregulation.[56] For example, it has been increasingly difficult to assess the impacts of childcare services[57] and services for the elderly,[58] because the government has reduced its efforts to collect data and monitor these programs. In other cases, privatization can result in governments spending less for services and subsequent reductions in services.[59] Many concerns about adequacy and accountability are raised when private companies provide public social services.

The Reagan–Bush Finale

So what actually happened after twelve years of Reagan and Bush policies? Although everyone was supposed to benefit from supply-side economics, evidence mounted that the rich got richer and the poor got poorer. The Congressional Budget Office estimated that the lower and middle classes paid a higher net federal tax rate for 1990 than they paid in 1980 prior to tax reform.[60] Although personal income taxes had dropped, other taxes, primarily social insurance taxes, had increased. Poor Americans saw their income drop during the Reagan and Bush years, and their combined federal tax rate increased 16 percent. At the same time, the richest Americans enjoyed substantial increases in income, because their income tax rates dropped by 5.5 percent. The nonpartisan Citizens for Tax Justice found that only the very poor and the very rich saw tax decreases.[61]

Unemployment and inflation rates had once again abated, but the word "recession" was still being used, and the budget deficit had grown tremendously. Poverty rates were higher than before the Reagan years. Severe cuts in social welfare programs had hurt the poorest Americans, and the **underclass** (the most marginalized Americans) had fallen further behind. An assessment of the Reagan–Bush years may depend on one's own political perspectives, but after twelve consecutive years of Republican presidencies, it seemed that Americans were ready for a change.

THE PRESIDENTIAL YEARS OF BILL CLINTON

The 1992 presidential campaign turned out to be a three-way race between Republican President George H. W. Bush, Democratic candidate and governor of Arkansas William Jefferson "Bill" Clinton, and an independent candidate—Texas billionaire businessman H. Ross Perot. Independent presidential candidates are rarely considered viable opponents. Perot, however, garnered substantial support (19 percent of the popular vote, more than any third-party presidential candidate since Theodore Roosevelt ran on the progressive Bull Moose Party ticket in 1912), though not nearly enough to win the election. President George H. W. Bush failed to make strong showings in the presidential debates, and disillusionment among Americans with the state of the economy and other domestic matters gave way to the election of Bill Clinton. Clinton was the first "baby boomer"(those born post–World War II between 1946 and 1964) and the third-youngest president ever elected. Clinton chose Albert "Al" Gore, former senator from Tennessee, also a "boomer," as his vice president. The two set out to accomplish an ambitious set of goals. Among the most important were economic recovery, healthcare reform, welfare reform, and crime control.

Managing the Federal Debt

The budget deficit was a major issue in the 1992 presidential campaign. Upon taking office, President Clinton faced a $290 billion budget deficit, and the gross federal debt had grown from $909 billion in 1980 to $4 trillion in 1992. The gross federal debt equaled 64 percent of the gross national product (GNP). The gross federal debt is made up of two parts: the public debt (the amount the government owes the public from whom it borrowed money to pay for past annual budget deficits) and debt held by government accounts (the amount of money the federal government borrowed from itself, largely from government trust funds). Although both are important, it is public debt that takes the most direct toll on the economy.[62] In 1992, the public debt was $3 trillion and the debt held by government accounts was $1 trillion.[63] The biggest domestic worries of the federal government are how to manage spending and how to meet the needs of the American people within budgetary constraints, and at the same time keep the economy strong.

When the federal government spends more than it takes in, it must borrow money by selling U.S. Treasury bonds or bills to the public (or by taking money from its trust funds). The interest that must be paid to the public on these debts drains money that could fuel the economy through expenditures on transportation, education, technology, health, nutrition, or other public needs. With less money available for investment and for others to borrow, interest rates, and, in turn, inflation, are subject to increases, thus inhibiting economic growth.

Although some level of federal borrowing may be necessary or even desirable, the gravity of the federal debt that the Clinton administration inherited, and that we are seeing again under the George W. Bush administration, can be difficult to appreciate. Most of us cannot really comprehend what trillions of dollars mean. One way to put it is that in 1992 the national debt was mounting at a rate of $1 billion a day—a figure clearly too large to be sustained for long. Another way to look at it is that the federal government spent about $4,600 per American in 1993,[64] but it owed about $12,500 per American on the public debt alone (in 2004, the government spent an estimated $7,914 per American, but owed $15,088 per American on the public debt, or 39 percent of the GDP).[65]

Congress has tried to grapple with the deficit. It took a major step in 1985 with the Balanced Budget and Emergency Deficit Reduction Act, also known as Gramm-Rudman-Hollings after its sponsors, Senators Phil Gramm (R-Texas), Warren Rudman (R-New Hampshire), and Ernest Hollings (D-South Carolina). The act called for across-the-board spending cuts in defense and many domestic programs if Congress failed to meet specific deficit-cutting measures. More stringent deficit-cutting measures were enacted in the 1990 Budget Enforcement Act (BEA). But all this proved insufficient because some of the provisions were emasculated. Presidents Reagan and George H. W. Bush both were criticized for never proposing something that resembled a balanced budget, and Congress could not bring itself to enact a balanced budget. President Clinton revived the deficit-reduction measures contained in the BEA.

Congress's failure to balance the federal budget led to much talk about a balanced budget amendment to the U.S. Constitution to force its hand. Proponents believed it was the only way to insure that the government reduced its debt. Opponents felt it would hamstring the federal government in times of war or recession when deficit spending might be necessary. In 1996, a balanced budget amendment proved to be a real cliff hanger in Congress, but it and subsequent attempts have failed to be enacted.

During his first presidential campaign, Bill Clinton promised to cut the deficit in half during his four-year term if elected. In fiscal year 1994, President Clinton and Congress achieved a substantial deficit reduction. There are only three ways to decrease the deficit—raise taxes, decrease spending, or do both. After long hours of negotiation, a compromise was reached that included $241 billion in tax increases and $255 billion in spending cuts.

The booming economy of the 1990s, helped by Clinton's economic policies, did much to reduce the federal deficit from its $290 billion peak in 1992 to a $236 billion surplus in 2000.[66] Economic prosperity during this period boosted tax receipts and lowered borrowing and interest rates, which in turn reduced government's interest expenses. In addition, Medicare and Medicaid spending was restrained during this period by slower than normal growth in medical costs. Another contributor to the shrinking deficit was fiscal policy changes made by the 1990 and 1993 Budget

Enforcement Act (BEA), which tightened Medicare reimbursements to providers and increased income and excise taxes. For fiscal years 1991–1995, the BEA imposed two budget restrictions: (1) it capped discretionary spending at $550 billion during this period, effectively limiting defense and nondefense discretionary spending, and (2) it tied entitlement spending (such as Social Security) to tax increases and/or decreases. Tax reduction was prohibited without also reducing entitlement spending. Likewise, any increase in entitlement spending required an increase in taxes. A 1993 amendment to the BEA extended the life of the law to 1998.[67]

Although two things in life are certain—death and taxes—tax policy is not. The federal deficit was further reduced by raising taxes. Two higher tax brackets were added, bringing the total to five brackets of 15, 28, 31, 36, and 39.6 percent. Other important changes were subjecting all the wages workers earn to the Medicare payroll tax and taxing more of the Social Security benefits of higher-income recipients. The highest corporate tax bracket was raised by one percent for corporations earning over $10 million (making the highest corporate bracket 35 percent). Tax deductions for some business-related expenses, such as moving and entertainment, were restricted. Gasoline taxes were also increased. On the other side of the ledger, most luxury taxes were repealed. The earned income credit (EIC) was increased for working families with children, a smaller EIC was initiated for low-income workers without children, and deductions for certain equipment purchased by small businesses were increased. The Congressional Budget Office determined that the president would remain true to his pledge not to raise taxes on middle-income Americans—90 percent of the new taxes were estimated to fall on those earning $100,000 or more.[68]

As congressional control shifted from Democratic to Republican, the next years resulted in serious budget battles for President Clinton. In 1996, a bill that raised the minimum wage also ended up including tax provisions. It lowered some business taxes, gave homemakers the right to shelter money in tax-deferred individual retirement accounts, provided new options for people to save for retirement, and gave tax credits to many people who adopt children. Many federal workers got unexpected vacations when lack of agreement over the 1996 budget led to two shutdowns of many federal government operations. Welfare reform was at the heart of the differences. The president vetoed two major welfare reform bills before an agreement was reached on an overhaul of the public assistance programs (see Chapters 5, 7, and especially Chapter 6).

The next major budgetary event of great importance was the Balanced Budget Act (BBA) of 1997. Medicare cost containment was central in the BBA (see also Chapter 8). There were additions to some programs, notably an effort to insure more low-income children through state Medicaid programs, restoration of some public assistance benefits that had been taken away from immigrants during the 1996 welfare reform, and more money for states to use in helping people go from welfare to work. The budget deficit for fiscal year 1997 was $22 billion, the lowest in three decades.

The fiscal year 1998 budget reflected many provisions passed in the Taxpayer Relief Act of 1997.[69] On the tax-hike side, the act raised the federal cigarette tax by 15 cents. It also offered many tax cuts, making it the biggest cut since the Reagan years.

Many families got a new tax credit for children up to age 17. Also included were education tax credits of up to $1,500 for the first two years of college tuition and $1,000
for the third and fourth years and a $2,500 annual student loan interest deduction.
Even though this budgetary package did not increase federal revenues by much, when
all the recent budget measures were combined with the effects of a strong economy,
in 1999, the federal budget was back in black ink. For the first time since 1948, the
country was living within its means. When President Clinton left office, the budget
surplus was $236 billion. The gross federal debt was $5.6 trillion, or 58 percent of
GNP—down from 64 percent when he took office, and interest payments were reduced to 12.5 percent of the budget (down from 14.4 percent).[70]

Let's not forget that the Social Security Trust Funds and mechanisms like "off-
budget" items are still used to mask much of what the federal government owes.
People disagree on the importance of a balanced budget and the federal debt. Balancing the federal budget is not like balancing the household budget. Unlike you
and me, the federal government can print money and manipulate the economy. But
most people probably agree that the country is better off when the federal government is not constantly operating in the minus column. In good times, Congress and
the president like to indulge in self-congratulatory behavior. U.S. budgetary policy
and monetary policy (the work of the Federal Reserve Board) are important; however, some of the country's economic state depends on factors like the health of the
stock market and international events such as occurred on September 11, 2001, factors over which government has far less control.

One budgetary change that came as a particular surprise was that Congress made
Bill Clinton the first president to have line-item veto power, effective January 1997. It
allowed the president to cut particular line items from spending bills rather than veto
the whole bill.[71] The federal measure pertained to discretionary spending and new
spending (not to existing entitlement programs and not to interest on the federal debt).
It also permitted the president to veto tax breaks that benefit fewer than 100 people.
Congress did give itself the power to overturn the veto with a two-thirds vote in both
houses.[72] Governors of 43 states already had line-item veto powers.

The veto provision was quickly challenged as unconstitutional. A federal judge
ruled that it violated the separation of powers of the federal government because it
gave spending powers to the president that are reserved for Congress. Others believed
that Congress can legally delegate limited budget authority to the president, and that
the measure would cut some of the pork from the federal budget. Still others contended that the line-item veto restored rightful budgetary power to the president to
impound funds that had been stripped from the executive office by the 1974 Budget
Act—a power exercised by every president since Thomas Jefferson. Presidents
Kennedy, Johnson, and Nixon used it to cut federal appropriations by as much as
7 percent. The right to impound funds gave the president authority *not* to spend money
appropriated by the Congress if he felt that the spending was unnecessary. In 1998,
the Supreme Court agreed that the limited line-item veto as constructed was unconstitutional. As *Time* magazine noted, James Madison could now stop spinning in his
grave. A true line-item veto would require an amendment to the U.S. Constitution. In

its one-year existence, President Clinton used the line-item veto 82 times on 11 spending bills and cut $2 billion from projects that targeted special interests in both Republican and Democratic districts.[73]

Clinton and Social Welfare

During Clinton's presidency, the country enjoyed near full employment, low inflation, and the lowest misery index in three decades, owing largely to a strong economy that seemed to keep the president's popularity high despite the scandals that led to his impeachment trial. Like most other presidencies, the Clinton administration saw its share of failures and successes in promoting its social welfare agenda. In addition to economic reform, the president's domestic agenda included healthcare reform, welfare (public assistance) reform, and crime control.

The 1993 Budget Reconciliation Act squeaked by Congress without a single Republican vote for it. Vice President Al Gore broke the tie vote in the Senate. The economic reforms contained in the bill relied on investments in education, healthcare, science and technology, and opening foreign markets. The bill's passage helped to reverse 12 years of trickle-down economics and turned the largest deficit in history into the largest surplus in history, created 22 million jobs, increased wages, and brought homeownership to its highest rate on record. Under the Clinton economic plan, the country was predicted to be debt free by 2012.[74] According to Federal Reserve Chairman Alan Greenspan, the 1993 legislation was "an unquestioned factor in contributing to the improvement in economic activity that occurred thereafter."[75] The 1993 plan also contained the Empowerment Zones and Enterprise Communities initiative that provided $3.5 billion in job and wage credits and other incentives to build and revitalize economically depressed areas. By the end the of the Clinton Presidency, $10 billion had been invested in 135 communities (see Chapter 9).[76]

Probably most disappointing to the president was the rejection of his proposed Health Security Act, a plan that would have entitled all Americans to healthcare coverage (see Chapter 8). The plan failed because many thought it was too much government interference in healthcare. There has been a series of incremental steps to expand coverage to more individuals, but the number of uninsured has risen faster than the number obtaining insurance.

Bill Clinton pledged to end "welfare as we know it" by turning the welfare office into an employment office and by limiting the time families could spend on welfare. The president finally signed the major 1996 public assistance reform bill—the Personal Responsibility and Works Opportunity Reconciliation Act (PRWORA) of 1996—even though some its provisions disturbed him. Among them was cutting most aid to immigrants residing legally in the United States. Some of these provisions were later modified, but the president lost a number of allies as a result of signing the bill. Many thought the approach was an affront to the nation's children. Public assistance caseloads had begun to drop before the PRWORA due to the healthy economy.

In the years following welfare reform, the rapid fall of caseloads was seen as a sign of success. Since 1997 the TANF caseload has declined 63 percent;[77] however, outcomes are not all rosy. Many people leaving the welfare roles have not achieved self-sufficiency. In 1999, only about half of welfare leavers were employed. That number fell to 42 percent by 2002, partly due to tough economic times. Welfare reform may have reached its peak benefit. Those returning to welfare rose to 25 percent in 2002, up from 20 percent in 1999, and 14 percent had no source of income in 2002 (compared to 10 percent in 1999).[78] One in seven adults who left TANF were disconnected from the workforce—not working, without a working spouse, and not receiving other TANF cash assistance. Former recipients may be out of the program but not out of the poverty—not a ringing endorsement of the nation's social welfare system.

President Clinton got a major crime bill passed with provisions for more community police, bans on assault weapons, life sentences for three-time felony offenders, more prison funding, more crime prevention funds, and more attention to crimes against women (the Violence Against Women Act of 1994). Following the implementation of the crime bill, violent crime rates dropped 55 percent from 1994 to 2002.[79]

As the federal budget surplus grew and the bullish economy continued, Republicans insisted on returning the money to the American people through tax cuts, while Democrats demanded that the surplus be allowed to grow to insure the stability of Social Security for the soon-to-be-retiring baby boomers. As part of the fiscal year 1999 budget, Republicans tried unsuccessfully to pass more tax cuts that would have primarily benefited the upper classes. Tax cuts were a high priority for president George W. Bush as he took office in January 2001.

THE PRESIDENCY OF GEORGE W. BUSH

Presidential Election 2000

The 2000 presidential election between Republican candidate Governor George W. Bush of Texas and Democratic candidate U.S. Vice President Al Gore proved to be a dead-heat contest that came down to counting and recounting the last few votes in the state of Florida. The election outcome took five weeks to determine. Recounts in certain Florida counties raised serious questions about how votes were being interpreted (and whether many states' recount laws would be considered constitutional). Where punch cards were used, chads not completely removed from the ballot produced the "hanging chad" controversy, and marks ("dimples") left on ballots also caused ballot counters to question voters' intent. Investigations made it clear that there was no uniformity in how voter intent was interpreted across Florida counties and that these problems had occurred elsewhere. On December 12, 2000, the U.S Supreme Court halted the vote recount in Florida because voter intent was being interpreted differently from county to county. The court concluded that "it is obvious that the recount cannot be conducted in compliance with the requirements of equal protection and due process without substantial additional work." In the case of *Bush v. Gore*, the 5–4 Supreme Court decision gave the Florida election to Bush with a 537 vote margin.[80] This allowed Bush to win the electoral votes in Florida, and thus the electoral college election nationally, even though Gore had won the popular vote by 540,000.

The intense controversy over the 2000 presidential election outraged voters and awakened Americans to the reality that one of their basic rights, to vote and have that vote count, had been called into serious question. The votes of tens of thousands of Floridians were not counted because of errors in vote-counting procedures or because their names had been wrongly removed from voter registration lists.[81] The U.S. Commission on Civil Rights reported the most disturbing finding. According to its in-depth investigation, black voters were nearly ten times more likely than nonblack voters to have their ballots rejected.[82] The General Accounting Office (GAO) stated that 57 percent of precincts across the country experienced difficulties with voter eligibility, accessibility of polling places, technology, and poorly trained poll workers.[83]

Election Reform

The GAO and civic interest groups recommended election reforms in the areas of (1) voter registration; (2) absentee and early voting; (3) election day administration; and (4) vote counts, certification, and recounts. In the year following the election, more than 1,800 pieces of legislation were introduced to state legislatures, and 250 new laws were enacted. Nearly 50 bills were introduced in Congress.[84]

In October 2002, the Senate passed election reform legislation, the Help America Vote Act (HAVA). The bill provided about $3.9 billion over four years for upgrades to voting equipment, improvement of voting and voter registration procedures, and training for poll workers. Specific mandates of the bill include:

◆ By January 1, 2004, new registering voters must provide a driver's license number or the last eight digits of their social security number. For voters without either of these, state officials will assign a number.

◆ By the 2004 presidential election, states must provide provisional ballots to voters whose names do not appear on the registration list. When the voter's eligibility is verified, the vote will be counted.

◆ By 2006, all states must have a statewide computerized voter registration database, and all voting equipment must provide for "second chance" voting, to allow voters to correct errors on their ballots before casting them.

◆ All polling places must have at least one voting station accessible by individuals with disabilities.[85]

Many Americans choose not to vote, but those who do vote want to make sure their vote counts. As election 2004 approached, the bulk of the $3.9 billion Congress promised states to modernize their voting procedures had yet to be handed out, and members of the commission designated to help states reduce election problems were not confirmed until December 2003. Twelve states decided not to replace their punch-card or lever voting systems until after the 2004 election because of uncertainty about federal funding and equipment standards. States that had purchased and implemented touch-screen voting machines encountered problems. For example, in Fairfax County, Virginia, during the November 3, 2003, election, 10 voting machines locked up, calling into question the validity of the vote count. In Broward County, Florida, during a special House election in January, new touch-screen voting machines produced 137 blank ballots. The election was decided by 12 votes, but with no paper trail on the voting machines, it was not possible to trace voting error due to machine malfunction. Little research has been done on the failure rates of voting machines (see also Chapter 11).[86]

The United States at War

The election results may have been more than questionable, but as the 43rd president of the United States, George W. Bush won the confidence of substantial numbers of Americans. His overall approval ratings were generally high, soaring to 90 percent in response to his handling of 9/11.[87] But they dropped below 50 percent as the economy remained sluggish and in response to the situation in Iraq.[88]

During his campaign, President Bush promised to cut taxes, reform schools, and build the nation's defense, and his strategy of "compassionate conservatism" included leveling the playing field for faith-based groups to receive federal funds for social welfare services.[89] Soon after taking office, the president's domestic agenda took second priority to the war on terrorism and retaliation for the attacks on the World Trade Center and Pentagon and the war in Iraq.

9/11 and the War on Terrorism

This book is about social welfare, but it can hardly ignore sweeping events that have consumed much of the country's energy and resources and made it more difficult to concentrate on domestic concerns. Damage from the terrorist attacks on September 11, 2001, was massive. Nearly 3,000 airline passengers and crew members, workers in the World Trade Center and the offices of the Pentagon, and firefighters and rescue workers perished.[90] The World Trade Center's twin towers collapsed, and surrounding buildings were damaged or had to be destroyed. The Pentagon was also severely damaged. Human service workers' primary concerns for the marginalized in society shifted to caring for victims of the attack, helping families cope with losses, and stabilizing communities. They joined with the rest of the country in trying to process the attack on American values, the U.S. Constitution, and the country's way of life. The country was in mourning, and it responded with tremendous outpowerings of cash aid and volunteer services to those in New York City (though it diverted charitable giving from local communities).

President Bush called the attacks "The Pearl Harbor of the 21st century,"[91] declaring them "acts of war" against the United States.[92] Intelligence officials concluded that the Al-Qaeda terrorist organization was attempting to destroy the U.S. government.[93] On the evening of September 11, 2001, President Bush addressed the country and announced, "We will make no distinction between those who planned these acts and those who harbor them."[94] This message was intended for the Taliban regime in Afghanistan, comprised of extreme Islamic fundamentalist militias, who were harboring Al-Qaeda terrorists in exchange for substantial sums of money from Osama bin Laden.[95] Over the next few days, what appeared to be authentic threats on the White House continued. On September 14, 2001, Congress, with only one dissenting vote, authorized President Bush to use any necessary force in retaliation against the terrorists responsible for the attacks. When the Taliban refused to surrender bin Laden and his Al-Qaeda terrorists, President Bush ordered the capture and removal of the Taliban and Al-Qaeda terrorists from Afghanistan with military force.[96]

Between September 11, 2001, and October 30, 2002, Congress passed 19 pieces of legislation in direct response to the terrorist attacks. Legislation provided funds for victims and their families and money to help communities recovery. Security was a primary focus, as was economic support for airlines to get the nation flying again. To expedite the fight against terrorism, multiple pieces of legislation provided funds for intelligence gathering, law enforcement, and new rules for preventing terrorism. Appropriations made for the use of military force paved the way for rooting out the Al-Qaeda terrorist camps in Afghanistan. Funds for food, medical supplies, educational assistance, and other humanitarian aid were appropriated for Afghanistan's citizens.[97]

Perhaps the most controversial piece of post-September 11, 2001, legislation is the U.S.A. Patriot Act. It has been criticized for infringing on the civil liberties of Americans by expanding surveillance abilities (e.g., use of wiretaps and access to personal computers and library records) and reducing the checks and balances previously given to courts to guard against abuse of power. The expanded definition of "domestic terrorism" called into question the right of American citizens to legitimately stage public protests (see Chapter 11).[98] The current debate is whether to renew the Patriot Act or let it expire in 2005 and regain some of the civil liberties lost to the war on terrorism. Some communities have condemned parts of the act—for example, the way it treats noncitizens by denying them legal rights. Many groups, including the American Library Association, oppose provisions of the act. Attorney General John Ashcroft has toured the country to drum up support for Patriot Act II and to ensure Americans that it will not be used lightly. Americans certainly saw the need to institute new policies such as airport screenings in the wake of the terrorist attacks, but granting the government powers to detain American citizens and others without access to legal counsel and providing broad powers to survey patrons' library use are other matters.

The New Department of Homeland Security

As part of the response to terrorism, president Bush created the Department of Homeland Security (DHS) by consolidating 22 previously distinct domestic agencies for the primary purpose of protecting the nation against future terrorist attacks. A major function of the DHS is to assist states and cities in developing first-response teams in the event of attack. State and local governments have received nearly $4 billion to help meet the needs of first responders and to offset costs associated with extra security measures.[99]

DHS has been involved in many activities, such as working with the Centers for Disease Control to develop strategies against biological warfare, developing safeguards for the nation's financial system, working with scientists to implement new technologies for improved safety, and providing an advocate on immigration issues. One thing has become abundantly clear: Sealing the U.S. borders is nearly impossible, even with heightened security. Americans are concerned that more attacks may occur.

War on Iraq

During his 2002 State of the Union address, President George W. Bush declared Iraq, Iran, and North Korea "an axis of evil." He altered U.S. war policy when he said, "I will not wait on events," suggesting that he would act preemptively against perceived threats to the United States.[100] By April 2002, the president was openly advocating for a regime change in Iraq. Objections to the war were raised around the world. Bush called Iraq's leader Saddam Hussein a threat to national security because he and others believed that Hussein had stockpiled weapons of mass destruction (chemical, biological, and nuclear). Hard evidence supporting this position was limited and unconvincing to the international community.[101] The threat of an imminent attack on Iraq by the U.S. spawned antiwar and anti-Bush protests by millions of people around the world, and by the tens of thousands at home.

The talk of war with Iraq put world leaders on edge, especially those in the Middle East. Some feared that a war with Iraq could destabilize the whole region, and have staggering economic implications given the oil-rich countries in the region. Others believed that it could prompt more terrorist attacks and escalate the rising resentment toward the United States worldwide.[102] President Bush made the decision to invade Iraq in March 2003 with military support from Britain, Spain, and Australia.[103] Other allies (e.g., Germany, France, and Russia) objected, and there were massive antiwar demonstrations across Europe. Bush's intention was to "disarm Iraq of its weapons of mass destruction, and enforce 17 United Nations Security Council resolutions . . . [and to] liberate the Iraqi people from one of the worst tyrants and most brutal regimes on earth."[104]

U.S. and coalition forces declared victory three weeks later when the major military resistance in Baghdad fell, symbolized by U.S. Marines and Iraqi citizens toppling a statue of Saddam Hussein.[105] In December 2003, U.S. soldiers captured Hussein, but the hostilities in Iraq have not abated. The continued U.S. presence in Iraq has prompted Muslim militants to reenter Iraq and launch attacks against the occupying forces. Rumors are that Fundamentalist Islamic terrorist groups see Iraq as the battleground for Jihad, the Holy War against the Americans. Attacks continue on a daily basis, killing 40 to 80 military personnel a month and hundreds of civilians.[106] As the hostilities continue, President Bush faces growing criticism of his decision to invade Iraq, the prolonged American occupation of the country, and concerns that no weapons of mass destruction have been found. Particularly vexing are the intelligence failures upon which the war decision was made as detailed in a report by the U.S. Senate's Select Committee on Intelligence.[107] The United States spent billions to wage the war in Iraq. It will spend billions more to stabilize Iraq, rebuild the country, and engage in the difficult task of instituting democracy. Whether you supported the president's decision to invade Iraq or whether you opposed the war and even demonstrated against it, there is no question that the financial burdens of the invasion and the attention it has demanded from the executive, legislative, and judicial branches of the U.S. government are tremendous, draining time and resources from many aspects of the country's domestic agenda.

Economic Troubles at Home

At home, the precipitous drop in the stock market, the onset of a recession, the loss of millions of jobs, unprecedented exposure of corporate crime, and a rising unemployment rate called for President Bush's attention and action.

The Stock Market Bubble Bursts

The rapid growth of the stock market during the 1990s produced what has become know as the "stock market bubble." Such "bubbles" occur when favorable events (such as the invention of the World Wide Web, or the end of the Cold War) occur suddenly and unexpectedly, producing "irrational exuberance" about the stock market's future performance. A "bubble" such as occurred during the mid- and late-1990s makes the economy vulnerable to uncertainty. As economies around the world have grown increasingly interdependent, economic crises in one region of the world impact other regions.[108]

Two events in the late 1990s negatively impacted on the U.S. economy. First was the Asian financial crisis in 1997,[109] followed by the Russian default on foreign loans in 1998.[110] These economic events shook investor confidence in the global market. The technology market went from an after-tax profit of $21.6 billion in 1996 to an after-tax loss of $27.9 billion in 2000. From January 2000 to January 2001, the NASDAQ stock market dropped by 45 percent. The stock market bubble had burst.[111]

Then, in October 2001, Enron Corporation ushered in an era of corporate scandals when it unexpectedly announced a big quarterly loss and a huge write-down in shareholder equity. Indictments at Enron and of its accounting firm, Arthur Anderson, on fraudulent practices ensued. Other corporate scandals (including Adelphia Communications, ImClone Systems, Tyco International, and WorldCom Inc.) swept the business world. The illegal accounting practices, earning shortfalls, bankruptcies, and criminal indictments severely shook investor confidence in the stock market.[112]

Many workers lost their jobs, and many individual investors found themselves postponing retirement or other plans after their stock portfolios and investment accounts nosedived. Stock market investing, once reserved for the rich, is now used by many middle-class Americans, who were affected by these occurrences. Escalating federal defense and homeland security spending combined with a poor economy and joblessness was fast turning the federal budget surplus into a serious deficit. Even as the stock market improved, unemployment was slow to budge, perhaps due to practices like offshoring that can boost corporate profits without much effect on employment at home.

Boosting the Sluggish Economy

Economic policymakers used two major strategies to address the national recession and resistant economy from 2001 to 2003. First, the Federal Reserve progressively lowered interest rates, which boosted consumer spending for big-ticket items like homes and automobiles. Second, President George W. Bush convinced Congress to pass a series of tax relief measures. Relying on the principles of supply-side economics embraced by the Reagan administration, President Bush believed that: (1) tax cuts for individuals would return money to Americans to stimulate consumption and thus put a demand on production (although the biggest tax cuts were enjoyed by the top 1 percent of earners) and (2) tax relief for businesses would stimulate investments and job creation.[113]

The Economic Growth and Tax Relief Reconciliation Act of 2001 (EGTR) provided some of those tax cuts, giving American households money to stimulate consumer buying. Many Americans were probably surprised to see special tax refund checks in their mailboxes ($300 for an individual, and $600 for a couple), though some thought the government should have used the money to pay down the federal debt. EGTR also increased the child tax credit. The Job Creation and Worker Assistance Act of 2002 extended unemployment benefits for unemployed workers, provided tax credits to businesses impacted by the September 11th attacks, and continued tax credits that expired in 2001 to employers who hired workers belonging to underprivileged groups or participating in welfare-to-work programs.[114]

The Jobs and Growth Tax Relief Reconciliation Act of 2003 (JGTR) aimed to increase consumer buying through tax cuts, produce jobs using business incentives, and accelerate many EGTR provisions. JGTR provides temporary tax relief from 2003 to 2008. JGTR did the following:

♦ Increased the child tax credit from $600 to $1000 for 2003 and 2004. In 2005 it will fall back to $700 and will gradually rise to $1000 by 2010.

♦ Eliminated the "marriage penalty" by increasing the standard tax deduction for married filers to double that of single filers for 2003 and 2004. In 2005 the standard deduction for married filers will fall to 174 percent of single filers and gradually increase to 200 percent by 2009.

♦ Reduced tax rates to 10 percent for the lowest income earners and 35 percent for the highest income earners (15, 25, 28, and 33 percent for intervening tax brackets) for 2003 and 2004.

♦ Reduced capital gains taxes for 2003–2009.

♦ Provided business incentives through expanded expense thresholds and bonus depreciation.

♦ Extended tax payments for corporate taxpayers from September 15, 2003, to October 1, 2003.

♦ Appropriated $20 billion to be distributed among the 50 states as a tax relief measure.[115]

The combined tax relief provided in the EGTR, the Job Creation and Worker Assistance Act, and the JGTR disproportionately benefit the wealthiest 1 percent of earners. Families in the lowest 20 percent of earners could expect to see an average tax break of $87 in 2003, while the top 1 percent of earners could expect an average benefit of $51,627. Over the 10-year period (2001–2010), the average cumulative tax cut to the lowest-income earners is expected to be $827 compared to the top 1 percent, who will benefit by an average of $500,723 (see Table 2.2).[116] Given the tax cuts on dividends, interest, capital gains, and inheritance, more of the tax burden shifts to earned income, obviously benefitting the rich at the expense of lower-income wage earners.

Since the tax cuts, some economic indicators have begun to respond. The Gross Domestic Product (GDP) increased 3.1 percent in 2003, up from .5 percent in 2001, due largely to increased efficiency in productivity. The Consumer Price Index (CPI) remained stable at 1.9 percent, down from 2.4 percent in 2002. The stock market began to rebound, but remained somewhat volatile. Unemployment dropped from 6.4 percent in June 2003 to 5.7 percent in December 2003; however, job growth remained stagnant and the number of discouraged workers (those who have given up looking for work) continued to increase while the size of the labor force diminished.[117] With almost no job growth, this economic recovery earned the name of the "jobless re-

---

TABLE 2.2

Who Benefits from Bush's Tax Cuts?

Average tax cut by income group

	Avg. Income	2001	2002	2003	2004	2005	2001–10
Lowest 20%	$ 9,800	$ 57	$ 78	$ 87	$ 91	$ 77	$ 827
Second 20%	21,400	266	343	443	460	371	4,037
Middle 20%	35,300	403	557	827	863	563	6,516
Fourth 20%	57,400	572	860	1,469	1,544	971	10,453
Next 15%	97,500	742	1456	3,144	3,375	2,015	18,244
Next 4%	200,100	1,015	3,614	6,829	7,439	3,913	37,681
Top 1%	938,000	3,221	28,767	51,627	59,292	41,264	500,723
Total Tax Cuts		441	1,021	1,814	1,975	1,259	**13,520**

Source: CITIZENS for TAX JUSTICE. Institute on Taxation and Economic Policy Tax Model, June 2003, & Citizens for Tax Justice, *Average Tax Cuts under the 2001–3 Bush Tax Cuts by Calendar Year,* July 2003. Available at www.ctj.org.

covery." Many blame the North American Free Trade Agreement and other legislation for encouraging job loss and allowing corporations to export jobs to countries where they can hire workers at a pittance. It is questionable whether this does any good at keeping prices low at home.

States Struggle to Balance Budgets

Like the federal government, state budgets suffered under the declining economy, but like the federal government, all states except Vermont are required to balance their budget every year. States also experienced a fiscal insult from the tax cuts passed by Congress in 2001, 2002, and 2003. Some states' taxes (like state income taxes) are tied to federal tax rates, so as federal rates decline, state taxes often do the same. Other fiscal hardships for states included the rising cost of Medicaid and federal spending mandates to states for homeland security, education, and election reform. Almost every state experienced a budget crisis from 2001 to 2003.[118] States cut $20–40 billion from their spending from 2001 to 2003, with more expected in the 2004 fiscal cycle. Cuts in state spending have likely had a disproportionate impact on the poor.[119]

The Federal Budget—from Surplus to Deficit

Among the public's biggest concerns as they considered their vote in the November 2004 presidential election were the economy and jobs.[120] At the center of public discourse on the economy is the growing national budget deficit. Economic forecasts and American optimism that budget surpluses would continue to melt away the federal debt could not have been more erroneous. The federal balance sheet went from a surplus of $236 billion in 2000 to an estimated $475 billion deficit for 2004.[121] The Iraq war, creation of the Department of Homeland Security, tax cuts, and a sluggish economy are the major factors accounting for the growing federal deficit (see Figure 2.3).[122] Nevertheless, President George W. Bush pledged to cut the deficit in half over the next five years, while at the same time requesting that the temporary tax cuts enacted over the past three years be made permanent.

The Domestic Scene

Despite President Bush's attention to the war, he was able to push his domestic agenda forward on several fronts. On his first day in office, Bush rallied the support of anti-abortion groups when he reinstated a policy prohibiting any federal funding of family-planning groups that offer abortion services or abortion counseling overseas. This policy was first instated by President Ronald Reagan and rescinded by President Clinton in 1993.[123]

A success of President Bush's first year in office was passage of the No Child Left Behind Act of 2001 (discussed further in Chapter 9). This act provides some of the most sweeping school reforms since 1965, and redefines the federal role in K–12 education by targeting the achievement gap in reading and math between disadvantaged students

FIGURE 2.3

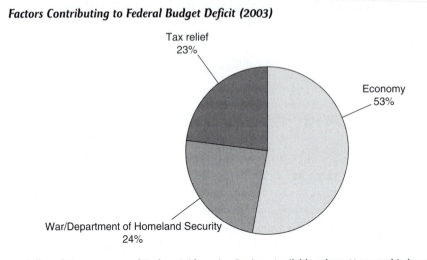

Factors Contributing to Federal Budget Deficit (2003)

Tax relief
23%

Economy
53%

War/Department of Homeland Security
24%

Source: Office of Management and Budget, Mid-session Review; Available at http://www.whitehouse.gov/omb/charts/msr-charts.html

and their peers.[124] The act is intended to increase standards and accountability for schools across the country.[125] States and schools are complaining that, among other things, federal funding for the act is insufficient to do the job, and that they are hard pressed to comply.

President George W. Bush campaigned on the concept of "compassionate conservatism" in helping the needy and underserved in the nation. As part of this approach, he launched his faith-based initiative during his first year in office. But funding priorities quickly shifted after September 11, 2001, and relatively little attention has been given to this initiative. With TANF reauthorization in the offing, the president is calling for tougher work requirements for recipients—40 hours per week—with no increase in childcare funding for working TANF parents.[126] He was also promoting state incentives to get couples to marry, believing that marriage is a key to addressing poverty and ending welfare dependency. Needless to say, promoting marriage is a controversial endeavor (see Chapter 6).

A major victory for George W. Bush was the passage of prescription drug benefits for Medicare recipients. On December 8, 2003, the President signed into law the Medicare Prescription Drug Improvement and Modernization Act of 2003.[127] This law provides prescription drug discount cards for Medicare beneficiaries who purchase their drugs through a private managed-care provider.[128] Critics of the legislation contend that the biggest benefit of the $400 billion (over 10 years) healthcare plan will go to drug companies and managed-care providers.[129] Just weeks after the landmark legislation, the Office of Management and Budget announced that the new estimated cost of the drug program is $534 billion. Legislators who voted for the bill under assurances that the cost would not exceed $400 billion were outraged. Democrats and disgruntled Republicans began drafting amendments to the prescription drug legislation.[130]

Polls tell us what the American public wants resolved: the economy, jobs, and unemployment; the war and terrorism; and healthcare.[131] Who wins the 2004 presidential election will likely to be determined by voters' confidence in the candidate to turn the economy around and the importance they place on guns versus butter.

SUMMARY

The roots of the U.S. welfare system can be traced back to Elizabethan times. Although the United States has developed its own unique brand of social welfare, some of this influence remains apparent.

In the early days of this country, welfare was largely provided by families, friends, private charities, and churches. But by the late nineteenth and early twentieth centuries, social problems had mounted, and state governments began to respond to the needs of the dependent and poor. Following the Great Depression, the federal government passed the Social Security Act of 1935 as part of America's New Deal. In the 1960s President Johnson declared "war on poverty" in an attempt to root out the significant poverty that remained in the United States.

During the twentieth century, the expansion of social welfare was shaped by the rural-to-urban migration, the elimination of residency requirements, the welfare rights movement, and cost of living increases in social welfare programs. The growth of the aged population and the increased number of single-parent families headed by women have also resulted in the need for more social welfare services.

Americans became disillusioned as they spent more on public assistance without the results they had expected. In the 1970s and 1980s a more conservative mood developed toward welfare. President Reagan tightened eligibility requirements in most public assistance programs, reduced spending growth in these programs, and consolidated many social programs. Reagan's program for economic recovery was intended to increase incentives to work and to slow inflation by reducing taxes and slowing the growth of the money supply. Another important aspect of Reagan's plan was to return to the states much of the decision-making power over how public assistance and social service dollars should be spent. Inflation decreased and more people went back to work during the Reagan years, but the number of poor remained high and federal budget deficits increased tremendously. President George H. W. Bush further encouraged the states to develop innovative solutions to reducing social problems, but he was unable to remain true to his pledge of "no new taxes" in light of mounting federal deficits.

After twelve years of Republican presidents, Democrat Bill Clinton assumed the presidency with ambitious ideas for reducing budget deficits, reforming healthcare and welfare, and controlling crime. But as Congress turned from Democratic to Republican control, the climate for public assistance became more austere. In 1996 Congress passed a sweeping reform of the public assistance programs. Since 1997, the number of families receiving public asistance has dropped precipitously. At the same time, market conditions (like the stock market's stellar performance), a strong monetary policy, and more attention to federal budget controls interacted to make life better for many Americans. By 1999 President Clinton had fulfilled his campaign promise of balancing the budget and had implemented a plan to completely eliminate federal debt by 2012. Even in light of this progress, many millions of Americans were still living in poverty. Advocates for the poorest Americans continued to press the federal government to do more for these individuals.

The election of President George W. Bush began with controversy as ballot disputes and polling policies came under attack in Florida and other states. These disputes led to the Supreme Court case *Bush v. Gore,* and its ruling that gave the election to George W. Bush. Soon after the election, reforms were enacted to protect the democratic election process.

Shortly after taking office, President George W. Bush faced the biggest challenge this country has seen since Pearl Harbor—the terrorist attacks on the World Trade Center and the Pentagon. Responding to these attacks and continued threats occupied most of his first term in office and continue to stir controversy. The removal of terrorist camps and the Taliban regime in Afghanistan, the creation of the Department of Homeland Security, and the Patriot Act are the primary strategies President George W. Bush has used to keep America safe. The threat of "weapons of mass destruction" believed to be in Saddam Hussein's possession led to the invasion and occupation of Iraq and the capture of Saddam Hussein, but also to controversy over intelligence failures and the legitimacy of the Iraq war. Even in light of those controversies, the president has generally received high marks on his leadership, and there have been no further attacks at home.

The president has been plagued with a struggling U.S. economy. The tax cuts he championed may have begun to help the economy, but new jobs are not being created. The American people, especially the poor, continue to struggle in this "jobless recovery."

The president was able to shepherd though landmark legislation in education reform and Medicare reform. Implementation of these reforms is meeting objections due to weak federal and state budgets.

NOTES

1. For more detailed descriptions of the history of social welfare in the United States, see June Axinn and Herman Levin, *Social Welfare: A History of the American Response to Need,* 3rd ed. (New York: Longman, 1992); Ronald C. Federico, *The Social Welfare Institution: An Introduction,* 3rd ed. (Lexington, MA: Heath, 1980); Blanche D. Coll, *Perspectives in Public Welfare: A History* (Washington, DC: U.S. Department of Health, Education, and Welfare, 1973).

2. Library of Congress, *Bill Summary and Status for the 100th Congress,* P.L. 100-485 (Washington, DC),

retrieved February 9, 2004, from http://thomas.loc.gov/cgi-bin/bdquery/z?d100:HR01720:|TOM:/bss/d100query.html

3. Library of Congress, *Bill Summary and Status for the 104th Congress,* P.L. 104-193 (Washington, DC), retrieved February 9, 2004, from http://thomas.loc.gov/cgi-bin/bdquery/z?d100:HR01720:|TOM:/bss/d100query.html

4. Children's Defense Fund, *President Bush's Welfare Reform Leaves Millions of Children Behind* (Washington, DC, March 14, 2002), retrieved January 28, 2004,

from http://www.cdfactioncouncil.org/analysis_welfare. htm. See also Office of the Press Secretary, *President Discusses Welfare Reform and Job Training* (Washington, DC, February 27, 2002), retrieved January 28, 2004, from http://www.whitehouse.gov/news/releases/2002/2/ print20020227-5.html; and *Fact Sheet: President Announces Welfare Reform Agenda* (Washington, DC, February 26, 2002), retrieved January 28, 2004, from http:// www.whitehouse.gov/news/releases/2002/2/print 20020226.html

5. See Federico, *The Social Welfare Institution*, p. 52; Coll, *Perspectives in Public Welfare*, pp. 1–2, for an elaboration of the role of the church and feudal landholders in the provision of welfare benefits.

6. Coll, *Perspectives in Public Welfare*, p. 2.

7. *Ibid.*, pp. 2–3.

8. Federico, The *Social Welfare Institution*, p. 104; Coll, *Perspectives in Public Welfare*, p. 4.

9. See Federico, *The Social Welfare Institution*, pp. 52–53, for further elaboration.

10. *Ibid.*

11. Philip Klein, *From Philanthropy to Social Welfare* (San Francisco: Jossey-Bass, 1968), p. 11, cited in Federico, p. 53.

12. See Federico, *The Social Welfare Institution*, p. 53; and Coll, *Perspectives in Public Welfare*, pp. 5–6, for elaboration on Elizabethan welfare.

13. Much of this section relies on Coll, *Perspectives in Public Welfare*, pp. 17, 20, 21–22, 27–28.

14. *Ibid.*, p. 17.

15. See P. Nelson Reid, "Social Welfare History," in Richard L. Edwards, ed., *Encyclopedia of Social Work*, 19th ed. (Washington, DC: NASW Press, 1995), pp. 2206–2225.

16. Thomas R. Dye, *Understanding Public Policy*, 4th ed. (Englewood Cliffs, NJ: Prentice Hall, 1981), pp. 116–117.

17. Reid, "American Social Welfare History."

18. Paragraphs describing the Great Depression rely on Thomas R. Dye and L. Harmon Zeigler, *The Irony of Democracy*, 5th ed. (Monterey, CA: Duxbury Press, 1981), pp. 100–101.

19. Cited in Richard Hofstadter, *The American Political Tradition* (New York: Knopf, 1948), p. 316.

20. Reid, "American Social Welfare History."

21. *Shapiro v. Thompson*, 394 U.S. 618; see Frances Fox Piven and Richard A. Cloward, *Regulating the Poor: The Functions of Public Welfare* (New York: Random House, 1971), for an elaboration on residency requirements, especially pp. 306–308.

22. National Center on Poverty Law, "Residency Requirements Case List" (Chicago), retrieved January 30, 2004, from http://www.povertylaw.org/ legalresearch/cases

23. This paragraph relies on Frances Fox Piven and Richard A. Cloward, *Poor People's Movements: Why They Succeed, How They Fail* (New York: Vintage Books, 1977); quote is from p. 275.

24. *Ibid.*

25. U.S. Social Security Administration, *Latest Cost-of-Living Adjustment* (Washington, DC, October 16, 2003), retrieved January 30, 2004, from http://www.ssa.gov/ OACT/COLA/latest COLA.html; U.S. Social Security Administration, "The History of COLA," retrieved June 28, 2004, from http://www.ssa.gov/cola/automaticcola. htm

26. Aaron Wildavsky, *Speaking Truth to Power: The Art and Craft of Policy Analysis* (Boston: Little, Brown, 1979), p. 98.

27. U.S. Social Security Administration, "The History of COLA."

28. U.S. Social Security Administration, *Latest Cost-of-Living Adjustment.*

29. U.S. Census Bureau, *Census 2000 Brief* (Washington, DC, October 2001), retrieved January 31, 2004, from http://www.census.gov/prod/2001pubs/; see also population estimates from U.S. Department of Commerce, *Population Projections of the United States by Age, Sex, Race and Hispanic Origin:1995–2050* (Washington, DC), retrieved January 31, 2004, from http:// www.census.gov

30. U.S. Census Bureau, *Statistical Abstracts of the United States: 2003* (Washington, DC), Table 66, retrieved February 10, 2004, from http://www.census. gov/prod/2003pubs/02statab/vitstat.pdf

31. *Ibid.*, Table 67.

32. Figures in this section rely on U.S. Census Bureau, *Poverty in the United States: 2002* (Washington, DC, September, 2003), retrieved January 31, 2004, from http://www.census.gov/prod/2002pubs/

33. U.S. Census Bureau, *Statistical Abstract of the United States: 1999* (Washington, DC, 1999), Table 607.

34. U.S. Census Bureau, *Statistical Abstract of the United States: 2003* (Washington, DC, 2003), Table 539.

35. *Ibid.*, Table 255.

36. Executive Office of the President, Office of Management and Budget, *Budget of the United States Government, Fiscal Year 2005; Percentage Composition of Receipts by Source*, Historical Tables (Washington, DC) Table 2.2, retrieved February 10, 2004, from http://www.whitehouse.gov/omb/budget/fy2005/ pdf/ist.pdf

37. Adam Carasso, C. Eugene Steuerle, and Mohammad Adeel Saleem, "How the 2001 and 2003 Tax Cuts Affect Hypothetical Families" (Washington, DC, Urban Institute: December 22, 2003); Tax Policy Center: A Joint Venture of the Urban Institute and Brookings Institution, Table T03-0164 & Table T03-0114,

http://www.taxpolicycenter.org/. See also Citizens for
Tax Justice, *Effects of the First Three Tax Cuts Charted*
(Washington, DC, June 4), retrieved January 28, 2004,
from 2003, http://www.ctj.org

38. Executive Office of the President, Office of
Management and Budget, *Budget of the United States
Government, Fiscal Year 2005: Percentage Composition
of Receipts by Source,* Historical Tables, Table 2.2.

39. Federation of Tax Administrators, *State Individual Income Taxes: Tax Rates for Tax Year 2003—as of
January 1, 2003* (Washington, DC, January 2003), retrieved January 31, 2004, from http://taxadmin.org/
fta/rate/ind_inc.html

40. Mimi Abramovitz, "Everyone Is on Welfare:
The Role of Redistribution in Social Policy Revisited,"
Social Work, Vol. 28, No. 6, 1983, pp. 440–445; Richard
M. Titmuss, "The Role of Redistribution in Social Pol-
icy," *Social Security Bulletin,* Vol. 39, 1965, pp. 14–20.

41. Library of Congress, *Bill Summary and Status
for the 107th and 108th Congress,* P.L. 107-16, "The Economic Growth and Tax Relief Reconciliation Act of 2001"
(Washington, DC), retrieved February 10, 2004, from
http://thomas.loc.gov/cgi-bin/bdquery/z?d107:
HR01836:|TOM:/bss/d107query.html and P.L. 108-27,
"The Jobs Growth and Tax Relief Reconciliation Act of
2003," http://thomas.loc.gov/cgi-bin/bdquery/z?d108:
HR00002:|TOM:/bss/d108query.html

42. Committee on Ways and Means, U.S. House of
Representatives, *Overview of the Federal Tax System,*
1993 edition (Washington, DC: U.S. Government Printing Office, 1993), p. 263.

43. Citizens for Tax Justice, *More Corporation Tax
Shelters on the Way* (Washington, DC, October 2003),
retrieved January 28, 2004, from http://www.ctj.org/
html/corp1003.htm. See also Citizens for Tax Justice,
*Surge in Corporate Welfare Drives Corporate Tax Pay-
ments Down to Near Record Low,* April 2002, retrieved
January 28, 2004, from http://www.ctj.org/html/corp
0402.htm, and Citizens for Tax Justice, *CTJ Director
Robert S. McIntyre Testimony on Corporate Tax Loopholes,* June 2003, retrieved January 28, 2004, from
http://www.ctj.org/html/corp0603.htm

44. Library of Congress, *Bill Summary and Status
for the 107th and 108th Congress,* P.L. 107-16, "The Economic Growth and Tax Relief Reconciliation Act of 2001"
and P.L. 108-27, "The Jobs Growth and Tax Relief Reconciliation Act of 2003," and "Jobs Creation and Worker
Assistance Act of 2002," http://thomas.loc.gov/cgi-
bin/bdquery/z?d107:HR03090:|TOM:/bss/d107query.
html (Washington, DC); and Congressional Budget Office, *An Economic Analysis of Taxpayers Relief Act of 1997*
(Washington, DC, April 2000), retrieved February 10,
2004, from http://www.cbo.gov/showdoc.cfm?index =
1959&sequence = 0

45. For example, see the websites of the following
watchdog groups, retrieved January 31, 2004, Citizens
for Tax Justice, http://www.ctj.org/; Center on Budget
and Policy Priorities, http://www.cbpp.org/; Tax Policy
Center, http://www.taxpolicycenter.org/home/; Tax
Foundation, http://www.taxfoundation.org/home.html

46. Joint Committee on Taxation, "List of Expired
and Expiring Federal Tax Provisions" (Washington, DC,
January 21, 2004).

47. President of the United States, *A Program for
Economic Recovery* (Washington, DC: U.S. Government
Printing Office, February 18, 1981), p. 4.

48. Eileen Shanahan, "President Signs Sweeping
Overhaul of Tax Law," *Congressional Quarterly,*
October 25, 1986, p. 2668.

49. See William Greider, "The Education of David
Stockman," *Atlantic Monthly,* December 1981,
pp. 27–54.

50. Executive Office of the President, Office of
Management of the Budget, *Budget of the United States
Government, Fiscal Year 2004, Summary of Receipts,
Outlays, and Surpluses or Deficits: 1789–2008,* Histori-
cal Table 1.1 (Washington, DC), retrieved January 26,
2004, from http://www.omb.gov

51. President Ronald Reagan, *State of the Union
Address* (Washington, DC: U.S. Government Printing
Office, January 26, 1982).

52. For a concise review and bibliography on the
issue of federalism, see Kenneth Jost, "The States and
Federalism," *Congressional Quarterly Researcher,* September 13, 1996, pp. 795–815.

53. This section relies on Executive Office of the
President, Office of Management and Budget, *Budget of
the United States Government, Fiscal Year 1991* (Washington, DC: U.S. Government Printing Office, 1990),
section IV; quotes are from p. 176.

54. Executive Office of the President, Office of
Management and Budget, *Management of the United
States Government, Fiscal Year 1990* (Washington, DC:
U.S. Government Printing Office, 1989), pp. 3–105.

55. Martin Rein, "The Social Structure of Institutions: Neither Public nor Private," in Sheila B. Kamerman and Alfred J. Kahn, eds., *Privatization and the
Welfare State* (Princeton, NJ: Princeton University
Press, 1989), pp. 49–71.

56. Marc Bendick, Jr., "Privatizing the Delivery of
Social Welfare Services: An Idea to Be Taken Seriously,"
in Kamerman and Kahn, *Privatization and the Welfare
State,* pp. 97–120.

57. Kamerman and Kahn, *Privatization and the
Welfare State,* p. 10.

58. Andrew W. Dobelstein with Ann B. Johnson,
Serving Older Adults: Policy, Programs, and Professional

Activities (Englewood Cliffs, NJ: Prentice Hall, 1985), pp. 125–128.

59. Bendick, "Privatizing the Delivery of Social Welfare Services"; for some interesting accounts of the problems raised by privatization, see Michael B. Katz, *The Price of Citizenship: Redefining the American Welfare State* (New York: Metropolitan Books, 2001).

60. "Study: Poor Get Poorer as Rich Find Wealth Less Taxing," *Champaign-Urbana News Gazette,* February 17, 1990, p. 5.

61. As reported in Tom Kenworthy, "15 Years of Cuts Said to Enrich the Rich," *Wall Street Journal,* September 13, 1991, p. A23.

62. Much of the next paragraphs on the federal deficit rely on Executive Office of the President, *Budget of the United States Government, Analytical Perspectives, Fiscal Year 1995* (Washington, DC: U.S. Government Printing Office, 1994), p. 186.

63. Executive Office of the President, U.S. Office of Management of the Budget, *Budget of the United States, Fiscal Year 2004: Federal Debt at the End of the Year: 1940–2008,* Historical Table 7.1 (Washington, DC), retrieved January 26, 2004, from http://www.omb.gov

64. Randolph E. Schmid, "Uncle Sam Doles Out More Dollars," *Austin American-Statesman,* April 4, 1994, p. A5.

65. Calculations for 2004 are based on Executive Office of the President, U.S. Office of Management and Budget, *Budget of the United States Government, Fiscal Year 2005,* Historical Tables 6.1 and 7.1, retrieved July 20, 2004, from http://www.omb.gov

66. *Ibid.,* Historical Table 1.1.

67. Alan D. Viard, "The New Budget Outlook: Policymakers Respond to the Surplus," *Economic and Financial Review,* 2nd Quarter, 1999, Federal Reserve Bank of Dallas.

68. Gilbert A. Lewthwaite, "1994 Brings Higher Taxes for Wealthy, Break for Poor," *Austin American-Statesman,* January 1, 1994, pp. A1, 8; Executive Office of the President, *Budget of the United States Government, Fiscal Year 1995,* p. 58.

69. Executive Office of the President, *Budget of the United States Government, Fiscal Year 1998* (Washington, DC: U.S. Government Printing Office, 1997).

70. Executive Office of the President, *Budget of the United States Government,* Historical Tables, Fiscal Year 2005 (Washington, DC, U.S. Government Printing Office, 2004).

71. "The Line Item Veto Act after One Year," Congressional Budget Office (CBO) memorandum, April 1998; http://www.cbo.gov/cgi-bin/menu.exe?nodelist = O + cfgfile = /www/bin/cbo2.cfg.

72. Testimony of Stephen Moore Director of Fiscal Policy Studies, the CATO Institute before the Committee on Judiciary U.S. House of Representatives, *The Line Item Veto* (Washington, DC, March 2000), retrieved January 31, 2004, from http://www.cato.org/testimony/ct-sm032300.html

73. *Ibid.*

74. *Ibid.* and White House Office of the Press Secretary, "President Clinton and Vice President Gore's Economic Plan: Building the Path to Prosperity for America's Families" (Washington, DC, August 2000), retrieved January 31, 2004, from http://www.ed.gov/PressReleases/08-2000/wh-0805.html

75. Alan Greenspan, Housing Committee Testimony (Washington, DC, February 20, 1996), as cited in White House Office of the Press Secretary, "President Clinton and Vice President Gore's Economic Plan: Building the Path to Prosperity for America's Families," *2000 White House Education Press Releases and Statements* (Washington, DC, August 5, 2000), retrieved February 2, 2004, from http://www.ed.gov/PressReleases/08-2000/wh-0805.html

76. White House Office of the Press Secretary, "President Clinton and Vice President Gore's Ecomonic Plan: Building the Path to Prosperity for America's Families," August 5, 2000, retrieved July 19, 2004, from http://www.ed.gov/PressRelease/08-2000/wh-0805.html

77. Elise Richer, Hedieh Rahmanou, and Mark Greenberg, "Welfare Caseloads in 27 States Decline in First Quarter of 2003: Most States Show Only Small Caseload Fluctuations" (Washington, DC, July 18, 2003); *Center for Law and Social Policy.*

78. Pamela J. Loprest, "Fewer Welfare Leavers Employed in Weak Economy," No. 5 in series "Snapshots of America's Families III" (Washington, DC: Urban Institute, August 21, 2003), retrieved February 11, 2004, from http://www.urban.org/template.cfm?Template =/TaggedContent/ViewPublication.cfm&PublicationID = 8550&NavMenuID = 95

79. U.S. Department of Justice, *Violent Crime Rates Have Declined since 1994, Reaching the Lowest Level Ever Recorded in 2002* (Washington, DC: Office of Justice Programs, Bureau of Justice Statistics, 2002), retrieved February 4, 2004, from http://www.ojp.usdoj.gov/bjs/glance/viort.htm

80. *Bush v. Gore* (00-949) Supreme Court of the United States (Washington, DC, December 12, 2000), retrieved February 11, 2004, from http://supct.law.cornell.edu/supct/html/00-949.ZPC.html

81. Thomas Mann, "An Agenda for Election Reform," *Brookings Institution Policy Brief No. 82* (Washington, DC, June 2001).

82. U.S. Commission on Civil Rights, *Voting Irregularities in Florida during the 2000 Presidential Election,* Executive Summary (Washington, DC, June 8, 2001), pp. 1–7, retrieved August 23, 2003, from http://www.usccr.gov/

83. U.S. General Accounting Office, *Elections: Perspectives on Activities and Challenges across the Nation,* GAO-02-3, (Washington, DC, October 15, 2001).

84. Kathy Koch, "Election Reform," *Congressional Quarterly Researcher,* November 2, 2001, Vol. 11, No. 38.

85. Edward Walsh, "Election Reform Bill Is Passed by Senate," *Washington Post,* October 17, 2002.

86. Doug Abrahms, *Accuracy in Voting Machines Remains Issue in Election Year,* January 2004, retrieved January 31, 2004, from http://wgrz.gannettonline.com/election2004/gns/200440116–37238.html; see also *Election Reform 2004* at Electiononline.com, retrieved February 5, 2004, from http://www.electionline.org/site/docs/pdf/ERIP_AR2004.pdf

87. Gallup Organization, *State of the Nation* (Princeton, NJ), retrieved August 23, 2003, from http://www.gallup.com/poll/stateNation/; PollingReport.com, "President Bush: Job Ratings" (January–February 2004), polls by Gallup, CNN, USA, and others, retrieved February 4, 2004, from http://www.pollingreport.com/BushJob.htm

88. "Poll: Iraq Taking Toll on Bush," CBSNews.com, May 24, 2004, retrieved June 28, 2004, from http://www.cbsnews.com/stories/2004/05/24/opinion/polls/main619122.shtml

89. Kenneth Jost, "The Bush Presidency," *Congressional Quarterly Researcher,* February 2, 2001, Vol. 11, No. 4.

90. Phil Hirschkorn, CNN New York Bureau, "New York Adjusts Terrorist Death Toll Downward," August 22, 2002, *CNN.com./US,* retrieved August 7, 2003, from http://www.cnn.com/2002/US/08/22/9/11.toll/

91. Bob Woodward, *Bush at War* (New York: Simon & Schuster, 2002), p. 37.

92. President George W. Bush, *Statement by the President in His Address to the Nation* (Washington, DC, September 11, 2001), retrieved August 7, 2003, from http://www.whitehouse.gov/news/releases/2001/09/200109/11–16.html

93. President George W. Bush, *Address to a Joint Session of Congress and the American People* (Washington, DC, September 20, 2001).

94. Bush, *Statement by the President.*

95. Woodward, *Bush at War,* p. 32.

96. Library of Congress, 107th Congress, *Joint Resolution to Authorize the Use of United States Armed Forces against Those Responsible for Recent Attacks Launched against the United States* [DOCID: f:pub1040.107], P.L. 107-40. (Washington, DC, September 18, 2001), [S. J. Res. 23], retrieved August 8, 2003, from http://frwebgate.access.gpo.gov/cgi-bin/getdoc.cgi?dbname= 107_cong_public_laws&docid = f:publ040.107

97. Library of Congress, *Thomas: Legislative Information on the Internet,* September 11th Legislation (Washington, DC); http://thomas.loc.gov/

98. Electronic Frontier Foundation *Analysis of the Provisions of the USA PATRIOT Act* (San Francisco, October 31, 2001), January 30, 2004, retrieved from http://www.eff.org/Privacy/Surveillance/Terrorism/20011031_eff_usa_patriot_analysis.html

99. *Ibid.*

100. President George W. Bush, *State of the Union Address* (Washington, DC, January 29, 2002), retrieved August 7, 2003, from http://www.whitehouse.gov/news/releases/2002/01/20020129–11.html

101. Michael Ratner, Jennie Green, and Barbara Olshansky of the Center for Constitutional Rights (New York: Seven Stories Press), pp. 14–19.

102. Woodward, *Bush at War,* p. 44.

103. U.S. White House, *Operation Iraqi Freedom, Iraq: Special Report: The Coalition* (Washington, DC, April 3, 2003), retrieved August 7, 2003, from http://www.whitehouse.gov/infocus/iraq/news/20030327–10.html

104. *Ibid.*

105. Woodward, *Bush at War,* p. 357.

106. Iraq Coalition Casualty Count, retrieved February 6, 2004, from http://lunaville.org/warcasualties/Summary.aspx; "The Human Toll," *Air Force Times,* September 20, 2004.

107. Select Committee on Intelligence, United States Senate, "Report on the U.S. Intelligence Community's Prewar Intelligence Assessments of Iraq" (Washington, DC: July 7, 2004).

108. United States Congress, Joint Economic Committee, Vice Chairman Jim Saxton (R-NJ), *Economic Repercussions of the Stock Market Bubble: A Joint Economic Committee Study* (Washington, DC, July 2003), retrieved August 25, 2003, from http://www.house.gov/jec/growth/07-14-03.pdf

109. *Ibid.*

110. "Commentary: Russian Default: Four Years Later," *On-line Pravda,* August 16, 2002, retrieved August 26, 2003, from http://english.pravda.ru/economics/2002/08/16/34706.html

111. U.S. Congress, *Economic Repercussions of the Stock Market Bubble.*

112. Kenneth Jost, "Corporate Crime," *Congressional Quarterly Researcher,* October 11, 2002, Vol. 12, No. 35, pp. 1–33.

113. Kenneth Jost, "Stimulating the Economy," *Congressional Quarterly Researcher,* January 10, 2003, Vol. 13, No. 1, pp. 1–34.

114. Library of Congress, *Bill Summary and Status for the 107th and 108th Congress*, P.L. 107-16, "The Economic Growth and Tax Relief Reconciliation Act of 2001."

115. Library of Congress, *Bill Summary and Status for the 107th and 108th Congress*, P.L. 107-16, "The Economic Growth and Tax Relief Reconciliation Act of 2001," and P.L. 108-27, "The Jobs Growth and Tax Relief Reconciliation Act of 2003."

116. Institute on Taxation and Economic Policy Tax Model, June 2003, and Citizens for Tax Justice, *Average Tax Cuts under the 2001–3 Bush Tax Cuts by Calendar Year*, July 2003, retrieved from www.ctj.org

117. Figures in this paragraph are from *Employment Situation Summary* for December 2003; Bureau of Labor Statistics at http://stats.bls.gov/news.release/empsit.nr0.htm; *Consumer Price Index Summary* for January 15, 2004, at http://bls.gov/news.release/cpi.nr0.htm; and Bureau of Economic Analysis, *Gross Domestic Product Summary for 2001–2003*, retrieved February 6, 2004, from http://www.bea.doc.gov/bea/newsrel/gdpnewsrelease.htm

118. Kenneth Jost, "Stimulating the Economy," *Congressional Quarterly Researcher*, January 10, 2003, Vol. 13, No. 1, pp. 31–34.

119. Louis Uchitelle, "Red Ink in States Beginning to Hurt Economic Recovery," *New York Times*, July 28, 2003, p. 1.

120. PollingReport.com polling reports, *Problems and Priorities*, polls conducted by Gallup, *Newsweek*, CBS News, CNN, *USA*, and others (January–February 2004), retrieved February 6, 2004, from http://www.pollingreport.com/prioriti.htm

121. Congressional Budget Office, *An Analysis of the President's Budgetary Proposals for Fiscal Year 2004* (Washington, DC, March 2003), retrieved January 30, 2004, from http://www.cbo.gov/showdoc.cfm?index = 4129&sequence = 0

122. Office of Management and Budget, *Mid-term Charts on Fiscal Situation* (Washington, DC, August 26, 2003), retrieved August 26, 2003, from http://www.whitehouse.gov/omb/charts/msr-charts.html

123. Kenneth Jost, "The Bush Presidency," *Congressional Quarterly Researcher*, February 2, 2001, Vol. 11, No. 4.

124. U.S. Department of Education, *No Child Left Behind Act of 2001* (Washington, DC, 2001), retrieved August 23, 2003, from http://www.ed.gov/offices/OESE/esea/

125. Paul E. Peterson and Martin R. West, eds., *No Child Left Behind? The Politics and Practice of School Accountability* (Washington, DC: Brookings Institution Press, 2003).

126. Children's Defense Fund, *President Bush's Welfare Reform Leaves Millions of Children Behind* (Washington, DC, March 14, 2002), retrieved January 28, 2004, from http://www.cdfactioncouncil.org/analysis_welfare.htm. See also Office of the Press Secretary, *President Discusses Welfare Reform and Job Training* (Washington, DC, February 27, 2002), retrieved January 28, 2004, from http://www.whitehouse.gov/news/releases/2002/2/print20020227-5.html; and *Fact Sheet: President Announces Welfare Reform Agenda*, February 26, 2002, retrieved January 28, 2004, from http://www.whitehouse.gov/news/releases/2002/2/print20020226.html

127. U.S. Department of Health and Human Services, Centers for Medicare and Medicaid Services, *Medicare Reform Implementation* (Washington, DC), retrieved February 4, 2004, from http://www.cms.hhs.gov/medicarereform/

128. U.S. Department of Health and Human Services, *Federal Register* (Washington, DC, December 15, 2003).

129. Edwin Park and Robert Greenstein, "The AARP Ads and the New Medicare Prescription Drug Law" (Washington, DC: December 11, 2003), Center on Budget and Policy Priorities, retrieved February 4, 2004, from http://www.cbpp.org/12-11-03health.htm

130. Kaisernetwork.org, Health Policy as It Happens, "Medicare: Cost Estimates of Medicare Legislation Rise from \$400B to \$534B over 10 years," *Daily Health Policy Report*, January 30, 2004, retrieved February 4, 2004, from http://www.kaisernetwork.org/daily_reports/rep_index.cfm?hint = 3&DR_ID = 21958. See also Amy Goldstein and Juliet Eilperin, "Medicare Drug Cost Estimate Increases," *Washington Post*, January 30, 2004, A01, retrieved February 4, 2004, from http://www.washingtonpost.com/ac2/wp-dyn/A61706–2004Jan29?language = printer

131. PollingReport.com polling reports, *Problems and Priorities*, polls conducted by Gallup, *Newsweek*, CBS News, CNN, *USA*, and others (January–February, 2004), retrieved February 6, 2004, from http://www.pollingreport.com/prioriti.htm

CHAPTER

Defining Poverty: Where to Begin?

WHAT IS POVERTY?

The very first obstacle to a rational approach to reducing poverty in the United States lies in conflict over the definition of the problem. Defining poverty is a *political* activity. Proponents of increased governmental support for social welfare programs frequently make high estimates of the number and percentage of the population that is poor. They view the problem of poverty as a persistent one, even in a generally affluent society. They argue that many millions of Americans suffer from hunger, inadequate housing, remediable illness, hopelessness, and despair. Given the magnitude of the problem, their definition of poverty practically mandates the continuation and expansion of a wide variety of public welfare programs.

In contrast, others minimize the number of poor in the United States. They see poverty as diminishing over time. They view the poor in America today as considerably better off than the middle class of fifty years ago and even wealthy by the standards of most societies in the world. They deny that people need to suffer from hunger or remediable illness if they make use of the public services already available. They believe that there are many opportunities for upward mobility in the United States and that no one need succumb to hopelessness or despair. This definition of the problem minimizes the need for public welfare programs and encourages policymakers to limit the number and size of these programs.

Political conflict over poverty, then, begins with contending definitions of the problem of poverty. In an attempt to influence policymaking, various political interests try to win acceptance for their own definitions of the problem. Political scientist E. E. Schattschneider explained,

> *Political conflict is not like an intercollegiate debate in which the opponents agree in advance on a definition of the issues. As a matter of fact,* the definition of the alternatives is the supreme instrument of power; *the antagonists can rarely agree on what the issues are because power is involved in the definition.*[1]

Although inadequate income has always been a concern during economic depressions, *poverty* has been a *political* issue only for the last 45 years. Prior to the 1960s, the problems of the poor were almost always segmented. According to James Sundquist, not until the Kennedy and Johnson administrations did the nation begin to see that these problems were tied together in a single "bedrock" problem—poverty:

> *The measures enacted, and those proposed, were dealing separately with such problems as slum housing, juvenile delinquency, dependency, unemployment, illiteracy, but they were separately inadequate because they were striking only at surface aspects of what seemed to be some kind of bedrock problem, and it was the bedrock problem that had to be identified so that it could be attacked in a concerted, unified, and innovative way. . . . The bedrock problem, in a word, was "poverty." Words and concepts determine programs; once the target was reduced to a single word, the timing became right for a unified program.*[2]

But even political consensus that poverty is a problem does not necessarily mean that everyone defines poverty in the same fashion. The following paragraphs elaborate on six different approaches to the conceptualization of poverty—as deprivation, as inequality, as lack of human capital, as culture, as exploitation, and as structure.

Poverty as Deprivation

One way to define poverty is as **deprivation**—insufficiency in food, housing, clothing, medical care, and other items required to maintain a decent standard of living. This definition assumes that there is a standard of living below which individuals and families can be considered "deprived." This standard is admittedly arbitrary; no one knows for certain what level of material well-being is necessary to avoid deprivation.

But each year the federal government calculates the cash income required for individuals and families to satisfy minimum living needs. The federal government calls its official calculations the **poverty thresholds.** It calls simplified versions of the poverty thresholds **poverty guidelines.*** The guidelines are used to determine who qualifies for federally supported public assistance programs. Many people use the term "poverty line," but the federal government does not provide a definition of this term like it does for the thresholds and the guidelines.

The Social Security Administration (SSA) first developed official poverty threshold calculations in 1964. Economist Mollie Orshansky was the key figure in developing these measures, and there was great debate over whether her conceptualization was too high or too low.[3] Several revisions have been made in the calculations over the years. For example, since 1981, lower poverty-level figures are no longer used to calculate poverty rates of female-headed households and farm families. Some distinctions based on whether a household is headed by an individual aged 65 or older are still made.

Originally, the poverty thresholds were derived by estimating a low-cost but nutritious food budget for households (similar to today's U.S. Department of Agriculture Thrifty Food Plan, described in Chapter 7). These figures were then multiplied by 3, since surveys indicated that about one-third of an average household budget was spent on food. Orshansky has said that her formula was intended only for the aged; nevertheless, it became the government's official definition.[4]

Since 1969, the previous year's poverty thresholds are simply adjusted to reflect changes in the Consumer Price Index (CPI). There are several variations of the CPI. The measure currently used to update poverty thresholds is the CPI for All Urban Consumers (CPI-U). It includes the living costs of more segments of the population than the measure previously used. Even so, the poverty level remains a crude measure of poverty. In 2002, the poverty threshold for a family of four was $18,392, up from poverty thresholds of $13,359 in 1990, $8,414 in 1980, and $3,968 in 1970.[5] Table 3.1 provides thresholds for families of varying sizes in 2002. Of all the families in the United States, 7.2 million, or 9.6 percent, of them were poor compared to 6.8 million, or 9.2 percent, in 2001.[6] In 2002, it would have taken an average of $7,205 to bring each family up to the poverty threshold (this is less than the $7,345 it would have taken in 2001). This figure is called the **income deficit** or, more informally, the poverty gap.

The poverty thresholds are an *absolute* measure of poverty because they provide one figure for the number of poor in the country, and individuals and families fall either above or below. According to this definition, 12.1 percent of all Americans were poor in 2002 compared with 11.7 percent in 2001. The nation's lowest poverty rate of

---

*In 2004, poverty guidelines for the contiguous states were $9,130 for one person and $18,850 for a family of four. These guidelines are based on prices in the previous calendar year, thus the poverty thresholds for 2003 and the poverty guidelines for 2004 are similar. The guidelines are usually published in February of each year in the *Federal Register* and can also be found with a great deal of other information about poverty measures at http://aspe.hhs.gov/poverty/index.shtml. The number and characteristics of people living in poverty are based on the poverty thresholds and are usually published in early fall of the following year. For example, in September 2003, the government issued figures on people living in poverty in calendar year 2002.

TABLE 3.1

Poverty Thresholds by Family Size: 2002^a

One person	$ 9,183
Two people	11,756
Three people	14,348
Four people	18,392
Five people	21,744
Six people	24,576
Seven people	28,001
Eight people	30,907
Nine people or more	37,062

Source: Bernadette D. Proctor and Joseph Dalaker, U.S. Census Bureau, Current Population Reports, P60-222, *Poverty in the United States: 2002* (Washington, DC: U.S. Government Printing Office, 2003), p. 4.

^{a}These are summary figures, referred to as "weighted average thresholds." There are actually 48 thresholds because thresholds for one- and two-person families vary by whether the head of household is under or over age 65, and thresholds also vary by the number of adults and children in families. The U.S. Census Bureau uses the 48 thresholds to compute poverty data.

11.1 occurred two decades ago in 1973. In 2002, an estimated 34.6 million individuals lived in poverty,* 1.7 million more than in 2001 (see Figure 3.1).

Even if we were to agree that poverty should be defined as deprivation, there are still many problems in establishing an official poverty threshold based on the federal government's definition as described earlier. First of all, this definition of poverty includes only cash income (such as wages, Social Security and public assistance checks, and interest from bank accounts, all *before* taxes) and excludes **in-kind benefits** such as medical care, food stamps, school lunches, and public housing. If these benefits were "costed out" (calculated as cash income), there would be fewer poor people in the United States than shown in official statistics. Also, many people (poor and nonpoor) apparently underreport their incomes.[7] Taking this into account would further reduce the number of people counted as poor.

There are other problems with this definition of poverty. It does not take into account regional differences in the cost of living, climate, or styles of living. It is unlikely that a family of four can live on $18,392 in New York City, even if it might be possible in Hattiesburg, Mississippi. It does not account for family assets. An older family that has paid off its mortgage does not usually devote as much to housing as a young family that rents or has recently purchased a home. It does not recognize

*The margin of error for this 2002 estimate is plus or minus 658,000 individuals and it is plus or minus .2 percent of the estimated 12.1 percent living in poverty.

FIGURE 3.1

Number in Poverty and Poverty Rate: 1959 to 2002

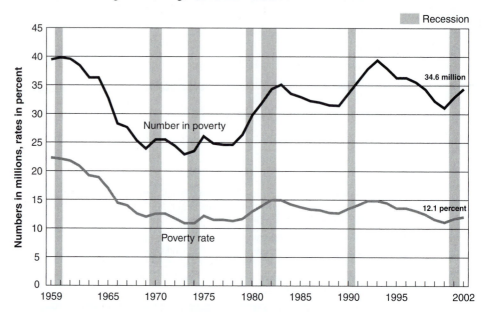

Source: U.S. Census Bureau, Current Population Survey, 1960–2003 Annual Social and Economic Supplements.
Note: The data points represent the midpoints of the respective years.

differences in the status of individuals or families—for example, whether family members are students or retirees. Some of these people may not consider themselves "poor," although they are counted as poor in official government statistics. This definition also does not recognize the needs of families that may have incomes above the poverty level but have special problems or hardships that drain away income—chronic illnesses, large debts, or other problems. Finally, the estimate that one-third of family income is spent on food is outdated. The high cost of housing, in particular, has changed the composition of the family budget. In 2001, the poorest 20 percent of Americans spent an average of $3,269, or slightly more than 17 percent (about one-sixth) of their income on food (the richest 20 percent spent an average of $9,101, or nearly 12 percent, of their income on food; the national average was $5,321, or 13.5 percent).[8] In 2004 the United States Department of Agriculture provided a maximum monthly food stamp allotment of $471 to a family of four (see Chapter 7). Multiplying the cost of this basic diet by 6 over the period of a year would yield a figure of $33,912—considerably higher than the current poverty threshold of $18,392. Illustration 3.1 describes the Self-Sufficiency Standard, an approach to determining how much it takes individuals and families to cover basic living expenses without government assistance.

ILLUSTRATION 3.1

Examples of the Self-Sufficiency Standard[a]

The Self-Sufficiency Standard calculates how much money working adults need to meet their basic needs without subsidies of any kind. Unlike the federal poverty standard, the Self-Sufficiency Standard accounts for the costs of living and working as they vary by family size and composition and by geographic location.

Two Adults, One Preschool Child, and One Schoolage Child

Monthly Costs, 2004	Philadelphia, Pennsylvania	Alamosa County, Colorado[b]
Housing	$791	$543
Child Care	$977	$772
Food	$565	$565
Transportation	$212	$467
Health Care	$267	$242
Miscellaneous	$281	$259
Taxes	$776	$389
Earned Income Tax Credit (−)	$0	$0
Child Care Tax Credit (−)	−$100	−$115
Child Tax Credit (−)	−$167	−$167
Self-Sufficiency Wage		
Hourly[c]	$10.23 per adult[d]	$8.40 per adult[d]
Monthly	$3,602	$2,955
Annual	$44,222	$35,463

Sources: Adapted from Diana Pearce, *The Self-Sufficiency Standard for Pennsylvania 2004* (Seattle: The University of Washington, June 2004); and Diana Pearce with Jennifer Brooks, *The Self-Sufficiency Standard for Colorado 2004: A Family Needs Budget* (Seattle: The University of Washington, 2004). The Self-Sufficiency Standard for all participating states can be found at www.sixstrategies.org.

[a]The Standard is calculated by adding expenses and taxes and subtracting tax credits. Taxes include federal and state income tax (including state tax credits except state earned income tax credit and child tax credit) and payroll taxes.

[b]Alamosa County is rural.

[c]The hourly wage is calculated by dividing the monthly wage by 176 hours (8 hours per day times 22 days per month).

[d]The hourly wage for families with two adults represents the hourly wage that each adult would need to earn, while the monthly and annual wages represent both parents' wage combined.

Note: Total may not add exactly due to rounding.

Economist Patricia Ruggles believes that, given current consumer spending patterns, the poverty level would have to be increased by at least 50 percent to bring it up to date.[9] Besides considering urban–rural and regional cost-of-living differences, she says that one poverty level may not be enough, depending on our purposes. But as the president of the Urban Institute once said:

> *However contentious, drawing a poverty line is essential. It is a way of knowing how much progress we are making in reducing the numbers of underprivileged in America and, in very practical terms, it is a standard used by federal and state governments to implement programs that aid the poor.*[10]

Of course, we do need some convention for measuring poverty. Others ask

> *Why is the poverty rate still the statistic of choice . . . despite its defects? One important reason may be the perception that better measures are too complex to be communicated to a wider audience. If the whole point of measuring poverty is to affect the policies that might affect poverty, then a poverty index that cannot be understood by the public and by policy makers is pointless.*[11]

The U.S. government has studied numerous ways to alter its official definition of poverty over the past four decades, and it still has not come to a conclusion about how to best measure poverty.

Measuring Poverty: Let Me Count the Ways

In 1992 Congress commissioned a major study of the poverty measure.[12] Most members of the study panel recommended changes to address long-noted problems with the current measure such as adjusting for costs across geographic regions and counting in-kind benefits like food stamps. John F. Cogan of the conservative Hoover Institution was the lone dissenter, calling the suggested measure "value judgments made by scientists—with a particular point of view."[13] Nevertheless, the government keeps experimenting with these and different ways to measure poverty.

One study the federal government conducted used 17 different calculations of income in addition to the official calculation and found that while official poverty was 13.3 percent in 1997, using these alternative definitions, poverty ranged from 10 percent to 21.4 percent.[14] Not surprisingly, the experimental measures being considered today "are more comparable in magnitude to official rates than those reported in earlier studies."[15] For example, using a revised measure of poverty that includes a more restrictive measure of inflation and considers the value of many government programs, including the value of Medicaid and Medicare as well as health benefits from employers, and also includes income from capital gains and subtracts federal and state income taxes, poverty in 2002 went from the official calculation of 12.1 to 8.2 percent.[16]

Much attention has been paid to how best to calculate the value of in-kind benefits, and most serious students of social welfare think they should be included.[17] Calculating the value of food stamp benefits is relatively straightforward. The cash value of benefits can be used, although it has been estimated that recipients would trade $1,500 of food stamp benefits for $1,400 in cash.[18]

Calculating the value of medical or healthcare benefits is much more difficult. Most experts agree that this benefit does not actually raise people's income. Without this benefit, people might have to use money that they would ordinarily spend on other things to cover medical expenses, but in-kind medical benefits cannot be spent for other items in the household budget. One position is that healthcare benefits should not be counted in determining income and poverty levels because they are not added to the incomes of those above the poverty line, and they are not included in the current poverty thresholds (although they could be included in both). If healthcare costs were included in calculating poverty rates, should we use the cash value of medical services received, or the value of employer- or government-provided healthcare benefits (premiums), or should only out-of-pocket costs be considered? Each of these methods produces very different estimates, and there has been little agreement about whether to include them at all or how to do so if they were included.

Calculating housing benefits presents another set of headaches. The Census Bureau does have a way of valuing housing subsidies.[19] It uses figures from the 1985 American Housing Survey and assigns values based on region and family size and income and adjusts for inflation using a rental price index. This method seems to underestimate the value of housing subsidies. One experimental method uses fair market rents. Since this method produces higher figures or subsidies, it results in lower estimates of the poverty rate.

Even though in-kind benefit programs have grown much faster than cash public assistance programs in recent decades,[20] including in-kind (and cash) benefits has only a modest effect on reducing poverty figures because "the reductions from any single program are generally quite small."[21] For example, in 2002, the poverty rate for children was 19.7 percent based on cash income before government transfers (benefits). After social insurance programs were considered, this rate fell to 17.4; after cash means-tested (public assistance) program transfers, it dropped by less than 1 percent to 16.7 percent, and after considering a number of means-tested noncash (in-kind) benefits, it dropped by almost two points to 14.8 percent. After adding benefits from the earned income credit and subtracting federal income taxes, the poverty rate dropped to 12.6 percent. Therefore, social insurance and tax benefits were the most effective in helping children out of poverty, followed by in-kind public assistance benefits; least effective were cash public assistance benefits.[22] In 2002, before any government transfers, the poverty gap for children was $37.4 billion; after government transfers it was $17.2 billion, a 54.1 percent reduction.

For those aged 65 and older, the picture is different. Poverty was an amazing 49.9 percent before any government transfers and fell to 11.5 percent after social insurance (primarily Social Security) was factored in; means-tested cash transfers reduced poverty to 10.4 percent, and means-tested noncash benefits reduced poverty to 9 percent; poverty remained at 9 percent even after factoring in tax benefits and deductions.[23] In 2002, the poverty gap for older people was $89.7 billion before any of these transfers and $7 billion after, a reduction of 92.2 percent! Obviously it is Social Security that makes the big difference. Means-tested benefits have only a modest effect. Public assistance may not reduce *national* poverty rates dramatically, but these programs can make a tremendous difference in the quality of life of those who are poor.

Who Is Poor?

Poverty occurs among many segments of the population and in all areas of the country; however, the incidence of poverty varies considerably among groups (see Figures 3.2 and 3.3). In absolute figures, more whites are poor than blacks. Of the 34.6 million people counted as poor by government definition in 2002, approximately 15.6 million were white (not of Hispanic origin) while 8.6 million were black.[24] However, the likelihood of blacks experiencing poverty is more than three times greater than it is for whites: *The 2002 poverty rate for the nation's black population was 24.1 percent compared to 8 percent for the white (non-Hispanic) population.* In other words, whites outnumber blacks among the poor, but a much larger percentage of the nation's black population is poor. There are 8.6 million poor people of Hispanic origin in the United States (they may be of any race). Their poverty rate is 21.8 percent. From 2001 to 2002, the poverty rate for blacks increased but did not change significantly for whites or those of Hispanic origin.

*The very highest poverty rates occur in families headed by women where no husband is present.** The poverty rate for these female-headed households is 26.5 percent compared to 5.3 percent for families headed by married couples. *For families headed by non-Hispanic white women, the rate is 20 percent; the rates for families headed by black women and women of Hispanic origin are much higher—38.2 and 36.4 percent, respectively.*

There are approximately 12.1 million poor children under age 18 in the United States, or 16.7 percent of this age group. In 1959 poverty among children was 27.4 percent. By 1969 it had reached a low of 14 percent, better than we could report for 2002. For children of Hispanic origin and black children, the situation is especially bad; *28.6 percent of all children of Hispanic origin and 32.3 percent of all black children in the United States live in poverty, compared to 9.4 percent of white children.*

There is some better news in the official poverty figures. Poverty rates for Americans 65 years of age and older have dropped substantially over the years—from 35.2 percent in 1959 to 24.6 percent in 1970 and 10.4 percent in 2002. Among these older Americans, poverty is 23.8 percent for blacks, 21.4 percent for those of Hispanic origin, and 8.3 percent for whites. More older women are poor compared to older men. Today, the 10.4 percent poverty rate for those age 65 and older is not statistically dif-

*Additional information on poverty among black and Hispanic Americans and among women is found in Chapter 11.

Poverty Rates by Selected Characteristics, 2002

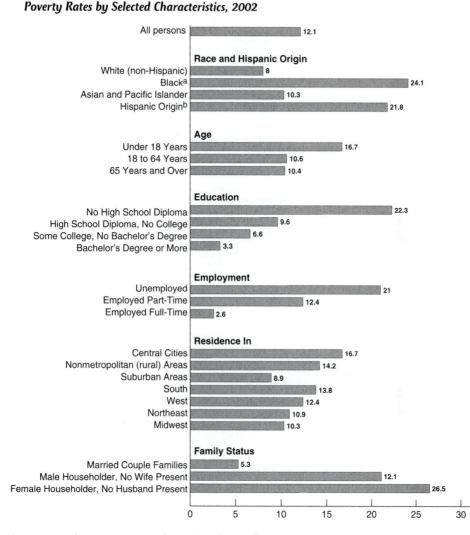

Source: Bernadette D. Proctor and Joseph Dalaker, U.S. Census Bureau, Current Population Reports, P 60-222, *Poverty in the United States: 2002* (Washington, DC: U.S. Government Printing Office, 2003).

[a]This is the figure for those who reported they were black and not of any other race. The combined rate for those who reported black alone or in combination with another race is 23.9.

[b]Hispanics may be of any race.

ferent from the 10.6 rate for those aged 18 to 64. Though poverty rates for older people have dropped substantially over the years, compared to the overall population, their incomes are concentrated more at the near-poor level (defined as income that is 25 percent higher than poverty thresholds), and remember that official poverty

FIGURE 3.3

Poverty Rates by Age, 1959 to 2002

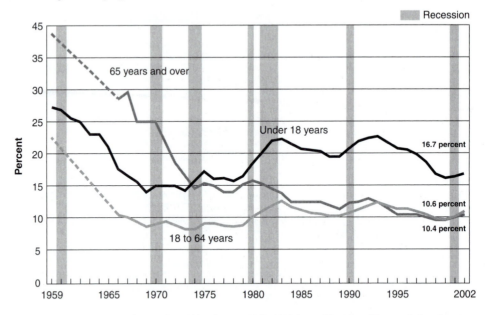

Source: U.S. Census Bureau, Current Population Survey, 1960–2003 Annual Social and Economic Supplements.

Note: The data points represent the midpoints of the respective years. Data for people 18 to 64 and 65 and older are not available from 1960 to 1965.

thresholds for households headed by someone aged 65 or older are lower than for younger people.

Education also figures prominently in the poverty equation. The poverty rate of those with less than a high school diploma was 22.3 percent and is far less for those who have a high school diploma or more education, as Figure 3.2 illustrates. As one might expect, work is also a substantial factor. The poverty rate for those who did not work at all was 21 percent compared to 2.6 for those who worked full time.

Poverty occurs not only in large, urban areas but in rural America as well. In 2002 about 16.7 percent of the residents of central cities were poor, and about 14.2 percent of rural residents were poor. Suburban areas have less poverty (a rate of 8.9 percent) because those with low incomes are unlikely to find affordable housing there. There is always more poverty in the South than in other regions of the country. About 13.8 percent of residents of southern states are poor compared to 12.4 percent in the West, 10.9 percent in the Northeast, and 10.3 percent in the Midwest.

An important question we must ask about poverty is whether it is a temporary or transient rather than a persistent, long-lasting problem. Information on this issue comes largely from the University of Michigan's Panel Study of Income Dynamics

(PSID), which has tracked nearly 8,000 U.S. families since 1968.[25] Two analyses of PSID data indicate that about 2.6 percent of the total population will be poor for at least eight out of ten years.[26] There is some consolation in the fact that the circumstances of most people who experience poverty will change—although they may lose their jobs, separate, divorce, or become ill, later they may find work, remarry, or get well, thus improving their financial condition. But there are clearly two groups of poor people, those who experience poverty for a relatively short period of time and those who are persistently poor. Other methodologically sensitive studies of "spells of poverty" indicate that persistent poverty is much more serious than once thought. Although the majority still experience poverty for a short time (one or two years), 60 percent of those classified as poor at any given time will experience poverty for seven years or longer.[27]

The Survey of Income and Program Participation (SIPP) allows for estimates of the transitions in and out of poverty. These poverty estimates differ somewhat from the official calculations used by the Bureau of the Census, but, according to the SIPP, the chances of escaping poverty diminish over time. The probability is .53 in the first year of a spell, dropping to .36 the second year, and .2 or less by the fifth year.[28] The most current SIPP study reports on the dynamics of poverty from January 1996 to December 1999 and includes those who were poor for at least two months during these years. The study found that 34.2 percent were poor for at least two months during the four-year period; only two percent were poor for all 48 months.[29] In total, 51.1 percent were in poverty 2 to 4 months, 19.3 percent were poor for 5 to 8 months, 9.2 percent were poor for 9 to 12 months, 11.2 percent were poor for 13 months to 24 months, 3.5 were poor for 25 to 36 months, and 5.7 percent were poor for 36 to 48 months. Since poverty declined among the U.S. population from 1996 to 1999, more people (14.8 million) exited than entered (7.6 million) poverty. The chances of escaping poverty varied by demographic characteristics. Those 65 years and older were more likely than younger people to be poor for the entire four years and were less likely to exit poverty, probably due to lower likelihood of change in their incomes over time. Blacks and Hispanics were more likely to enter poverty and less likely to exit poverty than whites.

The dynamics of poverty (i.e., poverty entries and exits) have changed over time.[30] The number of entries and exits were generally constant from 1975 to the early 1990s. In the early to mid-1980s poverty rates were high with low numbers of entries and exits. In the mid-1990s poverty rates were also high, but the number of entries and exits were also high, indicating that more people were cycling through poverty than remaining stuck in poverty. Also important are the major events, triggers, or situations that cause people to move into and out of poverty. Using PSID data from 1975 to 1996, researchers found that changes in unemployment rates and other general economic conditions influenced poverty transitions (entries and exits) only slightly. More important were changes in household composition, employment, and disability status. Poverty entries are most likely to occur when a household goes from being headed by two adults to being headed by a single female. But only a very small number of households experience this change or event. Many more people enter poverty due to unemployment. Conversely, employment is the most frequent event that triggers a poverty exit, followed by a transition from being a female-headed household to becoming a household headed by two adults. These findings are based on multivariate statistical analyses (i.e., they consider several factors simultaneously) and challenge previous research showing that a change in family composition is the strongest predictor of moving into and out of poverty.

Has the percentage of poor in this country changed substantially? Franklin D. Roosevelt said in his second inaugural address in 1937, "I see one-third of a nation ill-housed, ill-clad, ill-nourished." He was probably underestimating poverty; economic historians think that over 50 percent of the nation would have been classified as poor during the Great Depression. Since poverty levels account for the effects of inflation, there is no question that the U.S. political and economic system has succeeded in reducing the proportion of poor (as defined in official government statistics). Poverty declined dramatically during the 1960s and reached lows of 11 to 12 percent during the 1970s (see Figure 3.2). But in 1983 and again in 1993, the poverty rate exceeded 15 percent. Though good economic times brought a near record low of poverty in 2000 (11.3 percent), poverty began to increase in the new millennium as the economy soured. Given how low current poverty thresholds are, many Americans think that a poverty rate of 12.1 percent in 2002 is nothing to wink at. Particularly disturbing was that 4.9 percent of Americans had incomes that were less than half of poverty thresholds. One thing remains clear, millions of Americans are still poor by government definition.

Poverty as Inequality (or Who Shrank the Middle Class?)

Poverty can also be defined as **inequality** in the distribution of income. Unlike the federal government's official definition of poverty, which is tied to an absolute level of deprivation, inequality refers to **relative deprivation**—some people perceive that they have less income or material possessions than most Americans, and they believe they are entitled to more.[31] Even with a fairly substantial income, one may feel a sense of relative deprivation in a very affluent society where commercial advertising portrays the "average American" as having a high level of material well-being.* According to economist Victor Fuchs,

> By the standards that have prevailed over most of history, and still prevail over large areas of the world, there are very few poor in the United States today. Nevertheless, there are millions of American families who, both in their own eyes and in those of

*However, an international study of poverty (cited in Committee on Ways and Means, U.S. House of Representatives, *Overview of Entitlement Programs, 1993 Green Book* [Washington, DC: U.S. Government Printing Office], pp. 1451, 1453) that includes the Unites States, Canada, Australia, Sweden, Germany, the Netherlands, France, and the United Kingdom, showed that the United States poverty rate was nearly two to five times higher than these other countries. A more recent analysis (Lars Osberg, "Trends in Poverty: The UK in International Perspective—How Rates Mislead and Intensity Matters," Working Papers of the Institute for Social and Economic Research, Paper 2002-10 [Colchester, England: University of Essex, June 2002]. Retrieved March 5, 2004 from http://www.iser.essex.ac.uk/pubs/workpaps/pdf/2002-10.pdf) also indicates greater poverty intensity in the United States compared to Canada, the United Kingdom, Sweden, and Germany.

others, are poor. As our nation prospers, our judgment as to what constitutes poverty will inevitably change. When we talk about poverty in America, we are talking about families and individuals who have much less income than most of us. When we talk about reducing or eliminating poverty, we are really talking about changing the distribution of income.[32]

How can we measure poverty as inequality? One method, used often in cross-national comparisons of poverty, is to calculate poverty as a percentage (perhaps one-half or more) of each country's median income. In the U.S., economists frequently measure the distribution of total personal income across various classes of families. Since relative deprivation is a psychological as well as a social and economic concept, these classes or groups are difficult to establish, but a common method is to divide all American families into five groups—from the lowest one-fifth in personal income to the highest one-fifth. Table 3.2 shows the percentage of total personal income received by each of these groups for selected years since 1950. If perfect income equality existed, then each fifth of U.S. families would receive 20 percent of all family personal income, and it would not even be possible to rank fifths from highest to lowest. But clearly, personal income in the United States is distributed unequally.

The poorest one-fifth of U.S. families now receive less than 5 percent of all family personal income. This group's share of income, like that of the middle class, rose slowly for many years and then declined in recent decades. The opposite situation occurred for the wealthy, defined in Table 3.2 as the highest one-fifth of all Americans in personal income. This group's share of income declined for many years, then rose in recent decades. Those in the top 5 percent of income also lost ground for many years, but lately they too have captured more of the country's wealth.

TABLE 3.2

Share of Aggregate Income Received by Each Fifth and Top 5 Percent of Families, Selected Years

Quintiles	1950	1960	1970	1980	1990	2001
Lowest	4.5%	4.8%	5.4%	5.3%	4.6%	4.2%
Second	12.0	12.2	12.2	11.6	10.8	9.7
Third	17.4	17.8	17.6	17.6	16.6	15.4
Fourth	23.4	24.0	23.8	24.4	23.8	22.9
Highest	42.7	41.3	40.9	41.1	44.3	47.7
Total	100.0	100.0	100.0	100.0	100.0	100.0
Top 5 percent	17.3	15.9	15.6	14.6	17.4	21.0

Source: U.S. Bureau of the Census, *Historical Income Tables—Families.* Retrieved February 23, 2004, from http://www.census.gov/hhes/income/histinc/f02.html

The income gains made by America's poorest families have been lost. Between 1970 and 2001, the income share of those in the lowest quintile declined by 22 percent. The income shares of the middle classes have also declined. The income share of the lower-middle class (the second-lowest quintile) has dropped by 20 percent since 1970 and that of the third (middle) quintile by more than 12 percent. Meanwhile, the income of the wealthiest one-fifth of the population has increased by nearly 17 percent.

Income inequality can also be measured by the *Gini index,* with zero indicating perfect income equality and 1 indicating total inequality. As measured by the *Gini index,* income inequality has grown from .39 in 1970 to .46 in 2002.[33]

Although the hardships of some of the poor are mitigated by in-kind benefits (food stamps, public housing, Medicaid, and similar programs) that are not counted as income, even small reductions in their cash incomes can have serious consequences. Those who study income dynamics describe a shrinking middle class and increasing economic polarization in the United States. According to Greg Duncan of the Survey Research Center at the University of Michigan, a "tidal wave of inequality" has been occurring between those with more skills and work experience and those with less of both, and these trends have affected men and women and people of all ethnic groups.[34] The gap is reported to be the largest since World War II,[35] and the largest of any industrialized country.[36] The tidal wave is growing.

WHY ARE THE POOR, POOR?

Poverty is explained in many ways. We naturally assume that illness, old age, disability, lack of job skills, family instability, discrimination, unemployment, and general economic recessions all contribute to poverty. But how do these problems interact to create poverty?

Poverty as Lack of Human Capital

Perhaps the most popular explanation that economists use to explain poverty is the **human capital theory.** This theory explains income variations in a free market economy as a result of differences in productivity. The poor are poor because their economic productivity is low. They do not have the human capital—knowledge, skills, training, education—to sell to employers in a free market. As partial evidence for this theory, we observe that poverty among those with less than a high school education is 22.3 percent, while poverty among those who completed high school is 9.6 percent (see Figure 3.2). For those with some college education, it is 6.6 percent, and for those with at least a bachelor's degree, it is 3.3 percent.

Economists recognize that poverty may also result from inadequate demand in the economy as a whole, in a particular segment of the economy, or in a particular region of the nation. A serious recession and widespread unemployment raise the proportion of the population living in poverty. Full employment and a healthy economy improve opportunities for marginal workers, but these factors do not directly reduce poverty among people who have no marketable skills.

Absence from the labor force is among the largest sources of poverty. This is also demonstrated in Figure 3.2. Twenty-one percent of unemployed individuals were poor compared to 12.4 percent who worked part time and 2.6 percent who worked full time. The picture is worse when poverty is calculated for families. Families with no workers had a poverty rate of 32 percent compared to 7.9 percent of families with at least one worker. A substantial number of the poor are older people and those with severe disabilities who cannot reasonably be expected to be employed. No improvement in the national economy is likely to affect these people directly. They are outside the labor market and, therefore, are largely the concern of government rather than of the private economy. Many of the poor are children. There is hope of helping them out of poverty by improving their parents' employment opportunities and the opportunities for these children.

Finally, we must consider poverty that is the direct effect of discrimination against women and people of particular racial or ethnic groups. It is true that some differences in incomes are a product of educational differences between groups. However, even if we control for education among year-round, full time workers, we can see, for example, that black men and men of Hispanic origin at almost every educational level earn less than white men (see Table 3.3). If the human capital theory operated freely—without interference in the form of discrimination—then we would not expect differences between blacks and whites and between men and women at the same educational levels. But unfortunately this is not the case.

When in 1776 Thomas Jefferson wrote on behalf of the Second Continental Congress that "all men are created equal," he was expressing the widespread dislike for

TABLE 3.3

Mean Income of Men Who Worked Year-Round, Full-Time by Race or Ethnicity and Education, 2002

Education	White (non-Hispanic)	Black	Hispanic[a]
Less than 9th grade	$23,999	$19,702	$19,741
9th to 12th grade (no diploma)	23,106	19,189	23,698
High school graduate	34,909	25,582	27,992
Associate degree	44,099	36,028	37,365
Bachelor's degree	66,638	47,018	46,115
Master's degree	75,187	60,647	59,901

Source: U.S. Census Bureau, Current Population Survey, 2003 Annual Social and Economic Supplement, retrieved February 23, 2004, from http://ferret.bls.census.gov/macro/032003/perinc/new04_000.htm

[a]May be of any race.

hereditary aristocracy—lords and ladies, dukes and duchesses, and queens and kings. The Founding Fathers wrote their belief in equality of law into the U.S. Constitution. But their concern was **equality of opportunity,** not absolute equality. Indeed, the Founding Fathers referred to efforts to equalize income as "leveling," and they were strongly opposed to this notion. Jefferson wrote,

> *To take from one, because it is thought his own industry and that of his fathers has ac-*
> *quired too much, in order to spare to others, who, or whose fathers have not, exercised*
> *equal industry and skill, is to violate arbitrarily the first principle of association, the*
> *guarantee to everyone the free exercise of his industry and the fruits acquired by it.*[37]

Equality of opportunity requires that artificial obstacles to upward mobility be removed. Distinctions based on race, ethnicity, gender, birth, and religion have no place in a free society. But this is not to say that all people's incomes should be equalized. Andrew Jackson, one of the nation's first democrats, explained,

> *Distinctions in every society will always exist under every just government. Equality of*
> *talents, education or wealth cannot be produced by human institutions. In the full en-*
> *joyment of the gifts of heaven and the fruits of superior industry, economy, and virtue,*
> *every man is entitled to protection by law; but when the laws undertake to add to these*
> *national distinctions, to grant titles, gratuities, and exclusive privileges, to make the*
> *rich richer . . . then the humble members of society have a right to complain of the in-*
> *justice of their government.*[38]

Just how much equality should we try to achieve? Utopian socialists have argued for a rule of distribution: "From each according to his ability, to each according to his needs." In other words, everyone produces whatever he or she can, and wealth and income are distributed according to the needs of each person. There is no monetary reward for hard work, or skills and talent, or education and training. Since most people's needs are roughly the same, they will each receive roughly the same income. Collective ownership replaces private property. If such a Utopian society ever existed, then near-perfect income equality would be achieved.

But all societies—capitalist and socialist, democratic and authoritarian, traditional and modern—distribute wealth unequally. It is not likely that income differences will ever disappear. Societies reward hard work, skill, talent, education, training, risk taking, and ingenuity. Distributing income equally throughout society threatens the work ethic. The real questions we must confront are how much inequality is necessary or desirable for a society, and conversely, how much inequality can society afford to tolerate? We might argue about the fairness of the current distribution of income (as shown in Table 3.2), but virtually everyone recognizes that a country in which 12 million children are growing up in poverty cannot lead to positive outcomes for them or for society.

Of course, when defined as *inequality,* the problem of poverty is not capable of a total solution. Regardless of how well off poor individuals and families may be in absolute standards of living, there will always be a lowest one-fifth of the population receiving something less than 20 percent of all income. We can reduce income inequalities through less drastic political changes than communism or socialism (a more progressive personal income tax or more generous social welfare benefits, for example), but some differences will remain, and to the extent they do, someone will see them as a "problem."

Poverty as Culture

Some argue that poverty is a "way of life" passed on from generation to generation in a self-perpetuating cycle. This **culture of poverty** involves not just a low income but also attitudes of indifference, alienation, and apathy, along with lack of incentives and of self-respect. These attitudes make it difficult for people who are poor to use the opportunities for upward mobility that may be available to them. Increasing the income of poor people may not affect their joblessness, lack of incentives and educational opportunities, unstable family life, incidence of crime, and other social problems.

There are sharp differences between scholars and policymakers over whether or not a culture of poverty exists. The argument resembles the classic exchange between F. Scott Fitzgerald and Ernest Hemingway. When Fitzgerald observed, "The rich are different from you and me," Hemingway retorted, "Yes, they have more money." Observers who believe that they see a distinctive culture among the poor may say, "The poor are different from you and me." But opponents of the culture-of-poverty notion may reply, "Yes, they have less money." But are the poor undereducated, unskilled, poorly motivated, and "delinquent" because they are poor? Or are they poor because they are undereducated, unskilled, poorly motivated, and "delinquent"? This distinction has important policy implications.

One especially controversial view of the culture of poverty was set forth by former Harvard University government professor Edward C. Banfield, who contended that poverty is really a product of "present-orientedness."[39] According to Banfield, individuals caught up in the culture of poverty are unable to plan for the future, to sacrifice immediate gratifications in favor of future ones, or to exercise the discipline required to get ahead. Banfield admitted that some people experience poverty because of involuntary unemployment, prolonged illness, death of the family breadwinner, or some other misfortune. But even with severe misfortune, he claimed, this kind of poverty is not squalid, degrading, or self-perpetuating; it ends once the external cause of it no longer exists. According to Banfield, other people will be poor no matter what their "external" circumstances are. They live in a culture of poverty that continues for generations because they are psychologically unable to plan for the future. Improvements in their circumstances may affect their poverty only superficially. Even increased income is unlikely to change their way of life, for the additional money will be spent quickly on nonessential or frivolous items.

There are other controversial views of the culture of poverty. Nicolas Lemann attributed hard-core poverty in poor inner-city communities comprised largely of black residents to an anthropological cause—the rural southern heritage of many of its residents.[40] As sharecroppers, blacks were unable to own property, save money, maintain stable family relationships, or obtain an education, and he contends these patterns have carried over to the present day. Opponents of the culture of poverty idea argue that this notion diverts attention from the conditions of poverty that currently foster family instability, present orientedness, and other ways of life of the poor.

Social reformers are likely to focus on the condition of poverty as the fundamental cause of the social pathologies that afflict the poor. They note that the idea of a culture of poverty can be applied only to groups who have lived in poverty for several generations. It is not relevant to those who have become poor during their lifetimes because of sickness, accident, or old age. The cultural explanation basically involves parental transmission of values and beliefs, which in turn determines the behavior of future generations. In contrast, the situational explanation of poverty shows how present social conditions and differences in financial resources operate directly to determine behavior. Perhaps the greatest danger in the idea of a culture of poverty is that poverty in this light can be seen as an unbreakable, puncture-proof cycle. This outlook may lead to inaction or at least a relaxation of efforts to ameliorate the conditions of poverty.

If one assumes that the poor are no different from other Americans, then one is led toward policies that emphasize opportunity for individuals as well as changes in their environment. If poor Americans are like other Americans, it is necessary only to provide them with the ordinary means to achieve—for example, job-training programs, good schools, and counseling to make them aware of opportunities that are available to them. The intervention that is required to change their lives, therefore, is one of supplying a means to achieve a level of income that most Americans enjoy.

In contrast, if one believes in the notion of a culture of poverty, it is necessary to devise a strategy to interrupt the transmission of lower-class cultural values from generation to generation. The strategy must try to prevent the socialization of young children into an environment of family instability, lack of motivation, crime and delinquency, and so forth. One drastic means to accomplish this would be to remove children from lower-class homes at a very early age and to raise them in a controlled environment that transmits the values of the conventional culture rather than of the culture of poverty. This was done to some extent in the early part of the twentieth century (see Chapter 10). Such a solution is no longer realistic (although certain conservatives have suggested a return to the use of orphanages for children whose parents are unable to provide an adequate upbringing). More acceptable solutions today are special day care centers and preschool programs to remedy cultural deprivation and disadvantage such as Head Start (see Chapter 9). Theoretically, these programs should bring about change in young children through "cultural enrichment."

Poverty as Exploitation

Both Marxist and non-Marxist writers have defined poverty as a form of **exploitation** by the ruling class. Sociologist Herbert Gans contended that poverty serves many functions for the middle and upper classes in America such as providing a cheap source of labor.[41] In fact, a substantial number of poor people work (in 2002, more than one-third of people in poverty worked full or part time),[42] but obviously they do not make enough to escape poverty and hardship. Gans's implication is that poverty is maintained by ruling classes in order to make their own lives more pleasant. Poverty does not have to exist; it could be eliminated with the cooperation of the middle and upper classes. But it is unlikely that these classes will ever give up anything they believe they have earned through their own hard work, useful skills, or business enterprise. A substantial number of Americans think that they are insulated from financial disaster and poverty.

Other authors have also written about the class-based nature of poverty. Two of them have called our society the "upside-down welfare state" because "the welfare state is a complicated system in which those who need help the most get the least, and those who need it least get the most."[43] They say that all Americans, rich or poor, benefit from government welfare programs. The poor and near-poor receive government assistance through programs called Temporary Assistance for Needy Families, food stamps, Medicaid, and the earned income credit. The middle classes receive government assistance primarily in the form of home mortgage loans and associated tax deductions and educational grants. The rich receive government assistance through various income tax deductions, government contracts, and subsidies to business and industry. The difference is that government assistance to the poor is called "welfare," while government assistance to the rich is called "good business"—an investment in the economy and in the nation. In the final analysis, the poor receive only a pittance of all government assistance. Much more government assistance goes to the middle and upper classes.

Social scientists Frances Fox Piven and Richard A. Cloward have also commented on the economic, political, and social utility that the upper classes see in maintaining poverty. In 1971 they published *Regulating the Poor: The Functions of Public Welfare,* in which they claimed that "the key to an understanding of relief-giving is in the functions it serves for the larger economic and political order, for relief is a secondary and supportive institution."[44] Piven and Cloward argued, especially with regard to the former AFDC program, that welfare had been used as a device to control the poor in order to maintain social stability. Welfare programs were expanded in times of political unrest as a means of appeasing the poor, and welfare rules and regulations were used as a means of "forcing" the poor into the labor market during times of political stability, especially when there was a need to increase the number of people in the workforce. Piven and Cloward later updated their original ideas when they saw that this cyclical pattern of contraction and expansion of welfare had been replaced by a more permanent set of welfare programs, making people less dependent for their survival on business and industry and fluctuations in the labor market.[45] Piven and Cloward espoused the right to welfare, and they encouraged Americans to resist cuts in social welfare programs. The 1996 federal welfare reforms once again put social welfare programs on more shaky footing in another attempt to modify the behavior of the poor[46] (see Chapters 5, 6, and 7).

If poverty is defined as the exploitation of the poor by a ruling class, then it might be suggested that only a radical restructuring of society to eliminate class differences would solve the problem of poverty. Marxists call for the revolutionary overthrow of capitalist society by workers and farmers and the emergence of a new "classless" society. Presumably, in such a society there would be no ruling class with an interest in exploiting the poor. Of course, in practice, Communist-ruled societies have produced one-party governments that dominate and exploit nearly the entire population (most of these governments have now given way to more democratic governance). There are less radical means to achieving a more egalitarian society. Civil rights legislation is one example. Substantial numbers of people have benefited from such laws, but many people view the remaining class differences as still far too wide.

These perspectives help us to understand that there are indeed class differences in views on poverty. If the upper classes do not deliberately exploit the poor, they sometimes express paternalistic attitudes toward them. Although the upper classes generally have little understanding of the lives of poor people, they believe they "know what's best" for them. Moreover, the upper classes frequently engage in charitable activities and support liberal welfare programs to demonstrate their idealism and "do-goodism," whether the poor are actually helped or not.

Poverty as Structure

Poverty can also be considered by studying the **institutional** and **structural** components of society that foster its continuation. As already mentioned, some poverty can be attributed to the effects of discrimination. The term **institutional discrimination** refers to practices that are deeply embedded in schools, the criminal justice system, and other organizations that serve gatekeeper functions in society. For example, poor school districts generally receive fewer resources that can be used to promote educational opportunities for their young citizens than schools in wealthier districts. Such differences have become the bases for court challenges to the ways in which public school education is funded in a number of states. Health care institutions and other service organizations are generally not well organized in poorer communities. Lack of access to health care and other resources also contribute to circumstances that make it more difficult to avoid poverty. Another example of institutional discrimination occurs in the criminal justice system, since jails and prisons are overpopulated with those who are black or of Hispanic origin and poor. Problems of this nature can only be ameliorated by changing the structure of societal institutions that perpetuate them.

The economic structure of the country has also resulted in deep-seated poverty that arises from inadequate demand in a particular sector of the economy or in a particular region of the nation. For example, industrialization and technological development have bypassed large segments of Appalachia, one of the country's poorest areas. The closing of steel mills in large eastern cities and auto plants in midwestern cities also forced workers into poverty. The current threat is "offshoring," a euphemism for exporting more jobs than ever before to countries where labor is much cheaper, a practice that has been made increasingly possible by various trade agreements the United States has with other countries. Whether it is Brach's Confections, Inc., leaving Chicago or Levi Strauss & Co. leaving El Paso, working communities are deeply affected as more jobs make their way to Mexico, Asia, and other countries. More highly paid workers in sectors like the high-tech environment are also feeling the effects. Many workers are able to locate new jobs, but those with few marketable skills are least likely to secure jobs in other segments of the economy; neither are they able to relocate to find employment. The structure of work is also changing. Contract work is becoming more common, and it lacks benefits like health insurance and retirement plans, thus increasing poverty risks. Some former highly paid professionals are beginning to wonder if they will ever see the kinds of jobs, salaries, and benefits they once had. But this does not mean that these individuals with good educations and community status see that they have much in common with those who are poor.

Karl Marx used the term *lumpenproletariat* (the proletariat in rags) more than a hundred years ago to describe those who had, in essence, dropped out of society.[47] In the 1960s this concept reemerged to refer to those most severely affected by changes in community and economic structure. The term *underclass* was adopted to describe those individuals who had been unable to weather changes in the country's economic structure and who were not able to obtain jobs in a market that relied increasingly on more highly skilled and educated workers.

Today, the term underclass is used with particular reference to residents of poor, black, ghetto communities that are characterized by long-term unemployment, long-term welfare dependency, and overall social disorganization, including high levels of street crime.[48] The term is controversial because of its derogatory sound and because it fails to distinguish the diversity among the poor.[49] This so-called "underclass" is of considerable concern because it is outside the mainstream of the social, economic, and political institutions that are part of the lives of most citizens. Prior to the 1960s these inner-city communities were not as severely depressed as they are today.[50] In the 1940s and 1950s they were home to blacks of all social classes. Fair housing and other antidiscrimination laws had not yet evolved that would allow many middle- and upper-class blacks to move to more affluent city and suburban neighborhoods. Schools, businesses, and other social institutions in these neighborhoods were used by all residents, and the economic exchange in these communities provided jobs for many residents, including those with marginal job skills. But as professional and blue-collar workers were able to find better housing in the suburbs, the most disadvantaged were left behind. According to several authors, community leaders were no longer present to bring stability to these neighborhoods. Their departure also caused a severe decline in economic enterprises. At the same time, the job market in the cities underwent considerable change. Industrial and manufacturing jobs were being replaced by jobs in the financial, technical, and administrative fields, and these were not the kinds of jobs for which most poor inner-city residents were prepared. Jobs in the food and retail industries, which inner-city residents might have been able to fill more readily, were increasing in numbers in the suburbs, but those who needed these jobs the most could not find housing there. It has been said that these structural changes left open a path for social disorganization. As a result, inner-city neighborhoods deteriorated and problems such as unemployment, teen pregnancy, and drug dealing increased.

To remedy this type of severe or persistent poverty, recommendations are that multiple approaches be used; for example, that job training, relocation, and other types of services be coupled with efforts to bring the poor in touch with mainstream society. These solutions sound similar to those suggested to interrupt the culture of poverty. The important distinction is that the notion of a culture of poverty is concerned with changing *personal* characteristics of the poor that prevent them from functioning in the mainstream. Some have referred to this as a "blame the victim" mentality. Poverty viewed as a *structural* issue is quite different. It implies that the solutions to the problem lie in developing new social institutions or modifying existing ones to be more responsive to disadvantaged members of society. This is an important distinction in developing social policies. For example, rather than provide housing for the poor in ghetto communities, a structural approach would be to offer housing in middle-class communities to allow disadvantaged individuals to avail themselves of greater societal opportunities. Another suggestion to bring young people into the mainstream is a national service requirement for *all* youth. This type of universal program differs substantially from job programs that target only youth from disadvantaged backgrounds. The concept behind such a universal program is that it would provide for better integration of all members of society, but clearly such a requirement would meet with opposition from those who are already better off and feel that they would not gain by it.

POOR AND HOMELESS: NOT INVISIBLE ANY MORE

In an influential book of the 1960s, *The Other America*, Michael Harrington argued that most Americans were blind to the poverty of millions in their own country.[51] Harrington wrote of two nations within the United States—one a nation of comfortable and affluent Americans, the other a nation of the poor—those who suffer deprivation and humiliation because they are without access to adequate education, housing, employment, and healthcare. Harrington believed that most Americans were blind to poverty because the poor were "invisible"—they did not live, go to school, work, or socialize with the more affluent. Even today, rural poverty can be masked by a beautiful countryside. With mass production of clothing, a poor person may be relatively well dressed but unable to afford decent housing or healthcare. The elderly poor are invisible because they do not venture far from home. And finally, most poor people are invisible because they have no political power; in fact, they are often the victims of political action.

Since the 1980s, poverty has become more visible, primarily because of increased homelessness. Just how many people are homeless? There are a number of interesting accounts of how figures on homelessness have been derived.[52] Early estimates ranged from 250,000 in a 1984 study by the Department of Housing and Urban Development (HUD)[53] to suggestions of 3 million in a 1983 report published by the Community for Creative Non-Violence (CCNV).[54] Mitch Snyder was the controversial activist who led the CCNV. Snyder sued HUD over estimates he considered lowball.[55]

Of course, it is difficult to get an accurate count of homeless people when some are sleeping in alleys and under bridges and might rather be left alone. The process has been likened to "fly-fishing with a blindfold."[56] Furthermore, just what constitutes homelessness? Should the definition be reserved for those sleeping on the street? Should it include those in shelters, or should it be broadened to include those "doubled up" with family and friends because they cannot afford their own living quarters?[57] In conjunction with the 1990 national census, the Census Bureau conducted the S (street and shelter)-Night Enumeration using an innovative method of decoys and observers to determine the study's comprehensiveness.[58] The figure derived was 228,000 homeless individuals, an estimate that even conservative Rush Limbaugh thought was too low.[59] Among the flaws were serious deficiencies in counting people living on the streets. The Census Bureau declared that this was not an official count. The 2000 census did include people in emergency and transitional shelters, but the Census Bureau emphasized that it also does not represent an official count.

In an analysis of homelessness in America, social worker Joel Blau suggests that the best estimates come from the National Alliance to End Homelessness.[60] Using HUD data, the Alliance estimated that 735,000 people are homeless on a given day and that 1.3 to 2 million are homeless at some time during the year.[61] Others indicate that the best available estimate comes from the Urban Institute's 1987 study, which arrived at a figure between 500,000 to 600,000 during a week's time, with more homeless generally found in urban areas.[62] Other estimates from various sources indicate that during a year, the number of homeless people is much greater than previously thought, perhaps 2 to 3 million.[63] A more recent estimate of homelessness agrees with this assessment. Comparing the 1987 figures with those based on estimates from a 1996 study, Burt and Aron found that "even in a booming economy, at least 2.3 million adults and children or nearly 1 percent of the U.S. population are likely to experience a spell of homelessness at least once during a year."[64]

Another set of researchers used a telephone survey of a representative sample of U.S. households to study homelessness, which obviously underestimates the problem.[65] They still came up with figures that 12 million people had been literally homeless (e.g., living in an abandoned building or shelter) at some point during their lifetime because they could not afford another arrangement. The figure rose to 28 million when people who had moved in with family or others were included. Those literally homeless often reported deprivation (e.g., lack of food) and victimization (e.g., being robbed or even raped), and they spent considerable time with no place to live.

Who Is Homeless?

Most of the poor have some permanent residence. Although the quality of this housing may vary, they do have an address to call home. But some Americans have no address at all. Two groups have comprised most of the homeless population. One is alcoholics and drug addicts. Alcoholic men in particular have long been a significant portion of the homeless population, and an increase in other types of drug abuse has added to the homeless population.[66] The second group is those with severe mental illness.[67] Deinstitutionalization of people with mental illness beginning in the 1960s, combined with the lack of community-based mental health services, increased the homeless population, and substantial numbers have both mental illness and substance-use disorders (see also Chapter 10). Today homelessness has a third face—one- and even two-parent families with young children. High housing costs, combined with unemployment and low-paying jobs, contribute to families' inability to locate permanent shelter. Spousal violence also adds to the number seeking shelter, and some children are homeless because they have run away as a result of abuse, neglect, or other family problems.[68] Another group of homeless young people have been released from foster care on reaching adulthood without an appropriate transition to independent living.[69]

Generally consistent with previous studies, in 2001, the U.S. Conference of Mayors estimated that of the homeless population in cities, 41 percent were single or "unaccompanied" men and 13 percent were unaccompanied women, 41 percent were families with children, and 5 percent were unaccompanied youth.[70] Substance abuse (alcohol and/or other drugs) was the cause attributed to 32 percent of homeless cases and mental illness for another 23 percent. Twenty-two percent of the homeless population were employed and 10 percent were military veterans. The homeless population seems to be younger and more ethnically diverse than in the past.[71]

One couple who have ministered to homeless people suggest that the nation must overcome its "politics of denial" and recognize that alcoholism, drug addiction, and serious mental illness, accompanied by disaffiliation and alienation from family and friends, are the major causes of homelessness today.[72] They point to the population bulge created by the baby boomers and the growth of the underclass as having exacerbated the problem. Others contend that the increase in homelessness is caused by social factors (loosening of family and community ties), economic and structural conditions (unemployment, a more competitive work environment, low wages), and politics (cutbacks in public assistance and social services).[73] They believe that the root of homelessness is the lack of affordable housing, not mental illness or chemical dependency. One point on which everyone seems to agree is that the homeless need good, affordable housing, and that those with mental health and substance abuse problems also need treatment.[74] Martha Burt sums it up this way:

> It is clear that personal conditions such as poverty, mental illness, alcoholism, physical handicap, and drug addiction increase a person's vulnerability to homelessness; hence a large proportion of homeless people exhibit these characteristics. But many people have had these vulnerabilities in past decades. Only the changes in structural factors can explain why the vulnerabilities [have] led to a much larger homeless population.[75]

For years, alcoholics and others on "skid row" have sought shelter at the Salvation Army and church missions. Now almost all communities of any size have shelters for a broader cross-section of the homeless population (see Illustration 3.2). Some operate

ILLUSTRATION 3.2

"Pa Kettle" (Wesley Ernest Bryan) Talks about Homelessness

I've only been clean two years. Where was I livin' in New York? Behind Sardi's. Before that, I used to live in the tunnels. Remember when everyone was livin' down in the subway tunnels? I was stayin' in a tunnel right by the Port Authority, Thirty-fourth Street. They come in and ran everybody up out of there. Two o'clock in the morning. That's when I moved back to Sardi's. Eighteenth Street on the East Side. Yes. It's a big-time restaurant. It's super high society. A biscuit cost you fifty dollars. Yes. A glass of water would probably cost you about twelve dollars, and they want a tip when you leave. Yes. I wound up getting a job there, and that helped a lot. Took a lot of pressure off.

See, people can never really understand homelessness until they go through it, 'cause Americans have this problem: "As long as it's not one of my relatives and not in my backyard, I don't see it except on TV." You know? "I might catch it if it's on *Oprah.*" You know? "If it happens to be on the nightly news and it's around Christmas time, I might dig in my drawer and find somethin' to give that po' homeless guy, so I can feel guilty before the tax write-off man comes." You know? (Laughs.) People never really understand until it actually happens to them.

When we was in New Orleans, this lady used to come down every weekend and throw eggs at the homeless. I don't mean physical eggs. I mean verbally: "Why don't you bums get a job?!" She was one of those high, city council–type people. Then when they had that flood and her house got wiped out, now she's one of the biggest outreach workers they got down there. Now she can't do enough for

the homeless. Why? Because it took an act of God to get her off her high horse. You understand what I'm sayin'?

But they make big money off of you. All of the government organizations—the homeless industry. Most of it disappear in that little gray area called "operational overhead." You understand what I'm sayin'? They could do a lot more than what they're doing. They ain't that slow when it comes to building a prison! They can always seem to find prison room. Can't find no shelter, you know, buildings for battered and abused women. But they can always build a prison! You know, a lady gettin' beat up by her boyfriend. "Oh, we're sorry. We don't have bed space we got so many people." But they got that prison. Better go out and shoot that fool! You understand what I'm sayin'? It's all relative.

And what's the biggest thing now? What's the biggest thing now? Now, it's privatizing all of these institutions, so you absolutely have no rights. The ACLU [American Civil Liberties Union] can't do nothin'. Have your rights been violated? What rights? You have no rights! The only rights you have out here is the class you carry within yourself. Those are the only real rights you have out here.

Just hope that you never go through it. This is none of that Jack Kerouac thing where everybody decides "let's go Beatnik around the country." This is crap. See, back then, it was a movement to change things around. Now it's just somethin' that happens to your butt. You can't control the circumstances, but you can control how you live and operate within those circumstances. There's nothin' romantic about it. You can go to jail out here

continued

ILLUSTRATION 3.2 *(continued)*

just for bein' sleepy and tired. You can. You can be layin' up under that tree. Cop don't like you, you can go to jail for vagrancy or whatever he decides to come up with. In other words, just being honest, just being sober, just bein' safe ain't no guarantee that you ain't gonna get harassed.

When I'm playin' music, people come up and say, "Here's a buck." That may not be a lot to them, but to me it's a lot. Most of the time, when you give money to people on the street, you're participating in their genocide because you know they're going to go out and buy liquor. You know they're going to go out there and buy crack. When people come up and say, "I never see you drunk no more, here," "I know that you're really tryin', here," when somebody gives me money, they are helping with my liberation. Big difference. If I was strung out, then they would be participating in my genocide 'cause I'm actually fightin' not to die.

Another phenomenon now is a lot of people want to have shelters. A lot of people want to build soup lines and soup kitchens. All of sudden, there's a lot of government money out here. Everybody tryin' to do a shelter and become another movement hustler. You know?

In order to get that tax bracket. You have to watch out for them. You get to know one or two people on the city council and get you a zone in the right neighborhood, and you can have you a nice lil' shelter *too.* That's another trend you have to watch out for 'cause it may start out all meaning well, but you start gettin' all that government money, people change, boy! People like Jim Bakker. Straight-up swindlers.

See, I'm a dying breed: an honest bum in America. (Laughs.) I'm serious. You know, that's an enigma nowadays. You know? Politicians are crooked. Preachers are crooked. Cops are scary and crooked. You understand what I'm sayin'? Can't look to your leaders no more for leadership. Can't be a role model no more. You know? All the decent heroes and Lone Ranger croaked.

So what's left? Guys like me. See, at least when I go, God say, "Well, what have you got to say fo' yo'self?" I can say, "Yeah, I was a bum, but I was an honest bum. Run the tape." I ain't got to look over my shoulder. You understand? I did some really dumb stuff, which I pass on to the growin' up of my youth. But as I get older, I get straighter. So you can run this tape. At least I can go out like dat.

Source: From *Nomads of a Desert City,* by Barbara Seyda, © 2001 Barbara Seyda. Reprinted by permission of the University of Arizona Press.

with government assistance, others with private support, or a combination of the two. Although this humanitarian aid is welcome, there is a fear that shelters have become substitutes for permanent homes. The addition of families to the ranks of the homeless is perhaps the straw that motivated Congress to pass the Stewart B. McKinney Homeless Assistance Act in 1987, now reauthorized as the McKinney-Vento Homeless Assistance Act. The states receive some of this funding in the form of a block grant from the U.S. Department of Housing and Urban Development (HUD) and provide matching funds for most program components.[76] Communities also compete for much of this funding rather than receive it on a formula basis. The competitive programs are supportive housing, which includes additional services to alleviate homelessness, the Shelter Plus Care Program for homeless persons who have disabilities, and the Single Room Occupancy (SRO) Program, which provides rental assistance to individuals along with funds for "moderate" rehabilitation of SROs (often these are residential-type hotels that have been operated by groups like the YMCA). HUD promotes a continuum of care approach that requires communities to submit funding applications that show how they will coordinate services. The noncompetitive formula program primarily covers emergency shelter services.

President George W. Bush has pledged to end chronic homelessness, defining this population as about 150,000 individuals who suffer from addiction, mental illness, or a physical disability and experience multiple periods of homelessness. The president's 2005 budget says that research indicates that this group may be only 10 percent of the homeless population but that individuals in these situations use a large number of services because their needs are not addressed in a holistic way. To help this group, the president has proposed the Samaritan Initiative, with $50 million for housing from HUD's budget and $10 million each from the Veteran's Administration and the Department of Health and Human Services to provide other services. This initiative has been criticized for failing to include families and other segments of the homeless population.

A 2004 study commissioned by HUD highlights the efforts that some areas have made in addressing homelessness among groups considered most difficult to assist.[77] The city of Philadelphia uses an Outreach Coordination Center (OCC) to address street homelessness. The OCC relies on daytime outreach efforts using teams from several agencies who work together. There is a comprehensive database of information, and services are available from health, mental health, and substance abuse agencies. San Diego is using a different approach based on two strategies that involve the police department (and may be considered more coercive)—the Homeless Outreach Team (HOT) and the Serial Inebriate Program (SIP). HOT teams are composed of a police officer, a mental health worker, and a benefits eligibility technician. Homeless individuals are encouraged to accept services, but the officer is there as an authority figure who can involuntarily move the individual from the street if necessary. SIP is for those with chronic substance abuse problems, primarily alcoholism, who do not accept services. These individuals are often arrested for public drunkenness. Once they traverse the court system, they are offered treatment and transitional housing as an alternative to jail.

Some cities like Columbus, Ohio; San Diego, California; Seattle, Washington; and Los Angeles, California, are using various "housing first" approaches that may include access to "safe havens" and other "low demand" housing. In the lingo of service providers, these approaches generally do not require that residents be "housing ready," that is, they do not have to be abstinent (though HUD regulations forbid using illegal drugs on premises) or receiving mental health or substance abuse services to move in, but services are available and encouraged. By providing decent shelter first, service providers hope that homeless people with alcohol, drug, and mental health problems will be more likely to accept services. In addition to resolving substance use disorders and mental health crises, the approach aims to help these individuals maintain stable housing.

Affordable Housing

There are different views of the causes of homelessness, but there is more agreement that the United States has a serious shortage of affordable housing. The largest item in most household budgets is housing. Whether it is the monthly rent or mortgage payment, housing consumes an increased portion of the personal budget. As far back as the Housing Act of 1949, Congress acknowledged the need for a "decent home and a suitable living environment for every American family." It is difficult for many Americans to realize the American dream—owning a home. It is also difficult for many people to pay the rent. In 1995, using the federal government's definition that housing costs should not exceed 30 percent of the household budget, the Center for Budget and Policy Priorities found that three out of five poor renters used more than half their income to pay for rent and utilities and that they typically expended 60 percent of their income to cover these costs.[78] In the same year, HUD reported figures of 43 percent of very low-income renters paying more than half their income for housing.[79] A 2000 HUD report describes a "worsening crisis," with 5.4 million families who do not receive rental assistance earning less than half of the local median wage and paying more than half their income for rent or residing in substandard housing, while the pool of affordable housing available to them is shrinking.[80] Since 1989, the National Low Income Housing Coalition (NLIHC) has conducted studies of affordable rental housing. The NLIHC's 2003 report indicates that in 106 metropolitan statistical areas and 597 counties, more than half of renter households cannot afford a two-bedroom apartment at fair market rent (FMR).[81] Additionally, in 40 states, which include 90 percent of all renter households in the nation, it takes more than twice the prevailing minimum wage to afford an apartment. Even with two family members working full time at minimum wage, a family could not afford a two-bedroom apartment at FMR. In 11 states it takes more than three times the minimum wage to afford such an apartment.

Residents of publicly supported housing are generally expected to contribute 30 percent of their income for rent, even though the concept of "shelter poverty" indicates that this formula fails to take into account the various circumstances of individuals and families.[82] Some families may not have enough left for other necessities after they pay 30 percent of their income for housing, while others may be able to pay more than 30 percent. According to the Utah Issues Information Program, the

> *Shelter Poverty model demonstrates the material deprivation of poverty by showing how monthly income and expenses cannot realistically be reconciled by the poor, [yet] they must be paid if the danger of losing housing is to be avoided. As . . . homeless individuals and families will attest, being unhoused is highly disruptive of nearly all other aspects of life and the pathway from homeless to becoming housed once again is a difficult one.*[83]

The U.S. Department of Housing and Urban Development is the federal government's main agency for helping low-income Americans find housing. When Americans think of government-sponsored housing, they may think of the large, high-rise public housing projects that have gained much notoriety for being rodent-, drug-, and crime-infested dwellings. Much of the more recent construction has been lower density, but HUD has not funded new public housing developments since 1994.*[84] The strategy today is to disperse housing for low-income individuals throughout neighborhoods rather than concentrating publicly supported housing units together.

HUD's major approach for assisting very low-income families and individuals who are disabled or elderly is the Housing Choice Voucher Program, commonly called Section 8,[85] initiated in 1974 during the Nixon administration. HUD provides funds to local public housing agencies or authorities (PHAs) that administer the program locally. Vouchers generally go to those whose incomes are not more than half of the area's median income, and three-quarters of vouchers must go to those whose income is not more than 30 percent of the median. A small number of participants use their subsidies to purchase homes, but the vast majority use them to defray rent costs. The PHAs may give preference to certain types of applicants, for example, low-income families who are homeless, living in substandard housing, displaced, or paying an inordinate amount for rent. PHAs use fair market rent (FMR) calculations, which include utilities but not phone service, to determine what they will pay under the voucher program (Illustration 3.3 contains 2004 FMRs for selected cities). Families or individual generally pay 30 to 40 percent of their monthly adjusted gross income for rent and utilities, and the PHA pays the difference between this amount and fair market rent. Families or individuals must find their own housing and the housing must meet minimum health and safety standards. If the family or individual selects housing that exceeds the amount established by the PHA, the family must pay the difference. The voucher program is not an entitlement program, and in most places there are long waiting lists to participate.† In other cases, individuals and families have a hard time finding affordable housing or a landlord who will accept a voucher.[86] Some families also receive help with utility payments through the Low-Income Home Energy Assistance Program funded through the U.S. Department of Health and Human Services and administered by the states.

Two million households participate in the Section 8 voucher program, and the program's costs have risen rapidly in recent years.[87] Fiscal year 2004 appropriations were more than $14 billion. For housing advocates and poor individuals and families, the rub comes because President Bush's 2005 budget proposes to cut funds and alter the way the program is administered. According to the Center on Budget and Policy Priorities (CBPP), the proposal would chop more than $1 billion from the program in 2005 and more through 2009, potentially resulting in 250,000 fewer families served in 2005 and up to 800,000 fewer by 2009, or 40 percent of all those served.[88] Rather

*Since some HUD programs require long-term funding commitments, prior appropriations continue to support them, even though they may not receive new funding.

†A visit to the website of the Housing Authority of the City of Austin, Texas, on July 4, 2004, indicated that it was not accepting new applications for the Housing Choice Voucher Program until 2005, and there were well over 4,000 names on the waiting list.

ILLUSTRATION 3.3

Fair Market Rent in 2004 for Selected Cities

Fair Market Rents (FMRs) are used to determine standard payment amounts for the Section 8 Housing Choice Voucher program. The U.S. Department of Housing and Urban Development (HUD) annually publishes FMRs for 354 metropolitan areas and 2,350 nonmetropolitan county FMR areas.

FMRs are gross rent estimates. They include the shelter rent plus the cost of all utilities, except telephones. HUD sets FMRs to assure that a sufficient supply of rental housing is available to program participants. To accomplish this objective, FMRs must be both high enough to permit a selection of units and neighborhoods and low enough to serve as many low-income families as possible. The level at which FMRs are set is expressed as a percentile point within the rent distribution of standard-quality rental housing units. HUD sets FMRs at either the 40th or 50th percentile rent, the dollar amount below which 40 or 50 percent of the standard-quality rental housing

units are rented. These percentiles are drawn from the distribution of rents of all units occupied by recent movers (renter households who moved to their present residence within the past 18 months). Public housing units and units less than two years old are excluded. For most areas, the 40th percentile is used.

Cities	One-Bedroom Apartment
Mobile, Alabama	$455
Los Angeles, California	$807
Colorado Springs, Colorado	$526
Orlando, Florida	$687
Atlanta, Georgia	$810
Bloomington, Indiana	$514
Lawrence, Kansas	$457
Baltimore, Maryland	$727
Boston, Massachusetts	$1,135
Omaha, Nebraska	$496
Seattle, Washington	$729
Madison, Wisconsin	$547

Source: Retrieved March 10, 2004, from http://www.hud.gov; see also *Federal Register,* Vol. 68, No. 190, October 1, 2003, Department of Housing and Urban Development, Fair Market Rents for the Housing Choice Voucher Program and Moderate Rehabilitation Single Room Occupancy Program Fiscal Year 2004.

than cutting families from the program, the PHAs could give less assistance to each household. The CBPP estimates that in 2005 this could cost each family an additional $800 in rent. Another possibility is assisting more families that have higher incomes and can pay more rent, and leaving more poorer families to find other options. This strategy has been suggested before and has been lambasted in the *New Republic* as "tantamount to making Medicare solvent by denying coverage to the old and sick."[89] President Bush wants to turn the program into a block grant in order to achieve greater efficiency. The CBPP agrees that programs costs have grown rapidly, but growth has slowed considerably and CBPP argues that the proposed spending reduction cannot possibly be recouped through the president's plan.

In addition to the Section 8 voucher program and other HUD-sponsored programs, many states and communities offer additional assistance. There are also programs to help people with low and moderate incomes purchase housing. Considerable federal housing assistance goes to middle- and upper-income households in the form of mortgage assistance and income tax deductions, which amount to much more than the money spent on public and subsidized housing.

HUD and other governmental programs reach only a small proportion of those who could use help in obtaining safe, affordable, and permanent housing. Unhappy with the number of people living in substandard and unsafe housing, nonprofit groups such as Habitat for Humanity (its most prominent volunteers are former president and first lady Jimmy and Rosalyn Carter) are constructing or "rehabilitating" housing for low-income and poor individuals and families. Many of the beneficiaries contribute "sweat equity"—their own labor—to help build these homes. Most also make modest mortgage payments.

Not all the news about access to housing is bad. Since 1994 the national home-ownership rate has risen due to a strong economy during much of this period. With unemployment, inflation, and home mortgage interest rates low, home purchases were more affordable despite rising home prices. In addition to federal mortgage assistance, communities use bond monies to offer low-interest mortgages to low- and moderate-income first-time home buyers. Also being credited with increasing home ownership are the Community Reinvestment Act, which puts more pressure on banks to make loans in low-income communities, and the growth of community development corporations.[90] Another significant piece of legislation is the Cranston-Gonzalez National Affordable Housing Act of 1990, which provides housing block grants to state and local governments for housing assistance such as home ownership programs.[91] According to the U.S. Census Bureau, in the last quarter of 2003, the national home ownership rate was 68.6 percent, the highest it has ever been.[92] Of course, home ownership is not distributed equally among the population. For example, it is 49.4 percent for African Americans and 47.7 percent for Hispanic Americans compared to 75.5 percent for non-Hispanic whites. President George W. Bush has announced his goal of making an additional 5.5 million minority families homeowners by the end of the decade. His immediate plan is to spend $400 million ($200 million in 2004 and the same amount in 2005) on the American Dream Downpayment Act to help 80,000 families become homewners.

Homeownership is especially important in reducing **asset poverty.** A home is often a household's biggest asset. Assets like savings, investments, and home ownership provide a cushion when resources are needed due to unemployment or other hardships. As this chapter demonstrates, income inequality is substantial. Asset inequality is even greater. Adding assets to income provides a more realistic picture of how wealth is distributed in the U.S. Using the definition that a household is asset poor if it does not have sufficient resources to cover three months worth of expenses, a pair of economists found that based on net worth (the value of assets that could be turned into cash minus debt), nearly 26 percent of Americans were asset poor in 1999.[93] When home equity was excluded from net worth, the number that were asset poor increased to 40 percent. This is reason enough for governments to boost home ownership and encourage other forms of asset development.

The relatively modest amount of assistance provided to low-income people by the Department of Housing and Urban Development may be a result of the many difficulties the agency has faced. Republican Jack Kemp, HUD secretary during the George H. W. Bush Administration, was faced with changing the image of an agency tarnished by scandals. There were accusations that prominent Republicans and former HUD officials had raked in millions of dollars in consulting fees in order to steer HUD contracts to particular firms and that private escrow agents siphoned off millions from the sale of foreclosed homes. Kemp worked hard to instill pride in public housing projects, and he even managed to turn ownership of a few projects over to their residents.[94]

President Clinton appointed former San Antonio mayor Henry Cisneros HUD secretary. Cisneros worked hard to assist the homeless, to demolish ("blow up" is the term used) decayed public housing and rehabilitate other units under a program called HOPE VI, and to use the voucher program to integrate poor people into decent neighborhoods. HUD's budget shrank, however, amid calls to get rid of the financially troubled agency entirely, and eventually, amid his own personal problems, Cisneros left the agency. HUD's problems were also compounded by some local public housing authorities that were plagued by poor management. In 1999, the agency faced criticisms that it had left unspent more than $14 billion dollars that could have gone to assist poor renters.[95] HUD remains a relatively small agency with little political power.[96]

Housing is so integral to health and general well-being that it is surprising that it has not been the focus of more attention. Illustration 3.4 shows just how important decent housing is to one woman who grew up in the slums.

A FUNDAMENTAL SHIFT

This discussion of poverty and homelessness has considered contending definitions of the causes of these problems. In the 1920s the prevailing causes of poverty were attributed to the dominance of business interests and worker exploitation; in the 1930s national economic collapse was the cause, and in the 1960s discrimination (racism and sexism) and lack of opportunity were the prevailing explanations. During each of these eras, the solutions were generally agreed upon. Respectively, they were minimum wages and other fair labor standards; economic recovery, work programs, and a safety net of social insurance and public assistance programs; greater equality of opportunity through civil rights and gender rights legislation and access to nutrition, job training, health care, and early education programs. In the past three decades there have been increasing schisms about the causes of poverty in the United States. Our discussion turns to the contemporary view of conservatives or neoconservatives that public assistance programs promote poverty and that a philosophy of mandatory work will root out all but some small unavoidable vestige of the problem.

ILLUSTRATION 3.4

Pam Jackson's New Apartment

At first glance, Pamela Jackson's apartment looks like any ordinary place. Her living room is functionally appointed with cheap furniture: a black vinyl sofa, matching love seat, glass coffee table, and a TV. Everything appears fairly new. Adjacent to the living room is a perfectly immaculate galley kitchen. In each of two small adjoining rooms, the beds are neatly made. If not for the smattering of framed photographs, a child's drawings, houseplants, and stuffed animals, one might mistake this for a motel suite of above-average cheerfulness. A walk around the two-story red brick development in which the apartment is situated only exacerbates the pervasive sense of dull normality. Driving around the Chicago suburb of Palatine heightens it further.

But to Pamela Jackson, the apartment represents far more. To her, a clean, safe, affordable place to live still comes as such a surprise that it induces a kind of euphoria when she talks about it, some nine months after moving in. For her, a nondescript apartment in a middle-class neighborhood is the basis of a new life, vastly better than the one she knew before. It is a sanctuary, a safe haven from conditions so degraded that most of us can only imagine them. A slim, bright-eyed woman, wearing a sleeveless denim dress on a hot autumn day, Pam sits on the edge of her sofa and races, tripping over her words as she tries to explain what the apartment means to her: Here there are no crackheads trying to sell secondhand bus transfers for a quarter, no giant rats, random shootings, or playgrounds strewn with broken glass. Instead there's a good suburban school where her daughter is learning to play the clarinet, a parking lot

where she walks without fear at night, and a landlord who responds promptly to the complaint of a leaky faucet.

Jackson told me her story when I visited her in 1995. For the first thirty years of her life, she lived in a variety of public housing projects and privately owned slum apartments on Chicago's South Side. At twenty, she got pregnant and gave birth to a daughter, Porshá. Porshá's father, to whom Pam wasn't married, soon left, and she went on public assistance. For the next nine years, she was in and out of work, in and out of apartments, on and off welfare. The father of her daughter sometimes works, she says, but he will quit a job sooner than pay child support.

Poverty and danger turned mother and daughter into refugees in the city. Before moving to Palatine, they lived with the family of Pam's brother at Seventy-sixth and Union, sleeping on a sofa in the living room. Though she had a full-time job at Woolworth's, Pam couldn't afford a place of her own, even in a marginal neighborhood. In the last few years the area where she lived with her brother has gone from bad to intolerable. Seventy-ninth is "the street that never sleeps," Jackson says, with young men standing on the corner dealing drugs "all night, in every kind of weather." After getting off work at ten o'clock, she would have to cross that street to pick up Porshá at her babysitter's. Porshá's school, at Sixty-third and Dulles, was in a similarly menacing precinct, "with people hanging out under the El station, gangs and drug dealers," she says. Parkway Gardens, a blighted housing project, was the school's backyard. "On

continued

ILLUSTRATION 3.4 *(continued)*

Sixty-second Street anything can happen," Pam says. Although reconciled to a measure of risk herself, she was afraid for Porshá. "I wanted some stability in my daughter's life," she says.

When, after a long struggle to get it, Pam moved to her new place in Palatine, the first thing she did was take off all of her clothes. "I never felt I could walk around, you know, free before. My daughter asked, 'Mama, why you walking around without any clothes?' Where I was you just don't have the freedom." They moved in on December 17, 1994. Jackson decided the apartment was her Christmas gift and got a small tree. A few months later, she bought herself a set of living room furniture as a birthday present.

Source: Jacob Weisberg, *In Defense of Government: The Fall and Rise of Public Trust* (New York: Scribner, 1996), pp. 11–13. Jacob Weisberg is Chief Political Correspondent for *Slate* Magazine.

Doesn't Welfare Cause Poverty?

The belief that welfare programs can actually *increase* the number of poor people is certainly not new. Since Elizabethan times, welfare payments have been kept minimal (the principle of **less eligibility**) to discourage potential recipients from choosing welfare over work. The large numbers of people from all social classes who became poor during the Great Depression of the late 1920s and early 1930s made the country realize that poverty could befall almost anyone. Yet many people still believe that welfare should be made an unattractive alternative to earnings. A good deal of attention has been given to the argument that much of today's poverty is a *direct* result of the social policies and programs of the 1960s and 1970s. The argument is presented this way: from 1947 to 1965 the poverty rate was reduced by more than half without massive government social welfare intervention; by the mid-1960s many believed that the poverty that remained was due to lack of opportunities and bad luck.[97] The solution was government intervention to reduce poverty and create more opportunities for the disadvantaged. Welfare spending and the numbers of welfare programs increased, but the number of poor did not decrease. During the 1970s the poverty rate remained at about 12 percent.

The first book to receive widespread attention that claimed welfare was to blame for welfare dependency was George Gilder's *Wealth and Poverty*, published in 1981. Gilder boldly discusses what he calls "the devastating impact of the programs of liberalism on the poor":[98]

> What actually happened since 1964 was a vast expansion of the welfare rolls that halted in its tracks an ongoing improvement in the lives of the poor, particularly blacks, and left behind—and here I choose my words as carefully as I can—a wreckage of broken lives and families worse than the aftermath of slavery.[99]

Gilder believes that the expansion of the public assistance system led to an erosion of the work ethic and self-reliance. He contends that as these benefits increase, the value of a *man's* labor to his family decreases, especially if he earns low wages at his job. The welfare system saps his dignity by making him less necessary to his family. This in turn leads to family breakup and to further reliance on welfare. Gilder also criticizes antidiscrimination policies, which he says favor credentials over the drive to succeed. His book contains strong gender biases, because it focuses on the importance on jobs for men over those for women. Using many Horatio Alger–type success stories, Gilder pointed to examples of how poor Americans and immigrants to the United States were able to achieve prosperity through their hard work (the "bootstrap" approach). He is enamored of the advantages that a capitalistic economic system affords to those who are willing to "sacrifice to succeed."

In 1984 Charles Murray made much the same argument in his book *Losing Ground: American Social Policy, 1950–1980.*[100] Using statistical presentations, Murray concludes that there are more poor following the social programs of the Great Society; the underclass has fallen further behind, and social welfare policy is responsible. To make his point, Murray compared three measures of poverty. "Official poverty," as discussed earlier, is the amount of poverty as measured by the U.S. government each year. "Net poverty" is official poverty minus the value of in-kind benefits. "Latent poverty" is the number of people who would be poor if they did not receive social insurance and public assistance payments. Murray claims that in-kind benefits have reduced official poverty figures—but not as much as they should considering the amounts of money spent on these programs (e.g., food stamps and Medicaid). Even worse, he believes, is that latent poverty is so much higher than official poverty. In 1980 official poverty was 13 percent. Latent poverty increased after 1968, reaching 22 percent of the population by 1980. The War on Poverty was supposed to make people economically self-sufficient and get them off welfare. The unfortunate situation is that these programs failed to reduce the need for public aid.

Those critical of Murray's work contend that his statistics and analyses can be misleading, because poverty is a complex issue, and many factors must be presented in any discussion of the rising numbers of poor people.[101] For example, bad economic times result in higher unemployment (the lesson of the Great Depression). Lack of preparation for good jobs—not the desire to be on the dole—adds to the ranks of the poor. In hard times it is not surprising that the underclass will be unemployed and require social welfare assistance. Murray ignores many of the approaches to understanding the root causes of poverty suggested in this chapter—structure, exploitation, and discrimination. He blames "the system" for instituting federal welfare programs that have enticed low-income individuals to abandon work and family values.

The thrust of Murray's argument was directed toward public assistance programs like Aid to Families with Dependent Children (AFDC, now TANF), a program that is a small part of the social welfare system (see Chapter 6). Murray used a hypothetical couple named Phyllis and Harold who were unmarried and expecting a baby to describe how the system encouraged (1) them to remain unmarried, (2) Phyllis to keep her baby and to go on AFDC rather than work, and (3) Harold to quit his low-paying and unsatisfying job and collect unemployment insurance. Although few would deny the irrationality of many aspects of the welfare system, Murray went too far in his claims because he used some erroneous premises. For example, he assumed that Harold could easily get unemployment compensation. In fact, unemployment compensation is not available to those who leave their jobs voluntarily, and these benefits are generally available only on a short-term basis (see Chapter 4). Murray also implied that welfare officials would not ask Phyllis who the father of her baby is, that she would not be required to comply with the rule that applicants assist in establishing paternity, and that the state would not at least try to collect child support from Harold (also see Chapter 6). Even more damning is that Murray had little faith that either Phyllis or Harold, both high school graduates in his scenario, would ever get additional education or seek a better life. Many social welfare scholars have discounted much of Murray's arguments "about the effects of welfare or welfare state policies on the poor."[102] It is apparent, however, that Murray and Gilder continue to touch a nerve among the public, many of whom do not get the kind of governmental benefits known as welfare, but who are working hard and still struggle to make ends meet.

Poverty or Dependency? The Debate Rages On

Murray's view led him to advocate an end to all existing federally-supported public assistance programs for working-age people (AFDC, food stamps, Medicaid, and so on), and leaving the rest of welfare to private charities and state and local governments. Why he favors this solution is unclear, since federal intervention came about as a result of the inability of the local approach to respond to social welfare needs. TANF (formerly AFDC) benefits, which are determined by the states, have declined substantially in real dollar terms over the last few decades (see Chapter 6). Turning all public assistance programs back to the states would certainly mean severe cuts in these programs, thereby making welfare even less desirable and more degrading than it is now. But the approaches suggested by Gilder and Murray have had a significant impact on public assistance programs, to an extent that may surprise even these conservatives. Most of us agree that being a productive member of society is important, but there are some public assistance costs to be paid in a highly competitive, technological society, and we continue to struggle with what should be done.

Gilder and Murray have been followed by others writing in the neoconservative vein. In a book published by the Libertarian Cato Institute, Michael Tanner calls the solutions proposed by most neoconservatives insufficiently radical to bring about change. Most conservatives, he believes, think that they can alter the government's approach to achieve their ends. Tanner believes there is no hope at all for government welfare: "Welfare has failed and cannot be reformed. It is time to end it. In its place, the civil society would rely on a reinvigorated network of private charity."[103] Like journalism professor Marvin Olasky,[104] who inspired Newt Gingrich, Tanner writes about "the bond" or the personal relationship that develops between those in need and those who wish to help—a relationship that the welfare bureaucracy finds difficult to emulate. Private charities can pick and choose whom they want to help, and they can hold those helped accountable for the assistance they receive. Sounding very much like Ronald Reagan and his supply side economic approach (see Chapter 2), Tanner says that high taxes and excessive regulatory policies are standing in the way of job creation and economic growth that provide opportunities for people to rise out of poverty.

Coming from an evangelical Christian perspective, Olasky emphasizes "abstinence and adoption" as keys in reducing welfare. Olasky calls governmental programs "too stingy in what only individuals can give: time, love, and compassion."[105] He makes three suggestions to increase "effective compassion": (1) allow states, rather than the federal government, to levy most of the taxes, and have states give citizens generous tax breaks for philanthropy and volunteerism; (2) allow religious groups to utilize government funding without restricting their religious activity, since change from within, including spiritual change, can help people transcend poverty; (3) allow organizations that help the poor redeem vouchers for the services they provide—but only if they show that the individual being helped has improved. Obviously, Olasky's views are deeply akin to those of President George W. Bush, who has promoted the use of religious or faith-based organizations to deliver social welfare services as well as initiatives to promote marriage as a solution to social problems.

These ideas have varying degrees of appeal to Americans, but is it realistic to think that private citizens and organizations can accomplish so much? As we saw in Chapter 1, many people who are well entrenched in serving the poor through the nonprofit and religious sectors do not believe that their organizations, let alone individuals of good will, can do it all, even with the government's support.[106] Rather than decreased dependency, they see increased misery without government involvement in helping the poor.

Americans have not rejected government intervention to reduce poverty. Instead, through their elected officials, they have placed their hopes on "welfare reform." In particular, their bets are on the view expressed by political scientist Lawrence Mead.[107] Mead contends that the welfare state has been too permissive by failing to "set behavioral standards for the poor."[108] Mead rejects notions that low wages, lack of jobs, discrimination, and lack of access to child care and health care are what cause people not to work and to consequently fall into hard core poverty. He believes that liberals have failed the country because they do not give poor people "credit to advance their own interests." With increased public assistance benefits, poor people simply were no longer motivated to work, and poverty became personal, not structural. Complacency developed by thinking of the poor as "victims" rather than "workers." Mead describes the poor as "dutiful but defeated," and he says:

> To a great extent, nonwork occurs simply because work is not enforced. Overall, I think conservatives have the better of the barriers debate—the chance to get ahead is widely available. But liberals have the more realistic view of the psychology of poverty—the poor do not believe they have the opportunity, and this still keeps them from working.[109]

Espousing a "new paternalism," Mead's analysis is that the poor respond well to structure, including the structure imposed by work programs. For Mead and those like him, poverty has gone from being a problem of too little income to a problem of dependency, requiring that the poor become motivated to be like most Americans who toil at jobs to try to better themselves and their families. "Work, not welfare," is the order of the day. Others contend that most poor people are motivated to work when work can be found and that explanations of poverty like structure and exploitation are as relevant as ever. They point to changes in the economy (e.g., offshoring) and the work environment (e.g., part-time and contract labor) and the slow growth of jobs even as the economy has rebounded. Jobs that fail to pay a living wage, lack health-care benefits, and do not allow people to amass assets like retirement accounts, leave even working people in jeopardy.

As Mead also notes, in America's ongoing discourse about the causes and solutions to poverty, communication between liberals and conservatives has broken down.[110] For many who have devoted themselves to theorizing about poverty, advocating for the poor, or helping the poor directly, the latest round of welfare reform, particularly the transformation of AFDC to TANF, has been a bitter pill to swallow. Though conservatives have clearly won the latest round in the poverty debates, a look at websites of liberal, conservative, libertarian, and religious groups on the World Wide Web is clear indication that this debate rages on.

SUMMARY

Defining poverty is a political activity rather than a rational exercise. This chapter included six approaches to defining poverty—as deprivation, as inequality, as a lack of human capital, as culture, as exploitation, and as structure. Americans have not agreed on any best approach for defining this social construct.

Using the official government poverty thresholds as our arbitrary measure of deprivation, there were 34.6 million poor people in the United States in 2002, or about 12.1 percent of the population. If we add in-kind welfare benefits to the official definition, the number of poor people is somewhat lower. Since the government began counting around 1960, poverty has declined substantially, but the lows of 11 percent achieved in the 1970s have yet to be achieved again. Poverty is more frequently found among black and Hispanic Americans and in households headed by women. Poverty remains higher among children than among older Americans and other adults. Homelessness is another concern.

There will always be differences among people in economic wealth, so it is particularly difficult to define poverty for public policy purposes as inequality. The real concern of society is the inequality that results in squalor. Poverty has many causes. Some people are poor because they lack the human capital, i.e., the resources and opportunities of the nonpoor, and some, such as the elderly, children, and those with severe disabilities, are not able to work. Discrimination is another source of poverty. Equality of opportunity remains an obstacle to the elimination of poverty in the United States.

The way in which poverty is defined has important implications for strategies to alleviate the problem. Human service professionals have a commitment to increasing opportunities for poor people as a means of reducing poverty. They reject the definition of poverty as culture, believing that disadvantaged people will make use of opportunities if only given the chance.

Increases in the number of poor people may also be defined by structural changes in social institutions such as the economy that leave people without jobs or other adequate means for survival. If this is the case, then solutions should not be directed at individual inadequacies. Educational, economic, and social institutions should be made more responsive to those who are disadvantaged.

Others view poverty as a form of exploitation by the ruling classes. The dominant classes maintain poverty in order to produce a source of cheap labor and to "use" the poor economically, socially, and politically. This definition magnifies class conflict and also suggests a restructuring of social systems to reduce poverty.

Several well-publicized books blame the worsened condition of the poor on social welfare policies. Their conservative or neoconservative authors believe that public assistance programs in particular have destroyed incentives to self-sufficiency and undermined the spirit of the poor, making welfare a more attractive alternative than low-paying jobs. Congress and the Clinton administration moved to "end welfare as we know it." George W. Bush had tried to move further in this direction by increasing work requirements for participants. But fluctuations in poverty rates that have occurred in recent years seem to be related to the state of the economy as much as they are to changes in the welfare system. The topics of poverty and dependency, their causes, and their solutions continue to compose one of the great debates of the American people.

NOTES

1. E. E. Schattschneider, *The Semi-Sovereign People* (New York: Holt, Rinehart, & Winston, 1961), p. 68.

2. James L. Sundquist, *Politics and Policy* (Washington, DC: Brookings Institution, 1968), pp. 111–112.

3. Patricia Ruggles, *Drawing the Line: Alternative Poverty Measures and Their Implications for Public Policy* (Washington, DC: Urban Institute Press, 1990), p. 36.

4. Dana Milbank, "Old Flaws Undermine New Poverty-Level Data," *Wall Street Journal,* October 5, 1995, pp. B1, 8.

5. U.S. Census Bureau, "Poverty Thresholds," retrieved February 21, 2004, from http://www.census.gov/hhes/poverty/threshld.html

6. Poverty figures for 2000 are based on U.S. Census Bureau, Current Population Reports, P60-222, *Poverty in the United States: 2002* (Washington, DC: U.S. Government Printing Office, 2003).

7. See U.S. Bureau of the Census, *Measuring the Effect of Benefits and Taxes on Income and Poverty: 1992,* Current Population Reports, Series P60-186RD (Washington, DC: U.S. Government Printing Office, 1993), Appendix F.

8. Bureau of Labor Statistics, "Consumer Expenditures in 2001," April 2003, retrieved February 21, 2004, from http://www.bls.gov/cex/home.htm# overview

9. Ruggles, *Drawing the Line,* see pp. xiii–xiv, 2, 167.

10. Cited in *ibid.,* p. xiii.

11. Lars Osberg, "Trends in Poverty: The UK in International Perspective: How Rates Mislead and Intensity Matters," Working Papers of the Institute for Social and Economic Research, Paper 2002-10 (Colchester, England: University of Essex, June 2002), retrieved March 5, 2004, from http://www.iser.essex.ac.uk/pubs/workpaps/pdf/2002-10.pdf

12. Contance F. Ciro and Robert T. Michael, Eds., *Measuring Poverty: A New Approach* (Washington, DC: National Academy Press, 1995).

13. As cited in *ibid.,* p. 386.

14. Joseph Dalaker and Mary Naifeh, *Poverty in the United States: 1997,* Bureau of the Census, Current Population Reports, Consumer Income P60-201 (Washington, DC: U.S. Government Printing Office, 1998), p. A-3.

15. Kathleen Short, U.S. Census Bureau, Current Population Reports, P60-216, *Experimental Poverty Measures: 1999* (Washington, DC: U.S. Government Printing Office, 2001), p. 1.

16. Committee on Ways and Means, *2003 Green Book*, Appendix H-Data on Poverty, Table H-11, posted February 11, 2004, retrieved February 21, 2004, from http://waysandmeans.house.gov/Documents.asp? section = 813

17. Committee on Ways and Means, U.S. House of Representatives, *Overview of Entitlement Programs: 1993 Green Book* (Washington, DC: U.S. Government Printing Office, 1993), p. 1317.

18. U.S. Bureau of the Census, *Estimates of Poverty Including the Value of Noncash Benefits: 1987,* Technical Paper 58 (Washington, DC: U.S. Government Printing Office, August 1988).

19. Short, *Experimental Poverty Measures: 1999.*

20. Committee on Ways and Means, *Overview of Entitlement Programs: 1993 Green Book.*

21. Short, *Experimental Poverty Measures: 1999,* p. 1.

22. Committee on Ways and Means, *2003 Green Book,* Appendix H—Data on Poverty, Table H-20, p. H-39.

23. *Ibid.,* Table H-19, p. H-36.

24. Bernadette D. Proctor and Joseph Dalaker, U.S. Census Bureau, Current Population Reports, P 60-222, *Poverty in the United States: 2002* (Washington, DC: U.S. Government Printing Office, 2003).

25. Information on the University of Michigan's Panel Study of Income Dynamics can be found at http://psidonline.isr.umich.edu

26. These studies are summarized in Ruggles, *Drawing the Line,* Chapter 5.

27. Mary Jo Bane and David T. Elwood, "Slipping into and out of Poverty: The Dynamics of Spells," *The Journal of Human Resources,* Vol. 21, No. 1, 1986, pp. 1–23, especially pp. 11–13. Also see Martha S. Hill, "Some Dynamic Aspects of Poverty," in M. S. Hill, D. H. Hill, and J. N. Morgan, Eds., *Five Thousand American Families: Patterns of Economic Progress,* Vol. 9 (Ann Arbor, MI: Institute for Social Research, University of Michigan Press, 1981); Mary Jo Bane, "Household Composition and Poverty," in Sheldon H. Danziger and Daniel H. Weinberg, Eds., *Fighting Poverty: What Works and What Doesn't* (Cambridge, MA: Harvard University Press, 1986), pp. 209–231 and p. 398, note 3; William Julius Wilson and Kathryn Neckerman, "Poverty and Family Structure: The Widen-ing Gap between Evidence and Public Policy Issues," in Danzinger and Weinberg, especially p. 241; William Julius Wilson, *The Truly Disadvantaged: The Inner City, the Underclass, and Public Policy* (Chicago: University of Chicago Press, 1987), pp. 9–10.

28. Ann Huff Stevens, "The Dynamics of Poverty Spells: Updating Bane and Ellwood," *American Economic Review,* Vol. 84, No. 2, 1994, pp. 34–37; see also T. J. Eller, "Who Stays Poor? Who Doesn't?," *Dynamics of Economic Well-Being: Poverty, 1992–1993,* Current Population Reports, Household Economic Studies, P70–55 (Washington, DC: U.S. Bureau of the Census, June 1996).

29. John Iceland, *Dynamics of Economic Well-Being, Poverty 1996–1999.* Current Population Reports, P70-91 (Washington, DC: U.S. Census Bureau, 2003).

30. This discussion relies on Signe-Mary McKernan and Caroline Rateliffe, "Transition Events in the Dynamics of Poverty" (Washington, DC: Urban Institute, 2002).

31. On the subject of relative deprivation, see Edward C. Banfield, *The Unheavenly City Revisited* (Boston: Little, Brown, 1974), especially chapter 6.

32. Victor R. Fuchs, "Redefining Poverty and Redistributing Income," *Public Interest,* No. 8, Summer 1967, p. 91.

33. Carmen Denavas-Walt, Robert W. Cleveland, and Bruce H. Webster, Jr., U.S. Bureau of the Census, *Income in the United States: 2002,* Current Population Reports, Consumer Income, P60-221 (Washington, DC: U.S. Government Printing Office, 2003), Table A-4.

34. Testimony of Greg Duncan Before the House Select Committee on Children, Youth and Families, February 1992, based on Greg J. Duncan, Timothy Smeeding, and Willard Rodgers, "W(h)ither the Middle Class: A Dynamic View?" University of Michigan, Survey Research Center, 1991, cited in Committee on Ways and Means, *1993 Green Book,* pp. 1447–1448; also see Greg J. Duncan, Timothy Smeeding, and Willard Rodgers, "Why the Middle Class Is Shrinking," December 1992, cited in Committee on Ways and Means, *1993 Green Book,* pp. 1448–1450.

35. Jared Bernstein, Lawrence Mishel, and Chauna Brocht, "Any Way You Cut It" (Washington, DC: Economic Policy Institute, 2000), retrieved March 6, 2002, from http://www.epinet.org/content. cfm/briefingpapers_inequality_inequality

36. John Balzar (Los Angeles Times), "The Demise of the Middle Class," *Austin American-Statesman,* May 25, 2002, p. A15.

37. Cited in Richard Hofstadter, *The American Political Tradition* (New York: Knopf, 1948), p. 42.

38. *Ibid.,* p. 45.

39. Edward C. Banfield, *The Unheavenly City* (Boston: Little, Brown, 1968); Banfield, *The Unheavenly City Revisited;* also see William A. Kiskanen, "Welfare and the Culture of Poverty," *Cato Journal,* Vol. 16, No. 1, 1996, pp. 1–15.

40. Nicolas Lemann, "The Origins of the Underclass," *Atlantic Monthly,* June 1986, pp. 31–55, and July 1986, pp. 54–68.

41. Herbert J. Gans, "The Uses of Poverty: The Poor Pay All," *Social Policy,* Vol. 2, No. 2, July–August 1971, pp. 20–24.

42. Proctor and Dalaker, *Poverty in the United States: 2002.*

43. Thomas H. Walz and Gary Askerooth, *The Upside Down Welfare State* (Minneapolis: Elwood Printing, 1973), p. 5.

44. Frances Fox Piven and Richard A. Cloward, *Regulating the Poor: The Functions of Public Welfare* (New York: Random House, 1971), quote from p. xiii.

45. Frances Fox Piven and Richard A. Cloward, *The New Class War* (New York: Pantheon Books, 1982); on the relationship between social welfare and labor force participation see also John Myles and Jill Quadagno, Eds., *States, Labor Markets, and the Future of Old-Age Policy* (Philadelphia: Temple University Press, 1991).

46. Frances Fox Piven and Richard A. Cloward, *The Breaking of the American Social Compact* (New York: The New Press, 1997); also see Frances Fox Piven and Richard A. Cloward, *Regulating the Poor: The Functions of Public Welfare,* updated ed. (New York: Vintage Books, 1993).

47. This paragraph relies on Michael Harrington, The New American Poverty (New York: Penguin Books, 1984).

48. For discussion of the term underclass, see Wilson, *The Truly Disadvantaged,* especially p. 7.

49. *Ibid.*

50. The remainder of this section relies on Wilson, *The Truly Disadvantaged,* and Lemann, "The Origins of the Underclass."

51. This paragraph relies on Michael Harrington, *The Other America: Poverty in the United States* (New York: Macmillan, 1962).

52. See Christopher Hewitt, "Estimating the Number of Homeless: Media Misrepresentation of an Urban Problem," *Journal of Urban Affairs,* Vol. 18, No. 3, 1996, pp. 431–447; Anna Kondratas, "Estimates and Public Policy: The Politics of Numbers," *Housing Policy Debate,* Vol. 2, Issue 3, 1991, pp. 631–647.

53. U.S. Department of Housing and Urban Development, Office of Policy Development and Research, *Report to the Secretary on the Homeless and Emergency Shelters* (Washington, DC: U.S. Department of Housing and Urban Development, 1984).

54. Mary Ellen Hombs and Mitch Snyder, *Homelessness in America: A Forced March to Nowhere* (Washington, DC: Community for Creative Non-Violence, 1983), p. xvi.

55. James D. Wright and Joel A. Devine, "Housing Dynamics of the Homeless: Implications for a Count," *American Journal of Orthopsychiatry,* Vol. 65, No. 3, 1995, pp. 330–329, especially p. 320.

56. Kim Hopper, "Definitional Quandaries and Other Hazards," *American Journal of Orthopsychiatry,* Vol. 65, No. 3, 1995, pp. 340–346, especially p. 340.

57. Robert C. Ellickson, "The Homeless Muddle," *The Public Interest,* No. 99, Spring 1990, pp. 45–60.

58. See James D. Wright, ed., *Evaluation Review,* Vol. 16, No. 4, August 1992, which is devoted to S-Night surveys; and Wright and Devine, "Housing Dynamics of the Homeless: Implications for a Count."

59. Rush Limbaugh, *The Way Things Ought to Be* (New York: Pocket Star Books, 1992).

60. Joel Blau, *The Visible Poor: Homelessness in the United States* (New York: Oxford University Press, 1992), p. 24.

61. Alliance Housing Council, *Housing and Homelessness* (Washington, DC: National Alliance to End Homelessness, 1988), also cited in Institute of Medicine, *Homelessness, Health, and Human Needs* (Washington, DC: National Academy Press, 1988), see pp. 171–172.

62. Martha R. Burt and Barbara E. Cohen, *America's Homeless: Numbers, Characteristics, and Programs That Serve Them* (Washington, DC: Urban Institute, 1989), chapter 2.

63. See Martha Burt, "Critical Factors in Counting the Homeless: An Invited Commentary," *American Journal of Orthopsychiatry,* Vol. 65, No. 3, 1995, pp. 334–339.

64. Martha K. Burt and Laudan Y. Aron, "America's Homeless II: Population and Services" (Washington, DC: Urban Institute, January 1, 2000), retrieved March 8, 2004, from http://www.urban.org/url. cfm?ID = 900344

65. Bruce Link, Jo Phelan, Michaeline Bresnahan, Ann Stueve, Robert Moore, and Ezra Susser, "Lifetime and Five-Year Prevalence of Homelessness in the United States: New Evidence on an Old Debate," *American Journal of Orthopsychiatry,* Vol. 65, No. 3, 1995, pp. 347–354.

66. Gordon Berlin and William McAllister, "Homelessness," in Henry J. Aaron and Charles L. Schultze, Eds., *Setting Domestic Priorities: What Can Government Do?* (Washington, DC: Brookings Institution, 1992), p. 64.

67. See, for example, *Outcasts on Main Street* (ADM) 92-1904 (Washington, DC: U.S. Department of Health and Human Services, Interagency Council on the Homeless, and Federal Task Force on Homelessness and Severe Mental Illness, 1992).

68. *A Report on the 1988 National Survey of Shelters for the Homeless* (Washington, DC: U.S. Department of Housing and Urban Development, 1989).

69. Blau, *The Visible Poor*, p. 29.

70. U.S. Conference of Mayors, "Hunger, Homelessness on the Rise in Major U.S. Cities," December 18, 2002, retrieved March 1, 2004, from http://usmayors.org/uscm/news/press_releases/documents/hunger_121802.asp

71. See also Blau, *The Visible Poor*, chapter 2; Berlin and McAllister, "Homelessness"; Committee on Ways and Means, *1993 Green Book*, pp. 1233–1238; Alice S. Baum and Donald W. Burnes, *A Nation in Denial: The Truth about Homelessness* (Boulder, CO: Westview Press, 1993), chapter 1; Martha R. Burt, *Over the Edge: The Growth of Homelessness in the 1980s* (New York: Russell Sage, 1992).

72. Baum and Burnes, *A Nation in Denial*.

73. See Blau, *The Visible Poor*; Paul Koegel, "Mental Illness among the Inner City Homeless," *Journal of the California Alliance for the Mentally Ill*, Vol. 1, No. 1, 1989, rev. 1992, pp. 16–17.

74. Koegel, "Mental Illness Among the Inner City Homeless"; Berlin and McAllister, "Homelessness," p. 67; Burt, *Over the Edge*, chapter 2.

75. Burt, *Over the Edge*, p. 226.

76. This description relies on Department of Housing and Urban Development, "Homeless Assistance Programs," retrieved March 6, 2004, from http://www.epinet.org/content.cfm/briefingpapers_inequality_inequality

77. This paragraph and the next rely on Martha R. Burt, John Hedderson, Janine Zweig, Mary Jo Ortiz, Laudan Aron-Turnham, and Sabrina M. Johnson, *Strategies for Reducing Chronic Street Homelessness: Final Report* (Washington, DC: U.S. Department of Housing and Urban Development, 2004).

78. Center on Budget and Policy Priorities, "In Search of Shelter: The Growing Shortage of Affordable Rental Housing" (Washington, DC, June 10, 1998), retrieved March 7, 2004, from http://www.cbpp.org/615hous.htm

79. "Why America's Communities Need a Department of Housing and Urban Development," Issue Brief #10, June 1995, Washington, DC: U.S. Department of Housing and Urban Development, retrieved from gopher://huduser.org:73/00/2/briefs/issbr10a.txt

80. U.S. Department of Housing and Urban Development, "Rental Housing Assistance: The Worsening Crisis" (Washington, DC, March 2000), retrieved March 7, 2004, from http://www.huduser.org:80/publications/affhsg/worstcase00/toc.html

81. National Low Income Housing Coalition, *Out of Reach 2003: America's Housing Wage Climbs* (Washington, DC: NLIHC, 2003), retrieved March 7, 2004, from http://www.nlihc.rog/oor2003/

82. Michael E. Stone, *Shelter Poverty: New Ideas on Affordable Housing* (Philadelphia: Temple University Press, 1993).

83. "Shelter Poverty: A Real-Life Way to Measure Inadequate Incomes," Utah Issues Information Program, Poverty Paper Series, retrieved December 30, 1997, from http://www.xmission.com/~ui/shelter.html

84. This paragraph relies on U.S. Department of Housing and Urban Development, "Public Housing Development," updated December 5, 2000, retrieved March 7, 2004, from http://www.hud.gov/progdesc/pdev.cfm

85. U.S. Department of Housing and Urban Development, "Housing Choice Voucher Fact Sheet," updated July 19, 2001, retrieved March 7, 2004, from http://www.hud.gov/offices/pih/programs/hcv/about/fact_sheet.cfm

86. Committee on Ways and Means, *2003 Green Book*, p. 15-9.

87. Office of Management and Budget, *Budget of the United States Government, Fiscal Year 2005*, "Department of Housing and Urban Development" (Washington, DC: Office of the President, 2004).

88. Much of this paragraph relies on Center on Budget and Policy Priorities, "Administration Seeks Deep Cuts in Housing Vouchers and Conversion of Program to a Block Grant," revised February 24, 2004, retrieved March 7, 2004, from http://www.cbpp.org/2-12-04hous.htm

89. Jonathan Chait, "HUD Sucker Proxy," *The New Republic*, June 23, 1997, p. 12; also see Special Report, "Issue: Housing," *Congressional Quarterly*, December 6, 1997, pp. 3017–3018.

90. Neal Peirce, "Community Reinvestment Act: Victory for Smart Regulation," *Austin American-Statesman*, July 8, 1996, p. A7.

91. Committee on Ways and Means, *1996 Green Book*, pp. 915, 917; Committee on Ways and Means, *1998 Green Book*, pp. 989, 991–992.

92. U.S. Census Bureau, Press Release, "Housing Vacancies and Homeownership, Fourth Quarter 2003," Table 7, retrieved March 7, 2004, from http://www.census.gov/hhes/www/hvs.html; see also Frank Nothaft, "Homeownership Rate Now Approaching 70 Percent," July 7, 2003, retrieved March 7, 2004, from

http://www.freddiemac.com/news/finance/commentary/070703_homeown_rate.htm

93. This paragraph relies on Asena Caner and Edward N. Wolff, *Asset Poverty in the United States: Its Persistence in an Expansionary Economy*, Public Policy Brief No. 76 (Annandale-on-Hudson, NY: Levy Economics Institute of Bard College, 2004).

94. Jeffery L. Katz, "Rooms for Improvement: Can Cisneros Fix HUD?" *Congressional Quarterly*, April 10, 1993, pp. 914–920.

95. Stephen Koff (Newhouse News Service), "Billions Intended for Poor Go Unspent," *Austin American-Statesman*, November 11, 1999, pp. A1, A13; "HUD Needs to Get Own House in Order," *Austin American-Statesman*, November 15, 1999, p. A10.

96. Chait, "HUD Sucker Proxy," pp. 11–12.

97. See James Gwartney and Thomas S. McCaleb, "Have Antipoverty Programs Increased Poverty?" (Tallahassee, FL: Florida State University, 1986).

97. George Gilder, *Wealth and Poverty* (New York: Bantam Books, 1981), p. ix.

99. *Ibid.*, p. 13.

100. Charles Murray, *Losing Ground: American Social Policy, 1950–1980* (New York: Basic Books, 1984).

101. Robert Kuttner, "Declaring War on the War on Poverty," *Washington Post*, November 25, 1984, pp. 4, 11; see also Daniel Patrick Moynihan, "Family and Nation," Godkin Lectures, Harvard University, April 8–9, 1985.

102. See, for example, the critique of the Phyllis and Harold story and the references to other works challenging Murray in Theodore R. Marmor, Jerry Z. Mashaw, and Philip L. Harvey, *America's Misunderstood Welfare State: Persistent Myths, Enduring Realities*

(New York: Basic Books, 1990), especially pp. 104–114; quote is from p. 105; also see Rino Patti, Mimi Abramovitz, Steve Burghardt, Michael Fabricant, Martha Haffery, Elizabeth Dane, and Rose Starr, *Gaining Perspective on Losing Ground* (New York: Lois and Samuel Silberman Fund, 1987).

103. Michael Tanner, *The End of Welfare* (Washington, DC: Cato Institute, 1996), quote from p. 148.

104. Marvin Olasky, *The Tragedy of American Compassion* (Washington, DC: Regnery Gateway, 1992); Marvin Olasky, *Renewing American Compassion* (New York: Free Press, 1996); Marvin Olasky, *Compassionate Conservatism: What It Is, What It Does, and How It Can Transform America* (New York: Free Press, 2000); see also Myron Magnet, *The Dreams and the Nightmare: The Sixties' Legacy to the Underclass* (San Francisco: Encounter Books, 2000, reprint).

105. Olasky, *Renewing American Compassion*, p. 152.

106. "Assertion that Charities Can Go It Alone Is Untested and Unreasonable," Twentieth Century Fund report, January 12, 1998, retrieved from http://www.epn.org/tcf/julrel.html.

107. See Lawrence M. Mead's books: *Beyond Entitlement* (New York: Free Press, 1986); *The New Politics of Poverty* (New York: Basic Books, 1992); *The New Paternalism* (Washington, DC: Brookings, 1997).

108. Quotes in this paragraph rely on Mead, *The New Politics of Poverty*.

109. *Ibid.*, p. 134.

110. Lawrence M. Mead, "Conflicting Worlds of Welfare Reform," *First Things*, August/September 1991, pp. 15–17, retrieved from http://www.firstthings.com/ftissues/ft9708/mead.html

CHAPTER

*Preventing Poverty:
The Social Insurance
Programs*

PREVENTING POVERTY THROUGH COMPULSORY SAVINGS

*O*ne way to address poverty is to have people insure themselves against its occurrence, much as they insure themselves in the event of death, accident, or property loss. In the social welfare arena, this preventive strategy is called **social insurance.** Social insurance programs compel individuals or their employers to purchase insurance against the possibility of their own indigency, which might result from forces over which they have no control—loss of job, death of a family breadwinner, advanced age, or disability. As statesman Thomas Paine said in 1795, "Were a workman to receive an increase in wages daily he would not save it against old age. . . . Make, then, society the treasurer to guard it for him in a common fund."[1] Social insurance is based on many of the same principles as private insurance—the sharing of risks and the setting aside of money for a "rainy day." Workers and employers pay "premiums" in the form of Social Security taxes, which are recorded by the government under each worker's name and Social Security number. When age, death, disability, or unemployment prevents workers from continuing on the job, they or their dependents are paid from Social Security trust funds. Social insurance offers one relatively simple and rational approach for addressing poverty.

Social insurance differs from another government approach for addressing poverty called **public assistance.** If (1) the beneficiaries of a government program are required to make contributions to it before claiming any of its benefits (or if employers must pay into the program on behalf of their workers) and if (2) the benefits are paid out as legal entitlements regardless of the beneficiaries' personal wealth, then the program is called social insurance. However, if (1) the program is financed out of general tax revenues and if (2) the recipients are required to show that they are poor in order to claim benefits, then the program is called public assistance.

Although the history of helping people in need in the United States began with public assistance approaches, social insurance programs have become the more viable political strategy.[2] Today most Americans have come to believe that social insurance is merely enforced savings, and they hope to get their money back during retirement. Americans feel entitled to receive Social Security because they have paid taxes into a Social Security trust fund. On the other hand, public assistance programs are paid out of the general tax revenue fund. There is no "public assistance" trust fund. Though most of us pay taxes into the general tax fund during our lifetimes, this is not a requirement for receiving public assistance benefits. Despite any taxes that the poor may have paid, there is much less perception that they have the right to public assistance. Moreover, while the vast majority of Americans expect to live to see some Social Security benefits returned to them, they do not expect to become public assistance recipients.

The concept of government sponsored social insurance originally appealed to conservatives because it represented a form of thrift. Social insurance programs also appeal to liberals because these programs can be used to redistribute income from current workers to former workers in economic need—those who are aged, sick, disabled, or unemployed—or their dependents.

The Social Security Act

Government old-age insurance, the first social insurance program, was introduced in Germany in 1889 by the conservative regime of Chancellor Otto von Bismarck. The idea spread quickly and most European nations had old-age insurance pension programs before the beginning of World War I in 1914. In the United States, many railroads, utilities, and large manufacturers instituted private old-age pensions at the beginning of the twentieth century. The U.S. government began its own Federal Employees Retirement program in 1920. By 1931 seventeen states had adopted some form of compulsory old-age insurance for workers, although eligibility requirements were strict and payments were small.[3]

During the Great Depression, Francis E. Townsend, a California dentist, began a national crusade for very generous old-age pensions of $200 a month to be paid by the government from a national sales tax. The politically popular but very expensive "Townsend Plan" was perceived by government and business leaders as totally unfeasible, even radical, but the combination of economic depression and larger numbers of older people in the population and in the workforce helped to develop pressure for some type of old-age insurance.[4] Despite fears that social insurance would foreshadow a socialist state, during the presidential campaign of 1932, Franklin D. Roosevelt advocated a government insurance plan to protect the unemployed and the aged. This campaign promise and party platform plank actually became law—the Social Security Act (Public Law 74-271), signed by President Roosevelt on August 14, 1935.

One might attribute the Roosevelt administration's political success in gaining acceptance for the Social Security Act to several factors:

1. The weakening of ties among family members and the increasing inability of urban families to care for their aged members.

2. The economic insecurities generated by the Great Depression of the 1930s, including the increasing fear of impoverishment, even among the middle class.

3. Political movements of different ilks, from the Townsend Plan to socialism and communism, that threatened the established order.

Roosevelt's skills as a national leader should also be added to these factors. Social Security was presented to the Congress as a *conservative* program that would eventually eliminate the need for public assistance programs. For the first time, Americans would be compelled to protect themselves against poverty.

The Social Security Act of 1935 established the country's basic social welfare policy framework. Although Americans tend to think of Social Security mostly as retirement benefits, the original act contained social insurance, public assistance, social service, and public health programs. Today, the social insurance programs it includes are

♦ Federal old-age and survivors insurance (OASI)

♦ Federal disability insurance (DI)

♦ Federal health insurance (HI) for older people, called Medicare

♦ Unemployment insurance (also called unemployment compensation) programs in the states

The public assistance programs it includes are

♦ Federal aid to people who are aged, blind, or disabled under the Supplementary Security Income (SSI) program

♦ Federal–state aid to families with dependent children under the Temporary Assistance for Needy Families program (formerly Aid to Families with Dependent Children)

♦ Federal–state medical assistance for the poor, called Medicaid

The social service programs it includes are

♦ Child welfare

♦ Maternal and child health

♦ Additional social services to a number of vulnerable groups

This chapter examines most of the social insurance programs—the old-age, survivors, and disability insurance programs (collectively known as OASDI or OASDHI when Medicare is included), and unemployment insurance. The state-operated workers' compensation programs are also discussed. Subsequent chapters examine the public assistance programs, the health care programs, and social services.

Social Security: The World's Largest Social Welfare Program

Originally, the Social Security program covered only retirement benefits for workers in about half of the labor force; many farm and domestic workers and self-employed people were exempted, as were state and local government employees. This old-age insurance program was financed by employer–employee contributions of 1 percent each on a wage base of $3,000, or a maximum contribution by workers of $30 per year plus a $30 contribution by their employers. It paid for retirement benefits at age 65 at a rate of about $22 per month for a single worker, or $36 per month for a married couple. Benefits were paid as a matter of right, regardless of income, as long as a worker was retired. Thus retired workers were spared the humiliation often associated with public charity. Actually, no taxes were collected until 1937, and no benefits were paid until 1940, to allow the trust fund to accumulate reserves.

Since 1935 there have been scores of amendments to this social insurance legislation. The first major amendments came in 1939 when Congress made dependents and survivors of retired workers and survivors of insured workers who died before age 65 eligible for benefits. In the early 1950s, farmers, domestic workers, and self-employed people were added to the program, bringing the total number of covered workers to over 90 percent of the labor force. In 1954 the "earnings test" for retired workers was liberalized so that those engaged in some employment could earn more without losing Social Security benefits. In 1956 women in the labor force were permitted to retire at age 62 rather than 65 on the condition that they accept 80 percent of the monthly benefit otherwise available at 65; men were allowed to retire at age 62 beginning in 1961. In 1956 disability insurance was approved for totally and permanently disabled workers aged 50 and older; benefits for their dependents were added in 1958. Disabled workers younger than age 50 were added to the disability program in 1960. In 1965 Medicare was adopted, and in 1972 Congress enacted COLAs—automatic cost-of-living adjustments (measured by rises in the Consumer Price Index)—to help Social Security payments keep pace with inflation.

Social Security soon became the nation's largest social welfare program. Today, the U.S. Social Security system may rightfully be called the world's largest government program. By 2003, 153 million workers (about 96 percent of the workforce) plus their employers paid Social Security taxes, and nearly 47 million people collected benefits totaling more than $40 billion per month.[5] The public assistance programs pale in comparison to the scope and effects of Social Security.

OASDHI is a completely federal program administered by the Social Security Administration (formerly part of the Department of Health and Human Services and now an independent agency). But it has an important effect on federal, state, and local public assistance programs: by compelling people to insure themselves against the possibility of their own poverty, Social Security has reduced the problems that governments might otherwise face.

The growth of OASDHI in numbers of recipients (beneficiaries), average monthly benefits, and as a percentage of the federal government's total budget is shown in Table 4.1. Social Security taxes are the second largest source of income for the federal government; these tax revenues are exceeded only by the federal personal income tax. The Social Security tax is marked on the paycheck stubs of many workers with the abbreviation FICA, which stands for the Federal Insurance Contributions Act. Self-employed people pay under SECA, the Self-Employment Contributions Act. By 2004, the *combined* maximum annual Social Security contribution for the employee and the employer had grown to nearly $13,500.[6]

TABLE 4.1

Social Security Growth

	1950	1960	1970	1980	1990	2000	2003
Number of OASDI beneficiaries (in millions)	3.5	14.8	26.2	35.6	39.6	45.3	47.0
Annual expenditures for OASDI (in billions)	$1.0	$11.8	$33.1	$123.6	$253.1	$415.1	$479.1
Average monthly benefit for retired workers (in dollars)	$44	$74	$118	$363	$579	$869	$941
Social insurance taxes (OASDHI) as a percentage of all federal revenue	11.0	15.9	23.0	30.5	36.8	32.2	40.0
Medicare expenditures (in billions of dollars)[a]	—	—	$7.1	$35.0	$109.7	$219.0	$277.9

Sources: Committee on Ways and Means, U.S. House of Representatives, *Overview of Entitlement Programs: 1993 Green Book* (Washington, DC: U.S. Government Printing Office, 1993); Committee on Ways and Means, U.S. House of Representatives, *2003 Green Book: Social Security: The Old Age, Survivors, and Disability Insurance* (OASDI) programs (Washington, DC, January 9, 2004) p. I-4, retrieved from http://waysandmeans.house.gov/Documents.asp?section = 813; Social Security Administration (SSA), *Social Security Accountability Report for Fiscal Year 1997*, November 21, 1997, http://www.ssa.gov; SSA's FY 2003 Performance and Accountability Report (Washington, DC: SSA, 2003), retrieved from http://www.ssa.gov/finance/; Executive Office of the President, *Historical Tables 2.2 and 16.1, Budget of the United States Government, Fiscal Year 2005* (Washington, DC), retrieved from http://www.whitehouse.gov/omb/budget/fy2005/pdf/hist.pdf; Social Security Administration, *Monthly Statistical Snapshot* (Washington, DC: SSA, December 2003), retrieved from http://www.ssa.gov/policy/docs/quickfacts/stat_snapshot/index.html; Social Security Online, *Beneficiary Data,* retrieved from http://www.ssa.gov/OACT/ProgData/benefits.html and *Trust Fund Data,* retrieved from www.ssa.gov/OACT/STATS/table4a3.html

[a]Program began in 1965.

Social Security is considered a regressive tax, because it takes a larger share of the income of middle and lower-income workers than of the affluent. That is because

1. OASDHI taxes are levied only against wages and not against other types of income such as dividends, interest, and rents, which are more frequently sources of income for wealthier Americans.

2. OASDI taxes are levied on a fixed amount of earnings; wages in excess of that amount are not subjected to these taxes.

3. Unlike the federal personal income tax, Social Security taxes make no allowance for situations such as number of dependents or high medical expenses.

Social Security taxes were not a concern when they amounted to very little, but what began as a very modest "insurance premium" is now a major expense for both employers and employees. Today, the size of OASDHI alone—approximately 40 percent of the federal government's income and about one-third of its expenditures—has an important impact on the overall equity of the country's revenue structure. However, the regressive nature of the Social Security tax on current workers is offset at retirement, because benefits are figured more generously for those who earned less, and because retirees in higher income brackets must now pay taxes on part of their Social Security benefits.

Even the Best-Laid Plans

The original strategy of the Social Security Act of 1935 was to create a trust fund with a reserve that would be built from the insurance premiums (Social Security taxes) of working people. This trust fund reserve would earn interest, and both the interest and principal would be used in later years to pay benefits. Benefits for insured people would be in proportion to their contributions. General tax revenues would not be used at all. The Social Security system was intended to resemble private, self-financing insurance. But it did not turn out that way.

Roosevelt's planners quickly realized that building the reserve was taking money from the depressed economy and slowing recovery. The plan to build a large, self-financing reserve was soon abandoned in 1939 under political pressure to pump more money into the economy. And over the years, Congress encountered pressure to increase benefit levels to retirees, even though these retirees never paid enough money into their accounts to cover these benefits. Moreover, benefits under Social Security were no longer proportionate to contributions; they were figured more generously for those whose wages were low than for those whose wages were high. Political pressure to raise benefits while keeping taxes relatively low reduced the trust fund reserve to a minor role in Social Security financing. Social Security taxes were lumped together with all other tax revenue in the federal government's budget. The accounts of workers were simply IOUs—promises to pay—not money specifically set aside in separate accounts for each contributor. Automatic COLAs, adopted in 1972 legislation and effective since 1975, proved to be another very popular feature of the program because of their hedge against inflation, but Social Security ran into trouble. It could no longer cover these regular increases, especially in times of high inflation.

Social Security mushroomed into such a large program because Americans came to view these ever increasing benefits as a right. As the number of workers grew and their wages increased during the affluence of the 1950s and 1960s, no one worried much about the program. But during the 1970s and 1980s, the growth in Social Security rolls and payments was accompanied by economic recession.[7] Income from the "pay-as-you-go" Social Security system (about $200 billion per year) matched the outgo in Social Security benefits. The program was on the verge of bankruptcy.

As the problems of Social Security intensified, it became clear that something would have to be done to fix the ailing retirement system. In 1977, for the first time in the program's history, benefits were cut, and taxes were increased again. In 1981, the Reagan administration took measures to reduce program spending. As a result, the floor on the benefit minimums was removed; benefits for children of workers (deceased, retired, or disabled) who were ages 18–22 were eliminated; and a national commission chaired by Alan Greenspan (chairman of the Federal Reserve Board since 1987) was established to study the problems of the Social Security system to make recommendations for reform.

The commission's work was called "a remarkable achievement in political statesmanship," as were Congress's actions. The report was issued with bipartisan support, and in 1983 Congress enacted many of the commission's recommendations. "The bill moved through both houses of Congress in just over ten weeks."[8] Among the most important reforms was a delay of the popular cost-of-living adjustment (COLA) and a "stabilizer" that was placed on future COLAs. COLAs are now provided if there is at least a 0.1 percent increase in the Consumer Price Index for Urban Wage Earners and Clerical Workers (CPI-W); however, if Social Security trust funds fall below certain levels, benefits are indexed according to the CPI-W or the average increase in wages, whichever is lower. Since inflation has varied considerably over the years, so have COLAs. For example, the COLA was 14.3 percent in 1980, 5.4 percent in 1990, and 2.1 percent in 2003.[9]

The 1983 amendments also raised the age at which full retirement benefits can be received. Although about 79 percent of all retirees now opt to retire before reaching their full retirement age (FRA), formerly age 65,[10] the age that one may collect full retirement benefits is gradually increasing to age 67. This change began in 2003 and affects those born in 1938 (who were 65 in 2003) and later. Those born in 1938 had to be 65 years and 2 months old to receive full benefits, and the regular retirement age is continuing to rise in 2-month increments until the new regular retirement age reaches a full 67 years in 2027. (Those born in 1960 will be 67 in 2027 and among the first Social Security beneficiaries required to be 67 years old before receiving full retirement benefits). Beneficiaries can still retire earlier, at age 62, but the amount of benefits is gradually falling from 80 percent to 70 percent of full retirement benefits by 2027.

Another measure enacted in 1983 to make Social Security more fiscally viable was to reduce so-called windfall benefits. This means that those who receive Social Security and other government pensions (such as military retirement), but who paid into the Social Security system for only a short time, may receive lower Social Security benefits under a new formula. Better news is that by 2008 those who choose to retire after the full retirement age will receive 5 percent more in benefits than they would today. Medicare benefits will still be available at age 65.

More workers were also included under the Social Security system as a result of the 1983 amendments. All new federal employees must participate as well as all members of Congress, the president and the vice president, federal judges, and all employees of nonprofit organizations, among others. Many of these people were formerly included under other systems. For example, federal employees were covered under a separate, more generous retirement system.

The commission made a few changes that primarily benefitted women. For example, divorced spouses may begin collecting benefits at age 62 if their former spouses are eligible even if they have not yet claimed benefits, and payments to disabled widows and widowers aged 50 to 59 were increased. Other major gender inequities were not addressed and remain unresolved today (see Chapter 11 for a further discussion).

Under former provisions, Social Security benefits were not counted as taxable income, but in 1983, and again in 1993 as part of the Clinton administration's deficit reduction plan, this change was instituted. Today, half of Social Security benefits are subject to regular income tax rates if combined income (taxable income plus nontaxable interest) plus one-half of Social Security benefits is between $25,000 and $34,000 for a single person and $32,000 to $44,000 for a couple. Singles whose combined income plus one-half of their Social Security benefits exceeds $34,000 and couples exceeding $44,000 are subject to regular income taxes on 85 percent of their benefits. Approximately 39 percent of retirees paid some income tax on their Social Security benefits in 2003.[11] It is really quite remarkable that changes such as this are no longer considered the "third rail" of American politics (touch it and one's political career is over). These taxes are returned to the Social Security trust funds. In the scheme of things, these taxes are fairly inconsequential to the overall Social Security system. In 2003, they amounted to only about 3 percent of OASDI benefits paid.

In 1983 and again in 1996 amendments increased the amount retirees could earn from employment without jeopardizing their Social Security benefits; then, in 2000, the Senior Citizens' Freedom to Work Act eliminated the Social Security retirement earnings test for beneficiaries after they attain full retirement age (FRA). The earnings of early retirees that exceed $11,520 are "taxed" by 50 percent (one dollar is withheld from benefits for every two dollars earned) until the retiree attains the FRA. During the year the FRA is attained, one dollar of benefits is withheld for every three dollars earned above the limit of $30,720. In the calendar year after the FRA is attained, no penalty is applied—retirees are free to earn as much income as they like or are able. This is a welcomed change for older Americans who need to or want to work. It also puts more money into the economy since taxes are paid on these wages.

Especially important among the 1983 amendments were increases in the Social Security tax rate and taxable wage base. The tax rate was increased gradually until it reached 7.65 percent for both employers and employees in 1990 (a combined rate of

15.3 percent). The 7.65 percent Social Security tax funds Social Security's three programs: 5.35 percent funds retirement and survivors' benefits under OASI; .85 percent funds benefits for disabled workers under DI; and 1.45 percent funds healthcare for the elderly under Medicare. In 2003, for every dollar of taxes paid to Social Security, 70 cents went to the OASI trust fund, 11 cents went to the DI trust fund, and 19 cents went to the Medicare trust fund.[12] In 1990 the taxable wage base was $51,300, but this was insufficient to finance Medicare, so in 1991 the taxable wage base for the HI part of the program was increased to $125,000. The wage base for HI was increased further in 1992 and 1993, and as of 1994 the HI tax is applied to all earnings. This change to the HI wage base supports the contentions of those who believe that Social Security taxes should be less regressive. Formulas are used to keep the OASDI taxable wage base in line with inflation. In 2004 the taxable wage base for OASDI was $87,900. This figure increases each year as inflation rises. Illustration 4.1 describes how one qualifies for Social Security benefits and how benefits are determined.

The 1983 reforms did a good job of putting Social Security on more stable footing.[13] Now, more than 20 years since the passage of the 1983 amendments, Social Security is taking in much more than it is paying out. For instance, in 2002, the OASDI trust funds paid out $454 billion and took in $627 billion, and had assets of $1.4 trillion,[14] while the HI trust fund took in $171 billion and paid out $141.7 billion (Medicare is also financed with general revenues).[15] However, this seemingly rosy financial picture of today belies the major financial difficulties facing the trust funds in the not too distant future as the "baby boomers" retire. Each year a board known as the Social Security Trustees (the Secretary of the Treasury, the Secretary of Labor, the Secretary of Health and Human Services, and two members appointed by the President with Senate confirmation to represent the public) determines the health of the trust funds by using optimistic, moderate, and pessimistic assumptions about the country's economic situation. This forecasting is always risky because not even economists can predict with certainty what will happen in the future, but these are the best "guesstimates" we have to help in planning rationally for the future.

In 2003 the Social Security trustees provided the following information based on moderate assumptions.[16] In the short run (the next 10 to 15 years), the OASI, DI, and HI trust funds are adequately funded to pay beneficiaries. A trust fund is adequate if the amount of money in the fund at the beginning of the year is sufficient to cover the benefits owed for the entire year. For example, at the end of 2001, the OASI trust fund had a balance of approximately $1.1 trillion and owed approximately $394 billion in benefits for the entire year of 2002. In other words, it had 2.8 times the amount needed to cover benefits in 2002. The DI trust fund reserves were 2.1 times the amount needed to cover benefits. The HI trust fund reserves were significantly lower, accounting for only 1.4 times its 2002 obligations.

In the long run, the health of the three Social Security trust funds is somewhat gloomy. The number of retired workers is expected to grow rapidly from 2010 to 2030, when the baby boomer generation (those born from 1946 to 1964) will be retiring, putting an enormous strain on the Social Security system. The strain will also occur because today's low fertility rates are expected to continue in the future, producing

ILLUSTRATION 4.1

Social Security—Who Qualifies, and How Much Do Beneficiaries Receive?

Approximately 96 percent of workers are now paying into the Social Security system. Employees and employers continue to pay equal amounts toward the employee's OASDHI insurance, and on retirement, workers receive benefits if they have enough *credits* (formerly called *quarters*) to qualify. For example, those born in 1929 or later need forty credits (generally equivalent to ten years of work). In 2003, workers accrued one credit if they earned $890 regardless of how much or how long they worked during the year. The maximum number of credits that can be earned in one year is four (equal to $3,560 in 2003). The amount needed to earn each credit rises gradually each year. At retirement, most workers have far more than the number of credits needed to qualify.

Once it is determined that the worker is qualified to receive Social Security benefits, his or her primary insurance amount (PIA) is calculated. This is the amount that retirees receive if they wait until the full retirement age (currently age 65 years and 4 months) to collect benefits. The formula is rather complicated, but it is based on the average amount earned during most of the individual's working years. Workers may retire as early as age 62, but benefits are reduced and calculated as a percent of the PIA. For a person who had *average* earnings, Social Security replaces about 42 percent of earnings. Replacement rates are higher for low-income earners and lower for high-income earners. In any case, payments to retirees are relatively modest—an average of about $941 a month in 2003; many retirees receive less, though some receive the maximum—now about $1,721 a month.

Insured workers may also be eligible for benefits if they become physically or mentally disabled prior to retirement. The disability must prevent work for at least one year or be expected to result in death. The average monthly payment to disabled workers in 2003 was about $937.

Although there are many complex rules, benefits (calculated as a percentage of the worker's PIA) are often also payable to the dependents of retired and disabled workers and to the survivors of deceased workers. The terms *survivors* and *dependents* refer to spouses and minor children, disabled adult children, and occasionally parents of covered workers. Survivors and dependents must meet certain qualifications, such as age requirements and definitions of disability. For example, a woman aged 62 or older who never worked in covered employment, or who worked but earned less than her spouse, is generally entitled to receive an amount that is 50 percent of her retired spouse's benefits. Widows or widowers may receive benefits, generally beginning at age 60 or at age 50 if they are disabled. Widows or widowers caring for children under age 16 can receive benefits at any age, and their children are also entitled to benefits. A lump sum benefit of $255 is also payable on the death of an insured worker to an eligible child or spouse.

Some additional types of benefits are also available. For example, a *special minimum*

continued

ILLUSTRATION 4.1 *(continued)*

benefit may be paid to people who had many years of covered employment but earned low wages. And virtually *all* people 65 years of age and over, regardless of whether they have ever paid into Social Security, are allowed to participate in Medicare.

Sources: Most of this discussion relies on Committee on Ways and Means, U.S. House of Representatives, 2003, *Green Book, Section 1, Social Security: The Old Age, Survivors, and Disability Insurance Programs*, retrieved from http://waysandmeans.house.gov/Documents.asp?section = 813; Social Security Administration, *Social Security Online: Lump Sum Death Benefit*, retrieved from http://www.ssa.gov/survivorplan/onyourown7.htm, and *Beneficiary Data*, available at http://www.ssa.gov/cgi-bin/awards.cgi

---

an insufficient number of workers to pay into the system. As soon as 2008, the DI trust fund is projected to spend more than it will collect in taxes. The same is projected for HI in 2013 and OASI in 2018. Interest earned on trust fund reserves will help keep the funds solvent for a few more years, but in 2018 both the DI and HI trust funds will begin paying out more in benefits than they will take in in taxes and interest combined. The same fate is slated for OASI in 2030. If nothing is done, by 2026, the HI trust fund will be exhausted—it will not have enough to pay the benefits due in that year. The DI trust fund will be exhausted in 2028, and OASI in 2044 (for critical dates for the OASDHI trust funds, see Table 4.2). In the years that the funds are projected

---

TABLE 4.2

Critical Dates for the OASDHI Trust Funds[a]

	OASI	DI	OASDI (combined)	HI
Year benefit payments exceed income (excluding interest)	2018	2008	2018	2013
Year benefit payments exceed income (including interest)	2030	2018	2028	2018
Year fund is exhausted	2044	2028	2042	2026

Sources: 2003 Annual Report of the Board of Trustees of the Federal Old-Age and Survivors Insurance and the Federal Disability Insurance Trust Fund, pp. 2–10; Committee on Ways and Means, U.S. House of Representatives, *2003 Green Book*, p. I-60; Social Security Administration, Performance and Accountability Report Fiscal Year 2003, retrieved from http://www.ssa.gov/finance/; and Social Security Administration, A Summary of the 2003 Annual Reports: Social Security and Medicare Boards of Trustees, retrieved from http://www.ssa.gov/OACT/TRSUM/trsummary.html

[a]These figures are based on current law and current assumptions.

to be exhausted, the HI and OASDI funds will be able to pay only 73 percent of the benefits owed, and by 2077 these percentages will drop to 30 percent and 65 percent, respectively. The HI fund is in the worse shape because healthcare costs are projected to rise much faster than wages.

While many of these dates seem like a long way off, no one wants to see the Social Security trust funds depleted. The funds need to be in good actuarial balance (the difference between annual income and outgo) for the country to breathe easy. Some action will be taken, and Americans must consider in advance how to ensure the health of these funds. The following discussion considers how the country might go about ensuring the security of retirees and former workers with disabilities as well as their dependents and survivors in the years ahead.

Achieving the Goals of Social Security: Adequacy and Equity

Participation in Social Security is a different experience for younger generations than for older ones. Current workers realize that they are paying a substantial tax to participate. Many Americans, young and old, support the concept of Social Security,[17] but confidence in the program has waned.[18] The Social Security Advisory Board reports that in a 2001 survey only 34 percent of respondents were "very or somewhat confident" of the program's future viability.[19] Among those aged 55 and older, 58 percent expressed such confidence compared to only 22 percent in the 25-to-34 age group. Social Security officials are undoubtedly tired of hearing that young people are more likely to believe in UFOs than think they will collect Social Security.[20]

The current system might not be viewed so pessimistically if (1) today's workers and employers did not view the Social Security tax as overly burdensome (lower-income workers today pay more Social Security taxes than income taxes) and (2) the number of aged people supported by the working population were not increasing so fast. These factors give pause to many younger people who are paying in but unsure of what they might get in return. The fact is that Social Security was never intended to support people fully during their "golden" years. The analogy of a three-legged stool has been used to describe what workers need to retire "comfortably": one leg is Social Security, the second is pension income, and the third is personal savings and investments. Many beneficiaries have at least a small income from sources other than Social Security, but most also receive Social Security retirement benefits that greatly exceed their original investment, and more if Medicare is considered. No wonder the program is so popular among the nearly 47 million current beneficiaries, most of them older people who comprise a very large bloc of the most active voters in the United States. With such strong support, it has been difficult to consider major changes in the program.

What about today's workers? Will they get their "money's worth" or a fair return on their investment? As Illustration 4.2 shows, a single worker born in 1910 who retired at the full retirement age of 65 in 1975 after earning average wages would have recouped the OASI taxes he or she paid plus interest before the age of 67. A single worker born in 1930 who retired in 1995 at the age of 65 after earning average wages would have recouped his or her taxes plus interest just before age 73, while a single

ILLUSTRATION 4.2

Will You Reap What You Sow?

The following examples show what individuals expected or might expect to get in Social Security retirement benefits if they retired at the full retirement age in 1975, 1995, and 2015. These hypothetical individuals would have been born in 1910, 1935, and 1949, respectively. It also shows how long it will take them to recoup their contributions and their contributions combined with those of their employer. Figures are also provided for those with a spouse of the same age who never worked outside the home, though in the future, more and more spouses will have their own Social Security record on which to draw. The figures are based only on the OASI portion of Social

Security taxes and benefits for three broad categories of wage earners: maximum wage earners who paid the full amount of Social Security taxes over their lifetimes, and those considered average and low wage earners. These illustrations do not consider those who need disability benefits earlier in life or those whose survivors draw or will draw on their benefits. In these examples, the base wage year is 1995. In 1995 the OASI tax was assessed on a maximum of $60,600 of earnings. Average wages were $23,900, and low wages were $10,800 for the year. These illustrations include the interest earned on the contributions made by the workers and their employees.

Workers who retired in 1975
The wage ceiling was $13,200; average, $8,000; low, $3,600.

		Single workers		Worker and spouse	
		Employee taxes only	Employee and employer taxes	Employee taxes only	Employee and employer taxes
Maximum	Your monthly benefit:		$316		$475
	Your lifetime contribution:	$7,670	$15,339	$7,670	$15,339
	Time to recover taxes paid:	2 yrs.	4 yrs., 1 mo.	1 yr., 5 mo.	2 yrs., 8 mo.
Average	Your monthly benefit:		$271		$406
	Your lifetime contribution:	$5,857	$11,714	$5,857	$11,714
	Time to recover taxes paid:	1 yr., 10 mo.	3 yrs., 7 mo.	1 yr., 3 mo.	2 yrs., 5 mo.
Low	Your monthly benefit:		$180		$270
	Your lifetime contribution:	$2,592	$5,183	$2,592	$5,183
	Time to recover taxes paid:	1 yr., 3 mo.	2 yrs., 7 mo.	10 mo.	1 yr., 9 mo.

continued

worker born in 1949 who retired at age 66 (remember, the full retirement age is rising slowly) in 2015 after earning average wages would not recoup his or her investment until just after age 78. If the taxes that these individuals' employers paid plus interest are added in, then payments for these workers are not recouped until ages 68 years and 7 months, 83 years and 6 months, and 95 years, respectively.

ILLUSTRATION 4.2 (continued)

Workers who retired in 1995
The wage ceiling was $60,600; average, $23,900; low, $10,800.

		Single workers		Worker and spouse	
		Employee taxes only	Employee and employer taxes	Employee taxes only	Employee and employer taxes
Maximum	Your monthly benefit:	$1,199			$1,798
	Your lifetime contribution:	$120,100	$240,472	$120,100	$240,472
	Time to recover taxes paid:	10 yrs., 6 mo.	25 yrs., 7 mo.	6 yrs., 7 mo.	15 yrs.
Average	Your monthly benefit:	$858			$1,287
	Your lifetime contribution:	$67,564	$135,245	$67,564	$135,245
	Time to recover taxes paid:	7 yrs., 11 mo.	18 yrs., 6 mo.	5 yrs.	11 yrs., 1 mo.
Low	Your monthly benefit:	$520			$780
	Your lifetime contribution:	$30,404	$60,860	$30,404	$60,860
	Time to recover taxes paid:	5 yrs., 8 mo.	12 yrs., 8 mo.	3 yrs., 7 mo.	7 yrs., 10 mo.

Workers who will retire in 2015
The projected wage ceiling will be $142,800; average, $59,600; low, $26,800.

		Single workers		Worker and spouse	
		Employee taxes only	Employee and employer taxes	Employee taxes only	Employee and employer taxes
Maximum	Your monthly benefit:	$3,283			$4,924
	Your lifetime contribution:	$557,648	$1,116,359	$557,648	$1,116,359
	Time to recover taxes paid:	17 yrs., 6 mo.	47 yrs., 1 mo.	10 yrs., 11 mo.	25 yrs., 4 mo.
Average	Your monthly benefit:	$2,074			$3,111
	Your lifetime contribution:	$258,824	$518,102	$258,824	$518,102
	Time to recover taxes paid:	12 yrs., 2 mo.	29 yrs.	7 yrs., 9 mo.	17 yrs., 1 mo.
Low	Your monthly benefit:	$1,254			$1,881
	Your lifetime contribution:	$116,471	$233,146	$116,471	$233,146
	Time to recover taxes paid:	8 yrs., 9 mo.	19 yrs., 7 mo.	5 yrs., 8 mo.	12 yrs., 1 mo.

Source: Social Security Administration as reported in Patterson Clark, "Will You Get Your Money's Worth?" *The Miami Herald*, August 13, 1995, p. 45. © The Miami Herald/Patterson Clark.

In the recent past, when there were unprecedented high returns on stock market investments and private funds were paying generous interest rates, some argued that people would fare much better by investing their money privately rather than in Social Security. However, with the precipitous drop in the stock market in 2000–2001, many retirees and near retirees lost significant amounts of their retirement nest egg almost overnight, effectively removing one leg of their three-legged stool. Some re-tirees returned to work to because their investment returns were insufficient to meet living expenses, and some nearing retirement postponed their retirement, perhaps in-definitely.[21] One advantage of the Social Security system is that, as long as the fund is solvent and benefits must be paid by law, workers are guaranteed a return on their investment, even if that return is small. Investing in the market is much more a game of chance—while some may win big, others will lose. Many believe that this is not the best way to plan for retirement. More stable investments are certificates of de-posit, individual retirement accounts (IRAs), and Treasury bills. While these invest-ment methods have a much smaller rate of return, they are more dependable than the stock market, and provide more security in retirement. Workers also need better pro-tection of private, employer-managed retirement funds. Poor management of these funds and recent company failures can mean the loss of monies that workers had banked on for their retirement. Governments' lax oversight of business has contributed to this problem.

Today, many workers take the three-legged stool analogy seriously and try to put away something more than Social Security for retirement, even though this takes an-other chunk out of current earnings. Others have such a tight cash flow situation that they find this very difficult. About half lack sufficient private pension income from their former jobs to secure their retirement.[22] Americans are notoriously poor savers (why save when you can shop?), and they grossly underestimate what they will need to retire. What if you are a young person today? What will it take for you to be able to retire? Illustration 4.3 provides a rough idea of what you might get in Social Secu-rity benefits and how much more you might need.

Despite its dilemmas, Social Security has been praised for achieving "a unique blend of adequacy and individual equity," two principles on which the program was founded.[23] It is adequate because it helps many older people escape poverty. It is eq-uitable because those who contributed more get higher benefits, while at the same time the benefits paid are proportionally more generous for those who contributed to the system at the same rate as others but earned smaller wages over their lifetimes.

Social Security is the major source of income for two-thirds of retired Americans. Thirty-four percent rely on it for at least 90 percent of their income and 32 percent more for at least half of their income. Social Security is highly effective at reducing poverty among older people and improving their quality of life. In 1959, the poverty rate among those aged 65 and older in the United States was 33.1 percent. By 1972, it was down to 18.6 percent, and in 2002 it was 10.4 percent—a 69 percent reduc-tion over a 43-year period. Experts agree that Social Security is the single most im-portant factor in lifting the elderly out of poverty.[24] The word "social" in Social Security is important because the program has important goals, such as redistribu-tion of income to those less fortunate, that differ from private pension and retire-ment programs.[25]

Since there is no individual asset-building account for each worker who contributes to Social Security, the program's adequacy and equity are directly affected by the **de-pendency ratio**—the ratio of beneficiaries to workers. In 1950 there were 16 workers

ILLUSTRATION 4.3

Will You Have Enough to Retire?

You might be thinking ahead to your own retirement and wondering how much money you will get from Social Security and how close it will come to allowing you to live comfortably during your "golden years." The Social Security Administration (SSA) helps people estimate their Social Security retirement benefits if they take early retirement at age 62, wait until the full retirement age, or retire later, at age 70. You can estimate your own Social Security retirement benefits at http://www.ssa.gov/planners/calculators.htm.*

Of course, these figures are only estimates, and the younger one is now, the riskier the calculations for retirement years are, but let's take an example. We used the SSA's quick calculation feature and entered wages of $30,000 for Joe, who was born in 1980 and was age 24 in 2004. Looking at Table A, the SSA must have assumed that Joe was in college in the years from 1998 through 2001, or otherwise earned little, and assigned Joe small amounts of earnings. It also must have assumed that Joe took his first regular job in 2002 and earned $26,485 that year. The SSA also estimated Joe's future earnings, which in 2042 at age 62 would be $134,775, based on 2004 earnings of $30,000. As Table B shows, if Joe retired early, at age 62 in 2042, his monthly Social Security benefit would be an estimated $3,569 (Joe may also have a spouse whose benefits are not shown here). If Joe waited until age 67 to retire in 2047, his benefit would be $5,943 a month, and if he retired at age 70 in 2050, his benefit would be $8,173.

This might sound like a substantial amount of money today, but even $3,569 a month today is just a modest salary of $42,828 annually. If Joe is still working in 2042, the SSA estimates that his earnings would be $134,775, or about 4.5 times what he is earning today. At age 62, Joe's annual Social Security benefit of $42,828 will not be nearly that much. Chances are Joe won't need as much to live in retirement as he did when he was working. He might have paid for his home by then, and he might not need as much money to cover clothing or automobile or other commuter expenses that he needed when he was working, but he is likely going to need substantially more than Social Security to cover his expenses at retirement. Let's say that at age 62 Joe can live on half of the wages he earned just before he retired. Half of $134,775 is $67,387, still considerably more than the $42,828 he can expect to get from Social Security. Perhaps Joe will have a retirement plan through his employer (or employers) that will help make up the difference. If Joe becomes disabled before retirement age, his benefits from Social Security will be lower because he will not have worked as long.

To make up the difference in any additional money needed, saving at a younger age is better than saving at an older age because interest (returns on your money) compound over time. For example, if Joe invested $5,000 at an interest rate of 5 percent, compounded once annually, in 10 years he would have $8,144 (1.63 times the original value, or a 63 percent increase); if he kept the same investment for 30 years, the total value would be $21,610 (4.32 times its original value, or a 332 percent

*The Social Security website has a vast array of user-friendly materials on its programs, including information on eligibility and benefits.

continued

ILLUSTRATION 4.3 *(continued)*

increase). An old saying goes something like, "life is short; enjoy it now," but Joe may live to a ripe old age, and he also wants to be able to enjoy life then.

Table A
Joe's Earnings

Past Earnings		Future Earnings (Selected Years)[a]	
Year	Taxable Amount	Year	Taxable Amount
1998	$2,655	2005	$31,269
1999	$2,859	2015	$46,990
2000	$3,077	2025	$69,970
2001	$3,213	2035	$104,681
2002	$26,485	2042	$134,775
2003	$28,216	2047	$156,818
2004	$30,000	2049	$166,569

[a]Adjusted for estimated national average wage growth (inflation).

Table B
Joe's Estimated Monthly Social Security Benefits[a]

Retirement Age	Monthly Benefit Amount
62 and 1 month in 2042	$3,569
67 in 2047	$5,943
70 in 2050	$8,173

[a]assumes future increases in prices or earnings

for each beneficiary. As the U.S. population grows increasingly older due to lower birthrates and longer life spans, the dependency ratio is plummeting. Today it takes about 3.3 workers to pay for every one person receiving benefits. If fertility rates remain as low as projected, the number of workers supporting each beneficiary will decline to 2.2 by 2030 as the last baby boomers reach full retirement age.[26] This is a heavy responsibility to place on younger generations of workers.

Social Security has been described as an "intergenerational compact" in which one generation of workers agrees to help current retirees with the promise of being helped themselves in retirement.[27] This was less of a problem when succeeding generations were much larger than preceding ones. A key to making everyone feel better about the program may be to promote "intergenerational equity," that is, to be as fair as possible to both the old and the young.[28] Largely as a result of OASDHI, the financial status of older people has improved over the years. Some argue that older Americans are now living a better life at the expense of the young. Others bristle at this thought, noting that many older people are not terribly well off. Others suggest that cuts in Social Security would not necessarily mean that more would be done to help younger people. The more salient issue to consider is why the country has been less successful at reducing poverty among younger Americans than it has among older citizens. (As we will see in Chapter 6, helping younger people is a different political issue than helping older Americans.)

The baby boomers made it possible for many younger individuals to enjoy a very nice standard of living as they were growing up, but will Generation X (and succeeding generations) see the boomers' retirement as a source of consternation? Economist Henry Aaron believes that the fuss about the boomers putting a strain on younger generations is ill founded.[29] After all, the boomers are now paying a substantial tax for their retirement while supporting retirees who are getting back more than their share. Everyone knows that the boomers will not be paid the same rate of return as older generations. The problem of too few workers in the future is not confined to the Social Security system. There will also be fewer workers to support all government activities.[30]

Another point of contention is whether the Social Security program is operating at unfair expense to members of certain racial and ethnic groups,[31] a growing concern as the country becomes more ethnically diverse. For example, since African Americans have shorter life spans than whites, they tend to collect benefits for shorter periods than whites. More members of ethnic minority groups are also employed at jobs requiring physical labor, which take their toll early. Social Security reforms, such as raising the retirement age, place them in an even more untenable position. Furthermore, on the average, these groups (particularly Hispanics) are younger than whites. This places an even greater burden on those who are generally poorer and who will reap fewer retirement benefits to support the growing retirement population that is disproportionately white and more affluent.

Others believe that the program is fair to African and Hispanic Americans. Granted, they pay a larger portion of their income in Social Security taxes, but they receive disability benefits and their dependents receive survivors' benefits more frequently than whites.[32] Although these factors may not be much consolation, the benefits paid to African and Hispanic Americans proportionate to their wages are also larger in all components of the program. More than one-quarter of today's Social Security recipients are disabled beneficiaries and their dependents and survivors of deceased workers. Without Social Security, many younger people of all racial and ethnic groups might be left with little or no income, since they may not have private disability insurance or large life insurance policies that would guarantee them or their families adequate income in the event of misfortune.

Still another crucial intergenerational aspect of the program is that it protects younger people from having to support their own elderly or disabled parents. Most workers would find it quite difficult to provide much financial support to their parents (although they may help in other ways), and older people do not want to burden their children with this responsibility. Kingson and his colleagues write that "When the program is examined from a long-term perspective, the benefits and costs . . . are shown to be distributed widely across the generations."[33]

Social Security is also a good investment because it is highly portable. It goes with the worker from job to job, a feature still not true of many other pension plans that are tied to a specific job and employer. Portability is important in a mobile society like ours where workers are likely to change jobs several times during their careers. And unlike virtually all current private pensions, Social Security adjusts for inflation.[34]

In addition to adequacy and equity, efficiency is a goal of the Social Security program. Slightly less than one cent per dollar collected is used to administer the program.[35]

Keeping the Wolves from the Door

Various methods have been used to monitor the Social Security system and make the reforms needed to ensure the continuance of the social insurance programs that have become an integral part of most Americans' lives. In 1969, the 13-member Advisory Council on Social Security was formed. The Advisory Council met every four years until 1994, and submitted its final report in 1996, offering three plans for averting the exhaustion of OASDHI trust funds. All three options involved some degree of privatization of Social Security through stock market investments.[36]

At the time that the Advisory Council issued its last report, the stock market was performing remarkably well, and many (either mistakenly or foolishly) thought this upward trend would just continue. In addition, other countries, such as Chile, had privatized their social security systems with seeming success. The council's report generated much discussion among economists, Congress, other policymaking bodies and individuals, and the public at large, but no action was taken. Since then, the economy and the stock market have undergone major changes. Stock market losses of billions of dollars put the brakes on privatizing Social Security. An incremental approach to policymaking may have saved the day, but some groups, the Libertarian CATO Institute strong among them, continue to contend that rich and poor alike would benefit from privatization.[37] According to the institute's Andrew Biggs, "even with the recent stock market decline, a worker investing only in stock would receive benefits 2.8 times higher than he would had he 'invested' the same amount of money in the current program."[38]

In 1996, the Advisory Council on Social Security was replaced by the Social Security Advisory Board. This bipartisan board was created by Congress and is appointed by the president and Congress. Much like the old Advisory Council, the Advisory Board is charged with monitoring the health of the OASDHI programs and trust funds and making recommendations to improve the system.[39]

Options for Reform

Fix the Current System

The most obvious suggestions for Social Security reform are those that have been made in the past: (1) raise payroll taxes, (2) increase the taxable wage base, (3) lower benefits, and (4) alter automatic cost-of-living adjustments. The sooner changes are made, the less dramatic and painful they will be.[40] The Social Security trustees concluded that, to bring the system into actuarial balance, an immediate 15 percent increase in revenues (payroll taxes, taxes on benefits, and interest on trust fund reserves) is necessary.

If the Social Security payroll tax were increased now by 1.92 percent, projections are that the OASDI trust fund shortfall would be resolved until 2075, when another tax rate increase would be needed. Waiting until 2020 to hike the tax would make the increase much larger because there would be fewer years in which to collect taxes in order to resolve the trust fund deficit. Increasing the tax rate puts more of the burden on lower- rather than higher-income workers.

The taxable wage base is already automatically adjusted every year based on changes in average U.S. earnings. To make a difference in the trust fund deficit, increases would have to be made over and above this annual adjustment, or the earning ceiling could be eliminated altogether as was done with the HI trust fund. Increasing the taxable wage base or taxing all wages puts more of the burden on higher-income workers.

Reducing Social Security benefits to retired workers is another consideration. To bring the OASDI trust fund into balance now would require an immediate 13 percent benefit reduction. An across-the-board benefit cut would hurt lower-income beneficiaries more because they generally have fewer alternative sources of retirement income. Another way to reduce benefits is to reduce the benefit formula. In 2003, the formula used to calculate benefits was 90 percent of the first $606 of average monthly earnings, 32 percent of the amount from $606 to $3,653 of earnings, and 15 percent of additional covered earnings. Each of these earning categories is referred to as a "bend" in the formula. This formula is applied to workers' 35 highest earning years. The graduated structure of the formula results in more favorable treatment of workers with lower earnings, remaining true to the program's goal of adequacy. There are three ways to reduce the benefit formula. The first way is to reduce the percentage of wages replaced at retirement. While benefits to all retirees would be reduced, lower-wage earners would still be treated more favorably. The Advisory Board reported that an immediate 5 percent reduction in wage replacement rates would eliminate one-third of the long-range financial deficits in the trust fund without affecting the equity structure of the formula. Another option is to increase the number of earning years used in calculating benefits, perhaps from 35 to 38 or 40. This would reduce workers' overall earning averages by capturing additional years where earnings were generally lower, thus producing lower benefit payments. A final approach to adjusting the benefit formula is to reduce the bend earning limits. Currently, these amounts are adjusted annually to account for earnings increases. While these adjustments could continue in the future, the base earning amounts could be reset to a lower amount. Benefit payments would again be lower because they would be calculated on smaller amounts of past earnings.

As noted earlier in this chapter, each year retirees see an increase in their benefit checks due to the automatic cost-of-living adjustments called COLAs. Some experts believe that the current method used to calculate the consumer price index (CPI) overstates the rate of inflation because it simply takes the same market basket of goods and recomputes prices rather than assuming that people will purchase cheaper goods or adjust spending in other ways when faced with higher prices.[41] The 1996 Advisory Council advised against adjusting COLAs downward because COLAs are so important for the neediest (and oldest) recipients.[42] However, the Social Security Advisory Board suggests that Congress and the president consider this option for bringing the trust funds into actuarial balance because COLAs have compounding effects. For example, for a worker retiring at age 65 today, a 1 percent reduction in COLAs would result in a 12 percent benefit reduction by the time the worker is age 75. By age 85 the worker's benefits will have been reduced by 20 percent, a savings for the Social Security program, but a substantial hit for America's neediest retirees.

All the approaches discussed thus far for securing Social Security are painful for individuals who need the benefits and for the country. These interventions would buy the system some time, but they only tinker around the edges of the problem. They would not provide a long-term fix for the pay-as-you-go system. Real reform will require a new program structure.

Create a New System

An often discussed alternative for making Social Security more structurally sound is to convert it to a prefunded system.[43] In the current pay-as-you-go system, one generation (current workers) pay taxes that are used to pay benefits for another (retired) generation. Since the retiring population is growing rapidly and the proportion of the working population is shrinking, the burden of supporting retirees is getting heavier and heavier. In a prefunded system, each generation funds its own retirement by investing today's Social Security taxes for tomorrow's retirement. Responsibility for supporting retirees does not fall on future generations. Under this system, the retirement fund never runs out of money. However, depending on how it is structured, a prefunded system could eliminate the more favorable treatment of low-income workers that exists under the current system. Prefunded systems can be created through the private market, but as mentioned earlier, this approach has inherent risks because the market is unpredictable and even volatile. In a market-driven system, *individuals* would bear the risks of their personal circumstances, personal investment choices, and general economic conditions. Under the current system, risks are shared by the all contributors and beneficiaries.

Another approach is to switch to a prefunded system that is government-based rather than market-based. Because the government could control the amounts that workers pay in and the amounts paid to beneficiaries, the adequacy and equity of the current system could be retained while simultaneously ensuring the trust funds' long-term solvency. The switch to a prefunded system comes with sticker shock—an estimated transition cost of $10 trillion (slightly less than three times the federal debt currently held by the public). While this is a hefty upfront price tag, it is a one-time fee to fix a very large problem that touches virtually all Americans. The cost could be phased in over time to ease the burden, but as with other solutions to fixing the current system, the longer the country waits to take action, the more that burden falls on fewer people. If action is taken soon, the burden can be carried over several working generations before the OASDI trust funds near exhaustion.[44]

What Happens if OASDI Becomes Exhausted?

It is highly unlikely that Congress will allow the Social Security trust funds to become exhausted, but if it did, one of two things will probably happen.[45] Benefit levels might be allowed to drop. The projected average monthly Social Security benefit for the year of exhaustion ($1,428) would fall to $1,041. Low-wage earners would likely feel these cuts most. Their benefits would drop from $864 to $631. These reduced benefits would replace significantly less of workers' pre-retirement wages. For example, at a retirement age of 65, one projection is that low-wage earners' replacement rate would immediately drop by 13 percentage points, average-wage earners by 10 percentage points, and high-wage earners by 8 percentage points.[46]

The government could also wait until funds are exhausted to raise payroll taxes. Remember that, currently, 12.4 percent (6.2 percent from employer and employee each) of the 15.3 percent payroll tax collected goes to the OASDI fund (the remainder goes to the HI fund). Waiting to raise payroll taxes until OASDI funds are exhausted would require a tax increase to 17.8 percent (8.9 percent each). For the average earner, this would mean paying about $1,300 more in Social Security taxes a year. (A payroll tax increase would have no impact on retired workers, since they are no longer in the workforce.) The heaviest tax burden would fall on young workers, as the increased taxes accumulate over a working lifetime. Enacting a payroll tax increase during the year the fund is exhausted would not assure that full benefits could be paid for an indefinite period of time.

As Congress, advisory boards, think tanks, and advocacy groups engage in what has become a never-ending debate about how to fix Social Security, valuable time is being lost. The magnitude of the problem continues to increase, and the resources needed to avert insolvency become greater. The Advisory Board has provided a convincing list of reasons why action should be taken *now:*

♦ More choices are available.

♦ Changes can be phased in more gradually, thus avoiding extreme changes that would be more burdensome for workers and beneficiaries.

♦ The cost of repairing Social Security can be spread more evenly over more generations of workers and beneficiaries. In delaying action, the burden of repairing the system falls disproportionately on younger generations.

♦ There will be more advance notice for those who will be affected, so they can better plan for their retirement.

♦ Confidence in Social Security's ability to continue to pay benefits to future generations of retirees will be strengthened.

♦ There will be less disruption in labor market participation. For example, benefit cuts may induce people to work longer; workers can plan ahead when deciding how long to remain in the labor force; and employers can make changes in the size of their workforce more gradually.

♦ Individuals and families will have to make less-abrupt decisions about consumption and savings.[47]

Congress has amended the Social Security Act many times to keep pace with the needs of Americans and to address financial and other important concerns of the Social Security system. It has never allowed the system to reach a point where it cannot keep its promises to the public, and it is unthinkable that it would ever do so. The Advisory Board recommended that any reforms to the Social Security system be integrated with measures to strengthen other parts of individuals' retirement plans, such as private pensions and private investments. Economists, advocates, and legislators all agree that Social Security needs change,[48] but whether change will come sooner or later has yet to be decided.

UNEMPLOYMENT INSURANCE

Another major social insurance program—unemployment insurance—was part of the original Social Security Act. The federal government and some states call it unemployment compensation (UC). This program provides some income to recently and involuntarily unemployed people and helps stabilize the economy during recessions. Again, the underlying rationale is to compel employers to contribute to a trust fund that would help employees in the event of job loss. The federal government does this by requiring employers to pay into state-administered unemployment insurance programs that meet federal standards. The federal standards are flexible, and the states have considerable freedom in shaping their own programs.

In order to receive benefits, unemployed workers must apply in person and show that they are willing, able, and ready to work. In practice, this means that unemployed workers must register with the U.S. Employment Service (usually located in the same building as the state unemployment insurance office), actively seek work, and accept a "suitable" job if found. Suitability is generally defined in terms of risks to health, safety, and morals, as well as the individual's physical capabilities; prior education, work experience, and earnings; the likelihood of obtaining employment in one's customary line of work; and distance to the job. But the longer the period of unemployment, the more pressure there is to take whatever is available.[49]

States cannot deny benefits to unemployed workers for refusing to work as strikebreakers or refusing to work for less than prevailing wages in the community. They also cannot deny benefits for refusing to take jobs that require union membership, and they cannot deny benefits solely because a woman is pregnant (an attempt to allow workers to obtain unemployment insurance benefits after having a child or adopting and taking time off from work under the Family and Medical Leave Act failed). Basic decisions concerning eligibility requirements, the amount of benefits, and the length of time that benefits are paid are largely left to the states, but, in all states, unemployment insurance is temporary, usually a maximum of 26 weeks of regular coverage financed by the states, and sometimes 13 weeks of extended coverage financed by both the federal and state governments. When unemployment is high, Congress generally extends UC benefits. For example, through much of 2002 and 2003 when unemployment was high and job opportunities were scarce, Congress extended unemployment benefits an additional 13 weeks (for a total of 39 weeks). A problem with these extensions is that they are a response to national unemployment rates. They are not sensitive to differences in unemployment across the country. Even in the midst of low overall unemployment, some areas may be hit hard. Without an extension by Congress, workers in these economically depressed areas have to do without. Unemployment insurance is not a protection against long-term or "hard-core" unemployment, but it is essential to keeping many families afloat between jobs, especially during hard economic times.

Under the Federal Unemployment Tax Act (FUTA), employers' taxes are placed in a federal unemployment trust fund that contains an account for each state plus accounts for groups such as federal employees. Currently, the federal government requires that employers pay 6.2 percent of the first $7,000 that each employee earns.[50] States with no delinquent federal loans get back 5.4 percent, generally making the federal tax rate 0.8 percent. Regardless of how much employees earn, employers typically pay $434 a year per employee ($7,000 × .062), with $56 (.08 percent) going to the federal UC account and the remainder going to the state account. Federal taxes are used to cover federal program administration costs and to pay for half the federal-state extended benefit program; they also cover a loan account that states can use if their trust funds become exhausted.

States fund their own programs and pay regular state unemployment claims and half of the claims for the federal-state extended benefits program. The states vary in both the taxable wage base and the tax rate they use to fund their programs. The states determine tax rates based on an employer's unemployment (lay off) history; these rates range from zero to 10 percent. In 2003, the estimated tax contributions of employers nationwide averaged 2.1 percent of their taxable payroll with a range from 0.2 percent in Virginia to 4.2 percent in Pennsylvania and New York. In 2003, maximum allowable weekly benefits ranged from $205 in Arizona to $760 in Massachusetts. States determine the weekly benefit amounts to be paid to unemployed workers and generally replace about 50 to 70 percent of a worker's pretax wages up to the maximum benefit level. Thus, unemployment insurance covers a higher proportion of lower-earners' wages than higher-earners' wages. In 2003, an estimated 10.3 million people received an average weekly benefit of $260.

Nearly all (99.7 percent) wage and salary workers have unemployment protection, but not everyone who is unemployed receives assistance. In 2002, the U.S. Department of Labor estimated that 56 percent of unemployed people did *not* receive benefits. Some of these individuals were "exhaustees" who had used all the benefits to which they were entitled (not a bad name since most people feel exhausted after pounding the pavement looking for work for 26 weeks or more). In 2003, 4.1 million unemployed workers exhausted their unemployment benefits. This was up from 2.3 million in 2000 and a reflection of the recession begun in 2001 and lethargic economy still plaguing the country. An earlier study of "exhaustees" found that many did not expect to be called back to their previous jobs, and many also had low levels of job skills.[51] Others are unemployed for short periods and either do not qualify or do not bother to apply for benefits. Still others did not earn enough or did not work at their last job long enough to qualify. Some people are fired for poor job performance or misconduct or leave their jobs voluntarily, including strikers; these situations are not covered by unemployment insurance.

What Is Unemployment?

Until unemployment insurance was first adopted in 1935, losing one's job could have resulted in sheer destitution. Most families depended on the support of one worker—usually the father. If he lost his job, the family's income was immediately reduced to zero. Today many American families benefit from the earnings of more than one worker. Unemployment is still serious, but a second income provides a buffer against economic disaster. Unemployment insurance and public assistance programs like Food Stamps can reduce hardship when unemployment lasts for more than a short time. These changes have had an important effect on the motivations and expectations of unemployed people. They may now decide to pass up, at least for a while, low-paying or undesirable jobs in the hope of finding better-paying, more satisfying employment.[52]

Considerable fluctuations in unemployment rates have occurred during the past century (see Figure 4.1). In 2000, unemployment rates dipped below 4 percent in some months, figures not seen since the late 1960s.[53] This is far better than 1982 and 1983, when unemployment rates exceeded 10 percent in some months, and certainly far below the 20 to 30 percent unemployment rate estimated during the Great Depression of the 1930s. But it is still more than the 2.5 to 3.5 percent lows achieved during the early 1950s. The most recent unemployment peak of 6.3 percent (more than 9 million people) occurred in June 2003 and has since declined.

Of course, there is some unavoidable minimum unemployment. In a large, free economy, hundreds of thousands of people move and change jobs and temporarily find themselves unemployed. This "frictional" unemployment is estimated to be about half of the total unemployment during normal (nonrecession) periods. But others are unemployed for long periods due to poor job skills, ill health, or limited intellectual capacities, or because they live in areas with few job opportunities. These "structurally" unemployed are estimated to be less than 20 percent of the total unemployed, but they face the greatest challenges in obtaining and maintaining employment.

A current concern is that the number of jobs being created each month (on average 100,000–125,000) is not keeping pace with the number (about 150,000 per month)

FIGURE 4.1

Seasonal Adjusted National Unemployment Rate, January 1948–February 2004

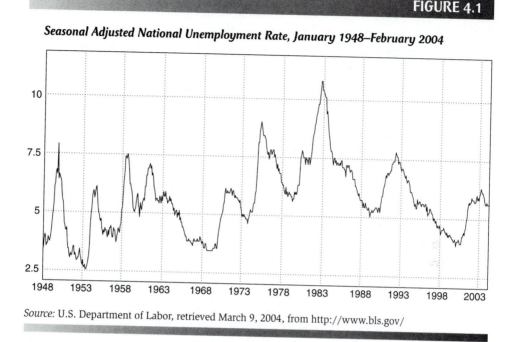

Source: U.S. Department of Labor, retrieved March 9, 2004, from http://www.bls.gov/

of new entrants into the labor force. The higher-paid manufacturing and information technology sectors have lost jobs, while low-wage sectors such as the service industry have seen gains.[54] Prolonged, fast-paced technical advances (as experienced over the past decade) seem to create both frictional and structural unemployment. Given changes in market demands, it may take workers longer to find the most desirable job (frictional unemployment), and some workers find that their skills have become obsolete (structural unemployment). Technological advances have affected three groups of workers the most: poorly educated workers, older workers, and women, especially those of child-bearing age.

Who Gets Counted as Unemployed?

Determining just who is unemployed has been a real bone of contention. Each month the U.S. Department of Labor estimates the percentage of the workforce that is out of work and actively seeking jobs (state and local unemployment figures are calculated differently). This official unemployment rate is based on a survey of about 60,000 households and includes those 16 years of age and older.[55] The Labor Department is frequently criticized because many of the downtrodden are never counted as unemployed. "Marginally attached" workers are people who want to work, are available for work, and have looked for a job some time in the prior 12 months. But only those who have actively looked for a job in the four weeks prior to the unemployment survey are included in the official unemployment rate. In June 2004, there were 1.5 million marginally attached workers.[56] Of these, 478,000 were "discouraged workers." This subset of marginally attached workers believe there are no jobs available for them and have given up even looking. Including all marginally attached workers would increase the official unemployment rate.

For years, the Labor Department was also criticized because it counted part-time workers as fully employed even if they wanted full-time work. In 1994, the household survey was modified to be more sensitive to this and other issues.[57] For example, in June 2004, 7.4 million workers held more than one job.[58] Their work may equal or exceed the 35 hours that define full-time employment, but they often work at lower wages and do not receive fringe benefits.[59] Multiple job holders were 5.3 percent of all employed workers. Most of these held a full-time job and a part-time job (3.7 million workers), or two part-time jobs (1.6 million workers).[60] Fewer workers (332,000) held two full-time jobs. An excess of part-time employment is an indicator that the economy is not performing as well as the country would like.

At any given time, the number of part-time workers (those working fewer than 35 hours per week) who are working for noneconomic reasons (in school, family obligations, etc.) outpaces the number of those who are working for economic reasons (slack work or business conditions). In hard economic times, the number of those working for economic reasons goes up, while those working for other reasons goes down. For example, in 2000, for every part-time worker employed for economic reasons, there were 3.3 part-time workers who were employed for noneconomic reasons. By January 2004, during the economic downturn, this ratio was down to 1:1.9. In other words, more people were working because of slack work or business conditions.[61]

If those working for part-time economic reasons were combined with marginally attached workers and included in official figures, the unemployment rate would be even higher.

A figure that remains totally unaccounted for is the number of people who are **underemployed.** Underemployment occurs when people work at jobs for which they are overqualified, but have taken due to need rather than preference. These jobs also tend to pay less than workers may be capable of earning.

How much unemployment is too much? There is an old saying: "When your neighbor is unemployed, it's a recession. When *you* are unemployed, it's a depression." Although most controversy centers on underestimates of unemployment, others believe that these figures are too high. For example, to qualify for programs such as food stamps, able-bodied individuals must sign up with the state employment office in their area. It has been argued that this artificially inflates unemployment, because some public assistance beneficiaries do not really intend to seek work.[62] Welfare reform has probably mitigated this effect, since many public-assistance recipients must now meet more stringent work requirements in exchange for their checks.

In addition to national unemployment, it is important to examine unemployment among subgroups of the population.[63] In good economic times or bad, the unemployment rate for African Americans is at least double that for whites. For example, in June 2004, the unemployment rate for whites was 5 percent, compared to 10.1 percent for blacks.[64] Hispanic Americans fared significantly better than African Americans (6.7 percent). The teenage (16 to 19 years old) unemployment rate is often three times higher than the rate for the general population. The highest unemployment rate of all is for African American teens. Their unemployment rate was 32.6 percent in June 2004.[65] Unemployment rates for women and men are often quite similar; sometimes women's rates are higher, and sometimes men's rates are higher, but women are concentrated in lower-paying jobs.

The unemployment picture would improve considerably if jobs and unemployed workers were better matched. This could be done in at least two ways. First, more job training and retraining programs could be offered to help workers with limited or outdated skills learn skills that employers are seeking. Efforts such as the Workforce Investment Act of 2000 (see Chapter 9) and some aspects of welfare reform (see Chapter 6) are intended to help with this problem. Second, those unable to find employment near their homes could be encouraged or assisted to relocate to areas where jobs are available. Relocation assistance is often provided for higher-paid workers by their employers but not for low-wage earners, who may need this assistance the most. President George W. Bush has proposed "Personal Reemployment Accounts" allowing workers who face difficulty in reentering the workforce to receive up to $3,000 for use in their job search.[66] The account could be used for job training, child care, transportation, or for relocation expenses for workers moving to a new city to accept a job. But today, U.S. companies are increasingly locating operations in other countries. A vigorous debate is occurring about the effects of this "offshoring" and the strategies need to ensure sufficient jobs for Americans in the increasingly global economic environment.[67]

Future demographic trends may help to ease unemployment. During the 1970s and 1980s, the large population of baby boomers entered the labor market, contributing to unemployment. But as the boomers retire, there will be more room for younger people in the workforce, particularly blacks, Hispanics, and immigrants, who will contribute substantially to new labor force additions. The preparation of future workers is crucial, because the bulk of new jobs with good salaries and fringe benefits will require a highly skilled workforce. Those without solid qualifications will continue to comprise the ranks of the poor and the unemployed.

WORKERS' COMPENSATION

Workers' compensation (not to be confused with unemployment insurance) is another social insurance program of the states. Direct federal involvement is generally limited to programs that cover federal employees. The program is mandatory for most private employers in all but Texas, where injured employees can sue employers who do not participate.[68] States vary considerably in how public, nonprofit, religious, and charitable employers are treated. About 90 percent of the workforce has coverage.[69] In 2001, that amounted to 127 million workers, slightly less than the number covered in 2000, reflecting recession and subsequent unemployment.[70] Most workers are protected against short-term illness and disability through sick time paid by their employers, but 30 percent of workers have no protection from temporary illness or disability other than workers' compensation.

The first state "workers' comp" programs were initiated in Wisconsin and New Jersey in 1911; all states had programs by 1948.[71] Each state's labor department oversees the program. The programs vary by state, but each provides cash payments and medical benefits to workers who sustain injuries on the job or develop job-related diseases. The intent "is to provide prompt, adequate benefits to injured workers, while at the same limiting employers' liabilities."[72] Workers' compensation is also intended to protect employees in the event of "occupational disabilities without regard to fault," not just when employer negligence is involved.[73] Employers are encouraged to improve workplace safety, and most programs exclude injuries resulting from employee's intoxication, willful misconduct, or gross negligence.[74]

Although intended to limit contentious legal cases, workers' compensation claims can be highly litigious because workers must still prove that their injury or illness is work related.[75] Compared to traumatic injury cases, disease-related cases are often more difficult to prove because the disease may have developed over a long time or may be due to other causes. Medical problems that take time to manifest are problematic because many workers' compensation programs include time limits on filing claims. Some special federally mandated programs include compensation for black lung disease for coal miners, illness and disease due to the production and testing of nuclear weapons, and a few other cases. New classes of injuries or disabilities have arisen, such as repetitive motion disorders like carpal tunnel syndrome. In 2000, states that paid the most claims were heavily involved in mining, forestry, and fishing—occupations with high injury rates.[76] States with the lowest rates were more heavily involved in technology, finance, and service industries.

Workers' compensation programs provide wages lost to injury or disease rather than "pain and suffering."[77] There is an emphasis on reducing fraudulent claims and encouraging workers to return to employment as quickly as possible using the vocational rehabilitation system (see Chapter 5) when needed. A quick return to work is seen as beneficial to the employee as well as to the employer. The longer an employee is out of work, the greater the costs to the employer and the lower the likelihood that the employee will return to work.[78]

Workers' compensation payments are usually calculated as two-thirds or more of the worker's weekly wages at the time of illness, injury, or death, although there are caps on these amounts.[79] Rather than attempt the difficult process of estimating lost wages, administrative and legal expediency has also resulted in the development of schedules that equate particular injuries with a given number of weeks of compensation at the employee's regular wage.[80]

Workers' compensation helps in cases of permanent, long-term disability, but it is especially important, because unlike Social Security, it also helps with short-term disabilities and longer-term partial disabilities.[81] Most individuals who receive unemployment compensation benefits recover from their disabilities.[82] Workers who sustain permanent disabilities are only 1 percent of beneficiaries; their benefits may continue for life, and they may also receive Social Security benefits. Immediate dependents of workers killed in job-related accidents are generally entitled to benefits.

Most employers insure their workers through a private insurance company; others self-insure; and, in some cases, the state insures employers. Employers' premiums are based on the hazardousness of the work involved. Due to the risks involved in some industries, employers may not be able to obtain private coverage and must resort to state operated "high-risk pools." Workers' compensation programs emerged as state efforts because business people wanted control closer to home, but as with other social welfare concerns, greater consistency could be achieved through a federal program.[83]

In 2001, employers paid $63.9 billion for workers' compensation programs in premiums, deductibles, benefits, and administrative costs of self-insurance.[84] Benefits paid to workers or their survivors totaled $49.4 billion. Approximately 55 percent of benefits were made as cash payments to workers and 45 percent went to medical care. Maximum weekly payments available to those who are disabled vary widely depending on whether they are covered by a federal or state program. Payments made to federal workers are usually calculated more generously than in state programs. In 2002, under state programs, payments to permanently and totally disabled former workers ranged from a high of $1,069 in Iowa to a low of $323 in Mississippi.

Though the federal government ended its regular collection of workers' compensation data in 1993, the Bureau of Labor Statistics survey of private-sector employees indicates that 5.2 million nonfatal workplace injuries and illnesses were reported in 2001, down from 6.3 million a decade ago. The decline may be due to several factors. Many workplaces have become safer, and there are stricter eligibility standards for obtaining benefits. Others indicate that a substantial number of injured workers never file for benefits. The Center for Policy Alternatives claims that too often workers do not file because they fear retaliatory action from their employer, such as being fired.[85] The Center calls most states' laws weak on protecting workers from such actions. The number of work-related fatalities increased from 5,920 in 2000 to 8,786 in 2001 due to the deaths of 2,886 workers from the terrorist attacks in September 2001. Though the number of claims has dropped overall, the dollar amount of claims has increased, with medical costs rising faster in workers' compensation cases than in general healthcare, perhaps owing to the types of services required by injured workers.[86]

One reason that states are concerned about their programs is that businesses consider the workers' compensation environment in deciding where to locate.[87] Programs are faced with balancing the interests of injured workers (and in some cases their attorneys), employers, insurers, medical providers, and states trying to keep their systems afloat. Some states have had difficulties operating their workers' compensation systems because of the increased costs of claims, rapidly rising insurance rates, and large program deficits.

> *Organized labor says too many injured workers are denied adequate compensation and face too much resistance from insurance companies on claims. Business complains that too many doctors and chiropractors play the system for maximum profit rather than focus on getting an injured worker back on the job. Doctors face so much hassle justifying treatment that many of them have simply quit accepting workers' compensation patients. The cost of health care itself—as it has for everyone—continues to climb rapidly.*[88]

A 2000 report on workers' compensation in California indicated that though the ratio of compensation costs to payroll costs and other economic indicators had decreased in the last decade, the value of workers' benefits had fallen substantially since the mid-1980s.[89] The report recommended that benefits be indexed to inflation. California, with reportedly the most expensive workers' compensation premiums in the nation, has made significant changes in its program to contain litigation and speed workers' return to work.[90] There were claims that medical providers, especially outpatient surgery centers, were charging much more for the same services when the patient was an injured worker than when the patient was treated under a regular group insurance plan.[91] Disputes often arise over appropriate medical treatment and the extent of workers' injuries. To avoid a ballot initiative decided by California voters, the state legislature passed a bill requiring, among other things, use of American Medical Association guidelines to ensure fair and consistent consideration of disabilities, use of employer-selected medical providers, measures to ensure that workers' compensation covers only work-related disabilities, guidelines for treating common injuries to reduce unnecessary care, and limits on chiropractic and physical therapy services. Permanent partial disabilities raise considerable concern. For example, in New York state, these disabilities reportedly accounted for 14 percent of claims but 77 percent of claim costs. Reforms in New York included limits on benefit duration in this type of case. Suggestions in other states have been to terminate workers' compensation for permanent benefits at age 70 and to set workers' compensation insurance rates at the anticipated actuarial level of claims and investment income.[92] Other suggestions are to coordinate or integrate workers' compensation with the group health care and disability insurance plans offered to all workers in the employment setting.[93]

SUMMARY

One strategy for preventing poverty in the United States is social insurance programs. Social insurance helps workers protect themselves and their dependents against poverty, which may result from advanced age, death, disability, or unemployment of a breadwinner. The major social insurance program in the United States is known as Social Security. The Social Security Act of 1935, signed by President Franklin D. Roosevelt, was the first major piece of federal social welfare legislation. This act has been amended many times; today it includes a number of social insurance programs including Old Age, Survivors, Disability, and Health Insurance, collectively called OASDHI or Social Security.

Social Security was originally intended to be a self-financing program, but it developed into a "pay-as-you-go" system because life expectancy increased, and payments were continually raised to keep pace with the cost of living. In order to finance the growing program, the amount of taxable wages increased over the years and the rate at which these wages were taxed also increased. Eventually it looked as if the program would be bankrupt.

In 1983, under President Reagan's leadership and with recommendations from a bipartisan commission, Congress passed legislation to reform Social Security. Reforms included raising the retirement age, increasing the taxable wage base and the Social Security tax rate, taxing part of the Social Security benefits of those with higher incomes, increasing benefits to those who retire later, decreasing benefits to those who retire early, allowing retirees to earn more while losing less in Social Security benefits, and changing the way cost-of-living adjustments are computed if trust funds run low.

The 1983 reforms have helped to keep Social Security afloat, but the system faces another major strain as the baby boomers begin to retire. The Social Security Advisory Board and the Social Security Board of Trustees have recommended immediate action to fix the system. Options include those used in the past—raising payroll taxes, increasing the taxable wage base, adjusting COLAs, raising the retirement age, and increasing income taxes on benefits. Even these efforts would only buy the system time. For long-term solvency, most agree that structural changes are needed. The challenge is how to switch from a pay-as-you-go system to a prefunded system without losing the adequacy and equity features of the current system, and without putting the trust funds at undue market risk. Privatization of all or some of the OASDI trust funds has been considered in the past. With billions of dollars lost in the stock market in 2001 and 2002, this is probably not a politically viable option at this juncture in the country's history. Another possibility is to convert Social Security to a government-funded prepaid system. This would require a hefty initial cost that could be spread over several generations if action is taken soon. Whatever Congress does, the longer it waits to act, the higher the cost will be, and the more extreme the adjustments that employees, employers, and beneficiaries will have to make.

Despite its problems, Social Security provides most workers some income during their retirement or in the event of disability during their working years. It also insures their dependents in the event of the worker's death. It relieves younger people of much of the burden of supporting their parents and grandparents, and it is a highly portable program that workers take with them from job to job. Social Security is the nation's largest government program and its most effective antipoverty effort. It will remain the country's most important social welfare program for years to come.

Unemployment insurance is another important social insurance program. While helpful in the short term when workers are between jobs, UC does not help with the long-term unemployment experienced by some vulnerable populations or during serious economic downturns. Workers' compensation, another social insurance program, assists workers who are injured or become ill in work-related situations. These programs also need a watchful eye to see that all parties are treated fairly. Social insurance programs are a preferred alternative for preventing poverty, but particularly important for the years ahead are ensuring a skilled workforce and flexibility in matching workers with job opportunities. The country must also address issues such as U.S. corporations moving operations to other countries and an excess of employment that offers low wages and few benefits.

NOTES

1. Thomas Paine, "Agrarian Justice," 1795, retrieved from http://www.mediapro.net/cdadesign/paine/agjst.html; and at Social Security Administration, "Social Security History Page," http://www.ssa.gov/history/quotes.html

2. For further discussion of this point, see Eric R. Kingson and Edward D. Berkowitz, *Social Security and Medicare: A Policy Primer* (Westport, CT: Auburn House, 1993), pp. 29–37.

3. *Ibid.*, p. 33.

4. Joseph A. Pechman, Henry J. Aaron, and Michael K. Taussig, *Social Security: Perspectives for Reform* (Washington, DC: Brookings Institution, 1968).

5. Committee on Ways and Means, U.S. House of Representatives, *2003 Green Book: Social Security: The Old Age, Survivors, and Disability Insurance* (Washington DC: January 9, 2004), p. 1-4, retrieved February 17, 2004, from http://waysandmeans.house.gov/Documents.asp?section = 813. See also Social Security Administration (SSA), *Monthly Statistical Snapshot* (Washington, DC: SSA, December 2003), retrieved February 5, 2004, from http://www.ssa.gov/policy/docs/quickfacts/stat_snapshot/index.html; Social Security Administration (SSA) *Performance and Accountability Report Fiscal Year 2003* (Washington, DC: SSA, 2003), pp. 8–9, retrieved from http://www.ssa.gov/finance/; and National Center for Policy Analysis, *Quick Facts about Social Security* (Dallas: National Center for Policy Analysis), retrieved February 6, 2004, from http://www.mysocialsecurity.org/quickfacts/

6. Committee on Ways and Means, U.S. House of Representatives, *2003 Green Book,* p. 1-39.

7. See Kingson and Berkowitz, *Social Security and Medicare: A Policy Primer,* pp. 48–50.

8. Wilbur J. Cohen, *Social Security: The Compromise and Beyond* (Washington, DC: Save Our Security Education Fund, 1983), pp. 4–5.

9. Social Security Administration, *Social Security Online: Cost-of-Living Adjustments, 1975–2003* (Updated October 16, 2003), retrieved January 30, 2004, from http://www.ssa.gov/OACT/COLA/colaseries.html

10. Committee on Ways and Means, U.S. House of Representatives, *2003 Green Book,* p. 1-47.

11. Committee on Ways and Means, U.S. House of Representatives, *2003 Green Book,* pp. 1-57–1-58.

12. Social Security Administration (SSA), *Social Security Online: Understanding Your Benefits* (Washington, DC: SSA, February 2003), retrieved February 8, 2004, from http://www.ssa.gov/pubs/10024.html#pgfId-1124569

13. For a more detailed description of these reforms see "Report of the National Commission on Social Security Reform," *Social Security Bulletin,* Vol. 46, No. 2, 1983, pp. 3–38. For more on House and Senate action, see "Social Security Rescue Plan Swiftly Approved," 1983 *Congressional Quarterly Almanac* (Washington, DC: Congressional Quarterly, 1984), pp. 219–226. For a concise consideration of the changes adopted, see Wilbur J. Cohen, "The Future Impact of the Social Security Amendments of 1983," *The Journal/The Institute of Socioeconomic Studies,* Vol. 8, No. 2, 1983, pp. 1–16.

14. Social Security Administration, *The 2003 Annual Report of the Board of Trustees of the Federal Old-Age and Survivors Insurance and the Federal Disability Insurance Trust Funds,* p. 2, retrieved February 13, 2004, from http://www.ssa.gov/OACT/TR/TR03/index.html

15. Centers for Medicare and Medicaid Services, *Medicare Operations of the HI Trust Fund: Selected Fiscal Years,* retrieved February 19, 2004, from http://www.cms.hhs.gov/researchers/pubs/datacompendium/2002/02pg20-21.pdf

16. Discussion of the Social Security trust funds relies on Social Security Administration, *The 2003 Annual Report of the Board of Trustees of the Federal Old-Age and Survivors Insurance and the Federal Disability Insurance Trust Funds,* pp. 2–10; Committee on Ways and Means, U.S. House of Representatives, *2003 Green Book,* p. 1-60; Social Security Administration (SSA), *Performance and Accountability Report Fiscal Year 2003* (Washington, DC: SSA, 2003), retrieved February 17, 2004, from http://www.ssa.gov/finance/; and Social Security Administration (SSA), *A Summary of the 2003 Annual Reports: Social Security and Medicare Boards of Trustees* (Washington, DC: SSA, 2003), retrieved February 19, 2004, from http://www.ssa.gov/OACT/TRSUM/trsummary.html

17. See Ben Wildavsky, "Poll Watchers Dress Down the Press," *National Journal,* September 13, 1997, p. 1786.

18. Jill Quadango, "Social Security and the Myth of the Entitlement Crisis," *The Gerontologist,* Vol. 36, No. 3, 1996, pp. 391–399.

19. Social Security Advisory Board, *Social Security: Why Action Should Be Taken Soon,* July 2001, retrieved July 4, 2004, from http://www.ssab.gov

20. Reported by Marshall N. Carter and Williams G. Shipman, *Promises to Keep: Saving Social Security's Dream* (Washington, DC: Regnery Publishing, 1996), based on a Third Millennium Survey by Frank Lutz and Mark Siegel; also referred to in Sam Beard, "Minimum-Wage Millionaires: The Capitalist Way to Save Social Security," *Policy Review,* No. 73, Summer 1995, http://www.heritage.org/heritage/library

21. American Association of Retired Persons, *Impact of Stock Market Decline on 50–70 Year Old Investors,* December 2002, retrieved July 10, 2004, from http://research.aarp.org/econ/market_decline.html

22. Eugene Steuerle and Jon M. Bakija, "Retooling Social Security for the 21st Century," *Social Security Bulletin,* Vol. 60, No. 2, 1997, pp. 37–60; see also Eugene Steuerle and Jon M. Bakija, *Retooling Social Security for the 21st Century: Right and Wrong Approaches to Reform* (Washington, DC: Urban Institute Press, 1994); James Moore and Olivia Mitchell, "Projected Retirement Wealth and Savings Adequacy in the Health and Retirement Study," NBER Working Paper 6240 (Cambridge, MA: Natural Bureau of Economic Research, October 1997); Bernard Wasow, "Promoting Retirement Savings: The Bush Plan vs. A Better Way" (New York: The Century Foundation, February 2004).

23. Eric R. Kingson, "Misconceptions Distort Social Security Policy Discussions," *Social Work,* Vol. 34, No. 4, 1989, pp. 357–362; Kingson and Berkowitz, *Social Security and Medicare: A Policy Primer;* Gordon Sherman, "Social Security: The Real Story," *National Forum, The Phi Kappa Phi Journal,* Vol. 78, No. 2, 1998, pp. 26–29.

24. Social Security Administration, *Performance and Accountability Report Fiscal Year 2003,* p. 9; and U.S. Census Bureau, *Current Population Reports: Poverty in the United States: 2002,* pp. 60-222 (Washington, DC: U.S. Department of Commerce, September 2003), retrieved February 19, 2004, from http://www.census.gov/prod/2003pubs/p60-222.pdf

25. Dorcas R. Hardy, "The Future of Social Security," *Social Security Bulletin,* Vol. 50, No. 8, 1987, p. 7, reprinted from Connecticut College Alumni Magazine, Spring 1987.

26. Social Security Administration, *Performance and Accountability Report Fiscal Year 2003,* p. 26.

27. See Kingson and Berkowitz, *Social Security and Medicare: A Policy Primer,* p. 23; J. Douglas Brown, *Essays on Social Security* (Princeton, NJ: Princeton University Press, 1977), pp. 31–32.

28. Martha N. Ozawa, "Benefits and Taxes under Social Security: An Issue of Intergenerational Equity," *Social Work,* Vol. 29, No. 2, 1984, pp. 131–137.

29. Henry J. Aaron, "Costs of the Aging Population: Real and Imagined Burdens," in Henry J. Aaron, ed., *Social Security and the Budget: Proceedings of the First Conference of the National Academy of Social Insurance* (Lanham, MD: National Academy of Social Insurance and University Press of America, 1990), pp. 51–61.

30. Philip J. Longman, "Costs of the Aging Population: Financing the Future," in Aaron, *Social Security and the Budget: Proceedings of the First Conference of the National Academy of Social Insurance,* p. 67.

31. This paragraph relies on Robert Gnaizda and Mario Obledo, "1983 Social Security Reforms Unfair to Minorities and the Young," *Gray Panther Network,* Spring 1985, p. 12.

32. This paragraph relies on Kingson, "Misconceptions Distort Social Security Policy Discussions"; Bernard Wasow, "Setting the Record Straight: Social Security Works for Latinos" (New York: Century Foundation, May 2002), retrieved March 8, 2004, from http://www.socsec.org; Bernard Wasow, "Setting the Record Straight: Two False Claims about African Americans and Social Security" (New York: Century Foundation, March 2002), retrieved March 8, 2003, from http://www.socsec.org

33. Eric R. Kingson, Barbara A. Hirshorn, and John M. Cornman, *Ties That Bind: The Interdependency of Generations* (Washington, DC: Seven Locks Press, 1986).

34. See Kingson and Berkowitz, *Social Security and Medicare: A Policy Primer,* p. 78.

35. Committee on Ways and Means, *2003 Green Book,* Table 1-38, p. 1-66.

36. Advisory Council on Social Security, *Report of the 1994–1996 Advisory Council on Social Security* (Washington, DC: January, 1997), retrieved February 20, 2004, from http://www.ssa.gov/history/reports/adcouncil/report/toc.htm

37. Michael Tanner, "The 6.2 Percent Solution: A Plan for Reforming Social Security" (Washington, DC: CATO Institute, February 17, 2004), retrieved March 12, 2004, from http://www.cato.org

38. Andrew G. Biggs, "Personal Accounts in a Down Market: How Recent Stock Market Declines Affect the Social Security Reform Debate," CATO Institute Briefing Paper No. 74 (Washington, DC: CATO Institute, September 10, 2002), p. 6, retrieved March 12, 2004, from http://www.cato.org

39. Social Security Advisory Board, *Annual Report: Fiscal Year 2002* (Washington, DC: December 2002), retrieved February 20, 2004, from http://www.ssab.gov/NEW/Publications/AnnualReports/annualreport2002.pdf

40. Much of this section relies on Social Security Board of Trustees, *Social Security: Why Action Should Be Taken Soon;* see also Alison Shelton and Laurel Beedon, *Improving Solvency Using the Social Security Benefit Formula* (Washington, DC: Public Policy Institute, AARP, 2003), pp. 1–15, retrieved February 19, 2004, from http://research.aarp.org/econ/ib63_solvency.pdf; and Laurel Beedon and Mitja Ng-Baumhackl, *The Social Security Benefit Formula,* (Washington, DC: Public Policy Institute, AARP, 2003), pp. 1–4, retrieved February 19, 2004, from http://research.aarp.org/econ/fs59r_ssbenefit.html

41. See Social Security Board of Trustees, *Social Security: Why Action Should Be Taken Soon,* pp. 15–16, 21–22.

42. See also Steuerle and Bakija, "Retooling Social Security for the 21st Century." These authors agree that cutting COLAs is not a good idea.

43. Social Security Board of Trustees, *Social Security: Why Action Should Be Taken Soon,* pp. 18–19; see also Alan D. Viard, "Pay-as-you-go Social Security and the Aging of America: An Economic Analysis," *Economic and Financial Policy Review* (Dallas: Federal Reserve Bank of Dallas, 2002), Vol. 1, No. 4, retrieved September 28, 2003, from http://dallasfedreview.org/pdfs/v01_n04_a01.pdf

44. *Ibid.*

45. Social Security Board of Trustees, *Social Security: Why Action Should Be Taken Soon,* pp. 12–13.

46. *Ibid.,* p. 13; see also Social Security Administration, *The 2003 Annual Report of the Board of Trustees of the Federal Old-Age and Survivors Insurance and the Federal Disability Insurance Trust Funds,* pp. 44–70.

47. Social Security Board of Trustees, *Social Security: Why Action Should Be Taken Soon,* pp. 14–15.

48. *Ibid.,* pp. 1–2.

49. Committee on Ways and Means, *1993 Green Book,* p. 497.

50. Some of this selection relies on Committee on Ways and Means, U.S. House of Representatives, *2003 Green Book: Unemployment Compensation* (Washington, DC: January 9, 2004), Section 4, retrieved February 17, 2004, from http://waysandmeans.house.gov/Documents.asp?section = 813

51. W. Corson and M. Dynarski, *A Study of Unemployment Insurance Recipients and Exhaustees: Findings from a National Survey,* Occasional Paper 90-3 (Washington, DC: U.S. Department of Labor), cited in Committee on Ways and Means, *1998 Green Book,* pp. 342–343.

52. For elaboration of the effects of social welfare programs on labor see Francis Fox Piven and Richard Cloward, *The New Class War* (New York: Pantheon Books, 1982).

53. U. S. Department of Labor, Bureau of Labor Statistics, *Employment Situation* (Washington, DC: January 2004), retrieved February 13, 2004, and July 5, 2004, from http://www.bls.gov/news.release/empsit.nr0.htm; for extensive unemployment data see http://stats.bls.gov/cps/cpsatabs.htm

54. William J. Baumol and Edward N. Wolff, *Protracted Frictional Unemployment as a Heavy Cost of Technical Progress* (New York: New York University, December 1996), Working Paper No. 179, retrieved February 20, 2004, from http://econwpa.wustl.edu/eps/mac/papers/9803/9803001.pdf; see also Quick MBA, *Economics Unemployment,* retrieved February 20, 2004, from http://www.quickmba.com/econ/macro/unemployment/; also at this website, see *Economics: The Business Cycle.*

55. Bureau of Labor Statistics, *Current Population Survey, Technical Paper 63RV, Design and Methodology* (Washington, DC: U.S. Department of Labor, March 2002), retrieved July 10, 2004, for http://www.bls.census.gov/cps/tp/tp63.htm

56. U.S. Department of Labor, Bureau of Labor Statistics, *Employment Situation,* p. 3.

57. See Sharon Cohany, Anne E. Polivka, and Jennifer M. Rothgeb, "Revisions in the Current Population Survey Effective January 1994," *Employment and Earnings,* Vol. 41 (Washington, DC: U.S. Government Printing Office, February 1994), pp. 13–35.

58. U.S. Department of Labor, Bureau of Labor Statistics, *Employment Situation,* Table A-13.

59. See "U.S. Job Count Is Revamped," *Austin American-Statesman,* January 14, 1993, p. B1.

60. U.S. Department of Labor, Bureau of Labor Statistics, Employment Situation, Table A-13.

61. U.S. Department of Labor, *Labor Statistics from the Current Population Survey* (Washington, DC: Bureau of Labor Statistics, 1994–2004), A Tables, retrieved February 21, 2004, from http://data.bls.gov/servlet/SurveyOutputServlet

62. Kenneth W. Clarkson and Roger E. Meiners, "Government Statistics as a Guide to Economic Policy: Food Stamps and the Spurious Increase in the Unemployment Rates," *Policy Review*, Vol. 1, 1977, pp. 27–51.

63. Unemployment figures for subgroups of the population are available from the Bureau of Labor Statistics at http://146.142.4.24/cgi-bin/surveymost?lf

64. U.S. Department of Labor, Bureau of Labor Statistics, *Employment Situation*, Table A-2.

65. *Ibid.*

66. *President Bush Pushes for Personal Reemployment Accounts Legislation*, Remarks by the President on Employment Training, Ernst Community Cultural Center, Northern Virginia Community College, Annandale, Virginia, June 17, 2003, retrieved September 19, 2003, from http://www.whitehouse.gov/news/releases/2003/06/20030617-3.html; Lerxst, *What Happened to the Reemployment Accounts?* (Economist for Dean, January 30, 2004), retrieved February 21, 2004, from http://econ4dean.typepad.com/econ4dean/2004/01/what_happened_t.html

67. Ken Moritsugu, "Few Jobs Lost As a Result of Offshoring, Study Says," *Austin American-Statesman*, June 11, 2004, pp. C1, 6; Gene Sperling, "The Effects of Offshoring," *Progressive Politics*, Vol 3.2, June 30, 2004, retrieved July 5, 2004, from http://www.americanprogress.org

68. Cecili Thompson Williams, Virginia P. Reno, and John F. Burton, Jr., *Workers' Compensation Benefits, Coverage, and Costs, 2001* (Washington, DC: National Academy of Social Insurance, July 2003), retrieved February 21, 2004, from http://www.nasi.org/usr_doc_/Workers_Comp_Report_2001_Final.pdf

69. "Workers Compensation," June 2004, Insurance Information Institute, retrieved July 3, 2004, from http://www.iii.org/media/hottopics/insurane/workerscomp/

70. The federal government ended its regular collection of workers' compensation data in 1993; currently, the only comprehensive database for workers' compensation is maintained by the National Academy of Social Insurance. Much of the information in this section relies on Cecili Thompson Williams, Virginia P. Reno, and John F. Burton, Jr., *Workers' Compensation: Benefits, Coverage, and Costs, 2001* (Washington, DC: National Academy of Social Insurance, July 2003), retrieved February 21, 2004, from http://www.nasi.org/usr_doc/Workers_Comp_Report_2001_Final.pdf; and Committee on Ways and Means, U.S. House of Representatives, *2003 Green Book*, Section 15, *Workers' Compensation* (Washington, DC: January 9, 2004), retrieved February 17, 2004, from http://waysandmeans.house.gov/Documents.asp?section = 813

71. Edward D. Berkowitz, *Disabled Policy: America's Programs for the Handicapped* (Cambridge, England: Cambridge University Press, 1987), p. 15. Reprinted with the Permission of Cambridge University Press.

72. Committee on Ways and Means, *1993 Green Book*, p. 15-1.

73. Committee on Ways and Means, *1996 Green Book*, p. 945; see also *2003 Green Book*, p. 15-1.

74. See, for example, U.S. Department of Labor, "When Injured at Work Information, Guide for Federal Employees," retrieved September 27, 2004, from http://www.dol.gov/esa/regs/compliance/owcp/ca = 11.htm

75. Berkowitz, *Disabled Policy*, pp. 15, 26; see also Committee on Ways and Means, *2003 Green Book*, pp. 15-1, 15-30.

76. Committee on Ways and Means, *2003 Green Book*, p. 15-10.

77. Committee on Ways and Means, *2003 Green Book*, p. 15-2.

78. "Workers Compensation," June 2004, Insurance Information Institute.

79. Committee on Ways and Means, *2003 Green Book*, p. 15-2.

80. Berkowitz, *Disabled Policy*, p. 28.

81. *Ibid.*, p. 39.

82. The remainder of this paragraph relies on Committee on Ways and Means, *1993 Green Book*, p. 1702; see also Committee on Ways and Means, U.S. House of Representatives, *Overview of Entitlement Programs: 1994 Green Book* (Washington, DC: U.S. Government Printing Office, 1994), p. 847.

83. Berkowitz, *Disabled Policy*, pp. 15–16.

84. Williams, Reno, and Burton, *Workers Compensation: Benefits, Coverage and Costs, 2001;* Committee on Ways and Means, *2003 Green Book*, Section 15, "Workers' Compensation."

85. "Worker's Compensation" (Washington, DC: Center for Alternative Policies, 2003), retrieved July 8, 2004, from http://www.cfpa.org/issues/work compensation/workercomp/index.cfm

86. "Workers Compensation," June 2004, Insurance Information Institute.

87. *Ibid.*

88. Bruce Hight, "Who Can Clean Up Workers' Compensation?" *Austin American-Statesman*, July 8, 2004, p. A11.

89. Commission on Health and Safety and Workers' Compensation, "Information Bulletin," December 14, 2000, retrieved July 3, 2004, from http://www.dir.ca.gov/chswc/Updatedcalifecon.html

90. Much of this paragraph relies on "Workers Compensation," June 2004, Insurance Information Institute.

91. "Workers' Compensation Notes" (Washington, DC: AFL-CIO Department of Occupational Safety and Health, August 2003), retrieved July 3, 2004, from http://www.aflcio.org/yourjobeconomy/safety/wc/wc_nhotes.cfm

92. *Ibid.*

93. "Workers Compensation," June 2004, Insurance Information Institute.

CHAPTER

Helping the "Deserving Poor": Aged, Blind, and Disabled

ndividuals who are aged or disabled are among those considered the "deserving poor"—groups that society generally feels morally and ethically obliged to aid. Four types of social policy provisions provide this assistance:

1. Social Security disability and retirement benefits for those with sufficient work histories (see Chapter 4)

2. Public assistance for those with little or no income whose conditions prevent them from pursuing gainful employment

3. Social service programs, since virtually all individuals who are disabled or aged can benefit from a wide range of habilitative, rehabilitative, or social services

4. Civil rights legislation aimed at reducing discrimination in employment, education, and housing, and at providing greater access to public and private facilities

PUBLIC ASSISTANCE FOR THE DESERVING POOR

Prior to the Social Security Act of 1935, many states had public assistance programs to aid the elderly poor. Massachusetts was among the first to appoint a commission to study the problems of the elderly.[1] In 1914 Arizona passed a law establishing a pension program for the aged,[2] and in 1915 the territory of Alaska did the same.[3] By 1935 thirty states already had old-age assistance programs. Eligibility requirements for these state programs were stringent. In addition to financial destitution, recipients generally had to be at least 65 years old, be United States citizens, and meet residency requirements in the location where they applied for benefits. In cases where relatives were capable of supporting an elderly family member, benefits were often denied. Elderly participants usually had to agree that any assets they had left at the time of their death would be assigned to the state.

Individuals who were blind were also considered "deserving." In fact, eligibility requirements were often more lenient in state pension laws for these individuals than they were for the elderly. By 1935, twenty-seven states had pension programs for people who were blind.[4] Individuals with other disabling conditions were also of concern, but early in the 1900s, policies to assist them varied considerably among states, and many states had no programs at all.

When the original Social Security Act was passed, its most far-reaching provision was the Social Security insurance program for retired workers. Not until 1956 were disabled workers included under social insurance, since many officials apparently preferred to aid them using public assistance programs.[5] Following the precedent established by many states, the original Social Security Act included three public assistance programs: Aid to Dependent Children (ADC), Old Age Assistance (OAA), and Aid to the Blind (AB). Disability policy continued to lag behind, but in 1950 Aid to the Permanently and Totally Disabled (APTD) was added. OAA, AB, and APTD were called the **adult categorical public assistance programs.**

Although these public assistance programs were federally authorized, each state could decide whether to participate. All states eventually adopted OAA and AB, but several states chose not to participate in APTD. The federal government shared costs with the states and set basic requirements for participation. Elderly individuals had to be at least 65 years old to receive federal aid. Those who were blind or otherwise disabled had to be at least 18 years old. The states had primary administrative responsibility and retained a good deal of discretion in determining eligibility requirements (definitions of disability and blindness, terms of residency, and income and asset limitations) and the amount of payments.

State administration of the OAA, AB, and APTD programs had serious ramifications for some beneficiaries. Those who moved to another state might have been denied benefits because they did not meet eligibility requirements in their new state of residence or because they were required to re-establish residency. Benefits were often meager and varied drastically by state. In the OAA program in 1964, West Virginia paid an average monthly benefit of $50, while Wisconsin paid $111.[6] Beneficiaries from poorer states generally received less because their states had less money to operate the program; other states had a tradition of limiting public assistance.

The Federal Government Steps In

When President Nixon took office in 1972 he wanted to clean up the "welfare mess." Nixon's welfare reform was to provide a minimum income to poor Americans that would replace the Aid to Families with Dependent Children (AFDC, formerly ADC), OAA, AB, and APTD programs and bring an end to the uneven treatment of welfare recipients from state to state. His **guaranteed annual income** proposal, known as the Family Assistance Plan (FAP), was the target of controversy in Congress. Liberals considered it too stingy. Conservatives believed that the reforms provided too much in welfare benefits and would reduce the incentive to work. Former Senator Daniel P. Moynihan (D-New York), then an adviser to President Nixon and supporter of the FAP, wrote in his book *The Politics of a Guaranteed Annual Income* about the controversy that focused primarily on reform of the AFDC program.[7] AFDC was not reformed, but, in the midst of the controversy, substantial revisions to the OAA, AB, and APTD programs went almost unnoticed.[8]

The major change Congress enacted in 1972 was to "federalize" the adult categorical assistance programs under a new program called Supplemental Security Income (SSI), Title XVI of the Social Security Act. Federalizing meant that Congress largely took the programs out of the hands of the states. Beginning in 1974, the states relinquished responsibility for determining basic eligibility requirements and minimum payment levels, and they also turned administration of most aspects of the programs to the federal government. These changes represented the most sweeping reform of the adult categorical assistance programs since APTD was added in 1950. SSI replaced the OAA, AB, and APTD programs by establishing a minimum income for participants and by standardizing eligibility requirements across all states. Under the change to SSI, no state could pay participants less than they had previously received. Today most states supplement the minimum payment to at least some participants.*[9]

How SSI Works

SSI is administered by the Social Security Administration, and since its name sounds like the Social Security program, some people think that these programs are the same. SSI, however, remains a means-tested public assistance program; it is not a

---

*Arkansas, Georgia, Kansas, Mississippi, Tennessee, West Virginia, and the Northern Mariana Islands (the only U.S. territory with an SSI program) provide no supplements.

social insurance program like Social Security. Individuals may receive SSI benefits in addition to Social Security retirement or disability benefits if their income from Social Security and other sources and their assets do not exceed SSI eligibility criteria. Despite its reputation as a guaranteed income for those who cannot earn it themselves, SSI is a "program of last resort"; that is, applicants must claim all other benefits to which they are entitled before they can qualify for SSI.[10] As its name implies, SSI is intended to supplement other income, but because people must be poor to qualify, they cannot have much. The number of SSI participants with Social Security income has declined from about half in the mid-1970s to about one-third today, and few participants have any earnings from work. It is not possible to describe all the details of the SSI program in a few pages, but the following paragraphs provide the basic idea.[11]

U.S. citizens and some immigrants residing legally in the U.S. may qualify for SSI. The minimum age to qualify for SSI to the aged is still 65. Adults (those 18 years or older) are considered disabled if they cannot work because of a "medically determined physical or mental impairment expected to result in death or that has lasted or can be expected to last for a continuous period of at least 12 months." Individuals are considered blind if they have no better than 20/200 vision or tunnel vision of 20 degrees or less in the better eye with a corrective lens. A less stringent definition of visual impairment may be used in the portion of the program for people with disabilities. Children whose disability is similar in severity to that of an adult with the same condition qualify in order to assist their families or others in caring for them.

Residents of public institutions like mental hospitals, nursing homes, or prisons generally cannot receive SSI, but there are some exceptions. For example, those residing in institutions for the primary purpose of acquiring vocational or educational training that can help them secure employment may qualify for SSI. Others may qualify if they reside in public facilities with no more than 16 residents, and those in public emergency shelters for homeless people may qualify temporarily. Patients in medical treatment facilities receive only a $30 monthly SSI payment if Medicaid pays more than half the costs of their care unless the state chooses to offer more.

SSI has strict assets limits. Since 1989 an individual's **countable resources** cannot exceed $2,000 and a couple's cannot exceed $3,000. Countable resources include such items as some types of real estate, savings accounts, and some personal belongings. Several types of resources are not included in determining eligibility. For example, the individual's home and normal household goods are not counted, and allowances are made for the value of a car.

Countable income is also restricted. Countable income includes most earnings from work, Social Security payments, other cash benefits, and interest income. It does not include the value of food stamps or most food, clothing, and shelter provided by nonprofit organizations, but some noncash assistance does count. Since some states supplement payments, the amount of income one may have depends on the state. In 2004, in states with no supplements, an individual who was not working generally could not have more than $584 in monthly income, and couples could not have more than $866. These figures are just $20 more than the federal maximum monthly SSI payment of $564 for an individual and $846 for a couple.[12] Those who cannot live independently may receive more. In the case of children, their parents' income is usually "deemed" (considered in determining benefits). Allowances are made for the parents' work expenses and the family's living expenses.

Income that is not counted (disregarded) in calculating benefits generally includes the first $20 a month from any source. In order to encourage employment, the first $65 of income from work plus half of all additional earnings are also disregarded until such point as the individual's countable income exceeds eligibility limits. Certain work- or disability-related expenses for individuals who are blind or otherwise disabled may also be disregarded in determining payments. These disregards are more generous for those who are blind. Scholarships and grants used for educational expenses are generally disregarded. Participants who are blind or disabled are also allowed trial work periods while still receiving benefits so they can determine if working is feasible. In 2004, individuals with disabilities who were working and had no unearned income were eligible for federal SSI payments if their income was no more than $1,213 monthly.

If an SSI participant lives in the home of someone who is contributing to his or her support, the SSI payment is reduced by one-third. However, SSI participants who pay their full share of expenses may receive the entire payment. Monthly payments are adjusted each year to keep pace with the cost of living using the same method as for the Social Security insurance programs (see Chapter 4).

Sometimes a person qualifies for benefits under more than one SSI component. For example, an aged person may also be disabled. Since there are additional income exclusions for participants with disabilities, it may be more advantageous for the individual to qualify as disabled rather than aged. Participants cannot receive SSI and TANF benefits simultaneously; when an individual qualifies for both programs, a determination should be made as to which provides the greatest benefits. Most SSI participants are eligible for Medicaid. SSI cases are generally reviewed at least every three years in order to determine if participants are still eligible. As in other federally funded welfare programs, attempts are made to reduce fraud and error by obtaining income and earnings information from the IRS and the Social Security Administration.

Determining Who Is Disabled

Individuals with disabilities (other than blindness) compose the largest number of SSI participants. To people unfamiliar with SSI, it may seem like deciding whether or not someone is disabled is a straightforward process, but in many situations that is not the case. Once SSI's income and assets tests are met, the more difficult part is deciding whether an applicant meets the definition of disabled.[13] The process of **disability determination** is the same in the Social Security Disability Insurance (SSDI) and the SSI programs. It includes five sequential steps. In step 1, applicants currently earning more than $810 per month (in 2004) from employment (called substantial gainful activity, or SGA) over and above disability-related work expenses are generally disqualified, even though earned income limits once one is in the program are higher than this. The SGA figure for those who are blind is higher ($1,350 in 2004). Applicants who are not employed or are earning less proceed to step 2 to determine if their condition is "not severe" (does not interfere with work). If it is not, they are disqualified; if it is severe, the applicant moves on to step 3. In this step, a determination is made as to whether the individual's condition meets the criteria described in a document called the *Listing of Impairments* or is of equal severity to these criteria and is expected to last at least 12 months. Cases that do are approved for SSI. Cases that do not are reviewed further in step 4 to determine if the applicant can perform the work he or she did previously. If the determination is that the individual can, the case is denied. If the individual cannot, step 5 is for the government to show whether the applicant can perform any SGA in the national labor force. The applicant's disability, age, education, work history, and skills are considered. Those unable to perform any work are awarded payments, while others are denied. SSI participants with disabilities may be required to accept vocational rehabilitation services. Cases are reviewed periodically to ensure that the individual continues to qualify for benefits. Reviews are more frequent when the individual's condition is expected to improve. The first review may occur from 6 to 18 months after the onset of disability. Following the outcry that arose after efforts to trim the welfare rolls during the Reagan years, criteria were established to help ensure that participants would not be cut from the SSI program unless their medical condition improved or they returned to substantial work. The Social Security Administration has greatly increased the number of disability reviews it conducts each year.

A disability determination often takes months, not only because medical evidence must be obtained and reviewed, but because of the backlog of cases. In 2003, it took an average of 97 days to process initial disability claims; there were 592,000 hearings and 582,000 initial claims were pending.[14] But when an applicant is obviously disabled and in financial need, SSI benefits may be issued prior to a formal decision.

Many SSDI and SSI claims are initially denied. Those who wish to contest a denial or other decision have recourse to four levels of appeals, culminating with the U.S. district court. Appeals are made frequently. As a result, or perhaps a cause of this litigation, some lawyers specialize and advertise their services in this area. Since many decisions are reversed on appeal, those who believe they are disabled may have to be persistent and patient. In 1997 the average processing time for disability claims appeals was 398 days.[15] President Clinton promised to reduce the time to 284 days and implemented changes to reduce processing time for initial claims, hearings, and appeals. In 2003 the appeals processing time was down to 294 days, but this is still nearly nine months.[16]

SSI in Figures

Participants

Individuals who are blind comprise the smallest group of SSI particpants. The number of participants in this component of the program has been relatively stable over the years due to advances in the prevention and treatment of blindness and to larger numbers of those who are self-supporting. As seen in Table 5.1, about 78,000 people currently receive benefits under this part of the program.

Participation by aged individuals has declined (see Table 5.1). In 1950 about 2.8 million people received old-age assistance. In 2002, 1.25 million older people received assistance on the basis of age. Despite the growth in the older population, their participation continues to decline for two good reasons. First, most older Americans now receive Social Security, and second, Social Security benefits have risen due to COLAs, thus fewer older people are in poverty (see Chapters 3 and 4). But a third factor is that many eligible older Americans (46 percent of them) do not participate in SSI. Some suggest that the costs of SSI participation—the lengthy eligibility process, the cost of transportation to and from Social Security offices, the time involved, sharing of personal information, and the stigma associated with welfare—outweigh the benefits that many might receive.[17] The average cash benefit for participants is $220, while it would be $155 for eligible nonparticipants if they enrolled in the program. When differences between participants and eligible nonparticipants are examined, nonparticipants still tend to be better off than participants.[18] For example, more nonparticipants own their homes (49 percent vs. 30 percent of participants), and 40 percent of nonparticipants compared to only 6 percent of participants have private health insurance. Since SSI participation is often a ticket to Medicaid (health insurance for many low-income individuals), older people without private health insurance might

TABLE 5.1

Number of Adult Public Assistance and SSI Program Participants for Selected Years (in thousands)

Year	Aged	Blind	Disabled	Total
1940	2,070	73	a	2,143
1950	2,786	97	69	2,952
1960	2,305	107	369	2,781
1970	2,082	81	935	3,098
1980	1,838	79	2,276	4,193
1990	1,484	84	3,320	4,888
2000	1,289	79	5,234	6,602
2002	1,252	78	5,459	6,788

Sources: U.S. Bureau of the Census, *Historical Statistics of the United States, Colonial Times to 1970* (Washington, DC: U.S. Government Printing Office, 1975), p. 356; Social Security Bulletin, *Annual Statistical Supplement, 1996,* Table 7.A3; Social Security Administration website at ftp://ftp.ssa.gov/pub/statistics/2a2; Social Security Administration, *SSI Annual Statistical Report 2000,* Table 4, retrieved from http://www.ssa.gov/policy/docs/statcomps/ssi_asr/2000/sect2.html#t4; Committee on Ways and Means, *2003 Green Book: Supplemental Security Income,* p. 3-42, retrieved from http://waysandmeans.house.gov/Documents.asp?section

a Program did not begin until 1950.

be more likely to apply in order to get healthcare coverage for things that Medicare does not cover, like prescription drugs and copays.

Researchers suggest that by raising benefits even modestly, SSI participation would increase significantly. Two studies are worth noting. In one study, researchers estimated that a $100 increase in benefits would increase participation by 15 percent. Another reported that by increasing the amount of income that is automatically disregarded in determining eligibility from $20 (an amount that has not changed since 1972) to $80, and adjusting this disregarded amount for inflation, the increase in SSI payments would lift 300,000 older Americans out of poverty.[19]

The older segments of the elderly population are more likely to experience poverty and more likely to participate in SSI. The fastest-growing segment of elderly SSI participants is those age 70 and older. In 1993 this group comprised 79 percent of participants who received SSI on the basis of age. By 1999 this proportion had increased to 84 percent. This shift will probably continue for some time into the future as the population (aged 70 and older) is projected to increase 178 percent by 2080.[20]

SSI growth is largely the result of increases in the number of participants with disabilities. When SSI began, a standard definition of disability was adopted that helped many new recipients join the rolls. More recent growth can be explained by factors such as laws, regulations, and court decisions that have expanded eligibility; the small number of participants who leave the rolls to work; and baby boomers reaching the age at which disabilities are increasingly likely. The number of participants with disabilities grew from about 369,000 in 1960 to about 5.5 million in 2002. Approximately 23 percent of adult participants aged 18 to 64 qualify due to intellectual disability (mental retardation) and 34 percent because of psychiatric disorders; the remainder have a wide range of physical diseases and disorders.[21] Children are 914,821 of the nation's 6.8 million SSI recipients. Most children are eligible because of a psychiatric disorder (37 percent) or intellectual disability (27 percent).[22] Some of the increase in children's participation is likely due to prenatal alcohol, drug, and HIV exposure and to premature babies saved through modern technology.[23] Boys are almost twice as likely as girls to receive SSI. Hispanics, and especially African Americans, are over-represented among children receiving SSI benefits.[24]

Payments and Costs

Average SSI payments to participants have increased but remain modest (see Table 5.2). In 2002, elderly recipients received an average of about $330 a month (many also receive some income from Social Security). Participants who are blind received payments averaging about $445 monthly, and those with other disabilities averaged about $425 monthly (see Table 5.3). In 2002, federal SSI payments constituted about 76 percent of the poverty level for individuals and about 90 percent for couples.[25] When the value of Social Security and food stamp benefits is added, the percentages increase to about 85 percent for individuals and 102 percent for couples.

Under SSI for the aged, the total costs of payments rose from $2.7 billion in 1980 to about $5.1 billion in 2002 (see Table 5.3). The smaller number of SSI participants

TABLE 5.2

Average Monthly Payments for the Adult Public Assistance and SSI Programs for Selected Years

Year	Aged	Blind	Disabled
1940	$ 20.25	$ 25.35	a
1950	43.05	46.00	$ 44.10
1960	58.90	67.45	56.15
1970	77.65	104.35	97.65
1980	131.75	215.70	200.06
1990	218.81	345.17	339.43
2000	299.69	413.22	397.92
2002	330.04	444.54	424.75

Sources: U.S. Bureau of the Census, *Historical Statistics of the United States, Colonial Times to 1970* (Washington, DC: U.S. Government Printing Office, 1975), p. 356; Social Security Bulletin, *Annual Statistical Supplement, 1996,* Table 7.A5; Social Security Administration (SSA) website at ftp://ftp.ssa.gov/pub/statistics/2a2; Social Security Administration, *SSI Annual Statistical Report, 2000* (Washington, DC: SSA, May 2001), Table 5, p. 12; also Social Security Administration, *SSI Annual Statistical Report, 2002* (Washington, DC: SSA, August 2003), Table 5, p. 21. SSI Statistical reports are available at http://www.ssa.gov/policy/docs/statcomps/

aProgram did not begin until 1950.

TABLE 5.3

Total Federal and State Adult Public Assistance and SSI Payments for Selected Years (in millions of dollars)

Year	Aged	Blind	Disabled	Total
1940	$ 473	$ 22	a	$ 495
1950	1,485	53	$ 8	1,546
1960	1,922	83	287	2,303
1970	1,866	98	1,000	2,964
1980	2,734	190	5,014	7,941
1990	3,736	334	12,521	16,599
2000	4,811	394	26,198	31,564
2002	5,086	426	28,996	34,567

Sources: U.S. Bureau of the Census, *Historical Statistics of the United States, Colonial Times to 1970* (Washington, DC: U.S. Government Printing Office, 1975), p. 356; Social Security Administration, *Social Security Bulletin, Annual Statistical Supplement, 1997,* Table 7.A4; Social Security Administration, *SSI Annual Statistical Report, 2002,* Table 2, p. 16; retrieved from http://www.ssa.gov/policy/docs/statcomps/ssi_asr/2002/table02.pdf

aProgram did not begin until 1950.

who are blind means that total payments in this component remain more modest; they were $190 million in 1980 and $426 million in 2002. Given the increases in the number of recipients with other disabilities, the most dramatic growth in expenditures has been in this program component. Total payment costs were $5 billion in 1980 and nearly $29 billion in 2002.

SSI Hot Spots

Many contentious issues have arisen in the SSI programs. One concerned participants who were not citizens. Not only were their numbers growing rapidly, their SSI benefits were often higher than those of citizens because many had not worked in the United States or had not worked long enough to qualify for Social Security benefits.[26] As part of the broad package of welfare reforms that Congress passed in 1996, most immigrants legally residing in the U.S. were made ineligible for benefits even if they were already receiving SSI (undocumented immigrants have never been eligible). Exceptions were made for some categories of immigrants such as refugees and asylees (who had fled their countries of origin for political reasons). Also exempt were those who had worked in the U.S. and paid Social Security taxes for 10 years or more.

The battle over immigrants in the SSI program was fought again in 1997. The *Congressional Quarterly* called it "the most protracted struggle" in the debates over what should be changed in the 1996 welfare overhaul.[27] Perhaps better economic times helped to quell the backlash. This time, the decision was to allow those who were in the United States as of August 22, 1996 (the day the welfare reform bill was signed) to receive benefits regardless of when they became disabled, even though House Republicans had urged that benefits be available only to those already disabled as of that date. In cases of immigrants with sponsors, the sponsor's income is considered in determining the immigrant's eligibility for several years after entry into the country. The specifics of an applicant's immigration status are carefully considered to make sure that they fall within the definitional boundaries. In some cases, eligibility for refugees and asylees is restricted to 7 years unless the individual becomes a citizen. Immigrants were 3.3 percent of all SSI recipients in 1982, and 12.1 percent in 1995. After the welfare reform changes of 1996, the number of noncitizen participants fell to 10 percent in 1997 and rose slightly to 703,515, or 10.4 percent, in 2002. Fifty-two percent of these immigrants were aged and 48 percent were blind or disabled.[28]

Most SSI hot spots concern individuals with disabilities other than blindness. A primary example is those with alcoholism and drug addiction. These individuals were required to use a third party (called a "representative payee") to receive their benefits since they were generally considered unable to manage their own money, and they were supposed to be enrolled in treatment programs. Apparently the treatment provision was not well monitored, and resentments toward this group of recipients grew. In addition to the feeling that most could work if they would stop using alcohol or drugs, some believed "that SSI checks were fueling addiction."[29] In 1994 benefits to alcoholics and drug addicts were limited to three years. Then, in 1996 as part of welfare reform, individuals disabled solely due to alcohol or drug use were made ineligible for SSI and SSDI, and were also cut from Medicare and Medicaid. If individuals with alcoholism or drug addiction have another disability, they may still qualify for SSI. Following the 1996 welfare reform, Social Security Disability Insurance and SSI benefits to more than 200,000 addicts were terminated. Many (43 percent) were reinstated based on another disability or because of old age.[30] Studies indicate that after two years, addicts who lost their benefits had higher rates of substance abuse than those who retained benefits, and the percentage of those participating in treatment dwindled from less than half to 10 percent.[31] Those who lost their SSI benefits were also more likely to commit drug-related crimes than those who requalified. A study of addicts in Chicago who lost their SSI benefits found that nearly half did not have access to healthcare because they also lost their Medicaid benefits.[32]

Another group that drew the ire of welfare reformers was a less likely target—children. In 1990 the U.S. Supreme Court issued a decision in *Sullivan v. Zebley*.[33] Prior to this decision, children who did not meet the criteria in the Listing of Impairments were disqualified, and some serious childhood conditions were missing from the list. The Zebley decision required that children be afforded the additional functional tests given to adult applicants. According to this ruling, a child was considered impaired if he or she was substantially unable to function as children of the same age are generally expected to do (i.e., unable to engage in "age-appropriate" activities). When the ruling came down, the Social Security Administration had to try locating and reassessing 452,000 children denied benefits as far back as 1980.[34]

Following *Zebley,* the number of children enrolled in SSI more than doubled.[35] The major increase was due to an expanded category of mental disorders, including intellectual disability and attention deficit hyperactivity disorder. Concern was that these children might remain on the rolls throughout their lifetimes. Later, reports emerged of parents coaching children to seem more impaired than they were in an effort to get benefits. It was difficult to prove this, but some government-sponsored studies recommended "strengthened" definitions of disability and eligibility criteria. As part of the 1996 welfare reform, Congress decided to again change the definition of disability for children, saying that children must have "marked and severe functional limitations" to qualify. The functional test for children was eliminated, and children must again meet criteria in the Listing of Impairments or have disabilities equal to them. The current listing reflects the new definition of disability for children.

In 1996 over one million children were receiving SSI benefits, a 14-fold increase from 1974. Following the 1996 welfare reform law, 288,000 children were slated for eligibility redetermination. Benefits to 101,000 of these children were terminated because they did not meet the more stringent eligibility definition included in the new law. By December 2000 the SSI child caseload had fallen to 846,784, but by December 2002 caseloads had begun to rise again to 914,821.[36] Children who were receiving SSI prior to the new law (August 22, 1996) continued to be eligible for Medicaid even if they lost their SSI benefits as a result of the new disability definition.

New rules are being considered for determining psychiatric and intellectual disabilities for children and adults. Concern is that the criteria for disability determination have not been updated to reflect new definitions of these conditions and advances in treatment and technology that could help people engage in gainful employment. As generally occurs when federal agencies propose new rules, the Social Security Administration solicited comments on the proposals by posting a notice in the *Federal Register.* Among the responders was the Depression and Bipolar Support Alliance.[37] Its opinion was that the current listings were working well. The Alliance cautioned against some of the rule changes. For example, new medications that may improve functioning and help people maintain employment may not be available to individuals with disabilities because they can be costly and Medicare and Medicaid may not cover them.

Many homeless individuals who are disabled or aged are not receiving SSI benefits. Based on a national study, estimates are that less than 1 percent of them are currently receiving SSI benefits, compared to 2.3 percent of the housed population.[38] Homeless individuals face many barriers to program participation: confusion about eligibility criteria, missing personal or third-party contact information on the application, lack of required documentation, and failure to complete enrollment following application. Homeless individuals are often terminated from public benefit programs because they do not receive their redetermination notices.[39]

Once they apply for SSI, homeless applicants are also disproportionately denied benefits.[40] In some states, 95 percent of SSI claims made by homeless applicants are denied. Even in states that do comparatively well in enrolling individuals who are homeless, such as Massachusetts, their denial rate is nearly twice the rate of the housed population. One reason that Massachusetts does better than other states is that it has created *Homeless Claims Units* that employ representatives who are sensitive to homeless individuals and knowledgeable about procedures for processing their claims. In response to President George W. Bush's Samaritan Initiative to end chronic homelessness in ten years, Congress appropriated $8 million in 2003 for outreach demonstration projects to enroll eligible disabled and aged homeless individuals in the SSI program.[41]

One group that previously had difficulty qualifying for SSI benefits is people living with HIV/AIDS. In 1985, AIDS was added to the impairment categories for "presumptive" eligibility, meaning that benefits could be paid to an the applicant for up to six months before a final eligibility decision was made.[42] In 1991, this status was extended to people with HIV if their disease was of a "listing-level" severity (the Social Security Administration provides a list of HIV-related impairments considered severe). For example, a person with HIV who has Kaposi's sarcoma, herpes simplex, Hodgkin's disease and all lymphomas, or HIV Wasting Syndrome would qualify for benefits. The standards set by the Social Security Administration for HIV presumptive eligibility have been challenged in court on the grounds that they discriminate against women. This is because the listing of impairments reflects a course of HIV disease most often seen in men and does not reflect the symptoms that women tend to have.

There are also concerns that factors other than disability, such as race, affect disability determination. A study by the General Accounting Office (GAO) found that in cases that go to an administrative law judge, African Americans who were not represented by an attorney were less likely to be approved for benefits than whites who were not represented.[43] Members of other racial or ethnic groups were approved as often as whites. In cases where applicants were represented by an attorney, blacks and whites were approved at equal rates. Also less likely to receive benefits were males, those with lower incomes, and non-English speakers who *had* a translator at the hearing. The study did not address whether these different approval rates are due to racial or other bias or other factors not accounted for in the study. SSA has provided training to employees to limit the possibility of racial bias, but it is not collecting sufficient data to determine whether members of racial and ethnic groups are continuing to be approved at different rates.

Efforts to contain the growth of SSI are primarily accomplished through disability determination and review processes. The GAO reported that these methods would probably do little to help in the long run, and suggests that "if SSA is to decrease long-term reliance on these [SSI and SSDI] programs . . . it will need to rely less on assessing medical improvement and more on return-to-work programs."[44]

EMPLOYMENT SUPPORTS FOR INDIVIDUALS WITH DISABILITIES

The first institutions for care of people with disabilities in the United States were established in the early nineteenth century. Training and education programs to assist those living in the community with potential for employment did not emerge until the twentieth century.[45] One of the first of these educational programs began in Massachusetts in 1916, and the U.S. Congress soon followed with its own legislation.[46]

Vocational Rehabilitation and Employment Services

In 1920 Congress passed the Vocational Rehabilitation Act (also called the Smith-Fess Act) to assist vocationally disabled civilians and disabled veterans returning from World War I by providing funds through a federal—state matching formula. The federal and state governments shared costs of the Vocational Rehabilitation (VR) program on a fifty–fifty basis. The program was appealing from conservative and economic viewpoints because rehabilitation is generally less costly than long-term care and income maintenance payments. In fact, it has been said that

> *people do not regard vocational rehabilitation as a welfare program. . . . Where welfare fosters dependence, rehabilitation promotes independence. Welfare represents a net cost to society; vocational rehabilitation is an investment in society's future.*[47]

Although originally intended for individuals with physical disabilities, in 1943 individuals with mental illness and intellectual disability were included in the VR program, and in the 1960s those with socially handicapping conditions, including adult and juvenile offenders, were added.[48]

Today, the Rehabilitation Services Administration of the U.S. Department of Education continues to provide formula grant funding for state-operated vocational rehabilitation agencies. These agencies "help individuals with physical or mental disabilities obtain employment and live more independently through the provision of such supports as counseling, medical and psychological services, job training, and other individualized services."[49] The formula funding covers the majority of VR program costs, and the states have latitude to operate their programs as they wish as long as they follow federal guidelines.

In the earlier days of the program, VR was charged with a practice called creaming—focusing on applicants who can achieve rehabilitation most easily. Critics claimed that most of the program's clients were young white males whose disabilities were neither chronic nor severe.[50] This did not sit well with potential consumers (clients) and rehabilitation advocates. Pressure developed to serve those with more severe disabilities. The 1973 amendments to the Vocational Rehabilitation Act helped to accomplish this change. Today the emphasis is on helping those with severe disabilities.

Applicants for VR services are evaluated by a doctor or other experts to determine whether they have a bona fide disability. Individuals who have a reasonable chance of becoming employed or reemployed and remaining so qualify for services. Each applicant accepted for services is assigned a VR counselor, and each consumer develops an individualized plan for employment, which includes the consumer's employment goal and the services needed to reach the goal. Although this sounds like a rational way to optimize services, VR is not an entitlement program. Available funds cannot be stretched to meet the needs of all those who want services. For those who are served, counselors may not be able to procure all the funds and services needed. In addition, because each state administers its own program, individuals with the same or similar disabilities may receive different types and amounts of services depending on the state in which they live.

VR and other employment programs for individuals with disabilities have not achieved all their intended successes. VR programs place about 200,000 individuals in jobs each year, but this has "never made a noticeable impact on the employment rate nationwide."[51] The number of new applications processed by state VR agencies has actually declined over the years. In 1975, 800,000 new applications were processed. In 1999, the figure was only 608,000.[52] In 1975, a total of 1.4 million clients were served by state VR agencies. Fewer than 1 million were served during the 1980s and early 1990s. In 1999, the number served grew again to nearly 1.2 million. Eighty-four percent of clients had severe disabilities. About 63 percent of all clients are considered successfully rehabilitated. The rehabilitation rate is similar for clients with severe disabilities. Federal and state funding for the VR program was $1.1 billion in 1980, $1.9 billion in 1990, and $3.1 billion in 1999.

There are other provisions for assisting individuals with disabilities to obtain employment. The state employment offices have a legal responsibility to assist those with disabilities. Individuals may also qualify under the Workforce Investment Act (see Chapter 9) or other programs.

Eliminating Work Disincentives, Supporting Work

Originally, there was to have been a strong link between the state and federal cash disability assistance programs and vocational rehabilitation. This never materialized as intended. A perverse feature of public policy is that individuals with disabilities who worked risk losing all government-sponsored benefits. This is also the case in the pension program for disabled military veterans and in the private insurance programs that some people purchase to protect themselves against loss of income in the case of disability. In 2002, only 341,000, or 6.5 percent, of all SSI recipients who were disabled or blind worked.[53]

Keeping More Cash Benefits and Health Benefits

For many years, disabled SSI recipients who earned more than the substantial gainful activity earnings limit of $300 a month after a trial work period generally lost their SSI benefits and Medicaid healthcare coverage. In 1990 this amount was raised to $500, and in 1999, to $700. Between 2001 and 2003 it gradually increased to $800, and in 2004 it was $810, still a modest amount of earnings on which to support oneself. Today, workers with disabilities are allowed some income exclusions from earnings (as described earlier in our discussion of SSI) when they engage in work. To further support SSI participants in their efforts to work, Congress amended the Social Security Act in 1980 and again in 1984 and 1986 with a provision known as section 1619. It allows SSI participants who are blind or disabled to keep more earnings from work even if they exceed the substantial gainful earnings limit as long as the disabling condition that qualified them for SSI does not improve. Cash benefits are gradually reduced until a participant's countable earnings reach the SSI standard or "breaking point." In 2004, this breaking point limit was $1,213 per month for participants with disabilities who had no unearned income such as Social Security. This may not seem like a lot, but it is an improvement over previous policy. In 2002 the average earnings for all SSI participants who worked was $495 a month, but those qualifying under section 1619 averaged between $1,043 and $1,094 (a substantial increase from 1987, when disabled earners covered by section 1619 averaged earnings between $494 and $739).[54]

Another benefit is that SSI participants who are disabled or blind remain eligible for Medicaid healthcare coverage even if they exceed the earnings "breaking point." Medicaid eligibility continues until earnings reach a higher level of income that takes into account the individual's ability to afford healthcare and normal living expenses. Considering the high costs of private health insurance, and considering that individuals with disabilities may have substantial medical expenses, this, too, is a welcome change. Medicare benefits for those receiving them are also continued.

Plan to Achieve Self-Support (PASS)

Another effort to help individuals with disabilities work includes Plans to Achieve Self-Support (PASS), which allows workers receiving SSI to save a specified amount of money toward a goal such as attending school or starting a business. The PASS is a formal agreement with the government. The money saved is disregarded in calculating a participant's SSI benefit. An example of what happens to an individual's SSI benefit when she works and when she uses a PASS are described in Illustration 5.1.

ILLUSTRATION 5.1

Working and Using a PASS under SSI

Denni Hunt receives an SSI payment of $564 each month and has Medicaid coverage. This is her only income. She was offered a job in a local fast food restaurant and contacted Social Security to see how this would affect her SSI payment. She was told that Social Security would not count the first $85 of earnings if she had no other income [$20 is automatically disregarded and another $65 is disregarded if the individual works].

Only half of the earnings over $85 would be counted against the SSI payment. Here is how her SSI payment would be affected:

Gross monthly earnings	$215
Subtract the $85 earnings deduction	– 85
	$130
Divide by 2 to get earnings we count	÷ 2
	$ 65
Subtract earnings we count from SSI payment	$564
	– 65
New SSI payment	$499
Add monthly earnings	+ 215
Total income	$714

Note that before she started working, Denni's total income was her SSI check of $564. Now that she's working, she has that extra income in addition to her SSI check ($499), so her total income is $714, even though her SSI payment is reduced.

Denni's pay increased to $367 a month after 18 months. She purchased an electric wheelchair, which cost $52 a month, to help her move better at work. Here's how the work expense deduction helps her:

Gross monthly earnings	$367
Subtract the $85 earnings deduction	– 85
	$282
Subtract work expenses	– 52
	$230
Divide by 2 to get earnings we count	÷ 2
	$115
Subtract earnings we count from SSI payment	$564
	–115
New SSI payment	$449
Add monthly earnings	+ 367
Total income	$816

So, even though her earnings went up by $152 (from $215 to $367), her SSI payment was reduced by only $50 (from $499 to $449) because of the work expense deduction. And her total income now is $816, substantially more than the $564 she had before she started working.

Denni decided that she wanted to get a college degree. Her sister helped her write a PASS, which described her plans to work and save money for school. She wanted to save $75 each month for school. Here's how the PASS helps her:

continued

ILLUSTRATION 5.1 *(continued)*

Gross monthly earnings	$367		Subtract earnings we count from SSI payment	$564
Subtract the $85 earnings deduction	– 85			– 40
	$282		New SSI payment	$524
Subtract work expenses	– 52		Add monthly earnings	+ 367
	$230		Total income (SSI plus earnings)	$891

Divide by 2 to get earnings we count   ÷ 2

                                            $115

Even though her earnings continue as high as they were in the previous example, her SSI checks are increased because we don't have to count the income she is setting aside to go to school. Her total income is now $891 monthly ($367 in earnings plus $524 in SSI).

Subtract PASS   – 75

                     $ 40

Source: Social Security Administration, *Social Security: Working While Disabled . . . How We Can Help,* SSA Publication No. 05-10095, January 1997, updated to reflect 2004 SSI payment amount.

Ticket to Work

In 1999, Congress enacted the Ticket to Work and Self-Sufficiency program. Under the new program, the traditional VR service system has been revamped for some participants and service providers. Ticket to Work is intended to be a comprehensive, "wraparound" program to help individuals with disabilities make the transition to work and sustain work and earnings over the long run. The intent is to improve participants' quality of life while decreasing SSI and SSDI program use.

Ticket to Work contains additional incentives for individuals with disabilities. Individuals can volunteer to participate in the program and receive vocational rehabilitation, employment services, and other support services. The Ticket to Work program was gradually implemented until all states were included in January 2004. Services are provided through "employment networks" (ENs). EN service providers are selected through a competitive bidding process and can be composed of one entity or a group of providers that collaborate with one another. The program attempts to attract more private rehabilitation providers by streamlining the reimbursement process. The Social Security Administration (SSA) provides eligible SSI and SSDI participants with a Ticket to Work document or voucher (see Illustration 5.2). SSI participants can use their tickets to obtain services from the state VR agency or from private EN service providers who are approved to offer employment services or other services the consumer needs to return to work. Competition among services providers is increased, and consumers can choose from more than the state VR agency. Individuals who do

ILLUSTRATION 5.2

Ticket to Work

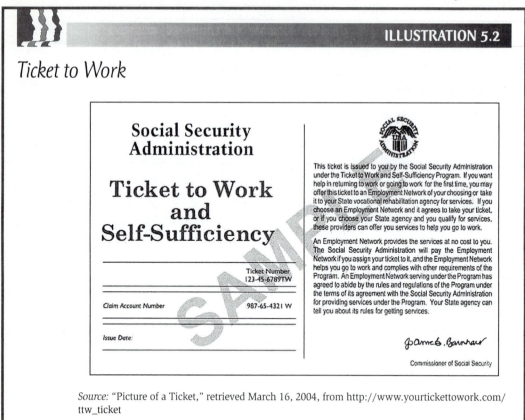

Source: "Picture of a Ticket," retrieved March 16, 2004, from http://www.yourtickettowork.com/ ttw_ticket

not qualify for a ticket may still request services through the traditional state VR eligibility process.[55]

Under Ticket to Work, service providers are reimbursed much differently than in the traditional state VR program. In the traditional program, state agencies must demonstrate outcomes, but once certain outcomes are achieved, services are paid on a cost reimbursement basis. EN providers are reimbursed only if the SSI or SSDI recipient makes a successful return to work. There are two ways providers can be paid. Under the "outcome payment" option, for any month the client receives *no* SSI or SSDI check because of work earnings, the EN gets 40 percent of the average monthly SSI or SSDI benefit for up to 60 months. Under the "outcome milestone payment" option, the EN can receive partial payments based on progress (milestones) the participant achieves in terms of months of work—one month, three months, and seven months in a 12-month period, and 12 months in a 15-month period in which the participant earns at least the amount considered substantial gainful activity. Providers selecting the milestone method begin collecting payments for services earlier than under the outcome option, but they also receive less in total than they would for a client under the outcome option. Private providers must choose one option or the other for all clients they serve. State VR agencies who serve clients with a ticket can opt for cost reimbursement for any client rather than the outcome or milestone option.

To enhance access and coordination of vocational rehabilitation and employment services, SSA has established a corps of "incentive specialists" who provide a program of grants, cooperative agreements, and contracts for benefit planning and assistance to assist individuals with disabilities. They also conduct outreach to identify potential program participants. Another benefit of Ticket to Work is that participants who are unable to continue working because of a medical condition can have their SSI benefits reinstated without filing a new application if benefits were terminated due to excess earnings, and if they file the request within 60 months of the benefit termination date.

Ticket to Work represents a form of privatization, and it could result in creaming, also known as "selection bias" or "favorable risk selection."[56] For example, individuals with severe mental disorders may face substantial obstacles to earning amounts sufficient for EN providers to obtain payments; the Ticket program fails to recognize the benefits of helping people earn more modest amounts.[57] When it comes to assisting individuals with intellectual disability, a case can also be made for paying service providers at some level, even when consumers' earning do not cause them to leave the SSI program.[58] Ticket to Work is a marked change from most government approaches to aiding individuals with disabilities. Evaluations are being conducted to determine its effectiveness.

Making sure that workers with disabilities who have "excess" earnings have healthcare is also important. Under Ticket to Work, states can raise their Medicaid income and asset eligibility limits for participants. States may require that participants "buy in" to the program by sharing in the cost of their coverage. In states with Medicaid buy-in programs, maximum eligibility income ranged from 100 percent of the federal poverty threshold in Wyoming to no income limit in Minnesota.[59] Most participating states set income limits at 200 percent of the poverty threshold or greater. Rather than connect income limits to the poverty threshold, Connecticut capped income at $75,000. Participants buy into the Medicaid program by paying premiums and co-payments for services. Premiums ranged from $26 to $82 per month, and co-payments ranged from $.50 to $3.00 a visit.

THE ERA OF CIVIL RIGHTS FOR INDIVIDUALS WITH DISABILITIES

If vocational rehabilitation constitutes one wave of a more enlightened public response to disability, and income maintenance through public assistance and social insurance programs a second, then the third and most recent wave is surely civil rights reform.[60]

The disability rights perspective views people with disabilities as a minority group that has been subject to discrimination and unfair treatment—in legal terms, a class of people. It stands in contrast to a charitable perspective which views people with disabilities as unfortunate and deserving of pity and care. Likewise, it stands in contrast to a medical model, which views people with disabilities as needing to be "cured." It also stands in contrast to a rehabilitation perspective, which views people with disabilities as needing experts and professionals who can provide services to enhance the functioning of the individual.[61]

Disability is also viewed "as a natural and normal part of the human experience"; rather than "fixing" the individual, the "new paradigm" of disability focuses "on eliminating the attitudinal and institutional barriers that preclude individuals with disabilities from fully participating in society's mainstream."[62]

From Deinstitutionalization to Normalization and Inclusion

Among the first responses of modern society to people with severe physical and mental disabilities was "indoor" relief—the "warehousing" of these individuals in large institutions. Treatment in these places was frequently deplorable. Even with efforts to see that patients or residents had some decent level of care, beliefs mounted that one should not be subjected to a life in an institution. The movement toward **deinstitutionalization** eventually gained judicial backing when, in 1972, the U.S. Supreme Court ruled in the case of *Wyatt v. Stickney* that "No persons shall be admitted to the institution unless prior determination shall have been made that residence in the institution is the least restrictive habilitation setting."[63] Subsequent court decisions have reaffirmed this right, such as *City of Cleburne, Texas v. Cleburne Living Center* in 1985, which supported the rights of individuals with intellectual disabilities to reside in the community. Today the goal of deinstitutionalization has been taken further to include **normalization** and **independent living.**

The concept of normalization apparently emerged in Scandinavia, particularly in Denmark as part of its 1959 Mental Retardation Act.[64] It was adopted in other countries and has been broadened to include those with other disabilities. Normalization means that regardless of the severity of an individual's disability, he or she should have the opportunity to live like other citizens.[65] Individuals with disabilities should have homes located in regular residential communities that resemble other homes in the community, and they should have equal opportunities for shopping, recreation, and other everyday activities.[66] Individuals with disabilities should also have the right to occupy the same social roles—spouses, parents, workers, etc.—as others.[67]

Although it seems logical from humanistic, cost savings, and civil rights perspectives, individuals with disabilities continue to face obstacles to normalization. These obstacles include negative attitudes from the general public, employers, and even human service professionals who underestimate their abilities; architectural and other barriers that continue to prohibit or restrict the use of buildings; and public transportation and other facilities and programs that still provide minimal assistance and foster dependence rather than promote integration.[68] Neighborhood residents frequently cite deed restrictions, declining property values, and safety issues as reasons for "not in my backyard," but "constitutionally, . . . people [with disabilities] have a right to live anywhere they want."[69]

The Independent Living Movement

Along with deinstitutionalization and normalization has come the movement for independent living. Important to this movement are **independent living centers**

(ILCs), which are "private non-profit self-help organization[s] that provide a range of basic services that help individuals with disabilities live independently in the community."[70] Advancements in educational techniques, technology, and medicine have made it possible for many more individuals to live independently. Equally important is that individuals with disabilities have begun to force the issue of their civil rights. ILCs developed through local efforts. They empower individuals with disabilities via their own self-help movement. A prototype is the Center for Independent Living in Berkeley, California. The centers break with the professional model of care in that individuals with disabilities are in charge. They teach others with disabilities how to get all the services to which they are entitled such as social insurance, public assistance, rehabilitation, education, attendant care (also called personal assistance services), and other services that will allow them to live as independently as they can and wish. The group called ADAPT—American Disabled for Attendant Programs Today—focuses on obtaining these services. ADAPT's slogan is "free our people," and according to its home page on the World Wide Web, "There's no place like home, and we mean real homes, not nursing homes."[71] Advocates have also resisted any attempts to reduce funding for the Section 8 Housing Choice Voucher program (see Chapter 3) because it would have serious repercussions for individuals with disabilities who are seeking affordable housing in order to live independently. Many individuals with disabilities also want real jobs in the competitive workforce that pay real wages.[72] They want the same choices and control over where they live, work, and spend leisure time as others in society.

A New Bill of Rights for Individuals with Disabilities

Persistent political efforts by individuals with disabilities, their families, and other advocates have resulted in legislation requiring increased access for individuals with disabilities. For example, the Architectural Barriers Act of 1968 includes specifications aimed at making buildings accessible and safe for individuals who are blind, deaf, using wheelchairs, or who have other disabilities. It requires that all buildings constructed in whole or in part with federal funds and buildings owned or leased by federal agencies have ramps, elevators, and other barrier-free access. Although it sounds as if the law would carry a considerable price tag, estimates are that the cost to the builder is "one-tenth of one percent of the total cost of a new building."[73] Another estimate is that an accessible entrance on a new house costs about $200.[74] The results of accessibility legislation are far from adequate. Many buildings today continue to fall short of the standards for restrooms, parking lots, doors, and warning signals. Locating suitable housing is particularly difficult for people with some types of disabilities. For example, individuals using wheelchairs find that few apartments or houses have accessible entrances, sufficiently wide doorways, or appliances that can be easily reached. To improve accessibility in new homes and apartments, the "visitability" movement works to ensure that all new home construction has a "zero-step" entrance, 36-inch-wide entry doors, and at least one wheelchair-accessible bathroom.[75] Eleanor Smith, a woman with a disability who was inspired through her work with ADAPT, started the movement in 1986 and founded the advocacy organization called *Concrete Change.* Twelve states and many communities have passed visitability legislation for new construction that incorporates at least some of the organization's recommendations. In 2003, a visitability bill was introduced to the U.S. Congress.

The Rehabilitation Act

One of the most important pieces of civil rights legislation for individuals with disabilities is Title V of the Rehabilitation Act of 1973. Under this act,

1. Federal agencies and businesses, organizations, and institutions holding contracts with the U.S. government must have affirmative action programs to hire and promote qualified individuals with disabilities.

2. Discrimination against qualified individuals with disabilities—employees, students, and consumers of healthcare and other services—in all public and private institutions receiving federal assistance is prohibited.

3. The Architectural and Transportation Barriers Compliance Board was established to enforce the 1968 Architectural Barriers Act, and now includes addressing communication barriers.

The Rehabilitation Act was the first to provide specific protections for individuals with disabilities in programs receiving federal funding. Though passed in 1973, implementing regulations were not issued until 1977. Offices of civil rights within agencies such as the U.S. Department of Education and the U.S. Department of Health and Human Services have responsibility for enforcing federal laws that prohibit discrimination against individuals with disabilities.

The Americans with Disabilities Act

Perhaps no piece of legislation, court decision, or administrative ruling holds more significance for individuals with disabilities than the Americans with Disabilities Act (ADA), passed with overwhelming Congressional support in 1990. The bill defines an individual with a disability as one who has "a physical or mental impairment that substantially limits one or more major life activities, a record of such an impairment, or being regarded as having such an impairment." This definition is consistent with those contained in the Rehabilitation Act and the Fair Housing Act. The ADA's goals are "equality of opportunity, full participation, independent living, and economic self-sufficiency." The act goes much farther in requiring private sector compliance than any previous legislation. For example, retail establishments such as restaurants, hotels, and theaters must be accessible. In debates over the bill, businesses argued that not only were the costs to adopt the new measures unrealistic and outrageously expensive, but that they were also unclear and potentially unsafe. For example, in testimony to the Senate, a representative of the National Association of Theater Owners argued against allowing patrons in wheelchairs to sit where they want, because "it is not only reasonable, but it is essential from a safety standpoint that wheelchair patrons be seated near an exit."[76]

Telecommunications provisions of the ADA require that telephone companies provide relay services for customers with hearing and speech impairments. In the area of transportation, all new buses and trains must be made accessible to wheelchair users, but existing vehicles were exempted. Representative Steny Hoyer (D-Maryland), the bill's chief sponsor, called the bill an "Emancipation Proclamation" for individuals with disabilities.

Airlines are not included in the ADA because they are covered under the 1986 Air Carrier Access Act, which prohibits airlines from discriminating against travelers with disabilities. Directives issued in 1990 by the U.S. Department of Transportation state that if an airline requires that an individual with a disability be escorted, the escort must be allowed to fly free. Another directive is that many planes must have moveable armrests and that wide-body planes must have an accessible lavatory. In addition, individuals with disabilities must be allowed to select any seat, except where this might be a safety hazard.

The act also broadened prohibitions on employment discrimination for businesses with 15 or more employees (including Congress but not federal agencies!). It includes bans against discrimination in hiring, firing, compensation, advancement, and training, and also requires employers to make "reasonable accommodations" for individuals with disabilities unless this would case "undue hardship." Reasonable accommodations may include providing readers or interpreters, modifying buildings, adjusting work schedules, and purchasing needed devices. Hardship is defined as "requiring significant expense." Some social welfare theorists complained that the ADA "was legislation on the cheap, mandating new responsibilities for private employers without offering any new financial assistance either to the employers or to the disabled people themselves."[77] The Equal Employment Opportunity Commission helps employers comply with the ADA (see Illustration 5.3), but just how far must employers go to make "reasonable" efforts, and how much is a "significant" expense? According to the U.S. Chamber of Commerce, "this language is an invitation to litigation,"[78] and it has indeed spawned many lawsuits.

With a more conservative Supreme Court, White House, and Congress, recent decisions have diluted the ADA. Between 1999 and 2003 rulings have favored business defendants rather than plaintiffs.[79] In a number of cases, the court has concluded that individuals whose impairment can be corrected with medication or eyeglasses are not "truly disabled" and therefore are not entitled to protection against employment discrimination under the ADA. The "catch-22" is that some people are not "disabled enough" to receive protection under the ADA, but they are disabled enough to be refused a job or fired from a job because their physical or mental limitations, in the employer's opinion, keep them from safely and/or effectively fulfilling job requirements. To date, courts have ruled against individuals with visual impairments, high blood pressure, carpal tunnel syndrome, and liver disease, and a stroke victim. In a Tennessee case, a judge ruled that a 9-year-old with spina bifida, a deformity of the spinal column, did not have a disability as defined by the ADA and therefore was

ILLUSTRATION 5.3

Guidance from the EEOC in Implementing the Americans with Disabilities Act in Cases of Psychiatric Impairment

Some of the examples offered by the Equal Employment Opportunity Commission to help employers implement the Americans with Disabilities Act of 1990 in cases of psychiatric disabilities are found below.

Example: An employee was distressed by the end of a romantic relationship. Although he continued his daily routine, he sometimes became agitated at work. He was most distressed for about a month during and immediately after the breakup. He sought counseling and his mood improved within weeks. His counselor gave him a diagnosis of "adjustment disorder" and stated that he was not expected to experience any long-term problems associated with this event. While he has an impairment (adjustment disorder), his impairment was short term, did not significantly restrict major life activities during that time, and was not expected to have permanent or long-term effects. This employee does not have a disability for purposes of the ADA.

Example: An employee with a psychiatric disability works in a warehouse loading boxes onto pallets for shipment. He has no customer contact and does not come into regular contact with other employees. Over the course of several weeks, he has come to work appearing increasingly disheveled. His clothes are ill-fitting and often have tears in them. He also has become increasingly antisocial. Co-workers have complained that when they try to engage him in casual conversation, he walks away or gives a curt reply. When he has to talk to a co-worker, he is abrupt and rude. His work, however, has not suffered. The employer's company handbook states that employees should be courteous to each other. When told that he is being disciplined for his appearance and treatment of co-workers, the employee explains that his appearance and demeanor have deteriorated because of his disability which was exacerbated during this time period.

The dress code and co-worker courtesy are not job-related for the position in question and consistent with business necessity because this employee has no customer contact and does not come into regular contact with other employees. Therefore, rigid application of these rules to this employee would violate the ADA.

Example: A reference librarian frequently loses her temper at work, disrupting the library atmosphere by shouting at patrons and co-workers. After receiving a suspension as the second step in uniform, progressive discipline, she discloses her disability, states that it causes her behavior, and requests a leave of absence for treatment. The employer may discipline her because she violated a conduct standard—a rule prohibiting disruptive behavior towards patrons and co-workers—that is job-related for the position in question and consistent with business necessity. The employer, however, must grant her request for a leave of absence as a reasonable accommodation, barring undue hardship, to enable her to meet this conduct standard in the future.

Source: Excerpted from Equal Employment Opportunity Commission, *EEOC Enforcement Guidance on the Americans with Disabilities Act and Psychiatric Disabilities* (Washington, DC: The Commission, March 25, 1997), retrieved March 14, 2004, from http://www.eeoc.gov/policy/guidance.html

not permitted to keep her service animal. The U.S. Supreme Court has supported a strict definition of disability, indicating that it must interfere with essential tasks such as brushing one's teeth or washing one's face.

Plaintiffs are also filing ADA law suits against states, but they are losing and states are winning based on the notion of "sovereign immunity" provided under the 11th Amendment to the U.S. Constitution. This amendment holds that it is unlawful to sue a state without the state's permission; consequently, individuals with disabilities have been denied punitive damages in suits against negligent states. For example, in the Garret decision (a ruling on two cases), Patricia Garret was denied punitive damages when she sued her employer, a state hospital, for demoting her after being diagnosed and treated for breast cancer; and Milton Ash was denied damages he sought from his state employer for not providing reasonable workplace accommodations for his asthma condition. Dissenting judges in the decisions argued that the ADA transcends sovereign immunity. Others infer from the rulings that the ADA and the Rehabilitation Act are unconstitutional because Congress overstepped its authority by telling states what to do. Some advocates fear that opponents of the law—particularly businesses—will not be satisfied until the U.S. Supreme Court rules that the ADA is unconstitutional and overreaches the powers of Congress. In fact, the majority opinion issued by U.S. Supreme Court Chief Justice William Rehnquist indicated that "efforts to open states to lawsuits exceeded Congress's authority."[80]

Some news has been more positive for individuals with disabilities. One of the most significant cases concerns the U.S. Supreme Court's 1999 Olmstead decision.[81] The court ruled that states violated the ADA by serving people in institutions when they could be served more appropriately in community-based settings. Since this decision, states have had to move more people out of institutions and into community-based care settings when treatment professionals determine that this is more appropriate, and the person affected desires it.

Much has been achieved under the ADA, including changes that we now take for granted—wheelchair-accessible curbs, lifts on public transportation, ramps to public and private buildings, and sign language interpreters for public speeches and events. Individuals with disabilities are more visible in the workplace and other public places. These signs of progress do not assure that individuals with disabilities have achieved equal protection under the law. Many civil rights concerns persist, such as the right to obtain as well as to refuse treatment and to informed consent, guardianship, fair treatment if accused of a crime, and voting rights and zoning restrictions on community residences.[82]

Additional issues confront advocates of the rights of individuals with intellectual disability (mental retardation). In 2002 the U.S. Supreme Court finally ruled that execution of death row inmates who are mentally retarded constituted cruel and unusual punishment, but it left the states to determine what constitutes mental retardation. There have been outcries against a decision by the Iowa Supreme Court that once again gives courts in that state the power to decide whether individuals who are intellectually disabled can be sterilized. The institutionalization of individuals with intellectual disability has been particularly vexing because they are often denied the same rights as individuals who are mentally ill to have their cases reviewed for discharge.

The New Freedom Initiative

To move further in achieving the goals of the ADA, in 2001, President George W. Bush used Executive Order 13217 to launch his *New Freedom Initiative*. This initiative is designed to further remove barriers to community living for individuals of all ages with disabilities and long-term illnesses.[83] Departments throughout the federal government have been directed to work in partnership with states to provide individuals who are elderly or disabled with the supports needed for full participation in community life. The initiative aims to move more individuals with disabilities into the workforce and to move people out of nursing homes and other institutional living settings to community living, when appropriate, with a five-year, $1.75 billion budget. States are to develop demonstration projects for meeting the initiative's objectives. Funding to help individuals with severe disabilities has favored institutional settings. Under the president's initiative, money would "follow the individual," allowing individuals with disabilities more choices and allowing states more options for serving them. Demonstration projects are also focused on providing respite care for caregivers and providing community-based-care alternatives for children with disabilities, including those residing in psychiatric residential treatment facilities. Another aspect of the legislation concerns Medicaid eligibility for spouses. Under current law, individuals with disabilities might be discouraged from returning to work because their earnings could jeopardize the eligibility of a spouse who receives Medicaid. The proposal would provide spouses the same Medicaid coverage protection now offered to workers with disabilities. U.S. Secretary of Health and Human Services Thompson created a new Office on Disability within HHS to coordinate activities across the department. The office will be a focal point for addressing disability. But now the concern is that with a weaker economy the president is backing off some of his spending promises.[84] Illustration 5.4 contains a commentary on the New Freedom Initiative.

DISABILITY POLICY FOR CHILDREN

Many advancements in assisting individuals with developmental disabilities (DD) stem from efforts in the 1960s.[85] Advocates gained a valuable ally in President John F. Kennedy, who had a sister with intellectual disability. The original, federal definition of developmental disabilities appeared in the Developmental Disabilities and Facilities Construction Act of 1970 and was expanded in the Developmental Disabilities Assistance and Bill of Rights Act of 1975. In 1987, the Rehabilitation Comprehensive Services and Developmental Disabilities Amendments eliminated specific diagnostic categories such as mental retardation, cerebral palsy, epilepsy, and autism in favor of a broader definition of developmental disability. Amendments to the act continue to foster the evolution of a more acceptable definition.

ILLUSTRATION 5.4

Dubya's New Freedom Initiative

JUST HOW MUCH "FREEDOM" IS THAT, ANYWAY?

by Marta Russell

"My Administration is committed to tearing down the barriers to equality that face many of the 54 million Americans with disabilities."

President-Select George W. Bush was unveiling his "New Freedom Initiative." The feel-good "equality" and "freedom" speech was well received, even by liberals like Sen. Ted Kennedy.

Disability in many ways has been a bipartisan issue in Washington politics, largely because it is nonthreatening to either party. Both parties have found ways to use it to fit their agendas. The GOP can put the emphasis on empowerment and ending dependency on government entitlements, while the Democrats can focus on civil rights and equal opportunity. Both parties get political mileage out of it. That doesn't mean that the disability movement has made substantial gains, however, especially when it comes to income equality.

In his New Freedom Initiative, Bush says that "new technologies" are essential to disabled people's participation—new technologies like text telephones for those with hearing impairments, computer monitors with braille displays for those with visual impairments, infrared pointers for people who cannot use their hands, lighter wheelchairs, lighter artificial limbs. "These modern wonders make the world more accessible, yet they are often inaccessible to people who need but cannot afford them," says the President.

But what does the President propose to do to remedy this situation? He is asking Congress to create a new fund—a federal investment—that would go directly to rehabilitation centers and businesses to develop and produce such equipment. Here's the clincher: These organizations will get money to pay staff and develop products, while disabled people, who absolutely need them, will have to purchase the equipment by taking out low-interest loans. The developers get the government money outright; the disabled person must find a way to pay for those products.

How does this tear down barriers to equality?

Harris Poll surveys commissioned by the National Organization on Disability in the decade since the Americans with Disabilities Act became law have found persistent gaps between disabled and nondisabled Americans in employment, education, voting and political participation, and in involvement in community, social, and religious life.

In 1998 the NOD/Harris Survey found that fully a third (34 percent) of adults with disabilities live in a household with an annual income of less than $15,000 compared to one in eight (12 percent) of those without disabilities. The gap between disabled and nondisabled persons living in very low-income households has remained virtually constant since 1986. Disabled people are twice as likely not to finish high school (22 versus 9 percent). A far higher percentage live in households that are below the poverty level (29 versus 10 percent).

continued

ILLUSTRATION 5.4 *(continued)*

Disabled people suffer from watered-down legislation and middle-of-the-road approaches which satisfy both political parties, don't accomplish much in the way of equality of results and keep us as vulnerable as ever to the capitalist economy. Disabled peoples' advancement has suffered from both the New Democrats' and GOP's unwillingness to address the relationship between "equality" and redistribution.

"For Americans without disabilities, technology makes things easier," says the National Council on Disability, but "for Americans with disabilities, technology makes things possible." In other words, it is necessary from the get-go for a disabled person to have this technology in order to function.

Yet assistive technology is an expense on top of and beyond what a nondisabled person must spend to accomplish similar tasks. To fulfill any notion of "equality" would require taking into account this difference. For equality to exist in this particular situation, the disabled person would have to have the technology to experience any freedom. It is not "optional."

Yet Dubya's New Freedom Initiative would make that freedom contingent upon a person's being able to take out loans and pay for it themselves.

How likely is it that a disabled person who has been surviving on the average Social Security benefit of $786 a month (for SSDI; for SSI it is an even skimpier $372) will be in the position to risk taking out a loan—with no guarantee of a job? How can a disabled person without the assistive technology, in fact, even be job-ready? A disabled person needs the technology just to function, whether or not she ever has a job. But without a job, how likely will they be to spring for a loan, low-interest or not?

The New Freedom Initiative does not mention alleviating the poverty of those trying to struggle by on SSDI or SSI below-poverty checks. It does not address the problems disabled people face daily in dealing with Medicaid, which is cutting back what it will pay for all the time; nor access to an attendant, a grossly underpaid job that no one wants; nor Medicare, which has never been designed to provide services of the type disabled persons need. By omitting such realities, the New Freedom Initiative becomes simply more useless talk about "freedom" in a country where people's material needs do not get met.

BUSH GIVETH, AND TAKETH AWAY . . .

The Commerce Department's proposed budget for the fiscal year starting Oct. 1 cuts the Technology Opportunities Program set up in the Clinton administration by about 65 percent, according to a story in the Wall Street Journal Interactive.

Bush FCC head Michael Powell reportedly likened the digital divide to "a Mercedes divide—I'd like to have one, I can't afford one."

The budget move signals what the Journal called a "federal retreat from efforts to encourage Internet use among minorities, the poor and people in rural areas." Not to mention disabled people.

Source: Ragged Edge Online, retrieved March 18, 2004, from http://www.raggededgemagazine.com/0501/0501ft3.htm

Marta Russell is author of *Beyond Ramps: Disability at the End of the Social Contract.*

© 2001 by The Advocado Press

Developmental Disabilities Assistance and Bill of Rights Act

The current definition of developmental disabilities is found in the Developmental Disabilities Assistance and Bill of Rights Act Amendments of 2000.

> *"Developmental disability" means a severe, chronic disability of an individual that is attributable to a mental or physical impairment or a combination of mental and physical impairments; is manifested before the individual reaches age 22; is likely to continue indefinitely; results in substantial functional limitations in 3 or more of the following areas of major life activity: self-care, receptive and expressive language, learning, mobility, self-direction, capacity for independent living, and economic self-sufficiency; and reflects the individual's need for a combination and sequence of special, interdisciplinary, or generic services, supports, or other forms of assistance that are of lifelong or extended duration and are individually planned and coordinated. Children younger than age 9 may also be considered developmentally disabled if they do not meet three of the criteria but have a condition that could cause them to do so if they do not receive services or supports.*

Most families and professionals believe that this definition is more functionally oriented, less stigmatizing, and does not restrict services to only those with specific diagnoses. Concern is that the definition may leave too much room for interpretation and prevent individuals with less severe disabilities from receiving services that could substantially improve the quality of their lives.

The amended definition of developmental disabilities has expanded the array of services to which individuals with disabilities are entitled. In addition, every state has either a separate commission or a special unit in its Vocational Rehabilitation office to serve individuals who are blind, and a number of schools provide education and training at the kindergarten through twelfth-grade levels specifically to children who are blind. At the federal level, the Deafness and Communicative Disorders Branch of the Rehabilitation Services Administration provides consultation to the states in developing services for individuals who are deaf or have other communication disorders. It also works on developing technological devices to assist individuals with disabilities. Designated publicly funded schools throughout the country provide residential programs for children who are deaf from infancy through high school. In 1972 the Economic Opportunity Act was amended to include a goal that 10 percent of Head Start enrollees be children with disabilities.

Inclusion for Children with Disabilities

Once a controversial issue, mainstreaming (also called inclusion) is now an accepted right of children with disabilities and their families, thanks to the Education for All Handicapped Children Act of 1975, P.L. 94-142, renamed the Individuals with Disabilities Education Act (IDEA) in 1990. The act states that every child with a disability is entitled to an "appropriate elementary and secondary education." If a child must be placed in a private school by the local education authority in order to obtain an appropriate education, this service must be provided at no cost to the child's family. Other services, including transportation and special devices, must also be provided. In 1997 IDEA was reauthorized with various amendments, including provisions to expand mediation services when parents and schools disagree on what a child needs and will get.

Inclusion has been hailed as a sensible and effective way to ensure that children with physical and mental disabilities are afforded full opportunities to learn and to interact with other children. It allows for the integration of children with disabilities into the mainstream of society and prepares them to be part of the community. Children who are mainstreamed may attend some special education classes, but most children with disabilities spend the majority of their time in regular classrooms.[86] Today, over 13 percent of students in public schools have a disability, and about 6.5 million children between the ages of 6 and 21 who have disabilities received special education services under IDEA in 2003. About 76 percent of teachers report that they instruct children with disabilities at least some of the time.

Early efforts at mainstreaming met with resistance as the number of children requiring services grew and states had to bear to majority of the cost of their education. Small, poor school systems were particularly hard pressed to meet the demands of the law. Advocates have long contended that Congress has never come close to providing the 40 percent funding for the additional costs of educating children with disabilities it promised in the 1975 act. In 2003 Congress provided an estimated 18 percent.[87]

Another issue for students with disabilities and teachers is the No Child Left Behind (NCLB) Act of 2001.[88] The NCLB law requires that all students—including students with disabilities—perform proficiently on reading and math tests. This is a new challenge for students in special education and their teachers. Until now, children in special education have largely been excluded from state testing. On one hand, teachers and parents welcome increased expectations for students with disabilities; on the other hand, they are concerned that expectations to perform at the same level as nondisabled students may invite unintended and harsh consequences. For the first time, federal law requires public schools to demonstrate how well they are serving children with disabilities, but making this assessment in a fair and appropriate manner is a concern. For example, 67 percent of children with disabilities in the public school system have specific learning disabilities or speech or language impairments. Twelve percent have significant cognitive impairments such as intellectual disability or head injuries. In the first year of testing since the passage of the new law, special education and general education students were compared on test outcomes. In 30 of 39 states with complete data, there was an achievement gap between special education and general education students of 30 percentage points or more on fourth-grade reading tests. In December 2003, the U.S. Department of Education responded by issuing a rule that states may use alternative forms of assessment for no more than 1 percent of students who have the most "significant cognitive disabilities," but states can appeal the 1 percent cap.[89]

A FAIR DEFINITION OF DISABILITY, A FAIR POLICY

There are many types of disabilities—amputations, arthritis, blindness, brain injuries, cerebral palsy, deafness, diabetes, mental illness, epilepsy, heart disease, mental retardation, multiple sclerosis, respiratory disorders, stroke, and stuttering among them. Disabilities may also be classified in terms of degree of impairment. Some individuals have disabilities so severe or significant that they can perform few activities of daily living, yet others function quite well even with significant disabilities. The traditional definition of disability is health-related problems that prevent an individual from working.[90] A more contemporary definition is limitations on any role or task a person usually performs in society, especially if these limitations exist for a long period of time.[91]

A fair or rational policy on disability may start with a fair definition, but the definitions of disability in various federal and state laws are not always consistent. During the 1980s, there were controversies over how HIV status fit into the definition of disability. Court decisions supported that HIV and AIDS were disabling conditions included under federal law. As noted earlier in this chapter, alcoholism and drug addiction are no longer sufficient conditions for receiving SSDI and SSI, but the ADA protects people with alcohol and drug addictions from discrimination when they receive medical or other services. Like other social problems, disability is a social construction, "a social judgment,"[92] and these constructions are subject to change.

No definition written on paper can really capture the abilities or the limitations of an individual with a disability, but disability-determination personnel are expected to weigh the evidence and make these decisions every day about individuals whom they generally have never seen. Is it the right of individuals with disabilities to receive social welfare benefits, or is it their obligation to make whatever contributions they can?[93] Does society prefer to pay benefits to individuals with disabilities rather than do what is necessary to include individuals with disabilities in the mainstream of U.S. life? Is our goal to make individuals with disabilities fit the workplace and other social institutions, or is it to make society accommodate individuals with disabilities? From the start, there was controversy over whether SSDI would stifle rehabilitation, but today the question is why there is not a more rational policy that supports individuals with disabilities in their efforts to work and live independently. The goals of the different waves of disability policy—financial assistance, rehabilitation programs, and civil rights—are often at odds with one another. In fact, the growth of SSDI and SSI is paradoxical given medical, technological, and civil rights advances that are supposed to make it easier for individuals with disabilities to function in the workplace.

Part of the importance of the ADA is that it is applicable across the United States, but some states already have more stringent legislation or include provisions not found in the ADA. "For example, California's Fair Employment and Housing Act provides for compensatory and punitive damages [in addition to other payments] where the ADA [generally] does not."[94] Monitoring and enforcement are keys to assuring that the rights of individuals with disabilities are upheld.[95] The EEOC reports that in fiscal year 2002, it received nearly 16,000 charges of disability discrimination, resolved nearly 19,000 charges, and recovered $50 million in monetary benefits for aggrieved parties (not including compensation obtained through litigation).[96] The U.S. Department of Justice is the agency primarily responsible for enforcing the ADA. Disability advocates have complained that the DOJ is not aggressive enough in pursuing cases. The disability rights movement has become increasingly strident and even militant, with some members subjecting themselves to arrest as in the days of the civil rights movements for racial equality.[97] *Mouth* magazine, which calls itself the "voice of the disability nation,"complains that DOJ is not aggressive enough in enforcing the ADA and prefers to "educate, negotiate, and mediate" rather than take cases to trial.[98]

Given the many and often contradictory disability policies and programs, disability historian and expert Edward Berkowitz recommends a congressional oversight committee and a federal agency dedicated to bringing together the many experts [including individuals with disabilities] needed to see disability as a whole.[99] The oversight committee would address the national budget for disability and serve as the conduit for disability policy. He suggests expanding the scope of the independent federal agency called the National Council on Disability so it could do more to insure that public policy "recognizes the capabilities" of individuals with disabilities. Berkowitz also recommends flexible policies that provide the supports needed by those who can and want to remain in the labor force (similar to the Ticket to Work) and that help others retire with dignity and a decent standard of living. He advocates the creation of "independence initiatives," which individuals could use to purchase attendant care or to make environmental modifications, and "independent living block grants" to localities to establish ILCs along with the guarantee of healthcare and the "vigorous enforcement" of civil rights protections.

GENERAL ASSISTANCE: THE STATE AND COMMUNITY RESPONSE TO WELFARE

Most of the major social welfare programs for the "deserving poor" discussed thus far are now totally or partly the responsibility of the federal government. The SSI and VR programs are cases in point. But some social welfare programs continue to be developed, administered, and financed by state and local governments, independent of the federal government. The term used to describe many of these programs is General Assistance (GA). General Assistance predated the New Deal, when local and state governments were the major suppliers of public assistance. Although the New Deal and subsequent developments at the federal level created many important social welfare programs, they do not include many needy people who were covered under the original General Assistance programs.[100] General Assistance exists today because the United States continues to use a fragmented approach to meeting social welfare needs. Some poor people do not meet the criteria for *any* of the major federal or federal–state welfare programs. They may not be aged or disabled, at least not according to federal standards; they may not have dependent children; they may not be entitled to unemployment benefits, or they may have exhausted them. They may need immediate assistance, unable to wait for federal benefits, which may take 30 days or more to begin. In other words, being "needy" is not always enough to qualify for social welfare assistance.

Although most Americans have heard of the TANF (formerly AFDC), Food Stamp, and Medicaid programs, and many have heard of the SSI program, General Assistance is not as well known. In some places it is referred to as "county welfare," "county aid," or "general relief." General Assistance programs are administered differently from state to state and even from one locality to another within the same state. The types and amounts of services also vary considerably, as do the types of recipients served. In some cases, the state government is entirely responsible for the General Assistance program. It determines the policies and procedures for General Assistance, and state workers accept applications and provide assistance to recipients. In other areas, the state may set policies and determine eligibility requirements, but General Assistance is administered by local governments. In these cases, the state may provide all the funding, or the state and local governments may share funding responsibilities. Other states have no involvement in General Assistance. Local governments are free to establish programs if they desire. If not, no General Assistance is available.

General Assistance has many uses. Historically the program has aided people who receive little or nothing from other social welfare programs and who need help, especially in emergencies. TANF and SSI beneficiaries are usually ineligible for GA except while waiting for these public assistance payments to begin. In some areas the emphasis is on helping poor people cover medical expenses. Other uses have been to assist people who are elderly or disabled, especially before improvements in the SSI program, and also to help the unemployed and those who earned very little.[101]

Some programs provide cash assistance; others rely on in-kind assistance such as medical care, and some use a combination of the two. GA has been called "the last strand in the safety net," especially for childless adults who have few other places to turn, but GA continues to be very sensitive to budget pressures.[102]

Immediately following passage of the Social Security Act, General Assistance expenditures decreased sharply as recipients transferred to the new federal-state public assistance programs.[103] In the last few decades, GA expenditures increased from $1.4 billion in 1980 to $3.7 billion in 2000, but budget pressures have again taken their toll. In 2001, GA expenditures were $3.3 billion.[104] These figures and virtually all aggregate data on GA programs should be interpreted cautiously, because there are no federal reporting regulations, "recordkeeping is notoriously lax,"[105] and information is difficult to obtain.[106] It has been suggested that some counties do not collect or report GA data because they fear that the information might be used to mount legal challenges to the amount of aid provided and the way it is provided.[107]

The Urban Institute sponsored the most recent comprehensive study of GA programs, focusing on changes in GA programs from 1989 to 1998 (see Table 5.4).[108] This study showed that 23 states have uniform statewide eligibility rules as does the District of Columbia. In nine states every county must have a program, but each county sets its own eligibility rules. Two states provide funding and supervision for counties that decide to operate programs. In states with GA programs, funding is generally provided by the state only or the counties also contribute. Sixteen (primarily southern)

TABLE 5.4

General Assistance Programs at a Glance, by Number of States, Summer 1998

Availability of GA Programs

States with GA Programs (includes District of Columbia)	41
Program throughout entire state	33
Program in only portion of the state	8
States with no GA Program	10

Populations Served by GA Programs

Disabled, elderly, and/or unemployable individuals	34
Children and/or families with children	24
Employable individuals without children	13

Form of GA Benefits

Cash (6 use electronic benefit transfers)	24
Vendor Payments/Vouchers	6
Mix of Cash and Vendor Payments/Vouchers	11

Maximum Cash Benefits as a Percentage of Poverty (individual recipients)

Average	37%
Low (Missouri)	12%
High (Nebraska)	96%

Duration of GA Benefits

No time limits	27
Time limits for a portion of beneficiaries	8
Time limits for all beneficiaries	6

Source: Jerome Gallagher, Cori E. Uccello, Alicia B. Pierce, and Erin B. Reidy, "State General Assistance Programs 1998" (Washington, DC: Urban Institute, September 1, 1999), Series A, No. A-36, http://www. urban.org/url.cfm?ID=409066. Used with permission.

states have no involvement in GA programs. In six of these states, one or more counties offer GA. The county programs generally provide less assistance than state programs and are more likely to offer in-kind benefits only. Though no GA program is available in many jurisdictions, localities often offer some emergency assistance.

GA is apparently "in decline. Most states have eliminated part or all of their programs, many recipients now receive limited vouchers instead of cash benefits; and cash benefits have not kept up with inflation."[109] GA benefits generally fall well below SSI and TANF benefits, and to qualify, participants generally cannot have income that exceeds half the poverty level. Able-bodied adults without dependent children (ABAWDs) have been hurt the most. In 1989, 25 states assisted this population; in 1998, only 13 did. In Michigan, Illinois, and Ohio combined, nearly 200,000 ABAWDs lost benefits. In the handful of states where this population is still served, there is more emphasis on getting them back to work. GA recipients who are elderly or disabled have fared better but still face reduced benefits or time limits in many cases. Four states did cut their program for individuals with disabilities, and others ended aid for at least some individuals with temporary disabilities. Benefits for children and families were least affected, but three states did cut aid to them entirely and four states restricted eligibility. Since the passage of welfare reform in 1996, nine states have transferred families with children previously eligible for GA to TANF because TANF allows coverage for more two-parent families and pregnant women than were previously included under AFDC. These families have usually fared better because TANF assistance is more generous than GA. In keeping with the tenor of the 1996 welfare reform, many states now deny GA benefits to immigrants who are not citizens. Of concern is that even as states encountered better economic times after 1998, they did not shore up their GA programs to help those still in need.[110]

FEDERALISM AND SOCIAL WELFARE

At the country's inception, the founding fathers laid out the federal government's powers in the Constitution and retained many powers for the states.[111] They did not want too much power vested in a single government. Originally, the federal government concentrated on national defense, foreign affairs, and issues that cut across state lines, like interstate commerce and postal service. The states were the major government entities, and social welfare, like most domestic issues, was the states' concern. Martin Grodzins referred to the separate functions of federal and state governments as "layer cake" federalism, also known as "dual federalism."[112] Much has changed in regard to federalism since the U.S. Constitution was signed in 1787.

Several events began to transform the conception of federalism. Among them were economic changes brought about by the Industrial Revolution, the country's involvement in World War I, and the institution of the federal income tax, which greatly increased the federal government's coffers. The Great Depression and the New Deal were defining moments for federalism in the social welfare arena. As the twentieth century progressed, the United States engaged more and more in "cooperative federalism" ("marble cake" federalism, as Grodzins called it) in which the federal and state governments share functions like social welfare. With the inception of the Great Society programs—like Food Stamps, Medicare, and Medicaid—during the 1960s, the federal government's role in social welfare grew even larger, resulting in a more centralized federalism.

For many years following the New Deal, the trend was toward greater centralization or federalization of social welfare programs. But during the Reagan presidency, debate over the appropriate approach to federalism in social welfare took on new vigor. Reagan had some successes in turning more responsibility for social welfare services and other services back to the states, primarily by collapsing a number of small programs into several block grants. His successor, George H. W. Bush, continued this new federalism by allowing some states to experiment with reforms in AFDC and other programs, a practice expanded during the Clinton administration. Clinton did want to institute national health insurance (see Chapter 8), but even his plan called for a certain amount of state discretion in administering the program.

People feel differently about which brand of federalism best serves social welfare interests. Some people (generally liberals) believe that only greater federal involvement can assure fair treatment of those in need and that the federal government can muster more resources to provide a higher standard of payments or care. Others (generally conservatives) believe that public assistance and social service programs should be the responsibility of state (or local) governments—government closer to home. They feel that the fifty state governments can be more responsive to their residents and that they create more innovation. But at the state and local levels, politics over social welfare programs and other programs is more contentious because the costs are spread over fewer people than when Congress takes action and institutes a program directed at needy individuals across the nation.

This diversity of opinion has led to very different arrangements in the social welfare programs. Social Security and Medicare, the largest social welfare programs, are the sole responsibility of the U.S. government. Unemployment insurance is largely a state program, though the federal government does help to extend benefits when unemployment rates remain high. Workers' compensation is almost entirely the purview of the states.

Like the major social insurance programs, the major public assistance programs are administered and funded in different ways. Food stamps and SSI are primarily programs of the federal government. The federal government assumes responsibility for eligibility requirements and benefit levels in the Food Stamp Program. In the SSI program the federal government finances a basic benefit and establishes basic eligibility requirements, but most states make some effort to supplement federal SSI benefits for at least some categories of recipients. TANF and Medicaid are joint ventures of the federal and state governments, which share in funding the programs. The federal government sets administrative guidelines but the states play a major role in determining eligibility requirements and benefits. There are, however, important differences in the intergovernmental arrangements in these two programs. Medicaid remains an open-ended entitlement program available to all who qualify. As part of the new federalism or devolution, TANF (formerly AFDC) is now structured as a block grant program with capped federal funding, regardless of how many families meet eligibility requirements. Under TANF, states have considerably more discretion over program rules than they did under the AFDC entitlement program (see Chapter 6). There are continued calls to turn over Medicaid and other social welfare programs entirely to the states—and just as much effort to resist these kinds of actions by supporters of a more federalized approach. General Assistance is a highly discretionary type of program and is the major public assistance program funded and administered by state and/or local governments with no federal participation.

Most social service programs, like mental health, child welfare, and vocational rehabilitation, are jointly funded by the federal and state governments. The level of involvement in funding and administration by the federal government and the states varying substantially depending on the specific program.

Clashes over federalism in the social welfare arena occur not only in the cash and in-kind benefit programs, but in other areas as well. As this chapter illustrated, state and local governments become frustrated when they feel the federal government issues mandates without providing sufficient resources to meet them. Such is the case with achieving new educational standards under the No Child Left Behind Act. Even if states believe in the spirit of the law, they argue that funding is inadequate to do the job. Some states also argue that that the federal government has exceeded its authority by making them the subject of lawsuits under certain provisions of the Americans with Disabilities Act. We continue to debate the appropriate roles of the federal, state, and local governments in social welfare (and other domains), but the states have become dependent on the federal government for monies to meet social welfare needs. There is really no turning back here, even if the recent trend has been to shift more responsibility for public assistance decision making back to the states.

SUMMARY

Social insurance, public assistance, social and rehabilitative services, and civil rights legislation are all of importance to people with disabilities. The major public assistance program for individuals with disabilities is the Supplemental Security Income (SSI) program. Despite problems such as low payments and delays in determining eligibility, SSI has been one of the major improvements in providing social welfare benefits to Americans since the original Social Security Act became law in 1935.

An important social service program for people with disabilities is the Vocational Rehabilitation (VR) program. VR is a limited program because not everyone who is disabled is entitled to assistance. The primary criterion for participation is the individual's potential for returning to work. For years, the VR program was accused of creaming—taking on clients who are most easy to rehabilitate and rejecting others— but in recent years the program has focused on clients with more severe disabilities. The 2001 Ticket to Work program seeks to make vocational rehabilitation services more accessible to people with disabilities. It reduces work disincentives by increasing the amount of earned income disregarded in computing SSI benefits and extends Medicaid coverage.

Individuals with physical and mental disabilities face a number of obstacles in achieving independence. Laws which emerged in the 1960s and 1970s were important steps in recognizing the rights of people with disabilities. The most important achievement of this period was Title V of the Rehabilitation Act of 1973, which makes it illegal for programs and agencies that receive federal funds to discriminate against individuals with disabilities in employment, education, and use of services.

Another significant piece of legislation was the Developmental Disabilities Assistance and Bill of Rights Act of 1975. As a result of this act, an array of services are available to those whose disability is manifested before age 22. The Individuals with Disabilities Education Act guarantees all children, regardless of their disability, a free, publicly funded education. Under this act, children are "mainstreamed"—placed in regular schools and classrooms whenever possible. Today more than six million children with disabilities attend public schools, and most spend the majority of their time in regular classrooms. The No Child Left Behind Act now requires that public schools not only serve children with disabilities but also document that they meet the same education standards as other children.

No recent legislation has been more encouraging for promoting the inclusion of citizens with disabilities than the Americans with Disabilities Act of 1990 with its expanded provisions to prevent discrimination in public and private accommodations, employment, communications, and travel. Other recent successes, such as the Olmstead decision, helped move more individuals from institutional to community-based settings. However, the current conservative Supreme Court has favored employers over individuals with disabilities in ADA employment lawsuits. The ADA is also being challenged on grounds that it is unconstitutional because it violates states' sovereign immunity.

Despite civil rights advances that might lead to greater employment of people with disabilities, SSI and Social Security Disability Insurance rolls have soared. This is largely because the social welfare policies that affect people with disabilities are contradictory. Most publicly funded assistance for people with disabilities comes in the form of much needed cash payments. What is lacking are rehabilitative services, attendant care services, and other services that promote inclusion, independence, and meaningful activity like work. President George W. Bush's New Freedom Initiative provides funds to states and institutions to remove barriers to independent living for people with disabilities.

An important public assistance program for some individuals with limited financial resources is General Assistance. GA generally helps individuals who are not covered by other public assistance programs. GA programs are funded and administered by state or local governments with no federal government involvement. These programs vary considerably across states and communities with respect to eligibility and payment levels. Some states and communities have no GA program at all.

The United States lacks a consensus about the best methods for funding and administering social welfare programs. Although some believe that the federal government is best suited to perform these functions because of its large revenue base and its ability to treat recipients equally regardless of the state in which they live, the trend over the past 25 years has been toward greater state control of social welfare programs. One danger in this shift is the loss of national focus on the needs of the poor.

NOTES

1. John G. Turnbull, C. Arthur Williams, Jr., and Earl F. Cheit, *Economic and Social Security* (New York: Ronald Press, 1967), p. 83.

2. *Ibid.*

3. The remainder of this paragraph relies on Robert J. Myers, *Social Security* (Bryn Mawr, PA: McCahan Foundation, 1975), pp. 400–401.

4. This paragraph relies on *ibid.*, p. 401.

5. See Edward D. Berkowitz, *Disabled Policy: America's Programs for the Handicapped* (Cambridge, England: Cambridge University Press, 1987), p. 58. Reprinted with the permission of Cambridge University Press.

6. U.S. Bureau of the Census, *Statistical Abstract of the United States: 1965* (Washington, DC: U.S. Government Printing Office, 1965), p. 309.

7. Daniel P. Moynihan, *The Politics of a Guaranteed Income* (New York: Random House, 1973).

8. Robert A. Diamond, ed., *Future of Social Programs* (Washington, DC: Congressional Quarterly, August 1973), p. 15.

9. For additional information on state supplements, see Committee on Ways and Means, U.S. House of Representatives, *2003 Green Book,* Section 3, "Supplemental Security Income" (Washington, DC: December 18, 2003), pp. 3-56–3-57, retrieved February 17, 2004, from http://waysandmeans.house.gov/Documents.asp?section = 813

10. *Ibid.*, p. 3-15.

11. Much of the information in this section relies on *ibid.*

12. The website of the Social Security Administration, http://www.ssa.gov, provides the latest figures on SSI payments. Check with individual states for the amounts of state supplements.

13. Social Security Administration, *Disability Evaluation under Social Security* (also known as the "Blue Book") (Washington, DC: Social Security Administration, 2003), retrieved March 18, 2004, from http://www.ssa.gov; Social Security Administration, "Disability Planner, How We Decide If You Are Disabled," retrieved March 14, 2004, from http://www.ssa.gov/dibplan/dqualify6.htm

14. Social Security Administration, *Performance and Accountability Report Fiscal Year 2003* (Washington, DC: 2003), p. 67, retrieved February 17, 2004, from http://www.ssa.gov/finance/

15. Executive Office of the President, *Budget of the United States Government, Fiscal Year 1999* (Washington, DC: U.S. Government Printing Office, 1998), p. 232.

16. Social Security Administration, *Performance and Accountability Report Fiscal Year 2003,* p. 67

17. Paul Davies, "SSI Eligibility and Participation Among the Oldest Old: Evidence from the AHEAD," *Social Security Bulletin,* Vol. 64, No. 3, 2001/2002, pp. 38–63.

18. *Ibid.*, p. 46; see also Social Security Administration, *Social Security Online: Income of the Aged Chartbook 2001* (Washington, DC: SSA, 2002), retrieved February 26, 2004, from http://www.ssa.gov/policy/docs/chartbooks/income_aged/2001/iac01.html

19. *Ibid.*, p. 38; see also Michael A. Anzick and David A. Weaver, "Reducing Poverty among Elderly Women," ORES Working Paper Series, Number 87 (Washington, DC: SSA, January 2001), pp. 1–26.

20. Davies, "SSI Eligibility and Participation among the Oldest Old: Evidence from the AHEAD," p. 40.

21. Social Security Administration, *SSI Annual Statistical Report, 2002* (Washington, DC: SSA, August 2003), Table 28, p. 51, retrieved February 27, 2004, from http://www.ssa.gov/policy/docs/statcomps/

22. *Ibid.*, Table 27, p. 54.

23. "More Children Get Disability Benefits," *Austin American-Statesman,* March 9, 1993, p. A5.

24. Social Security Administration, *SSI Annual Statistical Report, 2002,* Table 35, p. 35, and Table 39, p. 73.

25. Committee on Ways and Means, U.S. House of Representatives, *2003 Green Book,* Section 3, "Supplemental Security Income," Tables 3-9, 3-10, pp. 3-36–3-37.

26. Committee on Ways and Means, U.S. House of Representatives, *2003 Green Book,* Section J, "Welfare Benefits for Noncitizens," pp. J-1–J-11.

27. "Issue: Welfare," *Congressional Quarterly,* December 6, 1997, p. 3013.

28. Committee on Ways and Means, U.S. House of Representatives, *2003 Green Book,* "Welfare Benefits for Noncitizens," Section J, Table J-5, p. J-23.

29. Melanie Conklin, "Out in the Cold: Washington Shows Drug Addicts the Door," *The Progressive,* Vol. 61, No. 3, March 1997, pp. 25–27.

30. Committee on Ways and Means, U.S. House of Representatives, *2003 Green Book, Section 3,* "Supplemental Security Income," pp. 3-45–3-47.

31. "Report Highlights Impact of Welfare Reform on Addicted Population," *Alcoholism and Drug Abuse Weekly,* Vol. 15, No. 31, August 18, 2003. For an in-depth

look at the "Multi-Site Study of the Termination of Supplemental Security Income Benefits for Drug Addicts and Alcoholics," see the complete issue of *Contemporary Drug Problems,* Vol. 30, Issue 1/2, 2003.

32. Patricia Hanrahan, Daniel J. Luchins, Lea Cloninger, and James Swartz, "Medicaid Eligibility of Former Supplemental Security Income Recipients with Drug Abuse or Alcoholism Disability," *American Journal of Public Health,* Vol. 94, No. 1, 2004, pp. 46–47.

33. For a further description of the Zebley decision, see Committee on Ways and Means, U.S. House of Representatives, *Overview of Entitlement Programs, 1996 Green Book* (Washington, DC: U.S. Government Printing Office, 1996), pp. 262–263.

34. Committee on Ways and Means, U.S. House of Representatives, *Overview of Entitlement Programs, 1993 Green Book* (Washington, DC: U.S. Government Printing Office, 1993), pp. 852–853.

35. Committee on Ways and Means, U.S. House of Representatives, *1996 Green Book,* pp. 297–298; Committee on Ways and Means, U.S. House of Representatives, *Overview of Entitlement Programs, 1998 Green Book* (Washington, DC: U.S. Government Printing Office, 1998), pp. 301–302.

36. Committee on Ways and Means, U.S. House of Representatives, *2003 Green Book,* Section 3, "Supplemental Security Income," pp. 3-42–3-44.

37. Depression and Bipolar Support Alliance, "DBSA Comments to the Social Security Administration (SSA)," July 16, 2003, and July 7, 2004, retrieved July 11, 2004, from http://www.dbsalliance.org/Advocacy/SSARemarks.htm

38. Social Security Administration (SSA), *U.S. Interagency Council on Homelessness 2003 Annual Report* (Washington, DC: SSA, 2003); "Social Security Online: Services to the Homeless," retrieved February 28, 2004, from http://www.socialsecurity.gov/homelessness/SSA%20Homelessness%20Report.htm

39. Patricia A. Post, *Casualties of Complexity: Why Eligible Homeless People are not Enrolled in Medicaid* (Washington, DC: National Health Care for the Homeless Council, May 2001), pp. 1–73, retrieved February 28, 2004, from http://www.nhchc.org/Publications/CasualtiesofComplexity.pdf

40. National Health Care for the Homeless Council, "Reducing SSI Enrollment Barriers for Homeless Claimants" (Washington, DC), retrieved February 28, 2004, from at http://www.hrsa.gov/homeless/pdf/pa4_post_handout_3.pdf

41. Committee on Ways and Means, U.S. House of Representatives, *2003 Green Book,* Section 3, "Supplemental Security Income," p. 3–47.

42. This paragraph relies on *ibid.,* pp. 3-12–3-13; see also National Association of Social Workers, "Social Security Benefits for People Living with HIV/AIDS" (Washington, DC), retrieved February 28, 2004, from http://www.naswdc.org/practice/hiv_aids/aids_ss.asp

43. General Accounting Office (GAO), *SSA Disability Decision Making: Additional Steps Needed to Ensure Accuracy and Fairness of Decision at the Hearings Level,* GAO-D4-14 (Washington, DC: GAO, November 2003), General Accounting Office (GAO), *SSA Disability Decision Making: Additional Measures Would Enhance Agency's Ability to Determine Whether Racial Bias Exists,* GAO-92-831 (Washington, DC: GAO, September 2002), retrieved March 14, 2004, from http://www.gao.gov

44. General Accounting Office, "Social Security Disability: Improvement Needed to Continuing Disability Review Process," Abstracts of GAO Reports and Testimony, HEHS-97-1, October 16, 1996, http://www.gao.gov/AIndexFY97/subject/Supple1.htm; see also U.S. General Accounting Office, *Supplemental Security Income: SSA Is Taking Steps to Review Recipients' Disability Status,* HEHS-97-17, October 1996, http://www.gao.gov/AIndexFY97/subject/Supple1.htm

45. For a history of programs and policies addressing disability, see Richard K. Scotch, *From Good Will to Civil Rights: Transforming Federal Disability Policy* (Philadelphia: Temple University Press, 1984); Berkowitz, *Disabled Policy;* E. Davis Martin, Jr., *Significant Disability: Issues Affecting People with Significant Disabilities from a Historical, Policy, Leadership, and Systems Perspective* (Springfield, IL: Charles C. Thomas, 2001).

46. Edward D. Berkowitz, "The American Disability System in Historical Perspective," in Edward D. Berkowitz, ed., *Disability Policies and Government Programs* (New York: Holt, Rinehart, & Winston, 1979), p. 43.

47. Berkowitz, *Disabled Policy,* p. 164.

48. Scotch, *From Good Will to Civil Rights.*

49. U.S. Department of Education, "Office of Special Education and Rehabilitation Services," retrieved March 15, 2004, from http://www.ed.gov/aboutoffices/list/osers/rsa/index.html?src=mr

50. Berkowitz, "The American Disability System in Historical Perspective," p. 45.

51. National Council on Disability, *Achieving Independence: The Challenge for the 21st Century* (Washington, DC: The Council, July 26, 1996), p. 63; on the effects of the vocational rehabilitation approach, also see Berkowitz, *Disabled Policy;* Eric Kingson and Edward D. Berkowitz, *Social Security and Medicare: A Policy Primer* (Westport, CT: Auburn House, 1993), pp. 144–146.

52. Figures in this paragraph rely on U.S. Bureau of the Census, *Statistical Abstracts of the United States, 2003* (Washington, DC, 2003), Section 11, Table 558,

p. 369, retrieved July 18, 2004, from http://www.census/gov/statab/www

53. Social Security Administration, *Annual Report of the Supplemental Security Income Program,* retrieved April 1, 2004, from http://www.ssa.gov/OACT/SSIR/SSI03/SSiTOC.html; Social Security Administration, *SSI Annual Statistical Report, 2002,* Table 30.

54. Committee on Ways and Means, U.S. House of Representatives, *2003 Green Book,* Section 3, "Supplemental Security Income," pp. 3-48–3-49; see also Social Security Administration, *Annual Report of the Supplemental Security Income Program,* pp. 15–16, 49–71, 91.

55. Most information in this paragraph and the next is from Committee on Ways and Means, U.S. House of Representatives, *2003 Green Book,* Section 3, "Supplemental Security Income," pp. 3-49–3-50; Social Security Administration, *2003 Annual Report of the Supplemental Security Income Program,* pp. 15–16; Kalman Rupp and Stephen H. Bell, Eds., *Paying for Results in Vocational Rehabilitation: Will Provider Incentives Work for Ticket to Work?* (Washington, DC: Urban Institute, 2003).

56. Rupp and Bell, *Paying for Results in Vocational Rehabilitation.*

57. David Salkever, "Tickets Without Takers? Potential Economic Barriers to the Supply of Rehabilitation Services to Beneficiaries with Mental Disorders," in Rupp and Bell, *Paying for Results in Vocational Rehabilitation.*

58. Paul Wehman and Grant Revell, "Lessons Learned from the Provision and Funding of Employment Services for the MR/DD Population: Implications for Assessing the Adequacy of the SSA Ticket to Work," in Rupp and Bell, *Paying for Results in Vocational Rehabilitation.*

59. Information in this paragraph relies on U.S. General Accounting Office, *Report to Congressional Committees, Medicaid and Ticket to Work: States' Early Efforts to Cover Working Individuals with Disabilities,* GAO-03-587 (Washington, DC: June 2003), retrieved September 7, 2003, from www.gao.gov/cgi-bin/getrpt?GAO-03-587

60. Berkowitz, *Disabled Policy,* p. 186.

61. National Council on Disability, *Achieving Independence: The Challenge for the 21st Century,* pp. 19–20.

62. Robert Silverstein, "An Overview of the Emerging Disability Policy Framework: A Guidepost for Analyzing Public Policy," *Iowa Law Review,* Vol. 85, No. 5, 2000, pp. 1757–1802; quote from p. 1761.

63. *Wyatt v. Stickney,* 3195 U.S.3 (1972).

64. Eric Emerson, "What Is Normalisation?" in Hilary Brown and Helen Smith, Eds., *Normalisation: A Reader for the Nineties* (London: Tavistock/Routledge, 1992), pp. 1–18; Steven J. Taylor and Stanford J. Searl,

"Disability in America: A History of Policies and Trends," in Martin, *Significant Disability,* pp. 16–63.

65. Bengt Nirje, "The Normalization Principle," in R. Kugel and A. Shearer, Eds., *Changing Patterns in Residential Services for the Mentally Retarded,* rev. ed. (Washington, DC: President's Commission on Mental Retardation, 1976), p. 231.

66. *Ibid.;* Wolf Wolfensberger, Ed., *The Principle of Normalization in Human Services* (Toronto: National Institute on Mental Retardation, 1972).

67. For a discussion of the various conceptions of normalization, see Brown and Smith, *Normalisation,* especially Emerson's chapter, "What Is Normalisation?"

68. Roberta Nelson, *Creating Community Acceptance for Handicapped People* (Springfield, IL: Charles C. Thomas, 1978), pp. 12–22. See also Silverstein, "An Overview of the Emerging Disability Policy Framework; Stephanie L. Bernelly, "Theoretical and Applied Issues in Defining Disability in Labor Market Research," *Journal of Disability Policy Studies,* Vol. 14, No. 1, 2003, pp. 36–450.

69. Linden Thorn cited in Pat Harbolt, "The Fight against Community Programs," *Access: A Human Services Magazine,* Vol. 4, No. 4, February/March 1981, Florida Department of Health and Human Services, pp. 14–1. See also Denise Gamino, "Neighborhood Fights Home for Mentally Retarded," *Austin American-Statesman,* February 2, 1994, p. A7.

70. World Institute on Disability, *Just Like Everyone Else* (Oakland, CA: World Institute on Disability, 1992), p. 9.

71. ADAPT's website address is http://www.adapt.org.

72. Paul Wehman, W. Grant Revell, and Valerie Brooke, "Competitive Employment: Has It Become the 'First Choice' yet?" *Journal of Disability Studies,* Vol. 14, No. 3, 2003, pp. 163–173.

73. Shirley Cohen, *Special People: A Brighter Future for Everyone with Physical, Mental, and Emotional Disabilities* (Englewood Cliffs, NJ: Prentice Hall, 1977), p. 132.

74. "Myths and Facts," retrieved March 7, 2004, from Concrete Change, http://www.ConcreteChange.org/myth.htm

75. "Visitability: Becoming a National Trend?" *Ragged Edge Online,* January–February 2003, retrieved February 29, 2004, from http://www.raggededgemagazine.com/0103/visitability.html; see also RERC, "Visitability Initiative," at http://www.ap.buffalo.edu/idea/visitability/; and Urban Design Associates, "Strategies for Providing Accessibility and Visitability for HOPE VI and Mixed Finance Homeownership" (Washington, DC: Department of Housing and Urban Development, January 2000); "Office of Public Housing

Investments and Public and Indian Housing," retrieved from http://www.huduser.org/Publications/pdf/strategies.pdf; and Concrete Change's website, http://www.concretechange.org/. See also Jon Pynoos and Christy M. Nishita, "The Cost and Financing of Home Modifications in the United States," *Journal of Disability Policy Studies,* Vol. 14, No. 2, 2003, pp. 68–73.

76. Testimony of Malcolm C. Green, Chairman, National Association of Theater Owners, presented on May 10, 1989, before the Senate Subcommittee on the Handicapped on S.933, the "Americans with Disabilities Act," *Congressional Digest,* December 1989, Vol. 68, p. 309.

77. Kingson and Berkowitz, *Social Security and Medicare: A Policy Primer,* p. 148.

78. Testimony of Zachary Fasman, U.S. Chamber of Commerce, presented on May 9, 1989, before the Senate Committee on Labor and Human Resources on S.933, the "Americans with Disabilities Act," *Congressional Digest,* December 1989, Vol. 68, p. 299.

79. For a review of cases that challenge the definition of disability see "Spina Bifida 'Not a Disability,' " *Mouth: Voice of the Disability Nation,* September 2003, retrieved from http://www.mouthmag.com/news79pg3.htm. See also the following articles from the Center for an Accessible Society: "Supreme Court Hands Down *Cleveland* Decision"; "Court Says ADA Does Not Require Companies to Hire Those with Health Risks"; "Court Says ADA Does Not Take Precedence over Seniority Systems"; articles retrieved from http://www.accessiblesociety.org/index.shtml. See also the following articles by Joan Biskupic from the *Washington Post:* "Cases Could Affect Disability Law," February 21, 1999, p. A3; "High Court Focuses on 3 Disability Cases," April 29, 1999, p. A6; "Supreme Court Limits Meaning of Disability," June 23, 1999, p. A1; articles retrieved from http://www.washingtonpost.com. See the U.S. Supreme Court website at http://www.supremecourtus.gov/ for full opinions on the following cases: *Sutton v. United Airlines; U.S Airways v. Barnett; Echozabal v. Chevron; Albertsons v. Kirkingberg; Murphy v. United Parcel Services;* and *Cleveland v. Plicy Management Systems Corp.*

80. Linda Greenhouse, "Justices Give the States Immunity from Suits by Disabled Workers," *New York Times,* February 22, 2001. For a review of cases on sovereign immunity and the Americans with Disabilities Act, see also "Supreme New Threat to ADA," *Mouth: Voice of the Disability Nation,* September 2003, retrieved from http://www.mouthmag.com/news79pg3.htm; "Supremes: No Punitive Damages under ADA," *Ragged Edge Magazine News,* June 2002, retrieved from http://www.raggededgemagazine.com/drn/06_02.shtml; "Overview: Supreme Court Ruling in *Alabama v. Garrett,*" The Center for an Accessible Society, February

21, 2001, retrieved from http://www.accessiblesociety.org/topics/ada/garrettoverview.htm. For information on *Barnes v. Gorman* and *Garrett v. Alabama,* see also the U.S. Supreme Court website at http://www.supremecourtus.gov

81. For a review and analysis of Olmstead, see Mary Johnson, "What's Happening to our ADA?" *Ragged Edge Online,* Issue 1, 2002, retrieved from http://www.raggededgemagazine.com/0102/0102ft2.htm; see also Wendy Fox-Grage, Donna Folkemer, Tara Straw, and Allison Hansen, "The States' Response to the Olmstead Decision: Summary of a Work in Progress," World Institute on Disability, retrieved from http://www.wid.org/publications/pas/PASconference_articles/HTML/Fox_Grage_etal.htm; University of Houston Law Center, Institute of Health Law and Policy, "Supreme Court Rules on Olmstead Case," *Texas Medical Center News,* Vol. 22, No. 4 (Houston, March 3, 2004), retrieved from http://www.tmc.edu/tmcnews/03_01_00/page_06.html; Center for an Accessible Society, "Supreme Court Upholds ADA 'Integration Mandate' in Olmstead Decision" (Washington, DC, June 22, 1999), retrieved from http://www.accessiblesociety.org/topics/ada/suttonoverview.htm. View the complete court opinion at the U.S. Supreme Court website, http://www.supremecourtus.gov/

82. For an extensive consideration of these issues and others, see Bruce Dennis Sales, D. Matthew Powell, Richard Van Duizend, and associates, *Disabled Persons and the Law: State and Legislative Issues* (New York: Plenum Press, 1982).

83. Information on the New Freedom Initiative relies on U.S. Department of Health and Human Services, "President Will Propose $1.75 Billion Program to Help Transition Americans with Disabilities from Institutions to Community Living" (Washington, DC: HHS Press Office, January 23, 2003); retrieved from http://cms.hhs.gov/newfreedom/nfi12303pr.asp

84. Edmund L. Andrews, "Bush Budget Cuts a Variety of Programs," *New York Times,* February 4, 2004, retrieved March 18, 2004, from http://www.dimenet.com/hotnews/cgi/getlink.cgi?3599R; "Bush Budget Slashes Promised Initiatives," *Ragged Edge Online,* February 2004, retrieved March 14, 2004, from http://www.raggededgemagazine.com.drn/02_04.html#676

85. This paragraph relies on Kevin DeWeaver, "Developmental Disabilities: Striving toward Inclusion," in Diana M. DiNitto, C. Aaron McNeece, and contributors, *Social Work: Issues and Opportunities in a Challenging Profession,* 2nd ed. (Boston: Allyn and Bacon, 1997), pp. 149–167.

86. The remainder of this paragraph relies on "Special Education," *Education Week on the Web* (Pearson Education), March 3, 2004, retrieved from http://www.edweek.org/context/topics/issuespage.cfm?id =

63; Consortium for Citizen with Disabilities, information on IDEA, retrieved March 16, 2004, from http://www.c-c-d.org/ideafullfund.htm.

87. Consortium for Citizen with Disabilities, Letter to Senator, January 27, 2004, retrieved March 16, 2004, from http://www.c-c-d.org/ideafullfund.htm

88. This paragraph relies on "Quality Counts 2004: Special Education in an Era of Standards," *Education Week on the Web* (Pearson Education, January 8, 2004), retrieved from http://www.edweek.org/sreports/qc04/article.cfm?slug = 17exec.h23

89. *Federal Register,* Vol. 68, No. 236, December 9, 2003, pp. 68697–68708, retrieved March 15, 2004, from http://www.ed.gov/legislation/FedRegister/finrule/2003-4/12903a.html

90. Monroe Berkowitz, William G. Johnson, and Edward H. Murphy, *Public Policy toward Disability* (New York: Holt, Rinehart, & Winston, 1976), p. 7. An extensive consideration of disability policy issues is also found in Gary L. Albrecht, Katherine D. Seelman, and Michael Bury, eds., *Handbook of Disability Studies* (Thousand Oaks, CA: Sage Publications, 2001).

91. Berkowitz, "The American Disability System in Historical Perspective," p. 43. These definitional issues are also discussed in Bernell, "Theoretical and Applied Issues in Defining Disability in Labor Market Research."

92. Berkowitz, *Disabled Policy,* p. 3.

93. This paragraph relies on Berkowitz, *Disabled Policy,* pp. 161, 184, 188, 226, 227, 234, 236, 237, 239; Kingson and Berkowitz, *Social Security and Medicare: A Policy Primer,* especially chapter 8.

94. World Institute on Disability, *Just Like Everyone Else,* p. 13.

95. Silverstein, "An Overview of the Emerging Disability Policy Framework."

96. Equal Employment Opportunity Commission, "Disability Discrimination," January 6, 2004, retrieved March 15, 2004, from http://www.eeoc.gov/types/ada.html

97. Sharon Barnartt and Richard Scotch, *Disability Protests: Contentious Politics 1970–1999* (Washington, DC: Gallaudet University Press, 2001).

98. *Mouth* magazine, March–April 1998, p. 8.

99. This paragraph relies on Berkowitz, *Disabled Policy;* Kingson and Berkowitz, *Social Security and Medicare: A Policy Primer.*

100. James Patterson, *Congressional Conservatism and the New Deal* (Lexington, MA: Lexington Books, 1981), p. 63, cited in Hugh Helco, "The Political Foundations of Antipoverty Policy" in Sheldon H. Danzinger and Daniel H. Weinberg, Eds., *Fighting Poverty: What*

Works and What Doesn't (Cambridge, MA: Harvard University Press, 1986), p. 315.

101. For a discussion of how General Assistance has been used, see Duncan M. MacIntyre, *Public Assistance: Too Much or Too Little?* (Ithaca, NY: New York State School of Industrial and Labor Relations, Cornell University, 1964), p. 51.

102. L. Jerome Gallagher, "A Shrinking Portion of the Safety Net: General Assistance from 1989 to 1998" (Washington, DC: Urban Institute, September 1, 1999), retrieved July 12, 2004, from http://www.urban.org/url.cfm?ID = 309197

103. U.S. Bureau of the Census, *Statistical Abstract of the United States: 1943* (Washington, DC: U.S. Government Printing Office, 1943), p. 193.

104. *Statistical Abstracts of the United States, 2003* Section 8, State and Local Government Finances and Employment, Table No. 441, retrieved July 18, 2004, from http://www.census.gov/statab/www/

105. Joel F. Handler and Michael Sosin, *Last Resorts, Emergency Assistance and Special Needs Programs in Public Welfare* (New York: Academic Press, 1983), p. 81.

106. Urban Systems Research and Engineering, *Characteristics of General Assistance Programs 1982* (Washington, DC: U.S. Department of Health and Human Services, May 1983), pp. 1–2.

107. Ailee Moon and Leonard Schneiderman, *Assessing the Growth of California's General Assistance Program* (Berkeley, CA: California Policy Seminar, 1995), http://www.sen.ca.gov/ftp/sen/committee/STANDING/HEALTH/_home/rear02.htm

108. Gallagher, "A Shrinking Portion of the Safety Net: General Assistance from 1989 to 1998"; L. Jerome Gallagher, Cori E. Uccello, Alicia B. Pierce, and Erin B. Reidy, "State General Assistance Programs 1998" (Washington, DC: Urban Institute, June 1, 1999), retrieved July 13, 2004, from http://www.urban.org/urlprint.cfm.?ID = 6593

109. Gallagher, "A Shrinking Portion of the Safety Net: General Assistance from 1989 to 1998."

110. *Ibid.,* p. 8.

111. Some of this section relies on Thomas R. Dye, *Understanding Public Policy,* 9th ed.

112. Morton Grodzins, *The American System: A New View of Government in the United States,* Daniel Elazar, ed. (Chicago: Rand McNally, 1966); see also Thomas R. Dye, *American Federalism: Competition among Governments* (Lexington, MA: Lexington Books, 1990); Morris P. Fiorina and Paul E. Peterson, *The New American Democracy,* Alternate 2nd ed. (New York: Longman, 2002).

CHAPTER

Ending Welfare As We Knew It: Temporary Assistance for Needy Families

FROM MOTHERS' AID TO AFDC

*T*he family is the primary social unit, yet the United States has no broad policy that considers the economic, health, social, and psychological needs of families. Instead, a variety of programs address these needs. Since the early twentieth century, three main programs have assisted with financial difficulties faced by poor families with children. The first was state and local mothers' aid programs. Then came federal assistance under the Aid to Dependent Children program, later called Aid to Families with Dependent Children (AFDC). Congress passed legislation in 1996 that transformed AFDC from a categorical entitlement program into a block grant called Temporary Assistance for Needy Families (TANF). All of these programs have provided cash assistance so that children can continue to be cared for in their own homes. Today, one-sixth of children in the United States live in poverty. If there is any segment of society for whom people have compassion, it is children, who are completely dependent on others to meet their needs. Why then have these public assistance programs been mired in a sea of controversy? As we shall see, the conflict centers on the parents of poor children and whether these parents participate in the labor force and provide financial support to their children.

Mothers' Aid

In the early twentieth century, the states began formalizing laws to help children whose parents lacked the financial means to care for their physical needs. Local governments often provided the funds for these programs. The programs were intended to help children whose fathers were deceased; sometimes assistance was also provided to children whose fathers were disabled or absent through divorce or desertion. These early programs were called *mothers' aid* or *mothers' pensions.*[1]

Aid to Dependent Children

The federal government stepped in to share responsibility for dependent children in 1935, when the Aid to Dependent Children (ADC) program was included as part of the original Social Security Act. ADC was conceived of as a short-term device to assist financially needy children. The program was intended to diminish and eventually become outmoded as more and more families came to qualify for assistance under the social insurance programs of the Social Security Act.[2] According to Senator Daniel P. Moynihan (D-New York), the "typical beneficiary" was supposed to be "a West Virginia mother whose husband had been killed in a mine accident."[3] But the emphasis of the early ADC program was not on providing aid for widows; it was on providing help to mothers on behalf of their children.

Trying to Keep Families Together with AFDC

The ADC program grew slowly for many years with only minor changes made in some aspects of the program. Not until 1950 were the needs of the parent in an ADC family considered, and they too became eligible for assistance. Other improvements were also made. Medical services, paid in part by the federal government, became available to recipients. In 1958 a formula was developed so that states with lower per capita incomes received more federal assistance for their ADC programs than wealthier states.

But other parts of the program were becoming sore spots. One of the most stinging accusations leveled against ADC was that it contributed to fathers deserting their families. Although this argument was difficult to prove,[4] we can see how it arose. Under ADC, families with an able-bodied father residing at home were not eligible for benefits. In some cases, unemployed fathers qualified for other assistance—unemployment compensation, workers' compensation, Social Security Disability Insurance, or Aid to the Permanently and Totally Disabled. But it was quite likely that the father did not qualify for any of these programs or had exhausted his benefits. Consequently, an unemployed, able-bodied father who could not find work did not qualify for ADC and could not support his family. However, if he deserted, the family could become eligible for ADC assistance. It is not known how many fathers left so their families could receive aid. Parents may be absent for many reasons. They may be separated from their spouses because of incompatibility, or they may be in mental hospitals, nursing homes, or prisons. But the fact remained that when an able-bodied but unemployed father was at home, the family could not receive ADC.

To address this problem, two changes were made in ADC. First, in 1961 a new component called the ADC-Unemployed Parent (UP) program was enacted. This antirecession measure made it possible for children to receive aid because of a parent's unemployment.[5] Second, in 1962, the program's name was changed to Aid to Families with Dependent Children (AFDC) to emphasize the family unit. More importantly, a second adult was considered eligible for aid in states with AFDC-UP programs and in cases where one of the child's parents was incapacitated.

In 1967 the AFDC-UP program was changed to the AFDC-Unemployed Father program, but in 1979 the U.S. Supreme Court ruled that it was unconstitutional to provide benefits to unemployed fathers but not to unemployed mothers. Thus the program was changed back to AFDC-UP. Only half of the states voluntarily enacted AFDC-UP programs, and the number of fathers who received aid remained small. In 1988, the Family Support Act required all states to have an AFDC-UP program. Despite the commotion over it, relatively few families were added to the rolls.[6] This was probably because many states' eligibility requirements remained quite strict, and AFDC-UP programs had to favor parents who were recently unemployed, while excluding the "hard core" unemployed.

In retrospect, it may seem unfair to have excluded families with able-bodied unemployed parents from the ADC and AFDC programs. But for all the concern about welfare causing family breakup, a 1977 review of studies failed to show that AFDC-UP programs were associated with increased marital stability; in fact, evidence pointed in the opposite direction.[7] Although some data did show greater marital instability in states with higher AFDC payments, there was "little support" for higher payments "being a powerful destabilizer."[8] A decade later, researchers concluded that "the impacts of welfare on family structure are very modest. Comparisons of changes in family structure over time with changes in the welfare system and of differences in family structures across states both suggest that welfare has minimal effects on family structure."[9] Changes in family dynamics and family composition had occurred among all segments of the population and seemed to be a more reasonable explanation for the composition of families receiving AFDC. In the 1990s the evidence was the same: "While it is true that the system does provide adverse incentives for the formation of two-parent families, the empirical studies show conclusively that the magnitude of these disincentive effects is very small, such that our welfare system cannot explain the high rates of [female] headship and illegitimacy."[10] Despite the evidence, the myth that welfare is responsible for family demise persists, so much so that an explicit goal of the 1996 welfare reform law is to end welfare dependency by encouraging marriage.[11]

Man-in-the-House Rules

Even if public assistance is not the root cause of family instability, the number of able-bodied parents who receive benefits continues to fuel debate in a public concerned with the morality of welfare recipients. The work ethic, firmly entrenched in American culture, suggests that those capable of self-support should not be entitled to public aid. In the early days of ADC and AFDC, this belief was reflected in "man-in-the-house rules." It was clear that only in specific circumstances could able-bodied fathers be present while the family collected AFDC benefits. These concerns also carried over into welfare mothers' relationships with other men. The thought of welfare mothers allowing able-bodied men to spend time in their homes presented a threat to those who wanted to ensure that payments went only to the "right" people. The AFDC check was intended for the children and their mother, and in some cases, the children's father. It was considered immoral and illegal for the mother to allow anyone else to benefit from the welfare check. "Midnight raids"—home visits to welfare mothers late at night—were sometimes conducted. Their purpose was to ensure that no adult males resided in AFDC households, because these men could be considered "substitute fathers" responsible for the family's financial support. Although welfare "cheating" continues to be a concern (see Chapter 12), midnight raids are now eschewed by most professionals. More sophisticated means, often electronic checks of state and federal records, are generally used to monitor recipients' compliance with program rules.

MAKING PARENTS PAY: CHILD SUPPORT ENFORCEMENT

In 1968 the U.S. Supreme Court determined that man-in-the house rules could not be used as a method for "flatly denying" children public assistance. The emphasis shifted to methods of making legally recognized fathers and mothers support their children. Congress's first attempt to intervene in child support came in 1950. Subsequent and also largely futile efforts to improve child support collections followed in the 1960s.[12] From 1950 to 1975, the federal government limited its child support efforts to children receiving public assistance. Originally, most single-parent families resulted from the death of the father, but as the 1970s emerged, it became clear that the growing number of single-parent families was due to divorce or separation, or because the parents had never married. In 1975, Congress created part D of Title VI of the Social Security Act (called the IV-D program) to provide federal matching funds that states could use to collect child support and establish paternity. To keep more families off welfare, it also authorized Child Support Enforcement (CSE) agencies to help families that were not receiving public assistance, when they requested it.[13]

There is, however, controversy over whether helping nonpoor families detracts from collecting support for the poorest children. Though there is generally more to be collected for families not receiving public assistance, some blatantly note that it is families receiving TANF or other public aid that cost taxpayers money.

Because states were not collecting enough, and because their efforts were still considered too lax, the Child Support Enforcement (CSE) Amendments of 1984 toughened the methods that states could use to collect overdue support payments, and required states to pursue medical support awards (in addition to cash awards) to ensure that children of single parents have access to healthcare (see Illustration 6.1).[14]

ILLUSTRATION 6.1

Child Support Includes Medical Support

GETTING THE MESSAGE TO EMPLOYERS

Increasingly, legislation and government regulations have required that noncustodial parents provide "medical supports" in addition to cash child support to their children. Noncustodial parents generally provide healthcare coverage to their child through their employer's health plan or a private, individual health plan. They are also supposed to pay for out-of-pocket healthcare costs for ongoing and unusually high healthcare bills not covered by the child's healthcare policy. The 1984 CSE amendments require states to petition for medical support as part of any child support order when the cost to the noncustodial parent is "reasonable." Enforcing medical support increases the number of children covered by private insurance and reduces Medicaid costs. Medicaid is the federal-state program that provides healthcare coverage to a portion of the low-income population.

When some employers began refusing to cover children who did not reside with the employed parent or children born out of wedlock, Congress included provisions in the 1993 Omnibus Budget Reconciliation Act that required employers to insure these children on their parents' healthcare plans. To notify employers of the medical support order in a uniform way, and to impress upon employers that medical orders are in fact court orders that they are mandated to follow, the Child Support Performance and Incentive Act of 1998 provides a standard national medical support notice, and requires state CSE agencies to use the standardized form. Employers are required to accept the notices as "qualified medical support orders," but as of April 2003, only about half the states were using the national medical support notice. Despite ongoing legislative efforts to provide children of single parents with medical support orders over the past 20 years, only 49 percent received medical support orders in 2001, and only 18 percent of these orders were enforced.

Source: Office of Child Support Enforcement, *21 Million Children's Health: Our Shared Responsibility* (Washington, DC: U.S. Department of Health and Human Services, June 2000), retrieved March 6, 2004, from http://www.acf.hhs.gov/programs/cse/rpt/medrpt/executive_summary.htm; Committee on Ways and Means, U.S. House of Representatives, *2003 Green Book*, "Child Support Enforcement Program," pp. 8-29, 8-32, retrieved March 6, 2004, from http://waysandmeans.house.gov/documents.asp?section = 813

Parents whose payments are in arrears (usually 30 days late or more) may be subject to warning notices, reports to credit agencies, wage garnishment, civil and criminal charges, interception of federal and state income tax refunds, property liens, seizure and sale of property, and requirements that they post a bond. Unemployment checks can also be tapped. Even so, these measures prompted only a small amount of arrearage collections.[15]

Looking back on the last few decades, two things about child support enforcement are clear: much more is being collected, and collections still fall far short of what is owed. Particularly important to child support enforcement is the 1996 Personal Responsibility and Work Opportunity Reconciliation Act (PRWORA), which made 50 changes to CSE laws. The law requires states to operate a CSE program that meets federal standards in order to receive TANF funds. It gives states funds to create automated databases for locating parents and tracking and monitoring cases (though mandated in the 1988 Family Support Act, many states never met this requirement). In addition, CSE programs must give families leaving welfare top priority for collecting arrearages (past-due child support) to help them stay off welfare.[16] All states were required to adopt the model Uniform Interstate Family Support Act (UIFSA) to increase establishment and enforcement of child support orders for noncustodial parents living in a different state than their children. The 1996 law also established a National Directory of New Hires. Employers submit the names of newly employed workers, and government officials use the directory to determine if these individuals are in arrears on child support. In addition, Social Security Numbers (SSN) are required on applications for professional licenses, court records, and death certificates to make tracking noncustodial parents easier. CSE agency personnel now have authority to order genetic testing to establish paternity without seeking a court order. In 1996 and again in 1998, states were offered more help to increase the effectiveness and efficiency of their CSE programs.

CSE agencies now provide seven basic services: (1) locating parents, (2) establishing paternity, (3) establishing child support orders, (4) establishing medical orders, (5) collecting and distributing child support payments, (6) enforcing child support across state lines, and (7) reviewing and modifying support orders. In 2001, approximately 60 percent of eligible families received some form of government-funded child support service.[17]

Parent Locator and Interstate Services

When an absent, nonsupporting parent cannot be located with information from the custodial parent, additional efforts are made using state-operated parent locator services (required of all states) with information from tax, motor vehicle registration, unemployment compensation records, and similar sources. There is also the Federal Parent Locator Service (FPLS) with access to Social Security, IRS, veterans, and other national databases. In 2001 the FPLS provided information on 4.8 million noncustodial parents to help states find absent parents. The SSNs now required on various state applications are a big help in locating parents.[18]

Probably the most difficult child support cases to enforce involve parents who live in different states. Researchers found that in 1988 about 12 percent of parents lived in different states one year after the divorce or separation; seven years later, 40 percent of these same parents lived in different states.[19] The Office of Child Support Enforcement (OCSE) estimates that in 25 percent of cases parents live in different states.[20] In these cases, the states are supposed to cooperate in securing child support, but the task is complicated because not all states use the same approach to helping one another, and local courts exercise considerable autonomy in handling cases. There are several methods of enforcing interstate support cases. One is "long arm of the law" statutes, which allow the state in which the child resides to "reach out and grab" the noncompliant parent. To improve interstate support, all states passed some form of the Uniform Reciprocal Enforcement of Support Act (URESA), but it was apparently uniform in name only. The 1996 PRWORA and the Full Faith and Credit for Child Support Orders Act mandated that all states enact the Uniform Interstate Family Support Act (UIFSA) by January 1, 1998, to improve interstate enforcement of child support obligations. Under UIFSA, when more than one state is involved, only one valid child support order can be enforced. Another provision of the law allows a state to pursue an out-of-state delinquent noncustodial parent directly under certain circumstances. The OCSE has developed URESA procedures to expedite interstate cases, but complaints are that few states use them.[21]

Establishing Paternity

Over the last half-century, births to unmarried women have risen substantially. In 2001, about one-third of all births were to unmarried mothers, and in 2002, slightly more than 31 percent of all female-headed families with children under age 21 were headed by women who had never been married.[22] Children in these families are far more likely to live in poverty (see Chapter 3) and least likely to receive child support. In 2002, only about one quarter of never-married mothers had child support agreements or awards, and of those families, only 22 percent received any support payments in 2001. Unmarried mothers must cooperate in establishing paternity in order to receive public assistance, unless doing so is not in their child's best interest or puts the mother at risk of domestic violence. Those who do not cooperate can lose part or all of their TANF cash assistance.

In 2002, paternity was established for 7.5 million (74 percent) of the 10.1 million children with open Title IV-D cases. Twenty-nine states and the District of Columbia performed at the national rate or better in establishing paternities in 2002.[23] Changes in federal and state laws have helped to increase paternity establishment. For instance, the Family Support Act (FSA) of 1988 required states to adopt "a simple civil process for voluntarily acknowledging paternity," including efforts to have fathers acknowledge paternity at the hospital when their child is born.[24] One study suggested that the highest rates of paternity determinations are made in counties where fathers have more than one opportunity to acknowledge paternity voluntarily, rather than in counties that handle all cases through the courts.[25] The use of SSNs to locate missing fathers has also helped, as has granting more authority to CSE personnel to conduct genetic testing and streamlining paternity determination processes. Between 1994 and 2002, the number of cases for which paternities was established or acknowledged grew by 253 percent, from 592,000 to 1.5 million.[26]

In addition to the financial benefits, establishing paternity may provide children with social and psychological benefits. The opportunity to know the absent parent's medical history may also benefit the child. Research suggests that children who have a positive relationship with their father do better in school, develop better social skills, have fewer behavior problems, and use alcohol and drugs less.[27] Presidents Clinton and George W. Bush have supported initiatives to increase fathers' involvement in their children's lives. These initiatives provide incentives for establishing paternity, promote work opportunities for fathers, support visitation rights with their children, and offer educational programs to prepare fathers for responsible parenthood. Historically, child support and child visitation have been treated as separate legal issues. One political reason that fatherhood initiatives have shown up on the radar screen in that fathers are more likely to make child support payments if they have visitation rights or joint custody.[28] To increase fathers' involvement and child support, noncustodial parents (most of whom are fathers), also have increased access to mediation programs and can use the Federal Parent Locator Service to find absent children and their mothers. Of course, these cases can also open up cans of worms when the custodial parent does not wish the child to have contact with the noncustodial parent.

Child Support Orders and Payment Collection

A court-established child support order legally obligates the noncustodial parent to provide his or her child a specified amount of financial support. To make the child support award process more consistent within each state, states must adopt child support guidelines and make the guidelines available to all judges. States use one of three basic approaches to awarding child support: the *income shares* method, the *percentage of income* method, and the *Melson-Delaware* method.[29]

The income shares method, used in 34 states, is based on both parents' income. It rests on the assumption that children should receive the same share of their parents' income as if the family lived together. A percentage of the parents' combined income is used to determine the amount of support required. The higher the parents' income, the lower the percent they are assessed, but the total amount rises as income increases. The amount owed is apportioned between the parents based on their incomes. The actual child support award is the amount assessed the noncustodial parent.

The percentage of income approach also assumes that children should share in their parents' income, but it is based on the noncustodial parent's income and the number of children. The 12 states that use this approach differ in the percent assessed. Wisconsin, for example, assesses 17 percent for one child, rising to 34 percent for five or more children. While the percentage of income approach is based on a flat rate, with the income shares approach, the percent of income contributed declines as the noncustodial parent's income increases. Some people believe the income shares approach is inequitable because the child should have the same right to the noncustodial parent's income even if that income rises. Others believe the percentage of income approach is inequitable because it disregards what the custodial parent can afford to contribute.

Only three states use the Melson-Delaware approach. It begins with setting aside an amount deemed necessary for each parent to meet his or her subsistence needs. Next, a primary support amount is determined for each child and is apportioned between the parents. If the parents have additional income, a percentage of it is also allocated to the children. Massachusetts and the District of Columbia use variants of the three approaches.

There is no hard evidence that one approach is better than another; however, one research study found that the income shares formula generates higher awards for low-income families.[30] In addition, award amounts vary widely across states. For example, for a low-income family where the father has a monthly income of $530 and the mother has a monthly income of $300, the custodial mother would receive a child support award of $275 in South Dakota and an award of $0 in Connecticut. Table 6.1 shows the range of support awards for low-, moderate-, and upper-income families across states using the income shares and percentage of income methods.[31]

States must implement guidelines for reviewing and modifying child support orders. Once child support orders are established, custodial and noncustodial parents may request a review and modification of the support orders as often as every three years to address changing family circumstances, increases in either parents' incomes, or simply in response to the rising cost of living. Prior to the 1996 welfare reform law, states had to review support orders of TANF families every three years. In 1996, this mandate was dropped, and 32 states have discontinued this practice. States were also allowed to implement automatic cost-of-living adjustments on child support orders without reviews, but only three states (Minnesota, Iowa, and New York) have done this.[32]

Child support laws have helped increase the number of parents receiving child support orders. In 1991, 44 percent of custodial parents had a child support award granted to them. In 2002, 59 percent had awards, still well below the number of children who could benefit from them. Eighty-four percent of custodial parents receiving support orders were mothers, and 16 percent were fathers. Custodial mothers are more likely to receive an award than custodial fathers (63 vs. 39 percent), but never-married mothers are less likely to receive a support order (52 percent) than ever-married mothers (72 percent). Approximately 41 percent of all custodial parents (37 percent of mothers and 61 percent of fathers) do not have child support orders or agreements. Custodial mothers give various reasons for not pursuing child support. Some believe that they will get more support (financial and other forms of support) from the father if the legal system is not involved. Sometimes the father cannot be located. Other mothers do not to want the father involved in their life or their child's.[33]

Even when there is a child support order, most children do not receive all the money to which they are entitled. Of all families due support in 2001, only 45 percent re-

TABLE 6.1

Amount of Child Support Awarded to Custodial Mothers by Method of Award and Family Income

Family Income	Award Amounts Income Shares Method			Award Amounts Percentage Method		
Low-Income Family	High	$275	South Dakota	High	$210	Georgia
Father's income—$530	Low	$ 0	Connecticut	Low	$ 25	New York
Mother's income—$300						
Annual family income—$9,960						
Moderate-Income Family	High	$692	Indiana	High	$436	New York
Father's income—$2,500	Low	$ 26	Montana	Low	$251	Mississippi
Mother's income—$1000						
Annual family income—$42,000						
Upper-Middle-Income Family	High	$899	Indiana	High	$710	New Jersey
Father's income—$4,400	Low	$415	Oklahoma	Low	$427	Mississippi
Mother's income—$1,760						
Annual family income—$73,920						

Source: M. A. Pirog, M. Klotz, and K. V. Buyers, "Interstate Comparisons of Child Support Awards Using State Guidelines, 1997" (Bloomington, IN: Institute for Family and Social Responsibility, Indiana University, 1997), as cited in Committee on Ways and Means, *2003 Greenbook,* "Child Support Enforcement Program," Table 8-2, http://waysandmeans house.gov/documents.asp?section = 813

ceived the full amount due, down from 52 percent in 1991. No wonder the child support enforcement system has come under intense criticism. Custodial parents who received some payments did increase slightly from 38 percent in 1991 to 41 percent in 2001, and parents due awards who received no payments at all declined from 25 percent to 13 percent over the same time period. Mothers in poverty were less likely to receive child support payments (60 vs. 75 percent for all mothers). The average amount of child support due custodial mothers in 2002 was $5,138, and the average amount received was $3,192. Mothers who had less than a bachelor's degree, were never married, were black or of Hispanic origin, or were poor were least likely to have orders. Although the percentage of women who collect payments is similar regardless of demographic characteristics, women with the aforementioned characteristics collect less.[34]

Many noncustodial parents pay their child support voluntarily. Some pay directly to the custodial parent, although today payments are commonly made through a local government office. To further ensure that payments are made, the norm is now to require employers to withhold money directly from the noncustodial parent's paycheck. Since 1994, all states must use this method when a new support order is initiated (there are exceptions), regardless of whether the state's CSE agency is involved. In 2001, 65 percent of collections were made through wage withholdings.[35]

CSE offices have increasingly used the techniques available to them to collect arrearages, such as intercepting federal and state tax refunds and unemployment insurance checks. Some communities also print the names or pictures of nonsupporting parents in local newspapers and others use Internet web sites for this purpose. States are also required to have procedures for reporting child support debt to credit bureaus. Some communities conduct stings or roundups of "deadbeat" parents, as they are often called, and some judges don't hesitate to send parents to jail when they repeatedly fail to pay. In 1998, things got tougher when Congress passed the Deadbeat Parents Punishment Act, making failure to pay child support in the amount of $5,000 or more a felony with a two-year maximum jail sentence.[36] Some find the money on threat of jail, but many fathers, especially younger fathers, are poor themselves. Rather than punish them, more efforts are being made to help them prepare for work or obtain employment that will allow them to support their children. In some cases, fathers have begun new families, and this also strains their ability to support additional family members. Needless to say, it also raises the debate about responsible sexual behavior as well as responsibility for supporting one's dependents. On the other side of the argument, it raises issues of when we stop trying to get "blood out of a stone" and concentrate on assisting economically disadvantaged children in a society in which the tax system and income distribution heavily favors the wealthy. The Urban Institute found that 2.5 million fathers who do not reside with their children and do not pay child support are themselves living in poverty.[37] These fathers faced substantial employment barriers (lack of education, little recent work experience, health problems) and they lacked access to programs to improve their employment potential.

With these thoughts in mind, just how successful is the government in collecting child support for custodial parents and their children? In 2002, federal and state governments collected $20.1 billion, a 40 percent increase over 1998, and they spent $5.2 billion to collect this amount.[38] But remember that only 49 percent of all OCSE cases had collections. In cases that had child support orders, OCSE reported some child support payments in 69 percent of cases. Most collections (86 percent) were made for non-TANF families. Medical supports collected on behalf of children were equivalent to $89 million in 2002. This was up from $52 million in 1998, but down from $95 million in 1999. The Office of Child Support Enforcement estimated that in 2002, parents were in arrears on child support payments to the tune of $92 billion! This figure does not represent all support owed because it includes only cases handled by state agencies. It does represent unpaid obligations due since OCSE'S inception in 1975, and much of this will never be collected.[39]

States can suffer stiff penalties when they do not meet the federally set performance standards for child support enforcement. As in other areas of human services, private firms are being engaged to collect child support payment in the hope that they can meet federal mandates and in more cost-effective ways. States' child support enforcement offices have turned to the private sector for a number of reasons such as burgeoning caseloads. An early report from the U.S. General Accounting Office (GAO) indicated that fully privatized local offices generally did as well and sometimes better than public offices in collecting child support payments, locating parents, establishing orders, and establishing payments, perhaps because they often have more personnel flexibility and access to better technology.[40] As of March 2002, 16 states were using 38 private firms to deliver some or all of their child support enforcement services. A subsequent GAO report looked at private firms that take cases independently.[41] These firms performed comparably to state agencies, with collections in about 60 percent of cases. In addition to accepting cases selectively and generally not taking TANF clients, these independent firms had small caseloads and charged substantial fees that state agencies do not charge. The independent firms took on average 29 percent of the fees they collected and often had application and other fees.

TANF and Child Support

Before poor parents can receive TANF benefits, they must sign over their child support rights to the state, including arrearages. Any child support collected on behalf of TANF families is retained by the state and used to defray the cost of TANF benefits, until that debt is paid. As part of the 1996 welfare reform law, unemployed noncustodial parents who owe child support to a child receiving TANF must participate in work activities, and all states are required to pursue child support payments and medical supports on behalf of all children receiving TANF. Because the federal government shares the cost of providing TANF benefits, states are also required to share child support collections for TANF families with the federal government. To reduce TANF costs, many states have laws that make the noncustodial parent who is not paying child support legally responsible for the cost of the TANF benefits paid to the estranged family. Other states use what is known as the "common law principle," which holds that a father is legally responsible for reimbursing anyone who provides for his children.[42]

Every year states are required to report to the U.S. Secretary of Health and Human Services on how well their CSE programs have met federal requirements and performance standards. Failure to be in compliance costs states in TANF funds. For example, the first time a state is not in compliance, its TANF grant is reduced by 1 percent. On the second offense, the penalty is 2 to 3 percent, and on the third, 3 to 5 percent. The federal government audits each state's CSE program once every three years to ensure accurate reporting.

The total amount of child support collected for families receiving public assistance increased nearly six-fold (from almost $.5 billion to $2.8 billion) between 1978 and 1996 and then declined to $2.5 billion in 2000. Collections increased to $2.9 billion in 2002, but when adjusted for inflation, this constitutes a reduction in collections. Most concur that the drop in collections is directly related to the dramatic drop in the number of TANF cases since the 1996 welfare reform law was passed. Non-TANF collections have grown steadily and at a greater rate than TANF collections, from $.6 billion in 1978 to $17.2 billion in 2002.

In 2001, 16 percent of TANF families became ineligible for benefits as a result of child support collections, and 330,000 families were able to leave TANF. States must continue Medicaid coverage for four calendar months after the family leaves TANF if there is no medical support award or if it is not in force.

Does Child Support Enforcement Matter?

The greatest gains in child support enforcement over the past 25 years have been in locating parents and establishing paternities (up 156 percent). Successes in other areas have been modest. For example, the number of mothers receiving child support awards from 1978 to 2001 rose by only 4 percentage points (59 percent compared to 63 percent). Gains have been greater for *poor* women. The number receiving support awards rose from 38 percent to 56 percent, compared to a 3 percent decline for nonpoor women. From this perspective, the neediest women and children have gained the most, but poor women received only 63 percent of the child support owed them. For the most difficult cases, never-married mothers, the likelihood of them receiving child support payments rose from a mere 4 percent in 1976 to 18 percent in 1997. And while the number of women who received the full amount of support due decreased from 49 to 45 percent from 1978 to 2001, the amount collected through IV-D programs increased 631 percent. This is because many more families are being served by the IV-D program. Less than a quarter of all child support payments were collected through IV-D programs in 1978. By 2001, that number had grown to 87 percent, indicating that OCSE's efforts have been very successful in recruiting more and more families into the program. What is not known is how much collected is due to these efforts and how much would have been paid anyway.[43]

Child support payments have at least a modest impact on poverty. In 2001, 23 percent of all single parents lived in poverty, compared to 19 percent who received child support. About 3 percent of non-TANF families avoided poverty as a result of child support payments. Those not at risk for poverty also enjoyed a better standard of living because of child support payments.

CSE has also seen some successes in defraying public assistance costs. For example, in 1993, states showed a net gain of $482 million, the largest gain to date. But in 2000, states began to lose money. In 2002 the loss was $463 million. Historically, whatever money the federal government spent (lost) on CSE was made up for by the amount of child support the states collected on behalf of families receiving public assistance. Beginning in 1985, states were required to give the first $50 in child support collections each month back to families receiving public assistance (AFDC). This cut into states' savings. In 1996 that rule was made a state option. Most states wasted no time in revoking the "$50 pass through." Most likely, the loss of current savings is due to the sharp decline in the number of TANF cases since welfare reform was enacted in 1996. In 1998, states collected $11.7 billion in child support for non-TANF families; in 2002, these collections increased to $17.2 billion. The increase in collections for TANF families has been much smaller, from $2.6 billion in 1998 to $2.9 billion in 2002.

Some critics of the child support enforcement programs complain that too many mothers do not have awards, too many awards are not collected, and the size of awards is often too small. Nonetheless, in the past 25 years, these programs have had important impacts on public attitudes and expectations. The intent of the original CSE legislation was to collect child support in order to offset the cost of welfare. Later, Congress and the public-at-large recognized its importance in reducing poverty and insuring that noncustodial parents take responsibility for their children. A strong CSE program sends the message to noncustodial parents who would try to avoid paying child support that the system works and will track them down and hold them accountable. Philosophical debates and differences about social welfare aside, the American public has come to believe that paying child support is both a moral and a civic responsibility. Fathers have learned to pay, and mothers have learned to expect to receive financial support from their children's fathers.

Custodial and noncustodial parents have also had many complaints about the performance of CSE agencies. Mothers complain that CSE agencies do not try hard enough to get fathers to pay and that too often CSE agencies lose the checks. Fathers and mothers complain that they don't see the money because the state takes it to repay the welfare system, causing fathers to pay "under the table" instead.[44] Hope remains that the programs will continue to improve. Waiver programs and grants support state "laboratories" to explore, create, and test interventions in child support enforcement. Most states have had grants or waivers for implementing new CSE models, collaborating with existing agencies, developing new measures for performance outcomes, or testing new ways to review and modify existing orders. Other state initiatives funded by federal grants are exploring ways to better serve Native Americans, improve parenting, enhance fatherhood, and improve access and visitation rights and staffing standards. In Texas, for example, Project Bootstrap, a program of the state's Office of the Attorney General's (OAG) Child Support Division partners with the Texas Fragile Families Initiative to help young men in particular understand their responsibilities as fathers, obtain education and employment services, and pay their child support. The OAG is also helping to stem Texas's high teen pregnancy rate with the Parenthood/ Paternity (PAPA) Program to help teens make more responsible decisions.[45]

THE REINCARNATIONS OF WELFARE AND WORK

The original ADC program was designed when mothers were expected to stay home to care for their children. Requiring mothers to work or forcing fathers to pay child support had not yet entered the equation. But demographic, social, and economic changes caused the program to evolve in ways that no one had anticipated. As the 1960s emerged, the focus was no longer on providing financial support alone as a means of alleviating poverty. "Rehabilitating" people to help them escape poverty through greater opportunities became the order of the day. But as AFDC rolls continued to grow, Americans became increasingly unhappy about providing public assistance to those who seem capable of working. The focus shifted again, this time to decreasing welfare dependency through more incentives and tougher requirements to work.

Rehabilitation for Work

The first large-scale approach at rehabilitating people in order to break their ties with public assistance came in the 1962 social service amendments to the Social Security Act. This approach was designed to reduce poverty by treating personal and social problems that stood in the way of financial independence.[46] Services included counseling, vocational training, child management training, family-planning services, and legal services. States found a bonus in providing social services to public assistance recipients—for every dollar they spent, the federal government matched it with three more dollars, far more lucrative than the reimbursement formula for AFDC cash payments. To ensure the success of the social service amendments, worker caseloads were to be small—no more than 60 clients. But states were criticized for claiming federal matching funds for many services they were already providing to clients,[47] and it was difficult to find enough qualified social workers to provide services.[48] What had sounded good in theory could often not be put into practice.

Job Training and WIN

When social services were introduced as a way to help welfare recipients achieve financial independence, the AFDC caseworker was responsible for seeing that the family got its benefit check and its social services. In fact, AFDC mothers may have feared that if they did not accept social services, benefits might be terminated. At the same time, social workers complained that the time spent determining eligibility left little time to provide social services.[49]

In 1967 Congress separated payments from social services. A payments worker became responsible for matters related to the welfare check, while another worker was responsible for providing social services. This was the era of welfare rights, and this new approach recognized that poverty may be attributable to a variety of causes—some of them purely economic; not all poor families needed rehabilitation through social services. Families who wished to receive social services were still entitled and encouraged to do so. Social workers could devote more time to these cases.

Enthusiasm for the rehabilitation approach faded rapidly as welfare rolls continued to grow. A new strategy was needed, and the one chosen was tougher. Amendments passed in 1967 also emphasized work, and both "carrot" and "stick" measures were employed to achieve this purpose.[50] The "stick" included work requirements for unemployed fathers on AFDC, as well as for mothers and some teenagers. The "carrot" was the Work Incentive Now (WIN) program, established by Congress to train recipients for work and to help them locate employment. (The original name was the Work Incentive Program but the acronym WIP obviously could not be used.) The federal government threatened to deny AFDC matching funds to states that paid benefits to able-bodied recipients who refused to work or receive job training.

Other measures were also taken to encourage recipients to work. According to the "thirty plus one-third rule," welfare payments were not reduced for the first $30 of earned income, and one-third of all additional income was disregarded in determining eligibility until the limit on earnings was reached. Children of WIN participants were supposed to receive day care services, but shortages of licensed facilities often prevented placing children while their mothers worked or trained for jobs.

AFDC rolls were still climbing. Strategies aimed at encouraging welfare recipients to work once again failed to produce the results that rational planners had intended. Perhaps these failures had to do with the fact that participants did not earn enough in marginal, low-wage jobs to make work a rational alternative.[51] Short-term training programs generally do not enable recipients to substantially increase their earnings. Some find that in order to survive they must rely on a combination of "a little work and a little welfare." In fact sociologist Roberta Spalter-Roth and economist Heidi Hartmann found that 40 percent of AFDC mothers had rather substantial work effort over a two-year period, and that these women either combined paid work and welfare benefits or cycled between work and welfare.[52]

Workfare

The next reincarnation was workfare—mandatory employment in return for welfare payments. This concept is actually as old as the hills. In its most punitive forms, the workhouses of the Elizabethan period and similar institutions in the United States fit under the rubric of workfare.[53] As more women with young children joined the labor force, the argument was that mothers receiving public assistance should do the same. One author summed it up this way: after nearly four hundred years of various forms of these programs, both experience and empirical evidence indicate they have failed to improve the job skills of participants; they have failed to reduce the costs of welfare; they do not discourage malingering because the number of malingerers is already negligible; and welfare recipients who can would gladly take jobs if decent ones were available.[54] But as we shall see, work requirements have received increasing public and political support.

There was some evidence that work programs could work. For example, in the 1980s Massachusetts' voluntary employment and training program, called ET, got good reviews (albeit at a time when the state's unemployment rate was quite low and recipients could be more easily placed in jobs). Participants could choose between career counseling, education and training, on-the-job training, and job placement. Those in training got day care services for a year and Medicaid benefits for 15 months. Would a mandatory approach to work programs produce the same success?[55] Early controlled studies funded primarily by the Ford Foundation and conducted by the nonprofit Manpower Demonstration Research Corporation (MDRC) suggested that it might be possible, but participants generally worked at entry-level jobs and did not substantially increase their work skills.[56]

Studies on intensive long-term workfare programs conducted by MDRC showed similar results. For example, the Saturation Work Initiative Model (SWIM) in San Diego found higher employment rates and earnings for experimental group participants, and there were also welfare cost savings.[57] But again, net income for the experimental group did not change much—"gains in earnings were largely offset by reductions in government transfer payments."

In a five-year MDRC study of the SWIM program (created under WIN) implemented in Virginia, Arkansas, Baltimore, and San Diego,[58] researchers found that the programs made cost-efficient use of their limited resources; employment among AFDC recipients increased and short-term AFDC receipt was reduced; the portion of AFDC participants' incomes from earnings increased; and two of the four programs also resulted in public savings (San Diego and Arkansas) and one likely broke even (Virginia). Less positive was that participants in two of the programs had little or no net gain in income and only one site (Baltimore) showed clear indication of increased job pay; long-term AFDC receipt was not affected in two programs and in the other two reductions were "modest at best." The MDRC concluded that "The effectiveness of such services may hinge on the proper combination of program structure, rewards and sanctions, and support services and work incentives."

The JOBS Program

The evidence to support traditional work programs may have been weak, but Congress was not about to give up on work requirements, and it enacted what it hoped would be a better approach—the Job Opportunities and Basic Skills (JOBS) program. As part of the Family Support Act of 1988, JOBS was intended to be "a new social contract between government and welfare recipients," changing the AFDC program from a cash assistance program to a jobs and independence program.[59] It replaced WIN and was to be coordinated with the programs of the Job Training Partnership Act (replaced with the Work Investment Act of 1998 and discussed in Chapter 9). JOBS offered basic education; job skills and readiness training; job development, search, and placement; supportive services; on-the-job training; and community work experience "in areas where it was feasible."[60] Most states assigned "case managers" to determine what services AFDC recipients needed to make the transition from welfare to work, and to enroll them in the JOBS program.

States required that at least one parent in AFCD-UP households work a minimum of 16 hours a week, and single parents whose children were 3 years old or older were required to participate in JOBS, *if* state resources were available. States could draw 90 percent match for many services, but many did not draw their full allotment, claiming that state budgets were too tight.

The percentage of eligible AFDC recipients required to participate in JOBS varied widely. The state of Kansas placed its figure at 6 percent, while Nebraska estimated 73 percent; the national average was 15 percent. The federal expectation was that 20 percent of single AFDC parents would participate in JOBS. Nationally, this expectation was exceeded with 27 percent participating. The rate for AFDC-UP families was 38 percent, short of the expectation that 50 percent would participate. Under JOBS, teen parents without high school educations who were receiving AFDC were not required to work, but they were required to attend school.

The 1988 act also required states to provide child care to working AFDC families, increased earning disregards, and extended Medicaid healthcare coverage when families left AFDC. Unlimited federal matching funds for child care were available to states for AFDC parents who were working or in training, and also for working families not receiving AFDC, but at risk of doing so without child care.

The JOBS program redefined the "welfare problem" from poverty—being poor and lacking opportunity—to dependency—the need for greater incentives to work and self-sufficiency.[61] But did JOBS work better than previous efforts? The MDRC studied two JOBS program approaches over a two-year period.[62] One approach was called labor force attachment (short-term approaches to get participants to work quickly); the other was the human capital development approach (which focused on delaying work entry in favor of building job skills over a longer time period). The attachment approach produced a 24 percent increase in the number working, increased by 16 percent the number leaving AFDC, and raised earnings 26 percent. Still, 57 percent of the treatment group remained on AFDC and the group's *average* earnings were just $285 a month. The control group earned $226 a month on average and 66 percent stayed on AFDC. Perhaps because the two-year follow-up period was relatively short, the human capital approach did not produce consistent increases in earnings or employment. There was, however, a 14 percent AFDC cost savings. A survey of 453 JOBS administrators conducted by the General Accounting Office (GAO) found that less than half of the "job-ready" participants were employed, and that the JOBS programs lacked a strong employment focus.[63]

An extensive MDRC study of a model JOBS program, California's Greater Avenues for Independence (GAIN) program, also showed only modest improvements among participants.[64] The GAIN program emphasized basic education, and AFDC recipients were required to participate. After three years, single parents in the experimental group earned a total of $1,414 or 22 percent more than the control group, and they received 8 percent less in AFDC benefits than controls. A similar percentage of experimental (53 percent) and control (56 percent) subjects were still receiving AFDC. Riverside County (one of six counties included in the study) had the most impressive results. Experimental group participants there earned 49 percent more than controls, and AFDC payments made to experimental group participants were 15 percent less than for controls. Overall, Riverside participants produced $2.84 (in earnings, reduced AFDC payments, and taxes) for every $1 invested in the program. After reviewing results of many MDRC studies, it is not surprising that Senator Daniel Patrick Moynihan dubbed Judith Gueron, head of the MDRC, "Our Lady of Modest but Positive Results."[65]

WHY THE FUSS ABOUT WELFARE?

Public assistance, better known as welfare, is a "hot button" topic (see Illustration 6.2) even though many people are not well informed about the characteristics of people who receive TANF (see Illustration 6.3). As armchair quarterbacks, we can now review events that spawned the welfare reform of 1996.

ILLUSTRATION 6.2

Why Mother Slapped Me

by Ann Withorn

In our hot southern kitchen, as always, mother washed dishes. I dried while Sister Barbara put away.

I was a senior in high school, taking "Problems in American Democracy," finding out about a new issue every week that needed to be fixed, in time for Mr. Morrow's standard Friday paper. . . .

That week we were studying poverty. Usually, I avoided discussing politics with Mother. She was so sure of her beliefs, and we would fight so easily about so much. But this time I assumed, given the childhood poverty which had shaped her life, that we could have a discussion.

Wrong.

She was adamant that people who took welfare were lazy, and just didn't want to work hard like she and my father did. "Good people can find jobs if they aren't so picky. Women who have made their bed must lie in it," she insisted.

No radical yet, but I was always willing to react to that tone of dismissal in her voice, heard in so many criticisms of me: "Good girls who try to look pretty, and go to church, and don't read so much will be fine. They won't turn out weird like you."

So I took the bait. "But Mother, I thought you would be more sympathetic. After all, you grew up on welfare."

Mother was not a hitter. Words were her weapons. So when the slap in my face came it was almost an involuntary spasm, accompanied by words hissed between closed teeth. "Don't you *ever* say that again. My family did

not grow up on welfare. Your grandfather was ill, in the hospital, and received veterans benefits. We earned what we received from the government because he fought in the war. We were *never* on welfare." Then she left, yet another night when my "disrespect" left me with the washing *and* the drying of the dishes.

In our household of denial, the incident would never be discussed again. I was left alone to ponder how my grandmother's poverty—caused by Pop's mental illness after tough service in World War I, followed by his life-long hospitalization beginning when Mother was five—was so different from welfare. The Veteran's Administration never sent enough money, and the checks sometimes just did not come. Grandmother had to live, with three kids, in rummy apartments, share space with questionable relatives, and never have enough. People would look down on her; even her cousins would taunt that her children's father was a "crazy man." Why wasn't that like welfare?

I still wonder and still cannot discuss welfare with Mother.

But I can talk and teach and continually try to figure out why it is that welfare is such a hot zone for people. . . .

Once, on a bus, I sat behind two men who were talking about "welfare queens." Both agreed that it was pathetic that the government was giving them money to do nothing, raise criminals, and get fat. But as they talked, their voices got louder, echoing my mother's deep fury. "Who do they think they are?" one

continued

ILLUSTRATION 6.2 *(continued)*

man almost shouted to his friend as he left the bus, "having babies with no fathers, expecting *me* to pay for them?"

It has even affected me. An old friend was in my kitchen, trying to express his doubts to me about whether welfare is good for the Black community where he works. Somehow the idea that I have to defend women on welfare even in my own home, with my own friends, makes me furious. I yelled that he didn't know what he was talking about, how I wouldn't listen to such ignorance in my own kitchen.

I don't usually do this. But I, too, find it hard not to take welfare as a personal issue. When I hear people say cruel things about women on welfare, I want to jump up and scream about how they do not know Debby or Mary or Juanita (or my grandmother?). They work so hard, with so little, and manage so well, or sometimes not so well, in spite of stresses and pressures undiscussed by any "Problems in American Democracy" class.

Over the years of studying poverty, I have come to see that talking about welfare is not about public policy, about how much money should be or can be spent to provide basic economic security to families with children in an uncertain economy. It is about deeply based assumptions about how we view women, and work, and the meaning of the compromises we are supposed to make in this life. . . .

[It] is extremely dangerous to deny the reality to which welfare is such a meager response. Many families *do* fail women who can't survive with bodies and souls intact if they remain either with birth families or with the fathers of their children. Most jobs fail single mothers because they cannot provide the income, benefits, and flexibility they need to raise their children. So welfare, which also fails women, still becomes the best solution. At the cost of continued poverty, disrespect, and bureaucratic indignity, it provides at least time and some flexibility to face, and not deny, the life that one has.

Welfare is so personal because, if we think about it, we cannot escape thinking about how insecure jobs are within this capitalist economy and how so many families are not the source of love and support we wish them to be. It also suggests that there could be another way. . . .

Right now, almost the whole society is trying to slap down women on welfare, telling them, with a societal hiss stronger than any mother could conjure up: "Don't you *ever* say we could have chosen assistance rather than stay in bad marriages; don't you claim that we could have done anything besides take two jobs, never seeing our children and making ourselves sick; don't you *ever* say it because then nothing we've endured makes any sense."

Somehow I knew then, and I know even more clearly now, that even if I have to do the dishes and dry, and get slapped sometimes, it is better to try to say what has to be said, to make such claims, to cry out loud.

Source: Ann Withorn, "Why Mother Slapped Me," in Diane Dujohn and Ann Withorn, Eds., *For Crying Out Loud: Women's Poverty in the United States* (Cambridge, MA: South End Press, 1996), pp. 13–16.

ILLUSTRATION 6.3

Who's Driving a Welfare Cadillac?

Most people today have probably been dis-abused of the myth that some welfare recipi-ents drive Cadillacs, but other information about who receives TANF is not universal knowledge.

Most families receiving TANF are com-posed of one parent and one or two children. In 37 percent of TANF cases, payments go only to children and no adult. This may be be-cause the adult is receiving another type of as-sistance or because the child is being cared for by a relative or other adult who does not qual-ify for TANF. Slightly more than half of TANF families have a child under age 6 in the home. Despite relaxed rules that allow two-parent families to receive TANF, the number of two-parent families receiving assistance has de-clined. Only 3.5 percent of cases now include two (or more) adults (some states are using programs other than TANF to help families with two parents present).

An estimated 67 percent of adults receiving TANF have never married. About 12 percent of the adults were married and living together. Less than 1 (0.8) percent were wid-owed. The remaining adults (21 percent) were divorced or separated.

Adult TANF recipients are on average about 31 years old. Teen parents are just 2.3 percent of those who receive TANF. About half the adults receiving TANF do not have a high school education. The percent of adults receiving TANF who are employed has in-creased from about 5 percent in 1983 to about 11 percent in 1996 and nearly 26 percent in 2001 (see chart below).

Blacks are 39 percent of TANF recipients, non-Hispanic whites are 32.2 percent, Hispan-ics are 23.6 percent, Asians are 2.5 percent, and Native Americans are 1.3 percent. Partici-pation among non-Hispanic whites declined from 41.4 percent in 1994. Participation among blacks increased from 34.5 percent and Hispanic participation increased from 19.1 in 1994. Participation among Asians declined from 3.8 percent, and the percentage of Native Americans participating remained the same.

Under the former AFDC program, most families received aid for a relatively short time. In 1994, the median length of stay on AFDC was 23 months. In 1995, 34 percent had received AFDC for no more than 12 months; 17 percent had been in the program from 13 months to two years. An additional 28 percent had received payments for 25 months to five years, and the remaining 20 percent had received assistance for more than five years. Today, under TANF, time lim-its restrict the amount of time families can receive benefits. In an Urban Institute Study of those receiving TANF from 1997 to 1999, 23 percent had returned to the program, 26 percent were receiving TANF for the first time, and 47 percent had received TANF for the entire two years.

continued

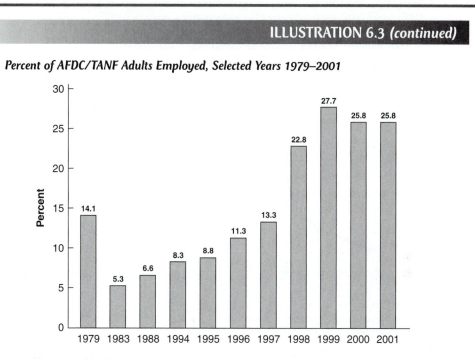

ILLUSTRATION 6.3 (continued)

Percent of AFDC/TANF Adults Employed, Selected Years 1979–2001

Source: Table prepared by the Congressional Research Service; 1979–1983 data are from studies by the U.S. Department of Health and Human Services (DHHS) of characteristics of AFDC families; 1994–1998 data are from Congressional Research Service tabulations of the FY 1988 TANF Emergency Data Report sample and FY 1994–1997 AFDC-Quality Control files; 1999–2001 data were compiled by DHHS.

Sources: U.S. House of Representatives, Committee on Ways and Means, *2004 Green Book,* retrieved March 26, 2004, from http://waysandmeans.house.gov/Documents.asp?section = 813; Department of Health and Human Services, Administration for Children and Families, "Characteristics and Financial Circumstances of AFDC Recipients, FY 1995," December 31, 1996, retrieved July 14, 2004, from http://acf.dhhs.gov/programs/ofa/content.htm; Committee on Ways and Means, U.S. House of Representatives, *1996 Green Book* (Washington, DC: U.S. Superintendent of Documents, 1996), pp. 473–474; Sheila R. Zedlewski and Donald Alderson, *Do Families on Welfare in the Post-TANF Era Differ from Their Pre-TANF Counterparts?* (Washington, DC: The Urban Institute, 2001).

Recipients and Costs

The number of ADC and AFDC recipients grew from 1.2 million individuals (349,000 families) in 1940 to 8.5 million individuals (2.2 million families) in 1970, and 11.5 million individuals (4 million families) in 1990 (see Figure 6.1).[66] Since some of this increase can be attributed to general population growth, another way to view the situation is to consider AFDC recipients as a percentage of the population. In 1950 recipients were 1.5 percent of the population; by 1970 they were over 4 percent.[67] At the peak number of 14.2 million individuals in 1994, recipients were 5.5 percent of the population. Perhaps this was a smaller percentage of the population than some people thought, yet the perception was that too many people were "on welfare."

FIGURE 6.1

Total Number of AFDC and TANF Recipients, 1960–2003[a]

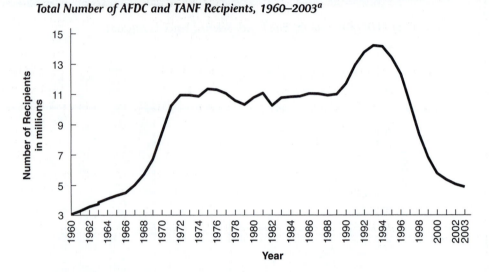

Sources: Social Security Administration, *Social Security Bulletin, 2003 Annual Statistical Supplement;* "Welfare Caseloads Drop Again," DHHS press release, March 30, 2004.

[a]2003 figure is for September.

AFDC costs had also grown. In 1940, AFDC benefits totaled $134 million; in 1970 they were $4.9 billion,[68] and by 1990 the total bill for AFDC benefits was $19.1 billion.[69] Even after controlling for inflation, costs seemed to spiral. But AFDC was only a very small part of governments' budgets. At its peak enrollment in 1994, less than 1 (.9) percent of all federal, state, and local expenditures went to the program.[70] Still, many people thought that a substantial number of adult recipients could work and that the public was needlessly providing benefits to many families.

Though total program costs were rising, maximum payment had dropped by 51 percent in purchasing power.[71] Benefits per family were always very modest. Just prior to "welfare reform" in 1996, maximum benefits for a three-person family ranged from a low of $120 per month in Mississippi to $703 in Suffolk County, New York,[72] a substantial difference even considering variations in the cost of living.

States decide what to offer in benefits. They generally started out in a rational manner by calculating a standard of need that considered what it would cost families of various sizes to meet basic food, shelter, clothing, and other needs. The most common methods for determining benefit levels were adoption of the federal government's poverty guidelines; a "market basket" approach in which living expenses were calculated for the area; and use of Bureau of Labor Statistics' poverty guidelines; a "market basket" approach in which living expenses were calculated for the area; and use of Bureau of Labor Statistics' figures for a modest standard of living.[73] Other methods were also used, but in some states need was not really determined. For example, in a few states the legislature determined the standard based on available funding, and another handful had used the same standard for so long that the method used to determine it could not be recalled!

Each state was then supposed to consider as eligible those families whose gross income did not exceed 185 percent of its standard of need, as long as their net income (after allowable deductions) did not exceed the standard of need. However, payment standards could be set below the standard of need, and only families with net incomes less than the payment standard were actually offered assistance. In 1996, most jurisdictions paid less than the need standard, and 16 also had a maximum benefit that was less than its payment standard.[74] For example, in Alabama, the need standard for a parent and two children was $673 a month, but both its payment standard and maximum benefit were $164.

Providing benefit levels below the standard of need seems more rational considering that families receiving public assistance usually get other benefits like food stamps that help to meet their survival needs. Under TANF (and previously under AFDC) families in states with lower payments receive more in food stamp benefits than families in states with higher TANF payments. This is because TANF benefits are considered in calculating food stamp benefits (but food stamps do not count against TANF benefits).

According to the Center for Budget and Policy Priorities, reports that welfare pays better than work rely on inflated estimates of benefits that assume that all recipients receive housing assistance, which few get. In the change to TANF, "most states . . . retained the same basic benefit levels that existed under AFDC, but all states have added provisions that lower or exclude benefits for certain groups of recipients."[75] Table 6.2 shows TANF benefit levels in 2003. Since 1994 Oklahoma has experienced the largest percentage drop in its maximum benefit payment and actually reduced its payment amount. In 1994 its maximum monthly benefit for a family of three was $324, well below the poverty threshold. In 2003, it was $292, more than a 25 percent reduction after considering inflation.

Rethinking AFDC

Substantive changes in the public assistance programs began during the Reagan administration. President Reagan wanted "to determine welfare needs more accurately, improve program administration, reduce fraud and abuse, and decrease federal and state costs."[76] Accordingly, various changes were made in the AFDC program, such as counting stepparents' income in determining eligibility, capping deductions for work-related expenses such as child care, and limiting the "thirty plus one-third" rule to four months. About 500,000 families were removed from the program,[77] with researchers suggesting that many children had been plunged deeper into poverty as a result.[78]

TABLE 6.2

Maximum AFDC/TANF Benefit[1] for a Family of Three and 1994–2003 Benefit Value Change

State	July 1994	January 2003	Percent Real Change[2]	State	July 1994	January 2003	Percent Real Change[2]
Alabama	$164	$215	−7.0	Nevada	$348	$348	−18.3
Alaska	923	923	−18.3	New Hampshire	550	625	−7.2
Arizona	347	347	−18.3				
Arkansas	204	204	−18.3	New Jersey	424	424	−18.3
California	607	679	−8.6	New Mexico	389	389	−18.3
Colorado	356	356	−18.3	New York– New York City	577	577	−18.3
Connecticut	680	636	−23.6				
Delaware	338	338	−18.3				
District of Columbia	420	379	−26.3	North Carolina	272	272	−18.3
Florida	303	303	−18.3	North Dakota	431	477	−9.6
Georgia	280	280	−18.3	Ohio	341	373	−10.7
Hawaii	712	570	−34.6	Oklahoma	324	292	−26.4
Idaho	317	309	−20.4	Oregon	460	460	−18.3
Illinois	377	396	−14.2	Pennsylvania	421	421	−18.3
Indiana	288	288	−18.3	Rhode Island	554	554	−18.3
Iowa	426	426	−18.3	South Carolina	200	205	−16.3
Kansas	429	429	−18.3				
Kentucky	262	262	−18.3	South Dakota	430	483	−8.3
Louisiana	190	240	3.2				
Maine	418	485	−5.2	Tennessee	185	185	−18.3
Maryland	373	473	3.69	Texas	188	201	−12.7
Massachusetts	579	618	−12.8	Utah	414	474	−6.5
Michigan– Washtenaw County	489	489	−18.3	Vermont	650	709	−10.9
				Virginia	354	389	−10.3
Minnesota	532	532	−18.3	Washington	546	546	−18.3
Mississippi	120	170	15.7	West Virginia	253	453	46.2
Missouri	292	292	−18.3	Wisconsin	517	673	6.3
Montana	416	507	−0.5	Wyoming	360	340	−22.9
Nebraska	364	364	−18.3				

Source: Committee on Ways and Means, U.S. House of Representatives, *2003 Green Book,* "Temporary Assistance to Needy Families (TANF)" (Washington, DC: March 17, 2004), Section 7, pp. 7-38–7-39, retrieved from http://waysandmeans. house.gov/Documents.asp?section = 813; table prepared by the Congressional Research Service on the basis of CRS surveys of state benefit levels.

[1]This table presents maximum benefits generally available to families without income. Some states pay larger benefits to certain categories of recipients. For example, Hawaii and Massachusetts have a separate benefit schedule for persons whom they exempt from work. Also, some states supplement benefits for families with special needs.

[2]The inflation factor used to convert July 1994 dollars to January 2003 dollars was 1.2244 (representing the change in the Consumer Price Index for all Urban Consumers).

Perhaps President George H. W. Bush's most notable contribution to welfare reform was to encourage more state innovation in the AFDC program. But what looked like a positive innovation to some was considered punitive by others. For instance, under Wisconsin's Learnfare program, working families could keep more of their pay without losing AFDC benefits, but if a teenage child dropped out of school, "defined as missing three days of school in a month without a valid excuse," the family faced a reduction in benefits.[79] In Wisconsin and New Jersey, women who had another child while receiving AFDC were denied additional payments. In Michigan, AFDC recipients who did not go to work or school or contribute volunteer service faced being docked $100 in benefits a month. A Wisconsin initiative, referred to as "Bridefare," encouraged young women to marry by allowing them to keep some benefits. More drastic changes were suggested by extreme right-wing conservatives, such as ending all government involvement in public assistance and placing poor children whose parents could not afford to care for them in orphanages.

By the time President Bill Clinton took office armed with the campaign pledge to "end welfare as we know it," the stage was set for dismantling the AFDC entitlement program and replacing it, predominantly with a work program. He also wanted to increase incentives to self-sufficiency through education and training, raise the earned income credit, and provide "seamless" child care and healthcare benefits. Clinton wanted to "make work pay" by increasing asset limitations and earnings disregards and permitting individual development accounts. Other parts of his proposal included improving paternity establishment and child support collections and promoting contacts between children and their noncustodial parents. The president also wanted to launch a national campaign to curb teen pregnancy. Clinton agreed with many conservatives that welfare payments should be limited to two years and that "welfare should not be a way of life."[80]

There was considerable concern about whether there would be enough jobs for all those who would have to work in lieu of receiving assistance and what would happen to those who might not find employment. Since JOBS had put only a portion of recipients to work, the assumption was that multiple employment strategies would be needed to end welfare. Suggestions included subsidized private employment, paying groups to place recipients in private-sector jobs, federal public works program like those used during the Great Depression, and placing recipients in public-sector jobs in the community. Unions were concerned that any large-scale job efforts would displace those already working in low-wage employment. Predictions were that it would be difficult to do better than JOBS unless substantial amounts were allocated for training and education.

While Congress hammered out its plan, the states were moving ahead with welfare reform. The Wisconsin legislature declared that it wanted to withdraw completely from the AFDC program by the end of the decade. It had already begun implementing a two-year moratorium on AFDC payments through its experiment called "Work, Not Welfare." Florida began a demonstration to hire welfare recipients and provide a minimum-wage job to those who did not locate work after two years on AFDC. By the time Congress and the president agreed on a welfare reform plan, about 40 states had already obtained waivers from the federal government so they could make changes to their AFDC programs that fell outside the current rules.

Has Welfare As We Know It Ended?

By 1994 the AFDC rolls had already started to drop, but conservatives and many others thought that the program still needed a radical restructuring. Congress twice delivered comprehensive welfare reform bills to President Clinton, which he vetoed, believing they were too punitive. Then, on the third try, the president relented and signed the Personal Responsibility and Work Opportunity Reconciliation Act of 1996 even though he disliked some of its components. Some of the nation's best-known welfare experts and the president's closest welfare advisers, Mary Jo Bane, David Ellwood, and Peter Edelman, quit in protest when Clinton signed the bill. Advocates for the poor criticized the president for selling out. David Ellwood wrote that the Republican takeover of Congress led welfare reform on a "remarkable political journey,"[81] and one columnist called the president's decision to sign the sweeping welfare reform bill "the biggest social accomplishment of his presidency, even though the Republican Congress wrote it and liberal Democrats hate[d] it."[82] The bill's most dramatic change was the end of the 61-year-old entitlement program known as AFDC and the birth of a block grant program called Temporary Assistance for Needy Families (TANF). The emphasis is on *temporary.*

The New Welfare Program—Temporary Assistance for Needy Families.

Under the Personal Responsibility and Work Opportunity Reconciliation Act of 1996 (PRWORA) public assistance shifted even further from a system historically focused on income supports to a system that emphasizes economic self-sufficiency through employment.[83] TANF's four main goals are to:

♦ Provide assistance to needy families

♦ End welfare dependency through job readiness, work, and marriage

♦ Reduce out-of-wedlock pregnancies

♦ Encourage the formation of two-parent families[84]

The new TANF program is composed of two block grants, which were originally authorized through 2002. Congress later extended them through March 31, 2004. As of August 2004, a new reauthorization bill had not been passed. The first block grant is the family assistance block grant, used to provide cash to families, to help families go to work, and to avert out-of-wedlock pregnancies. The money can also be used to encourage parents to establish or maintain two-parent families. This block grant combines the functions of the former AFDC and JOBS programs but caps funding levels. The other block grant is for child care to help families leave the public assistance rolls or avoid receiving public assistance without concern about their children's supervision. This block grant consolidates several government-supported child care programs and increases funding for them. In order to continue receiving federal funds, states had to replace AFDC with TANF by July 1, 1997. Federally recognized Native American tribes may operate their own TANF programs. Each state has almost free rein in defining those groups that will be included and those that will be excluded from TANF. Federal funds cannot, however, be used to pay TANF benefits to most immigrants legally residing in the United States during their first five years in the country. After the five years, states can continue to exclude immigrants who have not become citizens.

Under TANF, most families may receive cash assistance for no more than five years, while under AFDC, families were eligible until their youngest child was 18 years old. States may exempt 20 percent of their caseload from the five-year limit. Exemptions are determined by the state and may be granted in situations where family violence or disabilities may make it difficult for the adult head to care for the family without assistance. Able-bodied adults are expected to go to work and work toward self-sufficiency no later than two years after they begin receiving aid (a more stringent requirement than in previous incarnations of AFDC). Some states had already moved in this direction.

The family assistance block grant was fixed at $16.5 billion per year through March 2004. This is slightly more than what was spent for AFDC and JOBS in fiscal year 1995. The child care block grant increased funds previously spent for child care with $14 billion in entitlement funds and $6 billion in discretionary funds allocated over six years. Although the change to TANF received much of the attention in the welfare reform package, most *federal* savings comes from the Supplemental Security Income program (see Chapter 5) and the Food Stamp Program (see Chapter 7). These programs are mostly the responsibility of the federal government while TANF is more heavily financed by the states.

To receive its entire TANF allotment, a state must spend at least 75 percent of what it expended on AFDC in 1994. This is called the state's "maintenance of effort," or MOE. As Illustration 6.4 demonstrates, this formula continues to disadvantage families in poorer states. States that fail to meet federally established work participation rates in a given year must spend at least 80 percent of their 1994 expenditures the following year. States that experience more than average population growth or receive less than the national average amount of federal welfare funds for each poor resident were originally eligible for supplemental TANF funds through fiscal year 2001. Congress extended this provision until March 2004. Since 1998, 17 states have collected supplemental grants. About half of these qualifying states were poorer, southern states. The total grant amount across states increased from $79 million in 1998 to $319 million in 2001, where it remained for 2002 and 2003.[85] States that automatically qualified for these funds because of the low federal welfare funds they acquire for poor people are Alabama, Arkansas, Louisiana, Mississippi, and Texas. Alaska, Arizona, Colorado, Idaho, Nevada, and Utah qualified because of population growth. Six additional states (Florida, Georgia, Montana, New Mexico, North Carolina, and Tennessee) recently met both conditions and also received supplemental funds.

ILLUSTRATION 6.4

Short Takes on Welfare Policy

SHOULD STATES RECEIVE MORE EQUAL TANF FUNDING?

by David Merriman

Each year, all states and the District of Columbia receive a block grant from the federal government through the Temporary Assistance for Needy Families (TANF) program. But not all grants are the same size: 18 states receive grants of less than $2,000 per poor family, 19 states receive $2,000 to $4,000 per poor family, and 14 states get more than $4,000 per family. Some interstate differences are extreme. For example, Connecticut receives about $7,000 in TANF funds for every poor family—seven times the $1,000 allotment for Arkansas. Smaller disparities in public school funding have embroiled many states in vigorous legal challenges.

Why are some states less well funded? On TANF's inception, Congress based 98 percent of the federal allocation on states' historical expenditures under Aid to Families with Dependent Children (AFDC) and other smaller pre-TANF programs. The new distribution formula locked in preexisting differences in federal funding.

Under pre-1996 programs, expenditures per poor family varied because states' benefit levels, eligibility criteria, and population characteristics differed. The federal government's share of the AFDC bill also varied according to state median income. Low-income states and southern states generally had lower benefit levels and enrolled smaller shares of their poor families than other states. Thus, today, many of these higher-poverty states receive lower-than-average grants for each poor family.

The 2 percent of the TANF distribution formula not based on historical expenditures is too small to offset state funding differences. Congress allocated 1 percent of TANF funds to supplemental grants for states with historically low AFDC spending levels or high population growth. It allocated another 1 percent of TANF funds to performance bonuses rewarding states that had the greatest success in lowering nonmarital births (without increasing abortions) and raising employment among welfare clients. These supplemental and performance grants account for a small fraction of TANF funding. Thus, without legislative change, interstate inequities will persist.

WHY DO DISPARITIES MATTER?

TANF fundamentally altered the goals of the welfare system and states' spending priorities within the program. States now spend a much smaller share of welfare funds on cash assistance. In 1996, 76 percent of federal and state welfare spending financed cash benefits. By 2000, that share had dropped to 41 percent (Zedlewski et al. 2002). The rules and goals of TANF have required states to undertake new initiatives promoting employment and family stability.

Accordingly, states have shifted spending into job search and preparation activities, child care services, transportation, and other priorities. Recently, they have also begun directing limited funds to services targeting

continued

ILLUSTRATION 6.4 *(continued)*

hard-to-serve individuals, including substance abusers, domestic violence victims, and non-English speakers. Although the decline in cash assistance payments has freed up funds for some programs, pressure to find additional resources is high, especially among states that receive the fewest TANF dollars. Without increased TANF allocations, these states' employment-related achievements and service delivery improvements could fail to keep pace with TANF requirements.

RECOMMENDATIONS

No one with experience in the legislative process looks forward to a "formula fight," with states arguing over how to divvy up the federal pie. But reauthorizing the current distribution formula would again lock in state funding disadvantages. To ensure that all states can meet their TANF goals, Congress should consider the following options:

1. *Providing additional TANF funding to states with the smallest grants per poor family would help many high-need states.* This simple funding measure would leave states' maintenance-of-effort (MOE) requirements unchanged. The additional expenditures, though not insignificant, would represent a small share of TANF's overall costs. To bring the 10 states that receive the least funding per poor family to the U.S. median in 2000 ($2,296), TANF would require another $1.4 billion annually (about 8 percent of the program's total costs). An additional half-billion dollars (about 3 percent of funding) would bring all lagging states to the current median level.

2. *Reallocating TANF funds from states with above-average grants per poor family to states with the least funding would reduce interstate differences without increasing federal spending.* While more politically fraught than option 1, this approach is less costly. Gradually phasing in funding changes over several years might make the option more palatable to currently well-funded states.

3. *Offering to match spending initiatives in high-need, less-funded states with increased TANF funds would provide poorly funded states with an incentive to increase their spending.* For example, Congress could permanently increase federal grants to high-need states that agree to a permanent increase in their MOE requirements. This option would entail a smaller increase in federal funding than option 1, but it would require more state resources.

REFERENCE

Zedlewski, Sheila R., David Merriman, Sarah Staveteig, and Kenneth Finegold. 2002. "TANF Funding and Spending across the States." In *Welfare Reform: The Next Act*, edited by Alan Weil and Kenneth Finegold (225–46). Washington, DC: Urban Institute Press.

This series is funded by the David and Lucile Packard Foundation.

Assessing the New Federalism is also currently funded by The Annie E. Casey Foundation, The Robert Wood Johnson Foundation, the W. K. Kellogg Foundation, The Ford Foundation, and The John D. and Catherine T. MacArthur Foundation.

As of 1999, states with "high-performing" TANF programs are eligible for bonuses. The award criteria include job entry, job retention, and earning gains. There are also other stakes involved. Up to 25 states with the greatest reductions in out-of-wedlock births *and* greatest reductions in abortions could get a bonus payment. During the four years that nonmarital birth rate reduction bonuses were available (1999–2002), six states, the District of Columbia, and the Virgin Islands received bonus payments ranging from $.9 million in the Virgin Islands to $84.8 million for Alabama, Michigan, and the District of Columbia. Some states received awards every year they were available. However, the national nonmarital birth rate increased from 32.4 to 33.1 percent. Though the rate of growth declined in some states, only five jurisdictions actually saw a decline in nonmarital births (Connecticut, the District of Columbia, Michigan, Nevada, and New York).[86] Finally, states undergoing recession (measured by high unemployment and increased food stamp caseloads) can tap a $2 billion contingency fund if they have spent more than 100 percent of their 1994 AFDC levels on TANF.

After two years, or less if the state stipulates, adults must engage in work or work-related activities (as defined to some extent by each state) or be terminated from the program. Most single parents not participating in job skills or education programs were required to put in 20 hours a week at a work-related activity in 1998 and 25 hours in 1999. Since 2000 the number of hours has been 30. Single parents with children under age 6 are not required to work more than 20 hours a week. In two-parent families, one adult must work 35 hours weekly. If they receive federally funded child care, the other parent is supposed to work 20 hours per week unless that parent is disabled or caring for a child with disability. Parents who fail to work all the expected hours can be docked at least a portion of their benefits.

The highest work priorities are for parents in two-parent families and single parents whose children are in school, especially those who have older children. The states can use TANF funds to create a job in lieu of making cash payment to recipients. They can also require parents who have received aid for two months and are not otherwise working to perform community service, but states may exempt parents with a child under age 1 from all work requirements.

In 1997, the federal government required states to see that an adult was working in 25 percent of all TANF families. This figure increased by 5 percent each year so that, by 2002, 50 percent had to be working. For each percentage point that a state reduces its TANF rolls, its work participation rate is decreased by 1 percent, provided that the reduced rolls were not due to stiffer eligibility requirements. In 1997 and 1998, the requirement was that at least one parent in 75 percent of two-parent families had to be working. In 1999 this rate increased to 90 percent. The penalty for states that do not get enough people to work is 5 percent of TANF funds after the first year of failure. Each subsequent year of failure results in an additional 2 percent penalty up to a maximum yearly penalty of 21 percent.

States that do not comply with TANF expenditure levels or fail to limit families to five years face losing part of their block grant, and they must use state funds to replace the amount lost. The Secretary of the Department of Health and Human Services can waive penalties if states take corrective action. If a state's TANF program results in an increase of 5 percent or more in its child poverty rate, it must implement a plan to reduce this poverty if it wants to continue to receive TANF funds.

States can set a shorter time limit than five years for receiving benefits. If families need longer-term benefits, states can use their 20 percent exemption from the five-year rule to assist them, and they can use part of their Social Services Block Grant (see Chapter 10) to provide noncash assistance such as vouchers to needy families who reach the time limit. They can also use their own funds to assist families for longer periods if they wish.

Families cut from TANF due to increased earnings may retain Medicaid benefits for 12 months (6 months of full benefits and 6 months of subsidized benefits) if their income is no more than 185 percent of the poverty level. Families that leave TANF due to increased child support can get a four-month Medicaid extension. Some families that would have been eligible for cash assistance under AFDC rules but do not qualify under TANF may also be entitled to receive Medicaid.

To discourage out-of-wedlock births, states may eliminate all cash payments to unmarried teen parents. States that offer payments must require that the teen parent live with an adult and attend school. States can also choose to enforce a "family cap" by denying additional payments for a child born while the family is receiving TANF. The act also provides funds for abstinence education and urges states to consider methods of reducing teen pregnancy through prevention programs, statutory rape laws, and other strategies. States can also test recipients for illegal drug use and penalize those who test positive. Unless a state "opts out" by passing a new law, convicted drug offenders can be barred from the program forever; however, their children can receive benefits.

Other provisions allow states to contract with religious and private organizations to deliver public assistance services. This provision is controversial among those who feel that religion and public service functions may not mix well, and those who feel that governments should not abrogate their public responsibilities to enterprises that might be motivated by profit. More positive is that states may use TANF funds to establish individual development accounts (which are like savings accounts) for beneficiaries for specific purposes like starting a small business.

State TANF Programs.   Since the PRWORA, states have exercised considerable discretion in the following areas of the TANF program:

♦ Setting eligibility limits as well as cash benefits

♦ Setting income supplements for working families

♦ Offering additional incentives and sanctions

♦ Spending TANF funds on noncash programs and services aimed at meeting TANF goals

♦ Saving TANF block grant funds for economic downturns[87]

♦ Extending transitional Medicaid benefits beyond 12 months

♦ Designing new work and education programs[88]

To receive TANF funding, a state must submit a TANF plan every three years that tells the secretary of DHHS how it intends to structure its program and meet TANF requirements. The plan must describe (1) the state's cash assistance and work supportive services; (2) how it will require recipients to engage in work within 24 months; (3) how it defines "credible" work activities and sets participation goals; (4) methods for use and disclosure of TANF recipient information; (5) its goals and strategies for preventing nonmarital pregnancies; and (6) a program for education on statutory rape.[89]

As Table 6.2 on page 228 shows, most states have maintained cash benefit levels at the 1994 level. Some have increased TANF benefits, but five states and the District of Columbia actually reduced benefits below their 1994 level. Between 1994 and 2003, the real value of cash TANF benefits continued to decline in most states. The greatest decline (nearly 35 percent) was in Hawaii. In only six states (Alabama, Louisiana, Maryland, Mississippi, West Virginia, and Wisconsin) has the real value of benefits increased. In 2003, the maximum benefits for a family of three ranged from a low of $170 per month in Mississippi to a high of $923 in Alaska. Two states (Wisconsin and Idaho) no longer adjust cash benefits for family size, and 20 states use family caps so that a child born to a mother already receiving TANF will receive reduced or zero benefits. To balance these rather severe restrictions, 44 states have increased asset limits, and 47 have increased earnings disregards.

In 2001, 81 percent of TANF recipients also received food stamps ($288 per month on average), raising the monthly benefit package (cash plus food stamps) for a family of three to $525 in Mississippi (the state with the lowest TANF payment) to $1,157 in Alaska (the state with the highest TANF payment). Since 2002, states have had the option of providing five months of transitional food stamp benefits to families moving off TANF, but as of June 2003 only seven states were doing so. Many families with low incomes continue to qualify for food stamps.

To keep caseloads down, most states have also implemented temporary state emergency assistance programs or TANF diversion programs. In lieu of regular TANF cash assistance, these programs provide families who are eligible for TANF with short-term or lump sum assistance in cash or in-kind benefits on a case-by-case basis.[90] Because these lump sum payments may effect future TANF eligibility, potential recipients must make this choice carefully.

Under TANF, states must offer transitional Medicaid benefits for 12 months when families leave TANF. The DHHS reported that in 2001, nearly all (98.9 percent) of TANF families were enrolled in Medicaid. Eleven states have even extended transitional Medicaid eligibility beyond 12 months.[91] Twenty-two states apply sanctions to food stamps and Medicaid benefits for failure to comply with TANF requirements.

Forty-three states require that adult TANF recipients work before two years are up, and most states encourage a combination of work and welfare by disregarding some earnings or all earnings for a period of time. The number of families with a parent involved in work or work-related activities has grown. In 1997, only 28.1 percent of TANF families had a working adult. This percentage peaked at 38.3 percent in 1999 and declined to 34.4 percent in 2001 (see also Illustration 6.1). The rate was much higher for two-parent families (51.5 percent). Despite progress, work participation under TANF (calculated as a national average) has fallen far short of current federal participation requirements of 50 percent for single-parent families and 90 percent for two-parent families. In 2001, work participation ranged from 6.6 percent in Maryland to 80.7 percent in Kansas. Federal rules continue to allow for exempting up to 20 percent of caseloads from work due to hardship, and 17 states had waivers allowing them to use different rules to calculate work participation rates. With these adjustments for caseload reductions and waivers, most states have met federal work participation requirements.[92]

Congress appropriated $3 billion through September 2004 for the Welfare-to-Work (W-t-W) grant program specifically for TANF recipients with multiple barriers to employment, noncustodial parents, and TANF recipients facing the end of their five-year time limits within 12 months.[93] States reported that they served over half a million participants with W-t-W grant funds between 1999 and 2002. The core services most often provided to W-t-W participants were job readiness, intake, assessment, pre-employment case management, job development and placement, and postplacement follow-up. Job entry rates for W-t-W participants are comparable to national rates for other TANF work programs. For FY 2003, DHHS requested that W-t-W grants funds be used to focus on job retention, wage gains, and assistance to low-wage families. W-t-W grants also provide employers a 35 percent wage rebate of the first $10,000 paid to new hires who have been long-term welfare recipients. The rebate rate increases to 50 percent in the second year of employment.

TANF differs most markedly from AFDC in that it primarily focuses on providing supports to put families to work with a secondary focus on cash assistance; the reverse was true for AFDC. In addition to job-services, families can also receive child care and transportation and even short-term loans for work-related expenses.[94] TANF legislation recognizes 12 types of activities as work (see Table 6.3). To meet their 30 hours' weekly work requirement, adult TANF recipients must participate in one of these activities. In 2001, 382,853 TANF families participated in work activities, earning an average of $686 a month. Most (64.8 percent) participated in unsubsidized work activities (which costs states the least), followed by job search (13.5 percent), vocational education (10.9 percent), and work experience (9.4 percent). Compared to the former JOBS program, fewer TANF adults are engaged in educational activities. For example, in 1995, under the JOBS program, 47.2 percent of participants were involved in educational activities such as high school, GED classes, remedial education, English as a second language, vocational training, or higher education. In contrast, only 17 percent of TANF work participants were involved in educational activities. More than one observer has questioned the logic of trying to move poor people off TANF and into livable wage jobs when so little is committed to developing marketable skills through education and training.

States differ in how they treat earnings in their TANF programs. For example, three states (Alabama, Nevada, and North Carolina) ignore all earnings for the first four months of employment, and Connecticut disregards all earnings for as long as earnings fall below federal poverty guidelines. For the first 12 months of employment, earning limits ranged from $256 a month in Alabama to $1,933 in Alaska.[95]

TABLE 6.3

Average Number and Percentage of Adults Engaged in Work by Work Activity for Sufficient Hours to Be Counted in Work Participation Rates, 2001

Work Activity	Total Number of Participating Families	Percentage of Participating Families
Unsubsidized Employment	248,149	64.8
Subsidized Employment	4,884	1.2
Work Experience	35,875	9.4
On-the-Job Training	699	0.2
Job Search	51,832	13.5
Community Service	22,580	5.9
Vocational Education	41,762	10.9
Job Skills Training	7,513	2.0
Education Related to Employment	8,900	2.3
Satisfactory School Attendance	14,622	3.8
Providing Child Care	109	0.0
Additional Waiver Activity	28,098	7.3
Total	**382,853**	[1]

Source: Committee on Ways and Means, U.S. House of Representatives, *2003 Green Book,* "Temporary Assistance to Needy Families (TANF)" (Washington, DC, March 17, 2004), Section 7, pp. 7-63–7-64, 7-76–7-77, retrieved from http://waysandmeans.house.gov/Documents.asp?section=813

[1]Percentages add to more than 100 because some people participated in more than one work activity.

Seventeen states or jurisdictions have TANF time limits of *less* than five years; but nine states have, in effect, suspended the federal time limits by paying benefits to "timed-out" families using state funds only. Some states also stop the federal time limit clock by using state funds only to pay benefits to families who are working. The Department of Health and Human Services reported that by December 2001, 231,000 TANF families had reached their time limits. Most (138,000) continued to receive partial or full benefits either through a hardship extension or use of state funds. The remainder were dropped from TANF.[96]

Federal and State Tax Measures.   One tax measure available to low-income workers through the IRS is the earned income credit (EIC). The credit reduces the amount of federal income tax workers owe and can result in a tax refund if the credit amount is larger than the tax due. The EIC has been available to workers with children since 1975. The intent of the EIC was to help raise families with children out of poverty (since 1994, a smaller credit has also been available to low-income workers without children). The amount of the credit has increased in recent years. The 2004 credit ranges from $2,604 for a family with one child earning $30,338 or less to $4,300 for a family with two or more children earning $34,458 or less.[97] The EIC can be paid in a lump sum or spread out over the year and included in regular paychecks. For a single parent with two children working half time, the value of cash TANF and food stamp benefits combined with net minimum wage earnings and federal earned income credits raised the family's income to at least 70 percent of poverty and in some states to a high of 107 percent. For a family working full time at a minimum-wage job, the value increased family incomes from 107 to 129 percent of the federal poverty line. On average, across states, this is 86 percent of the poverty guidelines for TANF recipients who work half time and 113 percent of poverty guidelines for those who work full time (see Table 6.4). The EIC provides a maximum benefit of $2,972 for half-time TANF minimum wage workers and $4,204 for full-time earners.[98] Low-income workers not receiving public assistance also benefit from the EIC. Many more people receive the EIC than receive TANF.

TABLE 6.4

Earnings, Selected Benefits, and Resources as a Percentage of Poverty for a Single Parent with Two Children, Working Half-Time and Full-Time, January 1, 2003[a]

	Half-Time	Full-Time
Resource Value in Dollars		
Net Earnings	5,269	10,538
EIC (Federal)	2,229	4,110
TANF	2,893	688
Food Stamps	2,618	2,032
Combined Total	14,862	17,122
Resource as a Percentage of Poverty Guideline[b]		
Net Earnings	34	68
EIC (Federal)	17	24
TANF	19	4
Food Stamps	18	12
Combined Total	86	113

Source: Committee on Way and Means, *2003 Green Book,* Section 7, pp. 45–47, 49–51; retrieved from http://waysandmeans.house.gov/Documents.asp?section = 813

[a]Figures are averaged across states.

[b]The 2003 poverty guideline for a family of three was $15,260 in the 48 contiguous states and the District of Columbia ($19,070 in Alaska and $17,550 in Hawaii).

Nineteen states have also adopted state earned income tax credits to help TANF participants work and increase family resources.[99] States can decide whether to count EIC payments to TANF families as income. If they do, that reduces TANF benefits. Most states disregard EIC for the first two months, a few disregard all EIC, and still fewer do not disregard any of it.[100] Families can also take advantage of the federal child tax credit that was increased to $1000 with the passage of the 2001 federal tax cut. Twenty-three states now offer child credits on state income taxes as well. Seven states also have housing credits for low-income families.

How Have States Spent Their TANF Funds?   Total AFDC spending (state and federal) peaked in 1995 at $30.1 billion, and then began to decline under TANF. A sharp drop in spending occurred in 1997 with the start of welfare reform. In 1998, total welfare spending dropped again to 21.5 billion, but it began rising in 1999. In 2001 state and federal governments spent $24.5 billion on TANF. Since 1990 overall (state and federal) spending has dropped 18 percent or 30 percent after adjusting for inflation. However, the federal share of AFDC/TANF spending increased from 54 percent in 1995 to 60 percent in 2001.[101]

States' maintenance of effort (MOE) includes not only money spent on cash assistance to TANF families, but also expenditures on support services such as child care and work supports, and the cost of administrating the state's TANF program. Monies used as matching funds for the Child Care Development Fund (CCDF) cannot be counted as MOE expenditures, but funds for other services to low-income non-TANF families count toward MOE.[102]

As TANF cash assistance caseloads fell by about 50 percent between 1996 and 2000, this dramatic decline freed up TANF funds. Since 1997, states have generally increased child care spending and saved large portions of TANF funds for future needs.[103] Some states were accused of diverting the money for other purposes or not spending enough to help recipients. The savings have come in handy because economic downturns since 2001 have caused more families to apply for aid, and states have had to spend more than they received in TANF grants.[104] One-third of all TANF expenditures ($4.9 billion) came from reserved funds in 2001.

As funds spent on regular or basic TANF assistance declined, states have spent more on work supports, oddly referred to as "nonassistance." Nonassistance is non-cash or in-kind assistance that helps TANF recipients work and increase their earnings, such as earned income tax credits and child credits and work supports, such as child care, transportation, and work subsidies. In 1997, states spent 73 percent, or $13.9 billion, of TANF funds (state and federal combined) on basic (primarily cash) assistance (see Figure 6.2).[105] In 2002, states spent only 37 percent ($9.4 billion) of TANF funds on basic assistance. "Nonassistance" grew from 23 percent to 56 percent of TANF expenditures. Total *federal* spending for nonassistance increased from $2.3 billion in 1997 to $8.8 billion in 2002. Of nonassistance spending in 2002, 24 percent went to work-related activities and 17 percent to child care. States expended small amounts of nonassistance funds on pregnancy prevention (2 percent) and promoting the formation of two-parent families (1 percent). They spent large

FIGURE 6.2

Combined Expenditures of Federal Funds and State TANF MOE[a]
by Spending Categories in FY1997 and FY2002

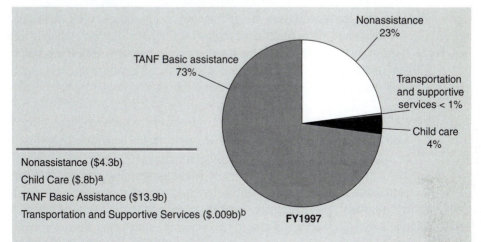

TANF Basic assistance
73%

Nonassistance
23%

Transportation
and supportive
services < 1%

Child care
4%

Nonassistance ($4.3b)

Child Care ($.8b)[a]

TANF Basic Assistance ($13.9b)

Transportation and Supportive Services ($.009b)[b]   **FY1997**

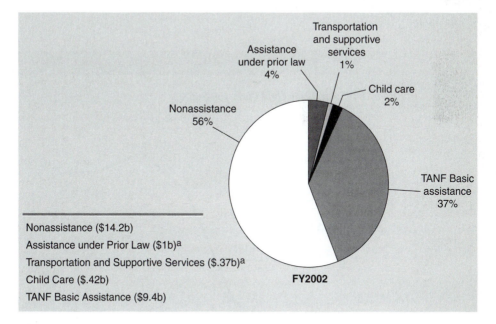

Assistance
under prior law
4%

Transportation
and supportive
services
1%

Child care
2%

Nonassistance
56%

TANF Basic
assistance
37%

Nonassistance ($14.2b)

Assistance under Prior Law ($1b)[a]

Transportation and Supportive Services ($.37b)[a]

Child Care ($.42b)   **FY2002**

TANF Basic Assistance ($9.4b)

Source: U.S. Department of Health & Human Services, TANF financial data, retrieved from http://acf.dhhs.
gov/programs/ofs/data/chart1_1997.html and http://acf.dhhs.gov/programs/ofs/data/chart1_2002.html

[a]MOE is maintenance of effort.

[b]These expenditures are counted in the Assistance category.

portions of nonassistance funds (80 percent in 1997 and 45 percent in 2002) on "other" supports (unfortunately, we know little about how these large amounts of funds were used). [106] The distinction between "assistance" and "nonassistance" is vital because many TANF regulations, especially time limits, apply to basic assistance but not to nonassistance. The issue is also complicated because of states' concerns that the federal government may not accept some of their uses of nonassistance and disallow federal funds used to pay for them. In addition, when federal funds are used, the clock is ticking on recipients' time limits on TANF. If the states play it safe and use only their own funds for nonassistance, they bear the full costs but they can stop the time limit clock for recipients. [107]

Child Care Spending.   Under AFDC, states were required to provide child care for recipients who worked or participated in work-related activities. TANF has no child care mandate, nevertheless, states' spending on child care grew dramatically between 1997 and 2000 from $249 million to nearly $4 billion (see Figure 6.3). This was largely because states could use TANF funds for child care. Nationwide, considerable amounts of "noncash" TANF funds are used to provide child care. Federal law allows states to use TANF funds for child care in two ways: (1) states may directly spend TANF funds on child care; and (2) states may transfer up to 30 percent of TANF funds to their Child

FIGURE 6.3

Use of TANF Funds for Child Care, 1997–2002

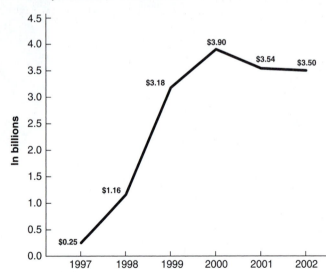

Source: U.S. Department Health and Human Service, Administration of Children and Families TANF Financial Data, www.acf.dhhs.gov/program/ofs/data/index.html

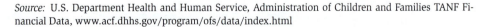

Care and Development Fund (CCDF). States transferred $2.6 billion in TANF funds to CCDF in 1999 but only $1.9 billion in 2002. In 2002, 38 states used this transfer mechanism to fund child care for needy families, down from 40 states in 2001.[108] Cuts in child care spending have been linked to the downturn in the economy and subsequent state budget crises.

From 1996 to 2000, the number of children receiving child care subsidies more than doubled. Even so, when child care spending peaked in 2000, only one out of seven eligible children was receiving child care assistance. In 2001, child care spending declined to $3.5 billion where it remained in 2002 (see Figure 6.3). More cuts are projected. As the economy has slowed, states have had to increase spending on TANF cash assistance to accommodate increasing caseloads. Unless the economy rebounds in the very near future, states expect to cut services to TANF families as means of contending with ongoing budget crises.[109]

Other Spending.   States may transfer up to 10 percent of TANF funds to their Social Service Block Grant (SSBG) for services to needy families. This allows states to provide services and benefits to low-income families who do not qualify for traditional cash assistance payments.[110] Like other TANF spending trends, the amount of funds transferred to SSBG increased each year until 1999, when it peaked at $1.3 billion. In 2002, about $1 billion were transferred to SSBG.[111]

Relatively small amounts of TANF funds have been used for education and training. For example, less than 2 percent ($462 million) were used to enhance skills in 2002. Similar amounts ($584 million) were spent on transportation and supportive services. Spending on pregnancy prevention programs grew from $102 million in 2000 to $726 million in 2002, constituting 2.6 percent of total TANF funds. Some states have started two-parent family formation programs, but nationwide, little funding ($284 million in 2002) has been used in this effort (perhaps because such programs are controversial). Spending for programs designed to put cash in the pockets of poor families, such as EIC and state funded tax credits, grew to $766 million in 2002,[112] only slightly more than was spent to prevent pregnancy.

An assets and investment program designed to complement welfare programs and help families save money for future needs is the Individual Development Account, or IDA. This approach allows for accumulation of "wealth" through government matching funds. Under the former AFDC program, recipients who accumulated even small amounts of cash or other assets were disqualified from assistance. But without assets, it is unlikely they will be able to leave welfare behind. IDAs can be used to help TANF and other low-income families save money, which is matched with government funds when families withdraw their own savings to buy a home, pay for education, or start a business.[113] Few states have taken advantage of IDAs, investing a mere $7.7 million in 2002.

Spending Forecast.   As states drew from their previous TANF savings, these rainy day funds dropped from $3.2 billion in 2000 to $2.7 billion in 2002.[114] Nationally, caseloads (total number of recipients) continued to decline, but slowly (by 2.3 percent from September 2002 to September 2003); 27 states reported caseload decreases.[115] For those still reporting decreases, the size of the decline has diminished significantly. States and welfare advocates are concerned about the ability to maintain cash benefits and work supports at current levels if the economy remains sluggish.[116] Many states have curtailed, or expect to cut, services and cash benefits to TANF recipients in response to state budget crises, complicated by rising Medicaid costs, eroding tax bases, and federal fiscal pressures through mandates such as homeland security.[117]

How Effective Has TANF Been?   By now, most of us have heard the success stories of the TANF program as measured by the number of people who have left the welfare rolls. Since welfare reform, more than two million families have left TANF, a decline of 54 percent.[118] Declining caseloads may be something to cheer about *if* families are doing well upon leaving TANF, but welfare reform began during the economic boom times of the late 1990s when the economy added 21 million jobs. Much of the decline in caseloads was likely a response not only to welfare reform policies, but also because more jobs were available. That having been said, it is also important to note that, before welfare reform, economic boom times did not result in substantial decreases in caseloads.[119] The Committee on Ways and Means said that factors that shrunk caseloads were "the new 'work first' culture, a rapidly growing economy, tougher work sanctions, . . . a lifetime limit for Federally funded benefits, and widespread adoption of diversion practices."[120] The Council of Economic Advisers attributed one-third of the drop to welfare policy changes, 8 to 10 percent to an improved economy, 10 percent to the increase in the minimum wage, and as much as 5 percent to the decrease in the value of cash welfare benefits.[121] The General Accounting Office agreed that the strong economy and changes in welfare policies, as well as changes in policies affecting low-wage earners, all contributed to the increase in work among low-income single mothers, and the decline in TANF caseloads.[122]

How have families fared after leaving TANF? Studies of recipients who leave TANF show that about 75 percent work at some point after leaving.[123] About one-half to two-thirds of welfare leavers are still working one to two years after leaving TANF. In 2002, welfare leavers earned an average of $7.72 an hour. The typical mother leaving welfare earns about $10,000 a year.[124] About a third of employed former TANF recipients work part time (less than 35 hours a week).[125] The real indictment of welfare reform is that many families who leave TANF remain poor and experience hardships because of low earnings. About 41 percent have incomes below the poverty threshold even when the value of EIC and food stamps is added to earnings.[126] Most people leaving TANF work in the low-wage service sector.[127]

In the face of a stagnant economy, life has gotten more difficult for TANF leavers. The Urban Institute's massive initiative called Assessing the New Federalism has been tracking the effects of devolution. It reported that the number of welfare leavers employed fell from 50 percent in 1999 to 42 percent in 2002.[128] Twenty-five percent of those leaving welfare in recent years have returned to TANF. Some are becoming disconnected from both the workforce and the welfare system. These individuals have no reported source of income—they are not working, do not have a working spouse, and are not receiving TANF or disability benefits. The Urban Institute reported that one in seven people who left TANF in recent years has become a disconnected welfare leaver (DWL), and that the percentage of DWLs increased from 10 percent in 1999 to 14 percent in 2002. Most disconnected welfare leavers face multiple barriers to employment, and thus incur more hardship than other TANF leavers. Sixty-three percent reported that they had run out of money to purchase food.[129] Less than half of those leaving TANF (43 percent) are receiving food stamps, only 15 percent are using child care supports, though 50 percent to 85 percent are receiving earned income credits.[130] Child care programs are underfunded, and low-income families are often unaware of the EIC.

The problems that led families to welfare remain as barriers to work for TANF recipients. Healthcare problems; lack of education and skills; mental illness, substance abuse, and other disabilities; and child care and transportation problems are the prominent barriers to getting and remaining employed. The Joyce Foundation found that the more problems people faced, the less likely they were to work, and that those with the severest problems often left welfare involuntarily due to sanctions for not meeting program demands.[131] Other problems remain in assessing the successes and failures of TANF policies and programs, particularly the difficulty in tracking TANF families after they leave the program.

TANF Reauthorization.   The Personal Responsibility and Work Opportunity Reconciliation Act of 1996 (PRWORA) was due to expire in 2002. Given the battles that ensued over initial passage of the PRWORA, it is no surprise that Congress has not been able to agree on reauthorization legislation. State TANF programs have been kept running through a series of stop-gap bills. Politicians on both sides of the political aisle do concur that federal TANF block grant funding should remain at the current level of $16.5 billion annually. Some advocates for the poor argue for increases to keep up with inflation and also because of the country's uncertain economic situation. Most of those close to the reauthorization process agree that, given unmet needs, more childcare funding is needed. Most bills being considered recommend increased childcare funding; however, President Bush's reauthorization proposal has not called for increased child care funding or an increase in the minimum wage, even though he wants work requirements increased to 40 hours per week. Rather than bonuses for reducing illegitimacy and funding to promote marriage, many people want a reauthorization bill that will reward states for reducing child poverty. Though families are generally better off financially when the parents are married, it can also be argued that a much more stable route to poverty reduction is to help women get education and better jobs (see Illustration 6.5).[132] An increase in the minimum wage would also be a big help. States are experimenting with everything from marriage counseling programs to bonus payments for married recipients; but little is known about the effectiveness of these approaches (whether they help or produce unintended problems).[133]

Most legislators want to keep the five-year time limit on TANF benefits.[134] Issues they do not agree on include:

♦ Whether states should receive bonuses for efforts at pregnancy prevention rather than actual declines in illegitimacy rates

♦ Whether states should improve tracking of welfare leavers to ensure that they continue to receive services for which they are eligible, such as food stamps and Medicaid

♦ Whether eligibility criteria for receiving foods stamps should be relaxed, and procedures for delivering benefits be altered to ensure that those who are eligible receive them[135]

♦ How states can how use demonstration programs to more effectively serve poor families with multiple barriers to work[136]

♦ Whether there should be improved reporting requirements for states to better account for "nonassistance" spending[137]

♦ Whether states should have to meet improved performance outcomes in measuring TANF successes

♦ Whether states should be required to invest in more effective education and training programs and allow more education and training as part of the work activity requirement under welfare reform[138]

States are complaining that it is increasingly difficult to budget for welfare spending when they do not know what future federal funding levels will be or what new mandates Congress may impose on them. One thing is certain: Those who believe in more work and less public assistance are having their way.

SUMMARY

No social welfare program has been as controversial as Aid to Families with Dependent Children. As AFDC caseloads rose due to divorce, desertion, and especially out-of-wedlock births and the lack of noncustodial fathers paying child support, concerns mounted that AFDC needed a major overhaul. There was a series of attempts to get mothers as well as the few fathers receiving AFDC to become self-sufficient through work, but none made more than a very modest dent in the program. Stronger enforcement of child support has also not resulted in the kind of success that politicians and the public had hoped.

AFDC was an entitlement program. Very poor families headed by single parents, and some headed by two parents in which a parent was unemployed or disabled, were eligible for AFDC as long as there was a minor child in the home. Many families received AFDC for a short time or vacillated between work and AFDC, but there was a group of recipients who never managed to shake free from the program. These highly welfare-reliant families used much of the program's resources and were the major target of concern. Liberals and conservatives alike hoped that

ILLUSTRATION 6.5

Bush Marriage Initiative Robs Billions from Needy

by Elizabeth Bauchner
WeNews commentator

A Bush administration proposal to divert almost $2 billion in scarce welfare funds to promote marriage should be squashed. As one state's effort shows, jobs and education lead to marriage, not the other way around.

Editor's Note: The following is a commentary. The opinions expressed are those of the author and not necessarily the views of Women's eNews.

(WOMENSENEWS)—A major goal of the landmark 1996 welfare reauthorization was "to end dependence of needy parents on government benefits by promoting job preparation, work, and marriage."

Seven years later, it seems our government is more concerned about promoting marriage than helping needy parents prepare for and find jobs.

The Bush administration proposes to spend almost $2 billion of scarce welfare funds over the next six years promoting marriage. Our total federal welfare budget is less than $17 billion per year, the same amount it was in 1996. In February, the House passed H.R. 4, a welfare reauthorization bill that diverts funds from basic economic supports such as job training and child care into experimental marriage-promotion programs. Currently, the bill is under consideration by the Senate.

Promoting healthy and stable marriages is not a bad idea as long as the programs don't take money away from helping welfare recipients obtain college degrees, which are proven to help boost women and children out of poverty.

However, H.R. 4 is littered with ineffective public policies that won't help the poorest among us. Marriage alone hardly ever gets women and children out of poverty. Education and job training do.

SOCIAL EXPERIMENT INSTEAD OF PROVEN HELP

If passed, H.R. 4 will divert $100 million per year from the federal Temporary Assistance for Needy Families budget as well as commit an additional $200 million per year in new funding to promote marriage. Additionally, states will be required to match $100 million per year in funding, which they could take out of their federal welfare budgets.

This money would be better spent on providing basic economic supports to enable recipients to pursue job training and education.

Studies show that a college education is the single biggest contributor to financial independence. "There is . . . no more well established link to economic well-being than educational attainment," according to a report by Avis Jones-DeWeever of the Institute for Women's Policy Research in Washington, D.C. Although a college education doesn't guarantee a life free from poverty, mothers who possess a bachelor's degree make up less than 2 percent of the welfare rolls.

Jones-DeWeever also cites research that shows that just one year of post-secondary education reduces poverty rates by half in households headed by women of color.

Acknowledging that not all women have the interest or ability to attend post-secondary schools, Jones-DeWeever recommends that such women be offered "other educational

continued

ILLUSTRATION 6.5 *(continued)*

supports and training opportunities . . . that lead to the types of jobs that provide stable employment, livable wages and access to benefits."

In order to do this, we need to forget diverting funds from federal welfare into marriage promotion programs and allow more welfare recipients access to education and job training.

MINNESOTA PLAN LED TO MORE MARRIAGES

Interestingly, education and job training would do more than just help families out of poverty. The Minnesota Family Investment Program helped families work their way out of poverty through three routes: job training, earned-income disregards and child care subsidies. They then discovered that leading families out of poverty led to increased marriage rates.

The Minnesota plan was successful in helping parents prepare for and find work. The earned-income disregards meant they could keep more of their federal welfare benefits in addition to their wages, eliminating an important work deterrent.

The child care subsidies helped take the burden off of the families transitioning from welfare to work. Although the Minnesota plan wasn't aiming to promote marriage, the marriage rates rose among welfare recipients, indicating that reducing economic stressors and meeting the basic needs of welfare recipients may lead to higher rates of marriage.

However, instead of addressing the basic needs of the poor, H.R. 4 would waste precious welfare dollars on experimental marriage-promotion programs, including programs that discriminate against single-parent families, preach biblical doctrine and appear to be for-profit businesses.

For example, the Department of Health and Human Services' Administration for Children and Families recommends about 40 possible marriage-promotion programs for states to adopt.

Their recommendations include two state programs already in existence. West Virginia offers monthly cash bonuses to couples after they marry, while Oklahoma penalizes cohabiting couples by reducing the children's welfare benefit if the couple doesn't marry. These two programs hurt the children of single-parent households simply because their mothers may be unable or unwilling to marry.

RECOMMENDED PROGRAMS TIED TO PROFIT MOTIVE

What's worse, many of the programs recommended by the Administration for Children and Families appear to be for-profit businesses that advocate against no-fault divorce and promise to "cure" marriage problems. Several of the programs teach strict biblical interpretations of marital conflicts. The Marriage Matters initiative of the Iowa Family Policy Center, for instance, claims to "help engaged couples prepare for marriage by instructing them in biblical roles." Is this the kind of marriage promotion we want to spend our tax dollars on?

If H.R. 4 passes, needy parents are not going to get the kinds of help they need to escape poverty. We will waste taxpayer money on programs that overlook what poor people really need: jobs that pay.

The surest way to a good job is through education and job training, and the surest way to keep the job is to have good child care and healthcare. If we focus on these issues first, marriage is more likely to occur.

Source: Women's eNews, http://www.womensenews.org

Elizabeth Bauchner lives in Ithaca, NY, and writes a weekly column, "Mothering Matters," in *The Ithaca Journal.* Reprinted with permission of Women's eNews.

they would be able to deter what came to be known as a cycle of dependence on public assistance.

During the George H. W. Bush administration, states began experimenting with welfare reform. Liberals thought that many of these ideas were ill-considered. Yet state applications to the federal government for waivers to deviate from AFDC program rules multiplied. While Congress and the president haggled over welfare reform, the states were busy changing the face of welfare. Finally, President Clinton signed a welfare reform bill that effectively "ended welfare as we knew it." The Personal Responsibility and Work Opportunity Reconciliation Act (PRWORA) changed AFDC from an open-ended entitlement program to a block grant program called Temporary Assistance for Needy Families, with fixed amounts sent to the states and more freedom for the states to do with welfare as they wish. Among the bill's many components are rather stiff requirements about how many TANF recipients must go to work or face losing benefits after two years. The maximum lifetime period that a family can generally receive benefits is five years.

The welfare rolls had begun dropping before Congress and the president agreed on the welfare reform plan. A healthy economy had put some people to work, and some believe that changes that states had already made in their programs also contributed to declining rolls. States have used the added flexibility offered by TANF to structure programs that primarily focus on providing work supports such as child care, job readiness training, case management, and transportation service to recipients, with a secondary focus on cash assistance.

There is controversy over TANF's success. While it is clear TANF rolls have shrunk by at least half there is disagreement as to how well TANF leavers are faring. Many are working, but in low-wage jobs, and many continue to live in poverty. Welfare leavers often do not receive the support services to which they are entitled. Some TANF recipients have multiple barriers to work and leave welfare involuntarily. A growing number of welfare leavers are disconnected from the workforce and the public assistance system. Many issues remain unresolved with the PRWORA and with TANF in particular. Legislators, scholars, and advocates continue to debate TANF reauthorization.

NOTES

1. For a history of mothers' aid, see Linda Gordon, *Women, the State, and Welfare* (Madison, WI: University of Wisconsin Press, 1990); Linda Gordon, *Pitied but Not Entitled: Single Mothers and the History of Welfare* (New York: Free Press, 1994).

2. Laurence E. Lynn, Jr., "A Decade of Policy Developments in the Income-Maintenance System," in Robert H. Haveman, Ed., *A Decade of Federal Antipoverty Programs: Achievements, Failures, and Lessons* (New York: Academic Press, 1977), p. 60; Martin Rein,

Social Policy: Issues of Choice and Change (New York: Random House, 1970), p. 311.

3. Quoted in Lynn, "A Decade of Policy Developments in the Income-Maintenance System," p. 73.

4. Gilbert Y. Steiner, *The State of Welfare* (Washington, DC: Brookings Institution, 1971), p. 81.

5. See Committee on Ways and Means, U.S. House of Representatives, *Overview of Entitlement Programs, 1993 Green Book* (Washington, DC: U.S. Government Printing Office, 1993), p. 623.

6. *Ibid.*, p. 733.

7. John Bishop, *Jobs, Cash Transfers, and Marital Instability: A Review of the Evidence,* Institute for Research on Poverty, University of Wisconsin, Madison, written testimony to the Welfare Reform Subcommittee of the Committees on Agriculture, Education and Labor, and Ways and Means of the U.S. House of Representatives, October 14, 1977, p. 9.

8. *Ibid.*, p. 8.

9. David T. Elwood and Lawrence H. Summers, "Poverty in America: Is Welfare the Answer or the Problem?" in Sheldon H. Danzinger and Daniel H. Weinberg, Eds., *Fighting Poverty: What Works and What Doesn't* (Cambridge, MA: Harvard University Press, 1986), pp. 92–93.

10. Hilary Williamson Hoynes, *Work, Welfare, and Family Structure: What Have We Learned?* Working Paper 5644 (Cambridge, MA: National Bureau of Economic Research, July 1996), p. 36.

11. Library of Congress, "Personal Responsibility and Work Opportunity Reconciliation Act (P.L. 04-193)," (Washington, DC: Thomas: Legislative Information on the Internet, August 22, 1996), retrieved September 19, 2003, from http://thomas.loc.gov/cgi-bin/bdquery/z?d104:HR03734:@@@L&summ2 = m&/TOM:/bss/d104query.html

12. See Alfred J. Kahn and Sheila B. Kamerman, *Child Support: From Debt Collection to Social Policy* (Newbury Park, CA: Sage, 1988).

13. Committee on Ways and Means, U.S. House of Representatives, "Child Support Enforcement Program," *2003 Green Book* (Washington, DC: December 30, 2003), Section 8, retrieved February 17, 2004, from http://waysandmeans.house.gov/Documents.asp?section = 813

14. *Ibid.*, p. 8-2.

15. Committee on Ways and Means, *1993 Green Book,* p. 776.

16. Committee on Ways and Means, U.S. House of Representatives, "Child Support Enforcement Program," *1993 Green Book,* pp. 8-77–8-81.

17. *Ibid.*, pp. 8-4, 8-11–8-12.

18. *Ibid.*, pp. 8-11–8-14.

19. M. S. Hill, *The Role of Economic Resources and Dual-Family Status in Child Support Payments* (Ann Arbor, MI: Institute for Social Research, University of Michigan, May 1988), as cited in Committee on Ways and Means, U.S. House of Representatives, "Child Support Enforcement Program," *2003 Green Book,* p. 8-43.

20. Committee on Ways and Means, U.S. House of Representatives, "Child Support Enforcement Program," *2003 Green Book,* pp. 8-44.

21. *Ibid.*, pp. 8-44–8-45; and U.S. Department of Health and Human Services, *Handbook on Child Support Enforcement* (Washington, DC: Office of Child Support Enforcement), p. 29, retrieved March 11, 2004, from http://www.pueblo.gsa.gov/cic_text/family/childenf/

22. Figures in this paragraph rely on U.S. Bureau of the Census, *Custodial Mothers and Fathers and Their Child Support: 2001* (Washington, DC: October 2003), Publication No. P60-225, Table B: Demographic Characteristics of Custodial Parents by Award Status and Payments Received: 2002.

23. Office of Child Support Enforcement, *FY 2002, Annual Statistical Report* (Washington, DC: Administration for Children and Families, November 2003), Table 49: Paternity Establishment, FY 2002.

24. Committee on Ways and Means, U.S. House of Representatives, *1996 Green Book* (Washington, DC: U.S. Government Printing Office, 1996), p. 539.

25. Freya L. Sonenstein, Pamela A. Holcomb, and Kristen S. Seefeldt, *Promising Approaches to Improving Paternity Establishment at the Local Level* (Washington, DC: Urban Institute, February 1993) cited in Committee on Ways and Means, *1993 Green Book,* pp. 756–757.

26. Committee on Ways and Means, U.S. House of Representatives, *2003 Green Book,* "Child Support Enforcement Program," pp. 8-15–8-17.

27. M. Robin Dion and Barbara DeVaney, "Strengthening Relationships and Supporting Healthy Marriage among Unwed Parents" (Princeton, NY: Mathematica, April 2003); Sara S. McLanahan and Marcia J. Carlson, "Welfare Reform, Fertility, and Father Involvement," *The Future of Children,* Vol. 12, No. 1, pp. 147–165, Winter/Spring 2002, retrieved July 15, 2004, from http://www.futureofchildren.org

28. This paragraph relies on the following sources: Committee on Ways and Means, U.S. House of Representatives, "Child Support Enforcement Program," *2003 Green Book,* pp. 8-8–8-15; Office of Child Support Enforcement, *HHS Fatherhood Initiative Fact Sheet* (Washington DC: Administration for Children and Families, June 21, 1999), retrieved from http://www.acf.hhs.gov/programs/cse/fct/fthr990621.htm; J. O. Teitier, "Father Involvement, Child Health and Maternal Health Behavior," *Children and Youth Services Review,* Vol. 23, No. 4/5, April/May, 2001; U.S. Department of Health and Human Services, *Fatherhood Initiative,* retrieved March 11, 2004, from http://fatherhood.hhs.gov/index.shtml

29. This discussion of methods used to award child support relies on Committee on Ways and Means, "Child Support Enforcement Program," *2003 Green Book,* pp. 8-21–8-23; see also Support Guidelines.com, "Child Support Guidelines on the Web," retrieved

March 13, 2004, from http://www.supportguidelines.com/links.html

30. Laura W. Morgan, "Child Support Models," in *Child Support Guidelines: Interpretation and Application* (Aspen Law & Business, 1996 & Supps.), retrieved March 13, 2004, from http://www.supportguidelines.com/book/chap1a.html

31. M. A. Pirog, M. Klotz, and K. V. Buyers, "Interstate Comparisons of Child Support Awards Using State Guidelines, 1997" (Bloomington, IN: Institute for Family and Social Responsibility, 1997) as cited in the Committee on Ways and Means, *2003 Green Book*, pp. 8-24–8-26.

32. Committee on Ways and Means, *2003 Green Book*, pp. 8-26, 8-28; and Office of Child Support Enforcement, *Automated Cost-of-Living Adjustments of Child Support Orders in Three States* (Washington, DC: U.S. Department of Health and Human Services, April 16, 2001), retrieved March 6, 2004, from http://www.acf.hhs.gov/programs/cse/pubs/reports/cola/index.html

33. This paragraph relies on Committee on Ways and Means, U.S. House of Representatives, *2003 Green Book*, pp. 8-24–8-25; see also U.S. Bureau of the Census, *Custodial Mothers and Fathers and their Child Support: 2001*, Table B.

34. U.S. Bureau of the Census, *Custodial Mothers and Fathers and Their Child Support: 1991*; U.S. Bureau of the Census, *Custodial Mothers and Fathers and their Child Support: 2001*, Table B; see also Committee on Ways and Means, *2003 Green Book*, pp. 8-71, 8-76.

35. Committee on Ways and Means, "Child Support Enforcement Program," *2003 Green Book*, pp. 8-33, 8-34.

36. *Ibid.*, pp. 8-38–8-40, 8-47.

37. Elaine Sorensen and Chava Zibman, "Poor Dads Who Don't Pay Child Support: Deadbeats or Disadvantaged?" (Washington, DC: Urban Institute, April 1, 2001).

38. Figures on child support enforcement rely on tables in Office of Child Support Enforcement, *FY 2002 Annual Statistical Report*.

39. General Accounting Office (GAO), *Child Support Enforcement: Clear Guidance Would Help Ensure Proper Access to Information and Use of Wage Withholding by Private Firms* (GAO-02-349) (Washington, DC: GAO, March 2002); retrieved July 16, 2004, from http://www.gao.gov

40. U.S. General Accounting Office (GAO), *Early Results on Comparability of Privatized and Public Office* (Washington, DC: GAO, 1996), Report HEHS-97-4, retrieved July 15, 2004, from http://frwebgate.access.gpo.gov/cgi-bin/useftp.cgi?IPaddress = 162.140.64.21&file name = he97004.pdf&directory = /diskb/wais/data/gao;

see also Committee on Ways and Means, *2003 Green Book*, pp. 8-5–8-51; and "Trends in Privatizing Child-Support Collections, *Privatization.org*, retrieved February 20, 2004, from http://www.privatization.org/database/policyissues/childwelfare_privtrends.html, Privatization.org at www.privatization.org and Reason Public Policy Institute at www.rppi.org

41. General Accounting Office, *Child Support Enforcement: Clear Guidance Would Help Ensure Proper Access to Information and Use of Wage Withholding.*

42. This section relies on Committee on Ways and Means, U.S. House of Representatives, *2003 Green Book*, "Child Support Enforcement Program."

43. Most of this section relies on *ibid.*

44. Frank F. Furstenberg, Jr., "Daddies and Fathers: Men Who Do for Their Children and Men Who Don't," in Frank F. Furstenburg, Jr., Kay E. Sherwood, and Mercer L. Sullivan, Parents' Fair Share Demonstration, *Caring and Paying: What Fathers and Mothers Say about Child Support* (New York: Manpower Demonstration Research Corporation, July 1992).

45. Clint Shields, "Father Friendly," *Fiscal Notes* (Newsletter of Texas State Comptroller), September 2002, pp. 5, 12–13.

46. Steiner, *The State of Welfare*, p. 36; Lynn, "A Decade of Policy Developments in the Income-Maintenance Programs," pp. 62–63.

47. Donald Brieland, Lela B. Costin, Charles R. Atherton, and contributors, *Contemporary Social Work: An Introduction to Social Work and Social Welfare* (New York: McGraw-Hill, 1975), p. 100; Steiner, *The State of Welfare*, p. 37.

48. Steiner, *The State of Welfare*, p. 37.

49. Andrew W. Dobelstein with Ann B. Johnson, *Serving Older Adults: Policy, Programs, and Professional Activities* (Englewood Cliffs, NJ: Prentice Hall, 1985), p. 126.

50. Lynn, "A Decade of Developments in the Income-Maintenance System," p. 74.

51. For further discussion of this point, see Sheldon H. Danzinger, Robert H. Haveman, and Robert D. Plotnick, "Antipoverty Policy: Effects on the Poor and the Nonpoor," in Danzinger and Weinberg, *Fighting Poverty*, pp. 50–77.

52. Roberta M. Spalter-Roth, Heidi I. Hartmann, and Linda Andrews, *Combining Work and Welfare: An Alternative Anti-poverty Strategy* (Washington, DC: Institute for Women's Policy Research, 1992); Heidi Hartmann, Roberta Spalter-Roth, and Jacqueline Chu, "Poverty Alleviation and Single-Mother Families," *National Forum*, Vol. 76, No. 3, 1996, pp. 24–27.

53. Leonard Goodwin, "Can Workfare Work?" *Public Welfare,* Vol. 39, Fall 1981, pp. 19–25.

54. *Ibid.*

55. Ellen Goodman, "Volunteer Workfare Program Proves Worth," *Austin American-Statesman,* March 5, 1985, p. A11.

56. Judith M. Gueron, *Reforming Welfare with Work* (New York: Ford Foundation, 1987).

57. Gayle Hamilton and Daniel Friedlander, *Final Report on the Saturation Work Initiative Model in San Diego* (Washington, DC: Manpower Demonstration Research Corporation, November 1989), quotes are from pp. x and vii.

58. This paragraph relies on Daniel Friedlander and Gary Burtless, *Five Years After: The Long-Term Effects of Welfare-to-Work Programs* (New York: Russell Sage Foundation, 1995), quote from p. 35.

59. Jan L. Hagen and Irene Lurie, "How 10 States Implemented Jobs," *Public Welfare,* Vol. 50, Summer 1992, p. 13.

60. Some of this section relies on Committee on Ways and Means, *1993 Green Book,* Section 7, especially pp. 624–644.

61. Robert B. Hudson, personal communication.

62. Stephen Freedman and Daniel Friedlander, *The JOBS Evaluation: Early Findings on Program Impacts in Three Sites,* Executive Summary (New York: Manpower Demonstration Research Corporation, 1995); also cited in Committee on Ways and Means, *1996 Green Book,* p. 428.

63. U.S. General Accounting Office, *Welfare to Work: Most AFDC Training Programs Not Emphasizing Job Placements* (GAO/HEHS-95-113) (Washington, DC: GAO, May 1995).

64. James Riccio, Daniel Friedlander, and Stephen Freedman, *GAIN: Benefits, Costs, and Three-Year Impacts of a Welfare-to-Work Program* (New York: Manpower Research Development Corporation, 1994).

65. Peter Passell, "Like a New Drug, Social Programs Are Put to the Test," *New York Times,* March 9, 1993, pp. C1, 10. For more in-depth information on welfare-to-work programs see Dan Bloom, *After AFDC: Welfare to Work, Choices and Challenges for States* (New York: Manpower Demonstration Research Corporation, 1997).

66. Administration for Children and Families, Department of Health and Human Services, "Temporary Assistance for Needy Families (TANF), 1936–1998," May 1998, retrieved from http://www.acf.dhhs.gov/news/tables.htm

67. Administration for Children and Families, U.S. Department of Health and Human Services, "Aid to Families with Dependent Children (AFDC), Temporary Assistance for Needy Families (TANF), 1960–1998," August 1998, retrieved from http://www.acf.dhhs.gov/news/tables.htm

68. Social Security Administration, *Social Security Bulletin, Annual Statistical Supplement, 1991* (Washington, DC: U.S. Department of Health and Human Services, 1992), p. 305.

69. Committee on Ways and Means, *1996 Green Book,* p. 459.

70. See U.S. Bureau of the Census, *Statistical Abstract of the United States: 1997* (Washington, DC: U.S. Government Printing Office, 1997), Table 477, p. 299.

71. Committee on Ways and Means, *1996 Green Book,* p. 442.

72. *Ibid.,* pp. 435, 437.

73. This description of methods used to determine standards of need is based on Center for Budget and Policy Priorities, *Enough to Live On* (Washington, DC), cited in "Study Faults State AFDC 'Need Standards,'" *NASW News,* Vol. 38, July 1993, p. 11.

74. Committee on Ways and Means, *1996 Green Book,* pp. 436–438, 451–453.

75. Center for Budget and Policy Priorities, "The Cato Institute Report on Welfare Benefits: Do Cato's California Numbers Add Up?" (Washington, DC, March 7, 1996), http://epn.org/cbpp/cbcato/html

76. Executive Office of the President, Office of Management and Budget, *A Program for Economic Recovery* (Washington, DC: U.S. Government Printing Office, 1981), p. 1-11.

77. John L. Palmer and Isabel V. Sawhill (Eds.), *The Reagan Record* (Cambridge, MA: Ballinger, 1984), p. 364.

78. "AFDC Cuts Hurt," *ISR Newsletter,* University of Michigan, Spring–Summer 1984, p. 3.

79. Executive Office of the President, *Budget of the United States Government, Fiscal Year 1991* (Washington, DC: U.S. Government Printing Office, 1990), p. 176.

80. Much of this section relies on Jeffrey L. Katz, "Clinton's Welfare Reform Plan to Be Out in Fall, Aides Say," *Congressional Quarterly,* Vol. 51, July 10, 1993, p. 1813; National Association of Social Workers, "Policy Recommendations of the Clinton Administration's Working Group on Welfare Reform, Family Support and Independence" (Washington, DC: May 6, 1994); also see Executive Office of the President, Office of Management and Budget, Budget of the United States Government, Fiscal Year 1995 (Washington, DC: U.S. Government Printing Office, 1994).

81. David T. Ellwood, "Welfare Reform As I Knew It: When Bad Things Happen to Good Policies," *The*

American Prospect, No. 26, May–June 1996, pp. 21–29, retrieved from http://epn.org/prospect/26/26ellw.html

82. Robert A. Rankin, "Clinton Steers to the Middle, and Traditional Welfare Falls," *Austin American-Statesman,* August 4, 1996, pp. D1, 6.

83. General Accounting Office, "Welfare Reform: Changing Labor Market and Fiscal Conditions," *Briefing to the Staff of the Senate Committee on Finance,* Washington, DC, May 13, 2003. This account of the new TANF program is largely based on Committee on Ways and Means, *1996 Green Book,* Appendix L; see also American Public Welfare Association, "Temporary Assistance for Needy Families (TANF) Block Grants (Title 1)," retrieved from http://www.apwa.org/reform/tanf.htm; David A. Super, Sharon Parrott, Susan Steinmetz, and Cindy Mann, "The New Welfare Law" (Washington, DC: Center on Budget and Policy Priorities, August 13, 1996), retrieved from http://epn.org/cbpp/wcpmfbl2.html

84. General Accounting Office, *Testimony to Committee on Finance, U.S. Senate: Welfare Reform* (Washington, DC, April 10, 2002), GAO-02-615T, p. 2.

85. Committee on Ways and Means, U.S. House of Representatives, *2003 Green Book,* "Temporary Assistance to Needy Families (TANF)" (Washington, DC March 17, 2004), Section 7, pp. 7-19–7-20, retrieved from http://waysandmeans.house.gov/Documents.asp?section = 813

86. *Ibid.,* p. 7-22.

87. Brookings Institution, "The Politics of TANF Reauthorization," *Welfare Reform and Beyond Initiative* (Washington, DC, January 25, 2001), retrieved September 19, 2003, from http://www.brook.edu/comm/transcripts/20010125_ii.htm

88. Margy Waller, "TANF Reauthorization: Options and Opportunities," *Presentation to the U.S. Conference of Mayors Annual Meeting,* June 15, retrieved September 21, 2003, from the Brookings Institution web page, http://www.brook.edu/es/urban/speeches/20020615 waller.htm

89. Committee on Ways and Means, U.S. House of Representatives, *2003 Green Book,* "Temporary Assistance to Needy Families (TANF)," pp. 7-14–7-15.

90. *Ibid.,* pp. 7-10, 7-12, 7-38, 7-39, 7-41; and Brookings Institution, "The Politics of TANF Reauthorization," *Welfare Reform and Beyond Initiative;* also see General Accounting Office, *Report to the Chairman and Ranking Minority Member, Committee on Finance, U.S. Senate: Supports for Low-Income Families* (Washington, DC, January 2004), GAO-04-256, p. 16.

91. Committee on Ways and Means, U.S. House of Representatives, *2003 Green Book,* "Temporary Assistance to Needy Families (TANF)," p. 7-11; Brookings Institution, "The Politics of TANF Reauthorization," *Welfare Reform and Beyond Initiative.*

92. Committee on Ways and Means, U.S. House of Representatives, *2003 Green Book,* "Temporary Assistance to Needy Families (TANF)," pp. 7-62, 7-64; Margy Waller, "TANF Reauthorization: Options and Opportunities."

93. Committee on Ways and Means, U.S. House of Representatives, *2003 Green Book,* "Temporary Assistance to Needy Families (TANF)," pp. 7-91–7-95.

94. General Accounting Office, *Testimony to Committee on Finance, U.S. Senate: Welfare Reform,* p. 8.

95. Committee on Ways and Means, U.S. House of Representatives, *2003 Green Book,* pp. 7-48–7-53.

96. *Ibid,* pp. 7-57–7-58.

97. H&R Block, "Rate Tables: Earned Income Credit and the Child Tax Credit," December 30, 2003, retrieved from http://www.hrblock.com/part 7856124con974632SI3647816/rate_tables/eic_ctc_ tables.html

98. Committee on Ways and Means, U.S. House of Representatives, *2003 Green Book,* "Temporary Assistance to Needy Families (TANF)," pp. 7-45, 7-51.

99. General Accounting Office, *Report to the Chairman and Ranking Minority Member, Committee on Finance, U.S. Senate: Supports for Low-Income Families,* p. 16.

100. Committee on Ways and Means, U.S. House of Representatives, *2003 Green Book,* "Temporary Assistance to Needy Families (TANF)," p. 7-12; and Brookings Institution, "The Politics of TANF Reauthorization," *Welfare Reform and Beyond Initiative.*

101. Committee on Ways and Means, U.S. House of Representatives, *2003 Green Book,* "Temporary Assistance to Needy Families (TANF)," pp. 7-58–7-60.

102. *Ibid.,* p. 7-118

103. Jennifer Mezey and Brooke Richie, *Welfare Dollars No Longer an Increasing Source of Child Care Funding: Use of Funds in FY 2002 Unchanged from FY 2001, Down from FY 2000* (Washington, DC: Center for Law and Social Policy, August 6, 2003).

104. General Accounting Office, *Report to the Chairman and Ranking Minority Member, Committee on Finance, U.S. Senate: Supports for Low-Income Families,* p. 31; Committee on Ways and Means, U.S. House of Representatives, *2003 Green Book,* "Temporary Assistance to Needy Families (TANF)," p. 7-60.

105. Much of this paragraph relies on U.S. Department of Health and Human Services, Administration of Children and Families, *TANF Financial Data* (Washington, DC), retrieved from http://www.acf.dhhs.gov/programs/ofs/index.html; in increase in employment supports and "nonassistance" is also discussed in Sheila R. Zedlewski, David Merriman, Sarah Stavetig,

and Kenneth Finegold, "TANF Funding and Spending across the States," in Alan Weil and Kenneth Finegold, (Eds.), *Welfare Reform: The Next Act* (Washington, DC: Urban Institute Press, 2002), pp. 225–246.

106. Mark Greenberg and Elise Richer, *How States Used TANF and MOE Funds in FY 2002: The Picture from Federal Reporting* (Washington, DC: Center for Law and Social Policy).

107. See Community Legal Services, Inc., "Public Benefits/Welfare Law Glossary," February 2001, retrieved July 16, 2004, from http://www.clsphila.org/Glossary.htm; Gordon L. Berlin, *Enhance States' Flexibility to Reward Work and Benefit Children* (New York: Manpower Development Research Corporation, 2002), retrieved July 16, 2004, from http://www.mdrc.org/Reports 2002/TANF/TANF/–Implications3.htm; Louisiana House of Representatives, "Issue Brief on TANF Program and Unobligated TANF Funds," December 2000, retrieved July 16, 2004, from http://house.legis.state.la.us/housefiscal/Publications/SCOFA/Briefs/tanf.htm

108. Much of this section relies on Mezey and Richie, *Welfare Dollars;* General Accounting Office, *Testimony to Committee on Finance, U.S. Senate: Welfare Reform*, p. 8.

109. General Accounting Office, *Report to the Chairman and Ranking Minority Member, Committee on Finance, U.S. Senate: Supports for Low-Income Families*, p. 27.

110. General Accounting Office, "Welfare Reform: Changing Labor Market and Fiscal Conditions," *Briefing to the Staff of the Senate Committee on Finance* (Washington, DC, May 13, 2003).

111. U.S. Department of Health and Human Services, Administration for Children and Families, *TANF Financial Data.*

112. Greenberg and Richer, *How States Used TANF and MOE Funds.*

113. Michael Sherraden, Mark Schreiner, and Sondra Beverly, "Income, Institutions, and Saving Performance in Individual Development Accounts," *Economic Development Quarterly*, Vol. 17, No. 1, February, 2003, pp. 95–112.

114. U.S. Department of Health and Human Services, *TANF Financial Data.*

115. Administration for Children and Families, "Welfare Rolls Drop Again" (March 30, 2004), retrieved July 15, 2004, from http://www.acf.hhs.gov/news/press/2004/TanfCaseloads.htm; Elise Richer, Hedieh Rahmanou, and Mark Greenberg, *Welfare Caseloads in 27 States Decline in First Quarter of 2003: Most States Show Only Small Caseload Fluctuations* (Washington, DC: Center for Law and Social Policy, July 18, 2003).

116. Mezey and Richie, *Welfare Dollars.*

117. General Accounting Office, "Welfare Reform."

118. U.S. Department of Health and Human Services, Administration for Children and Family Assistance, "Welfare Rolls Drop Again," HHS News Release, March 30, 2004, retrieved July 16, 2004, from http://www.acf.hhs.gov/news/press/2004/Tanfcaseloads.htm

119. Joyce Foundation, *Welfare to Work: What Have We Learned* (Chicago, March 2002), retrieved September 23, 2003, from http://www.joycefdn.org/pubs/pubsmain-fs.html

120. Committee on Ways and Means, U.S. House of Representatives, *2003 Green Book*, "Temporary Assistance to Needy Families (TANF)," p. 7-31.

121. *Ibid.*

122. General Accounting Office, "Welfare Reform."

123. Margy Waller, "TANF Reauthorization."

124. *Ibid.*

125. Pamela J. Loprest, *Fewer Welfare Leavers Employed in Weak Economy* (Washington, DC: Urban Institute, August 21, 2003), No. 5 in Series, "Snapshots of America's Families III," retrieved September 26, 2004, from http://www.urban.org/urlprint.cfm?ID = 8550

126. Joyce Foundation, *Welfare to Work;* General Accounting Office, "Welfare Reform."

127. General Accounting Office, "Welfare Reform"; see also *"Ten Things Everyone Should Know about Welfare Reform"* (Washington, DC: The Urban Institute, May 9, 2003), retrieved August 6, 2003, from http://www.urban.org

128. Pamela J. Loprest, *Fewer Welfare Leavers Employed in Weak Economy.*

129. Pamela J. Loprest, *Disconnected Welfare Leaver Face Serious Risks* (Washington, DC: The Urban Institute, August 21, 2003).

130. Waller, "TANF Reauthorization"; Michael Wiseman, "Food Stamps and Welfare Reform," Welfare Reform Policy Brief #19 (Washington, DC: Brookings Institution, March 2002).

131. Joyce Foundation, *Welfare to Work.*

132. See for example, Robert Lerman, "Should Government Promote Healthy Marriages?" *Short Takes on Welfare Policy, Number 5* (Washington, DC: The Urban Institute, May 2002), retrieved March 31, 2004, from http://www.urban.org

133. Courtney Jarchow, *Strengthening Marriage and Two-Parent Families* (Denver: National Conference of State Legislators, February 2003); Mary Parke and Theodora Ooms, *More Than a Dating Service? State Activities Designed to Promote Marriage*, Couples and Marriage Series, CLASP (Center for Law and Social Policy) Policy Brief No. 2, October 2002.

134. Waller, "TANF Reauthorization."

135. Wiseman, "Food Stamps and Welfare Reform."

136. Ron Haskins, "Welfare Reform: An Examination of Effects," *Testimony before House Committee on Education and the Workforce* (Washington, DC: Brookings Institution, September 20, 2001), retrieved September 24, 2003, from the Brookings Institution website http://www.brook.edu/views/testimony/haskins/20010920.htm

137. Greenberg and Richer, *How States Used TANF and MOE Funds in FY 2002.*

138. National Coalition for the Homeless, "New National Survey of the Nation's Poor Challenges Success of Welfare Reform; Two Thirds Unemployed, High Percentage Hungry, Homeless and Lacking Insurance."

CHAPTER

Fighting Hunger, Fighting Fat: Nutrition Policy and Programs in the United States

Consideration of nutrition and food assistance policy and programs in the United States puts us on two different tracks. One is the concern of anti-hunger advocates that poor Americans need more food assistance. The other is the concern that what most Americans need is a healthier diet and more exercise, not more food.[1]

NUTRITION PARADOXES

It is astounding that Americans and others in lands of plenty can sit in their living rooms and witness people starving in other countries around the world. The number of hunger-related deaths worldwide is declining (now estimated at 20,000 per day), but as many as one-sixth of the world's people suffer from *undernutrition* (malnutrition that occurs from too little to eat) that impairs health, productivity, and life expectancy.[2] Hunger is greatest in South Asia and sub-Saharan African, followed by Latin America and other parts of Asia. The Hunger Project reports that the vast majority of hunger-related deaths are due to persistent hunger; less than 10 percent are due to famine. The first nutrition paradox is that the planet has the capacity to feed everyone adequately, yet wars, political strife, red tape, and extreme poverty continue to prevent an end to world hunger.[3] The Hunger Project calls "democracy, the growth of civil society, and the broader emancipation of women" the keys to ending hunger. Reports, however, raise questions about whether world food production can keep pace with a world population that is expected to exceed 8 billion by 2025.[4] Much more could be said about agricultural production, price supports and subsidies paid to farmers, international food aid, and related politics, but this chapter concentrates on food and nutrition assistance policy in the United States, where other paradoxes abound.

Fat, Not Fit, in the USA

It might also be surprising that anemias and other nutritional deficiencies (from causes such as metabolic problems) result in approximately 3 deaths per 100,000 population annually in the United States.[5] But in the United States, where rail-thin models set the standard for beauty and special treatment programs assist individuals with anorexia nervosa and other eating disorders, the most glaring paradox is that most malnutrition is *overnutrition*. The first *Surgeon General's Report on Nutrition and Health* acknowledged that "for most of us the more likely problem has become one of overeating—too many calories for our activity levels and an imbalance in the nutrients consumed along with them."[6] The problem is getting worse (see Illustration 7.1) and growing globally.[7]

An article in the *Journal of The American Medical Association* predicts that "poor diet and physical inactivity may soon overtake tobacco as the leading cause of death" in the United States.[8] Body mass index (BMI) is a measure of the relationship between height and weight (weight in kilograms divided by height in meters squared) for adults. A BMI of 25 to 29.9 is considered overweight and 30 or greater is considered obese. The Surgeon cites a litany of health risks from obesity and overweight:[9]

♦ Obese individuals have a 50 to 100 percent increased risk of premature death from all causes compared to individuals with a BMI in the range of 20 to 25.

♦ An estimated 300,000 deaths a year may be attributable to obesity.

♦ Morbidity from obesity may be as great as from poverty, smoking, or problem drinking.

ILLUSTRATION 7.1

The Supersizing of America

♦ 61% of adults in the United States were overweight or obese in 1999.

♦ 13% of children aged 6 to 11 years and 14% of adolescents aged 12 to 19 years were overweight in 1999. This prevalence has nearly tripled for adolescents in the past two decades.

♦ The increases in overweight and obesity cut across all ages, racial and ethnic groups, and both genders.

♦ In women, overweight and obesity are higher among members of racial and ethnic minority populations than in non-Hispanic white women.

♦ In men, Mexican Americans have a higher prevalence of overweight and obesity than non-Hispanic whites or blacks.

♦ Women of lower socioeconomic status (income < 30 percent of poverty threshold) are approximately 50% more likely to be obese than those of higher socioeconomic status.

♦ 300,000 deaths each year in the United States are associated with obesity.

♦ Overweight and obesity are associated with heart disease, certain types of cancer, type 2 diabetes, stroke, arthritis, breathing problems, and psychological disorders, such as depression.

♦ The economic cost of obesity in the United States was about $117 billion in 2000.

Source: The Surgeon General's Call to Action to Prevent and Decrease Overweight and Obesity 2001, Overweight and Obesity: At a Glance, retrieved July 5, 2003, from http://www.surgeongeneral.gov

♦ A weight gain of 11 to 18 pounds increases a person's risk of developing type 2 diabetes to twice that of individuals who have not gained weight. Those who gain 44 pounds or more have four times the risk of type 2 diabetes.

♦ A gain of approximately 10 to 20 pounds results in an increased risk of coronary heart disease (nonfatal myocardial infarction and death) of 1.25 times in women and 1.6 times in men.

♦ Higher levels of body weight gain of 22 pounds in men and 44 pounds in women result in an increased coronary heart disease risk of 1.75 and 2.65, respectively.

♦ In women with a BMI of 34 or greater, the risk of developing endometrial cancer is increased by more than six times.

♦ Overweight and obesity are also known to exacerbate many chronic conditions such as hypertension and elevated cholesterol and are associated with increased risk for certain musculoskeletal disorders, such as knee osteoarthritis.

Many children and adolescents also suffer from overweight and obesity and incur significant health risks as well as stigmatization. Healthier diets might save $71 billion in costs associated with these conditions.[10]

The purpose of the National Nutrition Monitoring and Related Research Act of 1990 is to better track nutrition. The Act also requires that dietary guidelines be issued every five years and be reviewed by the Secretaries of Agriculture and Health and Human Services. The latest monitoring report did not give Americans high marks. Americans may be eating more, but across most age, gender, race, and ethnic groups, they registered less than recommended intakes of vitamins A, E, and B6, zinc, copper, and calcium. Certain groups also had insufficient iron, magnesium, and folate intakes. Although low-income adolescents and adults had lower intakes of vitamins and minerals than those from higher income groups, their levels were not more likely to fall below recommended standards. Low-income children did not have lower intakes than other children. Low income continued to be a major risk for nutrition-related health problems such as anemia, high cholesterol, hypertension, and overweight.[11] Evidence has surfaced that low-income individuals might become overweight or obese because they may purchase low-cost, nonnutritious, fattening food to stave off hunger, and "the body can compensate for periodic food shortages by becoming more efficient at storing more calories as fat."[12]

Serving Up Nutritional Advice

The federal government, through the U.S. Department of Agriculture (USDA), has been serving up nutrition advice almost since the agency's creation in 1862.[13] The USDA's first advice was to eat more to prevent dietary deficiency. When the federal government embarked on providing food aid during the Great Depression, people needed help getting food and most any food available would do. The government's early surplus commodity distribution programs were closely tied to agricultural policy and were placed under the auspices of the agriculture committees of Congress and the USDA. Needless to say, commodity distribution programs enjoyed strong support from the powerful farm lobby, the American Farm Bureau Federation, and the nation's farmers because they provided a much needed market for food they could not otherwise sell.

Today, the food business looks a lot different than it did in the 1930s. Mega corporations that now dominate the industry produce or manufacture many foods that come in cans, jars, and boxes. These businesses compete fiercely with each other for "brand share." Though someone must be eating the fresh fruits and vegetables displayed in grocery stores, Americans have become conditioned to consume foods high in fat, sugar, and salt. While many Americans were busy consuming non-nutritious, high calorie foods, an "epidemic," or "crisis," was apparently occurring. Americans were not only busy eating calorie-laden foods, they were busy working mostly at sedentary jobs, driving to work, and being couch potatoes during leisure time. They were also fueling the weight loss industry.

Obesity has increased despite the USDA food guide pyramid (see Figure 7.1) intended to help Americans make healthy, balanced dietary choices. The pyramid has undergone several contentious revisions and is set to undergo another. The sectors of the food industry contend for a place in the government's nutrition advice. Like all major industries, the food industry makes campaign contributions and lobbies. Sims contends

FIGURE 7.1

The Food Guide Pyramid: A Guide to Daily Food Choices

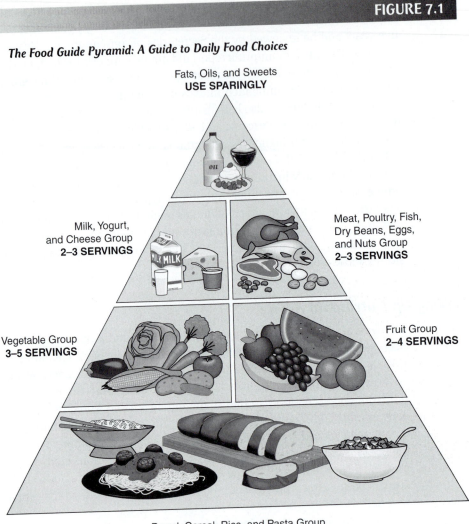

Source: U.S. Department of Agriculture and the U.S. Department of Health and Human Services, retrieved August 12, 2004, from http://www.usda.gov/cnpp/images/pyramid.gif

that, in many cases, advice to eat healthier and lower-fat foods directly contradicts "federally supported marketing orders and pricing structures [that] reward the promotion and sale of high-fat foods to consumers."[14] In addition, emphasis on physical fitness in the schools has declined and most American families own at least one car. Children used to walk or ride their bikes to school and play outdoors. Now, safety concerns compel hurried parents to accompany their children, and generally that means driving them wherever they need to go. Television programming and computers add to sedentary pursuits and growing waistlines,[15] and a periodic survey is conducted pointing fingers at the fattest cities in America.

Who's in Charge of Nutrition?

Both the Senate and the House of Representatives have a committee and subcommittee with primary responsibility for nutrition legislation. In the Senate they are the Committee on Agriculture, Nutrition, and Forestry and its Subcommittee on Research Nutrition and General Legislation. In the House, the Agriculture Committee and its Subcommittee on Department Operations, Oversight, Nutrition and Forestry are the major entities. Advocacy groups, particularly the Food Research and Action Center (FRAC) and the Center on Budget and Policy Priorities, are also key players in nutrition legislation. The Food Stamp Program (FSP) for poor and low-income Americans is the country's largest nutrition program. Economists Ohls and Beebout note that FSP legislation is primarily influenced by about thirty people who have the most intimate knowledge of the program; furthermore, food stamp legislation tends to be very detailed, with little discretion left to administrators, because of the importance legislators attach to this program.[16] They also note that food assistance tends to generate a strong emotional response that has generally resulted in expanded aid.

But in the federal bureaucracy, nutrition programs have been largely divorced from exercise and other aspects of health care policy. The USDA operates 15 food assistance programs for low-income individuals (described later in this chapter) that comprise about half of the agency's budget and serve about 20 percent of the population at some time in a given year.[17] The Food Stamp Program, which does not utilize surplus agricultural commodities, reaches millions of Americans. It might be argued that the U.S. Department of Health and Human Services (DHHS) should administer nutrition programs. One reason is that the DHHS already administers other major public assistance programs, like Temporary Assistance to Needy Families (TANF). Rossi conducted an evaluation of the major federal food programs and noted, "the issues identified are not to imply that USDA's administration . . . is in any way defective."[18]

Others have not been so kind to the USDA with the respect to its role in protecting consumers. One agricultural columnist writes:

> The USDA . . . really exists to promote the sale of U.S. farm products, at home and abroad. A recent General Accounting Office report faults the meat inspection system for relying too much on voluntary industry compliance and employing scientific methods that members of the understaffed inspection force don't even understand.[19]

The identification of the first U.S. case of mad cow disease in December 2003 and previous *E. coli* outbreaks may be cases in point.

Sims also suggests:

> In the United States . . . powerful economic interests are represented in the U.S. Department of Agriculture (USDA) and their allied constituents in major farm and food

enterprises. Health interests, especially those supportive of preventive health services, in contrast, have a yet fledgling, but growing, "home" in the Department of Health and Human Services (DHHS). . . . Despite the fact that the U.S. Department of Agriculture was named the "lead agency" for nutrition in the 1977 Farm Bill, the Department of Health and Human Services has repeatedly disputed this claim because of its extensive array of research and educational programs in nutrition and health.[20]

Regardless of which government agency might do a better job of promoting health, it is unlikely that any of the nutrition programs, which constitute a very substantial part of the USDA, would be willingly relinquished to another department. Perhaps the primary reason to keep the food stamp program (and other nutrition programs) under USDA auspices is that it "can maintain a unique identity that distinguishes it from other cash welfare programs run by different agencies."[21] Without this identity, support for all the food assistance programs might be considerably weaker.[22]

The View from Anti-Hunger Advocates

Given rampant overnutrition, can a case be made that there is hunger in the United States? In a developed country like the United States, it has been suggested that individuals "should be considered malnourished if for economic or other reasons beyond their control, they experience repetitive periods of hunger, even though their total intake of nutrients is sufficient to protect them from symptoms of deficiency disease."[23] Rather than hunger, the U.S. Department of Agriculture now focuses on measuring *food security and insecurity.* In food-secure households, members had continuous access to sufficient food for an active, healthy life.

> *Food insecurity means that a household had limited or uncertain availability of food, or limited or uncertain ability to acquire acceptable foods in socially acceptable ways (i.e., without resorting to emergency food supplies, scavenging, stealing, or other unusual coping strategies). Many food-insecure households were worried or unsure whether they would be able to get enough to eat, and most reduced the quality, variety, or desirability of their diets. They may have resorted to emergency food sources or other extraordinary coping behaviors to meet their basic food needs.[24]*

In 2002, the USDA found that 11 percent of U.S. households were food insecure at some time during the year and that individuals in 3.5 percent of households experienced involuntary hunger at some point because they were unable to afford sufficient food.[25] About half of food-insecure households experienced these problems even though they participated in a major government food assistance program; 3 percent went to a food pantry, food bank, or church, and members of about 395,000 households went to an emergency food kitchen (this figure does not include homeless individuals).

If Americans had all the food they needed, food banks and other nontraditional sources of food might not be so popular. Anti-hunger advocates contend that we must do more to shore up the government's nutrition assistance programs. Scores of community- and church-sponsored food banks operate to fill in the gaps in the federal food assistance programs (see Illustration 7.2). America's Second Harvest is the largest of these groups in the United States, serving 26 million people (8 million of them children) across the country. Among the many other groups is the Food Bank of North Carolina, serving people in 34 counties in the central and eastern parts of the state. MAZON, the Hebrew word for food, obtains funding primarily from Jews in the United States, who donate 3 percent of celebrations (e.g., weddings, bar mitzvahs), which is used to support food banks and kosher meals-on-wheels programs for homebound elderly individuals. Many anti-hunger groups are politically active. The Food Research and Action Center is among the best known national organizations promoting improved food assistance in the United States. State and local groups also work hard for the cause. Project Bread works to prevent or alleviate hunger in Massachusetts and to improve public policy with regard to hunger and food aid. The country's major nutrition paradoxes might be solved by getting food assistance to those in financial need and helping everyone eat a healthier diet. Much of this chapter focuses on getting assistance to those in need.

ILLUSTRATION 7.2

Filling the Food Assistance Gap

Hundreds of nonprofit groups like America's Second Harvest work to fill food assistance gaps through food gleaning efforts, which have grown substantially in the United States. There is certainly a lot to be gleaned. According to the USDA, a July 1997 "study showed that 96 billion pounds of food—over one quarter—of the 356 billion pounds of goods produced for human consumption was lost at the retail and food service levels."[a] Second Harvest, composed of 200 regional food banks, distributes one billion pounds of food each year to 50,000 organizations that help needy individuals.[b] The USDA encourages gleaning, and Congress passed the Bill Emerson Good Samaritan Food Donation Act of 1996 to limit the liability of those who donate and distribute the food.[c] In 2002, more than four million low-income families with children reported using a food pantry at some time during the proceeding year.[d] Nearly half also received food stamps.

NOTES

[a]USDA, "USDA Food Recovery and Gleaning Initiative," *Nutrition Program Facts,*" May 1998.

[b]*America's Second Harvest Fact Sheet,* retrieved July 6, 2003, from http://www.secondharvest.org

[c]*Together We Can!, A What, Why, and How Handbook for Working to End Hunger in Your Community* (Washington, DC: United States Department of Agriculture, 2000), FNS-315, retrieved July 4, 2003, from http://www.fns.usda.gov

[d]Sheila R. Zedlewski and Sandi Nelson, Snapshots of America's Families III, No. 17, *Many Families Turn to Food Pantries for Help,* November 2003, retrieved January 20, 2004, from http://www.urban.org

The View from Nutrition Advocates

Why aren't more Americans—rich and poor—eating a healthier diet and exercising more? Americans have become accustomed to eating foods that appeal to the taste buds but aren't necessarily nutritious. Adults and children alike are exposed to heavy-duty advertising. Children are attracted to brand name foods, often those associated with popular cartoon characters and celebrities, and they are being courted to be loyal consumers. Children may be rewarded with nonnutritious treats or a trip to their favorite restaurant that often serves a high calorie meal with a little toy included. Low-income individuals may face additional obstacles to healthy eating. Poor neighbor-hoods often don't have a major grocery store that offers a variety of foods and has sales. Convenience stores, which generally stock a limited supply of healthy foods and charge more, may be the only readily available shopping source. With housing and utilities consuming an increasing portion of the household budget, something has to give, and that may be the food budget. In Chapter 6, we saw that it is still difficult to make ends meet when TANF is combined with food stamps. Some contend that healthy foods often cost more[26] (others find that fruits and vegetables can be pur-chased economically). People may resort to nonnutritious food products that can be purchased more inexpensively.

Some nonprofit groups are teaming up to encourage a healthier diet. The national 5 A Day for Better Health Program enourages Americans to eat at least five servings of fruits and vegetables every day to improve health. The program is jointly sponsored by the National Cancer Institute and the Produce for Better Health Foundation, a con-sumer education foundation representing the fruit and vegetable industry. Special campaigns are directed at members of different ethnic groups. Other groups are pro-moting exercise.

Can, or should, public policy be used as a tool to promote healthier diets and more exercise? Policies that require foods to be labeled with nutrition information have apparently had little impact on Americans' waistlines. In promoting health-ier eating, public health expert and nurse Nancy Milio calls information, research, and evaluation more politically feasible, less costly, and less effective, and struc-tural changes (controls over subsidies, prices, production, and advertising) less po-litically feasible but more effective.[27]

A growing number of individuals have exposed the tactics that the food industry and its representative organizations use to encourage consumers to purchase non-nutritious foods and to ward off attacks by nutrition advocates. These authors are helping to set the public policy agenda on nutrition. In his book *Food Fight*, Yale psy-chologist Kelly Brownell discusses how far government should go to promote healthy eating. Among his many recommendations are taxing foods with little nutritional value in order to raise money to improve nutrition education, limits on fast food advertis-ing in schools, and zoning restriction on fast food restaurants near schools.[28] The medical journal *Lancet* also recommended "taxing soft drinks and fast foods; subsi-dising nutritious foods, like fruits and vegetables; labeling the content of fast food; and prohibiting marketing and advertising to children."[29]

Some foods may be fattening and nonnutritious, but consumed judiciously, they will not likely result in health risks. Individual responsibility is a factor in the health equation, and some people believe that a lack of individual responsibility is where much of the problem lies. After all, it is just as easy to eat a piece of fruit on the run as is it to consume a fat-laden meal from a drive-through window. Attempts to sue companies like McDonald's for contributing to obesity have been unsuccessful.[30] Nevertheless, fast food chains and other food companies are becoming more concerned that they will face lawsuits like the tobacco industry, and they are trying to offer healthier fare.

The nutrition concerns presented thus far are much different than those prevailing over much of the country's history. There is still concern about helping those in need purchase an adequate diet.

SERVING UP NUTRITIONAL POLICY

Prior to the 1930s, states and communities played the major role in feeding the "deserving poor," but with the advent of the Great Depression, more and more people were unable to obtain enough to eat. Scores stood in bread lines or waited at soup kitchens to obtain their only means of survival. Despite the effort, these methods of feeding the hungry were clearly inadequate for meeting the country's needs.

Commodity Food Distribution

By 1930 farmers had successfully encouraged the federal government to stabilize farm prices by buying their surplus agricultural commodities. The USDA and the Federal Emergency Relief Administration were authorized to purchase the commodities. In 1933 the Federal Surplus Relief Corporation was established to aid in the process. This new agricultural policy was intended to help farmers. It also provided an opportunity to distribute large amounts of food to poor people. Unfortunately, perishable foods were difficult to preserve, recipients still waited in long lines to receive whatever foods were available, and at least some public officials felt that this method of food distribution only added to the poor's degradation.[31] A better method of providing food was needed.

As a solution, in 1939, the nation attempted its first food stamp program in some parts of the country, this time with added encouragement from grocery store operators.[32] Participants could purchase from $1 to $1.50 of orange stamps per person, which could be exchanged for foods at regular grocery stores.[33] For each dollar of orange stamps purchased, participants received fifty cents worth of blue stamps free. Blue stamps could be exchanged only for designated surplus foods. The new program provided farmers a market for their surplus foods, preserved normal channels of trade through grocery stores, and gave recipients greater food choices.[34] However, the program was available only to public assistance recipients, not to others in need, many eligible individuals could not afford the orange stamps; there was also criticism that products other than surplus foods were being purchased with the blue stamps.

The country's first food stamp program ended in 1943, largely because of the increased demand for agricultural surpluses created by World War II. Given this demand, it was ironic that the country abandoned the use of food stamps in regular grocery stores and returned to commodity distribution. The new commodity program, called the Needy Family Program, utilized surplus farm goods and products purchased specifically for the program.[35] This new program did little to rectify problems such as large containers of food that were not easily preserved. Interest in a better method remained strong, and new food stamp program bills were introduced in every session of Congress.[36] In 1959 Congress authorized a discretionary two-year food stamp program, but the Eisenhower administration did not implement it.[37]

A New Food Stamp Program

In 1961, under the Kennedy administration, a new food stamp program was tested in several areas of the country.[38] Evidence that the approach resulted in recipients purchasing more foods and those of higher nutritional quality helped to spur passage of the Food Stamp Act of 1964.[39] Communities could still use commodity distribution if they wished.

The new Food Stamp Program was also the responsibility of the USDA, but each state determined eligibility criteria, and state and local welfare agencies certified eligible recipients and provided them with the stamps. The federal government determined how much recipients were charged for the stamps based on their income. The stamps, like paper money, came in various denominations and were exchanged at their face value for food products in regular retail grocery establishments that chose to participate in the program. The difference between the amount recipients paid and the total value of the stamps was called the "bonus value."

Politics Discovers Hunger

The extent of hunger in America was exposed in several ways during the 1960s. Particularly poignant is Nick Kotz's description of the visit of Senators Robert F. Kennedy and Joseph Clark in 1967 to the filthy shack in Cleveland, Mississippi, where Annie White and her six children lived.[40] The senators' trip was at the request of Marian Wright Edelman (now head of the Children's Defense Fund), and they were stunned at what they saw. One of the children, a girl about 2 years old, had a swollen stomach and was so listless that Senator Kennedy was never able to get her to respond to his cajoling. White said she could not afford to buy food stamps, and all the family had to eat at that time was the last rice and biscuits from its surplus commodity allotment. A study by the Citizen's Board of Inquiry into Hunger and Malnutrition in the United States called *Hunger U.S.A.* (supported by the Field Foundation of Chicago's Marshall Field department store) and a CBS television documentary also helped the country to "discover hunger."

In 1968 Congress responded by establishing the U.S. Senate Select Committee on Nutrition and Human Needs, chaired by Senator George McGovern. In 1969 President

Richard M. Nixon called a White House Conference on Food, Nutrition, and Health, and the USDA established the Food and Nutrition Service (from 1994 through 1997 it was known as the Food and Consumer Service) to administer its federal food assistance programs.

As described in the 1964 Food Stamp Act, the program was to be broader than previous efforts. States were to make stamps available not only to public assistance recipients, but also to low-income or near-poor people unable to afford an adequate diet. Instead, as the change from commodity foods to food stamps took place, program participation dropped precipitously. "In theory," says Kotz, "the food stamp plan sounded simple and workable, and should have been an enormous improvement over commodity distribution," but what really happened was "extortion":

> It was no accident that the stamp payment formula produced the outcries "We can't afford the stamps" and "The stamps run out after two weeks." Following their congressional leaders' twin desires of helping the farmers but not providing welfare to the poor, Agricultural Department bureaucrats had designed a Food Stamp program so conservative that reformers called the plan "Scrooge stamps."[41]

Political activism by groups such as the Poor People's Campaign helped to spur reforms.[42] Amendments passed in 1971 during the Nixon administration required that the program provide a "nutritionally adequate diet." Benefits were increased and eligibility criteria and application procedures were standardized so that applicants would be treated similarly, regardless of where they lived. Participants could not be charged more than 30 percent of their income for the stamps, based on the estimate that low-income families devoted 30 percent of their income to food (as described in Chapter 3, the poverty level is based on a calculation whereby the minimum amount needed by a family to acquire an adequate diet is multiplied by three). Unemployed adult recipients capable of holding jobs became responsible for registering for work and accepting employment if a "suitable" job could be found. In determining eligibility, income deductions for work-related expenses, housing, and medical expenses were introduced. Stamps were provided free to the poorest participants, and benefits were to be automatically adjusted (indexed) each year for changes in food costs.

By 1973, all communities had to adopt food stamps as their official nutrition program. Coupon allotments were to be indexed for inflation twice a year. Recipients still had to buy their stamps, and they had to buy all the stamps to which they were entitled at one time. Beginning in 1974 recipients could purchase a portion of the stamps. A series of lawsuits resulted in a 1975 court order to increase outreach efforts to make potentially eligible people aware of the program.

Eliminating the Purchase Requirement

Despite the benefits that were to be reaped (no pun intended), purchase requirements were just too high for some people. In 1977 during the Carter administration, the purchase requirement was eliminated. Recipients no longer had to put up cash to receive food stamps—they were simply given the bonus value of the stamps to which they were entitled. This spurred greater participation in some of the poorest areas of the country. However, national poverty guidelines were adopted as the income eligibility standard. Those with net incomes greater than these amounts could no longer participate. Income deductions were also tightened; benefits were reduced more rapidly as income rose (by 30 cents for every dollar of income), and requirements for student participation were made tougher. At the same time that elimination of the purchase requirement helped add needy people to the roles, others were being disqualified.

Politics Rediscovers Hunger

The 1980s began with more tightening of the Food Stamp Program and disagreement about the extent of hunger in America. Cost of living adjustments were changed from twice to once a year. President Reagan felt that the program had grown too large because families with greater than poverty-level incomes were allowed to participate, "divert[ing] the Food Stamp Program away from its original purpose toward a generalized income transfer program, regardless of nutritional need."[43] Eliminating the purchase requirement had indeed made food stamps more like an income maintenance program,[44] an effect that others applauded. In fact, benefits exceed TANF benefits in some states, making food stamps an important source of family income. Income deductions and income limitations, were made more stringent, including calculating family income partly on past income rather than on current income alone. Using federal funds to conduct outreach was prohibited, and the program was monitored more closely to reduce fraud and error. Program participation began to drop (see Figure 7.2).

New charges emerged that hunger was on the rise due to Reagan's social program cuts and also to rising unemployment. Concerned that reports of hunger were exaggerated,[45] Reagan appointed the President's Task Force on Food Assistance. Its general conclusion, published in 1984, was that undernutrition was not a serious problem in the United States. Social action groups lambasted the report,[46] and leading nutrition experts charged, "Despite their almost total lack of qualifications, the task force members did manage to find that hunger has reappeared in America. But because of their ineptitude, they were unable to qualify its extent, or to discern the presence of chronic malnutrition."[47] Meanwhile, the Food Research and Action Center publicized results of its own work indicating that infant mortality had increased in some areas of the country due to nutritional deficiencies. The Citizens' Commission on Hunger in New England also concluded that malnutrition and hunger again confronted America, and the Physician Task Force on Hunger in America identified 150 "hunger counties" in which substantial numbers of poor people were not receiving food stamps.[48] The Reagan task force recommended replacing the Food Stamp Program with a block grant, monitoring spending more closely, and beefing up efforts to detect fraud and

FIGURE 7.2

Food Stamp Program Participants and Costs

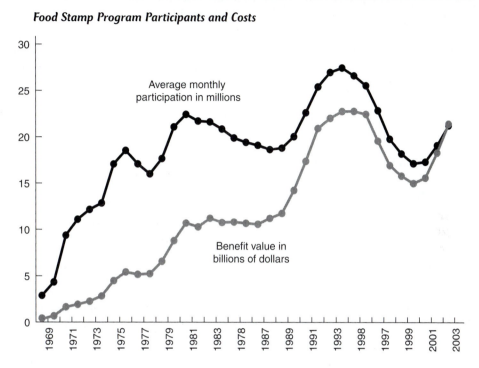

Sources: Food and Nutrition Service, U.S. Department of Agriculture (data as of December 19, 2003, 2003 figures are preliminary), retrieved January 23, 2004, from http://www.fns.usda.gov/pd/fssummar.htm

abuse, while the other groups encouraged increased food stamp spending, making it easier to obtain and use benefits, and forming a bipartisan commission to put an end to the country's hunger.

During the mid- and late-1980s food stamp legislation became kinder to recipients. AFDC and SSI recipients were declared automatically eligible. States that charged a sales tax on food could no longer tax food stamp purchases. Homeless people could apply even though they had no fixed address, and they could use their stamps to purchase low-cost meals in participating restaurants. Food stamp allotments were increased. States could use federal funds for outreach (although outreach was optional). On the other side of the ledger, states were also required to establish an Employment and Training (E&T) program in order to reduce Food Stamp Program participation.

In 1990 the Mickey Leland Memorial Domestic Hunger Relief Act, named after the late representative from Texas, reauthorized the Food Stamp Program through 1995. Leland's efforts to bring attention to the problem of world hunger were well known, and he chaired the House Select Committee on Hunger. The committee's efforts were highly respected, but it had only an advisory role, and the House abolished it in 1993 despite strong outcries. A USDA-sponsored hunger forum was held in 1993 to help the Clinton administration set its nutrition agenda. People with various interests in food programs, including food stamp participants, testified at the forum. During this period, Congress increased income deductions and disregards. The 1996 farm bill reauthorized the Food Stamp Program through 1997, but bigger changes were in store.

FOOD STAMP PROGRAM OPERATIONS

The Welfare Reform of 1996

The history of the Food Stamp Program continues to be one of expansion and contraction. In keeping with the country's mood to reform welfare, the Personal Responsibility and Work Opportunity Reconciliation Act (PRWORA) of 1996 reauthorized the Food Stamp Program through 2002 along with substantial program changes.[49] The program was saved from being converted into a block grant, which might have resulted in a cap on the number of eligible people who could be assisted, but many eligibility rules were made more stringent. For example, in determining household eligibility, some income deductions were frozen rather than adjusted annually. The Center for Budget and Policy Priorities estimated that the changes would reduce food stamp benefits from an average of 80 cents provided per person per meal to 66 cents (try eating on that); half of food stamp cuts would be borne by those with incomes of less than half the poverty line.[50] Many states began using their own funds to assist at least some elderly, disabled, and child recipients whose benefits were terminated.

The act made it easier for states to operate Food Stamp Employment and Training programs but increased work requirements for recipients. For example, unless exempt due to reasons such as physical or mental disability, able-bodied adults (aged 18 to 50) without dependents (ABAWDs as they are called) who do not meet work or other job program requirements can receive food stamps for only three months in a three-year period. They may regain eligibility by working or participating in a work program for 80 hours in a thirty-day period. In lieu of giving a household its food stamp allotment, the states may use the funds to subsidize a job for a household member participating in a work supplementation or support program. Other provisions "delete lack of adequate child care as an explicit good cause exemption for refusal to meet work requirements" and establish minimum disqualification periods for those who fail to meet work or workfare requirements. Thus, those who do not have dependents and who cannot find work where they live may be denied a benefit to which they were once entitled. (States can request exemptions from work requirements in areas with high unemployment, and they have the option of exempting 15 percent of those covered under the new work rule.)

The PRWORA eliminated some provisions that standardized the operation of food stamp offices across the country, like use of a uniform national application. Protections for participants took a beating. States are no longer required to waive office interviews for elderly and disabled applicants, and they no longer have to assist applicants in obtaining necessary information or completing applications.

The act severely limited the number of legally admitted immigrants who could receive food stamp benefits, such as certain refugees and asylees. The number of immigrants receiving benefits fell by half from 1996 to 2000, and another one-quarter were receiving fewer benefits.[51] In 2002, eligibility for some immigrants residing legally in the United States was restored, including those who have lived in the United States for at least five years and children regardless of date of entry.

Food Stamp Program Participation

The Food Stamp Program (FSP) operates in all fifty states, the District of Columbia, Guam, and the U.S. Virgin Islands. Recipients use their benefits to purchase food at regular retail stores. The FSP needs a new name because every jurisdiction has now replaced the paper coupons or stamps with electronic benefit transfer (similar to a debit card).

Means testing is the basis for determining food stamp eligibility.[52] Eligibility determination is complicated and is done by "household units." In fact, it takes more than five pages of small print in the Federal Register to spell out what constitutes a food stamp household![53] At the risk of oversimplification, a food stamp household generally consists of an individual or a group of individuals who live together and prepare meals together, regardless of whether they are members of the same family. Illustration 7.3 summarizes food stamp program eligibility requirements, and Illustration 7.4 describes food stamp program benefits.

In 1982, a block grant replaced the Food Stamp Program in the Commonwealth of Puerto Rico in an effort to control error, abuse, and rapidly rising costs.[54] By that time, 56 percent of Puerto Rico's population was receiving food stamps.[55] The Commonwealth exercises a great deal of discretion in designing its program. American Samoa operates a nutrition program for individuals who are elderly or disabled. The U.S. territory of the Northern Mariana Islands also receives a block grant. Participants must spend a portion of benefits on locally produced foods. In the territories, income eligibility limits are more stringent than what is allowed in the 48 contiguous U.S. states.

Some of the increase in Food Stamp Program participation is due to U.S. population growth, but, as shown in Figure 7.2, the number of participants has fluctuated. These fluctuations reflect a variety of factors, primarily economic recession and unemployment[56] and also tightening and loosening of eligibility requirements. Recipiency rates vary by state. Naturally, poorer states have the highest rates.

In March 1994 average monthly Food Stamp Program participation reached an all-time high, just short of 28 million individuals, nearly 11 percent of the U.S. population.[57] By July 2000, food stamp participation had dropped to 16.9 million.[58] An improved

ILLUSTRATION 7.3

Food Stamp Program Eligibility

COUNTABLE ASSETS

♦ Most households are limited to $2,000 in countable assets (e.g., bank accounts).

♦ Those aged 60 or older or disabled may have countable assets totaling $3,000.

♦ A home, personal effects, and some other items are not counted.

♦ In most cases, the value of a vehicle cannot exceed $4,650.

♦ Some vehicles are not counted (e.g., if its primary use is to earn income).

GROSS AND NET INCOME TESTS

♦ Households in which all members receive TANF, SSI, or in some places General Assistance, are exempt from gross and net income tests.

♦ Households with at least one person who is aged 60 or older or disabled do not have to meet the gross income test.

♦ For most households, gross income (which includes most cash received, e.g., earnings, cash public assistance, social insurance) cannot exceed 130 percent of federal poverty guidelines (in fiscal year 2004, $1,994 a month for a family of four, except in Hawaii and Alaska, where poverty guidelines are higher).

♦ Certain cash income is disregarded in calculating gross income (e.g., federal education aid, income earned by children attending school, income tax refunds).

♦ Net income for all households cannot exceed 100 percent of poverty guidelines ($1,534 a month for a family of four in fiscal year 2004).

DEDUCTIONS FROM NET INCOME

In determining net income, certain amounts of money are deducted to cover some household expenses. These include:

♦ A standard income deduction of $134 a month (higher in Alaska, Hawaii, and Guam, and lower in the Virgin Islands).

♦ 20 percent of all income earned from work.

♦ Costs of child or other dependent care while household members work or participate in training or education (the maximum allowable deduction is $200 per month for each child under age 2 and $175 for each other dependent). Few households use this deduction because they cannot afford this type of care.

♦ Many more households use the income deduction for excess shelter costs, calculated by determining the amount of the household's housing costs (mortgage or rent, utilities, property taxes, and insurance) that exceeds 50 percent of their remaining income after all other disregards or deductions are made. There is no cap on this deduction for households with elderly or disabled members. For other households the maximum deduction in 2004 was $378 per month (higher in Alaska, Hawaii, and Guam, and lower in the Virgin Islands). Some states use a standard utility cost rather than actual utility costs.

♦ Individuals who are elderly or disabled may deduct all but $35 of the medical expenses that they pay themselves.

♦ States can exclude legally owed child support payments in determining food stamp eligibility, or they can treat it as a deduc-

continued

ILLUSTRATION 7.3 (continued)

tion from net income (treating it as an income exclusion is of greater benefit to those who pay child support).

GROUPS THAT ARE INCLUDED OR EXCLUDED

◆ Included
- Victims of natural disasters.
- People living in some types of not-for-profit facilities (e.g., alcoholics and drug addicts in halfway houses, homeless people living in shelters, women and children in battered women's shelters, and people who are disabled or elderly and residing in group homes).

◆ Optional
- Native Americans living on or near reservations or in Oklahoma may participate in the Food Distribution Program on Indian Reservations (a commodity program) as an alternative to the Food Stamp Program if they wish, because it may be difficult to get to grocery stores.

◆ Excluded
- Most people living in large institutions.
- People who have quit a job without good cause.
- Strikers.
- Individuals not legally residing in the United States.
- Most immigrants legally residing in the U.S. for less than five years unless they are receiving disability benefits. (Immigrant children are eligible regardless of when they entered).
- Those convicted of federal or state felony drug offenses.
- States can exclude others such as those disqualified from other public assistance programs and those in arrears on child support.

Source: U.S. Department of Agriculture, http://www.fns.usda.gov

economy explained at least 20 percent of the decline in FSP participation; changes in the TANF program may have explained another 21 percent, and excluding noncitizens (who were only about 7 percent of FSP recipients just before welfare reform) and time limits on participation of adults without children might have added another 10 percent.[59] In 2003, with a weakened economy, monthly participation increased to an average of 21.3 million individuals.[60]

The FSP has important interactions with other public assistance programs. Prior to welfare reform in 1996, analysts found that food stamps and Medicaid (both in-kind types of programs) were used to substitute for increased AFDC payments (paid in cash) to recipients.[61] Food stamps continue to help equalize TANF and SSI payments across state lines. Since public assistance recipients in states with lower TANF and SSI payments have less countable income, they receive more in food stamp benefits. Food stamps may serve to ease the consciences of state lawmakers because they have allowed the real value of cash public assistance benefits to decline in recent decades. Furthermore, most food stamp households' income remains well below federal poverty guidelines, even if the cash value of food stamps is counted.[62]

ILLUSTRATION 7.4

The Thrifty Food Plan—How Much Is It Worth?

Food stamp benefits used to be based on the U.S. Department of Agriculture's (USDA) Economy Food Plan (EFP), but in the 1975 case of *Rodway v. USDA,* the U.S. Supreme Court found the EFP inadequate to meet nutritional needs. It was replaced with the Thrifty Food Plan (TFP) and updated in 1983.

The TFP is the most economical of the USDA's four plans, which also include the Low-, Moderate-, and Liberal-Cost Plans. Each plan has the same nutritional value, but there is a wide variation in the monthly dollar value of the plans. In August 2002, for a prototype family of two adults, aged 20 to 50, and two children, one aged 6 to 8 and the other aged 9 to 11, they were, from lowest to highest, $465.80, $593.60, $740.10, and $891.30.[a] Food stamp benefits are determined using this prototypical family and adjusted for households of different sizes and economies of scale (larger households can buy in larger quantities and make more efficient use of food products).

Except for family size, the TFP is not sensitive to family composition and needs, such as families with teenage members who might require greater food consumption or those (perhaps with older members) who may consume less. But all food stamp households receive benefits based on the prototypical family.

Advocacy groups have long criticized the TFP's adequacy.[b] The House Committee on Agriculture fended off criticisms of the TFP,[c] though the USDA conceded that the TFP "relies heavily on economical foods such as dry beans, flour, bread, and cereals. It includes smaller amounts of meat, poultry, and fish than families typically use."[d] In 1990, stamp allotments were increased to 103 percent of the TFP. In 1996, federal welfare reform legislation returned allotments to 100 percent of the TFP.

An analysis conducted in 1995 found that that the 1983 TFP did "not meet current nutritional recommendation for several nutrients and dietary components,"[e] and in 1999, the USDA issued an updated TFP based on the 1989 RDAs, the *1995 Dietary Guidelines for Americans,* the National Research Council's Diet and Health Report, and the servings recommended in the USDA Food Guide Pyramid.[f] The new TFP contains more fruits, vegetables, grains, and milk products, but fewer fats, oils, sweets, meat, and meat alternatives (e.g., beans, nuts) than the 1983 version.

Based on the revised TFP, in fiscal year 2004, the monthly food stamp allotment for a family of four on the U.S. mainland with no countable income was $471, or about $1.27 per person per meal for a typical 31-day month. As countable income rises, 30 percent of it is deducted from the maximum allowable payment of $471. For example, a family of four with $500 of countable income received a monthly food stamp allotment of $321. Food stamp allotments are higher in Hawaii, Alaska, Guam, and the Virgin Islands due to higher food costs in those locations. Nutrition benefits are also higher in the Mariana Islands, but lower in Puerto Rico.

Concerns about the TFP remain. According to a 2003 report:

The amount households spend for food is an indicator of how adequately they are meeting their food needs. In 2002, the typical (median) U.S. household spent $37.50 per person for food each week. Weekly food spending by the typical household

continued

ILLUSTRATION 7.4 (continued)

was about 25 percent higher than the cost of USDA's Thrifty Food Plan. . . . The typical food-secure household spent 32 percent more than the cost of the Thrifty Food Plan, while the typical food-insecure household spent 2 percent less than the cost of the Thrifty Food Plan.[g]

The TFP is based on all foods being prepared at home. The USDA provides menus and other information to help food stamp recipients keep their food purchases within budget. Here is the suggested menu for one day for a family of four receiving food stamps:

Breakfast: Orange juice (3 cups), *baked French toast, cinnamon sugar topping (4 teaspoons), 1% low-fat milk (2 cups)

Lunch: *Potato soup, snack crackers (low salt, 5 each), apple and orange slices (2 apples, 2 oranges, 2 cups), *rice pudding, 1% low-fat milk (2 cups)

Dinner: *Saucy beef pasta, white bread (4 slices), canned pears (2 cups), orange juice (3 cups), 1% low-fat milk (2 cups)

Snack: Lemonade (4 cups)

*Item was tested by households and/or in a food laboratory and a recipe is available.[h]

It takes a very careful shopper to stretch food stamp benefits over an entire month, and most of us probably don't eat every meal at home. Other factors also affect how far food stamp benefits can be stretched. Benefits are indexed for inflation each October based on food prices in the previous June. This lag has some negative effect on the amount of food that can be purchased. Since the TFP is based on average food prices, it also disadvantages those who live in areas where food prices are higher, as well as those who cannot get to stores offering the best buys.

NOTES

[a]United States Department of Agriculture, "Official USDA Food Plans: Cost of Food at Home at Four Levels, U.S. Average, October 2003," retrieved January 28, 2004, from http://www. cnpp.usda.gov

[b]Physician Task Force on Hunger in America, *Hunger in America: The Growing Epidemic* (Middletown, CT: Wesleyan University Press, 1985), pp. 106, 134.

[c]Subcommittee on Domestic Marketing, Consumer Relations and Nutrition, Committee on Agriculture, U.S. House of Representatives, *A Review of the Thrifty Food Plan and Its Use in the Food Stamp Program,* April 1985, p. viii.

[d]USDA, Human Nutrition Information Service, *Home and Garden Bulletin,* Number 183, rev. September 1984, p. 3.

[e]Shirley Gerrior, "Does the 1983 Thrifty Food Plan Provide a Nutritionally Adequate Diet at the Cost Level Currently Used?" *Family Economics and Nutrition Review,* Vol. 8, No. 3, 1995.

[f]Center for Nutrition Policy and Promotion, *The Thrifty Food Plan, 1999, Administrative Report* (Washington, DC: U.S. Department of Agriculture).

[g]Mark Nord, Margaret Andrews, and Steven Carlson, *Household Food Security in the United States, 2002* (Washington, DC: United States Department of Agriculture, 2002), p. iii.

[h]Center for Nutrition Policy and Promotion, *The Thrifty Food Plan, 1999.*

The USDA periodically compiles descriptions of households and their members that receive food stamps. In 2001:

♦ Half (51 percent) of participants were children.

♦ 10 percent were age 60 or older.

♦ 28 percent were working women and 12 percent working men.

♦ The average food stamp household had two or three members; households with children tended to be larger, and households with elderly members were smaller.

♦ The countable monthly resources of food stamp households averaged $148, and 68 percent had no countable resources.

♦ The average gross monthly income of food stamp households was $624.

♦ Only 11 percent of food stamp households had incomes in excess of the poverty line; 34 percent had incomes that were half of the poverty line or below.

♦ On average, food stamps constituted about one-fifth of the households' income.

♦ About 27 percent of food stamp households had earned income.

♦ Only 23 percent received TANF, 32 percent received Supplemental Security Income, 6 percent received General Assistance, and about 25 percent received Social Security.

♦ 41 percent were white, 35 percent were African American, 18 percent were Hispanic, 3 percent were Asian, and 2 percent were Native American.

♦ The average monthly food stamp benefit was $163. [63]

Since 1990, children have been 50 to 51 percent of participants, and the elderly have been 7 to 10 percent of participants. The percentage of participants that are disabled has grown from 4 percent in 1990 to 13 percent in 2001. In 1990, 42 percent of participants received AFDC; in 2001, 23 percent received TANF. The percentage of households with earned income increased from 19 percent in 1990 to 27 percent in 2001.

The states share most administrative costs of the Food Stamp Program equally with the federal government, but the federal government bears all costs of the value of the food stamps. Not counting for inflation, the total bonus value of food stamps increased from $550 million in 1970 to $8.7 billion in 1980, $14.2 billion in 1990, and $21.4 billion in 2003 (see Figure 7.2). An average of $50 million is paid in benefits each day. Total federal costs (including administration) were $15.5 billion in 1990 and $20.7 billion in 2002.

Despite changes that have restricted eligibility, the Food Stamp Program remains available to a broader cross-section of the population than any other public assistance program. It can still be described as the nation's only noncategorical public assistance program (i.e., although recipients must be poor to qualify, they need not be aged, disabled, or have dependent children). The program reaches many of those in greatest need, but about 40 percent of eligible individuals did not participate in 2000.[64] Almost 93 percent of individuals in households with incomes of half or less of the poverty guidelines participated, compared with about 77 percent of those with incomes of 51 to

100 percent of poverty guidelines. Participation for other subgroups varies substantially; although 72 percent of eligible children were enrolled, only 31 percent of eligible elderly individuals participated. About 91 percent of individuals in eligible single-parent households participated compared to 41 percent of individuals in two-parent households. About 76 percent of individuals in eligible households headed by African Americans participated, compared to 56 percent of eligible households headed by whites, and 44 percent headed by Hispanics. Larger households are more likely to participate than smaller households. Estimates are that enrollees use 82 percent of the benefits that would be available to the total pool of eligibles.[65]

Reasons cited for nonparticipation include the stigma of receiving welfare benefits, lack of knowledge of the program, and inability to reach a food stamp office to apply.[66] To this list, the General Accounting Office adds "limited office hours, unnecessary screening forms, failure to help applicants obtain necessary documents . . . and failure to consider applicants for expedited benefits."[67] Those who work traditional daytime hours are less likely than those working nontraditional hours to apply, perhaps because working 8 to 5 makes it more difficult to get the food stamp office to apply and recertify.[68] In other cases, people do not realize they are eligible, they do not think they need the benefits, the amount of benefits to be received is small and may not be worth the hassles involved in compiling the necessary information and going to the office, or mistakes by program staff lead people to believe they are not eligible.[69] Ohls and Beebout suggest that administrative requirements may be less burdensome than some people realize, but in some localities, they seem to be a greater obstacle to participation than stigma.[70] These deterents may be greatest for those whose food stamp allotments would be minimal.[71] Simplified reporting was adopted in 2001 (such as longer times between recertifications) to encourage greater participation.

NUTRITION PROGRAMS ACROSS THE LIFE SPAN

The Food Stamp Program reaches a broad cross-section of those in need. Other nutrition programs target specific segments of the population, particularly younger and older individuals.

Meals for School Children

School Lunches

The first federal legislation to help schools serve lunches to students was passed during the Great Depression in 1933. In 1946, the National School Lunch Act, signed by President Harry Truman, established permanent legislation to provide children from low-income families free or low-cost hot lunches as "a measure of national security." The program was prompted by concerns that during World War II, many potential recruits for the armed forces from poor families were rejected because of poor health related to nutritional deficiencies.[72] Today, the federal government, through the USDA's Food and Nutrition Service, provides cash assistance and food commodities to state departments of education to operate the National School Lunch Program (NSLP).[73] These departments then distribute the funds and food to participating public and private nonprofit schools and residential child-care institutions. Since 1998, funds have also been available to provide snacks to children in afterschool educational and enrichment programs. Children whose family income is not more than 130 percent of poverty guidelines receive free lunches, and reduced-price lunches are available to those with family incomes between 130 and 185 percent of poverty guidelines. Schools cannot charge more than 40 cents for reduced-price lunches, but they determine the amount that children from families with incomes greater than 185 percent of poverty guidelines are charged for full-cost meals (the average cost of a full-price meal is about $1.50). Schools get some reimbursement for full-cost meals, but programs must operate on a nonprofit basis. During the 2003–2004 school year, the federal government reimbursed most schools $2.19 for each free meal, $1.79 for each reduced-price meal, and 21 cents for each full-priced meal (subsidies are higher in Alaska and Hawaii). Slightly more is also paid to schools where 60 percent or more of students received free or reduced-price meals the previous year. States can also select from a number of "entitlement" commodities that add to the assistance they receive. The federal government provides additional "bonus" commodities as they become available.

Almost all public schools and many private schools participate in the NSLP; 99,000 schools and residential institutions participate. In 2002, an average of 28 million children participated each school day: 48 percent received their lunch free and 9 percent at reduced price. Total program expenditures (cash and commodities) were $6.8 billion in 2002 compared to appropriations of $3.7 billion in 1990 and $3.2 billion in 1980.

Initial controversies over the lunch program centered on whether the aid went to children who needed it most since schools that did not have kitchens—generally those in poor districts—were not allowed to participate.[74] Catered meals could have been used by these schools, but school lunch administrators had been known to lobby against earmarking funds for free meals to poor children for fear that private caterers would take their jobs.[75] They contended that they could adequately provide for these children with general school lunch aid, although criticisms were that they provided free lunches to only half of eligible children. When some schools on Indian reservations were still not allowed to participate due to lack of equipment, the Physician Task Force on Hunger charged that the federal government had enough of the necessary equipment in storage to solve the problem.[76] The Committee on Ways and Means reports that more than 90 percent of federal school lunch aid now goes to pay for the meals of children in low-income families.[77] The Reagan administration was successful in tightening income eligibility criteria and in reducing subsidies for the NSLP, but it was not successful in deducting the value of school meals from a household's food stamp allotment or in eliminating the subsidies for full-price meals (and ketchup was not declared a vegetable).

The Healthy Meals for Healthy Americans Act of 1994 requires that school meals meet Dietary Guidelines for Americans (the federal government's own nutrition standards). Schools now select from five approaches to menu planning, and the USDA provides educational assistance to children and school meal personnel to improve food choices. A major concern is that school meals are still too high in fat, cholesterol, and sodium and fail to meet guidelines. Schools determine what foods to serve and how the foods are prepared, but lunches must provide one-third of the recommended RDAs for protein, calcium, iron, Vitamins A and C, and calories, and contain no more than 30 percent of calories from fat and less than 10 percent from saturated fat.

The USDA has been developing more healthful school meals (including products like low-fat cheese and turkey sausage) and offering students more choices, especially ones that are appealing to children and reflect ethnic preferences of the locality. More fresh fruits and vegetables are also being served. Lunch programs can "offer" rather than automatically serve children foods in order to reduce waste. Nutrition experts continue to criticize school lunches on many counts: low participation; too much waste; and poor food choices, preparation, appearance, and taste (parents and students agree).[78] Students who obtain free and reduced-price meals no longer receive different color meal ticket than students who pay full price, but eating school meals may be regarded as stigmatizing regardless of family income; students prefer "choosing à la carte items, bringing lunch from home, or leaving school for lunch."[79] Serving all school meals free would make for less work and expense in determining who qualifies for meals, allow staff more time for meal planning, and reduce stigma associated with public assistance.[80] However, it would reduce targeting to low-income children and increase other program costs.[81] Apparently, one-quarter of low-income-eligible children are not enrolled and another one-quarter that are enrolled do not eat the lunches.[82]

While school lunch administrators are under pressure to make meals healthier and more appealing to often hard-to-please young people, commercialism is making the job more difficult. Nutritionist Marion Nestle describes how some caterers and fast food companies are taking advantage of the opportunity to peddle higher cost but not necessarily nutritious foods in the schools and that some schools, primarily those with low NSLP participation rates, would prefer to get out of the cumbersome lunch business.[83] By offering brand-name foods and using the "food court" concept, the companies and schools make more money. Students are less likely to avoid the school cafeteria, and cafeteria workers are getting more respect![84] Channel One provides free video equipment and news programming accompanied by advertising, including advertising for nonnutritious foods to schools and school children.[85] Schools' desires to help their coffers are apparently not improving children's health.

"Pouring rights"—soft drink company contracts—that pay schools substantial sums to hold exclusive rights to sell their products in schools, add to the concern about children's nutrition.[86] Schools districts in need of cash have succumbed to the "soft drink wars." Texas schools have made about $54 million a year from vending machine contracts.[87] A battle has ensued between nutrition advocates and those who profit from these "competitive" foods sold by commercial enterprises. USDA rules ban soft drink sales in school cafeterias until the lunch period ends, but sodas (and other foods of "minimal nutritional value") can be sold at all other places and times in the school. States and school districts can impose more stringent rules on competitive food sales. As nutrition advocates become more vocal in the popular press and Americans become increasingly cognizant of the price of too much food and too little exercise, more school districts are forgoing the profits.

School Breakfasts

The School Breakfast Program (SBP) began as a pilot program under the Child Nutrition Act of 1966 and became permanent in 1975.[88] Eligibility criteria are the same as the school lunch program. Schools cannot charge more than 30 cents for a reduced-price breakfast, but they determine the price of full-cost breakfasts. The regular subsidy for a free breakfast during the 2003–2004 school year was $1.20, 90 cents for a reduced-price breakfast, and 22 cents for a full-priced breakfast. Schools that served at least 40 percent of lunches free or at reduced price the previous year may obtain a "severe need designation" and receive up to 23 cents more for breakfasts if their meal costs exceed the standard subsidy. In 2002, nearly three-quarters of children participating received their breakfasts free and about 9 percent at reduced price,[89] making it a program that largely targets low-income children. The breakfasts must provide 25 percent of the recommended RDAs for protein, calcium, iron, Vitamins A and C, and calories.

All schools that participate in the NSLP may operate a breakfast program. Over time, more schools have chosen to participate; currently about 75,000 schools and institutions, or 76 percent of those with lunch programs have a SBP. Most everyone agrees that a nutritious breakfast can improve attention and learning, but not everyone agrees about why all schools do not participate. Some blame the extra administrative responsibilities and personnel costs involved in adding this program to the school day. One study found that although on average school lunch subsidies are somewhat more than the cost of the meals, school breakfasts cost more than the subsidy; but schools are most likely to say that they do not participate because the program is not needed.[90] Most students eat breakfast at home.[91] Offering breakfast free to all students and offering it in the classroom seems to increase participation without the need to track who gets a free or reduced-price meal; administrative savings can be applied to cover food costs.[92] One estimate is that less than one-third of those certified to participate actually eat the breakfasts.[93] The 1996 welfare reform legislation eliminated funds for starting and expanding breakfast programs.

In 2002, daily SBP participation averaged 8.1 million children, an increase from the 4 million children who participated in 1990 and the 6.3 million in 1995. Federal costs of the breakfast program were $1.6 billion in 2002 compared to $1 billion in 1995.

Special Milk Program

The Special Milk Program (SMP) was established in 1954 because the federal government had more surplus milk than it could use.[94] In 2001, about 7,000 schools and residential child-care institutions, 1,300 summer camps, and 562 nonresidential child-care institutions participated.[95] In 2002, the program provided nearly 113 million half-pints of milk at a federal cost of $16 million. Since the school lunch and breakfast programs include milk, schools participating in the these programs can offer the SMP only to pre-kindergarten and kindergarten children who do not have access to school breakfasts and lunches. Thus, the SMP has dwindled in size (in 1969 it provided about 3 billion half-pints of milk). Under the SMP, schools may provide milk free to all children, provide it free only to poor children, or charge all children, but the program must be operated on a nonprofit basis. The Food and Drug Administration specifies the levels of Vitamins A and D that the milk should contain, but the milk may be unflavored or flavored, whole, low-fat, skim, or cultured buttermilk. During the 2002–2003 school year, schools were reimbursed at the net purchase price for milk provided free to children, and they were reimbursed 13.5 cents for each half-pint of milk sold.

Summer Food Service Program

Since 1968, the Summer Food Service Program (SFSP) has provided free lunches and snacks to children in poor communities while schools are on summer recess. Schools or health or social service agencies administer the program, and camps and nonprofit organizations may participate. There were more than 31,800 program sites in 2000. In 2002, an average of 1.9 million children benefited each day (down from 2.2 million in 1998) with program expenditures of $262 million.[96] Children generally receive one or two meals through the program each day. Programs serving migrant children may serve up to three meals. People over age 18 with physical or mental disabilities who participate in school programs may also be served by the SFSP. Concerns are that many communities are not participating in the SFSP and that eligible children in participating communities are not getting the meals due to families' lack of knowledge about the program.

WIC

The Special Supplemental Nutrition (formerly Food) Program for Women, Infants and Children, commonly called WIC, is a highly regarded, federally supported nutrition program.[97] WIC was initially introduced in 1969, not through legislation, but by Secretary of Agriculture Orville Freeman.[98] Legislation established WIC as a pilot program in 1972 and it was made permanent in 1975.

WIC is intended to improve the nutrition of low-income women who are pregnant or postpartum, infants, and children up to age 5 who are certified by a health professional to be at nutritional risk based on federal guidelines. Risks include medical conditions such as anemia or a history of pregnancy complications; they may also include inadequate diet. Participants must also meet state residency requirements and receive TANF, food stamps, or Medicaid, or have income that does not exceed 185 percent of poverty guidelines. The USDA administers WIC in conjunction with state health departments, Indian tribal organizations, and local agencies operating at 9,000 sites. The states use their own standardized measures and cut off points to determine risk. The Institute of Medicine (IOM) reported that no good risk classification systems are currently available and that nutritional assessments are unnecessary given evidence that the entire WIC income-eligible population is at dietary risk.[99] There are also no data on the number of applicants deemed ineligible due to lack of nutritional risk.[100] Money being spent on nutritional assessments could be used to increase the food allotment or other purposes.

Most participants receive WIC coupons that allow them to purchase food in regular grocery stores (in some cases food is distributed through warehouses or delivered to participants). The foods, designed to supplement participants' diets, are specified in "packages" according to the recipient's age and nutritional needs. The packages contain items high in protein, calcium, iron, and vitamins A and C, such as infant formula, dairy products, cereals, juices, milk, cheese, peanut butter, tuna, beans, peas, and carrots. Each participant receives a set benefit that does not vary with income. Besharov says WIC packages rely too much on high calorie and high cholesterol foods rather than foods like fruits and vegetables. He calls nutritional counseling "WIC's biggest disappointment," and recommends increasing time devoted to instruction on healthful eating and cooking.[101] WIC participants can decline nutritional counseling. There has been increased alcohol and drug education and screening to prevent problems like fetal alcohol syndrome.

WIC participants who are able are encouraged to breastfeed because it benefits their babies, but much of WIC's budget pays for infant formula. States negotiate rebates with formula manufacturers to reduce costs and increase the numbers who can be served. To get the best price, each state selects only one manufacturer's bid. Scandals have a risen over price fixing by manufacturers due to the lucrative contracts involved—$620 million was spent on infant formula in 1996 (after subtracting rebates of $1.2 billion). State rebates were projected to be nearly $1.6 billion in 2002. WIC recipients also receive referrals to other health and social services.

Clearly, adequate nutrition in pregnancy is related to lower infant mortality and morbidity. Proper nutrition during childhood is also crucial in promoting normal development and in preventing life-threatening illnesses and problems that may affect health throughout life. A number of studies have been conducted over the years to assess WIC's effectiveness in promoting these outcomes. Nutrition advocates take delight in describing the positive benefits these studies demonstrate,[102] while researchers take pains to point out the studies' methodological shortcomings (primarily the difficulties in finding suitable comparison groups).[103] A qualified summary of study results indicates that (1) WIC improves birth outcomes (birth weight and gestational age) and reduces medical, particularly Medicaid, costs; and (2) infants and children benefit from improved diets, in particular reductions in iron-deficiency anemia and increased zinc intake, that promote behavioral and cognitive development.[104] Some say that WIC's real benefits may be in getting women earlier prenatal care.[105] In addition, compared to low-income children not enrolled in WIC, those in WIC are more likely to be immunized and have a source of preventive care.[106]

WIC is not an entitlement program. Funds are divided among the states using a need formula, and states give preference to recipients at greatest nutritional risk based on federal guidelines. When an agency reaches maximum participation, a priority system is used to fill vacancies; at the top of the list are pregnant and breastfeeding women and infants with a nutrition-related medical condition. Estimates are that WIC now reaches 90 percent of all those eligible to participate, including virtually all eligible infants and that 47 percent of all babies born in the United States participate.[107] In 1980, the program served 1.9 million women and children with a federal appropriation of $750 million. In 1990 appropriations were $2.1 billion with about 4.5 million participants. In 2002, there were 7.5 million participants at a cost of $4.3 billion. In 1996, welfare reform legislation eliminated requirements that the USDA promote the WIC program through public service announcements and other activities.

The Farmers' Market Nutrition Program (FMNP), begun in 1992, now provides additional coupons to some WIC participants or those waiting to receive WIC so they can purchase fresh produce.[108] The FMNP is also intended to increase use of farmers' markets. It serves a relatively small number of individuals (about 1.9 million in 2000) with a very modest annual benefit of $10 to $20 per participant decided by the state. Federal appropriations have increased from $6.8 million in 1997 to $17.5 million in 2000 with about 13,000 farmers and 1,600 farmers' markets certified to participate. States must pay at least 30 percent of program costs, and about 35 states participate. To support farmers in their own area, states may specify the foods that can be purchased.

Nutrition Programs for Older Adults

Many of the nutrition benefits available to older people are provided through programs established in 1972 amendments to the Older Americans Act of 1965[109] (see Chapter 10). Under this act, the Administration on Aging provides funds to states, which in turn channel these monies to local programs in order to serve meals to older Americans at "congregate sites" (e.g., community centers and churches) and to deliver meals to those who are homebound. Services such as nutrition assessment and education are also provided. The USDA participates in the meal programs by providing cash and some commodities. Individuals aged 60 or over and their spouses of any age are eligible as are disabled individuals under age 60. American Indian, Alaska Native, and Native Hawaiian tribal organizations can set lower minimum age limits due to their lower life expectancy or higher rates of illness. There is no means test and no set price for meals, but the focus is on serving those with the greatest need. Cash donations or food stamp payments for the meals are welcome. Each meal must generally provide one-third of the RDAs.

The program for homebound individuals is known as "Meals on Wheels." In many communities volunteers give their own lunch hours one or more times a week to deliver meals. In addition to improved nutrition, the positive spillover effects of these programs are that they provide support of independent living, social contacts with other members of the community, and the opportunity for referral should an older or disabled person need additional assistance.

In 1999, nearly 250 million meals were provided to 2.6 million older people.[110] Funding for the nutrition programs for the elderly was about $716 million in 2003. Considerable funds to support these programs also come from state, local, and private sources. About half the meals are served at congregate sites and half are delivered. Many communities have waiting lists for the home-delivered meals. Some elderly and disabled people are also allowed to use their food stamps to purchase low-cost meals in restaurants.[111] In 2002, $5 million was also provided for the Senior Farmers Market Nutrition Program.

More Nutrition Programs for Those in Need

Child and Adult Care Food Program (CACFP)

The CACFP provides meals and snacks year round to preschool children in day care facilities, children served in homeless shelters, children participating in afterschool programs in low-income areas, and adults with disabilities who participate in structured day care programs.[112] In addition to public and not-for-profit facilities, for-profit facilities may be eligible if they serve a substantial number of low-income participants. The number of meals or snacks varies depending on the facility or participants' ages. Reimbursement rates also vary. In 2001, average daily participation was 2.6 million children; 74,000 adults also participated. In 2002, total participation was 2.8 million at a federal cost of $1.8 billion.

Commodity Supplemental Food Program

The Commodity Supplemental Food Program (CSFP) operates in some states to serve low-income pregnant and breastfeeding women, infants, and children as well as poor older Americans. To qualify, women, infants, and children must be participating in another public assistance program. Elderly individuals cannot have incomes that exceed 130 percent of poverty guidelines. The states have considerable discretion in determining eligibility and operating the program. In some areas this program is used instead of WIC coupons. In 2002, the CSFP provided commodity foods to 427,000 individuals each month at a total cost of $111 million.

The Emergency Food Assistance Program

The Temporary Emergency Food Assistance Program was introduced under the Reagan administration in 1981. In 1990 it became the Emergency Food Assistance Program (TEFAP). The program reduces federal food inventories and storage costs and helps needy people. Due to changes that reduced subsidies in the federal agricultural price-support programs, the USDA is acquiring less surplus food; therefore, since 1988, TEFAP has been allowed to purchase nonsurplus products to assist those in need. The amount each state receives depends on the size of its low-income and unemployed population.

States determine eligibility criteria. The foods may go directly to people in need or to organizations that assist them like food banks and soup kitchens. In 2003, $190 million was appropriated, up from $150 million in 2002.[113] Food is purchased with these funds and surplus commodities are provided. These commodities were valued at about $288 million in 2002. Participants in other nutrition programs may also be eligible for TEFAP. The former Soup Kitchens/Food Banks Program was combined with TEFAP. The USDA also operates a commodity program to help people following natural disasters.

Community Food and Nutrition Program (CFNP)

The CFNP falls under the Community Services Block Grant and is administered by the U.S. Department of Health and Human Services. State and local governments, Indian tribes and nonprofit agencies, including faith-based organizations, are eligible to receive funding. Funds can be used for a variety of purposes such as encouraging improved diets, increasing nutrition program participations among targeted groups, and improved coordination of nutrition programs. In 2003, $2.1 was available in amounts of up to $50,000 per program.

EBT AND THE CASH VERSUS IN-KIND DEBATE

Public assistance benefits fall along a continuum from in-kind to cash. Commodity food distribution uses the in-kind strategy, because participants are given specific food products. Cash benefits are used in programs such as TANF and SSI. Food stamps, which are now delivered through electronic means in the form of a debit-type card, are often referred to as in-kind benefits. They actually fall in the middle of the continuum, representing a compromise between those who prefer cash benefits and those who prefer commodities.[114]

Advocates of the commodity approach, generally those with very conservative viewpoints, contend that this method can assure that nutritious food will be provided to participants (though it does not assure that the food will be consumed). They criticize the cash approach because it does not ensure that recipients will purchase food. The money can be used for other purposes. Commodity proponents also argue that food stamps do not ensure that nutritious foods will be purchased. Some people would prefer to see all the cash benefit programs converted to in-kind benefits because of the control they afford.

Advocates of cash benefits, generally those of the liberal persuasion, say that commodities rob people of their dignity because they do not allow them the food choices that other citizens have. They believe that most recipients are responsible people who use cash benefits wisely and that stamps, as well as electronic benefit cards, unnecessarily embarrass or stigmatize participants in grocery stores. In addition, food stamp benefits cannot be used to purchase cleaning supplies, paper goods, and other household necessities that most people purchase at the grocery store.[115] Since many food stamp recipients also receive TANF or SSI, advocates of cash benefits believe that nutrition benefits should simply be added to their public assistance check, allowing them to determine how best to allocate their funds.

Whether cash or stamps really make a difference has been the subject of USDA-supported studies. In an assessment of the Food Stamp Program, noted evaluation researcher Peter Rossi's general conclusion was that each food stamp dollar resulted in 30 cents more spent on food, while each cash dollar in benefits adds about 10 cents.[116] Identifying the effects on improved nutrition is more difficult. Most people consume sufficient nutrients. Available evidence does not clearly demonstrate that the FSP improves nutrition. Where advantages are indicated, they may accrue for some groups, like the very poor and children.

The evidence from USDA studies does clearly suggest that the bulk of cash benefits would be used to purchase food.[117] We also know that neither commodities, stamps, electronic benefits, nor cash can ensure that recipients will consume nutritious foods. Nevertheless, the USDA's position is that there are "no advantages to cashing out and that "because the Food Stamp Program was designed as a nutrition assistance program . . . many people . . . were concerned that cash-out would not ensure that food stamp benefits will be used to buy food."[118] The 1996 federal welfare reform legislation prohibits waivers to cash out food stamps, but some demonstrations are continuing in which the value of food stamps is combined with SSI or TANF benefits.

The older welfare programs, AFDC, now TANF, and SSI (and its forerunners) are cash benefit programs, but the preference among policymakers during the last few decades has not been cash benefits. The more recent public assistance programs, Food Stamps and Medicaid, are more like in-kind benefits. At the beginning of the 1960s, about 90 percent of welfare benefits were paid in cash; only 10 percent were in kind; by the 1980s, 70 percent were in kind; only 30 percent were distributed in cash.[119] Since recipients prefer cash to in-kind benefits, cashing-out might add to the rolls a substantial number of eligible people who are not participating in the Food Stamp Program.[120] But in-kind benefits seem to be integral to the political support of the Food Stamp Program; a cash-out might result in far less support, lower benefits,[121] and stricter eligibility requirements. The value of cash benefit programs (AFDC and TANF) has eroded (see Chapter 6), while food stamp benefits have done a better job of keeping up with inflation.[122] Combining food stamps with cash benefit programs like TANF would likely erode benefits further and negate the Food Stamp Program's effects in increasing overall public assistance benefits in states with low TANF payments.

Cash versus in-kind may still provide for a satisfying debate, but technology has really rendered the debate moot. Electronic benefit transfer (EBT) has emerged as the most expeditious and politically feasible way to provide public assistance benefits. EBT operates on the same principles as a debit card. The welfare agency places the amount of the individual's benefits in an account. In the grocery store checkout line, the recipient's EBT card is "swiped" through a reader or "point-of-sale" terminal, and recipients punch in their personal identification number (PIN). The cost of the purchase is deducted immediately from the recipient's account.

In 1984, Reading, Pennsylvania, was the first location to test EBT for food stamp benefits, and Maryland was the first to use EBT statewide. All states were to complete the transition to EBT by 2002, but not until mid-2004 did all areas make the change. Almost all states use on-line systems. Ohio and Wyoming have off-line ("smart card") systems. More than half the states are also using EBT to provide cash public assistance benefits.[123]

EBT is widely regarded as a useful alternative to the cumbersome process of using food stamps for program participants, grocery stores, and program administrators. The cards may also make participants less conspicuous when paying for grocery purchases. EBT provides additional security features. A lost or stolen card is more difficult for someone else to use than cash, a check, or stamps, because the PIN is supposed to be known only by the recipient. The electronic record of each transaction also makes it easier to identify illegal use of benefits. EBT may eliminate the reputation of food stamps as the "second U.S. currency," a reference to the use of food stamps in trafficking.

Initially, states incurred the costs of converting to EBT systems. In the long run, EBT may result in cost savings for recipients and governments. It costs governments less to do an electronic benefit transfer than to handle food stamps, and recipients avoid travel or time off work to get their stamps. EBT combines added efficiency with greater assurances that benefits will be used for food purchases, but as social scientist Jodie Allen once wrote, the Food Stamp Program "should not be viewed as an alternative to broader reform of our tax and transfer programs" and noted that Americans who need food assistance but are able to work would prefer lower taxes, lower inflation, and jobs to direct food assistance.[124]

SUMMARY

One irony of nutrition problems in the United States is that Americans, regardless of their income, are eating too many high-fat, nonnutritious foods, not getting enough exercise, and being sucked into quick-fix, fad diets. Perhaps more ironic is that some poor Americans lack the resources to obtain an adequate diet in a country that could easily feed everyone in need. The current Food Stamp Program and its predecessors have contributed to the nutrition of poorer Americans, but it can be difficult to stretch food stamp benefits over the course of a month. Though federal welfare reforms of 1996 have constrained the Food Stamp Program, it continues to reach a broader cross-section of Americans than any other public assistance program. A number of other federally supported and state and locally operated nutrition programs target children and their mothers and individuals who are older or disabled. Most of these programs also reach large numbers of recipients, though it is still surprising to see the number of eligible people who are not being helped or who are turning to food banks and soup kitchens. Some people reject government aid, but in many cases inadequate funding, administrative barriers, and inadequate outreach are to blame. The form nutrition benefits should take remains an issue in nutrition programs, though the use of electronic benefits seems to have quelled the issue in the Food Stamp Program. Using some methods may increase the likelihood that food will be purchased. It is more difficult to ensure that Americans improve the quality of their diets. To achieve this goal, nutrition education and greater availability of affordable, nutritious foods that appeal to the taste buds may be some of the keys to improving America's health, but too many of us fail to head the advice available. If only we could take the fat out of fattening foods!

NOTES

1. Douglas J. Besharov, "We're Feeding the Poor as If They're Starving," *Washington Post,* December 8, 2002, retrieved July 26, 2004, from http://www.aei.org/publications/pubID.31/pub_detail.asp

2. Most of this paragraph relies on the Hunger Project, *Frequently Asked Questions,* retrieved July 5, 2003, from http://www.thp.org/faq.html; see also Hester H. Vorster and Jo Hautvast, "Introduction to Human Nutrition: A Global Perspective on Food and Nutrition" in Michael J. Gibney, Hester H. Vorster, and Frans J. Kok, Eds., *Introduction to Human Nutrition,* pp. 1–11 (Oxford, UK: Blackwell Science, 2002).

3. See also, Frances Moore Lappé, *Diet for a Small Planet Tenth Anniversary Edition* (New York: Ballantine, 1982).

4. Curt Anderson, "By 2025, Population Growth May Outpace Food Production," *Austin-American Statesman,* December 11, 1997, p. A21.

5. U.S. Census Bureau, *Statistical Abstract of the United States: 2002* (Washington, DC: U.S. Department of Commerce, 2002), Table No. 101, p. 80.

6. U.S. Department of Health and Human Services, Public Health Service, *The Surgeon General's Report on Nutrition and Health,* DHHS (PHS) Publication No. 88-50211 (Washington, DC: U.S. Government Printing Office, 1988), p. 1.

7. World Health Organization, "Controlling the Global Obesity Epidemic," September 3, 2003, retrieved January 25, 2004, from http://www.who.int/nut/obs.htm

8. Ali H. Mokdad, James S. Marks, Donna F. Stroup, and Julie L. Gerberding, "Actual Causes of Death in the United States, 2000," *Journal of the American Medical Association,* Vol. 291, 2004, pp. 1238–1245; quote from p. 1238.

9. For the references on these risks see "Health Risks," *The Surgeon General's Call to Action to Prevent and Decrease Overweight and Obesity,* retrieved August 12, 2004, from http://www.surgeongeneral.gov:80/topics/obesity/calltoaction/1_2.htm

10. Elizabeth Frazão, "High Cost of Poor Eating Patterns in the United States," in Elizabeth Frazão, *America's Eating Habits: Changes and Consequences,*

Agriculture Information Bulletin No. 750 (AIB-750), pp. 5–32 (Washington, DC: Food and Rural Economics Division, Economic Research Service U.S. Department of Agriculture, 2000); retrieved June 4, 2003, from http://www.usda.gov

11. Life Sciences Research Office, Federation of American Societies for Experimental Biology, *Third Report on Nutrition Monitoring in the United States,* Vol. 1 (Washington, DC: U.S. Government Printing Office, 1995).

12. Center on Hunger and Poverty and Food Research and Action Center, *The Paradox of Hunger and Obesity in America,* retrieved June 4, 2003, from www.frac.org

13. Marion Nestle, *Food Politics: How the Food Industry Influences Nutrition and Health* (Berkeley: University of California Press, 2002).

14. Laura S. Sims, *The Politics of Fat: Food and Nutrition Policy in America* (Armonk, NY: M. E. Sharpe, 1998), p. 263.

15. Kelly D. Brownell and Katherine Battle Horgen, *Food Fight: The Inside Story of the Food Industry, America's Obesity Crisis, and What We Can Do about It* (Chicago: Contemporary Books, 2004).

16. Ohls and Beebout, *The Food Stamp Program.*

17. Economic Research Service, *The Food Assistance Landscape,* Food Assistance and Nutrition Research Report Number 28-2 (Washington, DC: USDA, March 2003), retrieved July 7, 2003, from http://www.usda.gov

18. Peter H. Rossi, *Feeding the Poor: Assessing Federal Food Aid* (Washington, DC: AEI Press, 1998), p. 103.

19. George B. Pyle, "The Dangers of Mystery Meat," *Washington Post,* August 17, 2002, p. A17.

20. Sims, *The Politics of Fat,* p. 47.

21. J. William Levedahl, "The Role of Functional Form in Estimating the Effect of a Cash-Only Food Stamp Program," *Journal of Agricultural Economics Research,* Vol. 43, No. 2, 1991, pp. 11–19; quote from p. 18.

22. Ohls and Beebout, *The Food Stamp Program,* p. 162.

23. Barbara Bode, Stanley Gershoff, and Michael Latham, "Defining Hunger among the Poor," in Catherine Laza and Michael Jacobson, Eds., *Food for People, Not for Profit* (New York: Ballantine, 1975), p. 301 (quote edited slightly).

24. Mark Nord, Margaret Andrews, and Steven Carlson, *Household Food Security in the United States, 2002,* Food Assistance and Research Report No. (FANRR35), Economic Research Service (Washington, DC: Department of Agriculture, October 2003), retrieved January 28, 2004, from http://www.ers.usda.gov/publications/fanrr35/

25. *Ibid.*

26. Brownell and Horgen, *Food Fight.*

27. Nancy Milio, *Nutrition Policy for Food-rich Countries: A Strategic Analysis* (Baltimore: John Hopkins University Press, 1990), p. 16.

28. Brownell and Horgen, *Food Fight.*

29. "Selling to—and Selling Out—Children," *Lancet,* Vol. 360, Issue 9338, p. 959.

30. Jesse J. Holland, "Bill Could Deflect Obesity Blame," *The Daily Texan,* August 12, 2004.

31. Lucy Komisar, *Down and Out in the USA: A History of Social Welfare* (New York: New Viewpoints, 1974), p. 51.

32. Maurice MacDonald, *Food, Stamps, and Income Maintenance* (New York: Academic Press, 1977).

33. Joan Higgins, "Feeding America's Poor," in Alice L. Tobias and Patricia J. Thompson, Eds., *Issues in Nutrition for the 1980s: An Ecological Perspective* (Monterey, CA: Wadsworth Health Science Division, 1980), pp. 271–275.

34. The remainder of this paragraph relies on Kenneth W. Clarkson, *Food Stamps and Nutrition* (Washington, DC: American Enterprise Institute for Public Policy Research, 1975); American Enterprise Institute for Public Policy Research, *Food Stamp Reform* (Washington, DC: The Institute, May 25, 1977).

35. Ohls and Beebout, *The Food Stamp Program,* p. 14.

36. Clarkson, *Food Stamps and Nutrition;* MacDonald, *Food, Stamps, and Income Maintenance.*

37. U.S. Department of Agriculture, Food and Nutrition Service, *Special Supplemental Nutrition Program for Women, Infants, and Children (WIC), History of WIC 1974–1999, 25th Anniversary, Activities Which Led to WIC's Establishment* (Alexandria, VA: USDA, 1999), retrieved June 4, 2003, from http://www.fns.usda.gov/wic/menu/new/wic25.htm

38. The history of the Food Stamp Program is described in a number of sources; see, for example, MacDonald, *Food, Stamps, and Income Maintenance;* Ellen M. Wells, "Food Stamp Program," in Anne Minahan,

Ed., *Encyclopedia of Social Work,* 18th ed. (Silver Spring, MD: National Association of Social Workers, 1987), pp. 628–634; Safety Net Reexamined Policy Research Project, *The Social Safety Net Reexamined: FDR to Reagan* (Austin: Board of Regents, University of Texas, 1989), chapter 2; Social Security Administration, *Social Security Bulletin,* Annual Statistical Supplement, 1991 (Washington, DC: U.S. Government Printing Office, 1991), pp. 95–97.

39. Clarkson, *Food Stamps and Nutrition;* MacDonald, *Food, Stamps, and Income Maintenance.*

40. This paragraph relies on Nick Kotz, *Let Them Eat Promises: The Politics of Hunger in America* (Englewood Cliffs, NJ: Prentice Hall, 1969).

41. *Ibid.,* pp. 52–53.

42. *Ibid.*

43. President of the United States, *America's New Beginning: A Program for Economic Recovery* (Washington, DC: U.S. Government Printing Office, February 18, 1981), p. 1.

44. Wells, "Food Stamp Program"; see also Rossi, *Feeding the Poor,* for more information on the income maintenance effects of the food stamps and other nutrition programs.

45. Mary Cohn, ed., "Hunger Reports Prompt Food Aid Expansion," *1983 Congressional Quarterly Almanac* (Washington, DC, 1983), pp. 412–416.

46. "Report on Hunger Overlooks Role of Cuts," *NASW News,* Vol. 49, No. 2, February 1984, p. 19.

47. Jean Mayer and Jeanne Goldberg, "New Report Documents Hunger in America," *Tallahassee Democrat,* March 29, 1984, p. 16E.

48. Physician Task Force on Hunger in America, *Hunger in America: The Growing Epidemic* (Middletown, CT: Wesleyan University Press, 1985), chapter 7.

49. Food and Consumer Service, *Summary of Food Stamp Provisions, Personal Responsibility and Work Opportunity Reconciliation Act of 1996* (Alexandria, VA: USDA, 1996), retrieved June 1, 1999, from http://www.usda

50. Center for Budget and Policy Priorities, "The Depth of the Food Stamp Cuts in the Final Welfare Bill," retrieved June 1, 1999, from http://epn.org/cbpp/food.html

51. Michael E. Fix and Randolph Capps, *Immigrant Well-Being in New York and Los Angeles* (Washington, DC: Urban Institute, 2002), retrieved July 6, 2003, from http://www.urban.org/

52. Eligibility criteria come from the United States Department of Agriculture website (www.usda.gov).

53. James C. Ohls and Harold Beebout, *The Food Stamp Program: Design Tradeoffs, Policy, and Impacts* (Washington, DC: Urban Institute Press, 1993), p. 23.

54. Wells, "Food Stamp Program"; U.S. Department of Agriculture, *Food Assistance Programs* (Alexandria, VA: USDA, 1992).

55. Food and Nutrition Service, "The Nutrition Assistance Programs in Puerto Rico and the Northern Marianas," *Food Program Facts* (Alexandria, VA: U.S. Department of Agriculture, May 1993).

56. Ohls and Beebout, *The Food Stamp Program*, p. 65.

57. Food and Nutrition Service, *Characteristics of Food Stamp Households: Fiscal Year 2001* (USDA: July 2002), retrieved June 22, 2003, from http://www.fns. usda.gov/oane/MENU/Published/FSP/Participation. htm

58. *Ibid.*

59. Robert Kornfeld, *Explaining Recent Trends in Food Stamp Program Caseloads, Final Report* (Cambridge, MA: Abt Associates, March 2002), retrieved June 22, 2003, from http://www.usda.gov

60. United States Department of Agriculture, Food and Nutrition Service, *Summary of Major Food and Nutrition Service Programs (Data as of May 23, 2003)*, retrieved June 22, 2003, from http://www.fns.usda.gov/pd/currentsum.htm

61. Robert Moffitt, "Has State Redistribution Policy Grown More Conservative?" *National Tax Journal,* June 1990, pp. 123–142.

62. Ohls and Beebout, *The Food Stamp Program*, p. 71.

63. Food and Nutrition Service, *Characteristics of Food Stamp Households: Fiscal Year 2001.*

64. Karen Cunnyngham, *Trends in Food Stamp Program Participation Rates: 1994 to 2000,* Final Report (Washington, DC: Mathematica Policy Research, June 2002), retrieved June 22, 2003, from www.fns.usda.gov

65. Committee on Ways and Means, U.S. House of Representatives, *1998 Green Book* (Washington, DC: U.S. Superintendent of Documents, 1998), pp. 940–941.

66. Physician Task Force on Hunger, *Hunger in America, Unfed America '85,* A Report of Hunger Watch U.S.A. Surveys (Washington, DC: Bread for the World Educational Fund, 1985).

67. Cited in Hunger Project, *Hunger Action Forum*, Vol. 2, No. 1, 1989, p. 2.

68. Signe-Mary McKernan and Caroline Ratcliffe, *Employment Factors Influencing Food Stamp Program Participation* (Washington, DC: Urban Institute, 2003), retrieved July 7, 2003, from http://www.urban.org/ANF

69. See also Ohls and Beebout, *The Food Stamp Program*, pp. 56–57, for a discussion of nonparticipation.

70. *Ibid.*, pp. 58–59.

71. Rossi, *Feeding the Poor: Assessing Federal Food Aid.*

72. *Ibid.*, p. 15.

73. Figures in this section rely on United States Department of Agriculture, Food and Nutrition Service, *National School Lunch Program,* August 2002, retrieved June 22, 2003, from http://www.fns.usda.gov/cnd/lunch/AboutLunch/faqs.htm; *Annual Summary of Food and Nutrition Service Programs (Data as of May 23, 2003),* retrieved June 22, 2003 from http://www.fns.usda.gov/pd/annual.htm

74. Dorothy James, *Poverty, Politics and Change* (Englewood Cliffs, NJ: Prentice Hall, 1972), pp. 58–59.

75. Kotz, *Let Them Eat Promises*, p. 59.

76. Physician Task Force on Hunger, *Hunger in America.*

77. Committee on Ways and Means, U.S. House of Representatives, *2000 Green Book: Background Material and Data on Programs within the Jurisdiction of the Committee on Ways and Means* (Washington, DC: U.S. Government Printing Office, 2000), p. 957.

78. Frederic B. Glantz, "Commentary" in Rossi, *Feeding the Poor: Assessing Federal Food Aid;* Marion Nestle, *Food Politics: How the Food Industry Influences Nutrition and Health* (Berkeley: University of California Press, 2002).

79. Glantz, "Commentary," p. 125.

80. "Meals for All," *Fiscal Notes,* newsletter of the Texas Comptroller of Public Accounts, February 1997, p. 5.

81. Glantz, "Commentary."

82. *Ibid.*

83. This paragraph relies on Nestle, *Food Politics: How the Food Industry Influences Nutrition and Health.*

84. Dan Morse, "School Cafeterias Are Enrolling as Fast-Food Franchisees," *Wall Street Journal,* July 28, 1998.

85. Brownell and Horgen, *Food Fight.*

86. *Ibid.*

87. "Schools Make Millions off Vending," *Austin American Statesman,* August 28, 2003, p. B2.

88. Figures in this section rely on United States Department of Agriculture, Food and Nutrition Service, *The School Breakfast Program,* August 2002, retrieved June 22, 2003, from http://www.fns.usda.gov/cnd/breakfast/AboutBFast/faqs.htm; *Annual Summary of Food and Nutrition Service Programs (Data as of May 23, 2003),* retrieved June 22, 2003, from http://www.fns.usda.gov/pd/annual.htm; Committee on Ways and Means, *2000 Green Book.*

89. Economic Research Service, *The Food Assistance Landscape.*

90. Frederic B. Glantz, Christopher Logan, Hope M. Weiner, Michael Battaglia, and Ellen Gorowitz, *School Lunch and Breakfast Cost Study, Final Report* (Cambridge, MA: Abt Associates, 1994), cited in Rossi, *Feeding the Poor.*

91. Johanna Dwyer, "The School Nutrition Dietary Assessment Study," *American Journal of Clinical Nutrition,* Vol. 61, No. 1(S), 1995, pp. 173S–177S.

92. Andrew Mollison, "Too Few Students Eat Breakfast at School, Research Center Says," *Austin American-Statesman,* November 20, 2002, p. A23.

93. Glantz, "Commentary."

94. U.S. Department of Agriculture, Food and Nutrition Service, *Special Supplemental Nutrition Program for Women, Infants, and Children (WIC), History of WIC 1974–1999, 25ᵗʰ Anniversary, Activities Which Led to WIC's Establishment,* 1999.

95. *Ibid.*

96. Figures in this section rely on Food and Nutrition Service, *About SFSP,* n.d., retrieved June 22, 2003, from http://www.fns.usda.gov/cnd/Summer/Administration/index.html; Summer Food Service Program Annual Summary, retrieved June 22, 2003, from http://www.fns.usda.gov/pd/sfsummar.htm; *Annual Summary of Food and Nutrition Service Programs (Data as of May 23, 2003),* retrieved June 22, 2003, from http://www.fns.usda.gov/pd/annual.htm

97. Some of this section relies on United States Department of Agriculture, Food and Nutrition Service, *WIC: The Special Supplemental Nutrition Program for Women, Infants and Children,* retrieved October 30, 2002, from http://www.fns.usda.gov

98. An interesting account of WIC's enactment by Rodney E. Leonard is excerpted in Food and Nutrition Service, *Special Supplemental Nutrition Program for Women, Infants, and Children (WIC).*

99. Food and Nutrition Board, *Dietary Assessment in the WIC Program* (Washington, DC: Institute of Medicine, 2002).

100. Rossi, *Feeding the Poor.*

101. Besharov, "We're Feeding the Poor As If They Are Starving."

102. Physician Task Force on Hunger, *Hunger in America.*

103. See Rossi, *Feeding the Poor.*

104. Barbara Devaney, "Commentary," in Rossi, *Feeding the Poor,* pp. 119–123; Barbara Devaney, Linda Bilheimer, and Jennifer Shore, "Medicaid Costs and Birth Outcomes: The Effects of Prenatal WIC Participation and the Use of Prenatal Care," *Journal of Policy Analysis and Management,* Vol. 11, No. 4, 1992, pp. 573–592; Lucinda R. Kahler, Robert M. O'Shea, Linda C. Duffy, and Germaine M. Buck, "Factors Asso-

ciated with Rates of Participation in WIC by Eligible Pregnant Women," *Public Health Reports,* Vol. 107, No. 1, 1992, pp. 60–65; Victor Oliveira and Craig Gundersen, "WIC Increases the Nutrient Intake of Children," *Food Review,* Vol. 24, No. 1, pp. 27–30.

105. Victor Fuchs, *How We Live: An Economic Perspective on Americans from Birth to Death* (Cambridge, MA: Harvard University Press, 1983).

106. Devaney, "Commentary."

107. Food and Nutrition Service, United States Department of Agriculture, *Annual Summary of Food and Nutrition Assistance Programs.*

108. Food and Nutrition Service, United States Department of Agriculture, *WIC Farmers' Market Nutrition Program,* July 30, 2002, retrieved October 30, 2002, from http://www.fns.usda.gove/wic/FMNP/FMNPfaqs.htm

109. *Fact Sheets, The Elderly Nutrition Program* (Washington, DC: Administration on Aging, 2003), retrieved July 8, 2003, from http://www.aoa.gov

110. "Elderly Nutrition Program Fact Sheet," n.d.; retrieved September 25, 2004, from http://www.frac.org/pdf/ENP.htm

111. Apart from some recipients who are elderly, disabled, or homeless, other food stamp participants cannot use their coupons to purchase meals in restaurants. The food stamp benefits of residents of approved not-for-profit facilities are used to offset the costs of their meals.

112. This section relies on Food and Nutrition Service, *Facts about the Child and Adult Care Food Program,* May 28, 2003; retrieved June 22, 2003, from http://www.fns.udsa.gov/cnd/Care/CACFP/cacfpfaqs.htm; Annual *Summary of Food and Nutrition Service Programs.*

113. Figures rely on Food and Nutrition Service, *The Emergency Food Assistance Program,* retrieved July 4, 2003, from http://www.fns.usda.gov/fdd/programs/tefap/; Annual *Summary of Food and Nutrition Service Programs.*

114. MacDonald, *Food, Stamps, and Income Maintenance.*

115. In addition to food products, stamps can be used to purchase seeds and plants to grow food for personal consumption, and in remote areas of Alaska, hunting and fishing equipment may be purchased with food stamps.

116. This paragraph relies on Rossi, *Feeding the Poor.*

117. For a discussion, see Diana DiNitto, *Social Welfare: Politics and Public Policy,* 5th ed. (Boston: Allyn and Bacon, 2000).

118. USDA, "Food Stamp Program," *Nutrition Program Facts,* October 1997, retrieved September 21, 1998, from http://www.usda.gov/fcs/

119. Gary Burtless, "Public Spending for the Poor: Trends, Prospects, and Economic Limits," in Sheldon H. Danzinger and Daniel H. Weinberg, Eds., *Fighting Poverty: What Works and What Doesn't* (Cambridge, MA: Harvard University Press, 1986), pp. 23–24.

120. Levedahl, "The Role of Functional Form."

121. Ohls and Beebout, *The Food Stamp Program,* pp. 48, 162.

122. Glantz, "Commentary."

123. Robert Pear, "Electronic Cards Replace Coupons for Food Stamps," *New York Times,* June 23, 2004, retrieved July 25, 2004 from http://www.nytimes.com

124. Jodie T. Allen, "The Food Stamp Program: Its History and Reform" *Public Welfare,* Vol. 51, No. 1, 1993, pp. 25–26, 46; first published in 1977.

CHAPTER

Improving Healthcare:
Treating the Nation's Ills

*H*ealth policy in the United States exemplifies many of the problems of rational policymaking. Political issues intervene at every stage of decision making—in defining the goals of health policy, in identifying alternative courses of action, in assessing their potential costs, and in selecting policy alternatives that maximize the quality and accessibility of healthcare while containing costs.

Healthcare is a basic human need. No one should suffer or die for lack of financial resources to obtain medical attention. But how much are Americans willing and able to pay for healthcare? If healthcare is a scarce resource, then how do we decide who will get what care and how? These are largely political questions that do not lend themselves easily to rational planning.

Before the 1940s, few people had private health insurance.[1] When they needed medical care, they arranged payment with their local doctor or hospital. Then companies such as Blue Cross and Blue Shield developed, offering the public health insurance; a monthly premium entitles the consumer to reimbursement for many healthcare services. With greater sophistication of medical practice and technology also came rapidly increasingly healthcare costs. Healthcare is among the most pressing social welfare issues in the United States. The cost of healthcare for all citizens is so high that policymakers can no longer be concerned about how to provide healthcare for the poor and elderly alone. Politicians, healthcare providers, employers, and citizens are concerned about healthcare for the entire nation.

GOOD HEALTH OR MEDICAL ATTENTION?

The first obstacle to a rational approach to health policy is deciding on our goal. Is health policy a question of good health—that is, whether we live at all, how well we live, and how long we live? Or are we striving for good medical care—that is, frequent and inexpensive visits to doctors, well-equipped and accessible hospitals, and equal access to medical attention by all citizens?

Good medical care does not necessarily mean good health. Good health is related to many factors over which medical personnel and facilities have no control—heredity (the health of one's parents and grandparents), lifestyle (smoking, eating, drinking, exercise, stress), and the physical environment (sewage disposal, water quality, conditions of work, and so forth). Of course, doctors can set broken bones, stop infections with drugs, and remove swollen appendixes. Anyone suffering from health problems certainly wants the careful attention of a skilled physician and the best of medical facilities. But in the long run, infant mortality, sickness and disease, and life span are affected surprisingly little by the quality of medical care.[2] If you want to live a long, healthy life, choose parents who have lived long, healthy lives, and then do all the things your mother always told you to do: don't smoke, don't drink too much, get lots of exercise and rest, don't overeat, relax, and don't worry.

Health Disparities

Historically, most reductions in infant mortality and adult death rates throughout the world resulted from improved public health and sanitation—including immunization against smallpox, clean public water supplies, sanitary sewage disposal, improved diets and nutrition, and improved standards of living. Many of today's leading causes of death, including heart disease, cancer, stroke, emphysema and other pulmonary diseases, accidents, diabetes, cirrhosis of the liver, suicides, and acquired immune deficiency syndrome (AIDS), are closely linked to heredity, lifestyle, or personal habits.

There have been major declines in the "crude" death rate (the number of deaths per 100,000 people) and the age-adjusted death rate (which accounts for changes in the age composition of the population) in the past century. Preliminary data for 2002 indicate that the crude death rate was 848.9 per 100,000 population, and the estimated age-adjusted death rate was at an all time low of 846.8 per 100,000 population.[3] Life expectancy reached a high of 77.4 years, but the infant death rate (measured per 1,000 live births) rose from 6.8 in 2001 to 7.0 in 2002, primarily due to preterm births and low birthweight. The largest percentage decrease (nearly 17 percent) in death rates was for homicide. Age-adjusted death rates for heart diseases and cancers, which account for more than half of all deaths, and in cerebrovascular diseases (e.g., strokes), accidents, and alcohol-related deaths also decreased. Increases occurred for deaths due to Alzheimer's disease, influenza and pneumonia, hypertension, septicemia, and kidney diseases. As addressed in Chapter 7, obesity now ranks at the top of the list as a primary cause of death along with smoking.

Health status and death rates differ considerably among segments of the population.

1. The poor and the aged, on the average, require more medical attention than the general population; indeed, "the prevalence of many chronic conditions is directly related to age and inversely related to financial status."[4]

2. Even though an ounce of prevention may be worth a pound of cure, preventive healthcare for many poor people is infrequent.[5] In addition to health risks facing the poor, even minor costs can delay treatment until health problems develop into major crises. Health problems are a major contributor to unemployment and poverty.

3. The healthcare delivery system (facilities and personnel) is particularly disorganized and inadequate in poor communities—both inner cities and rural areas.

4. There are major differences in health among racial and ethnic groups, even when income is controlled.

Infant mortality rates are considered to be especially sensitive to the adequacy of healthcare, and are frequently used as a general indicator of well-being. Figure 8.1 shows the wide discrepancies in infant mortality rates, ranging from 4.7 infant deaths per 1,000 live births for Asians and Pacific Islanders (the rate for Hawaiians is considerably higher) to 13.3 for blacks.[6] Even among American Indians, who have very high poverty rates, the infant mortality rate of 9.7 is considerably lower than it is for blacks. Also of interest is that Hispanics, who have much higher poverty rates and are far less likely to have health insurance than whites, have an infant mortality rate of 5.4, essentially the same as the 5.7 rate for non-Hispanic whites. This phenomenon is called the Hispanic paradox.[7] Hispanics are also more likely than other groups to go without seeing a doctor. In 2001, 27 percent of Hispanics had no visits to healthcare professionals, compared with 21 percent of American Indians, 21 percent of Asians, 16 percent of blacks, and 14 percent of whites.[8] We should note that among Hispanic subgroups, infant mortality rates ranged from 4.2 for Cubans to 8.5 for Puerto Ricans. Also of interest is that the infant mortality rate of 5.1 for mothers born *outside* the United States is *lower* than the rate of 7.2 for those born in the United States.

Blacks have been making greater gains in life expectancy than whites, but blacks' life expectancy is still about six years shorter than whites.[9] Harvard researchers have found that blacks do not always get the same level of care as whites, even

FIGURE 8.1

Infant Mortality Rates by Race and Ethnicity of Mother, 1995–2001

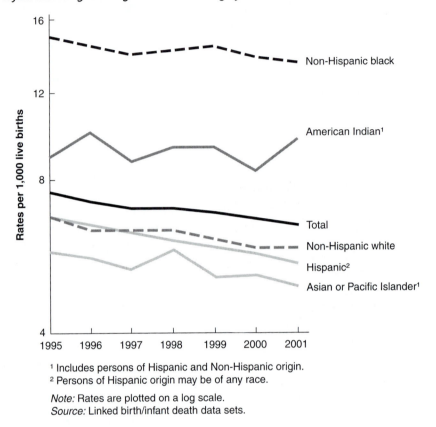

¹ Includes persons of Hispanic and Non-Hispanic origin.
² Persons of Hispanic origin may be of any race.

Note: Rates are plotted on a log scale.
Source: Linked birth/infant death data sets.

Source: T. J. Matthews, Fay Menacker, and Marian F. MacDorman, "Infant Mortality Statistics from the 2001 Period Linked Birth/Infant Death Data Set," *National Vital Statistics Reports,* Vol. 52, No. 2.

with insurance coverage.[10] In addition to infant mortality, Hispanics fare better on some health indicators, but they experience more problems in areas like obesity and are twice as likely to die from diabetes as non-Hispanic whites.[11] Asian Americans are among "the healthiest population groups in the United States. However, immigrant groups from Southeast Asia suffer disparities in . . . smoking, cancer, suicide, hepatitis B, tuberculosis, and heart disease."[12] Gender is also important. For example, women are less likely to survive a heart attack than men. Women have experienced greater improvements in life expectancy than men, but fewer medical research studies have included women. The overarching goals of the federal government's Healthy People 2010 initiative are to: (1) "increase quality and years of healthy life" and (2) "eliminate health disparities among different segments of the population."[13]

"Uninsurance"

In recent years the U.S. has made little progress in reducing what has been called the "uninsurance" rate. The number of uninsured fluctuates, primarily due to changes in unemployment. In 2002, 44.2 million Americans—more than 15 percent of the population—had no health insurance (see Figure 8.2).[14] Those least likely to have health insurance are young adults; nearly 30 percent of those aged 18 to 24 and nearly 25 percent of those aged 25 to 34 had no health insurance. Those most likely to have insurance are people aged 65 and over; less than 1 percent are uninsured. About 12 percent of children were uninsured.

There is a direct relationship between education and income and insurance—those with more education and income are more likely to be insured. As Figure 8.2 indicates, the poorer people are, the less likely they are to be insured. Those who did not work or worked part time were considerably less likely to be insured than those who worked full time. About one-third of Hispanics and one-fifth of blacks were uninsured. Whites had the lowest "uninsurance" rate (about 14 percent). People living in the South and West were more likely to be uninsured than those in the Midwest and Northeast. Border states with high immigrant populations have the highest uninsured rates. Texas, the home of President George W. Bush, had the highest uninsured rate (24 percent) followed by New Mexico (22 percent). Next are California and Louisiana (nearly 19 percent).

Most people get their insurance coverage through private means, in most cases an employer. Employer-sponsored group health plans are less expensive than individually purchased plans. In 2002, about 61 percent of Americans had employment-sponsored coverage and about 9 percent purchased private insurance directly. Of the nearly 26 percent with government-sponsored health insurance, about 13 percent had Medicare, about 12 percent had Medicaid, and about 4 percent had military healthcare (some had more than one type of coverage).

A study of health insurance coverage of children found that from 1999 to 2002, the number of uninsured children declined from 9.6 million to 7.8 million.[15] Most of this decline can be attributed to the expansion of government-sponsored health insurance programs for poor and low-income children. The decreases in uninsured children were greater for black and Hispanic children than white children, 4.8, 4.2, and 2.0 percentage points, respectively. But as Figure 8.3 shows, Hispanic children still fared the worst. Their uninsurance rate is about 21 percent, three times greater than white children and more than two times greater than black children. Children who had insurance were 1.5 times more likely to have had a well-child visit.

U.S. HEALTHCARE POLICY

A Brief History

At the turn of the twentieth century, Progressive-era reform groups first proposed a national health insurance plan.[16] Opposition from the American Medical Association

FIGURE 8.2

People without Health Insurance for the Entire Year by Selected Characteristics, 2002 (in percent)

	All	**People**	**In Poverty**
	15.2	Total	30.4
		Sex	
	16.7	Male	33.3
	13.9	Female	28.1
		Age	
	11.6	Under 18 years	20.1
	29.6	18 to 24 years	43.9
	24.9	25 to 34 years	48.6
	17.7	35 to 44 years	46.0
	13.5	45 to 64 years	33.1
	0.8	65 years and over	1.9
		Race and Ethnicity	
	14.2	White alone or in combination	31.2
	14.2	White alone[1]	31.4
	10.7	White alone, not Hispanic	25.4
	19.9	Black alone or in combination	26.1
	20.2	Black alone[2]	26.4
	18.0	Asian alone or in combination	37.9
	18.4	Asian alone[3]	38.7
	32.4	Hispanic (of any race)	42.8
		Nativity	
	12.8	Native	25.6
	33.4	Foreign born	55.3

(AMA) forced President Franklin D. Roosevelt to drop the idea of including health insurance in the original Social Security legislation for fear that it would endanger passage of the entire bill.[17] The AMA, already an important political force, contended that the plan would not work without support from the nation's physicians. President Harry S. Truman pushed hard for national health insurance, but it was again branded as socialized medicine by the medical community and defeated. Every year from 1935 until 1965, major health insurance bills failed in Congress, in large part because of AMA opposition. National health insurance was a major issue during the Truman administration in the late 1940s, but the medical establishment continually succeeded in calling it socialized medicine. Proposals for national health insurance generally

FIGURE 8.2 CONTINUED

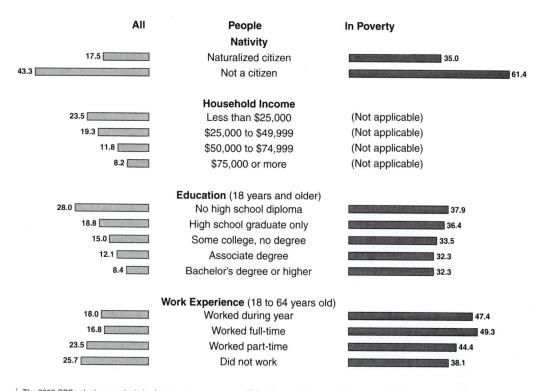

All	People	In Poverty
	Nativity	
17.5	Naturalized citizen	35.0
43.3	Not a citizen	61.4
	Household Income	
23.5	Less than $25,000	(Not applicable)
19.3	$25,000 to $49,999	(Not applicable)
11.8	$50,000 to $74,999	(Not applicable)
8.2	$75,000 or more	(Not applicable)
	Education (18 years and older)	
28.0	No high school diploma	37.9
18.8	High school graduate only	36.4
15.0	Some college, no degree	33.5
12.1	Associate degree	32.3
8.4	Bachelor's degree or higher	32.3
	Work Experience (18 to 64 years old)	
18.0	Worked during year	47.4
16.8	Worked full-time	49.3
23.5	Worked part-time	44.4
25.7	Did not work	38.1

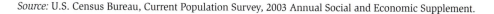

[1] The 2003 CPS asked respondents to choose one or more races. White Alone refers to people who reported White and did not report any other race category. The use of this single-race population does not imply that it is the preferred method of presenting or analyzing data. The Census Bureau uses a variety of approaches. Information on people who reported more than one race, such as "White *and* American Indian and Alaska Native" or "Asian *and* Black or African American," is available from Census 2000 through American FactFinder. About 2.6 percent of people reported more than one race in 2000.

[2] Black alone refers to people who reported Black or African American and did not report any other race category.

[3] Asian alone refers to people who reported Asian and did not report any other race category.

Source: U.S. Census Bureau, Current Population Survey, 2003 Annual Social and Economic Supplement.

tried to "socialize" health insurance but did not call for government ownership of hospitals and employment of physicians as in Great Britain. Even so, fear of government interference in medical practice and opposition from the medical community defeated major government health programs for 30 years.

In 1950, under the Truman administration, the federal government did authorize states to use federal and state public assistance funds for medical care for people who were poor and aged, blind, or disabled and poor families with dependent children. President Eisenhower rejected the idea of compulsory national health insurance,[18] but in 1957 the Kerr-Mills Act began a separate federal-state matching program for hospital care for the elderly and the poor, though not all the states participated.

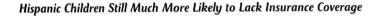

FIGURE 8.3

Hispanic Children Still Much More Likely to Lack Insurance Coverage

Child Uninsurance by Race/Ethnicity, 1999 and 2002

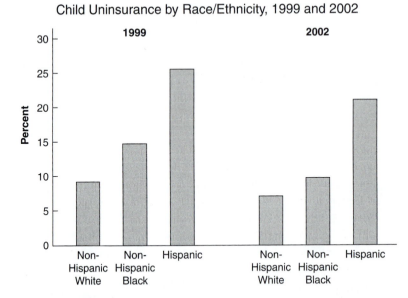

Source: Genevieve M. Kenney, Jennifer M. Haley, and Awith permisslexandra Tebay, "Children's Insurance Coverage and Service Use Improve" (Washington, DC: Urban Institute, July 31, 2003). Reprinted with permission of the Urban Institute.

For years, Congress debated the issue of subsidizing healthcare for poor people and older persons and made only modest gains in covering these vulnerable populations. In 1965, as part of the programs of the Great Society, President Lyndon B. Johnson finally succeeded in establishing major healthcare programs for both groups as part of the Social Security Act. Medicaid, the program for poor Americans, was established under Title XIX of the act. This combined federal and state public assistance program replaced and expanded earlier medical assistance under the Kerr-Mills Act. Medicare, established under Title XVIII of the Social Security Act, is a social insurance program operated by the federal government that covers virtually all people aged 65 years and older, as well as some younger people with long-term disabilities. These programs have given millions of Americans greater access to healthcare, but millions remain uninsured.

President Nixon advocated an expansion of public health insurance coverage along with some requirements that employers insure their workers. President George H. W. Bush advocated tax credits and tax deductions to help more people pay for health insurance premiums. Against strong opposition, Senator Edward M. "Ted" Kennedy (Democrat-Massachusetts), brother of President Kennedy, has continued to push for national health insurance for all Americans. Kennedy's efforts, and even much more limited plans, such as "Kiddie Care," a program to provide basic healthcare at reasonable costs for all the nation's children, have all been rejected.[19]

During his first race for the presidency, Bill Clinton's number one campaign promise was national health insurance. The president was so invested in the issue that he appointed Hillary Rodham Clinton, his wife, to chair the large task force that helped devise the plan. The 1,300-page plan, called the Health Security Act, was submitted to Congress on September 22, 1993. Advocates hoped that it would provide all Americans the opportunity to get preventive and early treatment while simultaneously keeping national health costs in check using expenditure controls.

Under the plan all citizens and legal immigrants would have received a "health security card" guaranteeing them comprehensive healthcare benefits, including preventive care, for life.[20] No one would have been denied coverage, and coverage would have been continuous regardless of employment. Eligibility and reimbursement rules would have been standardized across the country, replacing the myriad rules under the many healthcare policies and plans that exist today. Competition was a main theme of the plan, with participants buying into large purchasing pools (healthcare alliances) to get the best value for their healthcare dollar. Each alliance would have offered a choice of plans. Employers would have paid 80 percent of the premiums for the standard benefit package and workers would have paid the rest. Premium targets would have been set to protect against cost inflation. Poor individuals would have received premium discounts or would not have been charged. Medicaid would have covered premiums for poor individuals, who would also receive discounts on coinsurance payments. But everyone would have been served by an alliance. Medicare would have remained, but individuals could have chosen Medicare or a regional alliance. Prescription drug benefits would have been added to Medicare. A federal–state long–term care benefit including home- and community-based services for people with disabilities, regardless of age and income, would have been established.

About three-quarters of funding for the Health Security Act was expected to come from current sources—employers and the insured—with additional funding from cost-savings measures in Medicare and Medicaid. As healthcare expert Uwe Reinhardt aptly put it:

> The president's proposal . . . [was] not a clean, simple design tailored to a single dominant philosophy as are, for example, the Canadian and German health systems. True to American tradition, it . . . [was] a complex compromise that has been bent and twisted onto the Procrustean bed of a pluralistic set of ethical precepts and of an equally pluralistic set of narrow economic interests pursued by politically powerful groups.[21]

Dozens of competing proposals were offered.[22] Many of a more liberal ilk advocated greater government regulation, including a single-payer system in which the federal government would collect all funds used to pay for healthcare and would pay all claims. They wanted to eliminate the two-tier system of healthcare in which the rich receive the best treatment and the poor get second-class care. But the fear was that without competition, there would be no incentive for efficiency. At the other end of the spectrum were those who felt that the Clinton plan was too much government regulation. They complained that many healthcare decisions would be made by bureaucrats rather than between doctor and patient. Conservatives wanted to leave far more to the competition that flows from natural market forces, and they wanted to take a much more incremental approach. In the end:

> One need look no further than America's previous failures to reform the health system to recognize that it is a complex undertaking. The challenge is daunting because it must attract broad political support in a nation that has never achieved consensus on an overriding social ethic (universal coverage) to which all other worthwhile goals in healthcare must take second place. . . . The result of this ambivalence—open espousal of a lofty goal, but open hostility to the only means of achieving that goal—has led to the perennial stalemate that is the hallmark of congressional wrangling over universal health insurance.[23]

Any ray of hope for national health insurance quickly faded.

After 40 years of major federal government involvement in healthcare, Medicaid and Medicare remain the mainstays of public healthcare policy.[24] At the federal level, Medicaid and Medicare fall under the auspices of the U.S. Department of Health and Human Services (DHHS) and its Centers for Medicare and Medicaid Services or CMS (formerly the Health Care Financing Administration).

Several other important federally funded healthcare programs are not discussed in detail in this chapter but deserve mention. The Department of Veterans Affairs provides healthcare for those who once served in the armed forces. The Defense Department's health program, known as TRICARE, provides healthcare for active-duty military and their dependents and for military retirees and their dependents. The federally funded Indian Health Service serves members of the many Indian tribes in the U.S.

Also important are the programs of state and local health departments. Local governments and not-for-profit organizations also provide clinics or other avenues to healthcare. Some communities have voter-approved local hospital districts that levy a tax specifically to finance healthcare for those who cannot afford it.

Medicaid: Healthcare for Some of the Poor

Every state operates a Medicaid program, although Arizona held out until 1982. Medicaid rapidly grew to be the federal government's most expensive public assistance program. The costs of Medicaid now exceed the costs of any other "welfare" (public assistance) program, including the SSI, TANF, and Food Stamp programs. Combined federal and state Medicaid spending has even outpaced Medicare spending. Only the Social Security program now costs more than Medicaid.[25] In 1970, total Medicaid costs were about $5 billion; by 1990 they had risen to about $72 billion, and in 2002 the total bill was an estimated $258 billion.

The federal government pays its share of Medicaid costs from general tax revenues. The states also use their own revenues to fund Medicaid, and they are under constant pressure to raise more funds to pay their share and to draw down more federal matching funds. States may receive 50 to 83 percent of total Medicaid service expenditures from the federal government, with poorer states (as determined by per capita income) receiving the most. This percentage is calculated annually. In 2004, 11 states and the District of Columbia received at least 70 percent of their Medicaid benefit funds from the federal government; Mississippi received the highest rate at 77.08 percent. Thirteen states received 50 percent. The U.S. territories also received 50 percent for their Medicaid programs. All jurisdictions are reimbursed for 50 percent of administrative costs for most services rendered.

The House Committee on Ways and Means acknowledges that many people regard Medicaid as an *enigma*. Not only is the program complex, it does not serve most poor people. Each state administers its own program and sets it own rules, and each state has many different Medicaid components that may offer different services depending on the category under which one qualifies. This chapter can only hope to scratch the surface at describing Medicaid.

Each state must designate a single state agency (generally the state's health or welfare agency) to carry out its Medicaid program. The state can process its own claims or contract for this service. Each state determines the reimbursement rates it will pay for Medicaid services. Since 1989, federal guidelines say that reimbursement rates must be sufficiently adequate so that services will be as available to Medicaid recipients as they are to the general population in the area. Recipients are also supposed to have some freedom in choosing service providers. This does not mean that providers are anxious to accept Medicaid payments. Most physicians do not participate because payments are so low, the paperwork is quite burdensome, and reimbursement often takes too long.

Who Gets Medicaid?

Like SSI and Food Stamps, Medicaid is an entitlement program; everyone who qualifies must be served if they wish. Federal statutes actually define more than 50 distinct groups that can qualify for Medicaid. Without intimate knowledge of a state's Medicaid program, it would be difficult to say exactly who qualifies and who does not. Even in states with the most generous Medicaid programs, many poor people do not fit any of the eligibility categories and therefore have no claim to Medicaid. This is especially true for poor, able-bodied adults with no dependent children. In 2002, 11.6 percent of the U.S. population was enrolled in Medicaid. This included 40.5 percent of all those in poverty. Of all who received Medicaid, 42.5 percent had incomes below poverty, while 57.5 percent had incomes above poverty.

More detailed information is available by basis of eligibility for the 44.3 million individuals enrolled in Medicaid programs in 2000 (see Figure 8.4). About 51 percent of enrollees were under age 19, about 37 percent were 19 to 64 years old, and about 10 percent were 65 years of age or older. About three-quarters of enrollees were

FIGURE 8.4

Medicaid Enrollees by Basis of Elegibility, Fiscal Year 2000

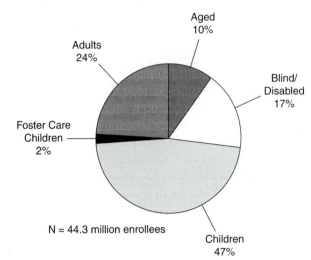

N = 44.3 million enrollees

Source: Committee on Ways and Means, U.S. House of Representatives, *2003 Green Book,* p. 15-12.

Note: Medicaid enrollees include all persons enrolled in Medicaid during the year regardless of whether any payments for services have been made on their behalf. Total enrollees include those in the 50 states and the District of Columbia.

children and their parents who are not disabled. At its inception, Medicaid was primarily intended for public assistance recipients. Those receiving AFDC or Old Age Assistance, Aid to the Blind, and Aid to the Permanently and Totally Disabled, which later became the Supplemental Security Income (SSI) program, automatically qualified for Medicaid. Nearly half of today's Medicaid enrollees entered through these traditional pathways—such as being an SSI program participant or qualifying based on guidelines applied to former AFDC recipients. Much of Medicaid's growth is due to newer pathways, primarily increased income limits enacted since the 1980s, which allow more people not receiving public assistance to participate. These newer pathways accounted for more than one-third of Medicaid enrollment in 2000.

People Who Are Aged or Disabled.   Although states determine many eligibility requirements, they must still cover certain categories of people, such as most SSI recipients. Should SSI recipients earn enough to make them ineligible for SSI, they can receive Medicaid for an extended period (also see Chapter 5). States may also cover individuals who are aged or disabled if their incomes do not exceed 100 percent of the poverty threshold and up to 250 percent of the poverty threshold for those with disabilities if they are working.

Through their Medicaid programs, states must pay Medicare premiums, coinsurance, and deductibles for "qualified Medicare beneficiaries" (QMBs). QMBs are Medicare beneficiaries (aged or disabled) with incomes below 100 percent of the federal poverty level and limited assets ($4,000 for an individual and $6,000 for a couple). States are also required to provide more limited assistance by paying Part B Medicare premiums (supplemental medical insurance largely for outpatient care) for other low-income Medicare recipients. States must also use Medicaid funds to pay Part A Medicare premiums (hospital insurance) for those who previously received Medicare and Social Security Disability Insurance but have returned to work, as long as they are still disabled, their income is not more than 200 percent of the poverty level, their resources do not exceed $4,000, and they are not otherwise entitled to Medicaid.

Children and Their Parents.   Prior to welfare reform in 1996 (see Chapter 6), states were required to cover all those receiving AFDC. AFDC was replaced with the Temporary Assistance for Needy Families Program (TANF). There is no automatic link between Medicaid and TANF, but in general, states must cover all those who meet AFDC financial eligibility criteria in place in their state on July 16, 1996. This provision was enacted so that low-income families would continue to have access to healthcare. There are some options that states can use to increase or decrease their previous AFDC income and resource standards if they wish. Most states have chosen to include more low-income families by loosening eligibility requirements.

States can terminate Medicaid benefits to adults who do not meet TANF work requirements, but their children must continue to be covered. Should TANF recipients earn enough or get sufficient income from child or spousal support to make them ineligible for TANF, they can continue to receive Medicaid for certain lengths of time so that their medical benefits are not abruptly terminated.

States must also cover pregnant women and children under age 6 with incomes up to 133 percent of official poverty guidelines. These women are entitled only to pregnancy-related services, but children receive all Medicaid benefits.

All children over age 5 and under age 19 in families with incomes less than 100 percent of poverty guidelines are also entitled to Medicaid. Medicaid must also cover a few other categories of poor children such as children under age 18 who are receiving adoption and foster care assistance, and they can extend this assistance to children leaving foster care until they reach age 20.

States may also provide Medicaid to other groups of children such as those living in certain types of institutions, and they may provide 12 months of continuous coverage to children once they become Medicaid participants even if their circumstances change.

Though children are more likely to receive Medicaid than those in other age groups, many eligible children are not enrolled (including an estimated 2 million children under age 6 in families with incomes less than 133 percent of poverty). These children may have other insurance, their families do not know they are eligible, or the families believe they do not need coverage.

Children under SCHIP.   An important development in healthcare coverage for low-income children is the State Children's Health Insurance Program, referred to as SCHIP or CHIP. SCHIP is related to Medicaid, but it is a block grant program established as Title XXI of the Social Security Act by the Balanced Budget Act of 1997. Children qualify for SCHIP if they are not eligible for Medicaid, are not covered by other health insurance, and live in low-income families.

The states can provide SCHIP to children whose family income is up to 200 percent of poverty guidelines. States that already covered children with incomes greater than 200 percent of poverty can raise their previously established income level by as much as 50 percentage points. States must submit a proposal to the federal government to obtain SCHIP funding. They can cover SCHIP-eligible children by expanding their Medicaid program, creating a new program, or using a combination of approaches.

There is some perversity in the relationship of SCHIP and Medicaid.[26] States get a bigger federal return for covering the higher-income children eligible under SCHIP than they do for covering poorer Medicaid-eligible children. SCHIP's funding formula reimburses states, in part, based on the number of uninsured children. This penalizes states that had already made more progress in insuring low-income children. However, states with higher per-capita incomes get a higher percentage increase to insure children under SCHIP than states with lower per capita incomes.

A primary concern about SCHIP is that many children are not enrolled and that some states are not doing all they can to draw down more matching funds or advertise the program to maximize enrollment. In Texas (the state with the highest "uninsurance" rate), there were claims of unwarranted delays in implementing SCHIP. Additionally, the state's Republican (and female) comptroller joined many child advocates and Democrats in complaining that federal funds were being left on the table after 107,000 children were dropped from the program.[27] (For every state dollar spent on SCHIP, Texas gets $2.59 in federal funds.) The Republican (and female) Chair of the House Select Committee on State Health Care Expenditures' response was that given the state's record budget deficit, the legislature did the right thing in tightening SCHIP's asset (not income) test (families with income up to 200 percent of poverty still qualify). She suggested that families with expensive vehicles purchase less expensive transportation instead.[28] The Comptroller suggested a $1 increase on each pack of cigarettes to raise money that would provide a needed transfusion to the state's healthcare budget.

In Texas, a lawsuit erupted over whether the state was providing sufficient access to preventive services for children under Medicaid. The state was also accused of ignoring Medicaid outreach while focusing on SCHIP outreach, and making SCHIP enrollment much easier than Medicaid enrollment (which has now been simplified). All this controversy came along with claims that the state had overpaid hospitals for services under Medicaid and might have to pay back $300 million.

Medicaid and SCHIP participation vary greatly by state. In Texas and elsewhere, many children do not get recertified once their initial enrollment period ends.[29] Reports indicate that "complex enrollment and re-enrollment procedures create barriers to participating in public insurance programs. More than half of the 7.8 million children uninsured in 2002 were actually eligible for Medicaid or SCHIP coverage but were not enrolled."[30] The Agricultural Risk Protection Act of 2000 encourages schools to use their federally subsidized school meal programs (see Chapter 7) to identify children who might be eligible for Medicaid or SCHIP. Of course, the more children enrolled, the more states have to pay. Many states may be dodging the budget bullet by not insuring more who are eligible.

Medically Needy.   Thirty-five states and the District of Columbia also provide Medicaid to people categorized as "medically needy." These individuals and families are similar to other groups covered by Medicaid except that their income and assets exceed eligibility requirements, within defined limits (this level is generally not more than 133 1/3 percent of the state's AFDC payment as of July 16, 1996). The states have some discretion in defining the groups considered medically needy, but if a state provides a medically needy program, it must include all children under age 18 who would qualify under a mandatory Medicaid category as well as pregnant women who would qualify under a mandatory or optional category, if their income and resources were lower.

Immigrants.   Many legally admitted immigrants are not eligible for Medicaid. Those admitted after August 22, 1996, cannot receive Medicaid for five years, though permanent residents who have earned 40 work credits under Social Security (see Chapter 4) can. States can opt to cover those in the U.S. before August 22, 1996, if they were receiving Medicaid as of that date or if they become disabled. States must provide Medicaid for up to seven years to those admitted as asylees or refugees. Immigrants with past or current U.S. military service and their dependents may also qualify. States must provide emergency Medicaid services to *all* noncitizens whether they are documented (legally admitted) or not, if they meet eligibility requirements.

Others.   States may also choose to cover certain low-income women while they are being treated for breast or cervical cancer if they do not have other healthcare coverage; 42 states do so. Eight states have also exercised the option to cover low-income individuals receiving tuberculosis treatment.

What Services Can Medicaid Beneficiaries Receive?

The federal government requires that states make certain services available to most Medicaid enrollees: inpatient and outpatient hospital care; physicians' services; laboratory and x-ray services; nursing home services for those over age 21; home healthcare (for those entitled to nursing home care); family-planning services and supplies; nurse midwife services; early and periodic screening, diagnosis, and treatment (EPSDT) services for those under age 21, which includes a variety of services; family and pediatric nurse practitioner services; dental surgery; and pregnancy and postpartum services. States can limit many services (e.g., the number of days of hospital care or the number of visits to physicians), but they cannot limit certain services to children.

States may offer other benefits to Medicaid beneficiaries such as prescription drugs, eyeglasses, psychiatric services to those under age 21 or over age 65, or special services to elderly people with disabilities or to others with developmental disabilities. States generally offer at least some optional services. In 2002, at least 40 states offered prescription drugs; dental services; optometrist services and eyeglasses; physical therapy; speech, hearing, and language therapies; occupational therapy; audiology services; intermediate care services for people with mental retardation; mental health services; podiatry; prostheses; skilled nursing facility care for those under age 21; case management; and transportation. The benefits used most often are prescription drugs and physician services, but the services that consumed the largest share of Medicaid spending were long-term care (about 35 percent) and inpatient hospital care (17 percent). Prescription drugs accounted for nearly 14 percent of Medicaid spending, and physician services for a little less than 5 percent.

In 2000, Medicaid services cost an average of $11,928 for each aged person, $10,559 for each blind or disabled recipient, $2,030 for each nondisabled adult recipient, and $1,237 for each nondisabled child recipient (see Figure 8.5). The higher costs for elderly and disabled recipients generally result because more of them reside in nursing homes or other facilities.

FIGURE 8.5

Medicaid Expenditures Per Recipient by Acute and Long-Term Care and Basis of Eligibility, Fiscal Year 2000

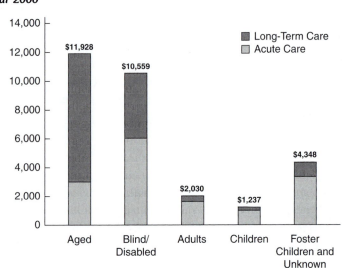

Source: Committee on Ways and Means, U.S. House of Representatives, *2003 Green Book,* p. 15-28.

How Are Medicaid Services Delivered?

Medicaid services are provided in-kind. Patients receive services from physicians and other healthcare providers, and the government directly reimburses providers. A number of states do use some type of program cost sharing, such as requiring recipients to pay small deductibles or copayments for services, but they cannot impose cost-sharing requirements on services for children under age 18, or for emergency, pregnancy, and family-planning services. People in custodial nursing facilities and intermediate-care facilities are not charged copayments, because virtually all their income already goes toward their care.

Most states use both fee-for-service arrangements and managed care plans to cover Medicaid recipients. In order to: (1) control costs and (2) improve service quality, more states have turned to managed care, but as the House Committee on Ways and Means notes, there is a good deal of uncertainty over whether either goal has been achieved. Managed care plans tend to come and go because of insurance company consolidations and bankruptcies. Some of the difficulties may be due to low reimbursement rates or unsuccessful risk-sharing methods (having many beneficiaries with high medical care needs). In 1991, only 9.5 percent of Medicaid beneficiaries were covered under managed care. In 2002 that number was nearly 58 percent, but Medicaid managed care growth is slowing.

Many states use more than one managed care arrangement. For example, to serve most children and families, who generally need only routine care, states may use a risk-based managed care organization (MCO). The MCO is paid a set fee to provide a defined set of benefits and is responsible for any additional costs incurred in serving the patient. States may also use a prepaid health plan for a particular type of service like mental health services. Some states are moving to primary care case management (PCCM) to coordinate services for recipients, especially those who have greater healthcare needs. This method can also provide more continuity when there is a turnover in plans. Fee-for-service arrangements are mostly used for aged or disabled recipients, who need more care, and for those who live in rural areas with limited access to managed care options.

States are testing various methods to improve healthcare delivery under their Medicaid programs. Some of this activity occurs under waiver programs (many under what is called Section 1115) that allow states to deviate from certain Medicaid rules. For example, states can offer a comprehensive benefit package to Medicaid-eligible individuals and other low-income individuals as well. The entire state of Arizona has operated under a waiver for two decades.

To help states make their Medicaid programs more efficient for people whom they are not required to cover, President George W. Bush wants to provide a cash infusion, actually a loan, that would reduce state's future funding. The proposal also involves turning more responsibility for Medicaid over to the states by transforming it into a block grant. (Ironically, a story on the president's proposal in a local newspaper preceded one discussing the results of his annual physical exam. This was a six-hour exam conducted by 14 physicians, not the 15 minutes most people get under managed care. The president's health was declared excellent.)

Other Routes to Healthcare for the Poor

Block grants are also used to provide medical care, primarily to low-income people. The Maternal and Child Health Services Block Grant, administered by DHHS's Health Resources and Services Administration, assists additional low-income pregnant women and young children. The Preventive Health and Health Services (PHHS) Block Grant, administered by DHHS's Centers for Disease Control, provides funds for a variety of services. States have a great deal of say in how they use the funds. Funds are often used for educational services and risk reduction programs, such as smoking cessation programs and nutrition advice; to treat those with specific health problems, such as hypertension and tuberculosis; and to provide some emergency medical services and rodent-control programs.[31] A portion of PHHS funds must be used for rape prevention and treatment.

The federal government offers many other health and health-related programs. States and communities also search for creative ways to meet health needs and stretch their healthcare dollars, but many Americans remain without a regular source of healthcare and without a ready means to pay for healthcare bills.

Medicare: Healthcare for Almost All Older Americans

Social welfare policy has come a long way in meeting the income and healthcare needs of older Americans. Older Americans have more restricted activity days and days in bed and in hospitals than the general population.[32] Prior to Medicare, less than half of elderly people had any health insurance. Even with Medicare, out-of-pocket healthcare costs for older Americans continue to increase. In 2003, this amount averaged $2,005 per enrollee, about twice as much as in 1990 after adjusting for inflation.[33]

Most Medicare beneficiaries are people aged 65 or older receiving Social Security retirement benefits (or who would be eligible for Social Security if they retired). Some younger people also qualify for Medicare, mostly former workers who have been receiving Social Security Disability Insurance (SSDI) for at least two years. The program also covers another group of people—those with end-stage renal disease (kidney failure). As part of the Social Security system, Medicare compels employers and employees to pay into the program during working years in order for workers to enjoy the benefits of health insurance after retirement or long-term disability. Since Medicare is a social insurance program and not a public assistance program, participation is not contingent on income. Even older people who do not qualify for Social Security can buy into Medicare.

About 35 million older individuals and 6 million disabled younger people were enrolled in Medicare in 2003. Federal spending was about $281 billion.[34] This is a huge increase from Medicare's $157 billion cost in 1995. Despite changes that subject all employees' wages to the Medicare tax, there is a constant concern about the Medicare trust fund's ability to keep up with healthcare costs (see Chapter 4). Concern mounts as the baby boom generation gets closer to claiming its Medicare benefits.

Medicare Part A: Hospital Insurance

The Medicare program has two basic parts—hospital insurance (HI), called Part A, and supplemental medical insurance (SMI), called Part B. Part A pays for beneficiaries' hospital care, skilled nursing care following a hospital stay, some (usually short-term) home healthcare, and hospice care, and is financed by a portion of the Social Security payroll tax (also see Chapter 4). This compulsory 1.45 percent tax is now levied on all the wages of current workers. Older people who do not qualify for Social Security and want to participate in Part A can pay premiums (in 2004 monthly premiums were either $189 or $343, depending on work history). Under Part A, beneficiaries incurring a hospital stay must pay a deductible ($876 in 2004), after which Medicare pays for the remainder of the first 60 days in the hospital and a portion of additional days. For days 61 through 90 in 2004, the patient's coinsurance payment was $219 per day, with the federal government paying the remainder; for days 91 to 150, the coinsurance payment was $438 a day (these 60 days are reserves that can only be used once in a lifetime). If more hospital days are needed, the patient must assume all the costs. There is also a $109.50 coinsurance fee per day for days 21 through 100 for skilled nursing home services during each benefit period.

Medicare Part B: Supplemental Medical Insurance

Medicare Part B, supplemental medical insurance, is a voluntary component that covers physician services, outpatient hospital services, certain home healthcare services, and durable medical equipment. Medicare Part A beneficiaries who wish to participate in Part B are assessed premiums. In 2004, monthly Part B premiums were $66.60. This cost is so low compared to private insurance that almost all Part A participants are enrolled in Part B. Part B premiums can be deducted automatically from Social Security retirement or disability checks. Even those aged 65 and older who are not insured under Part A can participate in Part B. Part B beneficiaries must pay for the first $100 of services themselves each year, after which Medicare pays 80 percent of most services and the patient pays the remaining 20 percent. General revenue funds are also used to fund Part B.

In 2003, Congress passed legislation to "modernize" Medicare that includes increases in Part B premiums. From 2004 through 2006, premiums for all Medicare beneficiaries are set at 25 percent of actual costs. Beginning in 2007, the percentage will increase gradually for those in higher income brackets, and they are scheduled to increase again in 2011. High income is defined as more than $80,000 in income per beneficiary, adjusted for inflation each year. By 2011, individuals with incomes from $80,000 to $100,000 will pay 35 percent of actual costs. Those with incomes greater than $200,000 will pay the most—80 percent of the actual costs of Part B premiums.

Both Parts A and B require patients to pay an initial charge in order to discourage unnecessary medical care and to recover some program costs. Medicare does not pay for custodial nursing home care, most dental care (including dentures), private-duty nursing, eyeglasses and eye examinations, most routine physician examinations, and hearing tests and hearing devices. Until 2004, Medicare did not help with prescription drug costs.

Covering "Medigaps"

A serious problem with the U.S. healthcare system is the inadequate coverage provided by most types of health insurance—both public and private. Private health insurance plans may limit payments to the first 30 or 60 days of hospital care; place caps on the dollar amounts paid to hospitals and physicians for a patient during her or his lifetime; exclude various diagnostic tests, outpatient care, or office visits; and so on. Moreover, private insurance often will not cover people initially found to be in poor health, who most need insurance. Perhaps the most serious concern about private insurance is that it frequently fails to cover "catastrophic" medical costs—costs that can easily run into the tens and even hundreds of thousands of dollars for serious, long-term illnesses. If such a catastrophe occurred, most people would lose everything they owned.

The gaps in Medicare coverage are referred to as "medigaps." In addition to prescription drugs, the most notable "medigaps" have been long-term custodial care and the costs of catastrophic illnesses. In 1998, Congress attempted to close some of these gaps, primarily long hospital stays and high prescription drug costs, with the Medicare Catastrophic Coverage Act. The added coverage was to be financed by a "surtax" on the incomes of Medicare recipients—$22.50 for each $150 dollars of federal income tax an individual or couple paid—and an additional $4 a month for SMI. The maximum surtax was set at $800. One year after it took effect, Congress repealed the law. In a nutshell, many older Americans were not willing to pay that much more for the increased coverage, and they successfully pressured Congress to repeal the law. The surtax was a major miscalculation in healthcare policy.

The act would have helped poorer older Americans with serious health problems the most, but many individuals who would have paid the surtax already had supplemental policies that cover some medigaps. Some policies cover medigaps better than others. To prevent unscrupulous individuals from taking advantage of older Americans' fears of impoverishment from illness, Congress passed legislation to regulate the sale of Medicare supplemental or "medigap" policies. Since 1992, medigap insurance carriers must offer 10 levels of policies from A to J. Only Plans H, I, and J have included any prescription drug coverage. At any given level, the same types of benefits are supposed to be offered (for example, all policies at level A have the same benefits). Level A offers the fewest benefits and costs the least, and level J offers the most benefits at the highest cost. This structure makes it easier to compare policies across carriers, but costs and coverage still vary widely depending on several factors, including the state in which the policy is purchased, with Florida residents paying the most.[35]

Most older Americans (56 percent) use private policies to supplement their Medicare coverage. Twenty-nine percent of them have supplemental coverage through an employer (though fewer employers are now offering this coverage); another 23 percent have a "medigap policy," and 4 percent have both. Thirteen percent were enrolled in a Medicare managed care plan that generally covered some medigaps. Sixteen percent were poor enough that they had Medicaid coverage to cover medigaps, and two percent had coverage from other public sources like the military's TRICARE program. Only 13 percent relied solely on the traditional Medicare fee-for-service program with no supplemental coverage.

Thoroughly Modern Medicare.   In 2003, Congress passed the controversial Medicare Prescription Drug, Improvement, and Modernization Act.[36] The House vote was 220 to 215; the Senate vote was 54 to 44. Under the law, older people will pay more for their Medicare coverage. The law also makes changes in private health plans and adds a voluntary prescription drug benefit.

Medicare Advantage (Part C).   As part of the Balanced Budget Act (BBA) of 1997, Medicare beneficiaries were given managed care options in addition to HMOs that might cover some "medigaps" and contain healthcare costs. These options were called Medicare + Choice or Part C. Under the 2003 Medicare legislation, Part C, now called Medicare Advantage, also offers Medicare beneficiaries various private managed care arrangements in addition to traditional fee-for-service Medicare. These plans vary substantially in terms of costs and benefits to participants, such as whether participants are limited to using "in network" physicians if they want costs covered. Every November, Medicare beneficiaries get information on Medicare's current benefits and the types of plans from which they can choose. A report by the Commonwealth Fund found that in 2004 these managed care arrangements will actually cost 8.4 percent more than traditional Medicare.[37]

Adding D (Prescription Drugs) to the A, B, Cs of Medicare.   The costs of prescription drugs are an increasing concern. One study in California found that about 20 percent of seniors failed to fill a prescription or skipped doses to make medications last longer.[38] Percentages were higher for those in poor health and without drug coverage.

When Medicare was enacted, drug costs were not the major expense they are today, and they were not included in Medicare. Momentum for a prescription drug benefit gained steam during the Clinton administration. Estimates vary, but among the highest is that as many as 40 percent of Medicare recipients lack prescription drug coverage.[39] Those enrolled in Medicare HMOs were most likely to have drug coverage, and those with medigap policies (the largest portion of Medicare beneficiaries) were least likely to have coverage.[40] Those with higher incomes were also more likely to have drug coverage, often through a former employer. Coverage was slightly greater for those below poverty than those just above poverty because many of the poorest individuals were receiving Medicaid, which often includes drug benefits. Those least likely to be covered were between 100 percent and 175 percent of poverty. They were least likely to have employer-based coverage and did not get Medicaid.

Since May 2004, a prescription drug benefit, called Part D, has been available to Medicare participants. This benefit is a drug discount card good through December 2005. Private pharmacy benefit management companies (PBMs) are offering the cards. Plans vary, and some are good only at specified pharmacies, so getting the best deal can take shopping around. A card is supposed to cost no more than $30 and provide prescription drug discounts of 10 to 25 percent. These cards are similiar to those already offered by some companies to the general population. However, Medicare participants whose income is less than about $12,000 for an individual and $16,000 for a couple can get their card free and receive an additional $600 benefit to cover drug costs. After the $600 is used, low-income beneficiaries will incur about a 5 to 10 percent copayment. Medicaid participants who have prescription drug coverage cannot get the discount card, and those participating in a Medicare + Choice plan that has a drug discount card are restricted to using that card. Those with coverage through a former employer may have better coverage and choose not to get a Medicare prescription drug card. Some "medigap" plans offer drug coverage, but the card may be preferable or provide additional help.

The discount cards are still new and a relatively small number of Medicare participants have signed up so far. One problem is that so many cards are being offered that it can be difficult to decide which, if any, to choose. Another issue is how much savings there are, especially for those who do not qualify for the $600 benefit. The Public Health Institute in Oakland, California, compared the prices of drugs using some cards against prices at the discount store Costco.[41] When it came to Lipitor, a cholesterol-lowering drug, and fluoxetine (Prozac), an antidepressant drug, prices were already slightly lower at Costco than with the Medicare drug cards used in the comparison.

In January 2006, prescription drug benefits will change. Medicare participants can join a private drug plan that includes a monthly premium. Though it is voluntary, not signing up during the first six months that one is eligible may result in higher fees. Exact costs are being determined. They will probably average $35 a month, but companies can decide what drug benefits to offer and how much to charge. Individuals will pay the first $250 of drug costs themselves (see Figure 8.6). After that, Medicare will pay 75 percent of the first $2,250 of drug costs, and Medicare beneficiaries will pay 25 percent. Then beneficiaries are solely responsible for the next $2,850 that they might incur. This gap in coverage has been dubbed the "doughnut hole." Medicare will not start paying again until beneficiaries have spent $3,600 of their own out-of-pocket money on the deductible, copayments, and the doughnut hole. After a beneficiary spends $3,600, the new catastrophic benefit kicks in—Medicare will pay 95 percent of drug costs, and the beneficiary pays $2 for generic drugs and $5 for brand-name drugs or 5 percent of drug costs (whichever is more). Medicare beneficiaries with limited income and assets will get more help, as shown in Figure 8.7. Beneficiaries' participation costs will likely increase each year.

The decision of which plan to purchase may also be difficult because drug plans do not have to cover the same drugs. They can have different "formularies" (preferred drug lists), but every plan must have at least one drug in each "therapeutic class." Participants may use an appeals process to try to get a drug not in the formulary.

FIGURE 8.6

Medicare Drug Benefit 2006 At-a-Glance

Prescription Drug Spending (no drug coverage other than Medicare)	Medicare Pays	Person Pays (no drug coverage other than Medicare)
0–$250	0	Up to $250 Deductible
$250–$2,250	Up to $1,500 (75% of drug costs)	Up to $500 (25% of drug costs)
$2,250–$5,100 Coverage Gap/Hole	0 (0% of drug costs)	Up to $2,850 (100% of drug costs)
Subtotal	Up to $1,500+	Up to $3,600 out-of-pocket = $5,100 total
Over $5,100 (Catastrophic Benefit)	95%	5% or $2 copay/generic $5 copay/brand name

Note: Your premium (about $35 per month/$420 per year in 2006) is not included

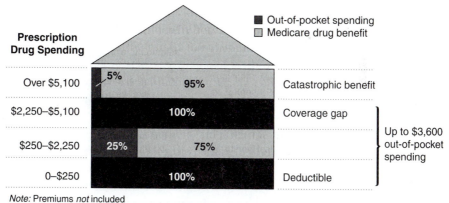

Note: Premiums *not* included

Source: American Association of Retired Persons, "Medicare Changes That Could Affect You." Used with permission of AARP, copyright 2004, AARP.

Once this new benefit program starts, "medigap" policies can no longer include prescription drug benefits, but all Medicare Advantage options except for fee-for-service plans must offer at least one plan with prescription drug benefits. States that help people who are older or disabled with prescription drug costs will have to decide whether to make any changes in their plans and could cover some or all of what Medicare does not pay. One consequence, which may be unintended and was not unanticipated, is that employers who offer retirees health benefits may drop

FIGURE 8.7

Medicare Prescription Drug Benefit

People with Medicare and full Medicaid coverage (Dual Eligible). Income below $9,360 single/$13,000 married couple:	Income below $13,000 single/$17,550 married couple. Assets* below $6,000 single/$9,000 married couple:	Income below $13,000 single/$17,550 married couple. Assets* below $10,000 single/$20,000 married couple:	Income between $13,000–$14,450 single/$17,550–$19,500 married couple. Assets* below $10,000 single/$20,000 married couple:
◆ No premium ◆ No deductible ◆ No coverage gap ◆ $1 copay for generic ◆ $3 copay for brand-name ◆ No copay if in nursing home ◆ No copay over the catastrophic limit ($3,600 out-of-pocket)	◆ No premium ◆ No deductible ◆ No coverage gap ◆ $2 copay for generic ◆ $5 copay for brand-name ◆ No copay over the catastrophic limit ($3,600 out-of-pocket)	◆ No premium ◆ $50 deductible ◆ No coverage gap ◆ 15% coinsurance ◆ $2 generic or $5 brand-name copay over the catastrophic limit ($3,600 out-of-pocket)	◆ Sliding-scale premium ◆ $50 deductible ◆ No coverage gap ◆ 15% coinsurance ◆ $2 generic or $5 brand-name copay over the catastrophic limit ($3,600 out-of-pocket)

Source: American Association of Retired Persons, "Medicare Changes That Could Affect You." Used with permission of AARP, copyright 2004, AARP.

*Assets that count include savings and investments. Assets that do *not* count include the home you live in, your car, a burial plot and/or life insurance policy up to $1,500 each. You can also keep $1,500 for burial funds.

Note: The income amounts in this chart are estimates for 2006. Real amounts are not yet set.

drug coverage for them. To encourage employers to continue drug benefits for retirees that are at least as good as Medicare's, the federal government will give employers a subsidy if retirees do not enroll in Medicare's new drug benefit. Medicare participants can stay with the plan a former employer continues to offer or choose the new Medicare option. Many older people are angry because they believe that their previous employer will dump drug coverage and they will end up with an inferior plan.

Prescription drug coverage is a major change in Medicare policy, and it has generated bitter battles. Many contend that the biggest beneficiaries are prescription drug companies and the insurance industry. The new law prohibits the federal government from negotiating prices with pharmaceutical companies, an obvious concession to the drug industry. Needless to say, drug companies lobbied to insure that any legislation Congress passed would benefit them. Under the new law, it will be up to private insurance plans to negotiate prices with the drug industry. Drug companies contend that prices will be regulated de facto, because insurance companies and HMOs will be using all their negotiation powers to keep drug prices down. But these insurers will also benefit because they will offer the plans. Others think that the government should just step in and regulate prescription drug costs and benefits like they do most other Medicare services.

AARP (formerly known as the American Association of Retired Persons) endorsed the prescription drug plan that was passed, causing a serious rift in the association's membership.[42] AARP is significant because it has more than 35 million members (every American gets an invitation to join at age 50). Older people show up at the polls in significant numbers, and they take their Medicare benefits seriously. Some criticized AARP for endorsing an inadequate prescription drug plan, and because the organization, which sells insurance, also stands to benefit from the new law.[43] AARP offered a prescription drug discount card before the new legislation, and it is offering one under the new Medicare law. Illustration 8.1 contains AARP's prescription for fixing the drug bill.

The Coalition of Wisconsin Aging Groups summarized the "good, the bad, and the ugly" of the Medicare Modernization law. Among the "good" are expanded Medicare services (e.g., some additional preventive care) and more help for low-income elderly individuals and those with large prescription drug bills. Some of the "bad" the group noted are a cap on general revenue spending for Medicare, the prescription drug "doughnut hole," inadequate prescription benefits for most older people, less help for elderly who previously qualified for Medicaid prescription drug benefits, and the introduction of means testing in Medicare. It called some of the "ugly" the "total capitulation to drug

---

ILLUSTRATION 8.1

AARP's To-Do List

AARP is promoting ways Congress can strengthen measures to contain prescription drug costs. Some goals:

♦ **Change the prohibition** on the government negotiating lower prices for Medicare beneficiaries.

♦ **Make it legal** for Americans to buy prescription drugs from licensed pharmacies in Canada and provide the U.S. Food and Drug Administration with the funds and authority to ensure that imported drugs are safe.

♦ **Fund research** comparing drugs used to treat the same conditions, to determine which work best for the least cost.

♦ **Require that pharmacy benefit managers (PBMs)** disclose to the government the rebates they receive from manufacturers to ensure that PBMs are passing on discounts to beneficiaries.

♦ **Require that customers are told** which medications are covered in any drug plan before they enroll in a plan.

♦ **Reform direct-to-consumer drug advertising** and require drugmakers to disclose gifts made to healthcare providers.

Source: Reprinted with permission of *AARP Bulletin*.

companies who will be able to sell more higher priced drugs while pocketing millions (maybe billions) of dollars in money that used to support Medicaid and other low-income programs."[44] Added to the controversy over Medicare "modernization" is an inquiry into whether the White House used estimated prescription drug benefit costs that were about $140 billion too low to get the bill passed.[45] Another scandal involved ads created by the Centers for Medicare and Medicaid Services extolling the benefits of the new prescription drug benefit. The ads appeared to be news reports by independent reporters. Instead the "reporters" were paid actors. The General Accounting Office ruled that the ads "violated the restriction on using appropriated funds for publicity or propaganda."[46] Before the new law even took effect, many were working to change it.

Long-Term Care.   Long-term care remains a major "medigap." People need these services when they cannot care for themselves due to difficulties with activities of daily living (ADL) like dressing, bathing, eating, or instrumental activities of daily living (IADL) like meal preparation, shopping, and money management. Long-term care services include both healthcare and supportive services and may be provided in institutional facilities such as nursing homes, community-care residences, or at home.

Nursing home care is provided at three levels—skilled, intermediate, and custodial. Skilled is the highest level and the only type reimbursed by Medicare. It is generally needed for a short time, for example, following some surgeries. Supplemental Medicare policies also usually do not cover intermediate and custodial nursing home care, yet this type of care is often needed.

Home healthcare includes a variety of services provided in the individual's own home or in homelike community-based programs. Home health is a fast-growing Medicare service. Medicare covers some in-home care, but not care needed on a 24-hour basis. Rather than paid services, spouses, children, and other informal caregivers provide the vast majority of in-home care. About 60 percent of those aged 65 and older who need such help rely exclusively on nonpaid assistance; only 7 percent use paid caregivers exclusively.[47] Chapters 5, 7, and 10 describe some of the publicly sponsored social services for individuals who are older or disabled and need help with meals (like Meals on Wheels), getting to the doctor, and so forth.

Individuals who need long-term care that is not covered by Medicare may pay out of their own pocket. The problem is that this care is expensive. Even a modest nursing home is beyond the financial reach of many people. The average cost of nursing home care is approximately $115 per day or $42,000 per year, with daily rates varying from less than $100 to more than $300 (but the quality of nursing home care depends more on staff than on the cost of care).[48] Many people enter a nursing home with some funds, but savings can easily be depleted.

Medicaid is the primary source of government funding for long-term care. To qualify for nursing home care under Medicaid, applicants must meet their state's definition of being poor. States' definitions vary considerably. Previously, when there was a spouse at home, both the nursing home patient and the spouse had to deplete their assets to qualify. Under Medicaid impoverishment provisions passed in 1988, the

spouse of a Medicaid nursing home patient is allowed to keep considerably more assets and income. The federal government sets a minimum and a maximum, and each
state then determines exactly how much it will allow (in 2003, the federally established minimum was $18,132, and the maximum was $90,660). States may recoup
Medicaid payments by taking proceeds from the sale of nursing home patients' homes
or other parts of their estate after their deaths, though little has actually been recovered in this way. One concern is older people transferring assets ("Medicaid estate
planning" as it has been called) in order to qualify for nursing home care at public
expense. An individual's eligibility may be delayed if assets were transferred or sold
for less than fair market value in the three years prior to application.

As people become more worried about needing care in their old age, sales of
long-term care insurance have grown.[49] These policies may cover nursing home
and home healthcare. According to the Health Insurance Association of America
(HIAA), between 1987 and 2001, 8.3 million policies were sold. Eighty percent were
sold to individuals and group associations, 16 percent were employer-sponsored,
and the rest were part of life insurance policies. Those buying individual policies
are getting younger; in 1990 their average age was 72, and in 2001, 62.[50] As one
ages, the policy price gets steeper. According to the HIAA, in 2001, to obtain a policy that pays a $100 per day benefit with 5 percent inflation protection and four
years of coverage, the average annual premium for a 50-year old purchaser was
$849; for a 65-year old purchaser, $1,726; and for a 79-year old purchaser, $5,821.
Low-income individuals are least likely to be able to afford the premiums, and
those who would quickly qualify for Medicaid upon entering a nursing home may
not think it is worth the cost. High-income individuals may assume the risk of
paying out-of-pocket should they need long-term care. Long-term care policies
might be most attractive to middle-income individuals who want to protect their
assets for family members. Employer-sponsored policies may be offered not only
to the worker, but also the worker's spouse, parents, and parents-in-law. Employer-
sponsored policies encourage younger people to participate, and spread the risk
over a larger group of people. The federal government is the largest employer to
offer long-term care insurance.

To make purchasing long-term care policies more attractive, employer contributions are excluded from employees' gross income, and benefits are now exempt from
taxes. In addition, long-term care expenses can be included with other medical expenses and taken as itemized tax deductions if they exceed 7.5 percent of adjusted
gross income. Long-term care insurance premiums can be included as part of this deduction, based on an amount that increases with an individual's age. These policies
are still relatively new, and people might be wary about what will and will not be provided should they need care.

In the hope of encouraging more people to buy long-term care insurance, some
states have experimented with a plan that allows long-term insurance purchasers
to protect a fixed amount of assets while still allowing them to participate in Medicaid once assets in excess of this amount are depleted. For example, if a person
buys coverage to protect $50,000 of assets, once the insurer pays out $50,000 for

the individual's long-term care, the individual would be allowed to participate in Medicaid as long as he or she has no more than $50,000 in assets. Linking private and public insurance like this might save public funds by delaying the time when a person qualifies for long-term care under Medicaid.

More common than long-term care insurance is disability insurance. A considerable number of workers purchase this coverage through their employer to protect them and their families should they become disabled during their working years.

In 2001, public and private expenditures for long-term care (nursing home, community, and home-based services) were $151.2 billion, or 12.2 percent of all personal healthcare expenditures. This includes funds spent for older people as well as intermediate care facilities for people with mental retardation (ICFs/MR). Medicaid paid for $73.1 billion, or 48 percent, of long-term care, consumers' paid for 22 percent of costs from their own pockets, Medicare paid for 14 percent, private health insurance for 10 percent, and other sources for 6 percent. In 2002, Medicaid expenditures for long-term care increased to $82 billion and constituted about one-third of all Medicaid spending. Of this amount, $57.4 billion, or 70 percent, was spent for institutional care—slightly more than 80 percent of it for nursing homes and the rest for ICFs/MR. There are about 1.6 million Medicaid nursing home beds.[51]

Some important changes in Medicaid spending for long-term care have been occurring. Due to other Medicaid commitments like prescription drug costs and more groups being served, the proportion of Medicaid funds spent for long-term care declined from 42 percent in 1990 to about 35 percent in 2002. In addition, more funding is being directed to home and community-based care, from 13 percent of long-term care funding in 1990 to 30 percent in 2002.

In 1999, about 9 million people aged 18 or older received long-term care services (about 5.5 million were aged 65 or older). Almost 80 percent received their care in community-based settings or their own home. Nearly 16 percent of the population aged 65 and older were receiving long-term care services, about 11 percent in the community, and only about 5 percent were in institutions (primarily nursing homes).

More could be done to help older people in their own homes by shifting more funding to in-home care. More could also be done with tax breaks and governmentally supported services like respite services to help families keep older and disabled members at home (see also Chapter 10). Studies suggest that home-based care may not result in cost savings, because elderly persons cared for at home may enter hospitals more frequently than those in institutions.[52] However, elderly people, their caregivers, service providers, and policymakers express satisfaction with home and community-based care. That may be reason enough to pursue these options.

Concerns about long-term care funding and the options available to provide this care mount with each passing year as the population ages. In 2010, the year before the first baby boomers turn 65, those aged 65 and older are projected to constitute 13.2 percent of the U.S. population.[53] By 2030 those aged 65 or older will constitute 20 percent of the population. The population aged 65 and older will double from 35 million in 2000 to 70 million in 2030; 33 million will be aged 75 and older, and almost 9 million will be aged 85 and older. Estimates are that by 2035 demand for institutional care like nursing homes and alternative living facilities (e.g., assisted living facilities) will increase by 70 percent and demand for home care by 85 percent.

Alternative living options have already increased.[54] **Assisted living facilities** offer help in accord with each resident's needs and desires, though they do not provide extensive medical or nursing care. These facilities vary in size and offer private space from a bedroom to a sizable apartment with kitchen. Services generally include meals, housekeeping, transportation, and perhaps assistance with personal care and medications and socialization and recreation. Assisted living facilities may be part of **continuing care retirement communities,** also known as **life care communities.** These communities are really multiple facilities located on the same property. Residents may start out in their own apartments, which may be purchased or leased and may include an entrance fee in addition to monthly fees. As residents' needs change, the level or amount of care they receive increases. Ultimately, they may require care in the community's skilled or custodial nursing component. Plans vary but can include options for lifelong care at fees that are established at the time of entrance. These alternative arrangements can be very expensive and require a clear understanding of costs and the legal commitment one is making. Some are more modestly priced because they are operated by religiously affiliated groups or other organizations with a desire to serve members. The solvency of the facility and the quality of its services as well as one's personal preferences about matters like privacy and decision making are also critical considerations in selecting these options.

WHAT AILS HEALTHCARE?

There is no doubt that Americans' access to medical care has increased with Medicaid, Medicare, and more employer-based coverage. Unfortunately, this increase in access to healthcare has not been met with a concomitant improvement in health. Evidence from the early 1970s on this point was particularly bleak—there seemed to be no relationship between increased healthcare expenditures and improved health for vulnerable groups.[55] Improvements in general health statistics were just as great prior to Medicaid and Medicare as they were following these programs' enactment.

Rather than more medicine, the U.S. needs a more rational means of distributing a scarce resource—medical care—in an efficient fashion to improve the nation's health. We cannot really hope to provide all the healthcare that everyone might want, but we could channel more funds to help Americans adopt healthier lifestyles. This might be one of the best uses of healthcare dollars. The greatest benefits to health and reductions in healthcare costs would accrue if people would eat healthier diets, exercise more, and stop smoking, all things that are apparently easier said than done.

Healthcare in International Perspective

Most people would expect a highly developed society to invest a substantial amount in healthcare. The United States does just that, exceeding spending over all other developed nations. Table 8.1 provides information on overall healthcare spending in several countries. No other country comes close to the $4,887 per person the United States spent on healthcare in 2001. The closest is Switzerland at $3,248, followed by Norway at $3,012. The United States also spends more on healthcare as a percent of gross domestic product (GDP) than other countries. At 13.9 percent in 2001, it exceeded Switzerland's 10.9 percent and Germany's 10.7 percent. Less than half (44 percent) of U.S. healthcare expenditures comes from public sources. Except for Switzerland, public funds account for more than two-thirds of healthcare expenditures in the other countries shown in Table 8.1. Nearly everyone in these other countries has publicly sponsored health insurance. The United States and South Africa are the only industrialized countries that do not have some form of national health insurance.

The cost of healthcare in the United States might not be so hard to swallow if Americans could boast that they were healthier than people in other countries, but this is

TABLE 8.1

Healthcare Expenditures per Capita and as a Percentage of Gross Domestic Product (GDP), and Public Expenditures as a Percentage of Total Healthcare Expenditures for Selected Countries

Country	Per Capita Expenditure in U.S. Dollars (2001)	Expenditures as Percent of GDP (2001)	Public Expenditures as a Percentage of Total Healthcare Expenditures (2001)
Australia	$2,350[b]	8.9%[a]	68.9[a]
Canada	2,792	9.7	70.8
Finland	1,841	7.0	75.6
France	2,561	9.5	76.0
Germany	2,808	10.7	74.9
Ireland	1,935	6.5	76.0
Italy	2,212	8.6[a]	74.8[b]
Japan	1,984[b]	7.6[a]	78.3[a]
Norway	3,012	8.3	85.5
Spain	1,600	7.5	71.4
Sweden	2,270	8.7	85.2
Switzerland	3,248	10.9	55.6[a]
United Kingdom	1,992	7.6	82.2
United States	4,887	13.9	44.4

Source: OECD in Figures, 2003 Edition, Statistics on Member Countries (Paris: Organization for Economic Cooperation and Development, September 2003). Reprinted with permission.

[a]Data are for 2000.

[b]Data are for 2002.

hardly the case. Despite access to the most advanced healthcare technology, Americans have a lower life expectancy than those in many other industrialized countries (ranking 21st for women and 22nd for men out of 30 countries) and higher infant mortality (ranking 26th).[56] Furthermore, the United States may be the only developed country in which "nearly half of . . . [people] are very or somewhat worried about being able to afford healthcare services (46 percent) and prescription drugs (41 percent), and over half of those with insurance coverage are worried about not being able to afford insurance (51 percent) or having their benefits cut back (50 percent) in the coming year."[57] Those with the greatest worries have lower incomes and no health insurance. *Time* magazine reported that medical bills are the primary reason for personal bankruptcy.[58]

The Nation's Healthcare Bill

It would be much easier to offer healthcare benefits to all Americans if medical costs were not so high. National healthcare expenditures have risen rapidly in the United States. In 1965, prior to Medicare and Medicaid, the country's total (public and private) healthcare bill was $42 billion; in 1990 it was $698 billion, and in 2001, healthcare expenditures (not counting construction and research) were nearly $1.4 trillion (see Table 8.2). Figure 8.8 shows that for every dollar spent on healthcare, private insurance and other private spending combined accounted for 40 cents, federal expenditures accounted for 33 cents, state and local spending for 11 cents, and out-of-pocket expenditures for 17 cents.

Employers are passing more health insurance costs on to employees, and some employees who have coverage cannot afford the additional premiums to insure their spouses and children. Some people work only in order to maintain healthcare coverage for their families because they are afraid to do without it.

Several factors have contributed to escalating medical costs:

1. Third-party financing, including the expansion of private insurance (especially through employers) and public insurance (Medicaid and Medicare), has contributed to these rapidly increasing health costs. All have increased the demand for healthcare.

2. The rapidly growing number of older people is another contributor, since those over age 65 use more healthcare services than the rest of the population.

3. Advances in medical technology also contribute. Amazing improvements have occurred in the diagnosis and treatment of many illnesses—including heart disease and cancer—which not long ago were invariably considered fatal. Equipment such as CAT scanners and magnetic resonance imaging and techniques such as organ transplants and other extraordinary means of sustaining life also add to costs. The technology that continues to be developed has allowed for increased survival rates of the tiniest infants and people with the most serious ailments.

4. There has been a vast expansion of medical facilities, including hospital beds that are expensive to maintain (though rural areas may not have a doctor, let alone a hospital).

TABLE 8.2

U.S. National Healthcare Expenditures, 2001 (in billions of dollars)

Spending Category	Amount
Health services and supplies	$1,372.6
Personal healthcare	1,236.4
Hospital care	451.2
Physician and clinical services	313.6
Dental service	65.6
Other professional services	42.3
Home healthcare	33.2
Nursing home care	98.9
Prescription drugs	140.6
Nondurable medical products	31.8
Durable medical equipment	18.4
Other personal healthcare	40.9
Government administration and net cost of private health insurance	89.7
Government public health activities	46.4
Research	32.8
Construction	19.2
Total	$1,424.5

Source: Centers for Medicare and Medicaid Services, Office of the Actuary; reprinted in U.S. House of Representatives, Committee on Ways and Means, *2004 Green Book,* Appendix C, retrieved from http:// waysandmeans.house.gov/ Documents.asp?section = 813

Medicaid funding has spawned many new nursing home facilities and resulted in many more people being placed in them.

5. Litigation is another contributor. The threat of malpractice suits results in doctors ordering more tests, even if their utility is questionable. Patients generally want all the best services available, and so do their physicians. Given the threat of lawsuits, malpractice insurance costs increase. Lawyers now place TV ads asking viewers if they or someone they know has contracted a particular disease or sustained an injury and encouraging them to pursue claims against employers, drug companies, or others involved. All these costs are also passed on to consumers.

6. Healthcare cost inflation remains a concern. The double-digit healthcare cost inflation of the 1980s has abated due to managed care, more competition, and providers' efforts to avoid greater government intervention in the healthcare arena.[59] In 1982, medical care cost inflation as measured by the consumer price index for all urban con-

FIGURE 8.8

Where the Nation's Healthcare Dollar Came From: 2001[a]

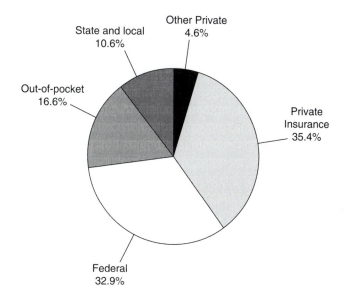

Source: Centers for Medicare and Medicaid Services, Office of the Actuary. Percentages caluculated by Congressional Research Service.

[a]Figures exceed 100% due to rounding.

sumers (CPI-U) was 11.6 percent, while the CPI-U for all items rose 6.2 percent.[60] In 1997, medical care cost inflation was 2.8 percent, the lowest in more than three decades.[61] But healthcare inflation is rising again, standing at 4.7 in 2002, while the general CPI-U was 1.6 percent. Health insurance premiums are rising much faster than general consumer inflation. They increased 11 percent in 2001, 13 percent in 2002, and 14 percent in 2003.[62]

Today, health economists generally note two main drivers of healthcare spending—the "march of science" (biomedical advances) and the aging population.[63] Even when technology drives down prices, more people utilize the technology and healthcare costs rise.[64] The pessimistic view shared by some healthcare experts "is that no approach our nation has tried, over the past thirty-five years, to control health costs has had a lasting impact."[65] But a study by two healthcare economists says that fully insuring the uninsured would cost less than many people might think: $34 billion to $69 billion in 2001 dollars, or 3 to 6 percent more in total healthcare spending, and the increase in the percent of the GDP devoted to healthcare would be less than one percent.[66]

Trying to Control Healthcare Costs

In the 1980s, the federal government took action to curb rapidly escalating public healthcare costs. Since Medicaid reimbursement rates are so low, the initial target of these efforts was the Medicare program.

Reining in Medicare

The major vehicles enacted to rein in Medicare were diagnosis-related groups (DRGs) and Medicare assignment. In 1983, Congress adopted its controversial DRG system. Prior to this, there were some restrictions on what Medicare would reimburse hospitals, but generally hospitals were reimbursed for the "reasonable" costs incurred in treating a patient. This was a *retrospective* (after-the-fact) method of paying for hospital care. Despite strong opposition, the DRGs introduced a *prospective* reimbursement method in which the federal government specifies in advance what it will pay hospitals for the treatment of 487 different illnesses, or diagnosis-related groups. A reimbursement formula was devised to include the average cost of treating a Medicare patient in the hospital, the average cost of treating the particular DRG, whether the hospital is in a large urban area or other area, and hospital wages in the area compared to the national average hospital wage. Greater reimbursement is provided for very costly cases, to hospitals that serve a large number of low-income patients or are the only providers in the area, and to regional referral centers and cancer treatment centers. Anyone who takes time to read the rules will be dazzled by the complexity of the DRG system. When a hospital spends more to treat a patient, it must absorb the additional costs, but when the hospital spends less than the DRG allows, it can keep the difference. Participating hospitals are not allowed to charge Medicare patients more than the DRG. Obviously, the purpose of DRGs is to make hospitals more cost efficient, and immediate drops in hospital stays along with cost savings were seen.

Containing physicians' charges was more difficult to achieve. Medicare traditionally paid physicians what was "usual, customary, and reasonable" in their community. Opposition from physicians and the AMA to controlling fees was a formidable obstacle to overcome.[67] Cost control provisions have included freezes on the amount that "participating" physicians can charge Medicare patients. Participating physicians and other participating providers agree to accept Medicare reimbursement as payment in full, while "nonparticipating" physicians may charge patients in addition to the amount covered by Medicare. Some physicians are not taking new Medicare patients, presumably because reimbursement is low and paperwork is high. Some providers (e.g., nurse practitioners, physician assistants, clinical laboratories) must accept assignment in order to receive Medicare reimbursement. Others (e.g., providers of durable medical equipment) are not compelled to accept assignment and can bill patients whatever they want. These providers have avoided price controls.

Each year the U.S. Department of Health and Human Services determines the fees that will be paid to physicians under the Medicare program. Incentives used to increase the number of participating physicians include higher payments, prompter reimbursement, and distribution of participating physician directories.

In 1989, Congress reckoned further with the AMA by instituting three major changes to control physicians' fees, largely borrowed from the Canadian national healthcare system. The first was "expenditure targets." If total Medicare costs are within the year's target, the increase in physicians' fees for the next year is larger than if the target is not met. If the target is not met, the excess costs are taken from the next year's budget. The second change limited "balance billing," which occurs when physicians charge the patient for the difference between their usual charge and what Medicare pays. Since 1993, nonparticipating physicians cannot charge Medicare patients more than 115 percent of Medicare's allowable charges, and they are reimbursed at 95 percent of the amount received by participating physicians. The third change was to pay physicians according to a fee schedule for about 7,000 different services beginning in 1992.

In spite of Congress's attempts to hold down expenditures, the government's share of healthcare costs increased substantially during the 1990s relative to that paid by the private sector and by households.[68] Most troubling was that the Medicare trust fund was headed for exhaustion even though Congress had taken measures to control costs and to raise more funds by levying the Medicare tax on all workers' earned income. As Congress searched for ways to bring the federal budget into balance, healthcare became a prime target of the Balanced Budget Act of 1997.

The Balanced Budget Act

The Balanced Budget Act of 1997, or BBA, made cost savings changes in Medicaid and Medicare. The vast majority of savings have come from smaller increases in payment updates to providers, including those exempt from the DRGS (such as rehabilitation facilities, long-term care facilities, psychiatric hospitals, children's hospitals, cancer centers, and hospice facilities). Medicare savings were projected to be $115 billion in the first five years compared to about $15 billion in Medicaid. The act also repealed the Boren amendment, which required states to make "reasonable and adequate" payments to hospitals and nursing homes. This gives states more flexibility but was particularly controversial because Medicaid nursing home reimbursement rates were already very low in many places.[69] Concerns continue to mount over the adequacy of nursing home care.[70]

Also controversial has been the savings to be gained from disproportionate share hospital (DSH) payments. In the past, hospitals and physicians made up for the costs of providing services to those who could not pay their bills by shifting these costs to third-party payers (government programs and private health insurers) and to patients who could afford the bills. Today, this is increasingly difficult to do because of public and private cost-containment strategies. DSHs serve many Medicaid enrollees and many poor people who have no health insurance. Disproportionate share payments have been used to compensate hospitals for this service. These payments became a sore spot for the federal government because states were taxing these hospitals, running the taxes through the state treasury, using the taxes to draw down federal DSH payments, and then returning the taxes and the DSH payments to the hospitals.[71] The BBA and previous legislation passed during the 1990s limit DSH payments in order to save the government money through more efficient service delivery.

Under the BBA, Medicare beneficiaries assumed more out-of-pocket costs, like higher Part B premiums. The BBA also sought to achieve savings through greater use of managed care and other healthcare options for poor and older people. According to the House Committee on Ways and Means, the BBA "achieved significant savings to the Medicare program by slowing the rate of growth in payments to providers and by enacting structural changes to the program."[72] The BBA might have done too good a job. Claims were that payment reductions were greater than intended, causing some facility closures and limiting some beneficiaries' access to care. Subsequent measures were taken to increase payment rates. But there have also been additional efforts to limit spending. For example, in 2003, Congress decided to reduce the amount of services that Medicare beneficiaries could get in a year from physical, speech, and occupational therapists.

The private sector also remains vitally concerned about healthcare costs. Healthcare benefits are an increasing cost of doing business, and employers are requiring employees to contribute an increasing amount to cover health benefits. In 2003, the Kaiser Family Foundation reported that employers paid 13.9 percent more for health insurance than they did in 2002—the largest increase since 1990. "The typical family health insurance policy now costs $9,068, with employers on average paying 73% and employees paying 27%."[73]

Managed Care: Good or Bad for the Nation's Health?

It used to be simple. When you needed healthcare, you went to a doctor, paid the fee on the spot, or negotiated payment arrangements with the physician. Doctors even came to the home when a family member was ill. Now consumers complain that a glossary is needed just to figure out what type of arrangement they should select to obtain healthcare, even before they see a physician. As both the demand for healthcare services and healthcare costs grew, the country's entrepreneurial spirit led to the development of various arrangements for obtaining healthcare benefits.

Among the first alternative arrangements that became widely available to Americans were **health maintenance organizations** (HMOs). To support the concept, Congress provided assistance with the Health Maintenance Organization Act of 1973. HMOs are membership organizations. Some hire doctors and other health professionals at fixed salaries to serve dues-paying members, often in a clinic-type setting (known as group HMOs). Many now contract with private physicians, who treat patients in their own offices (known as **individual practice associations** or IPA HMOs). IPA HMOs often use capitation—doctors are paid a set annual fee for each patient enrolled regardless of how much healthcare patients use. IPA HMOs can provide a greater choice of physicians than a clinic setting.

Both types of HMOs typically provide comprehensive healthcare for enrollees. Members pay a regular fee (the fee may be somewhat higher than the premium for traditional, private health insurance) that entitles them to hospital care and physicians' services at little or no extra costs (unlike traditional insurance, which pays a percentage of the bills after a deductible is met). Like traditional health insurance, HMOs vary in the services they offer. Some cover treatment for alcohol and drug disorders, prescription drugs, and eyeglasses; others do not. Many HMOs do require modest copayments to cover a portion of costs and deter unnecessary visits.

Advocates tout HMOs as being less costly than fee-for-service medical care, because physicians have no incentive to overtreat patients. Moreover, HMOs are supposed to emphasize preventive medicine, and therefore attempt to treat medical problems before they become serious illnesses. HMOs rapidly grew in popularity, covering an increasing number of employees as well as Medicaid and Medicare recipients. But some have come and gone because they were operating in the red (pun intended). Others have merged or been bought out by competitors. Enrollees sometimes find themselves covered by one HMO today and another one tomorrow, one not necessarily of their choosing. Many large employers offer their employees a selection of healthcare plans from which to choose. Others, especially smaller companies, may offer a single HMO.

The HMO concept was soon followed by **preferred provider organizations** (PPOs). Again the motive was cost containment. Under PPOs, employers or their insurance carriers reimburse a higher percentage of services—for example, hospital care—if employees use designated hospitals or other providers. Employees can use other services but their reimbursement level is lower (for example, 80 percent as opposed to 90 percent for preferred providers). PPOs developed as a result of competition among healthcare providers who want to keep their patient counts high and are willing to negotiate lower fees to do so.

Some large employers have opted for **self-insurance** in which companies directly cover employees' healthcare costs rather than contract with an insurance company. Under this option, companies may place more limits on the type and amount of services available to employees. These companies generally hire staff to shop for the best healthcare buys and monitor employees' use of services to keep costs down.

Still another option is **point-of-service** (POS) plans. These plans blend features of HMOs and PPOs. Each enrollee has a primary care physician, but patients can still be reimbursed when they see specialists without approval of their primary care physician if they are willing to pay more for the service. Furthermore, in almost all cases now, hospital stays and other extensive treatment, except in dire emergencies, must be preapproved by the health carrier regardless of the type of plan.

Medicare Part C was added to Medicare to give enrollees more managed care choices. In addition to HMOs, the Balanced Budget Act of 1997 gave Medicare participants options like preferred provider organizations and **provider sponsored organizations** (PSOs), in which doctors and hospitals group together to offer medical services. PSOs are similar to HMOs except that HMOs are run by insurance companies and PSOs are run by medical providers themselves. Still another option is a **private fee-for-service** (PFFS) plan, which utilizes a private indemnity health insurance policy; Medicare pays the insurer a per capita fee for each enrollee and providers are reimbursed at an agreed-upon rate.[74] Those who choose this option can see any provider participating in the arrangement. Few PFFS plans are available. **Medical Savings Accounts** (MSAs, also called medical IRAs after the individual retirement accounts that many people have) were also an option, but no provider established a MSA under Medicare + Choice (Part C).

Some people may enjoy sorting through all the options, but so many choices may be causing Americans stress. Others may not wish to obtain their healthcare through managed care arrangements, even if it might reduce out-of-pocket costs, because they want maximum say in their healthcare decisions.

Many Medicare HMOs did not make a financial go of it, and folded their tents entirely or reduced their service areas. Medicare + Choice simply failed to expand coverage in managed care. Prior to the BBA, 14 percent of Medicare participants were enrolled in managed care options; in 1999, 17 percent were enrolled, but by March 2003, this figure had dropped to 12 percent. According to the Committee on Ways and Means, Medicare managed care may have been less than successful "because the goal to control Medicare spending may have dampened interest by managed care entities"[75] (a nice way of saying that they were not able to make sufficient profits), and because Medicare regulations are onerous for the medical industry. Medicare managed care enrollment is expected to drop to 8 percent of enrollees by 2013.

A much higher proportion of Medicaid than Medicare recipients are enrolled in managed care arrangements. Perhaps this is because Medicaid is a public assistance program. Participants have less say in program features, and they are much less politically active. The state of Arizona has used managed care since it inaugurated its Medicaid program, called the Arizona Health Care Cost Containment System, in 1982, and Tennessee adopted its own managed care system called TennCare. Many states have obtained waivers (federal permission) allowing them to enroll Medicaid beneficiaries in managed care plans while restricting their choice of providers and waiving other Medicaid program requirements. The Balanced Budget Act of 1997 went further by allowing states to require many Medicaid beneficiaries to enroll in managed care plans without a waiver. The down side is that enrollee choice is restricted. The up side is that states have been able to use managed care to include more low-income people in their Medicaid programs.

Various permutations and combinations of managed healthcare options continue to emerge. If you have a choice of healthcare plans, which do you choose? To make the best decision, consumers must study the options carefully even though few people really want to read the fine print and it can be difficult to comprehend. If you want greater choice in selecting physicians, traditional insurance (fast becoming a thing of the past) or a preferred provider option may be the best choice. If an individual has high prescription drug costs, it is important to determine whether an HMO or another type of plan will provide better coverage. Families with young children generally need a series of routine care services, and HMOs usually cover them without a deductible. Becoming an informed consumer may be the best defense, but this has become an increasingly difficult task. Few consumers probably bother to study their policies unless a crisis arises.

At the same time that HMOs and other managed care arrangements have done their share to rein in healthcare inflation, they have generated more than their share of complaints. Some complaints concern limited numbers of service providers and the limited amount of time physicians spend with each patient. Other complaints come from patients who believe that they have been unfairly denied treatment. Specialists' services may be covered only if the patient's primary care physician makes a referral, raising concerns that HMOs may limit care in order to cut costs (you may have heard horror stories about treatment denied). Many managed care organizations now provide greater flexibility in seeking care from specialists. In 1996, the federal government issued rules telling HMOs serving Medicaid and Medicare participants that they cannot make payments to physicians as a reward for limiting treatment to a patient. The rules also make physicians responsible for carrying insurance to cover losses they might incur in treating HMO patients so they will be less likely to limit care. Now some HMOs are rewarding physicians who get high satisfaction ratings from patients. Other concerns about managed care organizations arose after patients were discharged too quickly from hospitals. When insurers told new mothers to leave the hospital almost immediately after delivery, Congress passed a law in 1996 requiring health plans to allow mothers to stay at least 48 hours when the delivery is natural and up to four days for a Cesarean delivery.

These situations lead to the vexing questions of who makes the decisions about patient care and who is responsible if something goes wrong. HMOs claim that they should not be liable for medical decisions because they pay for healthcare but do not make medical decisions. Others argue that HMOs have a tremendous influence on patient care decisions because they determine which services will be covered. There were also problems of "loyalty oaths" and "gag rules" that limited what doctors could tell their patients about HMO practices such as treatments not covered by their plans. The federal government issued rules telling HMOs to stop limiting what doctors can tell patients about treatment options. Texas and Missouri passed laws allowing patients to sue HMOs for malpractice. Minnesota tried to address the profit motive by requiring that all managed care plans be nonprofit.[76] Not so long ago, patients would never have dreamed that they would need to be protected from the healthcare system, but times have changed. President Clinton appointed an advisory commission that drafted a patients' bill of rights (see Illustration 8.2). Many health plans are utilizing these principles. Consumers are still waiting for broad federal action on patient rights and protections.

Shopping in Canada (Controlling Drug Costs)

The latest target of interest in controlling healthcare costs is the prescription drug industry. Most people who have private health insurance, especially employer-based insurance, have some kind of prescription drug coverage. Many Medicaid recipients also have prescription drug coverage. Even people with coverage are paying more from their pocket (generally in the form of a copay) when they go to the pharmacy. Health plans of all types try to negotiate to get the best prices on drug coverage because

ILLUSTRATION 8.2

A Proposed Consumer Bill of Rights and Responsibilities

1. Consumers have the right to receive accurate, easily understood information and some require assistance in making informed healthcare decisions about their health plan, professionals, and facilities.

2. Consumers have the right to a choice of healthcare providers that is sufficient to ensure access to appropriate high-quality healthcare.

3. Consumers have the right to access emergency healthcare services when and where the need arises. Health plans should provide payment when a consumer presents to an emergency department with acute symptoms of sufficient severity—including severe pain—such that a "prudent layperson" could reasonably expect the absence of medical attention to result in placing that consumer's health in serious jeopardy, serious impairment to bodily functions, or serious dysfunction of any bodily organ or part.

4. Consumers have the right and responsibility to fully participate in all decisions related to their healthcare. Consumers who are unable to fully participate in treatment decisions have the right to be represented by parents, guardians, family members, or other conservators.

5. Consumers have the right to considerate, respectful care from all members of the healthcare system at all times and under all circumstances. An environment of mutual respect is essential to maintain a quality healthcare system.

6. Consumers have the right to communicate with healthcare providers in confidence and to have the confidentiality of their individually identifiable healthcare information protected. Consumers also have the right to review and copy their own medical records and request amendments to their records.

7. All consumers have the right to a fair and efficient process for resolving differences with their health plans, healthcare providers, and the institutions that serve them, including a rigorous system of internal review and an independent system of external review.

8. In a health system that protects consumers' rights, it is reasonable to expect and encourage consumers to assume reasonable responsibilities. Greater individual involvement by consumers in their care increases the likelihood of achieving the best outcomes and helps support a quality improvement, cost-conscious environment.

Source: President's Advisory Commission on Consumer Protection and Quality in the Health Care Industry, "Consumer Bill of Rights and Responsibilities," July 17, 1998, retrieved from http://www.hcqualitycommission.gov/cborr/

prescription drug cost inflation has escalated much faster than healthcare inflation in general. Miraculously, prescription drugs have escaped the kinds of price controls that have been placed on physician, hospital, and other health providers.

Many Americans recall the day when the pharmaceutical industry did not run TV ads for prescription drugs like other companies do for laundry detergent and deodorant. Drug companies also spend a lot of time courting doctors and health plans, though they have been told to watch this practice, which could be viewed as involving illegal kickbacks.[77]

Compared to prices in the United States, prescription drug prices are cheaper not only in the Third World but in Canada and other developed countries. Though it is illegal for Americans to bring drugs from other countries into the United States, more Americans are "reimporting" prescription medications. "Reimportation" occurs when an American purchases a drug in another country that is produced by a U.S. manufacturer and is legally available in the United States. The U.S. government has generally not intervened when individuals "reimport" drugs for personal use.[78] Some states and communities are joining individuals in trying to make the practice legal. The 2003 Medicare law allows reimportation from Canada *if* the Secretary of Health and Human Services certifies that it is safe to do so and would reduce drug costs. Tommy Thompson, the current secretary, has refused to do so.

Retail drug prices are considerably lower in other countries because governments regulate drug prices. The way Canada does it, the price cannot exceed the highest price in Canada of other drugs to treat the same illness; if there is no competitor drug, the price cannot exceed the median cost in seven other countries (this includes the United States, Japan, the U.K., and four European countries); and drug cost increases cannot exceed Canada's general consumer price index.[79] Canada's Patented Medicine Prices Review Board reviews drug prices twice each year. Prices of generic drugs and brand name drugs with expired patents are not regulated. In Canada, everyone pays the same price for a drug, unlike the United States, in which prices vary. Canada's national health plan does *not* include prescription drugs like most others' countries national health plans do. Some Canadians have drug coverage through their employer, and most retired people get it through their provincial government. The provinces maintain drug formularies and decide which drugs to include.

On average, in 2001, Canadian drug prices were reportedly 69 percent lower than in the United States.[80] Illustration 8.3 shows some of the striking Internet mail-order price differences, the most amazing being the costs of generic versions of tamoxifen, a breast cancer drug, which costs an average of $233 in the United States, $61 in Canada, and $33 through the Minnesota Senior Federation (MSF). The MSF, which assists people of all ages, negotiates with a Toronto pharmacy to get lower than usual prices.

AARP reports that the Glaxo drug company stopped supplying Canadian pharmacies that sold to Americans, touching off senior citizen protests and prompting a full-page *New York Times* ad condemning Glaxo.[81] According to Representative Bernie Sanders (Independent-Vermont), Glaxo's 2002 profits were $10 billion and its CEO was paid more than $20 million.[82] Minnesota's state attorney general is trying to determine if Glaxo violated antitrust laws with its efforts to prevent Americans from buying drugs from Canada. One senator is reportedly donating his Senate salary to pay for bus trips to Canada for people who want to pick up their medications directly. AARP also reports that the Pfizer drug company has threatened to stop supplying Canadian pharmacies that in any way help Americans purchase drugs from them, and that Pfizer, which makes popular drugs like Lipitor to control cholesterol, Norvasc for

ILLUSTRATION 8.3

How Do Internet Mail-Order Prices Compare?

All prices in U.S. dollars, as of March 12, 2003, and subject to change.

	Strength/ Quantity	United States Mail Order	Canadian Mail Order	Minnesota Senior Federation
Celebrex Arthritis	100mg/100	$150.27	$72.27	$56.98
Glucophage Diabetes	500mg/100	$61.87*	$23.49†	$15.16†
Lipitor Cholesterol	20mg/90	$286.74	$164.78	$153.35
Norvasc Hypertension	10mg/100	$184.78	$161.16	$153.28
Paxil Depression	10mg/30	$74.21	$51.26	$43.48
Tamoxifen Breast Cancer	20mg/100	$232.96*	$61.38†	$32.90†

Source: Juan Velasco, 5W Infographic. Reprinted with permission.
*U.S. Generic
†Canadian Generic

high blood pressure, and Celebrex for arthritis, had revenues of $32 billion in 2002.[83] Pfizer and other drug companies may effectively thwart efforts by some U.S. states and communities to purchase drug supplies from Canada.

Drug companies contend that developing new medications is very expensive. Apparently it is Americans who are underwriting much of that cost. Drug companies also contend that importing drugs is not only illegal, it threatens safety. The counterarguments are that the Canadian drug supply is as safe as the U.S. supply, Americans' health is jeopardized when they cannot afford to purchase prescription drugs at home, and there is no justifiable reason for Americans to pay much more than people in other countries do. In November 2003, the 10th Circuit Federal Court ruled against a company called Rx Depot that was helping people purchase drugs from Canada.[84]

The state of Maine is locked in a battle with drug companies, not because it wants to obtain drugs from Canada, but because it wants to negotiate rebates with drug companies for all its residents.[85] Drugs manufactured by companies that agree to provide rebates would be placed on a preferred list. Physicians would need permission to prescribe drugs not on the list. The rebates would be used to compensate pharmacies providing discounted priced drugs to Medicaid and uninsured patients. Drug companies were incensed, charging that the government, rather than doctors and patients, would be making prescription decisions. The U.S. Supreme Court ruled in the case. The decision opened one door for Maine to proceed; it also opened another door allowing prescription drug companies to challenge the program by contending that Maine must get federal government approval to proceed with this change to its Medicaid program.

INCREMENTALISM AND THE FUTURE OF HEALTHCARE POLITICS

Nowhere is the United States' unique approach to social welfare policy more evident than it is in healthcare. The term *national health insurance* makes most people think of the type of socialized medicine practiced in Great Britain in which physicians and other healthcare providers are employees of the federal government and the government owns and controls hospitals and other medical facilities. The Canadian system is much different; physicians and hospitals are part of the private sector, but the government sees that all citizens have healthcare coverage. Canada adopted universal hospital insurance in 1958 and universal physician insurance in 1968. Care is considered quite good and the system reportedly functions efficiently by centralizing services and equipment.[86] Physicians maintain substantial incomes under the Canadian plan.

In Britain and Canada, healthcare is rationed in part by time rather than money. Patients may have to wait hours to see a doctor and months to undergo nonemergency surgeries. It is those who are willing and able to wait rather than to pay who are served. There is some dissatisfaction with these systems, and in Great Britain, some private practice by physicians has been permitted for patients willing and able to pay. But it is very doubtful that any country used to universal healthcare coverage would opt for a system like that in the United States. It is equally doubtful that the United States will ever adopt a system like Britain's. The free enterprise system prevails—physicians, drug companies, other healthcare providers, and insurance companies are powerful enough to resist that much government control. Americans are used to the status quo, and campaigns by these vested healthcare interests encourage Americans to fear greater government intervention in healthcare. In the 1930s President Franklin D. Roosevelt backed off from the idea of national health insurance when he thought it might endanger passage of the original Social Security Act. President Harry S Truman failed in his bid for national health insurance. So did President Bill Clinton.

The problems of the U.S. healthcare system are obvious. Costs are high. One-fourth of workers do not have employer-sponsored health insurance,[87] and many others are also uninsured. The expenses of providing healthcare to the uninsured are borne by the rest of society. Those without insurance often make expensive visits to emergency rooms for relatively minor problems like colds and the flu as well as serious problems that might have been prevented with earlier access to healthcare. In addition, the uninsured population is a moving target, because unemployment often leaves some without coverage. Public health insurance for all but older Americans is no better. An individual insured by Medicaid today may not be covered tomorrow due to increased income or other changes in circumstances.

But most Americans have a decent source of healthcare, and though they may complain about some facet of their health plan, the majority are satisfied with the current system. A poll conducted by three reputable groups found that "Americans favor building on the current system as a way of improving healthcare; they are not eager to make sweeping changes."[88] The Institute of Medicine (IOM) is trying to persuade Americans otherwise, saying that "incremental approaches to extend coverage are insufficient."[89] The IOM has offered several models for providing healthcare coverage to all Americans. Each is based on the following principles that the IOM believes are critical for the the country's health:

1. Healthcare coverage should be universal.

2. Healthcare coverage should be continuous.

3. The health insurance strategy should be affordable and sustainable for society.

4. Health insurance should be affordable to individuals and families.

5. Healthcare coverage should enhance health and well-being by promoting access to high-quality care that is effective, safe, timely, patient centered, and equitable.

The AMA and the Health Insurance Association of America have also joined the call for some type of universal health insurance. A number of years ago the AMA endorsed mandatory employer-supported healthcare. But these organizations criticized aspects of President Clinton's national health insurance proposal, especially spending controls.[90]

Even before Congress considered President Clinton's plan for national health insurance and the many other proposals offered by Congressmembers, the states had moved ahead to do something about the uninsured at their doorsteps. Arizona had already adopted a managed care system for low-income residents. Minnesota's Health Right had extended insurance to low-income residents without coverage, charging them on a sliding scale. Some states had obtained federal waivers to serve low-income people who had no healthcare coverage and were not eligible for Medicaid by allowing them to "buy into" Medicaid through premium payments. Hawaii was requiring employers to insure most of the workforce and has been working toward universal health coverage.

But most states have been struggling to insure more people. A 2003 report sponsored by The Commonwealth Fund titled *Expanding Health Insurance Coverage: Creative Solutions for Challenging Times,* a 2004 report published by the Robert Wood Johnson Foundation titled *State of the States: Cultivating Hope in Rough Terrain,* and a 2004 report by the Kaiser Commission titled *States Respond to Fiscal Pressure: A 50-*

State Update of State Medicaid Spending Growth and Cost Containment Actions all indicate that most states were working hard "just to maintain their health services."[91] In 2003, only a few states were able to expand coverage. Examples are Illinois and Idaho, which expanded SCHIP, and Wyoming, which increased Medicaid funding and added more participants.

Tennessee's managed care system called TennCare, implemented in 1994, fell on hard times as healthcare costs increased and the state's fiscal situation worsened. To help the system, Tennessee is focusing on reducing fraud and abuse and implementing cost controls.[92] Among the cost controls are exclusion of drugs with nonprescription alternatives and mandated use of generic drugs, more cost sharing for some enrollees, a foundation to review cases of enrollees who have reached their benefit limit, a comprehensive disease management program for some enrollees, and use of evidence-based medicine initiatives. Oregon's plan for covering more people while simultaneously rationing services was especially controversial. It, too, has faced financial difficulties. The state cut mental health and chemical dependency treatment for those not categorically eligible for Medicaid but later restored these benefits.[93] Oregon also ended its Medically Needy program because of financial constraints though it restored benefits for people with HIV/AIDS and transplant recipients.

As depressing as the outlook for expanded coverage seems, the state of Maine is trying an approach called "Dirigo" after the state's motto, the Latin word for "I lead."[94] Motivated by increasing healthcare costs and approved by the state legislature in 2003, the intent is to see that all Mainers are insured by 2009. Dirigo offers state residents the opportunity to obtain health insurance by expanding Medicaid, offering help to employers to cover more workers, and providing individuals the chance to purchase healthcare coverage at more reasonable costs. Individuals with gross incomes up to $28,000 and a family of four with an annual gross income of $56,500 will qualify for reduced insurance premiums on a sliding scale. Employers who participate and pay 60 percent or more of the costs of their employees' coverage are supposed to see lower rates due to better risk pooling. Prevention and disease management are important concepts in Dirigo's public–private partnership as is the coordination of various health insurance programs to negotiate better prices based on the number of people served. Financing is complicated, but the state is asking healthcare providers and insurers "to voluntarily limit their net revenues or charge increases in excess of 3 percent annually."[95] Perhaps even more controversial is that insurance companies will be charged a "savings offset fee." This fee represents the cost of serving the uninsured, which is passed onto to insurance companies and then to paying consumers. Since this practice drives up costs, the state believes that it is entitled to this fee to see that more people have insurance coverage. As more Mainers are insured, the overall costs of caring for the uninsured should decline. The offset payment will be based on how much savings are realized. Though there have been some criticisms of Dirigo, healthcare providers and insurers seem to be cooperating.[96] Many people will be looking toward Maine as the state tries to do something that has not been done in the United States—insure everyone.

As noted earlier, Congress has both required and encouraged the states to expand their Medicaid programs to more groups. As part of the Consolidated Omnibus Budget Reconciliation Act (COBRA) of 1985, Congress also allowed many former employees to keep their insurance coverage for a specified time after leaving their job if they could afford to pay the premiums themselves. The problem is, many cannot afford it while unemployed. According to Families USA, the average cost of individual coverage was about $225 a month in 2000 and $600 a month for a family.[97] Only one in five eligible for COBRA continued their health insurance through their previous employer. In 1996, three years after President Clinton unveiled his national health plan, Congress passed the Health Insurance Portability and Accountability Act (HIPAA), also known as the Kassebaum-Kennedy bill. It contained many provisions to increase healthcare coverage. The law's complexity has made for confusion about what it does and how it is to be implemented. It provides more opportunity for employees to get health insurance when they change jobs even if they have a preexisting condition, but there may be a waiting period if the employee did not have insurance coverage that included the condition for 12 months at their last job. Other caveats may also affect one's ability to get insurance under the act. For example, employees with a break of 63 or more days without insurance coverage may be excluded for 12 months before being able to obtain insurance through their new job, and nothing in the law requires a company to provide insurance to employees.

HIPAA increases health insurance tax deductions for self-employed individuals and provides tax benefits for those who pay or whose employer pays for long-term care insurance. It also contains *viatical* provisions that allow people with chronic or terminal conditions who have life insurance policies to sell these policies without paying federal taxes on the proceeds. They can use this money to pay for medical, living, or other expenses prior to their deaths.

HIPAA also tried to make medical savings accounts (MSAs) more attractive with tax deductions. The MSAs are coupled with insurance policies that have a high deductible but can be used in the event of illness or injury that results in major medical costs.[98] Demonstrations were also established to integrate acute and long-term care and Medicare and Medicaid benefits under managed care arrangements to see if a comprehensive set of services can be provided in a more rational manner.[99] President Clinton wanted to allow people as young as age 55 to buy into Medicare to help those who have lost their jobs and thus their healthcare coverage and younger retirees without access to coverage. Other ideas abound. The country continues to take a decidedly incremental approach to seeing that more Americans have healthcare coverage.

HEALTHCARE: SOME ETHICAL DILEMMAS

Healthcare Privacy

HIPAA not only concerns health insurance portability, it concerns healthcare privacy. Most people would probably prefer that their medical history be treated confidentially.

The DHHS website describes HIPAA as the first federal standards to provide a uniform floor of privacy protections for patients' medical records.[100] If you have received healthcare services or had a prescription filled since April 14, 2003, you have undoubtedly been asked to sign a HIPAA notice. But the law has as much to do with letting patients know how their medical information will be released to other parties (primarily to "coordinate," "manage," or seek reimbursement for treatment) as it does in protecting privacy.[101]

Healthcare Rationing

Bioethical dilemmas like healthcare rationing are also social welfare concerns. Since there are limits to the amount of healthcare that can be provided, what factors should be considered in rationing? For example, should we forgo life support for the very old in favor of more preventive healthcare for children? This is an extremely difficult question, and there is no consensus on how healthcare procedures should be ranked or rationed. In fact, some people insist that spending 14 percent or more of the country's GDP should not be an issue at all; the country should avoid rationing services. But healthcare is rationed by a number of factors—whether an individual has third-party coverage or can otherwise afford care; whether those who are ill present themselves for treatment; and whether the medical community treats indigent patients rather than refusing to treat or "dumping" them. Desperate parents have tried to influence rationing decisions by using television to plead for a transplant donor for their terminally ill child when they felt that existing networks were not responding quickly enough. Without a substantial amount of money up front, transplants are out of reach for many patients. Some Medicaid programs no longer pay for transplants.

The "Right to Die" or the "Right to Life"?

Other dilemmas include the "right to die"—who should be able to make such decisions and under what circumstances? Patients have asked the courts to permit them to remove life-sustaining devices such as respirators, but there is no consistent response to this issue, and state laws on the subject are generally unclear. **Living or penultimate wills** can help to clarify an individual's wishes when death is imminent. Another directive called a **durable power of attorney** can also clarify one's wishes and transfer legal powers to another to make medical decisions. For example, terminally ill individuals may request that they not be resuscitated (also called **passive euthanasia**), or they may request that certain methods be used to sustain their life. The patient Self-Determination Act of 1991 requires that many medical facilities receiving Medicare or Medicaid funds provide information to patients about advance directives. As few as 15 percent of patients may have these directives.[102]

The other side of the coin is the "right to life," as in the case of Terri Schindler-Schiavo.[103] Her husband contends that she is in a persistent vegetative state and believes that she should be allowed to die because she had expressed to him her desire not to be kept alive by artificial means. The Florida Supreme Court agreed with her husband's request to have her feeding tube removed. Schindler-Schiavo's parents disagree, calling it a "perfect crime" by her husband—court-sanctioned murder. Schindler-Schiavo did not have a written directive, but even if she did, the point may be moot. Her parents believe that their daughter is not in a persistent vegetative state, that she is responsive and might be helped with therapy that her husband refuses to provide. The case is complicated since her husband is the sole heir to what remains of a settlement won in a malpractice suit on his wife's behalf, and he now reportedly has a relationship with another woman,[104] but for some, these matters are beside the facts of the case. Florida Governor Jeb Bush supported Schindler-Schiavo's parents, and the Florida legislature passed an emergency law allowing the governor to order reinsertion of her feeding tube. Many religious groups agreed with the decision to reinsert the feeding tube. Advocacy groups for people with disabilities believe it is a victory for protecting the civil rights of people with severe disabilities and avoids the issue of who should be left to die.[105] In September 2004, Florida's Supreme Court declared the law a violation of the separation of powers guaranteed by the state's constitution.

In 1990, the U.S. Supreme Court reviewed the Cruzan case, which also received considerable media attention. But in this case, the parents wanted to stop feeding their unresponsive adult daughter, who was severely injured in a car crash. They believed it was their daughter's wish not to live in a vegetative state. The state of Missouri refused to comply with the parents' wishes on the grounds that it had no such instructions from the patient and that her treatment was not causing pain. The court upheld the state's position, stating there was not "clear and convincing" proof of the patient's wishes. The decision was the high court's first in a right-to-die case. The implications of the decision are that patients do have a constitutional right to reject medical treatment if their desires are made clear, but that states have considerable authority in determining how this right will be upheld. Most states allow family members more authority in making decisions on behalf of patients in vegetative states than is permitted in Missouri. Later, when presented with additional evidence, a Missouri probate judge allowed the feedings to stop. Ms. Cruzan died shortly thereafter.

Another reason that the proper limits of life are being debated is because life spans continue to increase. Several years ago, one governor gained national attention when he suggested that the elderly have a "duty to die." Medical technology may be able to sustain people, regardless of the quality of life, and the capabilities of medical technology continue to increase, making it even more difficult to decide between sustaining life and allowing death to occur. Recently identified diseases also present challenges. In one case an elderly Florida man was found guilty of murder and imprisoned after he shot to death his wife, who had Alzheimer's disease. He said he could no longer bear to see her suffer.

Futile Care

Even individuals with advance directives cannot be assured that their wishes will be carried out, because family members, medical professionals, or the courts might not know an individual's wishes, or they may not agree on what, if anything, should be done. An issue in point is "futile care policies" or "futile care theory" where hospitals reserve the right to refuse treatment to individuals who are terminally ill or in persistent vegetative states, even over their objection or their family's. The topic of what constitutes futile care is widely discussed in the medical literature. Apparently, "physicians do not have a responsibility to provide futile care even if a patient or surrogate insists on it."[106] Critics contend that decisions to stop treatment, despite the objections of patients and their families, are motivated by the high costs of providing such care.[107] These decisions raise even more suspicions under managed care.[108] In a survey of California hospitals, 24 of 26 hospitals reported that they have futile care policies.[109]

Most hospitals have an ethics committee that often includes community members such as clergy to help address the difficult decisions that patients, family members, and hospital staff face.[110] Medical personnel must also uphold their own codes of ethics and obey state laws.

Euthanasia and Assisted Suicide

Those who do believe in the individual's right to determine when life should end point to the Netherlands, which allows physicians to help patients with voluntary, active euthanasia in which the physician administers or prescribes drugs to promote death.[111] Active euthanasia was technically illegal but was practiced in the Netherlands for some time and seldom resulted in serious legal repercussions if the physician followed guidelines developed as a result of judicial decisions made in the 1970s. For example, the patient must make the request, the physician must have known the patient previously, and the physician is not compelled to honor the request. The Dutch parliament was deeply divided on the morality of the issue, but in 1993 it supported the practice, and in 2001, the parliament legalized it, making it the world's most liberal euthanasia policy.[112] It requires consultation with a second physician to ensure that all requirements are satisfied, and prison terms may be imposed for violations. Those opposed to the law believe that condoning the practice promotes the idea of social Darwinism (survival of the fittest) and could be used inappropriately. In 1995, the Northern Territory of Australia passed the world's first explicit voluntary euthanasia law. A few people used it to end their lives before the Australian parliament overturned it.

In the United States, the Oregon legislature passed a law in 1994 that allowed doctors to assist patients with lethal doses of medication. The law requires that an individual be mentally competent, have less than six months to live, make a written request that is witnessed, drink a cocktail of drugs rather than be administered an injection, and wait 15 days to be given the cocktail. Two physicians must concur, and a physician must discuss alternatives with the patient. In 1995, a federal judge ruled the law unconstitutional to prevent error, abuse, and discrimination. In 1996, the Ninth Circuit Court of Appeals overturned a Washington state law making it a felony to assist in a person's death by ruling that a mentally competent person who is terminally ill has a constitutional right to commit suicide with a doctor's help. In 1996 a federal appeals court found New York's law against physician-assisted suicide unconstitutionally discriminatory. Unlike the Washington decision, it did not find a constitutional right to assisted suicide based on the Fourteenth Amendment's guarantees of liberty and privacy. Instead, it said that while those on life support can hasten death by turning off machines that sustain their life, others in terminal situations have no such recourse, thus violating the Constitution's equal protection clause.

The U.S. Supreme Court agreed to hear appeals of the Washington and New York cases, a surprising move in that the high court usually tries to avoid the issue. In June 1997, it concluded that there is no constitutional right to physician-assisted suicide. The ruling allows states to ban physician-assisted suicides but does not stop states from allowing them in narrowly defined cases. The high court refused to hear an appeal of the Oregon law, but in November 1997, the issue was again put to Oregon voters. By a 20 percent margin, Oregonians affirmed approval of access to physician-assisted suicide. Oregon is the only U.S. state with such a law. The Drug Enforcement Administration tried to block the Oregon law by threatening to revoke the narcotics licenses of physicians who participate in suicides of terminally ill people. Janet Reno, then U.S. Attorney General, informed the DEA that the issue was not in its purview. Current U.S. Attorney General John Ashcroft and the U.S. Department of Justice also tried to block the law, but the 9th U.S. Circuit Court of Appeals said they did not have the right to do so.

Retired pathologist Dr. Jack Kevorkian devoted himself to the cause by assisting in suicides of ill individuals (or at least in helping them end their suffering). Kevorkian was prosecuted in a few of these cases and acquitted each time. A Michigan ban on assisted suicide and an attempt to invoke unwritten common law failed to stop him. Neither did the time he spent in jail. In late 1998, Kevorkian was charged and later convicted after a tape he provided to the TV show *60 Minutes* showed him administering a lethal injection of potassium chloride to a man with Lou Gehrig's disease. He is serving a 10- to 25-year sentence in the case, and the Supreme Court has refused to hear his appeal.

End-of-Life Choices (formerly the Hemlock Society), an organization interested in "the freedom to choose a dignified death and for individual control concerning death," states that it "support[s] the right of terminally ill, mentally competent adults to hasten death under careful safeguards."[113] On the other side of the issue, the National Right to Life Committee works to block efforts that support the right to choose death. Physician-assisted death has been likened to the issue of abortion, not only on constitutional grounds, but also because of the groups (like anti-abortion, "right to life" organizations) that have rallied around the issue and the fervor with which they have pursued their positions. Ethical, moral, and legal questions have been raised. Among them is the issue of discrimination. Many refer to it as a slippery slope bound to go further than most intend. For example, some fear that assisted suicide laws may turn into a duty to die, because in the United States a terminal illness, as well as a chronic, long-term illness, can bankrupt a family (unlike other countries where national health insurance protects families from financial disaster due to medical conditions). Another concern is that in many cases, patients' requests to end their lives are due to inadequate medical attention such as lack of sufficient pain medication and other palliative care that can ease suffering. In this case, the answer may lie in better education of medical professionals. Others contend that doctors fear repercussions for prescribing sufficient doses of potentially addictive pain-relieving narcotic medications.

The Assisted Suicide Funding Restriction Act of 1997 expressed the opinion of Congress and President Clinton by making it illegal to use federal funds to support physician-assisted suicide. The two largest physician organizations in the United States, the American Medical Association (AMA) and the American College of Physicians, also oppose physician-assisted suicide. On the issue of futile care, the AMA's Council on Ethical and Judicial Affairs also recognizes that "controversy arises when the patient or proxy and the physician have discrepant values or goals of care. Since definitions of futile care are value laden, universal consensus on futile care is unlikely to be achieved."[114] To address the problem, the council recommends a process for addressing futile care cases. But such a process cannot really resolve the issue when such deeply felt values are at stake.

As medical science advances further, the list of bioethical concerns grows. Stem cell research holds promise for curing many illnesses like Alzhiemer's disease, to which President Reagan and many others have succumbed, and offers hope to repair spinal cord injuries like the one that left actor Christopher Reeve paralyzed. Some people support stem cell research but draw the line at the use of embryonic stem cell research, which they believe denigrates the sanctity of human life. Another issue is cloning. Now that animals have been cloned, human cloning cannot be far behind, and that thought is especially disturbing.

SUMMARY

Many of the leading causes of death for those in all income brackets are related to heredity and lifestyle issues rather than lack of medical care. The United States spends more for healthcare than other industrialized nations, yet fewer Americans have health insurance, and U.S. adult and infant mortality rates exceed those of most of these countries. Black, Hispanic, Native Americans, and poor Americans continue to experience disparities in health insurance coverage and in many health outcomes.

Healthcare for aged and poor Americans has been on the social welfare policy agenda since the early twentieth century. Major federal healthcare proposals were introduced for fifty years before Medicaid and Medicare were adopted. The medical establishment worked to delay large-scale federal government involvement in medical assistance by branding it socialized medicine.

Medicaid is a public assistance program operated jointly by the federal and state governments. Most SSI and TANF recipients receive Medicaid. Other medically indigent people may also qualify, but Medicaid insures less than half of all poor Americans. Medicare is a social insurance program financed by the government through payroll taxes. It serves nearly all the nation's aged population as well as many former workers under age 65 with long-term disabilities.

President Clinton wanted to create a national healthcare program to ensure that all Americans have continuous healthcare coverage. The plan would have relied heavily on fees paid by employers. Employees would have shared costs and other enrollees would also have paid some premiums. The major opposition came from those who thought it was too much government interference in healthcare, but others advocated greater government involvement through a single-payer system like Canada's.

Healthcare makes up an increasing amount of public and private expenditures. Health maintenance organizations and other managed care arrangements are attempts at keeping these costs under control. Managed care is a major theme in providing healthcare coverage to Americans today, but it may be reaching its zenith.

The United States has used a decidedly incremental approach to increasing healthcare coverage. Some states are including more low-income people in their Medicaid programs, sometimes due to federal requirements and sometimes at their own discretion. Federal funding for the State Children's Health Insurance Program has helped to insure more low-income children. Efforts to provide some prescription drug coverage to older Americans are among the most recent changes to expand the program. Since U.S. residents pay very high prices for prescription drugs compared to those in other countries, many people could use help with the costs of medications.

Many other factors have contributed to rising healthcare costs that affect the ability to insure more low-income individuals. Rapidly growing technology and increased demand for healthcare that comes with insurance coverage are among the reasons that healthcare is so expensive. To rein in public healthcare costs, the federal government has made many changes in the Medicare program, such as controls on fees paid to healthcare providers and more charges to patients. Business and industry are also trying to check healthcare costs.

Healthcare ethics is another issue. Technology has also challenged us to consider how to extend life, but this opens the door to debates about who should have the right to decide when life-saving practices should be terminated or when they should be extended.

NOTES

1. For an extensive consideration of the history of healthcare, including health insurance, see Paul Starr, *The Social Transformation of American Medicine* (New York: Basic Books, 1982).

2. Although this point may seem arguable, the research literature is extensive. See, for example, Victor R. Fuchs, *Who Shall Live? Health, Economics, and Social Choice* (New York: Basic Books, 1974); Victor R. Fuchs, "The Clinton Plan: A Researcher Examines Reform," *Health Affairs*, Vol. 13, No. 1, Spring I, 1994, pp. 102–114; Nathan Glazer, "Paradoxes of Health Care," *Public Interest*, No. 22, Winter 1971, pp. 62–77; Leon R. Kass, "Regarding the End of Medicine and the Pursuit of Health," *Public Interest*, No. 40, Summer 1975, pp. 11–42; John B. McKinlay and Sonja M. McKinlay, "Medical Measures and the Decline of Mortality," in Peter Conrad and Rochelle Kern, Eds., *The Sociology of Health and Illness: Critical Perspectives* (New York: St. Martin's Press, 1994), pp. 10–23.

3. These data rely on Centers for Disease Control and Prevention, National Center for Health Statistics, *National Vital Statistics Report*, Vol. 52, No. 13, February 11, 2004, retrieved April 14, 2004, from http://www.cdc.gov/nchs

4. Committee on Ways and Means, U.S. House of Representatives, *2004 Green Book*, Appendix B, p. B-2, retrieved March 15, 2004, from http://waysandmeans.house.gov/Documents.asp?section = 813; see also Robert Sapolsky, "How the Other Half Heals," *Discover*, April 1998, pp. 46, 50–52.

5. "The Uninsured are Sicker and Die Sooner," "Uninsurance Facts and Figures" (Washington, DC: Institute of Medicine), retrieved March 29, 2004, from http://www.iom.edu/uninsured

6. "Infant Mortality Statistics from the 2001 Period Linked Birth/Infant Death Data Set," *National Vital Statistics Reports*, Vol. 52, No. 2, retrieved March 15, 2004, from http://www.cdc.gov/nchs/

7. Kyriakos S. Markides and Jeannine Coreil, "The Health of Hispanics in the Southwestern United States: An Epidemiologic Paradox," *Public Health Reports,* Vol. 101, No. 3, 1986, pp. 253–265.

8. U.S. Census Bureau, *Statistical Abstract of the United States: 2003* (Washington, DC: U.S. Government Printing Office, 2003), Table 165, p. 119, retrieved April 13, 2004, from http://www.census.gov/prod/www/statistical-abstract-03.html

9. Committee on Ways and Means, *2004 Green Book,* Appendix B, pp. B1, B2.

10. Eric C. Schneider, Alan M. Zaslavsky, and Arnold M. Epstein, "Racial Disparities in the Quality of Care for Enrollees in Medicare Managed Care," *Journal of the American Medical Association,* Vol. 287, No. 10, pp. 1288–1294.

11. Connie Goldsmith, "Vision of Health: New Prescription for the Nation's Well-Being," *Health Week,* Vol. 5, No. 5, 2000, pp. 1, 25.

12. *Ibid.,* p. 25.

13. U.S. Department of Health and Human Services, "Healthy People 2010, What Are Its Goals?" retrieved April 4, 2004, from http://www.healthy people.gov/About/goals.htm

14. U.S. Census Bureau, "Health Insurance Coverage in the United States: 2002," September 2003, retrieved March 29, 2004, from http://www.census.gov

15. This paragraph relies on Genevieve M. Kenney, Jennifer M. Haley, and Alexandra Tebay, "Children's Insurance Coverage and Service Use Improve" (Washington, DC: Urban Institute, July 31, 2003), retrieved March 28, 2004, from http://www.urban.org

16. For more historical information on healthcare policy in the United States, see Cynthia Moniz and Stephen Gorin, *Health and Health Care Policy* (Boston: Allyn and Bacon, 2003); Kant Patel and Mark E. Rushefsky, *Health Care Politics and Policy and America* (Armonk, NY: M. E. Sharpe, 1999); Starr, *The Social Transformation of American Medicine.*

17. For further discussion of the political history of healthcare in the United States, see Theodore R. Marmor, *Political Analysis and American Medical Care* (Cambridge, England: Cambridge University Press, 1983), especially Chapter 7.

18. Moniz and Gorin, *Health and Health Care Policy.*

19. Theodore R. Marmor, "The Politics of National Health Insurance: Analysis and Prescription," *Policy Analysis,* Vol. 3, No. 1, 1977, pp. 25–48.

20. This account of the Clinton proposal relies on *Budget of the United States Government, Fiscal Year 1995* (Washington, DC: Executive Office of the President, 1994), Chapter 4.

21. Uwe E. Reinhardt, "The Clinton Plan: A Salute to American Pluralism," *Health Affairs,* Vol. 13, No. 1, Spring I, 1994, p. 116.

22. See Walter A. Zelman, "The Rationale Behind the Clinton Health Care Reform Plan," *Health Affairs,* Vol. 13, No. 1, Spring I, 1994, pp. 9–29.

23. Uwe E. Reinhardt and John K. Iglehart, "From the Editor, the Policy Makers' Dilemma," *Health Affairs,* Vol. 13, No. 1, Spring I, 1994, pp. 5–6.

24. For an account of recent Medicaid and Medicare legislation, see David G. Smith, *Entitlement Politics: Medicare and Medicaid 1995–2001* (New York: Aldine de Gruyter, 2002).

25. Most of the remainder of this section relies on Committee on Ways and Means, U.S. House of Representatives, *2003 Green Book,* Section 15, "Medicaid," updated March 17, 2004, retrieved March 18, 2004, from http://waysandmeans.house.gov/Documents. asp?section = 813; see also *1996 Green Book: Background Material and Data on Programs within the Jurisdiction of the Committee on Ways and Means* (Washington, DC: U.S. Government Printing Office, 1996), pp. 879–914; Committee on Ways and Means, U.S. House of Representatives, *1998 Green Book: Background Material and Data on Programs Within the Jurisdiction of the Committee on Ways and Means* (Washington, DC: U.S. Government Printing Office, 1998), pp. 950–988.

26. Frank Ullman, Brian Bruen, and John Holahan, "The State Children's Health Insurance Program: A Look at the Numbers" (Washington, DC: Urban Institute, March 1, 1998).

27. "Federal Funds Left on the Table," *Fiscal Notes* (newsletter of the Texas Comptroller's office), March 2004, p. 4.

28. Dianne White Delisi, "Assets Test for CHIP Won't Hurt Texas' Neediest Children," *Austin American-Statesman,* April 2, 2004, p. A19.

29. Ian Hill and Amy Westpfahl Lutzky, "Is There a Hole in the Bucket?" Occasional Paper 67 (Washington, DC: Urban Institute, May 16, 2003), retrieved April 10, 2004, from http://www.urban.org

30. "Incremental Approaches to Extend Coverage Are Insufficient," Institute of Medicine of the National Academies, retrieved April 8, 2004, from http://www.iom.edu/uninsured

31. National Center for Chronic Disease Prevention and Health Promotion, "Preventive Health and Health Services Block Grant," National allocation of funds by Healthy People 2000/2010 health problem, retrieved March 30, 2004, from http://www.cdc.gov/nccdphp/blockgrant/hp2010.htm

32. U.S. Census Bureau, *Statistical Abstract of the United States: 2000* (Washington, DC: U.S. Government Printing Office, 2000), Table No. 211, p. 135; retrieved March 30, 2004, from http://www.census.gov

33. Committee on Ways and Means, U.S House of Representatives, *2004 Green Book,* Appendix B, p. B-19.

34. Centers for Medicare and Medicaid Services, "Medicare Data for Calendar Year 2003," Table 1.C1, retrieved April 10, 2004, from http://www.cms.hhs.gov

35. John Hendren (Associated Press), "'Medigap' Rates Vary Widely by State," *Austin American-Statesman,* July 8, 1997, p. D3.

36. The new law is nearly 700 pages long. A useful summary is provided in AARP, *Medicare Changes That Could Affect You,* retrieved April 1, 2004, from http://www.aarp.org; see also the website of the Centers for Medicare and Medicaid Services, http://www.cms.hhs.gov

37. Brian Biles, Lauren Hersch Nicolas, and Barbara S. Cooper, "The Cost of Privatization: Extra Payments to Medicare Advantage Plans," Issue Brief (New York: Commonwealth Fund, May 2004), retrieved July 23, 2004, from http://www.cmwf.org/media/releases/biles750_release05202004.asp

38. California Seniors and Prescription Drugs" (Menlo Park, CA: Kaiser Family Foundation, November 2002), retrieved April 13, 2004, from http://www.kff.org

39. "Pricey Drug Plans Offer Seniors Little Relief," *USA Today,* July 19, 2002, p. 12A.

40. Committee on Ways and Means, U.S. House of Representatives, *2004 Green Book,* pp. B15–16.

41. "Medicare Discount Card Worth It?" Kron 4, July 23, 2004, retrieved July 23, 2004, from http://www.kron.com/global/story.asp?S=1910245=nav=5D7vNZv4

42. David S. Broder *(The Washington Post),* "AARP's Reputation Rests with Outcome of Medicare Plan," *Austin American-Statesman,* March 19, 2004, p. A15.

43. "AARP to Reap Huge Profits from Flawed Medicare Drug Bill" (Chicago: Physicians for a National Health Program, November 26, 2003), retrieved April 12, 2004, from http://www.pnhp.org/news/2003/november/aarp_to_reap_huge_pr.php

44. Coalition of Wisconsin Aging Groups, "The Medicare Prescription Drug and Modernization Act: The Good, the Bad, and the Ugly," retrieved March 27, 2004, from http://www.cwag.org

45. "Republicans Block Effort to Force Testimony on Medicare Dispute," *Austin American-Statesman,* April 2, 2004, p. A16.

46. General Accounting Office, "Department of Health and Human Services, Centers for Medicare and Medicaid Services—Video News Releases," B-302710, May 19, 2004, retrieved July 23, 2004, from http://www.gao.gov/decisions/appro/302710.htm

47. "1994 National Long-term Care Survey," cited in U.S. House of Representatives, Committee on Ways and Means, *2004 Green Book,* Appendix B, pp. B-29–B-30.

48. "The Cost of Nursing Home Care"; retrieved April 18, 2004, from http://www.nursinghomereports.com/paying_for_care/cost_of_care.htm

49. Information on long-term care insurance relies on U.S. House of Representatives, Committee on Ways and Means, *2004 Green Book,* Appendix B, pp. B-40–B-44.

50. Health Insurance Association of America, cited in U.S. House of Representatives, Committee on Ways and Means, *2004 Green Book,* Appendix B, pp. B-40–B-42.

51. American Health Care Association, cited in U.S House of Representatives, *2004 Green Book,* p. B-35.

52. The remainder of this paragraph relies on William G. Weissert, Cynthia Matthews Cready, and James E. Pawelak, "The Past and Future of Home- and Community-Based Long-Term Care," *Milbank Quarterly,* Vol. 66, No. 2, 1988, pp. 309–386.

53. This paragraph relies on Committee on Ways and Means, U.S. House of Representatives, *2004 Green Book,* Appendix B, pp. B-27–B-29.

54. For information on these alternative living and care arrangements, see the websites of the AARP (http://www.arp.org) and ThirdAge (http://www.thirdage.com).

55. Paul Starr, "Health Care for the Poor: The Past Twenty Years," in Sheldon H. Danzinger and Daniel H. Weinberg, Eds., *Fighting Poverty: What Works and What Doesn't* (Cambridge, MA: Harvard University Press, 1986), pp. 106–137.

56. *OECD in Figures, 2003 Edition, Statistics on Member Countries* (Paris: Organization for Economic Cooperation and Development, September 2003).

57. "NPR/Kaiser/Kennedy School Poll on Health Care," June 5, 2002, retrieved April 12, 2004, from http://www.npr.org/news/specials/healthcarepoll

58. Jean Chatzky, "Cover Yourself," *Time,* April 21, 2003, p. 80.

59. Information from the Foster-Higgins consulting firm reported in Patricia Lamiell, "Health Benefit Costs Are Reported Up 8%," *Austin American-Statesman,* February 15, 1994, p. E1; see also Jon Gabel and Derek Liston, *Trends in Health Insurance: HMOs Experience Lower Rates of Increase than Other Plans* (Washington, DC: KPMG Peat Marwick, December 1993); Drew E. Altman and Larry Levitt, "The Sad History of Health Care Cost Containment As Told in One Chart," *Health Affairs,* January 23, 2002, retrieved April 18, 2004, from http://www.healthaffairs.org

60. U.S Bureau of the Census, *Statistical Abstract of the United States:* 1996 (Washington, DC: Superintendent of Documents, 1996), Table No. 746, p. 484.

61. U.S. Bureau of the Census, *Statistical Abstract of the United States, 2003,* Table No. 713, p. 475, retrieved April 18, 2004, from http://www.census.gov/statab/www/

62. *Employer Health Benefits, 2003 Summary of Findings* (Menlo Park, CA: Kaiser Family Foundation and Health Research and Educational Trust), retrieved April 12, 2004, from http://www.kff.org

63. Henry J. Aaron, "The Unsurprising Surprise of Renewed Health Care Cost Inflation," *Health Affairs,* January 23, 2002, retrieved April 18, 2004, from http://www.healthaffairs.org

64. *Ibid.*

65. Altman and Levitt, "The Sad History of Health Care Cost Containment."

66. Jack Hadley and John Holahan, "Covering the Uninsured: How Much Would It Cost?," *Health Affairs, Web Exclusive,* June 4, 2003, retrieved April 18, 2004, from http://www.healthaffairs.org

67. Starr, "Health Care for the Poor," pp. 109–110.

68. Cathy A. Cowan and Bradley R. Braden, "Business, Households, and Government: Health Care Spending, 1995," *Health Care Financing Review,* Vol. 18, No. 3, 1997, pp. 195–206.

69. Joshua M. Wiener and David G. Stevenson, *Long-Term Care for the Elderly and State Health Policy* (Washington, DC: Urban Institute, 1997).

70. Carole Fleck, "New Nursing Home Rules Stir Debate," *AARP Bulletin,* November 2003, p. 5; Richard Pérez-Peña, "Overwhelmed and Understaffed, Nursing Home Workers Vent Anger," *New York Times,* June 8, 2003, retrieved June 14, 2003, from http://www.nytimes.com

71. David Liska, *Medicaid: Overview of a Complex Program* (Washington, DC: Urban Institute, May 1997).

72. The remainder of this paragraph relies on Committee on Ways and Means, *2004 Green Book,* Appendix D—Medicare Payment Policies, p. D-2.

73. "2003 Annual Employer Health Benefits Survey" (Menlo Park, CA: Kaiser Family Foundation and Health Research and Educational Trust, September 9, 2003), retrieved July 25, 2004, from http://www.kff.org/insurance/ehbs2003-abstract.cfm

74. The remainder of this paragraph relies on U.S. House of Representatives, Committee on Ways and Means, *2004 Green Book,* Appendix E: "Medicare + Choice," retrieved April 1, 2004, from http://waysandmeans.house.gov/Documents.asp?section = 813

75. *Ibid.,* p. E5.

76. George J. Church, "Backlash against HMOs," *Time,* April 14, 1997, p. 37.

77. Robert Pear, "Drug Industry Is Told to Stop Gifts to Doctors," *New York Times,* October 1, 2002.

78. Patricia Barry, "Why Drugs Cost Less Up North," *AARP Bulletin,* June 2003, pp. 8, 10.

79. Information on Canada's price controls relies on *ibid.*

80. *Ibid.*

81. Patricia Barry, "More Americans Go North for Drugs," *AARP Bulletin,* April 2003, pp. 3–4, 6.

82. *Ibid.*

83. Much of this paragraph relies on Patricia Barry, "Crackdown in Canada," *AARP Bulletin,* February 2004, p. 18.

84. "Court Orders Rx Depot to Close," Consumer Affairs.Com, November 7, 2003, retrieved April 19, 2004, from http://www.consumeraffairs.com/news03/rx_depot.html

85. "Maine Launches Maine Rx Plus," Maine Rx Express, retrieved April 14, 2004, from http://www.rxmaine.com/; Charles Lane, "Justices Grapple with Maine Drug Plan," *Austin American-Statesman,* January 23, 2003, p. A6; Lyle Denniston, "Maine Gets Court's OK for Drug Plan," *Austin American-Statesman,* May 20, 2003, p. A3.

86. George Anders, "Canada Hospitals Provide Care as Good as in U.S. at Lower Costs, Studies Show," *Wall Street Journal,* March 18, 1993, p. B5.

87. "Incremental Approaches to Extend Coverage Are Insufficient," Institute of Medicine of the National Academies, retrieved April 8, 2004, from http://www.iom.edu/uninsured

88. "NPR/Kaiser/Kennedy School Poll on Health Care," June 5, 2002, retrieved April 12, 2004, from http://www.npr.org/news/specials/healthcarepoll

89. "Incremental Approaches to Extend Coverage Are Insufficient."

90. "Can Anything Resist Hillary Clinton? Time Will Tell," *New York Times,* October 3, 1993, Section 3, p. 2; Robert Pear, "Insurers End Opposition to Health Reform," *Austin American-Statesman,* December 3, 1992, pp. A1, 17.

91. The remainder of this paragraph relies on AcademyHealth, *State of the States: Cultivating Hope in Rough Terrain* (Princeton, NJ: Robert Wood Johnson Foundation, January 2004), p. 11.

92. "TennCare Strategy," retrieved July 27, 2004, from http://www.sitemason.com/page/c52CpW; "Bresden Outlines 'Last Chance' Strategy to Save TennCare," News Release, Governor's Communications Office, retrieved February 17, 2004, from http://www.sitemason.com/page/c52CpW; TennCare Legislation Overview, April 5, 2004, retrieved July 27, 2004, from http://www.tnpharm.org/TNCRLEGISLATIVE_POWER_POINT.pdf

93. AcademyHealth, *State of the States.*

94. Maine Office of Health Policy and Finance, "Summary: Dirigo Health," retrieved July 27, 2004, from http://www.maine.gov/governor/baldacci/healthpolicy/what_is_dirigo_health/summary.htm

95. AcademyHealth, *State of the States.*

96. Glenn Adams, "Maine Universal Health Plan Takes Shape," *Common Dreams News Center,* December 27, 2003, retrieved April 13, 2004, from http://www.commondreams.org/headlines03/1227-05.htm; John Carroll, "Shining Light or Shipwreck," *Managed Care Magazine,* October 2003, retrieved April 13, 2004, from http://www.managedcaremag.comarchives/0310/0310.maine.html

97. Families USA, "Key Facts on Providing Health Insurance for Newly Unemployed Workers," *Health Policy Memo,* October 15, 2001, retrieved April 12, 2004, from http://www.familiesusa.org

98. See Margaret O. Kirk *(New York Times),* "A New Trend in Healthcare," *Austin American-Statesman,* February 23, 1997, p. J4; National Association of Social Workers, "Government Relations Update" (Washington, DC: NASW, October 4, 1996).

99. Rosalie A. Kane and Mary Olsen Baker, *Managed Care Issues and Themes: What Next for the Aging Network?* (Minneapolis: University of Minnesota and National Academy for State Health Policy, July 1996); Robert L. Mollica and Trish Riley, *Managed Care, Medicaid and the Elderly: Five State Case Studies* (Minneapolis: University of Minnesota and National Academy for State Health Policy, 1996).

100. Department of Health and Human Services, "Fact Sheet: Protecting the Privacy of Patients' Health Information," April 14, 2003, retrieved April 12, 2004, from http://www.hhs.gov/news/facts/privacy.html

101. Deborah C. Peel, "Reclaim Your Right to Medical Privacy," *Austin American-Statesman,* April 16, 2003, p. A19.

102. Henry Glick, Marie E. Cowart, and J. Donald Smith, "Advance Medical Directives in Hospitals and Nursing Homes: Limited Success for the Federal Patient Self-Determination Act," *Viewpoints on Aging,* newsletter of the Pepper Institute on Aging and Public Policy, Vol. 2, September 1995, Florida State University.

103. Sarah Foster, "Life and Death Tug of War: Florida Governor, Lawmakers Defend 'Terri's Law,'" *WorldNetDaily,* November 12, 2003, retrieved March 28, 2004, from http://www.worldnetdaily.com/news/article.asp?ARTICLE_ID = 35559

104. Nedd Kareiva, "Schindler's Wish List," *Washington Dispatch,* October 15, 2003, retrieved March 28, 2004, from http://www.washingtondispatch.com/cgi-bin/artman/exec/view.cgi/24/6866

105. "A joint statement on the Terri Schindler-Schiavo Case from the Arc of the United States, UCP [United Cerebral Palsy], and AAPD [American Association of People with Disabilties]," October 2003, retrieved March 28, 2004, from http://www.aapd.com/cods/terrisignon.html; "Florida Supreme Court Imposes Death Penalty for the Crime of Disability," *Mouth: Voice of the Disability Nation,* September 2003, retrieved September 25, 2004, from http://www.mouthmag.com/news.htm

106. J. M. Luce, "Making Decisions about the Forgoing of Life-Sustaining Therapy," *American Journal of Respiratory and Critical Care Medicine,* Vol. 156, No. 6, 1997, pp. 1715–1718; quote from p. 1715.

107. "Hospitals Reserve the Right to Refuse Service," *Mouth: Voice of the Disability Nation,* September 2003, retrieved September 25, 2004, from http://www.mouthmag.com/news.htm

108. Luce, "Making Decisions about the Forgoing of Life-Sustaining Therapy."

109. "Hospitals Reserve the Right to Refuse Service"; Wesley J. Smith, "'Doc Knows Best,'" *National Review Online,* January 6, 2003, retrieved March 28, 2004, from http://www.nationalreview.com/comment/comment-smith010603.asp

110. Arlene Orhon Jech, "Hard Choices: Ethics Committees Grapple with Complex Issues," *Health Week,* Vol. 5, No. 18, 2003, pp. 20–21.

111. Alan L. Otten, "Fateful Decision: In the Netherlands, the Very Ill Have Option of Euthanasia," *Wall Street Journal,* August 21, 1987, pp. 1, 6; Carol J. Williams, "Netherlands Legalizes Euthanasia," *Austin American-Statesman,* April 11, 2001, p. A5.

112. Tamara Jones, "Dutch Set Euthanasia Guidelines," *Austin American-Statesman,* February 10, 1993, p. A12; on the case of the Netherlands and on assisted suicide and euthanasia in general, see Michael M. Uhlmann, Ed., *Last Rights? Assisted Suicide and Euthanasia Debated* (Washington, DC: Ethics and Public Policy Center, 1998).

113. End-of-Life Choices, retrieved March 28, 2004, from http://www.endoflifechoices.org; see also Derek Humphry, *Final Exit* (New York: Dell, 1991).

114. Council on Ethical and Judicial Affairs, American Medical Association, "Medical Futility in End-of-Life Care, Report of the Council on Ethical and Judicial Affairs," *Journal of the American Medical Association,* Vol. 281, 1999, pp. 937–941.

CHAPTER

Changing Paradigms: The Poverty Wars

American confidence in government's ability to solve social problems was once so boundless that President Lyndon Johnson was moved to declare in 1964, "This administration today, here and now, declares unconditional war on poverty in America." And later, when signing the Economic Opportunity Act of 1964, he added, "Today for the first time in the history of the human race, a great nation is able to make and is willing to make a commitment to eradicate poverty among its people."[1] Ten years later, Congress abolished the Office of Economic Opportunity. Although poverty declined during the 1960s, many thought that the effects of the "war" itself had been minimal, and throughout the 1970s, 25 million people remained poor. The government had passed a law, created a new bureaucracy, and spent $25 billion dollars. But according to critics, nothing much had happened.

An especially scathing critique of the social welfare policies of the 1960s and 1970s is that they spawned more poverty (also see Chapter 3). The federal government was accused of creating additional misery through antipoverty programs that actually encouraged welfare dependency instead of self-sufficiency.[2] Today some of the programs, and just about all the enthusiasm, of the War on Poverty have gone by the wayside. Head Start, the Job Corps, and some other programs do continue. Other important programs that were not contained in the Economic Opportunity Act but were part of this era called the Great Society have grown in importance. In particular, it would be difficult to imagine U.S. social welfare policy without food stamps (see Chapter 7) and Medicaid and Medicare (see Chapter 8).

Nonetheless, as described in Chapter 3, the paradigm in the wars against poverty has changed. The New Deal of the 1930s, the first major war on poverty in the U.S., was a war of moderates with its centerpiece of social insurance and dabs of public assistance. The war on poverty of the 1960s and 1970s was waged by liberals. The war itself tried to employ a curative strategy with aid to depressed and disadvantaged communities and efforts to make people self-sufficient through work and education programs. There was also a vast expansion of public assistance. The strategy of the third major poverty war embedded in the 1996 federal welfare reform legislation is one of conservatives. It ups the ante on work requirements and cuts aid for failure to comply. This chapter looks at the victories, defeats, and stalemates of the poverty wars and discusses current strategies intended to reduce poverty in the twenty-first century.

THE CURATIVE STRATEGY

The War on Poverty of the 1960s was an attempt to apply a **curative** strategy to the problems of the poor. In contrast to the **preventive** strategy of social insurance, which compels people to save money to relieve economic problems that are likely to result from old age, death, disability, sickness, and unemployment, and in contrast to the **alleviative** strategy of public assistance, which attempts only to ease the hardships of poverty, the curative strategy stresses efforts to help the poor become self-supporting by bringing about changes in these individuals and in their environment. The curative strategy of the War on Poverty was supposed to break the cycle of poverty and allow economically disadvantaged Americans to move into the country's working classes and eventually its middle classes. The strategy was "rehabilitation and not relief." The Economic Opportunity Act of 1964, the centerpiece of the War on Poverty, was to "strike at the causes, not just the consequences, of poverty."

The first curative antipoverty policies originated under President John F. Kennedy. Kennedy had read socialist Michael Harrington's *The Other America*—a sensitive description of continuing poverty that most Americans did not notice (see also Chapter 3).[3] Kennedy, the Harvard-educated son of a multimillionaire business investor, was visibly shocked when, during his 1960 presidential campaign, he saw the wooden shacks of West Virginia's barren mountains. In 1958, Kennedy's economic advisor,

John Kenneth Galbraith, published another influential book, *The Affluent Society,* which called attention to poverty in the midst of a generally affluent society.[4] Galbraith distinguished between **case poverty** and **area poverty.** Case poverty was largely a product of some personal characteristic of the poor—old age, illiteracy, inadequate education, lack of job skills, poor health, race—which prevented them from participating in the nation's prosperity. Area poverty was a product of economic deficiency relating to a particular sector of the nation, such as West Virginia and much of the rest of Appalachia. "Pockets of poverty" or "depressed areas" developed because of technological change or a lack of industrialization—for instance, decline in the coal industry, the exhaustion of iron ore mines, and the squeezing out of small farmers from the agricultural market. Area poverty has also resulted from declines in the automobile, steel, and petroleum industries in regions that came to be called the country's "rust belt," and in deteriorated inner city neighborhoods as economic enterprise moved to the suburbs. Illustration 9.1 provides a history of approaches to address area poverty.

A significant approach to area poverty is community development corporations (CDCs). These locally controlled nonprofit organizations operate to revitalize decaying areas, both urban and rural. Most CDCs require that the majority of board members reside in the community. CDCs bring together the relevant actors and community stakeholders necessary to do things like renovate or build new housing, develop business and industry that can benefit area residents, and provide a range of social and economic services (e.g., credit unions). The nonpartisan Urban Institute indicates that CDCs may offer a more "comprehensive and coordinated" approach to the community than other organizations and describes CDCs as "an alternative (but not replacement) to public or for-profit development efforts."[5] An advantage of CDCs over government programs is that they may be able to more quickly mobilize relevant parties when opportunities arise. Urban Institute researchers have been studying CDCs, relying on a decade of research in 23 cities that received funding from the National Community Development Initiative, now called Living Cities: National Community Development Initiative (NCDI). The NCDI is a public–private consortium comprised of the U.S. Department of Housing and Urban Development, foundations, and corporations. The NCDI funded two organizations, the Local Initiatives Support Coalition (LISC) and the Enterprise Foundation, to be the intermediaries for its initiatives by providing technical support and financial assistance from NCDI to local CDCs. The researchers' assessment is that CDCs' operations generally improved during the 1990s. With respect to commercial or business development, the growth of CDC industries varied widely across the cities studied because of the differences in the CDCs' capabilities. One of the main areas in which community improvements occurred was housing. Some CDCs are struggling in areas where gentrification (replacement of low-priced housing with expensive housing) is occurring, because low-income residents are displaced.[6] There has also been study of CDCs that have folded. Among the sad stories is that of Eastside Community Investments, Inc. (ECI) in Indianapolis. ECI was founded in the 1970s, became very successful, but shut down in 2001.[7] ECI's demise has been attributed to various causes. CDCs

ILLUSTRATION 9.1

Four Approaches to Community Development

by John Foster-Bey

Community development probably began in the 1960s with the Ford Foundation's Gray Areas Programs and Mobilization for Youth, both of which became prototypes, or models, for the War on Poverty. At that time, the War on Poverty started what was called the community action approach, a new concept that ran into problems with the political establishments in most cities almost immediately. By the late 1960s, community action programs had evolved into the economic development model exemplified by community development corporations (CDCs).

Community development works to stem the resource leakage that can destroy the local economy by ensuring that businesses are controlled by local organizations. Community development organization (CDO) intervention also attempts to improve the community's social foundations. The Bedford-Stuyvesant Restoration Corporation is generally thought of as the first of these groups. Though they are funded by the government as well, funding from foundations is important, because it comes with fewer restrictions. Early CDCs were large, multifunctional organizations that employed many community people.

The first wave of CDOs were replaced in the 1980s by "lean and mean" groups, focused on one or two activities, such as housing and commercial real estate development. These groups abandoned the involvement in direct business activities and social development that characterized the older wave, because of the loss of federal support for their activities. Public support dwindled as the neighbor-

hoods of the CDCs continued to decline. To attain the support of business, quantitative documentation of the success of the CDCs was needed. So, in the early 1980s, the Ford Foundation tried to move the field forward by creating a national financial intermediary called the Local Initiative Support Corporation (LISC). LISC focused on providing financial capital and raising money from the for-profit sector and foundations. There are probably about three thousand CDCs nationally, mostly single-purpose entities, focusing primarily on brick and mortar projects.

The second major category in the field is community empowerment and organizing, which also has roots in the community action work early in the War on Poverty. It owes much of its current work to activists such as Saul Alinsky, and his Industrial Areas Foundation in Chicago. Their core belief is that people in poor places are poor because they lack the power to force the system to respond to their needs and concerns. The response, then, is to form organizations that will press for their interests with these powerful establishments. In this context, community organizing is both confrontational and consensus building or collaborative. Many CDCs actually started as this type of community organization. This part of the field is not well funded, with most support coming from small, socially progressive foundations, and from funding by church-based philanthropy, such as the Campaign for Human Development.

The third category is neighborhood-based social development, or human capital devel-

continued

ILLUSTRATION 9.1 *(continued)*

opment. The roots of these efforts are again the War on Poverty, but also the settlement house movement that began in the early part of this century. In this model, the poor must become acculturated to the values and norms of the mainstream in order to improve their skills and ability to succeed. Social services and social programs help to meet and address immediate needs and problems, but they also provide the opportunity to develop skills, attitudes, and values necessary for success. This strategy resulted in an array of programs delivered at the neighborhood level. Much of the funding for these programs comes from community and family foundations and from corporate giving, including the United Way.

The last category is an emerging one: the comprehensive, or community-building approach, a new interpretation of another War on Poverty strategy, Model Cities. Model Cities sought to collaborate and coordinate programs and sectors to encourage a multifrontal attack on poverty in particular poor places, and to coordinate a whole range of services to do that. This strategy emphasizes more collaboration and less confrontation. While many consider the Model Cities program to have failed from an operational and political point of view, the comprehensive approach grew out of a recognition that conditions in poor communities were not improving. This strategy represents a merging and synergy among the three strategies, and a tailoring of them to local needs.

Community development is still struggling to achieve its promise. A major area of concern is whether revitalizing poor places is still relevant. With population growing much more rapidly outside than inside center cities, it may not be possible to revitalize poor communities by focusing on place-based strategies alone. We have begun to explore approaches that are less dependent on local, or even metropolitan, approaches.

William Julius Wilson, now at Harvard, has talked about healthy communities as being places that are organized around work and production, a sharp contrast to the conditions in most poor places now. The only way to get rid of poor places and poverty is to ensure that poor people become fully functioning participants in the mainstream economy. The economy is not neighborhood-based. Some of us have been exploring ways to increase access for poor job seekers to the entry-level jobs being created in many suburbs, in a process known as reverse commuting, or worker mobility. Funders also have a growing interest in finding ways to connect employment programs for the poor to private employers. We're also beginning to look at ways to more equitably distribute low-income housing around metropolitan regions, rather than concentrating it in poor neighborhoods. Most funders continue to support traditional CDCs, although I do think there's a shift toward a comprehensive, or community-building approach. Foundations are only beginning to examine whether these two approaches may be in conflict, or whether there may be a way of creating a more synergistic strategy.

If community development is not placed within a regional or metropolitan framework, it will only achieve modest results at best. If the focus on the needs and concerns of the poor, which should be the hallmark of a good community development approach, is not integrated into regional approaches, the potential benefits of regionalism will continue to elude the poor, and the conditions in the core cities will only get worse.

Source: Excerpted from Institute on Race and Poverty, "Linking Regional and Local Strategies to Create Healthy Communities," Conference April 12–13, 1996. Reprinted with permission. John A. Foster-Bey.

are complex business operations that require diversified funding, strong business management, and financial accountability as well as a concern for the community. Other models like the Neighborhood Preservation Initiative, funded by the Pew Charitable Trusts, focus on middle- to working-class neighborhoods to prevent them from declining.[8]

The initial forays in the War on Poverty begun in the Kennedy administration included the fight against area poverty. The Area Redevelopment Act of 1961, for example, authorized federal grants and loans to governments and businesses in designated "depressed areas" to promote economic activity. This program was later revised in the Public Works and Economic Development Act of 1965. Over the years, this legislation has been criticized as a trickle-down approach to alleviating poverty, with most benefits going to business and not the poor. Republicans have also called it a pork barrel program to aid Democrats in getting reelected. The Economic Development Administration (EDA), part of the U.S. Department of Commerce, defends its work, saying that its "programs pay for themselves by helping create jobs and generating tax revenues in distressed communities."[9] President Reagan tried to abolish the EDA, and the agency's annual appropriations continue to dwindle under the George W. Bush administration. A much larger program, the Community Development Block Grant (CDBG), begun in 1974, also provides funds to local Community Development Corporations to aid depressed areas with economic development and a variety of other neighborhood revitalization activities.[10] The CDBG, administered by the Department of Housing and Urban Development, has come under the same criticisms as the EDA for poor targeting. The George W. Bush administration has said that while the CDBG was "designed to boost low-income communities, its effectiveness is diluted by the inclusion of some of the richest cites in the country."[11] CDBG funding has also declined. The EDA and CDBG are just two federal efforts to address area poverty.

The fight against case poverty began with the Manpower Development and Training Act (MDTA) of 1962—the first large-scale, federally funded job training program. Eventually, MDTA was absorbed into the Comprehensive Employment and Training Act of 1973 and later into the Reagan administration's Job Training Partnership Act of 1982. Today, these program fall under the Workforce Investment Act, discussed later in this chapter.

LBJ AND THE ECONOMIC OPPORTUNITY ACT

When Lyndon B. Johnson assumed the presidency in 1963 after the assassination of President Kennedy, he saw an opportunity to distinguish his administration and to carry forward the traditions of Franklin D. Roosevelt. Johnson, a former public school teacher, believed that government work and training efforts, particularly those directed at youth, could break the cycle of poverty by giving people the basic skills to improve their employability and make them self-sufficient adults. In order to do this, he championed the Economic Opportunity Act.

The multitude of programs created by the Economic Opportunity Act were to be coordinated in Washington by a new, independent federal bureaucracy—the Office of Economic Opportunity (OEO). OEO was given money and authority to support varied and highly experimental techniques for combating poverty in both urban and rural communities. As evidence of its priority, OEO's first director was Sargent Shriver, brother-in-law of the late President Kennedy and later Democratic vice-presidential candidate with George McGovern in 1972. OEO was encouraged to bypass local and state governments and to establish new programs throughout the nation, with the poor participating in their governance. OEO was generally not given authority to make direct, cash grants to the poor as relief or public assistance. Most OEO programs were aimed, whether accurately or inaccurately, at curing the causes of poverty rather than alleviating its symptoms.

Community Action

The core of the Economic Opportunity Act was grassroots **community action programs** to be carried on at the local level by public or private nonprofit agencies, with federal financial assistance. Communities were urged to form community action agencies composed of representatives of government, private organizations, and, most importantly, the poor themselves. OEO was originally intended to support antipoverty programs devised by the local community action agency. Projects could include literacy training, health services, legal aid, neighborhood service centers, vocational training, childhood development activities, or other innovative ideas. The act also envisioned that the community action agencies would help organize poor people so that they could become participating members of the community and could avail themselves of the many programs designed to serve them. Finally, the act attempted to coordinate federal and state programs for the poor in each community.

Community action programs were to be "developed, conducted, and administered with the maximum feasible participation of the residents of the areas and members of the groups served." This was perhaps the most controversial phrase in the act. The more militant members of the OEO administration frequently cited this phrase as authority to "mobilize" the poor "to have immediate and irreversible impact on their communities." This language implied that the poor were to be organized as a political force by government antipoverty warriors using federal funds. Needless to say, neither Congress nor the Johnson administration really intended to create rival political organizations that would compete for power with local governments.

The typical community action agency was governed by a board consisting of public officials (perhaps the mayor, a county commissioner, a school board member, and a public health officer), prominent public citizens (from business, labor, civil rights, religious, and civic affairs organizations), and representatives of the poor (in some cases selected in agency-sponsored elections, but more often hand-picked by ministers, social workers, civil rights leaders, and other prominent community figures). A staff was hired, including a full-time director, paid from an OEO grant. A target area was defined—a low-income area of the county or the ghetto of a city. Neighborhood centers were established in the target area, perhaps with counselors, employment assistance, a recreation hall, a child care center, and a health clinic. Staff also assisted the poor in their contacts with the school system, the welfare department, employment agencies, the public housing authority, and so on. Frequently, the centers and the antipoverty workers who staffed them acted as advocates for the poor and as intermediaries between the poor and public agencies.

Youth Education

Community action agencies also devised specific antipoverty projects for submission to OEO's Washington offices for funding. The most popular of these projects was Operation Head Start. Preschool children from poor families were given six to eight weeks of special summer preparation before entering kindergarten or first grade. The idea was to give these children a "head start" on formal schooling. Congress (and the public) was favorably disposed toward this program and favored it in later OEO budget appropriations. In addition to education, Head Start emphasized social skills, nutrition, health and mental health services, and parental participation. A program called Follow Through was added in 1967 to continue comprehensive Head Start efforts for poor children through the third grade, and Upward Bound provided educational counseling.

Other youth-oriented OEO programs also attempted to break the cycle of poverty at an early age. The Job Corps was designed to provide education, vocational training, and work experience in rural conservation camps for unemployable youth. Job Corps trainees were to be "hard core" unemployables who could benefit from training away from their home environment—breaking habits and associations that were obstacles to employment while learning reading, arithmetic, and self-health care, as well as auto mechanics, clerical work, and other skills. The Neighborhood Youth Corps was designed to provide work, counseling, and on-the-job training for young people in or out of school who were living at home. The Neighborhood Youth Corps was to serve young people who were more employable than those expected in the Job Corps. The Work-Study program helped students from low-income families remain in high school or college by providing them with federally paid, part-time employment in conjunction with cooperating public or private agencies.

Legal Services

Still another antipoverty project was legal services to assist the poor with rent disputes, contracts, welfare rules, minor police actions, housing regulations, and so on. The idea was that the poor seldom have access to legal counsel and are frequently taken advantage of because they do not know their rights. Antipoverty lawyers using federal funds have brought suits against city welfare departments, housing authorities, public health agencies, and other government bodies. Congress amended the Economic Opportunity Act in 1967 to ensure that funds would not be used to assist defendants in criminal cases (public defenders assist poor clients in criminal cases).

In order to protect legal services from political pressure, President Nixon proposed making it an independent corporation. In 1974, a separate Legal Services Corporation (LSC) was established, financed with federal tax dollars and governed by an eleven-member board (no more than six members may be from the same political party). LSC programs also receive funding from other public and private sources. Despite efforts to insulate it, the LSC became a political hot potato. Conservatives argued that it is ridiculous to fund a government agency that sues other government agencies. They claimed that the LSC had gotten into issues well beyond its appropriate purview.[12] Particularly controversial were the LSC's "lobbying" activities and its involvement in class action suits (on behalf of groups of people). Defenders counter with claims that the poor deserve legal representation and that most LSC cases involve survival issues (e.g., child support, family violence, divorce, separation, eviction, housing discrimination, income maintenance, consumer finance, employment, health, safety, education, farm foreclosures). LSC attorneys are paid very modest salaries; they serve clients at a fraction of the cost of private attorneys; and they utilize the services of private attorneys who assist *pro bono*. Defenders also note that the country's private attorneys have failed to provide anywhere near the free legal services needed by those who have no access to legal assistance.

Congressional authorization for the LSC expired in 1980, but annual Congressional appropriations have kept the agency alive. Controversy over the LSC reached a boiling point during the Reagan administration.[13] None of President Reagan's 25 appointments to the LSC board was approved by Congress, because all were viewed as hostile to the agency's mission. In order to circumvent the approval process, Reagan made 19 board appointments while the Senate was in recess. The Senate retaliated by limiting the board's power to cut funds to LSC programs until such time as it confirmed the president's nominees. President George H. W. Bush continued to make recess appointments.

The Legal Services Act was amended in 1977 to prohibit assistance involving non-therapeutic abortions and school desegregation and to limit lobbying, class action suits, and political activities.[14] Since 1991 the LSC has also been prohibited from using federal funds in any cases involving abortions or undocumented immigrants. LSC advocates contended that since these restrictions are not contained in the Legal Services Act itself, nonfederal funds the agency receives could be used for these activities. An additional 19 restrictions on LSC activities were added in 1996, including a ban on participation in any class action suits and in partisan activities related to redistricting.[15] LSC lawyers are prohibited from pursuing cases involving these 19 restrictions even if nonfederal funds are used. By 1996, LSC lawyers had already restricted their class action work. In that same year, a New York state judge ruled it unconstitutional for Congress to tell the LSC how to spend nonfederal funds. The ruling has had little effect.

Another challenge to the LSC has been its use of interest on lawyers' trust accounts (IOLTA). This is the interest accrued on the monies that attorneys hold in trust for clients (like real estate escrow). Some contend that it is taking money illegally from clients, but each client's funds are so little or held for such a short period that they would have accrued little if any interest. Pooling the funds allows for substantial sums to be earned, and banks generally waive their fees on the accounts. Almost all the states raise money for legal services using this method. In 2003, the Supreme Court ended years of debate on the issue by ruling that the use of these funds is legal.

The presidency of Bill Clinton must have been some comfort to the LSC. Both Clinton and his wife, Hillary Rodham Clinton (now a U.S. senator), are lawyers, and she is a past chair of the LSC board. But the 1996 restrictions on LSC activities prevailed. Apparently the LSC is playing by the rules. Its 2000–2001 annual report stresses that it is "demonstrating its commitment to enforce the will of Congress."[16] Today, the LSC is on stronger footing. President George W. Bush's support for legal services has helped the agency reverse a series of previous budget cuts.

More Office of Economic Opportunity Projects

Other antipoverty projects originated under the OEO were family-planning programs (advice and devices to facilitate family planning by the poor), homemaker services (advice and services on how to stretch low family budgets), and additional job training programs (such as special outreach to bring the hard-core unemployed into established workforce programs). There were also programs to help small businesses and to provide direct economic assistance to residents of rural areas. Finally, Volunteers in Service to America (VISTA), which continues today, was modeled after the popular Peace Corps. VISTA volunteers work in domestic, poverty-impacted areas rather than in foreign countries. Many of the volunteers are young people who want to serve their country.

The Great Society

The Economic Opportunity Act established many programs, but the act was only a portion of the Great Society. President Johnson's plan included a number of other programs. Among the most important are

- *The Elementary and Secondary Education Act of 1965.* This was the first major, general federal aid-to-education program. It included federal funds to "poverty-impacted" school districts and became the largest source of federal aid to education. The act continues today under its current version, the No Child Left Behind Act of 2001.

- *The Food Stamp Program.* This nutrition program was an important step in the development of major in-kind benefit programs. It remains a major source of relief to a broad cross-section of poor people (see Chapter 7).

- *Medicare.* This health insurance program was created as an amendment to the Social Security Act. It covers virtually all the aged in the United States, as well as many younger former workers with long-term disabilities (see Chapter 8).

- *Medicaid.* This amendment to the Social Security Act is still the major federal health care program for certain groups of poor people (see Chapter 8).

♦ *Job Training.* This array of programs expanded the Manpower Development and Training Act and has evolved into other job and training programs. Its current version is the Workforce Investment Act.

♦ *The Public Works and Economic Development Act of 1965 and the Appalachian Regional Development Act of 1965.* These efforts continue to encourage economic development in distressed areas.

POLITICS OVERTAKES THE WAR ON POVERTY

The reasons for the OEO's demise are complex. OEO programs were often the scene of great confusion. Personnel were young, middle-class, inexperienced, and idealistic, and there was a high turnover among administrators. Aside from Head Start, there were no clear-cut program direction for most community action agencies. Many of the poor believed that the program was going to provide them with money; they never really understood or accepted that community action agencies provided other services—community organization, outreach, counselling, training, and similar assistance. Many community action agencies duplicated, and even competed with, existing welfare and social service agencies. Some community action agencies organized the poor to challenge local government agencies. As a result, more than a few local governments called on the Johnson administration and Congress to curb community action agencies that were using federal funds to "undermine" existing programs and organizations. There were frequent charges of mismanagement and corruption, particularly at the local level. Some community action agencies became entangled in the politics of race; some big-city agencies were charged with excluding whites; and in some rural areas, whites believed that poverty agencies were "for blacks only."

Perhaps the failures of the War on Poverty can be explained by lack of knowledge about how to *cure* poverty. In retrospect, it seems naive to believe that local agencies could have found their own cures for eliminating or even reducing poverty. OEO became an unpopular stepchild of the Johnson administration even before LBJ left office, so the demise of the OEO programs cannot be attributed to political partisanship—that is, to the election of a Republican administration under Richard Nixon. Nor can the demise of the poverty program be attributed to the Vietnam War—since both "wars" were escalated and later de-escalated at the same time. The Nixon administration reorganized the OEO in 1973, transferring most of its programs to other government agencies. The Ford administration abolished the OEO in 1974, turning its remaining programs over to other agencies. Today, community action agencies around the country receive assistance through the Community Services Block Grant (CSBG), established in 1981 and currently administered by the Administration on Children and Families of the Department of Health and Human Services. Community action agencies continue to offer a variety of antipoverty, social, health, and related services. Whether one believes that the War on Poverty was more of a defeat or more of a victory, many other programs borne of the Great Society era, like Medicaid, Food Stamps, and Head Start, continue to serve millions of poor and low-income Americans.[17]

It has been argued that the War on Poverty itself was never funded at a level that would make a substantial impact. OEO funds were spread over hundreds of communities. Such relatively small amounts could never offset the numerous, deep-seated causes of deprivation. The War on Poverty raised the expectations of the poor, but it never tried to cope with poverty on a scale comparable to the size of the problem. Often the outcome was only to increase frustration.

In an obvious reference to public policies affecting the poor and blacks in America, in 1968, Aaron Wildavsky wrote,

> *A recipe for violence: Promise a lot; deliver a little. Lead people to believe they will be much better off, but let there be no dramatic improvement. Try a variety of small programs, each interesting but marginal in impact and severely underfinanced. Avoid any attempted solution remotely comparable in size to the dimensions of the problem you are trying to solve. Have middle-class civil servants hire upper-class student radicals to use lower-class Negroes as a battering ram against the existing local political systems; then complain that people are going around disrupting things and chastise local politicians for not cooperating with those out to do them in. Get some poor people involved in local decision-making, only to discover that there is not enough at stake to be worth bothering about. Feel guilty about what has happened to black people; tell them you are surprised they have not revolted before; express shock and dismay when they follow your advice. Go in for a little force, just enough to anger, not enough to discourage. Feel guilty again; say you are surprised that worse has not happened. Alternate with a little suppression. Mix well, apply a match, and run.[18]*

The quote also speaks to more recent events such as the 1992 Los Angeles riots that erupted following the acquittal of white police officers in the beating of Rodney King, an African American stopped for speeding. The rioting renewed the verbiage about a return to community and a revitalization of communities that sounds much like the ideas that the creators of the Economic Opportunity Act envisioned. Though as one commentator noted in the wake of the 1992 riots, many middle-class Americans were more concerned about restoring law and order than were with "coming up with money for the urban poor."[19]

WHY HASN'T HEAD START "CURED" POVERTY?

When the Economic Opportunity Act was first authorized, some local officials balked at giving poor people a substantial role in the programs and refused to participate. Within one year, the Johnson administration and the Washington Office of Economic Opportunity decided that Head Start programs were the most desirable antipoverty projects and could reduce opposition to participation.[20] OEO earmarked a substantial portion of funds for Head Start programs. Helping to prepare disadvantaged children for school was certainly more appealing to the middle classes than programs that provided free legal aid for the poor, helped them get on welfare rolls, or organized them to fight city hall. Nearly all the nation's community action agencies operated a Head Start program, and by the late 1960s over one-half million children were enrolled throughout the country. Some communities expanded Head Start to full-time programs and also provided children with health services and improved daily diets. Head Start became OEO's showcase program.

Politics, Evaluation, and Head Start

Head Start programs were very popular, but were they really making a difference? Understandably, Head Start officials within the OEO were discomforted by the thought of a formal evaluation of their program. They argued that educational success was not the only goal of the program, that child health and nutrition and parental involvement were equally important goals. After much internal debate, Sargent Shriver ordered an evaluative study, and in 1968 a contract was given to Westinghouse Learning Corporation and Ohio University to perform the research.

When Richard Nixon assumed the presidency in January 1969, hints of negative findings had already filtered up to the White House. Nixon alluded to studies showing the long-term effects of Head Start as "extremely weak," prompting the press and Congress to call for the release of the Westinghouse Report. The report stated that the researchers had randomly selected 104 Head Start projects across the country.[21] Seventy percent were summer projects, and 30 percent were full-year projects. Children who had gone on from these programs to the first, second, and third grades in local schools (the experimental group) were matched on socioeconomic background with children in the same grades who had not attended Head Start (the control group). The children were given a series of standardized tests covering various aspects of cognitive and affective development. The parents of both groups of children were also matched on achievement and motivation.

The unhappy results can be summarized as follows: summer programs did not produce improvements in cognitive and affective development that could be detected into the early elementary grades, and full-year programs produced only marginally effective gains for certain subgroups, mainly black children in central cities. However, parents of Head Start children strongly approved of the program.[22]

Head Start officials reacted predictably in condemning the report. Liberals attacked the report believing that President Nixon would use it to justify major OEO cutbacks. The *New York Times* reported the findings under the headline "Head Start Report Held 'Full of Holes.'" It warned that "Congress or the Administration will seize the report's generally negative conclusions as an excuse to downgrade or discard the Head Start Program"[23] (not unreasonable in light of the findings, but politically unacceptable to the liberal community). Academicians moved to the defense of the War on Poverty by attacking methodological aspects of the study. In short, scientific assessment of Head Start was drowned in a sea of political controversy.

Years Later

It is difficult for educators and the social welfare establishment to believe that education, especially intensive preschool education, does not have a lasting effect on the lives of children. The prestigious Carnegie Foundation decided to fund research in Ypsilanti, Michigan, at the Perry Preschool, that would follow disadvantaged youngsters from preschool to young adulthood. The study was conducted with a small sample consisting of 123 children whose scores on the well-known Stanford-Binet intelligence test put them at risk of school failure. Fifty-eight of these children (the experimental group) received a special Head Start-type education at ages 3 and 4 and continued to receive weekly visits during later schooling. The others (the control group) received no special educational help. Both groups came from low socioeconomic backgrounds; half their families were headed by a single parent, and half received welfare. Researchers have reported on the progress of this small, local sample through age 27.[24]

Initial results were disappointing. Most gains made by the children with preschool education disappeared by the time they had completed second grade (a phenomenon now called "fade out"[25]). As children in the experimental group progressed through grade school, junior high school, and high school, their grades were not better than those of the children in the control group, although they did score slightly higher (by about 8 percent) on reading, mathematics, and language achievement tests. More importantly, only 19 percent of those in the experimental group ended up in special education classes, compared to 39 percent of the control group. The former preschoolers also showed fewer delinquent tendencies and held more after-school jobs. The key to this success appeared to be a better attitude toward school and learning among those with preschool education. Finally, at age 27, compared to those who had not received the special preschool program, the female former preschoolers were more likely to have finished high school, less likely to have given birth out of wedlock, and more likely to be married and employed. The male former preschoolers had more years of marriage and earned more money. The former preschoolers also had fewer arrests and were more likely to have avoided welfare and to own their own homes. The researchers reported that the program reaped $7.16 for every dollar spent, four-fifths of it due to potential criminal justice and crime victim savings.

But even academics and researchers who support early childhood education programs like Head Start are concerned about naive acceptance of this sevenfold benefit because evaluations of model programs like the Perry Preschool Project (which spent far more per child than does the average Head Start program) indicate what *can* be achieved, not necessarily what *is* being achieved.[26] They also note that, since each program is locally managed, there is concern about the quality of some Head Start programs, that long-term benefits are far more modest than the public has been led to believe, and that much more innovation is needed to help current generations.

The Head Start children of today often have only one parent to support them, and they live in environments where substance abuse, poor education, violence, unemployment, and teen pregnancy are common. They also come from diverse cultures with various languages spoken in the home, providing additional challenges to the staff who operate programs.[27] As two people who have studied Head Start over the years stated:

> Head Start is not a panacea for poverty, and attempts to posture it as such will lead to an inevitable fall. Clearly, it will be unwise to strengthen our national investment in Project Head Start if this investment is not accompanied by the continuation, improvement, and expansion of the other services and institutions that affect Head Start children and families.[28]

Much more research than the widely cited Perry Preschool study has been conducted on early childhood education and other early childhood interventions. One meta-analysis of 35 experimental and quasi-experimental early childhood education studies gave these programs high marks in terms of effects on children's intelligence and academic achievement and personal and social problems.[29] Authors of another meta-analysis, this one of 13 state-funded preschool programs found more modest support for results, calling them "similar to evaluations of other large-scale preschool programs for low-income children, such as Head Start."[30] A synthesis of studies by the RAND Corporation considered evaluations of Head Start, Perry Preschool, Carolina Abecedarian, Elmira (New York) Prenatal/Early Infancy Project (PEIP), and several other promising models.[31] Abecedarian is an educational day care and preschool center program that begins shortly after the child is born with medical services provided at the center. Some children in Abecedarian received services that lasted through age 8 and included customized education and parental involvement in educational activities. In PEIP, mothers received visits by nurses from the time of their pregnancy until their child was 2 years old in order to improve pregnancy outcomes and parenting skills and provide referrals to social services. RAND concluded that early childhood interventions *can* help disadvantaged children "overcome the cognitive, emotional, and resource limitations" in their environments, but the number of methodologically rigorous studies is too small and the programs too diverse to make broad generalizations about what works and what doesn't. RAND notes that many questions remain, such as why programs work, whether to focus on parents, children, or both, and which children might be targeted to produce the greatest results. Many people have called for large-scale, national studies to provide more definitive answers to questions about early childhood education and other early interventions.

Leaving No Child Behind

Head Start was a part of President Ronald Reagan's safety net. President George H. W. Bush supported substantial increases for Head Start but stopped short of Congress's desire to increase funding to allow all eligible children to participate.[32] Head Start continued to grow under the Clinton administration. Head Start's growth was accompanied by additional programs like Early Start to aid the development of children up to age 3.

In 2004, $6.8 billion was appropriated for Head Start (up from $2.8 billion in 1993), and President George W. Bush proposed spending slightly more in 2005. In 2002, 912,000 children participated,[33] somewhat short of the one million goal that President Clinton had hoped to achieve.[34] Of the children participating, 33 percent were black, 30 percent were Hispanic, 28 percent were white, 3 percent were American Indian, 2 percent were Asian, and 1 percent were Hawaiian/Pacific Islander. About 13 percent of the children had physical, emotional, or learning disabilities. There were 49,800 Head Start classrooms with 198,000 paid staff and 1.4 million volunteers. Twenty-nine percent of the staff were parents of current or former Head Start children, as were many of the program's volunteers. The average Head Start cost per child was $6,934. Since its inception in 1965, Head Start has enrolled more than 21 million children.

Head Start funds have always been awarded directly by the federal government to the local agencies or school systems that operate them. Now President George W. Bush has proposed a demonstration in which eight states will be awarded grants to operate Head Start. Child advocates like Dr. Alvin Poussaint, professor of psychiatry at Harvard Medical School,[35] and organizations like the Children's Defense Fund and the Association for Childhood Education International are opposed to this devolution for fear that federal program standards will be diluted by stressing isolated academic skills rather than focusing on the children's full social development. According to the Pew Charitable Trusts, most states also provide some early education services, but 10 states account for three-quarters of the funding provided for this purpose.[36] Additional concerns were raised about turning programs over to states suffering from budget deficits, but under Bush's proposal states would have to promise not to spend less than they would otherwise provide for Head Start services. President Bush also wants to raise the educational requirements for Head Start teachers. He contends that a shortcoming of Head Start is that it has not been well coordinated with local school districts' expectations of children's readiness to learn. Research on the Chicago Child-Parent Center (CPC) *might* lead to that conclusion.[37]

Like Head Start, CPC is a comprehensive early childhood program. It began in 1967 through the Elementary and Secondary Education Act. CPC also differs from Head Start. It serves children longer—from age 3 to age 9. CPC is part of the regular school system, while Head Start programs are usually operated by community agencies. CPC's features reportedly provide greater stability and continuity as children transition from preschool to kindergarten to elementary school. CPC also has a more intense parent component.

Researchers have followed a group of 1,150 children who received CPC services and compared them with 389 children who did not receive CPC (since the students were not randomly assigned to the two groups, they are not a true control group). To compensate for the lack of a true control group, the researchers have statistically controlled for many factors, such as the children's gender and race, and their parents' education. In studies that have followed the children to age 14 (eighth grade), the CPC group outperformed the comparison group on reading and math achievement, although there was some fade out. Differences also favored the CPC group with regard to greater life skills, less grade retention, and less time spent in special education. Longer CPC participation was associated with better outcomes, especially when children participated for five or six years, which also mitigated fade out. Certain factors mediated the relationship or improved the pathways between CPC participation and educational outcomes that were consistent with the theories on which the program is based. One theory concerns cognitive (school) readiness—that CPC students enter school better prepared to learn. The other theory concerns parent involvement and support—that parental involvement early in their child's education will persist into the school years. However, the CPC children were still performing well below the national average for their grade, indicating the disadvantages that many of these low-income children face. CPC researchers agree with Head Start researchers that it will take more than even the best early childhood education and development programs to ensure children's success throughout life.

President George W. Bush's approach to improve education is his No Child Left Behind (NCLB) Act of 2001, which amended the Elementary and Secondary School Act of 1965. There are four basic parts of the act. First, the focus is on helping students, particularly disadvantaged students, in reading and math, and testing all students in third through eighth grades annually to determine progress. An important aspect of the president's educational plan is seeing that all children are reading at grade level by the end of the third grade. Under NCLB, parents of children in poor-performing schools can select from a range of supplemental services that their children might need. The states must demonstrate that disadvantaged children who fall into certain groups based on poverty, ethnicity, limited English proficiency, and disability meet standards so that "no child is left behind." Schools and school districts that do not meet goals are subject to corrective action and sanctions that could include replacing school personnel, changing the curriculum, or restructuring the school. The second part of the act concerns the use of scientifically based teaching techniques to produce results, though some have assailed the "science" on which these requirements are based.[38] The third part of the act expands parental options to move students out of schools that fail to meet goals. The fourth part of the act is intended to give states and school districts that meet goals greater flexibility in how they use federal funding.

While public assistance programs, most notably the Temporary Assistance for Needy Families program, are being devolved to the states, the NCLB increases federal involvement in elementary and secondary education, which has primarily been the terrain of states and communities. Critics have called it an unprecedented and unwarranted instrusion by setting teacher qualifications, focusing too narrowly on reading and math, preventing schools from selecting approaches to teaching reading that work best for them, and setting rigid standards for students and schools to meet. President Bush is the NCLB's major proponent, even though conservatives are the ones most likely to want decisions about public school education left to communities. Many Republicans have taken exception to provisions in the law. Liberals complain that NCLB is a means for allowing greater use of federal funds for faith-based organizations to provide educational services, since these organizations and other community-based groups may offer the supplemental services that students in poor-performing schools can utilize. Objections have been raised across the board that the act does not provide states sufficient funds to meet the mandates. Many school districts and states have balked at the NCLB. Utah wanted to opt out but there would have been repurcussions for other federal education aid.[39]

WORK AND THE POVERTY WARS

Unlike Head Start, which has maintained the same identity since its inception, the federal government's job programs have undergone several revisions. The U.S. Department of Labor is the federal agency responsible for the major public job training and employment programs.

In 1933 the U.S. Employment Service (USES) was established under the Wagner-Peyser Act to help the millions of Depression-era unemployed find jobs. Today, the USES consists of about 2,000 state-operated employment offices located in communities throughout the nation. Employment offices are funded from federal unemployment insurance taxes paid by employers on their employees' wages (see also Chapter 4). The federal government distributes these funds to states based on the state's share of the labor force and its share of unemployed workers. The USES accepts job listings from private and public employers, and it accepts applications from individuals seeking employment. Often these listings are for jobs that require few skills and pay low wages. For both employers and job seekers this is a public service, there is no charge. USES offices are coordinated with state's unemployment insurance programs. Those applying for unemployment benefits must generally register with the USES and actively seek employment. Food stamps and other public assistance benefits may be distributed to adults contingent on their registering with the USES, even if there is little likelihood of their finding a job. In order to increase the chances that public assistance recipients and others looking for a job will become employed, the federal government has embarked on a series of job training programs.

CETA

The Nixon Administration proposed the Comprehensive Employment and Training Act of 1973 (CETA) to consolidate job programs from the Manpower Development and Training Act of 1962 and the Economic Opportunity Act of 1964. The U.S. Department of Labor was given overall responsibility for consolidating these job-training programs and distributing funds to city, county, and state governments to administer them.

Initially, CETA was directed at the structurally unemployed—the long-term, "hard core" unemployed who have few job skills, little experience, and perhaps other barriers to employment. But later, particularly in response to the economic recession of 1974–1975, Congress included people affected by "cyclical" unemployment—

temporary unemployment caused by depressed economic conditions. CETA provided job training for over 3.5 million people per year. Programs included classroom training, on-the-job experience, and public-service employment. Prime sponsor local governments contracted with private community-based organizations (CBOs) to help recruit poor and minority trainees, provide initial classroom training, and place individuals in public-service jobs.

As it turned out, a major share of CETA funds was used by cities to pay individuals to work in regular municipal jobs. Estimates were that about half of all CETA jobs were formerly paid for by local governments. In some cases, cities facing financial stress used CETA funds to cut back on their own spending without laying off large numbers of their employees. As a result, CETA was criticized for failing to target those who needed the assistance most—the economically disadvantaged and long-term, hard-core unemployed. One estimate was that only one-third of all CETA workers came from families receiving public assistance. Prime sponsors tended to skim off the most skilled of the unemployed. Nonetheless, according to federal figures, about 45 percent of participants had less than a high school education, 39 percent were age 21 or younger, about 40 percent were minorities, and 73 percent were classified as "low income."[40]

The Humphrey-Hawkins Act of 1978 "guaranteed" jobs to every "able and willing" adult American. The ambitious language of the act reflects the leadership of its sponsor, the late Senator Hubert H. Humphrey (Democrat-Minnesota). The act viewed the federal government as "the employer of last resort" and pledged to create public-service jobs and put the unemployed to work on public projects. Lowering the unemployment rate to 3 percent was to be a national goal. But the Humphrey-Hawkins Act is more symbolic of liberal concerns than it is a real national commitment. Even in the strongest of economic times, it is unlikely that the national unemployment rate will ever be reduced to 3 percent. Rather than public service jobs, Congress is more concerned with the creation of what has been called "real," permanent, private-sector jobs.

JTPA

In order to address criticisms, the Reagan administration allowed CETA legislation to expire and replaced it with the Job Training Partnership Act (JTPA) of 1982. JTPA was coauthored by the unlikely team of Senator Edward Kennedy (Democrat-Massachusetts) and former Republican Vice President Dan Quayle while he was an Indiana senator. Funds were provided in the form of state block grants. JTPA's goals were familiar: to increase employment and earnings and thereby reduce poverty and welfare dependency among unemployed and underemployed people by providing them with skill training, job search assistance, counselling, and related services. About 600 Private Industry Councils (PICs) were established, composed of volunteers from the business sector with knowledge of job skills needed in their communities. The PICs advised job training centers established by state and local governments with federal funds.

Did JTPA work? Early evidence, which compared program results with federal performance standards, showed that the number of adults who obtained jobs exceeded the federal standard and that placement costs for adults and youths were lower than the standard.[41] These positive results contrasted with findings that adult participants earned less than the federal standard and that fewer youth participants attained employment competencies, entered training programs, returned to school, and completed school than the standards stipulated. The report also indicated that creaming remained a concern. In 1995, 38 percent of youth who participated in the year-round JTPA program became employed at an average hourly rate of $5.80. Of adult participants leaving JTPA, 63 percent were employed, and they earned an average of $7.26 an hour,[42] a figure substantially higher than the minimum wage.

Although some of these results sound encouraging, they are based on federally determined performance standards; they do not compare JTPA participants with similar individuals who did not participate in JTPA. A later study of about 17,000 adult and youth JTPA applicants provides information eighteen months and thirty months after they made application to the program.[43] Sixteen sites across the country participated. Although the sites were not chosen randomly, they represent a cross section of programs, and applicants were assigned randomly to control and treatment groups. At 18 months the earnings of adult women assigned to the JTPA services group increased by an average of $539 or 7.2 percent more than the control group (those not assigned to JTPA services), and employment among the women assigned to JTPA was 2.1 percent higher. Although modest, the gains were statistically significant. The earnings of adult men assigned to receive JTPA services increased by $550, and they had 2.8 percent greater employment than the control group men. These improvements did not differ statistically from men in the control group.

Many applicants assigned to the JTPA group never actually enrolled in the services, although they are included in the results. The impacts were greater for those who actually enrolled. Those enrolled in on-the-job training (OJT) and job search assistance showed the greatest increases in performance over controls. However, subjects were assigned to services based on staff assessments and recommendations. They were not randomly assigned to the various services. People who received OJT and job search services tended to be the most employable of the applicants. It cannot be determined if these services would have similar effects on less employable adult applicants. Evidence showed that employment barriers (welfare receipt and limited education and work experience) negatively affected adult employment rates. The greatest difference between adult assignees and controls was found among those with fewer employment barriers.

The youth in the study (ages 16 to 21) were not in school at the time of assignment. Over the 18-month period, the earnings and employment rate of the female youth assigned to receive JTPA services did not statistically differ from controls, but many of the young women assigned to JTPA were participating in classroom education rather than paid employment. The male youths assigned to JTPA services earned significantly *less* than controls. The lack of improvement in males assigned to JTPA services was attributed to the prior arrest record of 25 percent of this group. The male JTPA assignees with arrest records earned far less than controls. The male JTPA assignees without arrest records did not differ from controls. However more female and male youth in the JTPA services group received a high school diploma or General Equivalency Diploma (GED) certificate than the control group.

Results after 30 months were similar. The researchers concluded "that JTPA works reasonably well for adults," with $1.50 returned in earnings for every $1.00 invested in the program.[44] JTPA participation, however, had little effect on the AFDC benefits received by female members of the treatment group, and food stamp benefits were not affected for men or women. OJT and job search assistance seemed to be particularly successful for the AFDC mothers who received these services. The findings for youth continued to be disappointing. The males in the experimental group still had less earnings than controls, and the females had only small earnings gains that were not statistically significant compared to controls. For both groups of youths, JTPA produced net social *costs*. The researchers also considered subgroups of youths and could not find any group that had earnings gains from JTPA participation.

Youth are a primary consideration since job training and employment services could have lifelong impacts for them. The Job Corps serves nearly 70,000 youth aged 16 to 24 per year at 118 centers located throughout the country.[45] The Job Corps is the government's most expensive job training program for youth. Services are usually provided in residential programs and include rather intensive basic education, vocational training, and work experience as well as interpersonal skill development, healthcare, recreational, and other support services. The Job Corps is intended to be attractive to youth. Computer managed instruction is used to teach reading, math, writing, and thinking skills. Services and length of participation are geared to each youth's needs. The major jobs or trades participants prepare for are clerical, health-related, carpentry, masonry, building and apartment maintenance, food service, auto/truck mechanic, welding, painting, and electrician. Job Corps services are uniform across the nation, centers are evaluated by performance measures, and many have been operated by the same contractors and staff for many years.

The U.S. Department of Labor has commissioned two large studies of the Job Corps at different times in the program's history. The most recent study was published in 2001.[46] Of the 110 programs operating at the time of the study, 30 were Civilian Conservation Centers (CCCs) run by the federal government; the other programs were privately operated. The study utilized a random sample of 11,313 Job Corps applicants (not just those who actually received services) from late 1994 through 1995 and followed them for four years. The control group could not enroll in the Job Corps, but they were free to access other services. Study results are based upon all applicants who completed a four-year interview (this included about 80 percent of both experimental and control group members). Of these applicants, 59 percent were male; of the females, about one-third had children. Nearly half were black, 27 percent were white, 18 percent were Hispanic, and 4 percent were American Indian, with Asians and members of other ethnic groups comprising the remainder. Three-quarters had not completed high school, and 27 percent had had an arrest. Many read at a low level. Study participants stayed in the Job Corps an average of eight months, with

28 percent enrolled for less than three months and nearly a quarter enrolled for more than a year. Most Job Corps applicants (92 percent) received vocational and academic instruction, averaging 1,140 hours (three-quarters vocational and one-quarter academic), equivalent to about one year of high school. Many control group members (72 percent) received training from non–Job Corps sources (an average of 850 hours).

The study findings were:

♦ More Job Corps participants (42 percent) received a GED than controls (27 percent) and more (38 percent) received vocational certificates than controls (15 percent). However, slightly more controls (8 percent) than Job Corps participants (5 percent) earned a regular high school diploma. Few study participants received a two- or four-year college degree with no difference between the two groups.

♦ During year four of the study, the experimental group earned $1,150 (12 percent) more than the control group; about two-thirds of the difference was due to more hours worked and one-third to higher hourly earnings. Most of the increased earnings accrued to those who got a GED or vocational certificate. The hourly wage of employed Job Corps participants in year four was $7.55, compared to $7.33 for employed control group members. If these gains persist, the researchers estimate a $27,000 advantage per Job Corps participant over his or her working years.

♦ Employed Job Corps participants were only slightly more likely than controls to have a job with fringe benefits. Outcomes were similar for the young men and women. There were earnings gains for those most and least "at risk."

♦ Job Corps participants who received services in residence (about 88 percent of participants) as well as those in nonresidential services (often young women with children who were likely to receive public assistance) benefited.

♦ Job Corps participation was associated with modest reductions in crime (29 percent were arrested compared to 33 percent of controls; the impact was greater for less serious crimes), less welfare receipt ($640 less received than controls), and increased independent living, but there was no impact on illegal drug use or custodial responsibility for their children.

♦ Older participants and CCC participants were more likely to earn a GED or a vocational credential than younger participants and those in other Job Corps programs.

♦ Though 16- to 17-year-olds had increased earnings, 18- to 19-year olds and Hispanics did not have increased employment or earnings even though they spent at least as much time in the Job Corps and had similar characteristics to other participants. Hispanic students had similar outcomes whether their first language was English or Spanish.

The researchers estimated that the government spends about $14,000 per Job Corps enrollee, which produces benefits of about $31,000 over the enrollee's lifetime, a net gain to society of about $2 for every $1 spent. The Job Corps seems to serve participants with serious obstacles to employment, but participants' earnings (at least in the short term) remain modest. Longer follow-up periods would help to determine whether the benefits of program participation decrease, increase, or remain the same as the participants age.

Workforce Investment Act (WIA)

During his terms in office, President Clinton pledged to "make the welfare office look more like an employment office" and to "make work pay." To do this, Clinton, like President George H. W. Bush before him, endorsed the idea of "one-stop shopping"— multiservice centers that would consolidate the "crazy quilt" of "150 federal job programs run by twenty-four agencies."[47] Getting twenty-four agencies to consolidate or coordinate unemployment insurance claims, job training, job search, and other employment-related services is no easy feat. The task is made more difficult by the different work requirements of the Temporary Assistance for Needy Families programs (see Chapter 6) and the Food Stamp Program (see Chapter 7), as well as efforts to help people with disabilities receiving Supplemental Security Income secure employment (see Chapter 4).

The current version of the federal government's job training and employment programs is the Workforce Investment Act (WIA) of 1998, which supersedes the JTPA and amends the Wagner-Peyser Act. WIA includes adult programs and youth programs, including the Job Corps. WIA is intended to "increase employment, retention, and earnings of participants, and in doing so, improve the quality of the workforce to sustain economic growth, enhance productivity and competitiveness, and reduce welfare dependency."[48] WIA's seven principles are:

1. Streamlining employment services through an improved one-stop delivery system
2. Empowering individuals with services such as individual training accounts (ITAs) that can be used at qualified institutions
3. Universal access to services and information such as job search, resume writing, and interviewing skills for all job seekers
4. Increased accountability that requires providers of job services to show that they are doing their job with sanctions for those that do not meet performance levels and incentive funds for those exceeding performance levels
5. A strong role for workforce investment boards and the private sector, like the role of the best private industry councils under the JTPA
6. State and local flexibility to respond to local and regional labor markets
7. Improved youth programs, especially for those in high poverty areas

Under WIA, adults aged 18 or older can receive core services such as skills and need assessments, job search, and placement assistance.[49] More intensive services like training may be available to those who need them to obtain or maintain employment. In 2001, 72 percent of low-income adults who received intensive services were employed within three months after exiting services, and their average earnings in that quarter were $3,649. In 2003, nearly $900 million was spent to serve about 546,000 adults.

Youth services include tutoring, study skills training, alternative high school services, and summer activities. In 2003, about $994 million was spent to serve about 446,000 youth. An additional $1.5 billion was spent for the Job Corps. In 2001, 76 percent of enrollees exiting the Job Corps entered jobs, full-time education or training, or the military.

The Department of Labor also offers Trade Act Programs to help individuals "unemployed as a result of increased imports from, or shifts in production to, foreign countries"[50] and to other "dislocated" workers who have been terminated or laid off.[51] Other programs target groups such as Native Americans and individuals released from prison.

WIA's principles sound like a rational approach to assisting Americans who have job training needs, but not everyone agrees. As shown in Illustration 9.2, a professor who studies job training and employment takes exception to the job training strategy, saying it is not participants' fault that they don't do better at securing employment—structural and political forces, such as "outsourcing" or "off-shoring" (sending jobs overseas), are to blame.

Minimum Wages and Living Wages

The federal Fair Labor Standards Act of 1938 was intended to guarantee a wage that would sustain a decent standard of living for all workers. The minimum wage began at 25 cents per hour (see Table 9.1). The labor act also established a forty-hour work week; employees can work longer, but for hourly-wage workers, overtime usually requires additional pay. Over 90 percent of nonsupervisory personnel are covered by the law, with certain exceptions (e.g., some farmworkers, workers who receive tips, and students). In 2002, 2.2 million workers or 3 percent of the labor force aged 16 and older who were paid hourly wages earned at or below the federal minimum wage.[52] About half of them were over 25 years of age. Minimum-wage jobs generally lack benefits like health insurance that can help with a worker's cost of living.

Many believe that the minimum wage is the most direct and comprehensive way to increase the earnings of the working poor. But given today's minimum wage, if only one person in a household is employed, minimum-wage earnings generally fall well below the official poverty level. For example, the poverty threshold (see Chapter 3), for a family of four in 2003 was $18,400, while a full-time (40 hour per week) worker earning the federal minimum wage earned a gross salary of $10,300. Low-income workers often find themselves working two jobs to make ends meet. Today, twelve states and the District of Columbia already have minimum wage laws that exceed the federal level; in the contiguous states they range from $6.15 to $7.01 an hour.[53] In many other areas, prevailing wages also exceed the federal minimum. Certainly, a high minimum wage helps the person who has a job, particularly an unskilled or semi-skilled worker who is most likely to be affected by minimum-wage levels. The need for a higher minimum wage has been argued consistently. Concerns prevail, however,

ILLUSTRATION 9.2

Job Training Farce Gives False Hope to Unemployed Americans

by Gordon Lafer, University of Oregon

For those who follow employment policy, it was no surprise that President Bush's State of the Union address called for more job training as the solution to unemployment. For 20 years, every jobs crisis—whether inner-city poverty, jobs lost due to the North American Free Trade Agreement or loggers put out of work by the spotted owl—has been met with calls for retraining.

Whatever the problem, it seems, job training is the answer.

The trouble is, it doesn't work, and the government knows it. The most comprehensive evaluation of training programs, conducted by the Department of Labor, followed 20,000 people over four years. For the vast majority, the government concluded that training made no difference whatsoever.

People got the same kind of jobs whether or not they'd been through the program. The single most successful group was adult women. But here's what it means to be the single most successful group: Those who did not go through training ended up making 47 percent of the poverty line, and those who did made 54 percent of the poverty line.

It's tempting to think that these meager results are due to mismanagement in one program. However, every training program reports similar anemic outcomes, whether publicly or privately run, for welfare recipients, high school dropouts or laid-off union workers. Indeed, in studying more than 40 years of job training policy, I have not seen one program that, on average, enabled its participants to earn their way out of poverty.

Why doesn't training work? First, there simply are not enough decent-paying jobs. Any individual may benefit from education, but training by itself does not create more jobs.

Second, outside of the professional job market, most jobs just do not require much in the way of sophisticated training. Fully two-thirds of American jobs are in occupations that do not require a college degree.

This leads to the obvious question: Training for what? The president insists that "much of our job growth will be found in high-skilled fields . . . " But the biggest-growing occupations are jobs in fast-food preparation, customer service, retail and security. Of the 25 occupations projected to add the most positions between 2000 and 2010, more than two-thirds can be learned in a few days of on-the-job training. And almost half pay wages near the poverty line.

The truth is that more technology jobs are being sent out of the country than are being created for Americans, with the industry estimating that one-tenth of all high-tech jobs will be exported to places such as India by the end of this year.

These facts aren't secret; most of them come from the government. So if the president knows there are not enough jobs, why is he trumpeting training as the answer to unemployment?

Simple. It's a way of shifting responsibility away from the administration—and its corporate donors—and suggesting instead that workers have themselves to blame for their

continued

ILLUSTRATION 9.2 (continued)

misfortune. If only they had the right skills, Bush implies, they wouldn't be facing the crushing reality of joblessness.

Democrats have accused Bush of hypocrisy for promoting training after cutting the training budget for three years. And indeed, the president's new $250 million initiative would serve less than one-tenth of 1 percent of the 8.5 million Americans currently unemployed. But the hypocrisy is not that Bush is spending too little. It's that he's promoting training at all when he knows that it can't solve the problem.

There are any number of things the president could do that would help workers more.

He could demand a raise in the minimum wage, helping millions escape poverty. He could make it easier for workers to unionize; union workers make roughly 25 percent more than nonunion workers in the same occupations and industries. Or he could discourage American companies from laying off American workers and moving jobs overseas.

The president is doing none of these.

In this context, to promote training in order to make workers think that unemployment is their own fault is a cruel joke on the millions of American families struggling to make it through hard times. They deserve better.

Source: This article is based on Gordon Lafer, *The Job Training Charade* (Ithaca, NY: Cornell University Press, 2002). Reprinted with permission.

TABLE 9.1

The Minimum Wage since It Was Established in 1938 by the Fair Labor Standards Act

1938	$0.25	1975	$2.10
1939	0.30	1976	2.30
1945	0.40	1978	2.65
1950	0.75	1979	2.90
1956	1.00	1980	3.10
1961	1.15	1981	3.35
1963	1.25	1990	3.80
1967	1.40	1991	4.25
1968	1.60	1996	4.75
1974	2.00	1997 to present	5.15

Source: U.S. Department of Labor, http://www.dol.gov/esa/minwage/chart.htm

that increases in the minimum wage increase unemployment by discouraging employers from hiring additional workers who have limited skills and whose labor may not be "worth" the minimum wage. Evidence does not support this claim. Past increases in the minimum wage have not resulted in any substantial job loss.[54]

Those who might be excluded from jobs by a higher minimum wage are teenagers, whom some feel have not yet acquired the skills to make their labor commensurate with the minimum wage. A higher minimum wage might induce employers such as fast-food chains, movie theaters, and retail stores to reduce their teenage help to cut costs. At a lower minimum wage, more teens might be expected to find work. The teenage unemployment rate is about three times the adult rate. Some economists claim that youth unemployment is partly a result of the minimum wage, but there is no consensus about whether a reduction or elimination of the minimum for teens would substantially reduce youth unemployment. One approach to encouraging teenage employment is a "subminimum" or "training wage" that allows employers to pay teenagers less during their first few months of employment.

The minimum wage was one of the first major domestic battles of George H. W. Bush's presidential administration. Bush and Congress favored raising the minimum wage, but they could not agree on how much of a raise was justified. Congress agreed on $4.55, but President Bush stood firm on $4.25, the figure ultimately adopted. More controversial was Bush's insistence on a training wage of $3.40 for all workers in their first six months on the job. Congress vehemently opposed this training wage, claiming it would hurt those adult workers who earn the least and change jobs often in order to remain employed. The agreement finally reached included a temporary training wage for teenage workers of $3.35 in 1990 and $3.61 from 1991 to 1993. Employers could pay 16- to 19-year-olds the training wage for the first 90 days of employment if the teenager had not worked before and could extend it for another 90 days if the employer had a training program.

President Clinton favored another increase in the minimum wage, but with health care and welfare reform legislation on the table, it was not until 1996 that a serious effort to give the minimum wage another hike was mounted in Congress. By this time the minimum wage was reported to be at a near 40-year low in purchasing power. Proponents of a higher wage argued that it was needed to "make work pay," especially to encourage more people to leave welfare for work. They also argued that the pay of CEOs and other high-end workers had risen much more rapidly than for workers at the low end of the pay scale and that Congress has been far more generous in voting itself pay raises. One argument against the increase was that higher-wage workers would also demand a raise. All these raises would increase employers' costs and result in lost jobs, higher prices to consumers, or both.

There was much political maneuvering over the issue. Democrats tried unsuccessfully to tack the minimum wage measure on to a Republican-favored bill to increase the government's borrowing authority and on an immigration bill. Then Senate Majority Leader Bob Dole, who had voted for raising the minimum wage in the past, wanted to package the new minimum wage bill with other Republican-supported economic measures. President Clinton said he would veto the bill if it included an amendment to exempt new hires and businesses that make less than $500,000 a year. In the end, the bill that was passed raised the minimum wage to $4.75 initially and then to $5.15 in July 1997. A subminimum wage for those under age 20 in their first 90 days with an employer was set at $4.25 per hour. The additional costs to businesses were cushioned because the bill also included various tax breaks for them. A subsequent Congressional effort to raise the minimum wage failed in 2000 largely because it was tied to tax cuts that Democrats opposed. Thus, the minimum wage has not been raised since 1997.

A raise in the minimum wage would be welcomed by those who earn this rate, but the number who do is relatively small. More important and more controversial are other ways to raise the wages of the working poor. Some think that the earned income credit (EIC), which has seen some substantial increases, is a better mechanism. The EIC relies on the tax system rather than on employers to provide more money to employees (see Chapters 2 and 6). Other ideas to increase earnings of low-wage workers include indexing the minimum wage to inflation or setting it at half of the national average wage, which in 2003 was about $15 per hour for production workers in private industry.[55] This would boost the current minimum wage, but it is not clear why half the national average wage is an appropriate figure. It might make more sense to pay a *living wage.* An organization called Universal Living Wage (ULW) and many others believe that an individual working full time should be able to afford basic housing.[56] ULW calculates living wages based on fair market rental rates and the Department of Housing and Urban Development's guideline that housing should not consume more than 30 percent of low-income individuals' budget (see Chapter 3). Since housing costs vary from community to community, ULW's living wage calculations also vary. For example, in 2001, ULW estimated that the wage needed for a 40-hour a week worker to secure a one-bedroom apartment in Little Rock, Arkansas, was $8.44 per hour, and in Boulder, Colorado, $13.62 per hour.

Some nonprofit groups and state and local governments are trying to address the problem of low wages through self-sufficiency projects. The nonprofit organization Wider Opportunities for Women (WOW) has partnered with the Corporation for Enterprise Development, the Ms. Foundation for Women, and the National Economic Development and Law Center to work with state and local partners to promote self-sufficiency.[57] WOW's "six strategies"approach for low-income families begins with determining how much it takes to live in a given area (called the self-sufficiency standard, discussed in Chapter 3) and includes targeting higher wage employment, integrating literacy and basic education with occupational skills to make adult education more successful, helping women pursue nontraditional training and employment, microenterprise (small business) development, and promoting individual development accounts that allow low-income families to build assets. Along these lines, the Wyoming Department of Workforce Services (DWS) issued a call for proposals for "three statewide community-partnership programs that will help workers who are struggling to earn a livable wage."[58] The DWS defines livable as 220 percent of the federal poverty level. One call focuses on preparing women to enter jobs or professions traditionally held by males. The second focuses on providing vocational training that would allow an adult in a low-income family to earn a wage while obtaining the training to earn a livable wage. The third was to offer adult basic education to obtain a GED, increase literacy, obtain or enhance current employment, enter and complete college, or achieve citizenship. Self-sufficiency projects in other areas also targeting specific populations like low-income fathers who are required to pay child support.[59]

It may seem like a "no brainer" that workers deserve a living wage or a wage that is fair—as in Fair Labor Standards Act. The minimum wage will eventually get a modest boost. The EIC may also get one, but it is unlikely that a federal living wage will see the light of day.

Enterprise and Empowerment Zones

One effort to revitalize communities so they can create jobs for residents is called **enterprise zones,** and more recently, **empowerment zones.** Their purpose is to encourage businesses to locate in economically distressed areas in order to boost employment and the local economy and increase community services. One newspaper editorial referred to these zones as "mini tax havens" because of the financial incentives they provide to employers.[60] The same editorial called these zones a good idea, but only if the businesses that benefited from them were expected to meet some reasonable goals for hiring disadvantaged residents. Republicans have been strong supporters of this approach because of the business incentives they entail.[61] Enterprise zones have been adopted by state and local governments and were first introduced to Congress about 25 years ago, but Congress was slow to give the approach financial support because of the loss in federal tax revenue. The 1992 Los Angeles riots made Congress rethink its nondecisions.

In 1993 Congress funded nine empowerment zones or EZs (six in urban and three in rural areas) and 95 enterprise communities or ECs (65 in urban and 30 in rural areas), opening competition for $3.5 billion in federal funding. Each empowerment zone selected got tax incentives including as much as $20 million in tax-exempt bonds. For each area resident a business in the zone hired, it was able to deduct up to $3,000 (20 percent of the first $15,000 of the employee's income) and some training expenses from its taxes. Each urban empowerment zone also got a $100 million social service block grant (for services such as child development, drug treatment, and job training), and each rural zone got $40 million; the enterprise communities received about $3 million each for these purposes. Zone applicants were required to submit a plan for supplementing the federal funding with state and local resources.

After some delays, Congress appropriated the necessary funds for a second round of EZs and ECs in 1999 and a third round in 2001, bringing the total to 30 urban EZs, 10 rural EZs, 65 urban ECs, and 50 rural ECs. The 2001 legislation also designated 40 renewal communities (RCs) in place of ECs. In the last round, communities got federal tax incentives to hire residents and improve business operations, but no grant funding. A 1997 Standard and Poor's report gave the urban EZs high marks, saying that in Detroit, General Motors dedicated $1 billion for suppliers that relocated to the EZ and crediting the effort with creating more than 3,000 jobs.[62] Banks in the area also pledged $1 billion for businesses and home mortgages over a ten-year period.

Federal funding of this initiative may be coming to an end. President George W. Bush says, "EZs are helping to stimulate billion of dollars in private investment, reviving inner city neighborhoods and supporting jobs, and helping families move from welfare to work," but he has not proposed funding any more rounds.[63]

There are other ideas for boosting employment of disadvantaged individuals. For example, "targeted jobs credits" give employers in various segments of the economy a tax break for hiring economically disadvantaged workers. Other alternatives are apprenticeship programs for youth, especially for young people who do not go on to college, and other programs that do more to help non–college-bound students make the transition to employment with the necessary vocational education and skills.

BUILDING COMMUNITIES THROUGH SERVICE

In 1995, Robert Putnam published an essay entitled "Bowling Alone: America's Declining Social Capital," in which he lamented Americans' lack of "civic engagement" and "passive reliance on the state."[64] (Putnam cites many examples, the most whimsical being that while more Americans are bowling than ever before, many fewer are bowling in leagues, and many more bowl than vote.) There is a great deal of interest in how to foster a deeper sense of community. One way is through community service, as exemplified by AmeriCorps, a program established under the Clinton Administration.

AmeriCorps provides various options for Americans 18 years and older to earn money for college or vocational education in exchange for service within the United States. AmeriCorps subsumed the former VISTA program in a program now called AmeriCorps*VISTA. It also includes AmeriCorps*State and National (funding goes to nonprofit organizations that sponsor volunteers) and AmeriCorps*National Civilian Community Corps (participants, aged 18 to 24, live together in one of several designated communities to provide service, and they receive leadership training and team building similar to the military).[65]

When President Clinton first proposed AmeriCorps, many members of Congress as well as the public gave it a very warm reception. Some partisan detractors thought the plan far too ambitious. Others felt that the program did not target poor and low-income individuals, that national student loan programs and private initiatives were already available to assist with further education, and that volunteer efforts should not be paid efforts. They also worried that it would create yet another large federal bureaucracy. In addition to initiating AmeriCorps, the president wanted to change the privately administered student loan program into a federally administered program that would save millions of dollars. Needless to say, the banking industry balked at the potential loss to it in interest payments. The debate turned into a filibuster in the Senate. What emerged was a diluted version of the Clinton plan, the National and Community Service Trust Act of 1993, which established the Corporation for National and Community Service to administer these domestic volunteer programs. Clinton also got a direct, federal student loan demonstration program. President George W. Bush created the U.S. Freedom Corps, a White House initiative to coordinate volunteer services in the United States and abroad.

AmeriCorps participants can earn $4,725 for a year of community service (they may serve for two years), which they can use to pay for tuition or student loans. Service may be done before, during, or after their education. They also get a living allowance of $9,300 a year while serving full-time (1,700 hours of work in a nine- to twelve-month period). Part-time work is also permissible for half the stipend. Volunteers serve in educational, public safety, environmental, health, and social welfare positions. They get health care benefits and, if needed, child care benefits. There is no maximum age limit and no financial eligibility requirements to participate.

In addition to AmeriCorps, the Corporation for National and Community Service is responsible for the National Senior Service Corps, which includes the Foster Grandparent Program, the Retired Senior Volunteer Program (RSVP), and the Senior Companion Program, all designed to encourage Americans aged 55 and older to serve their communities. Another of the Corporation's programs is Learn and Serve America, which encourages community service by elementary, secondary, and college students. America Reads is an initiative to utilize volunteers from existing Corporation programs and other efforts to see that all children are reading independently by the end of the third grade. In 2002, the Corporation reported that there were nearly 58,000 AmeriCorps volunteers (the vast majority were serving in AmeriCorps*State and National) and nearly 500,000 Senior Corps volunteers.[66] In 2003, AmeriCorps ran into some accounting problems that affected its ability to enroll as many volunteers.[67] The Corporation also administers the Presidential Freedom Scholarship program, which helps high school students earn $1,000 college scholarships as a reward for outstanding community service. Half the funds are provided by the Corporation and half must be raised from other sources like schools and community groups.

SUMMARY

Since the New Deal of the 1930s the paradigms of the wars on poverty have changed. The curative strategy of the War on Poverty in the 1960s and 1970s was an attempt to eradicate many of America's social problems, but a decade later 25 million Americans remained poor. The War on Poverty sounded like a creative approach to remedying many social ills, but it was plagued by problems such as inexperienced staff and experimental programs without clear goals. Case studies of Head Start programs, the Comprehensive Employment and Training Act (CETA), and the Legal Services Corporation all illustrate how politics interferes with rational approaches to policymaking and program implementation.

Despite criticisms of the War on Poverty, many OEO-originated programs such as the Legal Services Corporation survive, and others like Head Start thrive. Programs that emerged from additional Great Society legislation, like the Food Stamp, Medicare, and Medicaid programs, continue to help millions. Other programs have been reincarnated in different forms such as CETA, which became the Job Training Partnership Act, and is now the Workforce Investment Act.

Today the cure for poverty, or dependency as the problem is framed, lies in demanding work behavior of public assistance recipients, but the current federal minimum wage does not ensure an escape from poverty. Concepts like enterprise zones may help revitalize depressed areas and renew what many feel is a lost sense of community. A better prepared workforce is also important. But even jobs requiring high levels of technological skill are being exported to other countries. This round of the poverty wars has not taken the bite out of poverty that the country would like.

NOTES

1. Cited in Daniel Patrick Moynihan, *Maximum Feasible Misunderstanding* (New York: Free Press, 1969), pp. 3–4; see this book for an account of the early history of the War on Poverty.

2. For an extensive elaboration of this argument, see Charles Murray, *Losing Ground: American Social Policy, 1950–1980* (New York: Basic Books, 1984).

3. Michael Harrington, *The Other America: Poverty in the United States* (New York: Macmillan, 1962).

4. John Kenneth Galbraith, *The Affluent Society* (Boston: Houghton Mifflin, 1958).

5. Much of this paragraph relies on Christopher Walker, *Community Development Corporations and Their Changing Support Systems* (Washington, DC: Urban Institute, December 1, 2002); Christopher Walker, Jeremy Gustafson, and Christopher Snow, *National Support for Local System Change: The Effect of the National Community Development Initiative on Community Development System* (Washington, DC: Urban Institute, December 1, 2002), retrieved July 29, 2004, from http://www.urban.org

6. David J. Wright, *It Takes a Neighborhood: Strategies to Prevent Urban Decline* (Albany: New York Press, 2002).

7. See David A. Reingold and Craig L. Johnson, "The Rise and Fall of Eastside Community Development Investments, Inc.: The Life of an Extraordinary Community Development Corporation," *Journal of Urban Affairs*, Vol. 25, No. 5, 2003, pp. 527–549; William M. Rohe, Rachel G. Bratt and Protip Biswas, "Learning from Adversity: The CDC School of Hard Knocks," *Shelterforce Online*, Issue #129, May/June, 2003, retrieved July 29, 2004, from http://www.nhi.org/online/issues/129/CDCfailures.html

8. Gordon Oliver, "Gentrification Threatens Community Development Groups," *Planning*, August 1, 2000, retrieved July 29, 2004, from http://static.highbeam.com/p/planning/august012000/gentrificationthreatens communitydevelopmentgroupsb/

9. Economic Development Administration, *1999 Fact Sheet,* January 1999, retrieved from http://12.39.209.165/xp/EDAPublic/AboutEDA/AbtEDA.xml

10. Information on the Community Development Block Grant is available at http://www.hud.gov

11. Office of Management and Budget, *Budget of the United States Government, Fiscal Year 2003* (Washington, DC: Executive Office of the President, 2002), p. 173.

12. See Bill Keller, "Special Treatment No Longer Given Advocates for the Poor," *Congressional Quarterly,* Vol. 39, No. 16, April 18, 1981, pp. 659–664.

13. This paragraph relies on David Masi, "As New Legal Aid Law Is Written, Old Battles Will Be Refought," *Congressional Quarterly,* Vol. 52, No. 3, January 22, 1994, pp. 123–125; Steven Pressman, "Reagan's Recess Appointments Rankle Hill," *Congressional Quarterly,* Vol. 42, No. 28, July 14, 1984, pp. 1698–1699.

14. Histories of the LSC are found in Henry Cohen, "The Legal Services Corporation," Congressional Research Service Report for Congress, May 7, 1996; Karen Spar, "Legal Services Corporation: Basic Facts and Current Status," Congressional Research Services Report for Congress, May 10, 1996.

15. For stories on the LSC and the judge's ruling on class actions, see Don Van Natta, Jr., "Legal Services Wins Suit for the Poor," *New York Times,* December 27, 1996, pp. B1, 8; and Don Van Natta, Jr., "Lawyers Split on Impact of Ruling on Suits for Poor," *New York Times,* December 29, 1996, Metro section, p. 27.

16. Legal Services Corporation, *2000–2001 Annual Report,* retrieved January 31, 2004, from http://www.lsc.gov

17. "War on Poverty—Victory or Defeat," Hearing before the Subcommittee on Monetary and Fiscal Policy of the Joint Economic Committee, Congress of the United States, 99th Congress, 1st Session, June 20, 1985.

18. Aaron Wildavsky, "The Empty Headed Blues: Black Rebellion and White Reactions," *Public Interest,* No. 11, Spring 1968, pp. 3–4.

19. Bob Greene (Tribune Media Services), "Middle-Class Demands for Police Likely to Be Legacy of L.A. Riots," *Austin American-Statesman,* May 12, 1992, p. A10.

20. Edward Zigler, Sally J. Styfco, and Elizabeth Gilman, "The National Head Start Program for Disadvantaged Preschoolers," in Edward Zigler and Sally J. Styfco, Eds., *Head Start and Beyond: A National Plan for Extended Childhood Intervention* (New Haven, CT: Yale University Press, 1993), pp. 1–41.

21. Westinghouse Learning Corporation, Ohio University, *The Impact of Head Start* (Washington, DC: Office of Economic Opportunity, 1969).

22. For additional information on an early study, see David P. Weikart, Dennis J. Deloria, Sarah A. Lawser, and Ronal Wiegerink, *Longitudinal Results of the Ypsilanti Perry Preschool Project* (Ypsilanti, MI: High/Scope Educational Research Foundation, August 1970).

23. See James E. Anderson, *Public Policy-Making* (New York: Holt, Rinehart, & Winston, 1975), p. 150.

24. Lawrence J. Schweinhart and David P. Weikart, "High/Scope Perry Preschool Program Effects at Age Twenty-Seven" in Jonathan Crane, Ed., *Social Programs That Work* (New York: Russell Sage Foundation, 1998), pp. 148–162; see also the series of monographs of the High/Scope Educational Research Foundation, Ypsilanti, Michigan, reporting the results of studies of the Perry Preschool Project.

25. See Deborah A. Phillips and Natasha J. Cabrera, (Eds.), *Beyond the Blueprint: Directions for Research on Head Start's Families* (Washington, DC: National Academy Press, 1996). An extensive annotated bibliography on Head Start and related preschool program research is available from the Department of Health and Human Services and can be found at http://www.acf.dhhs.gov.cgi-bin/hs/text_field_search

26. See Zigler, Styfco, and Gilman, "The National Head Start Program for Disadvantaged Preschoolers."

27. The challenges faced by Head Start programs are summarized in Valora Washington and Ura Jean Oyemade Bailey, *Project Head Start: Models and Strategies for the Twenty-First Century* (New York: Garland, 1995).

28. Washington and Bailey, *Project Head Start: Models and Strategies for the Twenty-First Century,* p. 141; also see John Hood, "Caveat Emptor: The Head Start Scam," *Policy Analysis,* No. 187, December 18, 1992, retrieved July 30, 2004, from http://www.cato.org/pubs/pas/pa-187.html; William Julius Wilson, *When Work Disappears* (New York: Alfred A. Knopf, 1996), p. xv.

29. Kevin J. Gorey, "Early Childhood Education: A Meta-Analytic Affirmation of the Short- and Long-term Benefits of Educational Opportunity," *School Psychology Quarterly,* Vol. 16, No. 1, 2001, pp. 9–30.

30. Walter S. Gilliam and Edward F. Zigler, "A Critical Meta-analysis of All Evaluations of State-Funded Preschool from 1977 to 1998: Implications for Policy, Service Delivery and Program Evaluation," *Early Childhood Research Quarterly,* Vol. 15, No. 4, 2000, pp. 441–473.

31. Lynn A. Karoly, Peter W. Greenwood, Susan S. Everingham, Jill Hoube, M. Rebecca Kilburn, C. Peter Rydell, Matthew R. Sanders, and James R. Chisea, *Investing in Our Children: What We Know and Don't Know about the Costs and Benefits of Early Childhood Interventions* (Santa Monica, CA: RAND Corporation, 1998).

32. Julie Rovner, "Full Funding for Head Start Approved by Senate Panel," *Congressional Quarterly,* June 30, 1990, p. 2072.

33. Head Start enrollment, program, and cost figures are based on Head Start Bureau, *Head Start Program Fact Sheet* (Washington, DC: Administration for Children and Families, February 2003), retrieved July 30, 2004, from http://www.acf.hhs.gov/programs/hsb/research/2003.htm

34. Executive Office of the President, *Budget of the United States Government, Fiscal Year 1998* (Washington, DC: U.S. Government Printing Office, 1997), p. 58.

35. Alvin F. Poussaint, "The Hope of Head Start," *New York Times,* July 22, 2003, retrieved July 26, 2003 from http://www.nytimes.com

36. The Pew Charitable Trusts, "Early Childhood Education," retrieved August 7, 2003, from http://www.pewtrusts.com

37. Arthur J. Reynolds, "The Chicago Child-Parent Center and Expansion Program: A Study of Extended Early Childhood Intervention" in Jonathan Crane, Ed., *Social Programs That Work* (New York: Russell Sage Foundation, 1998), pp. 110–147.

38. Gerald Coles, *Reading the Naked Truth: Literacy, Legislation, and Lies* (Portsmouth, NH: Heinemann, 2003).

39. See, for example, Laura Scott *(Kansas City Star),* "No Child Left Behind Unfunded Mandate," Spokesman-Review.Com, February 20, 2004; retrieved July 29, 2004, from http://www.spokesmanreview.com/breaking-news-story.asp?submitdate=2004220162323

40. Executive Office of the President, *Budget of the United States Government, Fiscal Year 1982* (Washington, DC: U.S. Government Printing Office, 1981), p. 220.

41. Grinker Associates, *An Independent Sector Assessment of the Job Training Partnership Act, Final Report, Program Year 1985* (New York: Author, 1986).

42. Committee on Ways and Means, U.S. House of Representatives, *1998 Green Book: Background Material and Data on Programs within the Jurisdiction of the Committee on Ways and Means* (Washington, DC: U.S. Government Printing Office, 1998), pp. 1003–1004.

43. Howard S. Bloom, Larry L. Orr, George Cave, Stephen H. Bell, and Fred Doolittle, *The National JTPA Study: Title II-A Impacts on Earnings and Employment at 18 Months* (Bethesda, MD: Abt Associates, 1993).

44. Larry L. Orr, Howard S. Bloom, Stephen H. Bell, Fred Doolittle, Winston Lin, and George Cave, *Does Training for the Disadvantaged Work? Evidence from the National JTPA Study* (Washington, DC: Urban Institute Press, 1996).

45. U.S. Department of Labor, Employment and Training Administration, "About the Job Corps," retrieved February 1, 2004, from http://jobcorps.doleta.gov/about.asp

46. This description of the Jobs Corps and the study's findings are based on John Burghardt, Peter X. Schochet, Sheena McConnell, Terry Johnson, R. Mark Gritz, Steven Glazerman, John Homrighausen, and Russell Jackson, "Does Job Corps Work? Summary of the National Job Corps Study" (Washington, DC: U.S. Department of Labor, 2002), retrieved February 13, 2004, from http://www.doelta.gov

47. Clinton Proposes Changes in Unemployment, Training," *Austin American-Statesman,* March 10, 1994, p. A2.

48. Employment and Training Administration, "The Seven Key Principles of WIA" (Washington, DC: U.S. Department of Labor, n.d.), retrieved July 30, 2003, from http://www.doleta.gov/usworkforce/resources/sevenkey.cfm

49. This paragraph relies on Committee on Ways and Means, *2003 Green Book,* Section 15, Other Programs, "Workforce Investment Act," posted December 10, 2003, retrieved February 18, 2004, from http://waysandmeans.house.gov/documents.asp

50. U.S. Department of Labor, Trade Act Programs, "TAA for Workers," retrieved February 18, 2004, from http://www.doleta.gov/tradeact

51. U.S. Department of Labor, "Dislocated Workers," retrieved February 18, 2004, from http://www.doleta.gov/laypff

52. Bureau of Labor Statistics, "Characteristics of Minimum Wage Workers, 2002," Table 1 (Washington, DC: U.S. Department of Labor), retrieved July 30, 2004, from http://www.bls.gov/cps/minwage2002tbls.htm#1

53. "Statement of Robert B. Reich Secretary of Labor before the Joint Economic Committee," Congressional Testimony, February 22, 1995, retrieved from http://www.dol.gov/search97cgi/s97-cgi.exe

54. Employment Standards Division, "Minimum Wage Laws in the States" (Washington, DC: U.S. Department of Labor, January 1, 2003), retrieved February 20, 2003, from http://www.doleta.gov/esa/minwage/america.htm

55. Bureau of Labor Statistics, "National Employment, Hours and Earnings" (U.S. Department of Labor), retrieved February 20, 2003, from http://data.bls.gov/cgi-bin/surveymost

56. See the Universal Living Wage website at www.UniversalLivingWage.org

57. See the website of Wider Opportunities for Women (WOW), http://www.wowonline.org, its "Six Strategies" website, http://www.sixstrategies.org/about/about.cfm, and *Setting the Standard for American Working Families: A Report on the Impact of the Family Economic Self-Sufficiency Project Nationwide* (Washington, DC: Wider Opportunities for Women, 2003), which contains examples of state programs.

58. Information about the Wyoming Department of Workforce Services self-sufficiency projects retrieved July 29, 2004, from http://www.wyomingworkforce.org/programs/etss/ETSSproposals.asp

59. For information on self-sufficiency projects for fathers paying child support, see the *Self-Sufficiency Project Implementation Manual* of the U.S. Department of Health and Human Services Office of Child Support Enforcement, retrieved July 29, 2004, from http://www.acf.hhs.gov/programs/cse/rpt/fth/lessons.htm

60. This paragraph relies on "Done Right, Enterprise Zones Can Benefit All," *Austin American-Statesman,* June 21, 1992, p. D2.

61. See also "Issue: Enterprise Zones," *Congressional Quarterly, Special Report,* Vol. 51, December 11, 1993, p. 3391.

62. Kenneth A. Gear, "Detroit's Turnaround," *Standard and Poor's Credit Week Municipal,* December 22, 1997, pp. 9–11.

63. Executive Office of the President, *Budget of the United States Government, Fiscal Year 2005* (Washington, DC: Office of Management and Budget, 2004), p. 527.

64. Robert Putnam, "Bowling Alone: America's Declining Social Capital," *Journal of Democracy,* January 1995, pp. 65–78; Robert D. Putnam, *Bowling Alone: The Collapse and Revival of American Community* (New York: Simon and Schuster, 2001).

65. Information on these programs was retrieved from the website of the Corporation for National and

Community Service, retrieved July 30, 2003, from http://www.nationalservice.org

66. Corporation for National and Community Service, *Performance and Accountability Report, Fiscal Year 2002* (Washington, DC, 2003), retrieved July 14, 2003, from http://www.nationalservice.org

67. Elizabeth Schwinn, "President Signs Law to Soften AmeriCorps Cuts," *The Chronicle of Philanthropy,* July 2003, retrieved July 14, 2003, from http://www.philanthropy.com

CHAPTER

10

Providing Social Services: Help for Children, the Elderly, and Individuals with Mental Illness

SOCIAL SERVICES IN THE UNITED STATES

Social welfare programs are often equated with programs for the poor, but there are many social services that people may need regardless of their income and social status. Developing a list of all the social services available in the United States is nearly impossible, but it would include a number of services for individuals, families, and communities.[1] Among the services for individuals are those that target children, including community youth centers, child protective services, foster home care, adoption assistance, and voluntary guidance programs such as Big Brothers and Big Sisters of America. Other services are for individuals who are disabled or elderly, such as transportation, homemaker and chore services, opportunities for socialization at senior citizen centers or other community programs, adult protective services, and long-term care. Social services may also benefit families. Services aimed at family units include family planning, marital and family counseling, day care and after-school care for children, assessments for courts and schools, family preservation and renunification services when abuse or neglect has occurred, and respite care to provide relief to caretakers of older or disabled family members. Still other services are called **community organization** because they involve mobilizing groups such as community residents concerned about drugs and crime, mothers receiving welfare, migrant workers, newly arrived immigrants, tenants, individuals with disabilities and their families, and even gang members, to achieve beneficial goals for themselves and their communities.

Some services, such as education, counseling, and rehabilitation, are offered in several types of settings—churches, schools, general hospitals, workplaces, community mental health centers, outpatient treatment centers for alcoholics and drug abusers, and residential facilities such as juvenile detention centers, psychiatric hospitals, and community residences and state schools for individuals with mental or physical disabilities. To this growing list of services we can add information, referral, advocacy, and consumer services of various types, and there are many more. During their lifetimes, virtually all Americans will use some type of social service.

Who Provides Social Services?

Social services are provided by five types of organizations: (1) public agencies, (2) private not-for-profit corporations, (3) private for-profit corporations, (4) self-help groups, and (5) religious organizations. Services such as day care may be provided by all these types of organizations. Other services, such as child and adult protection, are provided by public agencies because these agencies have the legal right to intervene in cases of neglect or abuse. But even public child welfare agencies are contracting with private entities to provide some services once thought to be solely in the public domain.

Public agencies are established by law and are operated by federal, state, or local governments. The U.S. Department of Health and Human Services (DHHS) is the major federal agency responsible for social welfare services, though other federal agencies also offer social services. Some states also have large umbrella agencies for the many departments that deliver the states' social services. In other states, several separate agencies administer the various social welfare programs. Many counties and cities also operate social welfare agencies.

Private not-for-profit corporations, also called **voluntary** agencies, are governed by boards of directors or trustees. These agencies may receive funds from endowments and donations; client fees; other community organizations such as the United Way; or local, state, and federal governments in the form of grants, contracts, or fees for service. Private not-for-profit agencies provide a multitude of services, such as day care for children, mental health services, and nursing home care. Many of these agencies charge clients fees on a sliding scale, based on their ability to pay for the service. Other not-for-profit agencies, such as rape crisis centers, generally do not charge their clients. Some not-for-profit corporations act as advocates for their clientele by informing policymakers and the public of their clients' needs. The Arc (formerly the Association for Retarded Citizens of the United States) and its local affiliates, the Child Welfare League of America, and the National Council on Alcoholism and Drug Dependence are examples of private not-for-profit organizations.

Private profit-making organizations are also called **proprietary agencies.** They too provide services like child care, nursing home care, and mental health care, but generally charge their clients for services at the current market rate. Government agencies sometimes purchase services from private agencies, because the government may not directly provide a service needed by a client and cannot obtain it from a not-for-profit agency more economically. A great deal of Medicaid funds are used to purchase long-term care from proprietary nursing homes.

Self-help groups also provide social services but generally do not rely on governmental funding at all. Their structure is less formal than other social service agencies. Alcoholics Anonymous (AA), the best known self-help group, was founded in 1935 and assists people with drinking problems. The only requirement for membership is the desire to stop drinking. The group relies solely on its members for financial support. The self-help category also includes **cooperatives** where people band together to share child care, to purchase groceries more economically, or achieve other mutual goals. Other self-help organizations have emerged to assist people with mental disorders and their families, including the National Alliance for the Mentally Ill and Recovery, Inc. Some of these groups may be organized as not-for-profit corporations, but their focus is on mutual aid provided by those who share a common problem, rather than reliance on professional service providers.

Finally, religious organizations have a long history of providing social services. Although their services are generally (but not always) provided by the clergy or lay members of a particular religious sect, they may be available to people regardless of their personal religious beliefs. Among the services religious groups offer are child care, crisis pregnancy counseling, adoption, mental health counseling, food and shelter for people who are homeless or poor, and outreach to those who are incarcerated. As discussed in Chapters 1 and 6, the Bush administration has encouraged religious organizations to pursue federal funding to provide social services and mandated that federal agencies "level the playing field" for religious organizations that wish to do so.

These different types of agencies allow consumers choice when it comes to selecting services. However, Chapter 2 discussed a blurring of the sectors as governments pursue policies of privatization. In addition, more privately operated social service organizations have come to accept public funds in order to fill service gaps and sustain their missions. Many alternative service organizations originally emerged because the public sector was not providing needed services (such as rape crisis or substance abuse services) or it was not sensitive to the concerns of particular clientele (such as African Americans, women, or lesbians and gay men). One effect public monies can have is to subvert the original intent of these alternative agencies, because they must now conform to the expectations of these funders.[2] In other words, the various types of social service agencies may look more and more alike.

The Development of Social Services

Before the 1900s, social services were provided by family members, neighbors, church groups, private charitable organizations, and local governments in the form of indoor and outdoor relief (see Chapter 2). In fact, the Charity Organization Societies of the late 1800s, which helped poor people, preferred to provide social services rather than financial aid. During the first half of the twentieth century, the federal and state governments largely provided cash and in-kind assistance to destitute people. Although child welfare services were part of the original Social Security Act of 1935, most social services remained outside federal purview until 1956 when Congress amended the Social Security Act to provide social services to families on relief.[3]

More social service amendments were added to the Social Security Act in 1962 and 1967 (also see Chapter 6). The rationale was to rehabilitate poor people, help them overcome their personal problems, and thereby reduce their dependence on welfare. The federal government began giving the states three dollars for every dollar the states spent on social services, with virtually no limit on spending. The federal government's willingness to subsidize social services was a boon to the states that were willing to increase the social services available to clients. But the costs of social services increased so fast—from $282 million in 1967 to $1.7 billion in 1973[4]—that Congress decided to curb spending. In 1976 Title XX was added to the Social Security Act to place a ceiling on expenditures and to ensure that the majority of federally funded social services went to the poor.

In 1981, the Reagan administration convinced Congress to replace Title XX with the Social Services Block Grant. The goals of the block grant are to increase economic self-support and self-sufficiency, reduce abuse and neglect of children and adults, reduce inappropriate institutional care, and secure institutional care when needed. The grant is based on the premises that economic and social needs are interrelated and that states know best what services their residents need. State matching requirements were eliminated, and block grant funds are now allocated to states on the basis of population. But under the block grant, federal contributions to social services have decreased considerably. Unlike the open-ended funding that social services received when it had "entitlement" status, the Title XX Social Services Block Grant (SSBG) is capped. The original cap was $2.9 billion in 1981, but funding has eroded substantially to $1.7 billion annually. Congress not only sets the spending cap for social services, it also has granted itself the power to appropriate more or less than the cap if it deems necessary, and in several years it has appropriated less.[5] Most funds do go to assist low-income clients, and states are most likely to use their block grant funds for child welfare and related family services as well as adult protective services.[6]

Since the Reagan era, block grants have become the federal government's primary tool for supporting social services. In addition to the Title XX Social Services Block Grant, the Preventive Health and Health Services Block Grant, the Maternal and Child Health Services Block Grant, the Substance Abuse Prevention and Treatment Block Grant, the Community Mental Health Services Block Grant, the Low-Income Home Energy Assistance Block Grant, the Developmental Disabilities Assistance and Bill of Rights Act, the Older Americans Act, and many other pieces of federal, state, and local legislation also provide social service funding.

A significant development in social welfare is the recognition that those who are not poor can also benefit from social services. The growth of private social service agencies that cater to middle- and upper-class groups is an indication that many Americans need social services. People with problems of mental illness, alcohol and other drug dependence, child abuse and neglect, and the frailties that may accompany old age are among those who have received increased attention from social service providers since the 1960s. Social welfare policies that affect these groups are discussed in the following pages.

SOCIAL SERVICES FOR INDIVIDUALS WITH ALCOHOL, DRUG, AND MENTAL DISORDERS

Among the many obstacles to rationalism in providing alcohol, drug abuse, and mental health services is a lack of consensus about how to define these problems, how to identify the number in need, how to determine the services best suited to remedying these problems, and assuring that those in need have access to services.

Defining the Problems

Mental health professionals have long debated the best way to define mental illnesses,[7] but as laypeople we may conceptualize mental health and mental illness as two ends of a continuum. At one extreme are people who behave in an acceptable manner. At the other extreme are people with psychoses who are unable to cope with reality and cannot function within the community. Depression is a common mental health problem that can range from mild and temporary to so severe that an individual may become dysfunctional and even suicidal. The American Psychiatric Association publishes a manual for mental health professionals called the *Diagnostic and Statis-*

tical Manual of Mental Disorders (*DSM*) that describes dozens of mental health and alcohol and drug problems. Even this guide is controversial, because it drives the way mental health professionals are paid for their services, and it promotes labeling and categorizing people even when they may not specifically fit these categories, or when labeling may be counterproductive for the individual.[8]

All people experience emotional stress at some time in their lives. Most do not need professional help. Time and the care and concern of family and friends is generally sufficient to see them through these difficult times. Today more emphasis is placed on preventing mental health problems and treating them before they become severe. Mental health professionals, particularly in the private sector, are as likely to see family members with temporary adjustment problems to divorce or the loss of a loved one as they are to see individuals who are severely depressed or suicidal, or have schizophrenia.

Many people who need professional assistance seek treatment voluntarily, but many Americans cannot locate affordable or free services. Others with severe mental illness may not recognize their need for treatment, and in these cases, state and local policies stipulate the conditions under which an individual may be judged mentally ill and in need of treatment. Involuntary admission to a psychiatric hospital is generally reserved for people who psychiatrists believe are dangerous to themselves or others and who may not perceive the need for treatment. Involuntary commitment laws are controversial because there can be a fine line between involuntary hospitalization and civil rights infringements.

Defining mental disorders, alcoholism, and other drug problems is also difficult because there is no proof of the cause of many of these problems. The disease or biological model of chemical dependency has been useful in reducing stigma and promoting treatment, but this model is just one of several that has been used to describe alcohol and other drug problems.[9] Psychological and sociocultural theories often seem just as convincing in explaining these conditions.

Estimating Problems and Services

Despite disagreements about definitions, governmental bodies do estimate the numbers of people who experience mental illness and substance abuse. According to a major national survey based on psychiatric interviews, 48 percent of those ages 15 to 54 have had at least one psychiatric disorder during their lifetimes, and almost 30 percent reported at least one disorder in the last year.[10] The most common diagnoses were major depression, alcohol dependence, and certain phobias. Among those with a lifetime addictive disorder, 41 to 66 percent also had a mental disorder, and among those with at least one mental disorder, 51 percent had an addictive disorder.[11] There is a special concern about the population with serious mental illness, generally defined as those having a mental disorder and severe impairment within the last year.[12] Using this definition, 5.4 percent of the population had serious or severe mental illness, with 2.6 percent meeting an even more stringent definition referred to as serious and persistent mental illness. Data also indicate that 9 to 13 percent of children ages 9 to 17 have serious emotional disturbance.[13] With a nearly 50 percent prevalence rate, mental disorders are the most frequently occurring chronic conditions. Most experts believe that mental illness, like other stigmatized conditions, often goes underreported and untreated. This is especially true for children.[14]

An estimated 27 percent of Americans have had a substance abuse or dependence diagnosis in their lifetime.[15] According to the National Survey on Drug Use and Health conducted by the federal agency called the Substance Abuse and Mental Health Services Administration (SAMHSA), in 2002 an estimated 22 million Americans (9.4 percent of the population) had an abuse or dependence diagnosis with nearly 15 million abusing or dependent on alcohol alone.[16]

In 2002, there were more than 670,000 drug-related hospital emergency department (ED) episodes nationwide, up from 519,000 in 1994.[17] Alcohol in combination with at least one other drug was the most often mentioned drug problem in these ED visits.

Alcohol and other drug use among young people continues to be a concern. According to the 2002 National Survey, 7.2 million (19.8 percent) young people ages 12–20 reported that they had engaged in binge drinking (they drank 5 or more drinks on at least one occasion in the last month), and 2.3 million (6.2 percent) were heavy drinkers (they drank 5 or more drinks per occasion on 5 or more days in the past month). Among youths aged 12–17, 11.6 percent used an illicit drug in the past month (the rate was 5.3 percent in 1992). An estimated 1.8 million Americans used hallucinogens for the first time in 2001. The recent rise in the use of hallucinogens has been driven by the drug Ecstasy. First-time users of cocaine doubled between 1996 and 2001 (from .67 million to 1.2 million). The number of heroin users grew, with the initiation rate for youth more than doubling since 1994 (18,000 vs. 44,000). In addition, more than half of all youth aged 12–17 reported that marijuana was easy to obtain. About 16 percent reported that heroin was easy to obtain. Youth were less likely to use illicit drugs if they believed their parents would disapprove, and most youth thought that their parents would strongly disapprove. Youth who perceived that their parents would somewhat disapprove or not care one way or the other were six times more likely to have used marijuana in the prior month than youth who believed that their parents would strongly disapprove (30.2 vs. 5.5 percent, respectively).

Since a substantial percentage of the population have mental or substance use disorders, service providers are particularly anxious to find successful treatment approaches. But only a small portion receive assistance. Studies show most people with diagnosable disorders get no treatment at all: "only four of every ten respondents with a lifetime history of at least one disorder ever obtained professional help, only one in four obtained treatment in the mental health specialty sector, and about one in twelve were treated in substance abuse facilities."[18] According to the National Household Survey, in 2002, 7.7 million individuals needed treatment for an illicit drug problem, but only 18 percent of them received treatment in a specialty drug treatment facility. Twenty-four percent of those who felt they needed treatment but did not get it said they were unable to obtain help. Of the 18.6 million who needed treatment for an alcohol problem, only 8 percent got help at a specialty treatment facility. Of those who said they needed alcoholism treatment and sought it, 35 percent said they were unable to get it. However, the overwhelming majority who did not receive alcohol or drug treatment did not think they needed help even though they met criteria for problem use. Of the 27.3 million adults with mental illness, only 13 percent received treatment, but of the 18.4 million with serious mental illness, nearly 48 percent got treatment. Of those who felt they needed help and did not get care, the most often cited reason was that they could not afford it. Many also said they did not know where to get help. Each year SAMHSA attempts to count the number of clients receiving substance abuse services in public, private nonprofit, and private for-profit facilities on a particular day as an estimate of the number of clients in treatment. Of the 15,459 facilities contacted, 13,720 (89 percent) responded. These facilities reported that on March 29, 2002, 1.14 million clients were in treatment for substance use disorders (8 percent were under the age of 18). Most were receiving care through private nonprofit facilities (61 percent), and most were in outpatient treatment (90 percent).[19]

Between 7 and 10 million people in the U.S. suffer from at least one mental disorder *and* one substance use disorder.[20] These individuals find it very difficult to get effective treatment, because there is one system to treat mental illness and another to treat substance use disorders. Clients with these co-occurring disorders often bounce back and forth between the mental health system and the substance abuse treatment system. If one disorder goes untreated, both are likely to get worse, but only about 19 percent are receiving treatment for both disorders, and 29 percent receive no treatment at all.

Achieving Treatment Parity

Mental illness and substance use disorders cost society dearly. The National Mental Health Association estimates that mental illness costs society $205 billion a year (51 percent due to the loss of productivity, 45 percent due to treatment costs, and 4 percent due to crime and welfare),[21] and the Office of National Drug Policy estimated that substance abuse costs in 2000 were $161 billion (69 percent to productivity loss, 22 percent to crime, drug control, and welfare, and 9 percent to treatment).[22] Given that so many do not get care, treatment advocates want to increase access to services and promote more adequate and earlier treatment. Many believe that more progress towards these goals could be achieved if health insurance plans included the same coverage for these problems as for health problems.

Private insurance coverage for mental illness emerged in the 1950s, and separate coverage for substance use disorders began in the 1970s.[23] The federal Mental Health Parity Act of 1996 generally prevents employers with more than 50 employees who offer health plans that include mental health coverage from imposing more restrictive annual or lifetime dollar limits on these services than they do on medical or surgical care. A closer look shows that the act does not solve the parity problem. It does not require an employer to offer mental health coverage; it does not pertain to those with less than 50 employees; it exempts employers if the costs of compliance are at least 1 percent of the health plan's annual costs; it does not prevent plans from limiting the number of visits covered or requiring copayments or deductibles; and care can be limited to that deemed "medically necessary."[24] Furthermore, the act does not include care for substance use disorders.

The 1996 mental health parity law "sunsetted" in 2001. An attempt to replace it with the Mental Health Equitable Treatment Act, which would have provided parity not only for lifetime dollar limits, but also for hospital days, outpatient visits, copays, deductibles, and out-of-pocket maximums, was narrowly defeated. The 1996 law continues to be extended despite continued attempts at expanding parity legislations. The primary opponents of expansion are insurance companies and employers who argue that it would be a "budget buster." Evidence contradicts this assertion. The Congressional Budget Office estimates that the Mental Health Equitable Treatment Act would add less than a 1 percent increase to private insurance premiums. Thirty-seven states now have parity laws, and of these, 16 offer full parity, some for both substance abuse treatment and mental health care.[25] State studies confirm that the costs of mental health parity are minimal.[26] The RAND Corporation estimated that overall, premium costs for unlimited mental health care under managed care would increase premiums by about $1 per employee per year.[27] The additional cost is so small because increased mental health benefits have not resulted in increased use of mental health services.[28] Lack of education about mental illness and social stigma may be to blame for low use of mental health services. It may also indicate that those with the greatest treatment needs are not those who are covered by employer insurance plans. Providing full parity for substance abuse treatment does result in additional use and a larger increase in insurance premiums of about 6 percent per employee per year.[29] This cost is offset by the savings accrued from a healthier and more productive workforce.

A more active mental health lobby has resulted in incremental gains in state parity laws. In 2001, 34 states introduced 76 pieces of parity legislation.[30] This lobby continues to try to make inroads, but in some states Medicaid is dropping "optional" mental health services to adults (services not required by the federal government).[31] In 2000 President Clinton issued an executive order giving federal government employees mental health insurance benefits equal to other health benefits. (If you have insurance, you might want to see how your mental health benefits compare.)

The differences between the public and private tiers of the health care system (see also Chapter 8) are often more pronounced in the mental health and substance abuse treatment delivery systems. But we should not forget that the public sector often offers clients a broader range of services than the private sector. For example, public mental health services may offer housing, child care, and other supportive services for clients and their families at low or no cost that the private sector may not offer at all, even if one can afford to pay for these services.[32]

Finding Better Prevention and Treatment Approaches

People with mental illness were once thought to be possessed by the devil and were hidden away from public view, but by the nineteenth century treatment began to take different forms.[33] Phillipe Pinel, a French physician, introduced "moral treatment," which consisted of caring for patients with kindness and consideration, providing the opportunity for discussion of personal problems, and encouraging an active orientation to life. This was a far more humane approach to treating mental illness, but it was not the treatment offered to most patients. Institutionalization or incarceration were the typical methods for dealing with mental illness. Dorothea Dix, a social reformer during the mid-1800s, sought to improve the plight of severely mistreated mental patients. Dix succeeded in improving conditions within mental institutions, but with increasing numbers of people being labeled mentally ill, institutions grew larger and less capable of helping patients.

The Industrial Revolution increased many social problems, including mental illness. People came to the cities seeking jobs and wealth; instead many found overcrowding, joblessness, and misery. Coping with urban problems was difficult, and new arrivals were often without the support of family and friends. Immigrants from other countries also flocked to the cities. Those who did not acculturate or assimilate quickly into U.S. society were often labeled deviant or mentally ill.[34] City dwellers, overwhelmed with problems, had little tolerance for behavior they considered abnormal. This increased the number of people sent to mental institutions.

Apart from state institutions, there was little in the way of social policies and public programs for people with mental illness. Following Dix's efforts, Clifford Beers introduced the "mental hygiene movement" in the early twentieth century. In 1909 he founded the National Mental Health Association. Beers knew well the dehumanizing conditions of mental institutions; he himself had been a patient. His efforts to expose the inhumane conditions of the institutions, like Dix's, resulted in better care, but the custodial and institutional philosophies of mental health treatment continued.

During World War II, a large number of young men were needed for military service. Part of the screening procedure for new recruits was a psychiatric examination. The number of young men rejected as unfit for military service or later discharged for psychiatric reasons was alarming. Although these psychiatric screening procedures have been criticized, the identification of so many young men with mental problems brought renewed concern for mental health. This concern was reflected in the Mental Health Act of 1946. The act established the National Institute of Mental Health (NIMH), with its focus on training, education, and research.

In the 1950s another important event occurred—the development of improved psychotherapeutic drugs that reduced many of the troubling symptoms (such as hallucinations) that patients experienced. This allowed hospital staffs to reduce restrictions placed on patients and made patients more acceptable to the community. Psychotropic medications can have serious side effects, and the appropriate use of drug therapy has been debated,[35] but it is evident that they have reduced the need for hospitalization for many patients. New and better drugs are being developed all the time, but they are often costly, thus prohibiting more people from obtaining them.

The use of psychotherapeutic drugs helped to lay the groundwork for the Community Mental Health Act of 1963. The act was a key element of an emerging community mental health movement. It emphasized more federal involvement in community-based care, better coordination between hospitals and community services, improved services to people with serious mental illness, a reduction in state hospital treatment, an increase in community treatment consistent with deinstitutionalization and normalization (also see Chapter 5), education and prevention services, and greater use of paraprofessional staff.

The Public Mental Health System

The Mental Retardation Facilities and Community Mental Health Centers Construction Act of 1963, often called the Community Mental Health Act, mandated that community mental health centers (CMHCs) provide five essential services: inpatient care, outpatient care, emergency services, partial hospitalization (day care), and consultation and education. CMHCs were to provide a "mental health safety net" and make mental health services available to community members, regardless of ability to pay.[36] In 1975 more essential services were mandated, including special programs for children and the elderly, aftercare and halfway house services for patients discharged from mental hospitals, and screening services to courts and related agencies to identify those in need of treatment. In 1977, NIMH began the Community Support Program which established federal-state partnerships to encourage long-term care for those with serious mental illness.

In the 1970s, a number of studies evaluated the success of community mental health centers.[37] The General Accounting Office discussed the positive effects of CMHC programs, including an increase in the availability of community care. In another report, the Senate Committee on Labor and Public Welfare also discussed the positive results achieved by community-based care. Some reports were not as complimentary. A 1974 report by Ralph Nader stated that CMHCs had not reduced the number of people admitted to state mental hospitals and accused psychiatrists of benefiting unfairly from the programs and of neglecting services to the poor.

To improve services, the Mental Health Systems Act of 1980 continued many provisions of the Community Mental Health Act and included recommendations of the President's Commission on Mental Health, appointed by Jimmy Carter in 1977 and headed by First Lady Rosalyn Carter. There were provisions for special groups, including people with serious mental illness, severely disturbed children and adolescents, and others who were unserved or underserved. The act was rescinded in 1981 shortly after President Ronald Reagan took office and attention was directed back to the states.[38] Today, CMHCs are no longer required to provide the essential services formerly identified, and federal funds are channeled through block grants. Each state must now develop a State Comprehensive Mental Health Services Plan. These three-year plans cover services to individuals with serious mental illness, individuals who are homeless and mentally ill, and children with severe disturbances. NIMH recommends one or more of the following services for them: residential services (e.g., short-term crisis stabilization units and supported housing options); client and family support (e.g., counseling, medication services, and emergency screening); psychosocial habilitation or rehabilitation (for developing vocational, social, and independent living skills); case management (coordination of multiple services needed by clients and outreach). Special initiatives such as the PATH and ACCESS programs are efforts to prevent or remedy homelessness among individuals with mental illness.

Though the funding structure of CMHCs has evolved over the years, their main goals remain the same—provide mental health services to low-income and uninsured people, especially community-based services to people with serious mental illness (SMI). Serving these goals became more challenging. In the 1980s, when federal funding changed from categorical grants made directly to CMHCs to block grants to states, federal funding shrank, falling behind inflation and remaining stagnant at around $435 million for the past several years.[39] CMHCs were supposed to become self-sufficient, and funding was originally provided for construction only. To keep their doors open and continue to serve the poor, CMHCs have had to balance serving clients unable to pay with serving "paying" clients. With the advent of Medicaid and Medicare in the 1960s, funding for low-income clients increased, but there was still a group that needed services and had no means to pay for treatment, those who were poor and uninsured, but who did not qualify for Medicaid or Medicare. Increasing pressure to make clients with SMI a service priority has also made it difficult for CMHCs to provide mental services to community members with less severe disorders. CMHCs remain committed to serving low-income community members, but they often have waiting lists and may turn people away.

Medicaid and Medicare effectively expanded the public mental health system beyond CMHCs to other mental health providers, many in private practice, who would accept these public payments. Today, the public mental health system is a mix of private providers who accept government payment for services, CMHCs, Veterans hospital psychiatric services, and state mental health facilities such as psychiatric hospitals and residential treatment centers.

The September 11, 2001, terrorist attacks, the ensuing war on terrorism,[40] and the war in Iraq[41] have placed increased demands on the mental health system. The public mental health system has been asked to develop crisis response plans in the event of future terrorist attacks, but CMHCs are already overwhelmed with serving clients who are poor and those who have SMI.[42] In response to increasing mental health needs, President George W. Bush established the New Freedom Commission on Mental Health in April 2002 and charged it with conducting a "comprehensive study of the United States mental health service delivery system, including public and private sectors providers, and to advise the President on methods of improving the system."[43]

After a year of study and input from nearly 2,500 people, including consumers, mental health professionals, and national experts, the commission issued its final report in July 2003. The commission concluded that the system is not oriented toward recovery. It recommended a transformation of the public mental health system based on two principles:

1. Services and treatments should be patient- and family-centered, geared to give consumers real and meaningful choices about treatment options and providers—not oriented to the requirements of bureaucracies.

2. Care must be focused on increasing consumers' ability to successfully cope with life's challenges, on facilitating recovery, and on building resilience, not just on managing symptoms.

To transform the mental health system, the commission outlined the following six goals and made the following nineteen recommendations:

Goal 1 Americans Understand That Mental Health Is Essential to Overall Health.

RECOMMENDATIONS **1.1** Advance and implement a national campaign to reduce the stigma of seeking care and a national strategy for suicide prevention.

1.2 Address mental health with the same urgency as physical health.

Goal 2 Mental Health Care Is Consumer and Family Driven.

RECOMMENDATIONS **2.1** Develop an individualized plan of care for every adult with a serious mental illness and child with a serious emotional disturbance.

2.2 Involve consumers and families fully in orienting the mental health system toward recovery.

2.3 Align relevant federal programs to improve access and accountability for mental health services.

2.4 Create a Comprehensive State Mental Health Plan.

2.5 Protect and enhance the rights of people with mental illnesses.

Goal 3 Disparities in Mental Health Services Are Eliminated.

RECOMMENDATIONS **3.1** Improve access to quality care that is culturally competent.

3.2 Improve access to quality care in rural and geographically remote areas.

Goal 4 Early Mental Health Screening, Assessment, and Referral to Services Are Common Practice.

RECOMMENDATIONS **4.1** Promote the mental health of young children.

4.2 Improve and expand school mental health programs.

4.3 Screen for co-occurring mental and substance use disorders and link with integrated treatment strategies.

4.4 Screen for mental disorders in primary healthcare, across the life span, and connect to treatment and supports.

Goal 5 Excellent Mental Health Care Is Delivered and Research Is Accelerated.

RECOMMENDATIONS **5.1** Accelerate research to promote recovery and resilience, and ultimately to cure and prevent mental illnesses.

5.2 Advance evidence-based practices using dissemination and demonstration projects and create a public–private partnership to guide their implementation.

5.3   Improve and expand the workforce providing evidence-based mental health services and supports.

5.4   Develop the knowledge base in four understudied areas: mental health disparities, long-term effects of medications, trauma, and acute care.

Goal 6 Technology Is Used to Access Mental Health Care and Information.

RECOMMENDATIONS   **6.1**   Use health technology and telehealth to improve access and coordination of mental healthcare, especially for Americans in remote areas or in underserved populations.

6.2   Develop and implement integrated electronic health record and personal health information systems.[44]

Many praised the commission's work, but some advocates for people with mental illness complained that the commission ignored the needs of those in crisis and those with serious mental illness, failed to recommend treatment interventions known to be effective, ignored major funding issues, and perpetuated a myth that everyone with a serious mental health problem can recover[45] (see Illustration 10.1).

A War on Drugs or on Drug Addicts?

Concerted federal efforts to assist alcoholics did not occur until passage of the Comprehensive Alcohol Abuse Prevention, Treatment, and Rehabilitation Act of 1970. The act established the National Institute on Alcohol Abuse and Alcoholism (NIAAA). This was soon followed by the establishment of the National Institute on Drug Abuse (NIDA). These actions were the first major governmental attempts to recognize alcohol and drug dependence as treatable illnesses.

When Ronald Reagan collapsed funding for alcohol, drug abuse, and mental health services under a single block grant, the federal funds available to states were reduced. Critics continue to contend that this fiscal austerity has contributed to homelessness among people with mental and substance use disorders and to their inability to obtain treatment and other social services. Like community mental health centers, publicly funded substance abuse treatment programs are under increasing pressure to focus services on those with the most serious problems.

The nation's growing concerns about drug abuse did prompt the Reagan administration to establish the Office of Substance Abuse Prevention, with a focus on communities' efforts to halt drug use among their younger members. First Lady Nancy Reagan joined the effort, although her "Just Say No to Drugs" campaign, directed at children, was often criticized as being too simplistic to strike at the many causes of drug use and abuse. AIDS added to the concern about drug abuse with President Reagan's Commission on the Human Immunodeficiency Virus Epidemic calling for "treatment on demand" for drug abusers to help prevent the spread of HIV.[46]

ILLUSTRATION 10.1

Commission's Omission: The President's Mental-Health Commission in Denial

by Sally Satel and Mary Zdanowicz

Last week, the president's New Freedom Commission on Mental Health released its much-awaited report, "Achieving the Promise: Transforming Mental Health Care in America." President Bush had charged the 22-member group with making a "comprehensive study" that would "advise [him] on methods of improving the system."

Unfortunately, the report is woefully incomplete. The commission did not take on the most difficult cases.

Andrew Goldstein was a hard case. In 1999 the 29-year-old New Yorker killed Kendra Webdale by pushing her in front of a subway train. Goldstein suffered from schizophrenia and according to his court-appointed attorney had stopped taking his antipsychotic medication. Every year thousands of people with psychotic illnesses stop taking their medications; often because they do not even think they are ill.

They do not all murder, of course, but the consequences are dire nonetheless. Severe and persistent mental illness is a factor in 10–15 percent of violent crimes, according to a 2000 Lewin Group report. This rate is much higher than the two percent of people with a psychotic condition (schizophrenia or manic-depressive illness) in the population and the incidents occur most often because they are untreated. They swell the ranks of the homeless and incarcerated as well. Taxpayer costs aside, the human toll is staggering.

The commission, however, ignored this hard-to-treat group. Instead it focused on "consumers"—the politically correct word for psychiatric patients—who are willing and able to make use of treatments, programs, and opportunities. The commission even prided itself on soliciting testimony revealing that "nearly every consumer . . . expressed the need to fully participate in his or her plan for recovery." But they did not hear from the sickest silent minority that is languishing in back bedrooms, jail cells, and homeless shelters. They are too paranoid, oblivious, or lost in madness to attend hearings, never mind testify.

Dubbing its vision the "recovery model," the commission believes that sufficient therapy, housing options, and employment programs will enable people with schizophrenia or manic-depressive illness to take charge of their lives. Many will, it's true. But thousands won't. Over half of all untreated people with a psychotic illness do not acknowledge there is anything wrong with them. These people aren't avoiding treatment because services are unattractive (though many are indeed dismal) or because of "stigma," as the report repeatedly claims, but because they don't even know they need care in the first place.

The problem with the recovery vision is that it is a dangerously partial vision. It sets up unrealistic expectations for those who will never fully "recover," no matter how hard they try, because their illness is so severe. What's more, exclusive emphasis on recovery as a goal steers policymakers away from making changes vital to the needs of the most severely disabled.

One long-overdue change is helping those who need intensive long-term institutional care. Not only does the report fail to recognize

continued

ILLUSTRATION 10.1 *(continued)*

the paucity of psychiatric hospital beds, it ignores a blatantly discriminatory aspect of federal law. The Medicaid Institutions for Mental Disease (IMD) exclusion law prevents states from receiving federal reimbursement for facilities with more than 16 beds, simply because its residents are treated for psychiatric disorders.

It is a policy with devastating consequences, especially considering the condition of state budgets. Just last month, the IMD exclusion forced the closure of several beds for mentally ill felons in Miami who may now be forced to live under far less-supervised conditions.

The commission also neglected to advise the president on how to manage severely mentally ill people who stop taking their medications. There was no mention, for example, of proven strategies, such as assisted outpatient treatment (civil court-ordered community treatment), which is often necessary for those who have a reliable pattern of spiraling into self-destruction or dangerousness when off medication. The commission's hesitancy to address this treatment mechanism is especially odd given the results from instituting such measures. For instance, in New York, of those placed in six months of assisted outpatient treatment, 77 percent fewer were hospitalized, 85 percent fewer experienced homelessness, 83 percent fewer were arrested, and 85 percent fewer were incarcerated.

Doubtless the timid commission was afraid of censure from mental-health groups who reflexively charge civil-liberties violations at the slightest hint of coercion. But in fact, anti-psychotic medication, even when taken by a resistant patient, restores personal liberty, freeing him to make his own decisions again. Studies consistently show that the majority of patients initially treated without their consent agree with the decision when asked about it in

retrospect. Newer mental-health courts, another coercive option, use judicial persuasion and the threat of jail to keep minor offenders with psychosis in treatment and on medications at least long enough for them to make informed decisions about treatment.

Last, we come to the matter of stigma. The commission thinks that irrational fear and disapproval of the mentally ill explain public indifference to their welfare. While many are indeed fearful their attitudes are not inexplicable—they come from reading lurid headlines or dodging menacing or hallucinating individuals on the street. "The perception of people with psychosis as being dangerous is stronger today than in the past," according to the 1999 U.S. Surgeon General's Report on Mental Health. Unfortunately, the logical conclusion eluded the commission—stigma will continue unabated until we stem threatening and erratic behavior.

Despite our dismay, the commission got many things right. Among them it urged integration of funding agencies, medical, and social services. It promoted evidence-based treatments and programs and condemned the awful double bind in which many are forced to remain on meager disability income because taking on paid work would mean losing Medicaid coverage.

These recommendations, while solid, are not enough to help a deeply troubled system recover. Ever since deinstitutionalization began closing doors to state hospitals in the late 1950s, we have abandoned the sickest of the mentally ill to the streets and jails. Four decades later, the commission opted for the safe route and abandoned them as well.

—Sally Satel, M.D., is at the American Enterprise Institute. Mary Zdanowicz is a lawyer and executive director of the Treatment Advocacy Center in Arlington, VA.

Since the Reagan years, the theme of drug abuse prevention has been that of a "war on drugs." In 1986 and 1988 Congress passed omnibus drug abuse legislation to further arm this war.[47] The 1988 Anti-Drug Abuse Act established the Office of National Drug Control Policy (ONDCP), headed by a cabinet-level "drug czar" in the Executive Office of the President. The emphasis has been on interdiction (stopping the flow of drugs into the United States) and on stiffer legal penalties for drug-related crimes (including the possiblity of the death penalty when a murder is involved). These provisions are said to strike at the *supply side* of the drug problem. Prevention, education, and treatment efforts were also included in the act in an attempt to influence the *demand side* of the drug problem. There are numerous other provisions in the 1988 act, including those for drug-free workplaces and eviction of public housing residents who engage in or permit drug use on or near the premises.

But even the most casual observer will probably agree that the law enforcement approach has not substantially stemmed drug trafficking. No matter how many tons of drugs are seized, the enticement provided by the lucrative drug trade causes more to be produced. Many people in the United States and elsewhere are lured into this underground economy. The country's prisons are bulging at the seams with inmates convicted of drug-related crimes. Drug crimes are the single greatest contributor to the phenomenal increase in incarceration in the United States. Over half (55 percent) of federal inmates were sentenced for drug-related offenses. Federal drug offenders increased 156 percent between 1986 and 1999, and in 2003 the federal government spent about $3 billion to incarcerate drug offenders.[48] State jails and prisons are also overwhelmed with an influx of people incarcerated for relatively low-level drug crimes. Prisons are responding with more drug treatment, and there are now prisons devoted entirely to rehabilitating drug offenders.

In 1985, while President Reagan was in office, 82 percent of the federal budget for drug control went to law enforcement efforts and 18 percent to treatment, education, and prevention.[49] Under the George H. W. Bush administration, treatment, education, and prevention garnered 30 percent, but social service advocates remained concerned that too little of Congress's efforts were aimed at these services. The Clinton administration directed slightly more (about one-third) of the federal drug control budget to these demand reduction efforts, with the remainder being used for law enforcement, interdiction, and other supply-side interventions.[50] The George W. Bush administration reports that 45 percent of the drug control budget is now being directed to treatment and prevention, although law enforcement and interdiction still command the largest part of the budget (55 percent).[51]

To help more nonviolent drug offenders get treatment, the Violent Crime Control and Law Enforcement Act of 1994 supports the use of diversion programs, including drug courts, and Title I of the Omnibus Crime Control and Safe Streets Act of 1994 provided funds to states, tribes, and local courts to create drug courts. These 1994 acts recognized that incarceration has little impact on substance abuse.[52] Drug courts provide an alternative to incarceration through extensive su-

ILLUSTRATION 10.2

Getting People Back on Track at Cincinnati's Drug Court

Dan Smith, a 32-year-old drifter, is arrested on charges of possession of cocaine and methamphetamine. Numerous prior arrests of a similar nature have been documented throughout his life, but this is the first time Dan has been detained in Cincinnati. In the Hamilton County Drug Court, he will be given the tools he needs to get on track to a law-abiding, drug-free life.

After his arrest, a public defender identifies Dan as a potential candidate for the drug court. For two weeks he undergoes an inpatient assessment period conducted by substance abuse professionals at Talbert House Treatment Center. Four probation officers are assigned to the site to foster coordination between the criminal justice system and the treatment providers.

After the center's clinical experts determine that Dan is dependent on illicit drugs, he goes before the Honorable Kim W. Burke. Dan is placed on probation and ordered to complete a treatment regimen that typically includes ninety days of residential treatment, followed by six weeks of intensive outpatient care, and a minimum of twelve months of continuing care.

Judge Burke keeps a close eye on the drug court's clients, meeting with all 400 of them at least once a month and some as often as weekly. Key to the drug court's success is creating an environment that is supportive but firm. Says Judge Burke, "At our evening status reports, I have the probation officer there, I have the treatment counselor there, and I have the attorney there. That avoids a lot of people saying 'My probation officer told me I could do this,' or 'My counselor told me I could do that'."

As long as Dan remains drug- and alcohol-free for the duration of this sentence, he will serve no jail time for the original charge. The program relies on Dan's knowledge that he will receive weekly drug tests; if he is found to have used illegal drugs, he can expect immediate consequences.

Judge Burke puts it this way: "If a person tests positive, I find out about it pretty quickly—usually the next day. Relapse is part of what we deal with, but when they come in with a dirty drug screen, they know that they're going to spend a couple of days in jail. The point of it is for them to have immediate consequences for their actions."

Source: Office of National Drug Control Policy, *National Drug Control Strategy, Update 2003* (Washington, DC: Executive Office of the President, 2003).

pervision and drug treatment (see Illustration 10.2). Key components of drug courts include:

♦ Creating nonadversarial relationships between the defendant and the court

♦ Identifying treatment needs and making referrals to treatment quickly after arrests

♦ Emphasizing rehabilitation services and a continuum of care

♦ Using drug testing and monitoring

♦ Maintaining court interaction with participants

♦ Evaluating participants' outcomes

♦ Forging partnerships with public agencies and community-based organizations

By November 2003, nearly 1,100 drug courts were operating across the 50 states, with another 414 projected to open in the near future. Twelve states have passed legislation supporting the formation and maintenance of drug courts, and the United Nations considered a bill encouraging the use of drug courts internationally.

Drug courts seem to be working. Up to 65 percent of drug court graduates reportedly ceased substance use, and recidivism rates one and two years after graduating from drug courts were 16 and 28 percent, respectively, compared to 44 and 59 percent for drug offenders who had been released from jail. Eighty percent of juvenile drug court participants returned to or remained in school full time. Drug court participants said three primary factors contributed to their success in staying clean and sober: (1) close supervision and encouragement by judges; (2) intensive treatment; and (3) ongoing monitoring.[53] According to Steven Belenko from the National Center on Addiction and Substance Abuse, "drug courts have been quite successful in bridging the gap between the court and the treatment/public health systems and spurring greater cooperation among the various agencies and personnel within the criminal justice system, as well as between the criminal justice system and the community."[54] Success of the drug court model has prompted the creation of similar courts for individuals arrested for driving under the influence (DUI) and domestic violence and individuals with mental illness arrested for relatively minor infractions. These courts are also creating new pathways between treatment centers and the criminal justice system.[55] Along these same lines, California voters approved Proposition 36, which diverts all first- and second-time nonviolent drug possession offenders to treatment rather than incarceration.

SAMHSA has called for "changing the conversation" through its National Treatment Plan Initiative by closing the very large gap between the number who need treatment and the number who get it. The plan says that there should be "no wrong door" (i.e., no matter where people enter the system, they should be identified, assessed, and directed to appropriate care).[56] Although treatment helps substantial numbers of people, there is still much to be learned about how to make treatment for mental and substance use disorders more effective. Many people fail to complete treatment, and though relapse is considered a natural part of the recovery process, treatment providers are looking at ways to prevent or reduce relapses from occurring.

SAMHSA's plan does not consider more radical approaches to addressing the nation's voracious appetite for drugs. "Harm reduction" strategies, adopted by other countries, have largely been eschewed by the U.S. government.[57] For example, needle exchange programs for injection drug users are designed to save lives by stopping the transmission of HIV. This approach has met with serious opposition in the United States, including a federal funding ban, despite evidence that it reduces HIV transmission and does not encourage new users. Needle exchange programs can also help drug users get into treatment. The British medical journal the Lancet has implored the

United States government to remove the federal funding ban, as did the President's Advisory Council on HIV/AIDS under the Clinton administration and other groups, but nothing has happened.[58] The federal government has basically left decisions about needle exchange to the states, but most state and local governments have not budged. A number of needle-exchange programs continue to operate underground in defiance of the law or with unofficial sanction because community officials may see the need for them even if official approval is hard to come by. Public policy impedes establishing needle exchange programs because the majority of states have drug paraphernalia laws that make it illegal to manufacture, possess, or distribute injecting equipment for nonmedical use, and in some states, a doctor's prescription is needed to purchase such equipment.

Another harm reduction approach, methadone maintenance, which began in the 1960s, is known to reduce crime and help heroin addicts maintain more stable lives, but it also remains controversial because addicts continue to be drug addicted rather than drug free. A newly approved drug for the treatment of opioid addiction, buprenorphine, can be obtained from regular doctors' offices (if the doctor wishes to become approved to offer it). Without the need to comply with the additional requirements of methadone maintenance programs, like required drug counseling and coming to the program every day, more people might participate in this form of treatment.

Foreign policy also plays a substantial role in the United States's drug control efforts. The United States gives "favored status," including considerable financial aid, to countries that cooperate in drug crop eradication, but there are questions about how much some of these countries actually cooperate. Stopping drug production in one place only means that it will crop up in another. Poppy production (heroin is produced from poppies) was prohibited under the brutal Taliban regime, but the poppy fields have sprung to life again with the Taliban's overthrow. Afghanistan is once again the world's largest opium producer.[59] Prohibition did not stop alcohol use and it has not curbed illicit drug use. Many people, including intellectuals and those on both sides of the political aisle, see that the United States has failed to win the drug war, despite the billions devoted to this goal each year in the country's drug control budget. A system of legal access to drugs for addicts through controlled sales and medical monitoring might help to curb the lucrative illicit drug trade, which spawns violence in the United States and other countries. Even the use of marijuana for medical purposes has largely been rejected. In the few states that have passed medical marijuana laws, doctors have been threatened with sanctions by the federal government if they make use of the law. This chapter could take a serious look at drug legalization. Instead, we refer the reader to other sources. There is no chance that such alternatives will be considered in the foreseeable future because the more viable position for politicians is that legalization condones drug use or encourages a deadly habit. Congress expressly added a subtitle to the 1988 Anti Drug Abuse Act stating its view against legalization. We also remind readers that Chapters 5, 6, and 7 include policies that prevent people with felony drug convictions or substance use disorders from participating in many social welfare programs. No other medical or mental health diagnosis carries this type of public policy stigma.

Treatment and Civil Rights

People with mental illness and chemical dependency problems are often unable to recognize their need for treatment. They may be subjected to involuntary hospitalization for short periods of time for observation and assessment, and if found in need of mandatory care, ordered by the courts to remain in treatment. For those currently experiencing severe and acute problems, treatment provided on an outpatient basis or in community facilities may not be sufficient. Community programs may not be equipped to assist these individuals (now referred to as mental health consumers), or specialized facilities may not exist in a community.

Inpatient treatment may be deemed a necessity by professionals, but it restricts an individual from moving about in the community and participating in normal, daily activities. These restrictions on one's liberties mean that great care should be taken to prevent unnecessary confinement. Although the U.S. Constitution is necessarily concerned with protecting individual liberties, the states have primary responsibility for providing mental health services, and it is often courts at the state level that have intervened to offer civil rights protections.

Until the mid-1880s, involuntary commitment was mostly done through informal procedures rather than state statute; then, in 1845, "the Massachusetts Supreme Court established the precedent that individuals could be restrained only if dangerous to themselves or others and only if restraint would be conducive to their restoration."[60] But in practice patients had few means to contest their confinement. Some remained hospitalized for decades, even if their placement was no longer necessary or they had been placed inappropriately (such as those confined because they were mentally retarded, not mentally ill). In 1960, California's Lanterman-Petric-Short Act, and in 1972, Wisconsin's *Lessard v. Schmidt* decision, restricted the grounds for involuntary commitment and established stringent due process procedures. Soon after, in 1975, the U.S. Supreme Court ruled in Florida's Donaldson case, reinforcing the view that it is unjust to confine patients who are not dangerous in psychiatric institutions when they are not provided treatment and they can survive on their own. In 1980, Congress passed the Civil Rights of Institutionalized Persons Act to protect people held in state and local institutions.

Liberty or Neglect?

Thomas Szasz, in his well-known book *The Myth of Mental Illness,* called psychiatric illnesses "stigmatizing" labels, phrased to resemble medical diagnoses and applied to persons whose behavior annoys or offends others.[61] Szasz took the position of the true libertarian in denouncing all involuntary treatment as "crimes against humanity." Most people do not share this position; every community contains individuals whom other members of society feel are in need of protection. But it is sometimes difficult to know when intervention is necessary. Mechanic's assessment is that except for previous dangerous behavior, the conditions that qualify as dangerous to self or others have not been clearly identified.[62] Psychiatry is hardly an exact science, and the "system" often fails even those who present for treatment as cases like Andrea

Yates, the Houston, Texas, mother who drowned her five children, and too many others illustrate.

During the late 1980s, the well-publicized story of Joyce Brown of New York City, a 40-year-old woman who had worked as a secretary, typified the dilemma of deciding who requires protection.[63] Brown was confined to Bellevue (psychiatric) Hospital against her will. According to media accounts, Brown's behavior would probably seem unusual to most of us. She relieved herself on the sidewalk, shouted obscenities, burned money, slept on a steam grate, and wore filthy clothing. Brown had been hospitalized previously, and her sisters said that her abusive behavior caused them to ask her to vacate their home. But controversy erupted over whether Brown should have been hospitalized involuntarily. During a court appearance to determine whether she should remain in the hospital, the judge decided that Brown did not appear to present a danger, and he blamed the lack of decent housing for her predicament. The judge's ruling was later reversed by an appellate court, but this court would not allow the city to medicate Brown against her will, and she was released. Brown did well for a period, working and even lecturing on the matter, but later reports indicated that she had returned to the streets. New York City is generally thought to have a higher tolerance for deviant behavior than many other cities, but its former mayor Ed Koch was criticized by some camps for his decision that freezing weather meant homeless people would be given shelter, even against their will. In his essay "When Liberty Really Means Neglect," Charles Krauthammer gave serious consideration to Koch's position and the dilemmas posed by citizens like Joyce Brown. According to Krauthammer:

> Why not make compassion an all-weather policy? Danger should not be the only warrant for giving someone, even an unwilling someone, shelter and care. Degradation—a life of eating garbage, of sleeping on grates, of recurrent illness and oppressive hallucinations—should suffice. . . .
>
> Liberty counts for much, but not enough to turn away from those who are hopelessly overwhelmed by the demands of modern life. To permit those who would flounder in the slowest lane to fend for themselves on very mean streets is an act not of social liberality but of neglect bordering on cruelty.[64]

Involuntary Outpatient Commitment

The controversy over involuntary inpatient confinement and the debate over civil liberties have contributed to an alternative type of care for some people with serious mental illness—involuntary *outpatient* commitment (IOC). IOC is court-ordered outpatient treatment for individuals who are mentally ill.[65] In recent years there has been a proliferation of state statutes authorizing IOC. IOC standards vary from state to state from more restrictive standards, such as being a threat of harm to self or others, to less restrictive standards. Many states include a "grave disability" provision that indicates that the person is unable to meet basic needs (food, shelter, or safety) or that failure to participate in treatment will likely result in severe mental or emotional deterioration. Some states use the person's prior treatment and be-havioral history to determine the need for IOC. This is a major shift from past in-voluntary commitment laws that focused on behaviors occurring at the time of commitment requests. In some states, IOC is only used for patients being discharged from a psychiatric inpatient setting and serves as a bridge to community living to help insure that patients are adequately supervised and receive necessary treatment. While 38 states have IOC mechanisms, most states use it infrequently. The amount of time that a mental health client can be ordered into IOC ranges from 45 days in Arkansas to one year in Georgia. Most states allow for a limited number of exten-sions of the original IOC order, but in Arkansas the court can issue an unlimited number of extensions. All states with IOC laws except Colorado require a hearing before an order can be issued. Arizona requires that a treatment plan be in place before an IOC can be ordered, and Oregon and Pennsylvania require that commu-nity-based treatment be available and accessible. A few states (Colorado, Nebraska, Oklahoma, and West Virginia) include the right to order substance abusers as well as those with mental health problems into IOC treatment. Opponents of IOC fear that such practices make it too easy to violate the civil rights of individuals with mental illness, while proponents believe that when used appropriately, it protects civil liberties because it allows the courts to mandate care in least restrictive set-tings, and provides a means of intervening with effective treatment *before* the per-son's mental health deteriorates to the point of harming self or others. The National Alliance for the Mentally Ill (comprised of individuals with mental illnesses) and the Treatment Advocacy Center support the expansion of IOC laws to include "grave disability" and encourage treatment for people who cannot make that decision for themselves before imminent danger occurs.[66]

A RAND Corporation report reviewed the limited amount of research on IOC and found that when intensive treatment is provided, the number of hospital admissions and the length of stay for individuals with schizophrenia and other psychoses is re-duced.[67] IOC may also result in reduced violent behavior among individuals with se-rious mental illness who exhibit this behavior, and fewer were victims of crime. Several issues remain.

For IOC to be effective, community services and supports must be in place, and many communities are woefully deficient in this area because mental health services are grossly underfunded. One model that has demonstrated success with people who have serious mental illness is Assertive Community Treatment (ACT).[68] ACT is pro-vided by an intensive multidisciplinary community-based treatment team. Typically at least some of the team members go to the person rather than expecting the person to come to them. The team provides psychiatric treatment, coordinates care with var-ious service providers, and helps the individual meet life's basic needs. ACT may help individuals engage in treatment, improve their social functioning, and reduce hospi-tal admissions. But ACT is costly, and therefore is usually reserved for individuals who are the highest users of mental health services. Other community-based treatment in-terventions for people with mental illnesses are case management, psychosocial in-terventions, supportive housing, and supportive employment. Evidence on the effectiveness of these methods is mixed.

Although the client under IOC is mandated to receive treatment, it may be unclear if the mental health system is mandated to provide treatment, especially if services are not available in a timely manner or cannot be easily accessed by patients or clients. A portion of clients do not comply with treatment. Monitoring IOC orders usually falls on mental healthcare systems that lack the resources to provide the level of supervision needed. Some mental health professionals complain that many IOC laws do not have any "teeth," making them difficult to enforce. Mental health courts are trying to address these unresolved issues. The community mental health system really cannot make people participate in treatment, and while the emphasis on community-based treatment sounds wonderful, for many people, jails and nursing homes have become the defacto mental health system that provides nothing resembling mental health treatment or even adequate legal representation.[69] Others are languishing in deplorable circumstances in board-and-care homes.[70]

A Mental Health Bill of Rights

Today, consumers in mental health hospitals and drug treatment facilities must be informed of their rights both to obtain and to refuse treatment. Those who cannot read must have this information explained to them. Despite these legal protections, major obstacles continue to prevent consumers from receiving the best treatment in these facilities. As David Mechanic, an authority on mental health policy, has noted "the welfare of patients depends more on excellent systems of care than on legal definitions."[71] Mental health consumers should always be treated in a way that respects their individual dignity, but this manner of treatment is contingent on the quality and resources of the treatment facility and of its staff. Facilities, especially public and not-for-profit ones, are often crowded. Some are located in remote areas where it may be difficult to recruit and retain qualified staff. Yet decisions about a consumer's day-to-day activities are largely staff decisions. Consumers may have little influence in choosing these activities, short of refusing to participate. Moreover, when mental health consumers refuse to participate, they are often considered to be uncooperative and resistant to treatment. This may serve to prolong their stay in the hospital.

Mental health consumers have the right to know the reason for their inpatient or outpatient commitment and what must happen before release will be granted. They must be provided legal representation and access to mental health laws. Inpatients should be afforded privacy when they have visitors, and visits should not be denied unless there is reason to believe that they might be harmful to the consumer or others. Unfortunately, when hospitals are located far from the consumer's home, it is more difficult for family to maintain ties and for the consumer to visit family on short leaves from the hospital. These leaves can aid in reintegration into the community.

The American Psychological Association publishes a *Mental Health Bill of Rights* that is endorsed by many mental health professional organizations, including the National Association of Social Workers (see Illustration 10.3). The bill covers a broad range of rights including insurance benefits, expertise of mental health service providers, confidentiality, appeals and grievance procedures, treatment determinations, treatment reviews, and accountability.

ILLUSTRATION 10.3

Spread the Word: Text of Mental Health Bill of Rights

PRINCIPLES FOR THE PROVISION OF MENTAL HEALTH AND SUBSTANCE ABUSE TREATMENT SERVICES

Our commitment is to provide quality mental health and substance abuse services to all individuals without regard to race, color, religion, national origin, gender, age, sexual orientation, or disabilities.

RIGHT TO KNOW BENEFITS

Individuals have the right to be provided information from the purchasing entity (such as employer or union or public purchaser) and the insurance/third party payer describing the nature and extent of their mental health and substance abuse treatment benefits. This information should include details on procedures to obtain access to services, on utilization management procedures, and on appeal rights. The information should be presented clearly in writing with language that the individual can understand.

PROFESSIONAL EXPERTISE

Individuals have the right to receive full information from the potential treating professional about that professional's knowledge, skills, preparation, experience, and credentials. Individuals have the right to be informed about the options available for treatment interventions and the effectiveness of the recommended treatment.

CONTRACTUAL LIMITATIONS

Individuals have the right to be informed by the treating professional of any arrangements, restrictions, and/or covenants established between third party payer and the treating professional that could interfere with or influence treatment recommendations. Individuals have the right to be informed of the nature of information that may be disclosed for the purposes of paying benefits.

APPEALS AND GRIEVANCES

Individuals have the right to receive information about the methods they can use to submit complaints or grievances regarding provision of care by the treating professional to that profession's regulatory board and to the professional association.

Individuals have the right to be provided information about the procedures they can use to appeal benefit utilization decisions to the third party payer systems, to the employer or purchasing entity, and to external regulatory entities.

CONFIDENTIALITY

Individuals have the right to be guaranteed the protection of the confidentiality of their relationship with their mental health and substance abuse professional, except when laws or ethics dictate otherwise. Any disclosure to another party will be time limited and made with the full written, informed consent of the individuals.

Individuals shall not be required to disclose confidential, privileged, or other information other than: diagnosis, prognosis, type of treatment, time and length of treatment, and cost.

Entities receiving information for the purposes of benefits determination, public agencies receiving information for health care planning, or any other organization with

continued

ILLUSTRATION 10.3 *(continued)*

legitimate right to information will maintain clinical information in confidence with the same rigor and be subject to the same penalties for violation as is the direct provider of care.

Information technology will be used for transmission, storage, or data management only with methodologies that remove individual identifying information and assure the protection of the individual's privacy. Information should not be transferred, sold or otherwise utilized.

CHOICE

Individuals have the right to choose any duly licensed/certified professional for mental health and substance abuse services. Individuals have the right to receive full information regarding the education and training of professionals, treatment options (including risks and benefits), and cost implications to make an informed choice regarding the selection of care deemed appropriate by individual and professional.

DETERMINATION OF TREATMENT

Recommendations regarding mental health and substance abuse treatment shall be made only by a duly licensed/certified professional in conjunction with the individual and his or her family as appropriate. Treatment decisions should not be made by third party payers. The individual has the right to make final decisions regarding treatment.

PARITY

Individuals have the right to receive benefits for mental health and substance abuse treatment on the same basis as they do for any other illnesses, with the same provisions, co-payments, lifetime benefits, and catastrophic coverage in both insurance and self-funded/self-insured health plans.

DISCRIMINATION

Individuals who use mental health and substance abuse benefits shall not be penalized when seeking other health insurance or disability, life, or any other insurance benefit.

BENEFIT USAGE

The individual is entitled to the entire scope of the benefits within the benefit plan that will address his or her clinical needs.

BENEFIT DESIGN

Whenever both federal and state law and/or regulations are applicable, the professional and all payers shall use whichever affords the individual the greatest level of protection and access.

TREATMENT REVIEW

To assure that treatment review processes are fair and valid, individuals have the right to be guaranteed that any review of their mental health and substance abuse treatment shall involve a professional having the training, credentials, and licensure required to provide the treatment in the jurisdiction in which it will be provided. The reviewer should have no financial interest in the decision and is subject to the section on confidentiality.

ACCOUNTABILITY

Treating professionals may be held accountable and liable to individuals for any injury caused by gross incompetence or negligence on the part of the professional. The treating

continued

ILLUSTRATION 10.3 *(continued)*

professional has the obligation to advocate for and document necessity of care and to advise the individual of options if payment authorization is denied.

Payers and other third parties may be held accountable and liable to individuals for any injury caused by gross incompetence or negligence or by their clinically unjustified decisions.

PARTICIPATING GROUPS

American Association for Marriage and
    Family Therapy (membership: 25,000)
American Counseling Association
    (membership: 56,000)
American Family Therapy Academy
    (membership: 1,000)
American Nurses Association
    (membership: 180,000)

American Psychological Association
    (membership: 151,000)
American Psychiatric Association
    (membership: 42,000)
American Psychiatric Nurses Association
    (membership: 3,000)
National Association of Social Workers
    (membership: 155,000)
National Federation of Societies for Clinical
    Social Work (membership: 11,000)

SUPPORTING GROUPS

National Mental Health Association
American Group Psychotherapy Association
American Psychoanalytic Association
National Association of Alcoholism and Drug
    Abuse Counselors
National Depressive and Manic Depressive
    Association

Source: American Psychological Association, *Spread the Word: Text of Mental Health Bill of Rights* (Washington, DC, 1997), retrieved from http://helping.apa.org/spreadtheword/rights.html. Copyright © 1997 American Psychological Association. All rights reserved. Reprinted with permission.

CHILD WELFARE POLICY

Americans place a high value on privacy, and governmental interference in the private matters of the home is generally considered an unwelcome intrusion. As a result, the United States has no official national family policy. Instead, a number of federal, state, and local laws govern various aspects of family relations. This section focuses on one area of family relations—child welfare, especially child abuse and neglect.

Discovering Child Abuse

Following the tradition of English common law, children in colonial America were considered chattels—the possessions of their parents.[72] Parents who severely punished their children, even beat them, were not defying community standards or breaking the law; they were merely making sure their children obeyed. Eventually case law allowed for criminal prosecution of parents in very severe cases, but in reality little was done to protect children. Children in need of care were subject to the same demeaning forms of social welfare as adults—often almshouses or poorhouses, and they were also subject to indenture. This tradition prevailed in America until the Industrial Revolution brought an abundance of new social problems. Among them were the conditions of urban cities, which were often overcrowded and unsanitary and where hunger and disease were not uncommon. During this period a prevailing philosophy was that children from poor homes might be better raised in separate institutions. Institutions such as the New York House of Refuge were established for neglected, abandoned, and delinquent youth. But the emphasis was not on protecting children from parents who harmed or neglected them. Institutional placement was intended to reverse the trend of poverty by teaching children proper social values and good work habits. Some organizations, like the Children's Aid Society founded by Charles Loring Brace in 1853 and the Children's Home Society founded by Martin Van Buren Van Arsdale in 1883, decided that children would best be served in rural areas, and they sent thousands of them to live and work with families, generally Christian families, away from the cities and their own families.

In 1874 the famous case of Mary Ellen brought public attention to the plight of severely mistreated children. The folklore surrounding the little girl's plight is that the laws protecting animals were stronger than those protecting children, and so Henry Bergh of the New York Society for the Prevention of Cruelty to Animals (NYSPCA) decided to plead her case on the basis that the child was a member of the animal kingdom. Historical records do reflect Mr. Bergh's intervention, but apparently as a private citizen who presented the girl as a child in need of protection, not as a member of the animal kingdom.[73] The story, however, has become woven into the history of child welfare and did raise public consciousness about child abuse (see Illustration 10.4).

Despite efforts of the settlement houses and eventually the Charity Organization Societies to focus on services to the family unit, the prevailing philosophy in the early twentieth century remained removing children from their homes rather than rehabilitating parents. The establishment of juvenile courts during this period did little to change this, but as the century progressed, more concern was expressed for the children themselves. Orphanages and foster homes became the preferred alternatives for child placement. New state mothers' aid programs provided some financial means to children in their natural homes, and slowly, child welfare philosophy in the twentieth century came to reflect "the great discovery . . . that the best place for normal children was in their own homes."[74] Still, abusive parents were not themselves the targets of social policies or social programs, and the public largely condoned parents' use of physical force on their children.

According to Stephen Pfohl, it was not the social reformers, nor the juvenile court authorities, nor the public at large who finally "discovered" child abuse.[75] It was pediatric radiologists who identified the problem or "syndrome," gave it legitimacy, and aroused public concern. Beginning in 1946, the work of pediatric radiologist John Caffey led to the identification of parents as the cause of many of the bone fractures seen in children. Although emergency room and family physicians (not radiologists) were the first to come into contact with abused children, at least four factors prevented them from recognizing the problem: (1) Child abuse was not a traditional diagnosis; (2) doctors may have found it difficult to believe that parents would perpetrate such acts; (3) if the family, rather than just the child, was the doctor's patient,

ILLUSTRATION 10.4

Little Mary Ellen

Before 1875, U.S. authorities had no legal means to interfere in cases of battered children. The laws were changed with the help of the Society for the Prevention of Cruelty to Animals (SPCA).

A 9-year-old named Mary Ellen became the exemplar of the battered children's plight. Indentured to Francis and Mary Connolly (and rumored to be the daughter of Mary's ex-husband), the girl was whipped daily, stabbed with scissors and tied to a bed. Neighbors reported the situation to Etta Wheeler, a church worker, in 1874. When Wheeler found that there was no lawful way to rescue the child from her brutal guardians, she went to Henry Bergh of the SPCA for help.

Under the premise that the child was a member of the animal kingdom, the SPCA obtained a writ of habeas corpus to remove Mary Ellen from her home. On April 9, 1874, she was carried into the New York Supreme Court, where her case was tried. She was pitifully thin, with a scissor wound on her cheek. Mrs. Connolly was sentenced to a year in prison. Mary Ellen was given a new home. The following April, the New York Society for the Prevention of Cruelty to Children (NYSPCC) was incorporated.

Before-and-after photos of Mary Ellen (as a pathetic waif upon her rescue and as a healthy child a year later) still hang at the New York SPCA, framed with Mrs. Connolly's scissors.

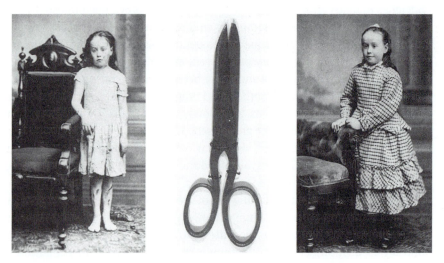

ASPCA's before and after photos of Mary Ellen, with scissors used to punish her.

Source: Reprinted with permission from Irving Wallace, David Wallechinsky, and Amy Wallace, "Significa," *Parade* magazine. Photos courtesy of ASPCA Archives.

reporting abuse may have constituted a violation of patient confidentiality; and (4) physicians may have been unwilling to report criminal behavior because of the time-consuming nature of criminal cases and their dislike for serving as witnesses in legal proceedings. Pediatric radiologists exposed child abuse because they did not deal directly with the child and the family. Issues regarding confidentiality and court proceedings were not their primary concerns. Their "discovery" also elevated the position of radiologists, who held lower status since they did not provide direct patient care.

To keep child abuse under the purview of the medical profession, it had to be viewed as a medical rather than a social or legal problem. In 1962, Dr. Henry Kempe and his associates labeled child abuse with the medical terminology "the battered-child syndrome," which legitimized its recognition by physicians.[76] Magazines, newspapers, and television programs, such as *Ben Casey* and *Dr. Kildare,* publicized the problem. Between 1963 and 1967 every state passed child abuse reporting legislation. Today, child abuse legislation is aimed more at rehabilitating parents than punishing them. Most cases are reported to social welfare rather than law enforcement agencies.

Extent of Child Maltreatment

Child maltreatment consists of both abuse and neglect. Abuse occurs when severe harm is inflicted on a child such as broken bones or burns, but it can also be emotional or sexual. Neglect occurs when a parent or caretaker fails to provide a child with the essentials needed to live adequately, including proper schooling, or it may result from psychological deprivation, such as isolating the child from others. Between 1986 and 1995, reports of child maltreatment increased by 42 percent.[77] Child abuse reports peaked in 1993 at 15.3 victims per 1,000 and then declined over the next six years to 11.8 per 1,000 in 1999.[78] This coincided with the economic boom that occurred during most of the decade and may have eased poverty and stress among low-income families, factors known to contribute to child maltreatment. As if on cue, as the economy began to slide, rates began to rise again. The overall growth in reports is due in part to public awareness of these problems. Child welfare authorities also believe there is an actual increase in the incidence of abuse due to factors such as poverty, violence, and drug (especially crack cocaine) use.

Professionals serving children (such as teachers, nurses, doctors, law enforcement personnel, day care providers, and social workers) are mandated by state laws to report even the suspicion of abuse or neglect to the local child protective services (CPS) agency. In 2002, professionals were responsible for 56 percent of the reports that were investigated (see Figure 10.1). Most remaining cases were reported by family and community members. CPS workers are supposed to respond to suspected cases within established time frames. High-priority cases require a response within 24 hours. Lower priority cases require a response within a few days to a few weeks, depending on the state. In 2002, the average response time to a report of abuse or neglect nationally was 52 hours.

FIGURE 10.1

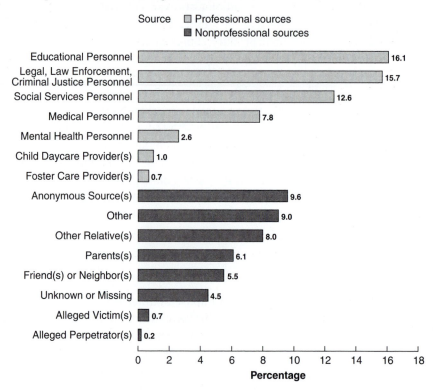

Alleged Child Abuse and Neglect, 2002

Source: Administration for Children and Families, *Child Maltreatment 2002* (Washington, DC: U.S. Department of Health and Human Services, 2004).

After CPS investigates, cases are categorized. In 2002, child protective services (CPS) agencies across the country received 1.8 million reports of suspected child abuse and neglect, representing more than 3 million children. After screening, approximately two-thirds of these cases were investigated, and of those, only half were substantiated (evidence of maltreatment was found) or indicated (there was reason to suspect maltreatment). This means that approximately 896,000 children were identified as victims of child abuse or neglect in 2002, a rate of 12.3 per 1,000 children. More than half (60 percent) of reports were not unsubstantiated because CPS investigations found no evidence or insufficient evidence to make a case.

Substantiation rates vary considerably by state. Sometimes reports are not investigated at all because the situation does not fall under the state's rules for investigation, or the case is not given a high priority and the state lacks the resources to follow up on every report. Data on the types of maltreatment in substantiated cases have been relatively consistent over time. In 2002, the National Child Abuse and Neglect Data System (NCANDS) reported that 57 percent of cases constituted neglect, including medical neglect; 17 percent, physical abuse; 10 percent, sexual abuse; 7 percent, emotional abuse; and 19 percent, other types of maltreatment such as abandonment or congenital drug addiction (some children are counted in more than one category). Younger children are more likely to be abused (see Figure 10.2). Slightly more than half (54 percent) of reported child victims are white, and about one-quarter (26 percent) are African American (see Figure 10.3). American Indian or Alaskan Native and African American children were overrepresented among reported abuse cases, with rates of 22 per 1,000 and 20 per 1,000, respectively. By comparison, white children's rate was 11 per 1,000. Children with a history of abuse were more than twice as likely to be reported. Most often, children were abused or neglected by one or both parents (81 percent). Usually this was the mother acting alone (40 percent), not surprising since mothers are often the only parent in the home. Fourteen hundred children died as a result of abuse or neglect in 2002. Most (76 percent) of these children were under 4 years of age. Seventeen of these deaths occurred in foster care. Many cases of abuse and neglect never come to the attention of authorities. The cases of child molestation by clergy members remind us that even the most trusted members of society can be responsible for harming children.

The figures on child abuse and neglect reported above are based on all states and the District of Columbia. Because states differ in their definitions of problems and the procedures they use to screen calls and investigate cases, there are inconsistencies or gaps in the picture these data present.

FIGURE 10.2

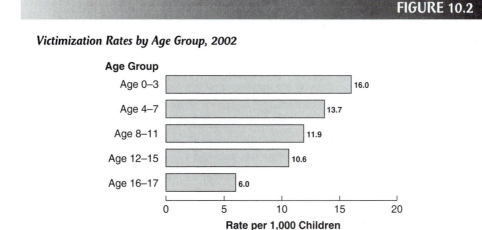

Victimization Rates by Age Group, 2002

Source: Administration for Children and Families, *Child Maltreatment 2002* (Washington, DC: U.S. Department of Health and Human Services, 2004).

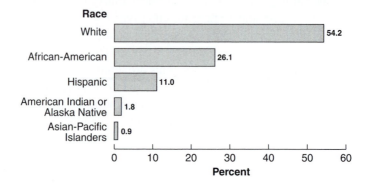

FIGURE 10.3

Percentage of Child Victims by Race, 2002[a]

Source: Administration for Children and Families, *Child Maltreatment 2002* (Washington, DC: U.S. Department of Health and Human Services, 2004).

[a] Total does not equal 100%. Some data are missing.

Services for Abused and Neglected Children

Children who come to the attention of child welfare agencies may receive a variety of services.[79] In 2002, 2.4 million children at risk for neglect or abuse or their parents received preventive services. Preventive services can be respite care, parenting education, housing assistance, substance abuse treatment, day care, home visits, individual and family counseling, homemakers' services, and transportation. Approximately 60 percent of children whose cases were investigated or their parents received services. Post-investigation services are meant to ensure against future episodes of abuse and neglect. They provide families with additional resources for raising their children in a healthier environment. These services may include individual and family counseling, family-based or in-home services (such as family preservation), family reunification services, court services, foster care, and adoption services.

Unfortunately, many children are not well served. There may not be enough services to go around, and states have different priorities about how to use child welfare services funding. Some states invest most of their funds in post-investigation services and fewer in preventive services. This may occur because states have large caseloads of children in need of foster care or family preservation services. Many services are offered on a voluntary basis, and the family has the right to refuse them. Children were more likely to receive services if they had prior episodes of maltreatment, were victims of multiple types of abuse, were 3 years old or younger, were identified as "other" or multiple races, or were reported by a social service or mental health professional.

A Brief History of Child Protection Legislation

The federal government's initial concern about the welfare of children began with the first White House Conference on Children in 1909 and the establishment of the Children's Bureau in 1912. The bureau addressed a broad range of child welfare issues, from health and child labor to delinquency and orphaned children. Under Title V of the original Social Security Act, the bureau was directed to cooperate with the states to develop child welfare services. Services were expanded, primarily during the 1960s. The AFDC-Foster Care program was established in 1961 to provide out-of-home care to poor children after the state of Louisiana dumped 22,000 black children from the AFDC program because it considered their own homes "unsuitable" to the children's well-being, a move which led to the growth of the foster care system. Child welfare services originally included under Title V of the Social Security Act were expanded under Title IV-B in 1967. In 1974 Congress passed the Child Abuse Prevention and Treatment Act (CAPTA) and established the National Center on Child Abuse and Neglect. In addition to assisting the states, the center conducts child abuse and neglect research. In 1975, Title XX allowed more child welfare services to be provided. The Title XX Social Services Block Grant has become another important source of child welfare service funding. In 1988 NCANDS was created as an amendment to CAPTA.

CAPTA expired in 2001, but Congress appropriated funds for 2002 and 2003, and CAPTA was reauthorized through 2008 under the Keeping Children and Families Safe Act of 2003. A number of new "assurances" were added to the law that states must follow if they want to receive CAPTA funding. These assurances focus on early intervention and prevention. States must:

♦ Require that healthcare providers involved in the delivery of a child exposed to illegal drugs report this to child protective services and develop a "safe plan of care" for the newborn.

♦ Develop triage procedures for reporting children at risk of maltreatment, but not *imminent harm,* to a community-based preventive service.

♦ Inform federal, state, and local government authorities of confidential information if it is needed to carry out lawful agency duties.

♦ Promptly inform suspected perpetrators of allegations against them.

♦ Develop state provisions for completing criminal background checks for prospective adoptive or foster parents.

♦ Develop provisions for improving the training (including training on legal responsibilities), retention, and supervision of caseworkers.

♦ Develop procedures for referring victims of child abuse less than 3 years of age to statewide early intervention programs.[80]

While pursuing early intervention and prevention is laudable, questions arise about too much interference in family matters and whether the mandates violate confidentiality and civil liberties, such as the right to privacy.

Perhaps the most significant recent development in the child welfare arena is the Adoption Assistance and Child Welfare Act of 1980, also known as the "permanency planning law." Amendments to the law were made by the Adoption and Safe Families Act of 1997. The 1980 law was a reaction to scathing indictments of the child welfare system, particularly the number of children who had been removed from their homes and who had become *lost* in the child welfare system. The law was intended to prevent the *drift* of so many children into foster care for long periods.[81] Federal policy had unwittingly encouraged the removal of children from their homes by providing much more funding for foster care and much less for in-home services. Some blamed the high levels of foster care utilization on a broadened definition of when intervention was needed—from "risk of harm to the child" to "vague notions of parental fitness or the child's best interests."[82] The 1980 and 1997 laws recognize children's rights to a permanent home. Financial penalties can be imposed on states that do not comply with the act. The components of these laws are Titles IV-B and IV-E of the Social Security Act, which are supposed to work in concert with each other.

The purposes of IV-B, Child Welfare Services and Promoting Safe and Stable Families Program (formerly the Family Preservation and Support Services Program), are

1. Protecting and promoting the welfare of all children, including handicapped, homeless, dependent, or neglected children.

2. Preventing or remedying, or assisting in the solution of problems that may result in the neglect, abuse, exploitation, or delinquency of children.

3. Preventing the unnecessary separation of children from families by identifying family problems, assisting families in resolving their problems, and preventing breakup of the family where the prevention of child removal is desirable and possible.

4. Restoring to their families those children who have been removed, by the provision of services to the children and the families.

5. Placing children in suitable adoptive homes, in cases where restoration to the biological family is not possible or appropriate.

6. Assuring adequate care of children away from their homes, in cases where the child cannot be returned home or cannot be placed for adoption.

Under IV-B, states must have written plans for every child and each case must be reviewed at least every six months. As a result of the 1997 amendments, within twelve months of placement (it was 18 months under the 1980 law), each case must have a permanency planning hearing to determine whether the child will be returned home, placed for adoption, or referred for another permanent living arrangement. With some exceptions, states must begin procedures to terminate parental rights if a child has been in foster care 15 of the past 22 months. Although states must make "reasonable efforts" to prevent foster care placement and to reunite children with their parents, there is no federal definition of reasonable efforts. States' interpretations vary.[83] The U.S. Supreme Court decision in *Suter v. Artist M.* failed to support the right to sue a state official or agency if reasonable efforts are not made. Congress convened a panel of child welfare experts to study reasonable efforts to keep families together. The panel concluded that despite the lack of a federal definition, reasonable efforts provisions had positive impacts and that existing federal requirements should be enforced.[84] Some panel members felt that a set of federally mandated services to promote reasonable efforts is unecessary because of the successes already achieved. They felt that this specificity should come from the local level, contrary to recommendations of the Child Welfare League of America.[85] In 2001, Congress amended the Promoting Safe and Stable Families Act. Mandatory federal funding was maintained at $305 million annually, but Congress may appropriate an additional $200 million each year. The amendments stress the importance of substance abuse treatment for parents when needed and post-adoption services for children who enter this arrangement.[86]

Title IV-E, Foster Care and Adoption Assistance Programs, now provide foster care services for children who would have been eligible for AFDC prior to its change to the TANF program (see Chapter 6) and adoption assistance for children with special needs (for example, older children, those with physical and mental disabilities, and sibling groups). It includes continued Medicaid eligibility for these children and grants to adoptive parents to encourage adoption.

In addition to Title IV-E adoption assistance, Congress has made other efforts to promote adoption, including tax credits to defray adoption costs. In 2001, this tax credit became a permanent part of the federal tax code, doubled the amount that parents could claim from $5,000 to $10,000, doubled the earning ceiling for full credit from $75,000 to $150,000, and provided a cost-of-living adjustment (COLA) for this credit. Since 2003, families who have finalized adoptions for special-needs children can claim the $10,000 tax credit even if their adoption expenses were less than this amount.[87] IV-E also provides services to help foster children make a better transition to independent living once they reach adulthood. To improve independent living services, the John H. Chafee Foster Care Independence Program (CFCIP) was established under the Foster Care Independence Act of 1999. Youth aged 18 to 21 can receive financial and housing assistance, counseling, and other supportive services to assist them in moving from foster care to independent living.[88]

Although the federal government has increased its role in remedying abuse and neglect, there is no single definition of these problems, and no single piece of legislation that uniformly addresses them throughout the nation. Child abuse and neglect statutes remain the states' prerogative. Available model legislation often serves as the basis for state statutes, but it is still difficult to achieve consensus on definitions. In April 2001, the Centers for Disease Control and Prevention (CDC) convened experts to discuss creating uniform definitions of child treatment for surveillance (data collection) purposes. Even if there were agreement on definitions, the best strategies for intervention are often unclear, and funding to provide all needed services is clearly inadequate to meet the needs of vulnerable children. This is true despite the federal government's 2004 allocation of $7.6 billion specifically for child welfare services. Other federal and state dollars are also spent for children welfare, including the Social Services Block Grant and funds from the TANF and Medicaid programs. A good many child welfare services are also provided by not-for-profit agencies and foundations devoted to improving the lives of children, such as the Annie E. Casey Foundation.

Trends and Projections in Child Welfare Services

Most federal child welfare funding categories are entitlements (although some are capped) and require state matching funds. The federal match ranges from 50 to 80 percent across child welfare programs, except for foster care assistance payments, which are matched at each state's Medicaid rate. This rate is inversely related to the state per capita income and may change over time. In 2002, this rate ranged from 50 to 83 percent across the states. Between 1995 and 2004, total federal child welfare spending increased nearly 200 percent, and is projected to be $8.7 billion by 2008.[89] The number of children in foster care grew dramatically from 133,000 in 1988 to 306,000 in 1998, but has since declined to 254,000 in 2002. The Congressional Budget Office projects that foster care caseloads will drop further to 228,000 by 2008. At the same time, federal foster care spending will increase by 14 percent. Adoption assistance caseloads are projected to increase 42 percent from 317,000 in 2003 to 451,000 in 2008. Federal spending for adoption services will increase by 66 percent.

Not all children in foster care are abused or neglected. Some are orphaned; others have parents who are too ill to care for them or are incarcerated. States pay foster parents to help cover the cost of caring for children until they are returned to their families or are adopted, although many remain in foster care until adulthood. Payment rates vary widely across states and generally increase as the child gets older because the expense of caring for a teenager is greater than that of caring for a toddler. In 2000, a foster parent caring for a 9-year-old child received as little as $254 a month in Alabama or as much as $690 in Connecticut. The average reimbursement was $404. States may also provide federal assistance in the form of a monthly subsidy check to families that adopt children with special needs, such as a disability, if the child is SSI eligible or would have previously been eligible for AFDC. These subsidies vary from $250 a month in Ohio to as much as $820 for some cases in Alaska. In 2002, subsidies were paid for 285,600 children every month.

The number of children in substitute care (not residing with their parent or parents) on September 30, 2001, was 542,000. Their average length of stay was just shy of three years. Many (48 percent) of these children were living in a nonrelative's home. Nearly a quarter were in relative foster family homes. The remainder were living in "pre-adoptive" homes, group homes, institutions, or supervised independent living. Two percent had run away from their substitute care setting.[90] During FY 2001, 290,000 children entered foster care, and 263,000 children exited foster care. Between 1998 and 2001, entries into foster care remained relatively stable, while exits increased by 15,000.[91]

Placements are affected by many factors, such as policies about removing children from their homes, the resources states allocate for care, the types of services they fund

FIGURE 10.4

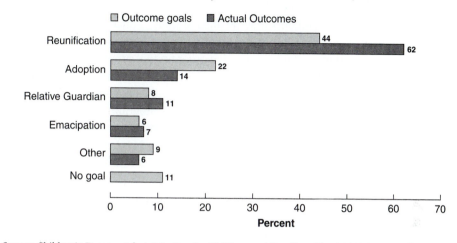

Outcome Goals and Actual Outcomes of Children in Substitute Care, 2001

☐ Outcome goals   ■ Actual Outcomes

Category	Outcome goals	Actual Outcomes
Reunification	44	62
Adoption	22	14
Relative Guardian	8	11
Emacipation	6	7
Other	9	6
No goal	11	

Source: Children's Bureau, Administration for Children and Families, The AFCARS Report (Washington, DC: U.S. Department of Health and Human Services, March 2003), retrieved March 30, 2004, from http://www.acf.hhs.gov/programs/cb

most heavily, and the extent of parents' problems. The 1997 amendments to the permanency planning law were intended to speed up the process by which children are placed for adoption and to provide financial incentives in the form of bonus payments for each adoption the state makes over previous levels ($4,000 for each regular foster care adoption and $6,000 for each special needs adoption).

In 2001, the case goals child welfare workers set for most children in substitute care were to reunify them with their families (44 percent) or to make them available for adoption (22 percent) (see Figure 10.4). Eleven percent of children had no goal established, but the number of children without an established goal decreased by 12 percent since 1998. Child welfare workers actually exceeded their reunification goal, with 62 percent of children reunified with their parents. Goals for emancipation and having a child live with a relative or guardian were also surpassed. In the area of adoptions, workers fell short of their 22 percent goal; only 14 percent of children in substitute care were adopted in 2001.

Preserving Families and Other Alternatives

Interest in family preservation has resulted in a number of studies to determine its efficacy. A 1987 review of permanency planning programs revealed that children reunited with their biological parents were as likely to return to foster care as were children prior to permanency planning legislation, and adjustment of children in permanent placements seemed no better than for those in temporary placement.[92] More encouraging was that the programs produced a "somewhat higher rate of adoption from foster care" and that these adoptions tended to be stable. Assessments indicate that intensive family preservation services improve family functioning and that out-of-home placements may be substantially reduced initially, but they apparently increase over time.[93] In a more recent review of outcomes from the Homebuilder family preservation model (an intensive program that provides services to biological families 24 hours a day for several weeks[94]), outcomes were inconsistent and placements increased over time.[95] This suggests that families may need continued follow-up services after completing a family preservation program. Child welfare advocates have long asserted that the goals of family preservation are derailed because only minimal services (usually education and monitoring) are provided to most families.[96]

Several states are now using Shared Family Care (SFC) to help families achieve permanency.[97] In SFC, a family (usually a single mother and her child or children) is placed in the home of another family. These family members act as mentors to help the mother in need acquire skills in parenting, budgeting, and life management. Placements last an average of eight months. Mentors work closely with a team of professionals who also provide intensive case management and resources to help the placed family achieve its goals and become self-sufficient. Birth parents retain the primary responsibility for parenting their children under the supervision and direction of their mentors. SFC began in Scandinavia and was first implemented in the United States in Minnesota and Philadelphia about a decade ago. In some states, SFC can be court ordered, but most families volunteer for the program. The first evaluations of SFC programs indicate that about three-quarters of families were living independently at graduation. Children's reentry rate into foster care was 8 percent, somewhat better than the 13 percent rate for reunified families who were not in an SFC program. SFC graduates' employment rates increased from 36 to 76 percent. Clients, social workers, and mentors are praising the program for its humane approach and effectiveness. SFC also appears to be cost effective, but it is not a panacea. SFC seems to work best for specific types of families—those who are motivated, committed to their children, and open to feedback and a mentoring relationship.

Removing children from their homes even temporarily can be traumatizing for the child, and finding an appropriate placement can be difficult. **Kinship care** is one approach that may lessen the trauma to children when they are separated from their parent or parents. Staying with Grandma or Auntie may not be unusual for a child, but being sent to stay with total strangers can be confusing to children at best, and deeply troubling at worst. Kinship care was once eschewed because it left the child unavailable for adoption or was believed to increase the risk of recurring maltreatment due to ease of access by the abusive parent. But kinship care has grown in use because it leaves the child in the context of his or her own family and it helps address the dire shortage of foster and adoptive families. Some rules prohibiting children's relatives from obtaining foster care payments have been removed, thus making this arrangement more financially viable for many family members who want to care for the child. Children cared for by relatives are apparently less likely to incur repeated maltreatment than children placed with nonrelatives.[98] Having undergone a major reversal of policy, almost all states now give preference to relative caregivers over nonrelatives.

According to the National Survey of American Families, many more children are in the care of relatives than are known to child welfare authorities.[99] **Private kinship care** is an arrangement family members make among themselves with no involvement of social welfare agencies or courts. More often than imagined, family members intervene on their own and make arrangements for children's well-being. Of the 2.3 million children reported to be in kinship care, the vast majority (76 percent) were in private kinship care. **Voluntary kinship care,** which accounted for 6 percent of relative placements, is another aspect of relative care. Voluntary kinship care occurs when social welfare agencies assist with a placement, but no court is involved. **Foster kinship care,** a formal placement involving courts and child welfare agencies, was the arrangement for only 17 percent of children cared for by kin.

Grandparents were the caretakers in half of all formal state-supervised kinship care cases. Census data provide a fuller appreciation of the role that grandparents are playing in raising their grandchildren. The Census Bureau reported that in 2000, 2.4 million grandparents had been the primary caregivers of at least one grandchild for five years or more. African American grandparents were more likely to be a primary caregiver than whites or Hispanics.[100]

It is fortunate that so many grandparents have assumed the primary caregiving role, but this presents a new family model and raises new concerns. Income usually diminishes as people retire, and these grandparent-headed families often live on fixed incomes and have economic hardships. Health and energy levels are often not what they were at a younger age. Grandparents may need support services such as respite care, transportation, in-home assistance, and in-kind or cash assistance to raise their grandchildren. In a study of grandparent caregivers in New York, grandparents suffered "extreme" levels of stress that they attributed to fears of not being able to raise their grandchildren into adulthood, or they feared that their grandchildren would be taken from them.[101]

Social workers and other professionals are searching for more effective ways to help children and their families. Federal and state governments are invested not only on humanitarian grounds but also because they foot most of the bill for remedying social problems. Federal grants and waivers (which allow states to bend established rules) are approved by Congress and provided through many government offices in order to test experimental approaches to address social problems. In 1994, Congress authorized DHHS to approve ten waivers for child welfare program demonstrations. The demonstrations were limited to five years with the possibility of a five-year extension, to allow sufficient time for determining that the programs were improving services to children and keeping children safer. More waivers were later approved and funded, and by December 2003, 25 projects were underway in 17 states. Innovative ideas are being tested in the following areas: new funding mechanisms for state agencies, services to caretakers with substance abuse problems, adoption services, intensive care systems, tribal administration, managed care payment systems, assisted guardianship/kinship permanence, and training for child welfare staff. Most projects are still being evaluated. Some completed projects demonstrated no improvement; others showed promising results.

Illinois tested an "assisted guardianship" program. The state provided some children and their guardians (the experimental group) with subsidy payments equal to that of adoption assistance payments along with a variety of services for a five-year period. Other children (the control group) continued in the usual state guardianship/kinship care program. Children in the new program were more likely to achieve a permanent home than children in the old program. Withdrawal of administrative oversight and casework services from the experimental group did not result in more child abuse and neglect. DHHS has extended the project for five more years.

The state of Indiana is trying to find alternative homes and community-based placements for children living in institutions. The state tested a capped IV-E program where counties were paid a maximum of $9,000 per child annually to provide intensive services to children in order to improve their well-being and the number of successful out-of-institution (community) placements. Since it began in December 2001, children in this program have had shorter institutional stays, higher reunification rates, and lower placement recidivism rates than children in the control group. A managed care program in Maryland designed to enhance exits from foster care demonstrated no difference between children in the experimental group and the control group; however, a surprising finding was that children in the experimental group were more likely to be adopted.

Child Welfare: Help or Harm?

Child welfare has had its share of problems and many question whether it sometimes does more harm than good. The goal of providing *every* child with a safe and happy home is laudable, but not easily achieved.

With high demands for services, state child protective service agencies cannot respond to the numbers of children and parents in need, so they resort to prioritizing cases. The more serious cases get the attention while others may not get addressed unless, or until, they become as serious. The public is particularly outraged when a child is not removed from the home and is later severely injured or dies as a result of abuse or neglect. This is a rare occurrence, but when it does happen, it captures media attention, and overshadows the successful cases that rarely make the news.

At the other end of the spectrum are stories of families destroyed by child welfare workers who removed children without an appropriate investigation or just cause. "Social workers" often take the blame in all these situations, but in reality, many child welfare workers are not professionally qualified and may lack the education necessary to do the job.[102] High caseloads, low pay, and stressful working conditions that result in staff burnout and high job turnover have also been blamed for problems in the child welfare delivery system. The threat of lawsuits also hangs over the head of child welfare workers. In 1989 the U.S. Supreme Court ruled six to three that public employees could not be held liable for failure to protect citizens from harm by other private citizens. The case involved the Winnebago County, Wisconsin, department of social services and Joshua DeShaney, who suffered severe, permanent brain damage as a result of abuse by his father after the department failed to remove him from his home.[103] Many child advocates were shocked by this decision, though it was surely a relief to child welfare workers who make tough decisions everyday about the lives of the children in their care. Greater threats of legal repercussions would likely cause an exodus of child welfare professionals. It is already difficult to find people who are willing to take or keep these jobs for long.

In 1994 the U.S. Supreme Court again granted protections to social workers by saying that they are immune from being sued even if their accusations against parents are wrong. The high court's ruling stemmed from a Kentucky case in which the 6th U.S. Court of Appeals stated that social workers should "not [be] deterred from vigorously performing their jobs as they might if they feared personal liability."[104] They can, however, be sued for clear civil rights violations.

A longstanding problem of the child welfare system is finding enough foster homes. Many foster families are well motivated to care for children, but they can be discouraged trying to meet the many special needs of foster children within the bureaucratic foster care system. As many as half the foster parents recruited drop out within the first year. Many leave before completing training or ever having a child placed in their home.[105] This may just be the weeding-out process to determine which families are up to the task, but it is a big expense to the child welfare system. The system is always in need of more good homes in which to place vulnerable children.

Child abuse and neglect generally do not remedy themselves. Child protection agencies and the courts usually mandate that parents who have perpetrated abuse and wish to keep their children or have them returned get professional help, but there are often long waits for services at community mental health and family guidance agencies, and private treatment is costly. The state of Florida repealed its "scarlet letter" law that required women to publish their sexual histories in the newspaper if they wanted to place their child for adoption but did not know the identity of the child's father.[106] To save infants' lives, some states have made it easier for women to turn newborns over to the state by designating places where they can leave the infant, like hospital emergency rooms or fire stations that have paramedics.

Finding adoptive homes for children who are permanently removed from their families can also be difficult. Child welfare agencies resort to placing pictures and stories of these children in the newspaper or on websites to attract interest. Many people are interested in adopting, but the preference is often for healthy, white infants. Children in foster care generally do not fit this description. Many are older, of ethnic minority backgrounds, and enter care with behavioral, developmental, medical, or other problems, and many of them live in a number of foster homes before they reach adulthood. There has been controversy over the placement of black, Hispanic, and Native American children in white homes.[107] The practice has been called "cultural genocide" and critics contend that nonwhites who wish to adopt have been treated unfairly by social service agencies. Others believe that given the disproportionate numbers of children of color in foster care, transracial and transcultural adoptions can ensure more children a permanent home. In response to this growing national controversy, Congress passed the Multi-Ethnic Placement Act in 1994 that prohibited states from delaying or denying adoption and foster placements on the basis of race or ethnicity, but allowed states to "consider" race in placement decisions. In 1996, the Inter-Ethnic Placement Provisions Act rescinded routine consideration of race and ethnicity in the placement of foster and adoptive children.[108] Of grave concern are reports that children of certain racial or ethnic groups bear a higher burden of mental health problems and have greater unmet mental health needs. The Surgeon General of the United States has called for rigorous empirical study and evidence-based interventions to support effective culturally competent practices, especially in settings where the highest needs go unmet, such as foster care.[109]

Most children enter placement due to abuse and neglect, and for more than 15 years, substance abuse has been a major contributor to removing children from their homes.[110] The introduction of crack cocaine in the 1980s has been blamed for the huge increase in the number of child maltreatment cases and of out-of-home placements. Substance abuse may put children at risk of in-utero drug exposure, as well as impair parents' judgment. It may also contribute to neglect when parents lose their jobs because of alcohol or illicit drug use, or spend money intended for housing and food on drugs. There is evidence that the effects of in-utero crack exposure have been exaggerated as part of the country's ill-conceived "war on drugs."[111] Substantial numbers also think that attempts to prosecute rather than help women who use drugs during pregnancy are ill considered. According to a DHHS-mandated study, about 8.3 million children lived with substance-abusing or dependent parents in 1999. DHHS recognizes the many barriers to providing child welfare services to substance-abusing parents. There is a shortage of substance abuse treatment facilities, and state and federal laws often make it difficult to coordinate substance abuse treatment and child welfare services. Child welfare may expect a cure, while chemical dependency professionals recognize that relapses are a part of the recovery process. DHHS identified key program features important to comprehensively attending to the substance treatment and child welfare needs of families. Among these needs are better training for caseworkers, more preventive services, and better access to substance abuse treatment and support during recovery.

Another group of concern is young adults transitioning from foster care to independent living. Take the case of Homer Bennett. *Time* magazine reported his case under the title "Fifteen Years in Foster Hell." Homer lived in 14 foster homes, most for less than one year. In some homes he was beaten. At age 20, Homer is a father who hopes to earn a GED. Given the chaotic life of many foster care children, they face an uphill battle when at age 18 or 21 they are simply told to make it on their own. Substantial numbers of foster youth reside in homeless shelters after leaving foster care.[112] Some ethnographic researchers suggest that the "drift" of youth in and out of homelessness after leaving foster care is a continuation of the drift they experienced in foster care.[113] Children who have the greatest difficulty transitioning have had multiple foster care placements, and they have less education. Independent living programs (IL) try to help with this transition. Ten years after IL programs began, DHHS found that large numbers of youth "aging out" of foster care had never received IL services. Even those who received IL services have had trouble maintaining employment and were often living on the streets or involved in the criminal justice system. Many children report that IL programs provide little concrete assistance, and they have difficulty recalling what the content of the IL program was.

In 1987, Congress appropriated $45 million for IL programs. Since then, federal and state government allocations to help prepare youth for adulthood have increased. In 2003 states spent $182 million, but the problems have not gone away. Youth who left foster care in the 1980s and late 1990s had similar outcomes. Twelve to 18 months after leaving foster care, large numbers were without a high school diploma and were unemployed and homeless; they also experienced unusually high rates of emotional problems, drug abuse, health problems, and pregnancy. One study in Wisconsin found that 40 percent of the young women and 23 percent of the young men received public assistance after leaving foster care, and 44 percent had problems getting healthcare. Whatever help these children received was apparently insufficient to compensate for the deficits they experienced during their developmental years.

Some child advocates contend that children are poorly treated because the U.S. lacks a comprehensive profamily policy that sees that every family has the basic resources it needs to help children become healthy, functioning adults. Others see these problems as rooted in the wanton acts of a group of parents who are too immature or too impaired by mental or substance use disorders to care for their children. Thus, the question becomes whether we should have a "child welfare system" focused on the basic needs of children and their families, or a "child protection system" focused on those who cause serious harm to children.[114] If it is to be a child protection system, should that system be in the hands of social welfare authorities who seek to make the family better, or in the hands of law enforcement officials who seek retribution and punishment from adults who harm children in their care? Of course, both approaches are needed—basic services for families when parents need help in performing their role, and legal intervention when they flagrantly violate society's standards. Of utmost importance is addressing the "best interests" of the child, but children have limited rights and the rights of their parents often take precedence.

When states fail to live up to their child welfare responsibilities, lawsuits are one course of action to gain compliance. New Jersey is one of several states that has come under intense scrutiny for the failings of its child welfare system. As the result of a federal lawsuit, the state has agreed to a major overhaul, including hiring 1,000 more child welfare workers (it had 3,000). This would bring the caseload to 15 children per worker, lower than the standard of 17 recommended by the Child Welfare League of America.[115] It has also promised to find 1,000 more foster homes for children in need.

SOCIAL SERVICES FOR OLDER AMERICANS

As Chapters 3 and 4 indicated, the quality of life of older Americans has improved considerably. But a significant number of older Americans still spend the last portion of their lives in economic need. As life spans increase, those in higher income brackets are also likely to need health care services, assistance in independent living, protection, and long-term care. The Social Security program (discussed in Chapter 4) is an important piece of legislation for older Americans; SSI (see Chapter 5) and Medicare and Medicaid (see Chapter 8) are also crucial in maintaining a high quality of life for older people. Another vital component in meeting the needs of older people is social services. Perhaps the most important legislation in this regard is the Older Americans Act (OAA) of 1965, last amended in 2000.[116]

The Older Americans Act

The goals of the OAA actually sound more like a wish list than a set of objectives that are likely to be achieved by government, but they include

♦ An adequate income in retirement in accordance with the U.S. standard of living

♦ The best possible physical and mental health that science can make available without regard to economic status

♦ Suitable housing that is independently selected, designed, and located, with reference to special needs and available at costs older citizens can afford

♦ Full restorative services for those who require institutional care

♦ Opportunity for employment with no discriminatory personnel practices because of age

♦ Retirement in health, honor, and dignity—after years of contribution to the economy

♦ Pursuit of meaningful activity within the widest range of civic, cultural, and recreational opportunities

♦ Efficient community services, including access to low-cost transportation, that provide a choice in supported living arrangements and social assistance in a coordinated manner, and that are readily available when needed

♦ Immediate benefit from proven research knowledge that can sustain and improve health and happiness

♦ Freedom, independence, and the free exercise of individual initiative in planning and managing one's own life

The 2000 amendments to the OAA give states more flexibility in designing services and using waivers to try new approaches. Legal services to protect the rights of older individuals continue to be a priority area. The amendments emphasize coordinating services with agencies and organizations that provide intergenerational activities and programs. The amendments permit states to ask older people to share in the costs of some services they receive, but not in a coercive way, and services cannot be denied for failure to share costs. Of particular concern is that the amendments eliminated a provision allowing states to obtain grants from the federal government to conduct outreach counseling and other assistance to help older people obtain publicly sponsored benefits. The OAA is due for reauthorization in 2005.

Although the country has yet to make a real dent in achieving many OAA objectives, the act does provide the framework for a modest array of services to older citizens. In order to qualify for services under the OAA, an individual must be at least 60 years old. Getting services to the poor elderly is of special concern.

The OAA created an "aging network" to express the concerns of older Americans (see Figure 10.5).[117] The network operates at the federal, regional, state, and local levels. At the federal level is the Administration on Aging (AoA), which is part of the U.S. Department of Health and Human Services. The AoA's primary function is to provide technical assistance to state and local governments in developing and implementing

FIGURE 10.5

National Aging Services Network

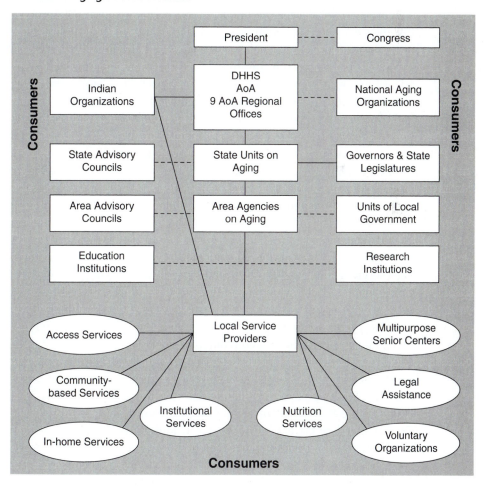

Source: Administration on Aging.

services for older people; it also conducts some program evaluations and research on aging and acts as a national clearinghouse on information about older people. To assist in its efforts, the AoA has nine regional offices across the United States.

At the state level, the entity concerned with services for older individuals may be part of the state's human services or welfare department or a free-standing cabinet-level agency or department. These state offices assist in implementing federal policies and act as advocates for older citizens. They make the needs and problems of the older people known to the AoA, and also to their own state legislatures, which determine how state programs to address these concerns will be funded and administered.

Actually, family and friends provide most help the elderly receive—about 82 percent of it.[118] But when families and friends cannot meet all these needs, local agencies try to respond. At the local level there are about 612 Area Agencies on Aging (AAAs). Each AAA is guided by an advisory council primarily composed of older people. The AAAs perform their advocacy function by assessing the needs of older people in their communities and distributing funds to community agencies. Of particular interest is that the OAA generally prohibits state agencies and AAAs from providing services directly. Instead, they must contract with local agencies to deliver services. Among the services local agencies provide are nutrition programs, senior centers, information and referral, transportation, homemaker and chore services, legal counseling, escort services, home repair and renovation, home health aid, shopping assistance, visitation, and telephone assurance (phone calls to the elderly for reassurance and to check on their needs). AAAs served 7.5 million older Americans in 2002. A fifth of those served were people of color and 28 percent were living in poverty.[119]

The OAA and the aging network are important adjuncts to the major cash assistance and health programs for older Americans. These social service programs provide important links to the community and help to keep the elderly involved in the mainstream of U.S. life and out of institutions. Advocacy groups for older Americans are concerned that services be well publicized to ensure they are used.

In addition to services for older citizens, family caretakers of the elderly may also need services if they are to continue to be a mainstay of support. For example, respite care provides relief to spouses, adult children, and other caretakers, so they can go shopping, have a few hours of free time, or take a vacation. Many families cannot afford or prefer not to purchase respite care and do without it or rely on other family members and friends when relief is needed. The Family and Medical Leave Act signed by President Clinton in 1993 (see also Chapter 11) allows many workers greater flexibility in taking time from work (although it is unpaid leave) to care for a parent. Public policies that might also encourage greater family involvement in elder care are allowing Medicaid and Medicare to cover more home health care costs. Other means are tax expenditures that would allow families to take more income tax deductions for providing care to their parents or grandparents, especially lower-income families who might otherwise be unable to provide this care. The 2000 OAA reauthorization makes $125 million available to establish the National Family Caregiver Support Program to increase services to those caring for ill or disabled family members.

There have been four White House Conferences on Aging, with older Americans from across the United States participating as delegates. The last one was held in 1995. Another is supposed to be convened by the end of 2005. The conferences have reiterated many of the goals of the OAA. In addition to support for Social Security, Medicare, Medicaid, long-term care services, the Older Americans Act, and research on aging, the 1995 conference focused on newer areas of concern.[120] Participants noted that the number of older people of color will double by the year 2030 and called for services that are sensitive to this dynamic as well as to the large number of women that comprise the older population. They also noted the growing number of grandparents who are raising grandchildren and called for better policies to assist them. Recognizing the contributions that older people make, participants called for the Corporation for National and Community Service (see Chapter 9) to recruit one million older volunteers to assist their communities.

The U.S. House of Representatives no longer funds its former Permanent Select Committee on Aging. The Senate has had a Special Committee on Aging since 1961. Special committees have no legislative authority, but they can bring attention to issues of concern. State legislatures generally have committees whose functions also include consideration of the needs of older individuals. Over the years about half the states have periodically convened "Silver Haired Legislatures" composed of older residents who discuss the needs of their age cohort and report to the governors and state legislatures. In addition to these advisory groups, older people throughout the country have organized in an effort to make their needs known. Perhaps the best known organization of older Americans is the nonpartisan AARP (formerly called the American Association of Retired Persons). With more than 35 million members, it can be called the country's largest advocacy group. A smaller but also vocal association is the Gray Panthers, which has a particular interest in intergenerational issues. Many more groups in states and communities are actively addressing the concerns of older people. As noted in Chapter 8, the Minnesota Senior Federation is working hard to help people of all ages obtain prescription drugs at more reasonable costs.

Although the goals of the Older Americans Act have remained largely the same, there has been increased emphasis on home and community-based services designed to reduce the need for nursing home and other institutional care.[121] When older people can no long care for themselves or when caretakers are unable to encourage them to eat or perform other self-care activities, their situation is termed "self abuse." Another serious situation is maltreatment by others. Most states have statutes that prohibit physical and psychological abuse of elders and exploitation of their resources (unauthorized use of their income or assets). These types of abuse may occur in the older person's home, the home of a caretaker, or in an institution such as a nursing home. Penalties for citizens who do not report elder abuse vary, and in many cases, there is no real penalty. The identification of elder abuse is complicated by several issues. For example, even those older people capable of reporting the abuse may not do so for fear that loss of their caretaker will result in their being placed in an institution. When the abuser is a loved one, the older person may not want to risk intervention by social service workers or legal action by law enforcement. Elder abuse laws are not as well developed as child abuse laws, but in most areas adult protective service workers or law enforcement officers can be asked to intervene. It is difficult to say how many older Americans are abused, neglected, or exploited each year. The National Elder Abuse Incidence Study indicated that about 500,000 were victims in 1996, but the Senate Special Committee on Aging estimates that more than 5 million individuals are victimized each year, with 84 percent of incidents going unreported.[122] The 2000 OAA amendments attempt to enhance state ombudsman programs that protect the elderly who reside in nursing homes and other facilities from abuse.

Guardianship

One civil rights issue for the elderly that is growing in scope is **guardianship** or **conservatorship**.[123] Guardianship may empower an individual to make personal and/or financial decisions for another individual, while conservatorship provides only for financial decisions.[124] The courts may appoint a guardian when it appears that an older person is no longer competent to manage his or her daily affairs. In most states these are probate courts that also deal with child custody and adults in need of treatment for mental illness. Once a guardian is appointed, the older person may be stripped of rights and decision-making power over where to live, how to spend money, whether to receive treatment, and so forth. Guardianship is defined under state law, and these laws have come under increasing scrutiny as more older people are subjected to guardianship. Concerns are that many guardianship decisions are made without sufficient information. Decisions may be based on the viewpoint of the individual who believes guardianship is needed rather than on any convincing evidence. The older person may not even be given an opportunity for legal representation. In many cases, supervision of guardians is also lax. The elderly can be robbed of assets and treated poorly by guardians who may be relatives or someone previously unknown to them.

In some areas, guardianship has become a new business for entrepreneurs because guardians may be paid a fee for their services. Some states have overhauled their guardianship programs to better protect older individuals. In many areas, guardianship is used only as a last resort. In some cases, bill-paying or other financial management services provided by volunteers can prevent the need for guardianship; or durable power of attorney (a voluntary process) is used, which can leave the older person with more rights intact by giving another individual limited powers such as in financial matters. Although useful in helping the elderly maintain their civil rights, these systems can also result in inappropriate use of an individual's financial resources, because many voluntary programs also lack oversight. At a minimum, closer supervision of existing systems is needed, since good alternatives seem to be few. Recall Mollie Orshansky, who developed the original federal poverty threshold calculation (see Chapter 3). More recently, Ms. Orshansky has been the subject of guardianship proceedings. Apparently, despite Ms. Orshansky's efforts to plan for her care, her wishes to place responsibility in the hands of family members were ignored. A court appointed a guardian and attorney for her and placed her in a hospital. In another case, a Seattle shop owner in her fifties testified that she was forced to spend her life savings to fight a guardianship petition intitiated by her children. In light of these stories and others, the chair of the Senate Special Committee on Aging called for a GAO report on guardianship.[125]

Two demonstrable effects of the total package of cash, health, and social services for older Americans have been "(1) an increase in the ability of the aged to maintain homes apart from younger relatives, and (2) an increase in proprietary nursing home beds for the sick aged."[126] Other demonstrable effects come from the Nursing Home Reform Act of 1987 (part of that year's Omnibus Budget and Reconciliation Act). For example, there is substantially less use of physical restraints and greater protections of nursing home patients' rights.[127] Still, patient abuses and violations of care procedures are too common. Tensions remain between the nursing home industry and regulatory bodies in trying to remedy problems. A major concern stems from low Medicaid reimbursement rates that restrict the number of employees that can be hired and the level of care they provide. The generally held view is that no one wants to go to a nursing home if he or she can avoid it. As Chapter 8 indicated, alternative living and care arrangements for older people are growing. The aging of the baby boomers will push the edge of the envelope with regard to social services, healthcare, residential opportunities, and legal rights.

SUMMARY

Social services include many types of programs, including child and adult day care, mental health care, treatment for alcohol and drug abuse, juvenile delinquency prevention services, child welfare programs, and nursing home care. Not all social services are directed toward those in financial need. People from all walks of life may require social services. Social services are provided by public agencies, private not-for-profit and profit-making organizations, religious organizations, and self-help groups. The Title XX Social Services Block Grant is a major vehicle for funding social services.

The Community Mental Health Act of 1963 was the landmark legislation that encouraged the building and staffing of community mental health centers across the country. The bulk of funds for these programs now comes from state governments, but the federal government does contribute. The current federal funding mechanisms are the Substance Abuse Prevention and Treatment Block Grant and the Community Mental Health Services Block Grant.

The United States has no comprehensive social policy for families and children, largely because of the belief that families should be relatively free from governmental intervention. However, state laws govern various aspects of family relations, such as intervention in cases of child abuse and neglect. The 1980 Child Welfare and Adoption Assistance Act, along with amendments to the act in 1997, is currently considered the most important child welfare legislation. This legislation focuses on keeping families together whenever possible and finding other permanent homes when children cannot be returned to their original families.

The most important legislation that recognizes the social service needs of the elderly is the Older Americans Act of 1965. The act emphasizes nutrition programs and services that increase the ability of the elderly to remain in the community. The Administration on Aging is the federal agency which administers this act by determining the needs of older Americans and by encouraging states and communities to provide services that address these needs.

NOTES

1. This overview of services relies on Alfred J. Kahn, *Social Policy and Social Services* (New York: Random House, 1979), pp. 12–13.

2. Steven Rathgeb Smith and Michael Lipsky, *Nonprofits for Hire: The Welfare State in the Age of Contracting* (Cambridge, MA: Harvard University Press, 1993).

3. See Robert Morris, *Social Policy of the American Welfare State: An Introduction to Policy Analysis* (New York: Harper & Row, 1979), p. 120.

4. U.S. Department of Health, Education and Welfare, *First Annual Report to Congress on Title XX of the Social Security Act* (Washington, DC: Department of Health, Education, and Welfare, 1977), p. 1; Martha Derthick, *Uncontrollable Spending for Social Services Grants* (Washington, DC: The Brookings Institution, 1975).

5. Committee on Ways and Means, U.S. House of Representatives, *2003 Green Book*, "Title XX Social Service Block Grant Program" (Washington, DC: September 22, 2003), Section 10, pp. 10-1–10-2, retrieved February 17, 2004, from http://waysandmeans.house.gov/Documents.asp?section = 813

6. *Ibid.*, pp. 10-6–10-8.

7. David Mechanic, *Mental Health and Social Policy*, 3rd ed. (Englewood Cliffs, NJ: Prentice Hall, 1989), Chapter 2.

8. For a critique of the DSM see Stuart A. Kirk and Herb Kutchins, *The Selling of the DSM: The Rhetoric of Science in Psychiatry* (Hawthorne, NY: Aldine de Gruyter, 1992); Herb Kutchins and Stuart A. Kirk, *Driving Us Crazy: DSM, the Psychiatric Bible and the Creation of Mental Disorders* (New York: Free Press, 1997).

9. C. Aaron McNeece and Diana M. DiNitto, *Chemical Dependency: A Systems Approach*, 3rd ed. (Boston: Allyn and Bacon, 2005).

10. Ronald C. Kessler, Katherine A. McGonagle, Shanyang Zhao, Christopher B. Nelson, Michael Hughes, Suzann Eshleman, Hans-Ulrich Wittchen, and Kenneth S. Kendler, "Lifetime and 12-Month Prevalence of DSM-III-R Psychiatric Disorders in the United States: Results from the National Comorbidity Survey," *Archives of General Psychiatry*, Vol. 51, No. 8, 1994, pp. 8–19.

11. Ronald C. Kessler, Christopher B. Nelson, Katherine A. McGonagle, Mark J. Edlund, Richard G. Frank, and Philip J. Leaf, "The Epidemiology of Co-Occurring Addictive and Mental Disorders: Implications for Prevention and Service Utilization," *American Journal of Orthopsychiatry*, Vol. 66, No. 1, 1996, pp. 17–31.

12. Ronald C. Kessler et al., "The 12-Month Prevalence and Correlates of Serious Mental Illness (SMI)," in Ronald W. Manderscheid and Mary Anne Sonnenschein, Eds., *Mental Health, United States, 1996* (Washington, DC: U.S. Government Printing Office, 1996), pp. 59–70.

13. Robert M. Friedman, Judith W. Katz-Leavy, Ronald W. Manderscheid, and Diane L. Sondheimer, "Prevalence of Serious Emotional Disturbance in Children and Adolescents," in Manderscheid and Sonnenschein, Eds., *Mental Health United States, 1996*, pp. 71–89.

14. Ronald C. Kessler, Elizabeth J. Costello, Kathleen Ries Merikangas, and T. Bedirhan Ustun, "Psychiatric Epidemiology: Recent Advances and Future Directions," in Ronald W. Manderscheid and Marilyn J. Henderson, Eds., *Mental Health, United States, 2000* (Washington DC: U.S. Government Printing Office), retrieved March 25, 2004, from http://www.mentalhealth.org/publications/allpubs/SMA01–3537/chapter5.asp

15. Kessler et al., "Lifetime and 12-Month Prevalence of DSM-III-R Psychiatric Disorders in the United States."

16. Findings from the National Survey on Drug Use and Health rely on Substance Abuse and Mental Health Services Administration, *2002 National Survey on Drug Use and Health* (Rockville, MD: Office of Applied Studies), retrieved March 26, 2004, from http://www.samhsa.gov/centers/clearinghouse/clearinghouses.html

17. Substance Abuse and Mental Health Services Administration, Drug Abuse Warning Network (DAWN), "Highlights," retrieved March 26, 2004, from

http://www.samhsa.gov/oas/nhsda/nhsdafls.htm; Substance Abuse and Mental Health Services Administration, Drug Abuse Warning Network (DAWN), "Trends in Drug-Related Emergency Department Visits, 1994–2002: At a Glance," *DAWN Report* (Rockville, MD, November 2003), retrieved March 26, 2004, from http://dawninfo.samhsa.gov/pubs_94_02/shortreports/

18. Kessler et al., "Lifetime and 12-Month Prevalence of DSM-III-R Psychiatric Disorders in the United States," p. 12.

19. Office of Applied Studies, *National Survey of Substance Abuse Treatment Services (N-SSATS): 2002* (Rockville, MD: Substance Abuse and Mental Health Services Administration, 2002).

20. Substance Abuse and Mental Health Services Administration, *Report to Congress on the Prevention and Treatment of Co-occurring Substance Abuse Disorders and Mental Disorders* (Washington DC: October 22, 2002), retrieved March 27, 2004, from http://www.samhsa.gov/reports/congress2002/index.html

21. National Mental Health Association, "Mental Health: Pay for Services or Pay a Greater Price," retrieved March 27, 2004, from http://www.nmha.org/shcr/community_based/costoffset.pdf. See also Dorothy P. Rice and Leonard S. Miller, "Health Economics and Cost Implications of Anxiety and Other Mental Disorders in the United States," *British Journal of Psychiatry,* Vol. 173, No. 34, pp. 4–9.

22. Office of National Drug Control Policy, *Economic Costs of Drug Abuse in the United States, 1992–1998* (Washington, DC: Executive Office of the President, September 2001), retrieved March 27, 2004, from http://www.whitehousedrugpolicy.gov/publications/pdf/economic_costs98.pdf

23. Bruce Lubotsky Levin, "Managed Mental Health Care: A National Perspective," in Ronald Manderscheid and Mary Anne Sonnenschein, Eds., *Mental Health: United States, 1992,* DHHS Pub. No. (SMA) 92-1942 (Rockville, MD: Center for Mental Health Services and National Institute of Mental Health, 1992), pp. 208–218.

24. See Mary Jane England, "The Mental Health Parity Act—Lifting the Benefit Plan Limits," *Health Insurance Underwriter,* January 1997, retrieved from http://nahu.org/hiu/1–97–16.htm; Congressional Budget Office, "CBO's Estimates of the Impact on Employers of the Mental Health Parity Amendments in H.R.3103," retrieved from http://www.fmhi.usf.edu/parity/cboestimate.html; Lawrence K. Cagney and Mary Beth Navin, "Compliance with the Mental Health Parity Act of 1996," September 30, 1997, Debevoise & Plimpton, retrieved from http://www.altavista.digital.com/cgi-bin/query?pg-q&what-web&kl-XX&9 = mental +

25. Russ Newman, "Professional Point: One Step (and 3 Votes) Away from Parity," *Monitor on Psychology,* Vol. 33, No. 3, March 2002, retrieved March 28, 2004, from http://www.apa.org/monitor/mar02/pp.html

26. Merrile Sing, Steven Hill, Suzanne Smolkin, and Nancy Heiser, *The Costs and Effects of Parity for Mental and Substance Abuse Insurance Benefits,* Substance Abuse and Mental Health Services Administration (Rockville, MD, March 1998), retrieved March 28, 2004, from http://www.mentalhealth.samhsa.gov/publications/allpubs/Mc99-80/Prtyfnix.asp

27. RAND Corporation, "How Does Managed Care Affect the Cost of Mental Health Services?" Research Highlights from *RAND Health* (Santa Monica, CA: 1998), Report RB-4515, retrieved March 28, 2004, from http://www.rand.org/publications/RB/RB4515/

28. Rosalie Liccardo Pacula and Roland Sturm, "Mental Health Parity Legislation: Much Ado about Nothing?" *Health Services Research,* Vol. 35, No. 1, April 2000, pp. 263–275, retrieved March 27, 2004, from http://www.findarticles.com/cf_dls/m4149/1_35/62162639/p1/article.jhtml

29. RAND Corporation, "How Expensive Are Unlimited Substance Abuse Benefits under Managed Care?" (Santa Monica, CA, 1998), Report RP-782, as cited in National Conference of State Legislatures, *State Health Lawmakers' Digest,* Vol. 1, No. 2, retrieved March 27, 2004, from http://www.ncsl.org/programs/health/forum/shld/12.pdf

30. National Alliance for the Mentally Ill, *State Parity Legislation 2001,* Tracking Report (Arlington, VA: August 2001), retrieved March 25, 2004, from http://www.nami.org/

31. Library of Congress, *THOMAS: Legislative Information on the Internet,* retrieved March 27, 2004, from http://thomas.loc.gov

32. I am indebted to Peggy Thweatt for reminding me of the benefits of public sector services.

33. Most of this section relies on Mechanic, *Mental Health and Social Policy,* pp. 83, 86–87, 96–97.

34. Gerald N. Grob, *The State and the Mentally Ill: A History of Worcester State Hospital in Massachusetts, 1830–1920* (Chapel Hill: University of North Carolina Press, 1966), cited in *ibid.,* p. 53.

35. Clara Claiborne Park with Leon N. Shapiro, *You Are Not Alone: Understanding and Dealing with Mental Illness—A Guide for Patients, Doctors, and Other Professionals* (Boston: Little, Brown, 1976), pp. 93–94.

36. David Hartley, Donna C. Bird, David Lambert, and John Coffin, *The Role of Community Mental Health Centers as Rural Safety Net Providers* (Portland, ME: Maine Rural Health Research Center, Edmund S.

Muskie School of Public Service, November 2002), Working Paper #30, retrieved March 27, 2004, from http://muskie.usm.maine.edu/publications/rural/wp30.pdf

37. See Lucy D. Ozarin, "Community Mental Health: Does It Work? Review of the Evaluation Literature," in Walter E. Barton and Charlotte J. Sanborn (Eds.), *An Assessment of the Community Mental Health Movement* (Lexington, MA: Health, 1977), pp. 122–123.

38. See E. Fuller Torrey, *Nowhere to Go: The Tragic Odyssey of the Homeless Mentally Ill* (New York: Harper & Row, 1988), Chapter 9.

39. U.S. Department of Health and Human Services, *Budget in Brief, 2005* (Washington, DC: Office of the Budget), retrieved March 29, 2004, from http://www.hhs.gov/budget/05budget/subabuse.html; see also General Accounting Office, "Mental Health: Community-Based Care Increases for People with Serious Mental Illness," Report to the Committee on Finance, U.S. Senate (Washington, DC, December 2000), GAO-01-224, retrieved March 28, 2004, from http://www.hhs.gov/budget/05budget/subabuse.html

40. "Briefing Sheet: The Psychological Impact of Terrorism on Vulnerable Populations," *APA Online* (Washington, DC: APA Public Policy Office, 2004), retrieved March 30, 2004, from http://www.apa.org/ppo/issues/terrorbrief603.html; see also "Many Americans Still Feeling Effects of September 11th; Are Reexamining Their Priorities in Life," *APA Online Practice* (Washington, DC, February 11, 2002), retrieved March 30, 2004, from http://www.apa.org/practice/poll_911.html

41. "Army Surveys Troops Mental Health," *Military.com* (Associated Press, March 26, 2004).

42. National Mental Health Association, *Investment in Community-Based Mental Health Services* (Alexandria, VA, 2004); retrieved March 28, 2004, from http://www.nmha.org/shcr/community_based/index.cfm

43. President George W. Bush, *President's New Freedom Commission on Mental Health: Executive Order* (Washington, DC: Office of the Press Secretary, April 29, 2002); retrieved March 30, 2004, from http://www.whitehouse.gov/news/releases/2002/04/text/20020429-2.html

44. President's New Freedom Commission on Mental Health, *Achieving the Promise: Transforming Mental Health Care in America: Executive Summary* (Washington, DC, July 2003), retrieved March 30, 2004, from http://www.mentalhealthcommission.gov/reports/Finalreport/FullReport.htm

45. E. Fuller Torrey, *Commission Report Offers Little for Severest Mental Illnesses* (Arlington, VA: Treatment Advocacy Center, July 23, 2003), retrieved March 30, 2004, from http://www.psychlaws.org/PressRoom/stmtNewFreedomCommissionfailssickest.htm; Sally Satel and Mary Zdanowicz, "Commission's Omission: The President's Mental-Health Commission in Denial," *National Review* (New York, July 29, 2003), retrieved March 30, 2003, from http://www.psychlaws.org/GeneralResources/article137.htm

46. *Report of the Presidential Commission on the Human Immunodeficiency Virus* (Washington, DC: U.S. Government Printing Office, 1988).

47. See U.S. House of Representatives, *The Anti-Drug Abuse Act of 1988: A Guide to Programs for State and Local Anti-Drug Assistance,* Report of the Select Committee on Narcotics Abuse and Control, 101st Congress (Washington, DC: U.S. Government Printing Office, 1989).

48. Paige M. Harrison and Allen J. Beck, *Prisoners in 2002* (Washington, DC: U.S. Department of Justice, Bureau of Justice Statistics, July 2003); John Scalia, *Federal Drug Offenders: 1999 with Trends 1984–99* (Washington, DC: U.S. Department of Justice, August 2001); Office of National Drug Control Policy, *National Drug Control Strategy: FY 2003 Budget Summary* (Washington, DC: Executive Office of the President, February 2002).

49. Data are from the General Accounting Office and the Office of Drug Control Policy and were compiled by the Drug Policy Foundation and reported in Julia Malone, "Clinton Shifts War on Drugs to Treatment, More Police," *Austin American-Statesman,* February 10, 1994, p. A4; see also Executive Office of the President, Office of Management and Budget, *Budget of the United States Government, Fiscal Year 1995* (Washington, DC: U.S. Government Printing Office, 1994), p. 206.

50. Office of National Drug Control Policy, *The National Drug Control Strategy, 1998* (Washington, DC: Executive Office of the President, n.d.), see Section V: "Supporting the Ten-Year Strategy: The National Drug Control Budget, FY 1999-FY2003," Table 2, retrieved from http://www.whitehousedrugpolicy.gov/policy/98ndocs/contents.html

51. Office of National Drug Control Policy, *Drug Control Funding Tables* (Washington, DC: Executive Office of the President, March 2004), retrieved March 30, 2004, from http://www.whitehousedrugpolicy.gov/publications/policy/budgetsum04/drug_control.pdf

52. U.S. Department of Justice, "Drug Court Resources—Legislation," and "In the Spotlight: Drug Courts—Summary" (Washington, DC: National Criminal Justice Reference Service), retrieved March 29, 2004, from http://www.ncjrs.org/drug_courts/legislation.html and http://www.ncjrs.org/drug_courts/summary.html

53. U.S. Department of Justice, "Drug Court Resources—Facts and Figures" (Washington, DC: National Criminal Justice Reference Service), retrieved March 29,

2004, from http://www.ncjrs.org/drug_courts/facts. html

54. Steven Belenko, "Research on Drug Courts: A Critical Review," *National Drug Court Institute Review,* Summer 1998, Vol. 1, No. 1, p. 47.

55. U.S. Department of Justice, "Drug Court Resources—Facts and Figures."

56. Substance Abuse and Mental Health Services Administration, *Changing the Conversation: Improving Substance Abuse Treatment: The National Treatment Plan Initiative* (Rockville, MD: U.S. Department of Health and Human Services, 2000).

57. For a discussion of treatment for substance use disorders and public policy, see McNeece and Diana M. DiNitto, *Chemical Dependency: A Systems Approach.*

58. "Needle-Exchange Programmes in the USA: Time to Act Now," *Lancet,* Vol. 351, January 10, 1998, p. 75.

59. Office of National Drug Control Policy, *National Drug Control Strategy Update* (Washington, DC: U.S. Government Printing Office, February 2003).

60. This paragraph relies on Mechanic, *Mental Health and Social Policy,* pp. 215–217; quote is from p. 215.

61. Thomas S. Szasz, *The Myth of Mental Illness: Foundations of Theory of Personal Conduct,* rev. ed. (New York: Harper & Row, 1974), pp. 267–268.

62. Mechanic, *Mental Health and Social Policy,* pp. 228–230.

63. This account of Brown's situation was described in Charlotte Low, "A Rude Awakening from Civil Liberties," *Insight,* March 21, 1988, pp. 8–9.

64. Charles Krauthammer, "When Liberty Really Means Neglect," *Time,* December 2, 1985, pp. 103–104.

65. This paragraph is based on Bazelon Center for Mental Health Law, *Summary of State Statutes on Involuntary Outpatient Commitment* (Washington, DC), retrieved March 29, 2004, from http://www.bazelon.org/ issues/commitment/ioc/iocchart.html; American Federation of State, County and Municipal Employees, AFL-CIO, *Issue Brief: Outpatient Commitment Laws* (Washington, DC, August 1999), retrieved March 28, 2004, from http://www.afscme.org/publications/ issueb/ib9908.htm; National Alliance for the Mentally Ill, *Outpatient Commitment Info* (Arlington, VA, 1995), retrieved March 28, 2004, from http://www.schizo phrenia.com/family/outpatient.html

66. M. Susan Ridgely, Randy Borum, and John Petrila, "The Effectiveness of Involuntary Outpatient Treatment: Empirical Evidence and the Experience of Eight States" (Santa Monica, CA: RAND Corporation 2001), retrieved March 27, 2004, from http://www. rand.org/publications/MR/MR1340/

67. The remainder of this section relies on *ibid.*

68. M. Marshall and A. Lockwood, *Assertive Community Treatment of People with Severe Mental Disorders* (Cochrane Review). Update Software, retrieved June 11, 2002, from http://www.cochrane.org/ cochrane/revabstr/ab001089.htm

69. "Study Criticizes Texas Legal System's Treatment of Mentally Ill Indigents," *Hogg Foundation News,* Vol. 34, Fall Quarter 2000, pp. 1, 3; Clifford J. Levy, "New York Stops Putting Mentally Ill in Lockups," *New York Times,* October 19, 2002.

70. Michael Winerip, "The Never-Promised Rose Garden and the Snake Pit," *New York Times,* May 5, 2002, retrieved August 2, 2004, from http://www. forensic-psych.com/artNYtimesSnakePit5.05.02.html

71. Mechanic, *Mental Health and Social Policy,* p. 222.

72. This historical account relies on Stephen J. Pfohl, "The Discovery of Child Abuse," *Social Problems,* Vol. 24, No. 3, 1977, pp. 310–323; Diana M. DiNitto and C. Aaron McNeece, *Social Work: Issues and Opportunities in a Challenging Profession* (Englewood Cliffs, NJ: Prentice Hall, 1990), Chapter 9; Sallie A. Watkins, "The Mary Ellen Myth: Correcting Child Welfare History," *Social Work,* Vol. 35, No. 6, 1990, pp. 500–503.

73. Watkins, "The Mary Ellen Myth."

74. Robert H. Bremner, Ed., *Children and Youth in America: A Documentary,* Vol. 2 (Cambridge, MA: Harvard University Press, 1974), pp. 247–248.

75. The remainder of this section relies on Pfohl, "The Discovery of Child Abuse."

76. C. Henry Kempe et al., "The Battered-Child Syndrome," *Journal of the American Medical Association,* Vol. 181, July 7, 1962, pp. 105–112.

77. See Michael R. Petit and Patrick A. Curtis, *Child Abuse and Neglect: A Look at the States, 1997 CWLA Stat Book* (Washington, DC: CWLA Press, 1997).

78. Unless otherwise noted, the figures in this section are from Children's Bureau, *Child Maltreatment, 2002* (Washington, DC: U.S. Department of Health and Human Services, 2001), retrieved April 1, 2004, from http://www.acf.hhs.gov/programs/cb/publications/ cm02/cm02.pdf

79. *Ibid.*

80. Emile Stoltzfus, *CRS Report for Congress: Child Welfare Issues in the 108th Congress* (Washington, DC: Library of Congress, August 11, 2003), Congressional Research Service, retrieved March 30, 2004, from http://www.thememoryhole.org/crs/RL31746.pdf

81. Henry Maas and Richard Engler, *Children in Need of Parents* (New York: Columbia University Press, 1959).

82. See Bruce Bellingham and Joseph Byers, "Foster Care and Child Protection Services," in Allen W.

Imershein, Mary K. Pugh Mathis, C. Aaron McNeece, and Associates, *Who Cares for the Children: A Case Study of Policies and Practices* (Dix Hills, NY: General Hall, 1995), pp. 101–121; quotes from p. 104.

83. See U.S. House of Representatives, Committee on Ways and Means, *1996 Green Book: Background Material and Data on Programs within the Jurisdiction of the Committee on Ways and Means* (Washington, DC: U.S. Government Printing Office, 1996), pp. 726–727.

84. American Bar Association and National Resource Center on Legal and Court Issues, *Reasonable Efforts Advisory Panel Meeting* (Washington, DC: American Bar Association, April 21, 1995); see also Committee on Ways and Means, *1996 Green Book,* pp. 727–728.

85. "CWLA on Reasonable Efforts," written comments to the Senate Committee on Labor and Human Resources hearing on reasonable efforts submitted by the Child Welfare League of America, January 27, 1998, retrieved from http://www.casanet.org/library/reasonable_efforts/cwla.htm

86. Kasia O'Neill Murray and Sara Gesiriech, *A Brief Legislative History of the Child Welfare System* (Washington, DC: Pew Commission on Children in Foster Care), retrieved March 30, 2004, from http://pewfostercare.org/research/

87. *Ibid.*

88. *Ibid.*

89. Unless otherwise noted, the information in this section relies on Committee on Ways and Means, U.S. House of Representatives, Child Protection, Foster Care, and Adoption Assistance, *2003 Green Book* (Washington, DC, February 27, 2004), Section 11, retrieved March 29, 2004, from http://waysandmeans.house.gov/Documents.asp?section = 813

90. U.S. Department of Health and Human Services, Administration for Children and Families, *The AFCARS Report* (Washington, DC: Children's Bureau, March 2003), retrieved March 30, 2004, from http://www.acf.hhs.gov/programs/cb/publications/afcars/report8.htm

91. National Clearinghouse on Child Abuse and Neglect Information, *Foster Care National Statistics* (Washington, DC: U.S. Department of Health and Human Services, June 2003), retrieved September 2004, from http://nccanch.acf.hhs.gov/pubs/factsheets/foster.cfm

92. For an extensive review of evaluations of the various types of child welfare services, see Alfred Kadushin and Judith A. Martin, *Child Welfare Services,* 4th ed. (New York: Macmillan, 1988); see also CWLA Best Practice Guidelines for Child Maltreatment in Foster Care (Washington DC: CWLA Press, 2003); see also B. Thomlinson, "Characteristics of Evidence-Based Child Maltreatment Interventions," *Child Wel-*

fare, Vol. 82, No. 5, 2003, pp. 541–569; Gina Alexander, Patrick A. Curtis, and Miriam P. Kluger, *What Works in Child Welfare* (Washington, DC: CWLA Press, 2001).

93. See Mark W. Fraser, Peter Pecora, and David A. Haapala, *Families in Crisis: The Impact of Intensive Family Preservation Services* (New York: Aldine de Gruyter, 1991).

94. Jill Kinney, David Haapala, and Charlotte Booth, *Keeping Families Together: The Homebuilders Model* (New York: Aldine de Gruyter, 1991).

95. Gary Cameron and Jim Vanderwood, *Protecting Children and Supporting Families: Promising Programs and Organizational Realities* (New York: Aldine de Gruyter, 1997), especially Chapter 6.

96. Bellingham and Byers, "Foster Care and Child Protection Services."

97. Information about shared family care is based on Christie Clovis, Amy Price, and Lauren Wichterman, *Annual Report on Shared Family Care: Progress and Lessons Learned* (Berkeley, CA: National Abandoned Infants Assistance Resource Center, August 2002); U.S. Department of Health and Human Services, *Promising Practices* (Washington, DC: Children's Bureau, September 2001), retrieved April 1, 2004, from http://cbexpress.acf.hhs.gov/articles.cfm?section_id = 4&issue_id = 2001–09; Amanda Bower, "Sharing Family Values: Troubled Parents Are Getting a Second Chance: Foster Care for Them along with Their Kids," *Time Archive* (February 17, 2003), retrieved April 1, 2004, from http://www.time.com/time/magazine/article/subscriber/0,10987,1101030217-421037,00.html; Amy Price and Lauren Wichterman, "Shared Family Care: Fostering the Whole Family to Promote Safety and Stability," *Journal of Family Social Work,* Vol. 7, No. 2, 2003, pp. 35–54.

98. Unless otherwise noted, information in this section relies on Committee on Ways and Means, U.S. House of Representatives, *2003 Green Book,* "Child Protection, Foster Care, and Adoption Assistance"; information in this paragraph also comes from Reid M. Jonson, "Foster Care and Future Risk of Maltreatment," *Children and Youth Services Review,* Vol. 25, No. 4, April 2003, pp. 271–294.

99. Urban Institute, *Assessing the New Federalism: Children in Kinship Care* (Washington, DC, 2003), retrieved April 2004, from http://www.urban.org/UploadedPDF/900661.pdf

100. U.S. Census Bureau, *Grandparents Living with Grandchildren: 2000* (Washington, DC, October 2003), retrieved April 2, 2004, from http://www.census.gov/prod/2003pubs/c2kbr-31.pdf

101. Gerard Wallace, "Grandparent Caregivers: Emerging Issues in Elder Law and Social Work Practice," *Journal of Gerontological Social Work,* Vol. 34, No. 3, 2001, pp. 127–136.

102. John V. O'Neill, "GAO Affirms Need for High-Quality Staff," *NASW News,* June 2003, p. 7.

103. See Rudolph Alexander, Jr., "The Legal Liability of Social Workers after DeShaney," *Social Work,* Vol. 38, No. 1, 1993, pp. 64–68.

104. David S. Savage (*Los Angeles Times* Service), "Court Gives Social Workers Immunity from Lawsuits," *Austin American-Statesman,* April 26, 1994, p. C20.

105. Kathryn W. Rhodes, John G. Orme, Mary Ellen Cox, and Cheryl Buehler, "Foster Family Resources, Psychosocial Functioning and Retention," *Social Work Research,* Vol. 27, No. 3, 2003, pp. 135–150; see also Enola K. Proctor, "Unmet Need, Safety Net Services, and Research," *Social Work Research,* Vol. 27, No. 3, 2003, pp. 131–134.

106. Dana Canedy, "Florida Repeals 'Scarlet Letter' Adoption Law," *New York Times,* May 31, 2003, retrieved May 31, 2004, from http://www.nytimes.com

107. See Arnold Silverman, "Outcomes of Transracial Adoption," in The Center for the Future of Children (Ed.), *The Future of Children* (Los Altos, CA: David and Lucille Packard Foundation, 1993), pp. 104–118; Ruth G. McRoy, "An Organizational Dilemma: The Case of Transracial Adoptions," *Journal of Applied Behavioral Science,* Vol. 25, No. 2, 1989, pp. 145–160.

108. Kasia O'Neill Murray and Sara Gesiriech, *A Brief Legislative History of the Child Welfare System.*

109. U.S. Department of Health and Human Services, Office of the Surgeon General, "A Vision for the Future," in *Mental Health: A Report of the Surgeon General* (Washington, DC, 1999); see also Ann F. Garland, John A. Landsverk, and Anna S. Lau, "Racial/Ethnic Disparities in Mental Health Service Use among Children in Foster Care," *Children and Youth Services Review,* Vol. 25, No. 5/6, 2003, pp. 491–507.

110. Unless otherwise noted, information about substance abuse and child welfare is taken from Committee on Ways and Means, U.S. House of Representatives, "Child Protection, Foster Care, and Adoption Assistance," *2003 Green Book;* see also U.S. Department of Health and Human Services, *Blending Perspectives and Building Common Ground: A Report to Congress on Substance Abuse and Child Protection* (Washington, DC, April 1999).

111. For an overview of this topic, see Diane R. Davis and Diana M. DiNitto, "Gender and the Use of Drugs and Alcohol: Fact, Fiction, and Unanswered Questions," in C. Aaron McNeece and Diana M. DiNitto, *Chemical Dependency: A Systems Approach, 3rd Edition,* pp. 503–546.

112. Unless otherwise noted, information on transitioning foster youth relies on Committee on Ways and Means, U.S. House of Representatives, "Child Protection, Foster Care, and Adoption Assistance," *2003 Green Book;* see also T. Reilly, "Transition from Care: Status and Outcomes of Youth Who Age out of Foster Care," *Child Welfare,* Vol. 82, No. 6, 2003, pp. 726–746; U.S. Department of Health and Human Services, *Title IV-E Independent Living Programs: A Decade in Review* (Washington, DC, November 1999); U.S. General Accounting Office, *Foster Care: Effectiveness of Independent Living Services Unknown* (Washington, DC, November 1999), GAO-HEHS-00-13.

113. Rose Marie Penzerro, "Drift as Adaptation: Foster Care and Homeless Careers," *Youth and Family Care Forum,* Vol. 32, No. 4, August 2003, pp. 229–244.

114. Bellingham and Byers, "Foster Care and Child Protection Services."

115. Richard Lezin Jones, "New Jersey Plan Would Hire 1,000 in Child Welfare," *New York Times,* February 19, 2004, retrieved February 20, 2004, from http://www.nytimes.com

116. For information on the Older American's act, see the website of the Administration on Aging, http://www.aoa.dhhs.gov

117. Also see Linda Hubbard Getze, "Need Help? What the Aging Network Can Do for You," *Modern Maturity,* March 1981, pp. 33–36.

118. University of California San Francisco, *Elderly Caregiving: Choices, Challenges, and Resources for the Family* (Berkeley, CA: Human Resources, 2003), retrieved April 1, 2004, from http://ucsfhr.ucsf.edu/assist/info.html?x = 1050

119. U.S. Department of Health and Human Services, Administration on Aging, "Characteristics of Persons Served under Title III of OAA: FY 2002" (Washington, DC, 2002), retrieved September 25, 2004, from http://www.aoa.gov/

120. "White House Conference on Aging Final Report Released," March 6, 1996, retrieved from http://www.aoa.dhhs.gov/aoa/pr/whcoarep.html; see also M. Fernando Torres-Gil, "Aging Policy in the Clinton Administration," *Journal of Aging & Social Policy,* Vol. 7, No. 2, 1995, pp. 113–118; Roberta R. Greene, "Emerging Issues for Social Workers in the Field of Aging: White House Conference Themes," *Journal of Gerontological Social Work,* Vol. 27, No. 3, 1997, pp. 79–87.

121. Robert B. Hudson, "The Older Americans Act and the Defederalization of Community-Based Care," in Paul H. K. Kim, Ed., *Services to the Aged: Public Policies and Programs* (New York: Garland Publishing, 1994), pp. 45–75.

122. National Center on Elder Abuse, "Fact Sheets about Elder Abuse" (Washington, DC, May 2003), retrieved April 4, 2004, from http://www.elderabusecenter.org

123. Paragraphs on guardianship rely on Fred Bayles and Scott McCartney, "Guardians of the Elderly, An Ailing System," a six-part Associated Press series appearing in the *Austin American-Statesman,* Septem-

ber 20–25, 1987, Section A; see also George H. Zimny and George T. Grossberg, *Guardianship of the Elderly: Psychiatric and Judicial Aspects* (New York: Springer, 1998).

124. Zimny and Grossberg, *Guardianship of the Elderly: Psychiatric and Judicial Aspects,* p. 9.

125. "Craig Calls for GAO Report on Guardianship after Listening to Abuse Horror Stories" (Washington, DC: U.S. Senate Special Committee on Aging, February 11, 2003), retrieved August 3, 2004, from http://aging.senate.gov/index.cfm?FuseAction = PressReleases.Detail&PressRelease_id = 55; "Written Statement of Michael S. Kutzin before the United States Senate Special Committee on Aging," February 11, 2003, retrieved August 3, 2004, from http://www.google.com; Government Accountability Office, *Guardianships: Collaboration Needed to Protect Incapacitated Elderly People,* GAO-04-655 (Washington, DC, July 2004), retrieved August 3, 2004, from http://www.gao.gov

126. Robert Morris, *Social Policy of the American Welfare State,* p. 150.

127. See Bruce C. Vladeck and Marvin Feuerberg, "Unloving Care Revisited," *Generations,* Vol. 19, No. 4, 1995–1996, pp. 9–13.

CHAPTER

Addressing Civil Rights and Social Welfare: The Challenges of a Diverse Society

*E*ighty-five years after women won the right to vote and more than 40 years after passage of the Civil Rights Act of 1964, the United States still struggles with racism and sexism. Perhaps Rip Van Winkle would be surprised at the progress that blacks, other people of color, and women have made, but frustration over inequality remains. Poverty and other social problems continue to be concentrated among particular groups—primarily women, blacks, Hispanic Americans, and American Indians. This chapter explores the history of discrimination in the United States and the quest for gender, racial, and ethnic equality through social policy.

GENDER INEQUITIES

The Feminization of Poverty

During the 1980s, "the feminization of poverty"[1] became a catch phrase, but this situation was hardly new. Most poor adults and public assistance recipients have always been women. Some of the earliest state and local welfare programs were mothers' aid and mothers' pension laws, which were followed by the federally assisted Aid to Dependent Children program and later the Aid to Families with Dependent Children program (AFDC) (see Chapter 6). These programs were originally intended to help mothers, not fathers. Even the AFDC-Unemployed Parent program, and later the Family Support Act of 1988 which extended AFDC to certain two-parent families in all states, did not change this emphasis. Traditionally, women "went on welfare" because they were expected to remain at home to care for their young children when their husbands were unable to support them due to death, disability, or unemployment, or unwilling to support them after divorce or desertion. When women did go to work to support themselves and their families, they were usually forced into low-paying jobs; many still are. These factors contributed to a pattern in which women are more likely to be poor and more likely to receive public assistance. The pattern was exacerbated in the 1970s and 1980s with the rapid increase in the number of female-headed households. The discussion of poverty in Chapter 3 clearly shows that female-headed households are most vulnerable to poverty, and that women who are members of certain ethnic groups are extremely vulnerable.

Women are about 58 percent of all Supplemental Security Income (SSI) recipients and 71 percent of aged SSI recipients.[2] Women are overrepresented in SSI for two reasons. First, they are more likely to be poor because their Social Security benefits are less than men's, and they are less likely to have other sources of income such as pensions. In 2001, the median income of males aged 65 and older was $19,436, compared to $11,406 for women,[3] and the percentage of women aged 65 and older living in poverty was 12.4, compared with 7 for men.[4] For older white women, the percentage was 11.1, compared with 6 for their male counterparts. For older Hispanic and black women, the percentages were 24.5 and 26.1, respectively, and for older Hispanic and black men, 18.1 and 18.6 percent, respectively (see Table 11.1). As women and men get older, poverty rates generally increase further, with the percentage of women in poverty remaining much larger. The situation is even worse for older women who live

TABLE 11.1

Poverty Statistics for Older Americans by Race, Gender, and Living Alone, 2001

Characteristic	Females				Males			
	All	White	Black	Hispanic	All	White	Black	Hispanic
	Percent Living in Poverty							
65 and Older	12.4	11.1	26.1	24.5	7.0	6.0	15.6	18.1
75 and Older	13.6	12.5	28.3	23.7	7.3	6.4	18.1	19.4
65 and Older and Living Alone	20.6	18.5	41.5	49.2	15.1	12.4	29.3	35.5

Source: U.S. Census Bureau, retrieved from http://ferret.bls.census.gov/macro/032002/pov/new22_003.htm; http://ferret.bls.census.gov/macro/032002/pov/new02_000.htm

alone, especially women of color. Older Hispanic women living alone had the highest poverty rate (49.2 percent) (see Table 11.1). The second reason that women are more likely to receive SSI is that they live longer than men. Therefore, they are more likely to encounter the chronic infirmities that accompany advanced age or disability and drain away resources.

Social welfare aid in the United States developed along two separate tracks: the less generous public assistance programs were instituted largely to help women and children while the more generous social insurance programs were targeted toward male workers.[5] Inequities caused by social policy are to blame for many of the economic problems of older women. When the Social Security system was first adopted, men's and women's roles were different than they are today. Women were less likely to work outside the home, and divorce was less common. The Social Security system reflected the social conditions of the 1930s when most women were considered "dependents" of their working husbands. Since women are poorer than men, they rely more heavily on transfer payments such as Social Security, but their benefits are often insufficient to meet their needs. In 2002, the average monthly Social Security retirement benefit paid to women was $713 compared to $1077 for men.[6] Unmarried women aged 65 and older are especially reliant on Social Security. In 2002, Social Security was 51 percent of their total income, compared to 37 percent for unmarried men. Social Security was the *only* source of income for 26 percent of unmarried older women.[7]

The Social Security system has not kept pace with the changing roles of men and women. Gender inequities persist for a number of reasons:[8]

1. Women's wages are generally lower than men's (even when they do the same work), resulting in lower Social Security benefits paid to women on retirement or disability.

2. Women are still likely to spend less time in the paid workforce than men because they continue to carry the major unpaid responsibilities for the home and family care. This also results in lower Social Security benefits paid to women.

3. A divorced woman who was married for at least ten years is entitled to a Social Security payment equal to half of her former husband's retirement benefits. If this is her only income, it is likely inadequate, and she cannot collect at all based on her former husband's earnings if they were married less than ten years.

4. Widows generally do not qualify for benefits until they are 60 years old unless they are disabled or have children under age 18.

5. Homemakers are not covered on their own unless they have held jobs in the paid labor force.

6. Social Security retirement benefits are often based on the earnings of the primary worker, generally the husband. The wages of a second earner, usually the wife, may not raise the couple's combined Social Security benefits.

7. Couples in which one worker (generally the husband) earned most of the wages may receive higher retirement benefits than those in which the husband and wife earned equal wages even if both couples' incomes were identical.

8. Married workers benefit from Social Security more than single workers. An individual who has never worked can benefit from Social Security payments based on the work of a spouse. Single workers do not receive additional benefits, even though they have made Social Security payments at the same rate as married workers.

There have been some efforts to reduce gender inequities in the Social Security programs, but most have had minimal impact. One measure allows divorced husbands to claim benefits based on the earnings records of their former wives. Another allows divorced spouses to qualify for benefits at age 62 based on a former spouse's earnings, even if the ex-spouse has not claimed benefits.

As we would expect, couples receive the highest Social Security retirement benefits. Widowed or divorced men receive more than widowed or divorced women, but never-married women now average more than their male counterparts (see Table 11.2).[9] The number of women who qualify for benefits based on their own work records has increased considerably, but many women still receive higher payments based on their husbands' earnings rather than on their own.

Several options have been suggested for remedying gender inequities in the Social Security system and bringing the program more in line with the times. The **earnings-sharing** option would divide a couple's earnings equally between the husband and wife for each year they are married. This option would allow benefits to be calculated separately for the husband and the wife whether they remained married or not and would eliminate the ideas of the "primary wage earner" and the "dependent spouse." This option would also recognize that a spouse with primary responsibility for care of the home and children is an equal partner in the marriage. A second option is to give women at least minimal Social Security earnings credits for each year they stay at home to raise children. A third option is the **double-decker plan.** Under this option, everyone would be eligible for a basic benefit, whether or not they had ever worked for pay. Individuals with paid work experience would receive a payment in addition to the basic benefit.

TABLE 11.2

Social Security Income of Those Aged 65 and Over by Gender, Marital Status, and Race, 2000

Characteristic	Federal Poverty Threshold	Median Social Security Income
Singles 65 and over	$8,259	
All Single Men		$9,916
Widowed		10,209
Never Married		7,909
Divorced		10,261
All Single Women		9,227
Widowed		9,487
Never Married		8,387
Divorced		8,088
Whites		
Single Women		9,439
Single Men		10,188
Blacks		
Single Women		7,366
Single Men		8,057
Hispanics		
Single Women		7,081
Single Men		7,955
Couples 65 and over	$10,419	
All Couples		16,467
White Couples		16,723
Black Couples		14,018
Hispanic Couples		12,863

Source: Social Security Administration, *Social Security Income of the Population 55 and Older, 2000,* retrieved from www.ssa.gov/policy/docs/statcomps/income_pop55/2000/sect5a.pdf

Now a fourth option requires women's careful consideration—the privatization of Social Security. As discussed in Chapter 4, privatization can take many forms. It could be combined with the double-decker and earnings-sharing plans. The Cato Institute (a zealous supporter of privatization) concludes that all women would be better off if Social Security was privatized, citing figures that married women earning $11,000 a year who placed their FICA payroll withholdings in an IRA-type account could more than double their Social Security retirement income.[10] Cato's argument is that private investments are sound and that even the lowest-risk investments (such as government bonds) have an annual return rate of 3–4 percent, compared to the

2 percent annual return rate that most people receive on the money they invest in the Social Security system. Most women (68 percent) surveyed by Zogby International said that they would support placing a portion of their Social Security taxes into a private IRA-type account.[11] Younger women were more likely than older women to support privatizing Social Security. But Democratic women in the U.S. House of Representatives have denounced incorporating private accounts into the Social Security system, claiming that such a move would be harmful to women, especially women who rely heavily on their husbands' earnings for Social Security retirement income.[12] Many groups argue that private investment accounts remove the safety net that Social Security provides.[13] It has also been noted that privatization might strain marriages in more ways than one, especially in one-earner families, if a working spouse was required to contribute to a stay-at-home spouse's private account. In today's system, stay-at-home spouses get a benefit with no additional contributions from the wage earner.[14] Regardless of what approach is used, the idea of women taking charge of their retirement income separate from their husbands makes sense, especially to young working women. Since women live considerably longer than men, aging is clearly a women's issue.

The Wage Gap

In 1955 the Bureau of Labor Statistics calculated that women earned 64 cents for every dollar earned by men; by 1961 the figure had dropped to 59 cents.[15] As it hovered there, "59 cents" became a well-known refrain of the equal rights movement. Not until the 1980s did the earnings ratio again consistently exceeded the 60 percent mark. In 2002, women's earnings were about 78 percent of men's. In the 25 to 34 age bracket, women working full time earned 85 percent of what men earned.

Over time, many reasons have been offered to explain the difference in earning power:

1. Traditionally, most women were not their families' major wage earners, nor did they earn salaries comparable to men's if they did work.

2. Women's wages were considered secondary or as a supplement to their spouses' wages.

3. Women were considered temporary employees who would leave their jobs to marry and have children; they were not seen as serious about careers.

4. Women's work outside the home was considered an extracurricular activity to fill free time.

5. Women had fewer opportunities to obtain education that would lead to better-paying jobs.

6. Women were forced into certain occupations on the low end of the wage scale.

7. Women had limited job choices because they were forced to accept employment that did not conflict with the routines of their husbands and children.

8. "Women's work"—cleaning and child rearing in their own homes—has not paid a wage.

9. Some argued that women "preferred" lower-level employment because these jobs were more compatible with characteristics they associated with women, such as nurturing qualities and lack of aggressiveness.

Although many of these explanations are readily dismissed, and even laughable today, there are elements of truth in some of them. Some women do terminate their employment on a temporary or long-term basis to raise families. The unfortunate term "mommy track" has been used to describe women who interrupt their careers or try to juggle both career and children. The term implies that women who want or need careers pay the price, because their multiple responsibilities diminish their chances of career advancement. For example, in 1994 Vassar College was found to have discriminated against a married woman with children who was denied tenure in the biology department. In the past 30 years, no married woman in the "hard sciences" had been tenured there.

Women's paid employment is often essential to their families' support. Eighteen percent of U.S. families are headed by women alone,[16] and many two-earner families would be in serious financial difficulty without the wife's economic contribution. Only a small number of American families fit the "ideal" or traditional perception of a mother at home caring for children and the father as sole wage earner. Most families today are made up of dual-earners. In fact, women married to high-income husbands are entering the labor force faster than women married to husbands with incomes in the lower half of the income distribution, suggesting that income is not the only force motivating women's increased labor force participation.[17] More and more, women are finding their work satisfying, challenging, and an integral component of their lives.

Women now comprise 47 percent of the civilian labor force.[18] A growing number have earned advanced degrees (in 2000, women were 56 percent of college students, and women aged 25 to 29 were slightly more likely than their male counterparts to have a college degree).[19] Many women also hold higher-level jobs, but women continue to earn less than men, even when they have the same education. Figure 11.1 shows that among full-time, year-round workers in 2003, women with a high school education earned more than $8,000 less than men with equal education; women with bachelor's or master's degrees also earned considerably less than men with equivalent education. Table 11.3 also shows that there are differences between women's and men's earnings among the major ethnic groups in the United States, with women consistently earning less. Earnings differences persist even among men and women in the same occupations who worked full–time, year-round, although inequality is greater in some professions than others (see Table 11.4). In the sales sector, women earned only 42 cents for every dollar earned by men. Even in traditional women's jobs such as nursing, women earned only 77 percent of men's wages. Among legal professionals (lawyers, judges), the earnings ratio was 67 cents to the dollar. Equality was by far the greatest in community and social service occupations (91 cents to the

FIGURE 11.1

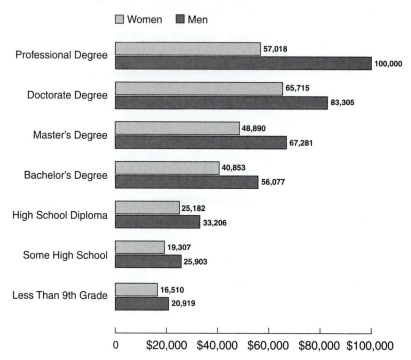

Median Annual Earnings of Full-Time, Year-Round Workers, 25 Years and Older, by Gender and Education, 2003

□ Women   ■ Men

	Women	Men
Professional Degree	57,018	100,000
Doctorate Degree	65,715	83,305
Master's Degree	48,890	67,281
Bachelor's Degree	40,853	56,077
High School Diploma	25,182	33,206
Some High School	19,307	25,903
Less Than 9th Grade	16,510	20,919

0    $20,000 $40,000 $60,000 $80,000 $100,000

Source: U.S. Bureau of the Census and the Bureau of Labor Statistics, *Current Population Survey: Annual Demographic Survey, March Supplement* (Washington, DC, March 2003), Table PINC-03, parts 136, 262, retrieved from http://ferret.bls.census.gov/macro/032003/perinc/new03_262.htm and http://ferret.bls.census.gov/macro/032003/perinc/new03_136.htm

dollar). Although a portion of the pay differentials between men and women may be explained by the number of years of work experience, gender discrimination and racial discrimination continue to explain part of the gap.

Women of "Generation X" (those born between 1966 and 1975) are making tremendous inroads in closing the wage gap and in gaining footing in nontraditional jobs. In 2000, 77 percent of women aged 25 to 34 were in the workforce, compared to 54 percent in 1975, and married Gen X women with children were significantly more likely to be working compared to their counterparts of 25 years ago.[20] Several factors have influenced this upshot in work participation, but two stand out. First, Generation X women are more highly educated (30 percent of women in the 25–34 age group had a college degree in 2000, compared to 18 percent in 1975). Second, Gen X women are delaying marriage or not marrying. In 1975, three out of four 25- to 34-year-old women were married, but in 2000, only three in five were married. In addition, the number

TABLE 11.3

Median Annual Earnings of Full-Time, Year-Round Workers, 25 Years and Older, by Gender and Race or Ethnicity, 2001

	Women	Men
All	$30,420	$40,136
White	30,849	40,790
Black	27,297	31,921
Hispanic[a]	21,973	25,271
Asian/Pacific Islander	31,284	42,695

Source: U.S. Census Bureau, *Current Population Survey, Annual Demographic Supplements, Historical Income Tables—People* (Washington, DC), Tables P-36, P-36a, P-36b, P-36c, P-36d, retrieved from http://www.census.gov/hhes/income/histinc/incperdet.html

[a]May be of any race.

TABLE 11.4

Median Annual Earnings of Full-Time, Year-Round Workers, 15 Years and Older in Selected Occupations, by Gender, 2002

Occupation	Men	Women	Women's Earnings as a Percentage of Men's
Chief Executives, General and Operations Managers	$79,734	$51,680	65
Computer Scientists, Analysts, Programmers, Engineers and Administrators	58,543	47,256	81
Community and Social Service Occupations	33,351	30,334	91
Lawyers, Judges and Magistrates	100,000	66,886	67
Postsecondary Teachers	48,035	26,177	54
Doctors	100,000	62,239	62
Nurses	50,109	38,389	77
Firefighters and Police	48,511	38,002	78
Sales and Related Occupations	33,641	14,065	42
Postal Workers	43,796	37,145	85
Farming, Fishing, and Forestry Occupations	16,225	9,958	61
Construction	26,622	18,463	69
Drivers	27,117	16,779	62

Source: U.S. Census Bureau, Current Population Survey, 2003 Annual Social and Economic Supplement, retrieved from http://ferret.bls.census.gov/macro/032003/perinc/new06_019.htm

of women who had never been married increased from 11 percent to 30 percent over the same time period. These changing demographic patterns explain why Gen X women earn 85 percent of men's wages, compared to 78 percent for all women. Though Gen X women still comprise most of the employees in their age cohort who hold traditional women's jobs (teachers, librarians, nurses), they now comprise 51 percent of all those aged 25 to 34 employed in executive, administrative, and managerial occupations. Whether Gen X women take this improved workforce status for granted is a question open to empirical examination, but older women know that the battle to help them get there has been hard fought. Women of color have also seen gains in wage earnings and occupational status over the past 25 years, but they still do not have parity with white women.

An obvious approach to narrowing the wage gap has been to press for equal pay for equal work. It is difficult, for example, to justify paying a male accountant more than a female accountant if their job responsibilities are the same. According to the Equal Pay Act of 1963, men and women who do the same work are supposed to be paid equally. The federal government established the Equal Employment Opportunity Commission (EEOC) to help employees address gender discrimination in the workplace.

Another effort to reduce the gap in earnings between women and men is **comparable worth**.[21] According to this concept, workers should be paid equally when they do *different* types of work that require the same level of responsibility, effort, knowledge, and skill. Many jobs done by men garner greater monetary compensation because the **dual labor market** creates a situation in which "women's professions" are regarded less highly than professions dominated by men. In discussing comparable worth, we are really asking whether the jobs in question are of equal value to society.

Some have called comparable worth a "truly crazy proposal."[22] Others argue that it is a truly rational approach to achieving equality. By 1985, twenty states had passed laws or resolutions making comparable worth a requirement or a goal of state employment. But states soon abandoned comparable worth efforts, stating that market-based wages are necessary to attract and retain workers.[23] Minnesota and Washington did establish equal pay systems for state employees. In Minnesota, state jobs are assigned points based on work requirements, skill levels, and the like in order to assess the comparable value of job categories. For example, in 1982, the state of Minnesota's job evaluation ratings for a delivery van driver (most were men) and a clerk typist (most were women) were the same—117 points; however, the monthly state salary for the van driver was $1,900 while the clerk typist salary was $1,400. The Minnesota legislature approved pay equity wage adjustments for state jobs found to be undervalued and underpaid, amounting to an average annual increase of $2,200 for these positions. Most of these salary increases went to women, though 10 percent went to men in undervalued jobs. Following implementation of this comparable worth policy, for state workers, the wage gap between men and women state employees closed by 9 percentage points.

The courts have generally not favored comparable worth, finding that paying prevailing market rate salaries is not illegal. For example, in a case against Brown University, a male faculty member accused the university of paying an equally qualified female faculty member a higher salary. The First Circuit Court ruled in favor of the university, which argued that the female professor was paid more because she had planned to take a position at another school that had offered her a higher salary. Brown wanted to retain her. The university contended that she had greater market value than the male professor, and the court agreed. In another case, nursing faculty at the University of Washington filed suit stating that they were paid less than male faculty in other departments. The Ninth Circuit Court ruled that under Title VII of the Civil Rights Act, suits cannot be brought before the court if salary inequities are due to labor market conditions.

Given court rulings, it may be surprising that comparable worth has seen a resurgence, with 26 state legislatures considering bills to close the wage gap between men and women. In 2001, the wage gap in 20 states exceeded the national wage gap. Wyoming had the greatest gender wage gap. Women there were earning only 69 percent of what men earned. Washington, DC, came closest to wage equity; women there earned 97 percent of men's wages. A 2002 study by the AFL-CIO's National Committee on Pay Equity estimated that it would take some states 20 more years to close the earning gap at the current pace, and in 16 states it would take until 2050 or longer. In 2000, the U.S Department of Labor instituted new affirmative action regulations to promote equal pay, requiring all federal contractors to report hiring, termination, promotions, and compensation by gender and minority status. This is the first time that these employers have been required to report compensation by gender and minority status to federal equal employment agencies.[24] The information will influence departments' decisions in hiring outside contractors.

Pay equity for women is long overdue, but some economists believe that such policies would wreak havoc with the supply and demand forces that regulate the free market. Others fear that it would reduce demand for female workers and increase unemployment among women. Some black women call the comparative worth movement a "white woman's movement" and others point out that comparable worth addresses gender only and ignores wage discrimination based on race, sexual orientation, or disability status.

Equality for Women

Women had been organizing to gain equality through political participation long before the suffragette movement, though it was not until 1920 that the Nineteenth Amendment to the U.S. Constitution finally gave women the right to vote. Even with this right, the percentage of women who hold political office remains small (see Table 11.5), but it has grown over time. In 1993, Carol Moseley-Braun (D-Illinois) become the first African American woman to serve in the U.S. Senate, and California became the first state to have two women senators simultaneously—Barbara Boxer and Dianne Feinstein (both Democrats). Women still have a long way to go if they want to claim the number of elected positions commensurate with their representation in the population. President Clinton's political appointments dramatically increased the number of women in

TABLE 11.5

Women in High-Level Federal and State Government Positions, 1999 and 2004

	1999		2004		
Office	Number of Women	Percent of Total	Number of Women	Percent of Total	Percentage Change
White House Cabinet	4 of 15	28	3 of 20	15	−13
U.S. Senate	9 of 100	9	14 of 100	14	+ 5
U.S. House of Representatives	56 of 435	13	59 of 435	14	+ 1
Governor	3	6	8	16	+ 10
Lieutenant Governor	18	36	17	34	−2
State Legislators	1,652 of 7,424	22	1,655 of 7,382	22	0
Secretary of State	14	28	10	20	−8
State Attorney General	10	20	5	10	−10
State Treasurer	10	20	8	16	−4
State Controller	4	8	3	6	−2
Overall Change					**−23**

Source: Center for American Women in Politics (CAWP), National Information Bank on Women in Politics Office, Eagleton Institute of Politics, Rutgers University. Reprinted with permission.

high-level posts. He appointed Madeleine Albright Secretary of State, making her the highest-ranking woman ever to serve in the federal government. He also appointed Janet Reno, the first woman to serve as U.S. Attorney General, and Ruth Bader Ginsburg, the second woman to serve on the U.S. Supreme Court. As the end of his first year in office approached, 37 percent of the more than 500 appointments he made were women, more than the 24 percent of the George H. W. Bush administration, and far more than other previous presidents.[25]

Since President George W. Bush took office in 2001, the number of women holding cabinet positions has dropped by 13 percent (see Table 11.5).[26] The most visible woman in George W. Bush's administration is Condolleeza Rice, National Security Advisor, who has been even more visible since the Iraq war began. Since 1999 there has been only a 5 percent gain in the number of women serving in the U.S. Senate and only a 1 percent gain in the U.S. House of Representatives. In 2002, Representative Nancy Pelosi (D-California) became the first woman to head a Congressional party caucus.

The proportion of women in statewide elected offices grew steadily for three decades from 7 percent in 1971 to 28 percent in 2000, but women have lost ground. In 2004 they held 25 percent of elected state offices. Though the number of women governors has increased and the number of women state legislators remained the same, there have been declines in other state posts, most notably in the number of women state attorneys general (see Table 11.5).

Equal Rights through Law

Since the 1960s, the federal government has attempted to address the inequities women face in employment, education, and the marketplace. The following list contains some of the most notable achievements:

1. The Equal Pay Act of 1963 requires employers to compensate male and female workers equally for performing the same jobs under similar conditions. The law does not cover all employment, but amendments have added to the types of jobs and employers that must comply.

2. Title VII of the Civil Rights Act of 1964 prohibits gender discrimination in employment practices and provides the right to court redress. The Equal Employment Opportunity Commission is charged with interpreting and enforcing Title VII.

3. Executive Order 11246, as amended by Executive Order 11375 in 1967, prohibits employers who practice gender discrimination from receiving federal contracts. Employers are also required to develop "affirmative action" plans to remedy inequities. The order established the Office of Federal Contract Compliance under the Department of Labor as an enforcement agency.

4. Title IX of the 1972 Education Amendments to the Civil Rights Act prohibits gender discrimination by elementary, secondary, vocational, and professional schools, colleges, and universities that receive federal funds.

5. The Equal Credit Act of 1975 prohibits discrimination by lending institutions based on gender or marital status.

6. The Pregnancy Discrimination Act of 1978, another amendment to the Civil Rights Act, protects women from employment discrimination as a result of childbearing.

A naïve observer would think that with all these pieces of legislation there should be no question that women are protected under the law. But battles over some of these pieces of legislation are fought and refought. Title IX is a prime example. Much of the debate concerns whether school's athletic programs continue to discriminate against female students or whether Title IX hampers men's athletics. U.S. Education Secretary Rod Paige appointed a commission to make recommendations on these matters. The committee's 2003 report just seemed to fuel the fire.

The Equal Rights Amendment

Official attempts to pass an equal rights amendment (ERA) to the U.S. Constitution for women began at the Seneca Falls Women's Rights Convention in 1923 when Alice Paul first introduced ERA language. Virtually every year thereafter the ERA was introduced into Congress, but it did not pass both houses of Congress until 1972. A Constitutional amendment requires ratification. Generally, there is no deadline for states to ratify an amendment (an amendment on Congressional pay raises was ratified in 1992—203 years after being passed by Congress).[27]

The ERA simply stated:

Section 1.   Equality of rights under the law shall not be denied or abridged by the United States or by any state on account of sex.

Section 2.   Congress shall have the power to enforce by appropriate legislation the provisions of this Article.

Section 3.   This amendment shall take effect two years after the date of ratification.

By 1978, the amendment still had not been ratified by the required 38 states. Congress extended the deadline to June 30, 1982. Despite the endorsement of 450 organizations with 50 million members—unions, churches, civil rights groups, legal associations, educational groups, medical organizations—ERA ratification fell short by three states.[28]

ERA proponents argued that this guarantee of equality under law should be part of the Constitution—"the supreme law of the land," and that until this happens, there is unspoken consent to discriminate on the basis of gender. While a number of federal and state laws already prohibit gender discrimination, many believe that these laws are inadequate to fully address the problem of gender inequality. ERA proponents contend that like many other social policy issues, gender discrimination is best addressed by a national policy rather than by a multitude of federal, state, and local laws, each subject to modification or repeal. Conservative Phyllis Schlafly founded the "Stop ERA Movement" shortly after Congress approved the ERA in 1972. The movement was based on fears about what might happen if the traditional roles of women in society were disrupted. There were rumors that the ERA would lead to a military draft and combat duty for women, and that restrooms would become unisex. There was concern about how an ERA would affect marital life. Conservatives blame the push for equal rights for changes in divorce laws that no longer give preferential treatment to women on issues of child custody, and for the near elimination of alimony. None of these concerns were specifically mentioned in the ERA. Schafly and the Eagle Forum continue to oppose the ERA, which continues to be introduced to almost every Congress. In 2003, when Representative Carolyn Maloney (Democrat-New York) and Senator Edward Kennedy (Democrat-Massachusetts) introduced the ERA to the 108th Congress, Anita Blair, the executive vice president and general counsel of the Independent Women's Forum (a conservative Republican organization) said, "Normal women don't want it and don't need it."[29] The United States is one of the few democratic nations without constitutional protection of women's rights.

Caring for the Family

More assistance with child care and other family responsibilities would certainly promote greater equality for women. In 1990 Congress passed several pieces of legislation that increased the federal government's participation in child care. Among them were the Child Care and Development Block Grant (CCDBG) and an expansion of child care services provided through the former AFDC JOBS program (see Chapter 6) so that families could maintain employment rather than risk joining the public assistance rolls.

In 1996, the Personal Responsibility and Work Opportunity Reconciliation Act (that instituted large-scale welfare reform) consolidated the CCDBG and AFDC child care programs into a single block grant called the Child Care and Development Fund (CCDF). An Urban Institute report determined that "states would have to put up on average an additional 70 percent of state dollars over and above" what they had been spending to draw down all the funds available to them.[30] Most states have taken advantage of a provision allowing them to transfer up to 30 percent of TANF funds into the CCDF. This has helped more TANF families go to work, and provided subsidized child care to other families to help divert them from the TANF roles (see Chapter 6). As Congress considers TANF reauthorization, a heated debate has ensued between the chambers on appropriating more child care dollars. The House bill includes an additional $1 billion in new child care funds. The Senate version includes an additional $6 billion, arguing that if work requirements for TANF families are going to increase to 40 hours a week as proposed, then Congress has an obligation to assure families that their children will be cared for while they are working.[31] Whether families receive subsidized child care has a lot to do with luck—the generosity of the state or community in which they live, the number of child care slots available, and the demand for those slots. In many other countries child care is a matter of entitlement.

Child care affordability, quality, and monitoring, as well as the low pay afforded child care workers that results in difficulties recruiting and retaining staff, are issues of concern to everyone who uses care or provides it. Many low-income parents must use whatever child care they can find, either because they must work to make ends meet or because TANF requires them to work. The "catch-22" is that many families cannot afford or find decent child care while they work, but they face sanctions if their children are injured or harmed if left inadequately supervised.

Congress has increased Head Start program expenditures and tax credits to help low-income working families obtain child care. Some proposals seek to increase the tax credit. Others claim that this approach is unfair to families that choose to use non-paid care while working, including those in which one parent stays at home with the children. They support a larger tax credit for dependents that would help families regardless of their employment and childcare choices.[32] This is what happened when the 1997 Balanced Budget Act included a modest child tax credit. The 2001 tax cut under the George W. Bush administration increased the child tax credit from $600 to $1000 (see Chapter 2).

Obtaining care for disabled adult and elderly family members also presents challenges, primarily to women who generally assume the major caretaker responsibilities. Community day care centers help alleviate some of this burden, and many families purchase home care through the private sector using Medicare, Medicaid, or their own funds.

During the George H. W. Bush years, Congress twice passed family leave bills that would have required some employers to provide twelve weeks of unpaid leave to family members when a new baby arrives or when a spouse, parent, or child had a serious illness. The same leave would have been extended to employees with an illness. Despite strong public support, Bush vetoed both bills, saying that while he favored family leave, the bills might force businesses to hire replacement help. Rather than preserve jobs, he feared that the bills might result in a net job loss. President Clinton felt very differently about family leave legislation. On taking office, he moved swiftly to sign the Family and Medical Leave Act of 1993. However, the law exempts businesses with fewer than 50 workers (thereby excluding half the workforce and the vast majority of businesses), and covered businesses are not required to provide leave to upper-echelon employees. In October 2002, President George W. Bush repealed a Clinton-era regulation that allowed states to use unemployment insurance to help people who take family leave.[33] Using unemployment insurance in this way might have been a stretch,[34] and no state exercised the option. About the same time, California became the first state to pass a family leave law.[35] The law entitles eligible workers to six weeks of paid leave at 55 percent of their salary, but no more than $728 per week, to care for a new child or a family member. To finance the program, about $26 of each employee's annual pay will be added to the state's insurance program for disabled workers. A common refrain of employers is that family leave is disruptive to business and costs too much money.[36] A United Nations study found that the United States had the least generous maternity benefits of all industrialized countries and that, of the 152 countries studied, only six—the United States, Australia, New Zealand, Lesotho, Swaziland, and Papua New Guinea—have no paid leave requirement.[37]

Addressing Sexual Harassment

The Equal Pay Act, the Equal Credit Act, the Family and Medical Leave Act, and similar policies are important to women, but other areas of public policy require attention if women are to enjoy true economic and social equality. One of these issues is sexual harassment. The definition found in the Code of Federal Regulations and employed by the Equal Employment Opportunity Commission is

> *Unwelcome sexual advances, requests for sexual favors, and other verbal or physical conduct of a sexual nature constitute sexual harassment when*
>
> 1. *Submission to such conduct is made either explicitly or implicitly a term or condition of an individual's employment or admission to an academic program,*
> 2. *Submission to or rejection of such conduct is used as the basis for decisions affecting an individual's employment status or academic standing, or*
> 3. *Such conduct has the purpose or effect of substantially interfering with an individual's performance on the job or in the classroom, or creating an intimidating, hostile, or offensive work or study environment.[38]*

Title VII of the Civil Rights Act of 1964 and Title IX of the 1972 Educational Amendments to the Act prohibit sexual harassment, but for many years, such behavior was considered harmless and was taken for granted. The damaging effects of such behavior on women as well as men have now come to be recognized in public policy. Under the Civil Rights Act of 1991, those who suffer sexual harassment may collect from $50,000 to $300,000 in damages, depending on the size of the company involved. But making accusations of sexual harassment is not without risks, as evidenced by law professor Anita Hill when she accused then Supreme Court nominee and now Supreme Court Justice Clarence Thomas of such behavior. Many people were outraged by the poor treatment Hill received during Thomas' Senate confirmation hearings. Some women said they were moved to run for public office because of their disgust with the hearings. Since then, the number of harassment suits has increased, extending even to the President of the United States.

Among the publicized cases of sexual harassment was that of Dr. Frances Conley, who resigned her position at Stanford University Medical School after becoming fed up with the sexual harassment she and female medical students had endured over the years (she did return to her job later). The Navy's Tailhook scandal demonstrated personal behavior unbecoming servicemen or any men, and such behavior can cross the line into sexual assault.[39] In its aftermath, the country learned of situations in other branches of the service in which women who did not go along with such behavior were denied career advancement or left the service altogether. It is probably no coincidence that exposing these scandals has been followed by significant promotions of female military personnel and expanded roles for women in duties once off limits to them. Sexual harassment has proved to be a very effective barrier to career advancement for women in all areas of employment.

The U.S. Supreme Court's first major decision in a sexual harassment case came in 1986 in *Meritor Savings Bank v. Vinson,* which stated that Title VII of the Civil Rights Act of 1964 does include sexual harassment. Some lower courts interpreted this decision rather narrowly, applying it only in situations where women were psychologically harmed or no longer able to work in that environment. The second major case came in 1993 when the Court broadened this interpretation. Teresa Harris first brought her sexual harassment case against Forklift Systems in the mid-1980s. Lower courts rejected her case because it did not meet the restrictive definition they had adopted. Supreme Court Justice Ruth Bader Ginsburg countered, arguing that those of one gender should not be subjected to conditions in which they are treated differently from the other gender in the workplace. And Justice Sandra Day O'Connor said that there should be recourse before the behavior becomes psychologically damaging. She added that sufficient proof should be that "the environment would be perceived, and is perceived, as hostile or abusive."

Today, sexual harassment cases are generally divided into two types: the "quid pro quo" type in which sexual favors are demanded or required as a basis for employment decisions, and the "hostile environment type" in which sexual conduct unreasonably interferes with work performance.[40] On the hostile environment type, controversial author, humanities professor, and self-described feminist Camille Paglia says, "the fanatic overprotection of women is fast making us an infantile nation."[41]

In 1998, the Supreme Court, in *Burlington Industries v. Ellreth* and *Farragher v. City of Boca Raton,* ruled 7 to 2 (Justices Thomas and Scalia dissented in both cases) that employers are liable for sexual harassment in both types of cases even if they did not know of the harassment and even if the threats or abuses were not acted on, as long as the harassment is pervasive or severe.[42] The rulings also indicate that employers may limit their liability by showing that they took care to prevent or correct harassment and that the worker was unreasonable in not trying to correct the situation. In another case, the justices ruled that schools receiving federal funds can be sued for damages if a student sexually harasses another student and if the school is "deliberately indifferent" to the situation. Title IX of the Civil Rights Act allows schools the opportunity to correct problems. Title VII does not grant this stipulation to employers.

While the definition of sexual harassment may be vague, court rulings have made many more employers take note by educating employees about the types of behaviors that may lead to lawsuits and by being less tolerant of employees who engage in these behaviors. Since 1997, eight women have accused football players at the University of Colorado of rape (three have filed suit). The football program has been accused of using sex and alcohol to recruit new players. The unanswered question is whether the football coach was aware of ongoing sexual harassment. He has been suspended pending the outcome of an investigation.[43]

No Middle Ground on Abortion Rights

Among the most contentious issues on the country's domestic agenda is abortion. Before the 1960s, abortions were rarely permitted in any states, except in cases where the mother's life was in danger. Then about a quarter of the states made some modifications in their abortion laws, extending them to cases of rape, incest, or when the physical or mental health of the mother was in jeopardy. Obtaining an abortion was still difficult because each case had to be reviewed individually by physicians and by the hospital where the abortion was to be performed.

In 1970, four states (New York, Alaska, Hawaii, and Washington) further liberalized their abortion laws, permitting women to obtain an abortion on the woman's request with her physician's agreement. In 1973 the U.S. Supreme Court made decisions that fundamentally changed abortion policy. In the cases of *Roe v. Wade* and *Doe v. Bolton,* the Court ruled that the Fifth and Fourteenth Amendments to the Constitution, which guarantee all people "life, liberty and property," did not include the life of the unborn fetus. In addition, the First and Fourteenth Amendments guaranteeing personal liberties were said to extend to childbearing decisions. The Court did stipulate some conditions under which abortions could and could not be restricted by the states: (1) during the first three months of pregnancy, the states cannot restrict the mother's decision for an abortion; (2) from the fourth through sixth months of pregnancy, the states cannot restrict abortions, but they can protect the health of the mother by setting standards for how and when abortions can be performed; (3) during the last three months of pregnancy, the states can prohibit all abortions except those to protect the mother's life and health.

Following the Roe and Doe decisions, poor pregnant women were able to obtain federally funded abortions under the Medicaid program. But in 1976, antiabortion groups, with the unflagging support of conservative Representative Henry J. Hyde (R-Illinois), were successful in pushing through "the Hyde Amendment." The amendment prohibited the federal government from paying for abortions except in cases where the mother's life is endangered. It did not prevent states from financing abortions with their own funds. The Hyde amendment also did not restrict women from obtaining privately funded abortions, but necessarily limited their ability to do so if they were unable to cover the costs. The U.S. Supreme Court upheld the Hyde Amendment, declaring that a poor woman does not have the right to a federally financed abortion except when her life is in danger. In 1977, the federal funding ban was lifted in promptly reported cases of rape and incest and in cases where "severe and long-lasting" harm would be caused to the woman, but in 1981 the language was again restricted to permit federally funded abortions only to save the mother's life. In 1989, Congress again approved legislation to add cases of rape and incest, but President George H. W. Bush vetoed it, and Congress could not muster the two-thirds vote needed in both chambers to override the veto.

In October 1993, Congress passed a law signed by President Clinton reinstating access to Medicaid-financed abortions in cases of rape or incest. Six states already permitted the use of their funds for abortions for poor women with certain restrictions, and 13 others provided state-funded abortions for poor women on request. The Clinton administration viewed abortions in cases of rape or incest as "medically necessary," and ordered all states to begin paying for them by March 31, 1994. A protest quickly arose over whether the intent of the law was to allow or to require states to pay for these abortions. Antiabortion activists called the directive an attempt to challenge laws in states with more restrictive abortion policies.[44]

Interpreting abortion rights kept the U.S. Supreme Court busy. In 1983, it reaffirmed the landmark 1973 decisions concerning the right to abortion and also extended some provisions. Abortions early in the second trimester do not have to be performed in hospitals, because medical advances now make it possible to conduct these procedures safely on an outpatient basis. The Court also struck down regulations adopted in Akron, Ohio, that made it more difficult to obtain an abortion, such as requiring minors to get parental consent and imposing a 24-hour waiting period between the time a woman signed an informed consent form and the time the abortion was performed. In 1986, the Court acted again. This time it struck down a Pennsylvania law aimed at discouraging women from obtaining abortions.

Eroding Abortion Rights

The tenor of the Court began to change. In its 1989 decision in *Webster v. Reproductive Health Services,* the Court upheld a Missouri law that (1) prohibits public hospitals and public employees from performing abortions and from counseling a woman to obtain an abortion unless her life is in danger; (2) requires physicians to determine whether a woman who is at least 20 weeks pregnant is carrying a fetus that is viable (able to survive outside the womb); and (3) declares that life begins at conception. The ruling opened the door for states to pass more restrictive abortion laws. Pennsylvania quickly adopted new regulations, including notification of husbands, 24-hour waiting periods, and prohibition of third-trimester abortions. A wave of additional attempts at more restrictive state laws ensued. In contrast, Maryland passed a law shoring up abortion rights. Although it met with some stiff opposition, abortion rights advocates hoped it might protect the right to abortion in Maryland should the Supreme Court fail to protect access to abortions in the future.

Abortion opponents, often referred to as "right-to-life" groups, were generally pleased with the 1989 ruling and hoped that it would be a major step in reversing *Roe v. Wade.* These groups oppose the freedom to obtain an abortion and generally base their arguments on religious, moral, and biological grounds, contending that abortion is tantamount to taking a human life. Prolifers demonstrate annually in Washington on the anniversary of the *Roe v. Wade* decision.

Abortion rights proponents, who often call themselves the "prochoice" movement, believe that a woman should have the right to make decisions about her own body, including abortion. Without recourse to legal abortions, they fear that women may turn to illegal abortions that can result in health risks or even death for the woman. Proponents believe that misery and suffering may be avoided when a woman can choose to end an unwanted pregnancy. Prochoice groups, including the National Abortion Rights Action League and Planned Parenthood, hold "speakouts" across the country to counteract the antiabortion movement.

Following *Roe v. Wade,* the number of abortions performed annually doubled from an estimated 745,000 in 1973 to about 1.6 million in 1980.[45] In 2000, the abortion rate hit a 25-year low at 16 per 1,000 women. Many reasons have been offered for the drop, including more use of contraceptives and fewer unplanned pregnancies, more decisions to give birth, changing attitudes about abortion, and lack of access to abortions, especially in rural areas (the vast majority of counties have no abortion provider).[46]

Prochoice groups grew increasingly concerned about abortion rights during the Republican administrations of the 1980s. The 1973 U.S. Supreme Court decision upholding abortion rights was supported 7–2, the 1983 decision 6–3, and the 1986 decision 5–4. In 1989, the restrictions in the Missouri law were also upheld 5–4. President Reagan made three appointments to the Court during his terms in office—Sandra Day O'Connor, the first woman ever to serve on the Supreme Court, and Anthony Kennedy and Antonin Scalia. All voted to uphold the Missouri law in 1989. It was the older members of the Court who defended abortion rights. President George H. W. Bush appointees to the high court, David Souter and Clarence Thomas, were choices that abortion rights advocates feared would further imperil their cause.

In 1992, the U.S. Supreme Court heard yet another case, this time concerning Pennsylvania's new abortion law. In another 5–4 decision, the Court again protected the right to an abortion, but in a 7–2 decision upheld the provisions requiring parental consent for women under age 18, 24-hour waiting periods for almost everyone, and requirements that physicians inform women of their options; it did, however, strike down provisions that required notification of husbands.

While in office, President Reagan tried hard to ban federal funding to family-planning clinics that so much as discussed abortion with patients through what came to be called the "gag rule." Planned Parenthood said it would give up its federal funding rather than obey the rule. The Supreme Court ultimately upheld the gag rule. Congress disagreed, but it was unable to override President George H. W. Bush's veto of its legislation. His administration did soften the rule by allowing physicians to discuss abortion if there was a medical need for it, but other personnel could make referrals only if women asked for information about abortion.

Other events in the history of abortion rights stem from the strident efforts of some prolife movement members to prevent women from obtaining abortions. Blockades of abortion clinics have resulted in the arrests of hundreds of members of antiabortion groups. Some clinics have been bombed or set on fire. Even if the vast majority of antiabortion activists decry violence, the shooting and bombing deaths of several physicians and staff members have raised serious concerns about how far the more fanatic members of the movement will go. Antiabortion activists have also used other tactics, such as Internet "wanted posters" with pictures of doctors who perform abortions. This activity was apparently protected by constitutional guarantees of free speech,[47] but Internet service providers have shut down various versions of the website because they were so threatening.[48] Another tactic is trying to entrap abortion clinic staff into agreeing to law violations such as keeping confidential that a minor had been impregnated by an adult boyfriend.[49]

In an effort to stop harassment at abortion clinics, the National Organization for Women (NOW) tried several strategies. It was unsuccessful in invoking an 1871 civil rights law that had been used in cases involving the Ku Klux Klan. But NOW filed another lawsuit to invoke federal racketeering and antitrust laws directed at organized crime (called the Racketeer Influenced, Corrupt Organization [RICO] Act of 1970) to prohibit protests at abortion clinics by Operation Rescue and similar organizations. The suit was initially dismissed because the protests involved a political activity, not a commercial activity for profit. Operation Rescue hailed it as a victory for free speech, but when the issue reached the Supreme Court, the justices unanimously agreed that RICO could be invoked if illegal activities are involved. In 1998, under RICO, a Chicago jury found three antiabortion activists guilty of using threats and violence in an attempt to prevent abortions at clinics. Believing that other Supreme Court decisions did not go far enough in protecting entrances to clinics, Congress passed a "buffer zone" law in 1994 that makes it a federal offense to block the entrances to abortion clinics and also to use or threaten force against those seeking or performing abortions. In 1994 Operation Rescue and another antiabortion group were ordered to pay $1 million in damages to a Planned Parenthood clinic in Texas, the largest such award to date. Rather than stem the efforts of antiabortionists, some feel that the efforts of antiabortionists have curtailed the number of medical professionals and clinics available to perform abortions.

The Democratic presidential administration of Bill Clinton pursued a far more liberal agenda on abortion than its Republican predecessors. On taking office, Clinton promptly lifted the gag rule. His failed plan for national healthcare included coverage for abortions. Clinton's appointment to the Supreme Court of Ruth Bader Ginsburg, a well-known advocate of women's rights, renewed hope for stronger support of abortion rights.

Will Abortion Rights Survive?

Prochoice advocates believe that the best way to protect abortion rights is through federal law. Since 1989, the Freedom of Choice Act has been introduced to every Congress in an effort to codify *Roe* into law and provide greater protection of women's right to choice.[50] It would prevent states from enacting their own restrictions on abortion prior to fetal viability, as has occurred with greater frequency under the George W. Bush administration. Efforts to curtail abortion rights have been fierce at state, national, and even global levels. The number of pieces of antichoice legislation considered across the states in 2003 was up 35 percent over 2002, and 45 antichoice measures were enacted. At the same time, the number of prochoice bills introduced in state legislatures declined.[51] Forty-four states now restrict minors' access to reproductive health services, requiring that they notify an adult or obtain consent before being allowed to obtain an abortion, and 26 states impose counseling against abortion and a mandatory waiting ("reflective") period before granting an abortion.

There have been many attempts to elevate the legal status of the fetus to personhood. One was President George W. Bush's proposal to allow pregnant women to obtain healthcare under the State Children's Insurance Program (SCHIP) (see Chapter 8) by calling the fetus a child. Under the Unborn Victims of Violence Act, Congress made it a crime to harm an "unborn child" during an assault of the pregnant mother. Several states have similar laws. These laws appear compassionate to many, but they undermine the *Roe* and *Doe* decisions that constitutional rights do not extend to the unborn fetus.

Another attempt to curtail abortions is the proposed Child Custody Protection Act, which would make it a federal offense to take a minor across state lines in order to avoid state laws that require parental involvement in abortion decisions. Still another piece of proposed federal legislation is the Abortion Non-Discrimination Act, which would prohibit discrimination against healthcare "entities" (such as physicians, hospitals, clinics, insurance companies, and other healthcare providers) that refuse to provide abortions.

A major blow to the prochoice movement came in November 2003, when the president signed into law the first ban on a specific abortion procedure. "Doctors call it intact dilation and extraction. Critics call it partial-birth abortion."[52] The ban makes it a criminal offense for doctors to perform the procedure, even to preserve the woman's health. The only exception is to save the woman's life. *Boston Globe* columnist Ellen Goodman called the law, which the American Medical Association and the American College of Obstetrics and Gynecology opposed, a "public relations coup," made worse by the picture of the bill's signing, showing the president and a group of legislators—all male.[53]

Efforts to impact women's reproductive rights extend globally. Like his father before him, George W. Bush has placed a gag rule on abortion, but this time on a global scale. Every year since taking office, he has cancelled the U.S. contribution to the

United Nations Family Planning program that provides reproductive health services (but *not* abortions) to the world's poorest women and has threatened to veto any attempt to overturn his global gag rule.[54]

Fed up with the curtailment of women's rights and attempts to overturn *Roe v. Wade*, Senator Barbara Boxer (D-California) introduced a sweeping new version of the Freedom of Choice Act in 2004 to reclaim abortion rights.[55] Under the act, women would have statutory reproductive rights articulated by the Supreme Court in *Roe v. Wade*. The act contains the following provisions:

♦ Poor women on Medicaid could not be denied an abortion.

♦ Public hospitals could not prohibit abortions.

♦ It would be unlawful to force anti-abortion lectures and materials on women or to make them wait for a predetermined amount of time for an abortion.

♦ Military women serving outside the United States would have access to abortions.

♦ Any woman denied access to an abortion or who is discriminated against in the process of seeking an abortion will be able to go to court to have the law enforced.

Boxer contends that "anti-choice is anti-woman and anti-equality."

Emily's List (Early Money Is Like Yeast; it helps the dough rise), which has been highly successful in raising funds, is the PAC dedicated to electing pro-choice Democratic women to office at all levels of government. Wish (Women In the Senate and House) List is the PAC dedicated to electing prochoice Republican women. Norma McCorvey, the plaintiff in *Roe v. Wade* and now a Born-again Christian, has been speaking out against abortion. (McCorvey never had an abortion because it took the courts so long to rule.)

Technology showing fetal development has advanced the anti-abortion agenda. Other advancements have made abortion access easier. In 1988 France granted women access to RU-486, a drug that induces an abortion in the early weeks of pregnancy. The United States did not approve its use until 2000, four years after it said the drug, called mifepristone in the United States, was safe. The drug allows women to avoid abortion clinics and to obtain a physicians' help to terminate a pregnancy more privately. To avoid boycotts of companies that made mifepristone available, the French drug company gave the nonprofit Population Council U.S. marketing rights. Medicaid does not provide the drug unless a woman would otherwise qualify for an abortion under Medicaid.[56]

Some women have had to sue their health plans to cover birth control, even though these plans cover men's sexual performance drugs like Viagra. It took a 2000 ruling by the Equal Employment Opportunity Commission to get some employer-sponsored health plans to cover birth control.

Confronting Violence against Women

Violence against women takes a number of forms. One form is spousal violence (which may be directed at husbands or other male partners), where most often wives and girlfriends are the victims. The U.S. Department of Justice estimates that 1.5 million women are physically and/or sexually assaulted by an intimate partner annually.[57] On average each of these women experiences more than three episodes of violence at the hands of her partner during the year. Many victims are young and it has become clear that teenaged girls are often victimized by boyfriends. Many high schools have instituted programs to prevent these occurrences. Witnessing intimate partner violence is also traumatic for children, and the children may also suffer abuse.

In the late 1970s, some states officially recognized that battered women were not receiving adequate legal protection, and they adopted the position that this amounted to gender discrimination.[58] All states have enacted some type of legislation to protect abused spouses. Battered spouses have two types of legal recourse: civil and criminal. Civil laws are used to "settle disputes between individuals and to compensate for injuries," while criminal laws are used to "punish acts which are disruptive of social order and to deter other similar acts."[59] Duluth, Minnesota, introduced a strategy for preventing additional incidents of domestic violence that has been adopted by many other jurisdictions:

> If a police officer has probable cause to believe that a person has, within the preceding four hours, assaulted a spouse, former spouse, or other person with whom he or she resides or has formerly resided, arrest is mandatory. The police officer still has the discretion in determining whether or not probable cause exists, but when there is visible sign of injury the officer has no choice but to arrest. A 1984 study conducted by the Minneapolis Police Department and the Police Foundation concluded that arrest was the most significant deterrent to repeat violence when compared to police use of mediation and separation.[60]

A more recent and controversial policy is "dual arrest" in which both parties in domestic violence cases are arrested. Many people believe such policies are unfair because often one party, usually the woman, was trying to defend herself and did not initiate the violence. Women's advocates have promoted the use of guidelines that can help law enforcement officers determine who initiated the attack.[61] Technology is helping prosecute domestic violence cases because digital photos can produce timely and sharp images of injuries that can be readily transmitted to prosecutors and judges.[62]

Protective or restraining orders are methods that victims often employ in an effort to protect themselves. There has been controversy over whether use of this tool further enrages male partners and promotes reassault. A Seattle study found that women with "permanent" orders (lasting about one year) were significantly less likely to report a subsequent assault to police than those with no order. Short-term orders were associated with greater likelihood of reporting psychological abuse (including stalking) to police.[63]

Other forms of violence against women are sexual assault, including rape, and the more recently defined category of stalking. Most women survive victimization with varying degrees of trauma, but this violence can also result in homicide, as media accounts indicate all too often. The most important and comprehensive piece of federal legislation for preventing and intervening in these problems is the Violence Against Women Act (VAWA), part of the Violent Crime Control and Law Enforcement Act of 1994. Prior to this law, the federal response to violence directed at women was considerably weaker.

The National Office on Violence Against Women, part of the Department of Justice, was created in 1995 and is responsible for oversight and implementation of the federal mandates included in VAWA. VAWA strengthens protective orders through interstate enforcement, prohibits those with restraining orders from possessing a firearm, and bolsters restitution orders and "rape shield" laws that prevent a victim's past sexual conduct from being used against her.

VAWA established the National Domestic Violence Hotline (1-800-799-SAFE) and has provided funds to strengthen and streamline the criminal justice system's approach to helping victims, including education for law enforcement officers, prosecutors, and judges, and the encouragement of pro-arrest policies and community policing techniques. Guidelines have also been developed to require sex offenders to register with local authorities.

VAWA encourages cooperation between the criminal justice system and agencies such as shelters for battered women, rape crisis programs, and victim-witness programs that have provided the front-line services to victims. The community response is crucial because women rely on local law enforcement agencies and courts for protection and to see that justice is served through setting appropriate bail, serving warrants, arresting suspects, and meting out appropriate punishment. Many social service agencies that assist women have small budgets and little consistent support. They can help only a fraction of those in need. Services are often crisis-oriented with insufficient long-term help in the form of transportation, housing, and other services such as psychotherapy for women, their children, and the perpetrators.

Originally, VAWA allowed victims to sue perpetrators for damages in federal court based on the premise that gender-based violence affects women's ability to engage in interstate commerce. In 2000, the U.S. Supreme Court overturned that provision saying that Congress had no business regulating "non-economic, violent criminal conduct based solely on [its] effect on interstate commerce." VAWA was reauthorized in 2000 under the Victims of Trafficking and Violence Protection Act of 2000 (also called the Violence Against Women Act of 2000).[64] Dating violence was added to the law, along with funds to educate and train law enforcement personnel about making arrests in dating violence cases. Cyberstalking was added to the definition of "interstate stalking." A new grant program was added to develop transitional housing assistance for victims of domestic violence. Elders who are abused, neglected, or exploited are now included as a protected group, along with funds for training law enforcement officers about elder abuse. New protections for battered immigrants were added, as well as a mandate for cracking down on human trafficking of persons, especially with regard to "sex trade, slavery and slavery like conditions." The president must create a task force to monitor and combat trafficking and establish new initiatives to enhance economic opportunities for trafficking victims. The law also requires the attorney general to establish a domestic violence task force. In 2002, the first annual symposium on Violence Against Women was held in Washington, DC.

In concert with the mandates of the reauthorized Violence Against Women Act, President George W. Bush launched a new Family Justice Center Initiative in October 2003.[65] This $20 million initiative will provide grants to 12 communities to establish pilot programs modeled after centers in San Diego and Indianapolis. The programs will provide domestic violence survivors a wide variety of services under one roof—medical care, counseling, law enforcement assistance, legal help, social services, employment assistance, and housing assistance. San Diego's Family Justice Center opened in 2002. After one year, 4,393 cases had been initiated with the city attorney; trial dates were set for 712 cases; 70 trials had been conducted; and 3,942 cases were reviewed in domestic violence court.[66]

Among the biggest obstacles women face in extricating themselves from domestic violence is economic security. Abusers often retain complete control of family finances and make it difficult for women to hold a job because the abusers harass, stalk, threaten, and even attack them at work. Bills have been introduced that would (1) allow victims time off work without penalty to make court appearances, get legal help, or get help with safety planning; (2) provide victims unemployment insurance if they are terminated from employment because of domestic violence; (3) provide a tax credit to employers who provide workplace safety programs; and (4) prohibit insurance companies and employers from making decisions based on a victim's abuse history.[67] This type of legislation would provide unprecedented economic support to women seeking to rebuild their lives.

GAY RIGHTS

Thirty-five years ago, there was no "gay rights" agenda in this country, only the taboos placed on gay and lesbian relationships. Then, in 1969, a police raid on a gay bar called Stonewall, in Greenwich Village, set off riots that culminated in the birth of the gay rights movement. For some people, gay rights is more a moral or religious issue than a legal or political issue, as evidenced by the struggles over accepting openly gay clergy that many churches are experiencing. No matter how one defines it, the gay rights agenda now has the attention of the media, the legislature, and the judiciary.

An End to Sodomy Laws

For almost 20 years, the U.S. Supreme Court refused to hear gay rights cases, leaving sodomy laws (which make certain types of sexual acts illegal) and other laws affecting gay men and lesbians to the states. But in 1985, the Court broke its silence and heard the case of *Oklahoma City Board of Education v. National Gay Task Force.* The case involved an Oklahoma law that permitted school boards to bar from employment teachers who publicly advocated homosexuality. The Gay Rights Task Force criticized the law as a First Amendment violation of free speech, while the Board of Education contended that the law was only concerned with those who publicly endorsed certain sexual acts between homosexuals. In its evenly divided 4–4 decision (Justice Powell was ill), the Supreme Court upheld a lower court's ruling that public school teachers cannot be forbidden from advocating homosexuality but that homosexuals can be prohibited from engaging in homosexual acts in public.

Shortly after, in 1986, the U.S. Supreme Court dealt a serious setback to the rights of gay men and lesbians in its decision in *Bowers v. Hardwick* by refusing to strike down Georgia's sodomy law.[68] In 1992, the Kentucky Supreme Court became the first since the *Hardwick* decision to overturn a state antisodomy law; the court ruled that the law violated its state's constitutional rights to privacy and equal protection.[69] A decade later, the U.S. Supreme Court decided to hear the case of *Lawrence v. Texas.* Lawrence was arrested when police responded to a call, made by a third party at a private residence. Upon arrival, the police discovered Lawrence in a sexual relationship with another man. Both were arrested for violating Texas's sodomy law. Two lower courts upheld the men's prosecution. Then in March 2003, the U.S. Supreme Court delivered its historic ruling, overturning *Bowers v. Hardwick* by invoking the constitutional right to privacy and the equal protection and due process clauses of the Constitution.[70] In doing so, the U.S. Supreme Court cited two previous decisions, *Romer* (1996) and *Casey* (1992). Drawing upon *Casey,* Justice Kennedy expressed the court's conclusion that "Our obligation is to define the liberty of all, not to mandate our own moral code," and that "It is a promise of the Constitution that there is a realm of personal liberty which the government may not enter." In *Romer,* the Court concluded that the case was "born of animosity toward the class of persons affected." The *Lawrence* decision asserted that "*Bowers* was not correct when it was decided, and it is not correct today. . . . Their [homosexuals'] right to liberty under the Due Process Clause gives them the full right to engage in their conduct without intervention of the government."

The decision was a major victory for the gay community. Civil rights groups hailed it as a huge step forward. At the time of the *Lawrence* decision, thirteen states still had anti-sodomy laws. The *Lawrence* decision invalidated these laws, giving consenting adults of the same gender the same rights of intimate sexual expression as heterosexuals.

Expanding the Gay Rights Agenda

Sexual behavior is only one aspect of gay and lesbian rights. Various municipalities have taken up the issues of gay and lesbian rights in employment, housing, and other matters, with cities such as San Francisco and St. Louis leading the way in passing antidiscrimination measures. In 1992 there was a flurry of state activity over gay rights, much of it, however, spurred by fundamentalist Christians and other conservative groups. A law passed in Colorado would have prohibited the state from enacting gay rights protections and would have caused the repeal of existing local laws supporting gay rights, but the Colorado Supreme Court declared it unconstitutional. The U.S. Supreme Court concurred that the law violated the U.S. Constitution's equal protection clause. This was "the first time the high court [had] treated gay rights as a matter of civil rights."[71] When Oregonians failed to approve a tough anti-gay state law that would have condemned homosexuality and forbidden protections to gay men and lesbians, some Oregon towns adopted their own anti-gay measures. In 1997, Maine joined ten other states and the District of Columbia with laws supporting gay rights. The measured added "sexual orientation to existing laws banning discrimination in employment, housing, credit and public accommodations."[72] In 1998 anti-gay forces were successful in overturning the Maine law at the polls.

But times change (often slowly). By 2004, 14 states had enacted some form of gay anti-discrimination laws covering public and private employment and housing, and 12 other states had implemented anti-discrimination practices for public employees based on executive orders, administrative rulings, or state court case law. Bill Clinton was the first president to address gay rights, and he issued a directive banning discrimination against federal employees who are gay. Most federal agencies already had nondiscrimination policies. The executive order was intended to make the policies uniform. A 1998 challenge to the order failed in the House of Representatives. The Employment Non-Discrimination Act (ENDA) has been introduced in every Congress since 1994. Each time it has gained sponsors and more companies have publicly endorsed it. In the 107th Congress, the bill was reported out of committee for the first time, but stalled there with a total of 225 House and Senate sponsors.[73] There is still no federal law prohibiting discrimination against gay men and lesbians, but given how far the gay rights agenda has advanced, this may not be far off.

Sexual orientation is not specifically included in federal hate crimes legislation. Twenty-nine states do have hate crime statutes that include sexual orientation (seven of these states also specifically include gender identity as a protected category). Many gay men and lesbians, as well as bisexual and transgender individuals, feel that the lack of laws protecting their rights and the laws that expressly deny them protections not only make them targets for discrimination but also for physical attacks or other hate crimes. The brutal murder of Matthew Shepard, a gay man, in Laramie, Wyoming, is a dramatic example. In 1991, the FBI began collecting data on hate crimes. Since that time, the number of reported hate crimes against gays and lesbians has increased threefold to a total of 12,000 between 1991 and 2002. In 2004, 14 states introduced hate crime legislation that includes sexual orientation, and in one case gender identity.[74]

Family Matters

Many other public policy issues are also of concern to gay men and lesbians, such as the right to child custody and adoption and the right to name a partner as "next of kin" in case of medical emergencies or other matters. The agenda also seeks to prohibit health insurance companies from asking lifestyle questions that may cause gay men and lesbians to be denied coverage. In the late 1980s, a handful of cities decided to extend bereavement leave to domestic partners not in traditional marriages, including gay and lesbian partners. Since then, the number of municipal governments and private companies (IBM, American Express, and Walt Disney Co. are among them) extending healthcare or other benefits to the live-in partners of employees, both gay and straight, has grown. In 1996 a judge ordered the state of Oregon to provide insurance benefits to the partners of its gay workers, saying that doing otherwise was discriminatory and violated the state's constitution. In June 2002 President George W. Bush signed the Mychal Judge Police and Fire Chaplains Public Safety Officers' Benefit Act of 2002, providing federal payments to beneficiaries of public safety officers killed in the line of duty on September 11, 2001. The bill was named after the New York Fire Department chaplain killed in the September 11th terrorist attacks. It allows benefits to be paid to same-sex partners if there is no surviving spouse or children. The inclusion of same-sex partners in this federal law was modeled after a similar state law passed in New York in May 2002. By 2004, seventeen states offered their employees some form of benefits or recognition for same-sex as well as opposite-sex domestic partners. The benefits most often extended were medical insurance, dental benefits, healthcare facility visitation rights, sick leave, and family leave. Vermont included all benefits traditionally offered to married couples.[75] In 2002, 5,698 employers across the country provided healthcare benefits for domestic partners.[76]

Most states recognize the rights of parents who are gay or lesbian to child custody and visitation. In 22 states sexual orientation cannot be used to terminate or limit a parent–child relationship unless there is demonstrable evidence that it can cause harm to the child, thus allowing gay men and lesbians in these states to adopt children.[77] Four states take a much dimmer view of this practice. For example, Florida and Mississippi have statutory laws prohibiting gays and lesbians from adopting, and Utah law states that children must be placed with a legally married man and woman. Arkansas uses state agency rules to prevent gays and lesbians from adopting. As recently as January 2004, the 11th U.S. Circuit Court of Appeals upheld Florida's ban on gay adoption, ruling that it did not violate the Constitution's due process and equal protection clauses.[78] Given the recent interpretation of civil rights involving due process and equal protection clauses in *Lawrence v. Texas,* the Supreme Court may take up Florida's adoption ban. In 2000, the New Jersey Supreme Court ruled that same-sex partners who raise a child have the same custody rights as other parents.

Same-Sex Marriage

Marriage between partners of the same gender has made its way to the public agenda. In 1991 two lesbian couples and a gay male couple sued the state of Hawaii because it refused to issue them a marriage license. Supporters believe that a marriage prohibition violates the U.S. Constitutions's equal protection provisions and is discriminatory. Alarmed that Hawaii might actually legalize such unions, in 1996, the U.S. Congress passed the Defense of Marriage Act (DOMA). Congress was concerned that the U.S. Constitution's "full faith and credit clause" might require other states to recognize marriages of same-sex couples performed in Hawaii or other states. DOMA does not prohibit states from recognizing or legalizing same-sex marriages. It says that states cannot be forced to recognize such unions performed in other states.[79] Although Hawaii's courts upheld same sex marriages, in 1998, voters in Hawaii and Alaska failed to approve them. The idea that gay marriages might be declared constitutional was a call to action to many individuals who oppose them. Thirty-seven states now ban same-sex marriages. Though more states were expanding civil rights protections to gays and lesbians, they wanted to protect the sanctity of marriage as a union between a man and a woman. Recent developments in Vermont, New Jersey, California, and, most notably, Massachusetts, are making that more difficult.[80]

In 2000, the Vermont Supreme Court ruled that denying homosexual couples the same benefits of married couples violated the Common Benefits Clause of the Vermont Constitution. Vermont's high court ordered the legislature to craft appropriate legislation to meet the constitutional mandate, warning that failure to do so would open the way for the plaintiffs to again petition the court for the right to marry. The legislature responded with a law that recognizes *civil unions* effective January 1, 2005, for gay and lesbian couples and provides them with all the "benefits and burdens" of married couples. Vermont's civil union for gays and lesbians is considered parallel to marriage. In 2003, seven same-sex couples petitioned the Massachusetts Supreme Court for the right to marry. Unlike Vermont, the Massachusetts Constitution does not have a Common Benefits Clause and therefore had to consider the case on the basis of marriage as an institution, and not marital benefits. The court denounced the exclusion of same-sex partners from the right to marry and concluded that assigning a different status to same-sex unions—civil unions—in effect relegates them to a "second-class status." The court's statement was strong: Denial of the right to marry "works a deep and scarring hardship on a very real segment of the community for no rational reason." The Massachusetts Supreme Court gave the state legislature 180 days to respond with appropriate legislation. The state legislature tried to sidestep the marriage mandate by passing a bill that provided the right to civil union with "all the benefits, protections, rights and responsibilities" of marriage, but the Supreme Court responded with a resounding "no." The court declared that there are certain intangible benefits to marriage, and without the right to marry, "same-sex couples are not only denied full protection of the laws, but are excluded from the full range of human experience." On May 1, 2004, the state of Massachusetts began issuing marriage licenses to same-sex couples; however, a state constitutional amendment prohibiting same-sex marriages may go before voters in 2006. Same-sex marriage opponents are also pushing for an amendment to the U.S. Constitution.

Cities, most notably San Francisco, have also taken up the marriage issue. In February 2004, San Francisco Mayor Gavin Newsom directed the county clerk to begin issuing marriage license to same-sex couples, claiming that to do otherwise violates due process and equal protection clauses of the state of California's Constitution. In the days following the directive, 3,000 same-sex couples were married. But Governor Arnold Schwarzenegger said that same-sex marriages are illegal because California's

Constitution clearly defines marriage as "a civil contract between a man and a woman." In addition, Proposition 22, approved by voters in 2000, declared that "only marriage between a man and a woman is valid in California." California courts are considering suits filed by opponents and proponents of gay marriage, which will determine the validity of the 3,000 gay and lesbian marriages that occurred in San Francisco. At the same time, California is set to expand its domestic partnership law recognizing same-sex relationships. As of January 1, 2005, same-sex couples will be entitled to the same benefits as married couples.[81]

The New Jersey Supreme court upheld that state's gay marriage ban in November 2003. The court's conclusion seemed contradictory. It stated that "the right to marry is fundamental, but the right to marry a same-sex partner is not," suggesting that there can be two standards of civil rights, one for heterosexual citizens and one for gay and lesbian citizens.[82] In New York, 13 same-sex couples sued the state in April 2004, claiming that denying them access to marriage denied their basic civil rights.[83] That case is yet to be settled. This rash of activity to allow same-sex couples the right to marry has invoked strong legal opposition. Twenty-four state legislatures have introduced bills that would amend state constitutions to ban them. Alaska, Nebraska, and Nevada have already amended their constitutions.[84]

With pressure from the far right, President George W. Bush publicly called for an amendment to the U.S. Constitution banning same-sex marriage, and the Federal Marriage Act was introduced to the Senate on March 22, 2004, calling for such an amendment.[85] Civil rights groups said that if such an amendment was ratified, it would be the first time that a discriminatory measure had been written into the U.S. Constitution. President Bush called "the union of a man and a woman . . . the most enduring human institution, honored and encouraged in all cultures and by every religious faith," claiming that "marriage cannot be severed from its cultural, religious and natural roots without weakening the good influence of society."[86] Since President George W. Bush has taken a stand against gay and lesbian marriage, there has been talk of the Log Cabin Republicans (a group of gay Republicans) pulling their support for him. The president was accused of using the issue to fuel his reelection campaign, but he did endorse the right of same-sex couples to form civil unions, causing some backlash from conservatives. Many liberals, on the other hand, believe that civil unions are discriminatory because couples joined under them cannot take advantage of many benefits that married couples enjoy.

Gays in the Military: Don't Ask, Don't Tell

Another vehemently debated gay rights issue is service in the military and in national security positions. In 1949, the U.S. Department of Defense implemented a rule intended to prevent gay men and lesbians from serving in the military, and for several decades there was no major policy change. In 1988 the U.S. Supreme Court did tell the Central Intelligence Agency that it could not dismiss a gay man without justifying the reason for its action, but the Court avoided the issue of whether gay men and lesbians have employment rights under the "equal protection clause" (Fourteenth Amendment) of the U.S. Constitution, including the right to military service.

Beginning in the early 1990s, some things began to change. In 1991 the case of Sergeant Perry Watkins, a gay soldier, was settled after years in court when he was awarded back pay, an honorable discharge, and full retirement benefits. In 1992 a federal judge ordered the Navy to reinstate Petty Officer Keith Meinhold, who had stated he is gay, but the ruling was based on a technicality and hardly settled the question of gays in the military. As the various branches of the military faced increasing pressure to stop discriminating against gay men and lesbians, President Clinton's desire to drop the ban caused a heated, national debate. Although everyone knows that there are gay men and lesbians in the military, there was considerable opposition both in the military and in Congress to lifting the ban. The president, who is also commander-in-chief of the armed forces, has the authority to lift the ban by executive order, although Congress could overrule him with a two-thirds majority. Those wanting to end the ban declared that sexual orientation has nothing to do with the ability to perform military jobs, while the opposition countered with arguments about close living quarters, security breaches, and low morale. There was some serious Democratic opposition to lifting the ban. So much furor arose over the issue that rather than lift the ban himself, President Clinton decided to go the route he often took in the face of opposition—the well-known political strategies of negotiation and compromise.

After much political wrangling, in July 1993, Clinton issued a watered-down policy. Under these new rules, applicants are not to be asked to reveal their sexual orientation, and investigations to determine sexual orientation without cause that sexual conduct codes have been violated are prohibited. As a result, the policy came to be called "Don't ask, don't tell, don't pursue." The guidelines also prohibit harassment of gay and lesbian military personnel, but homosexual conduct can be grounds for discharge. According to the Pentagon's guidelines, the definition of homosexual conduct includes acknowledgment of being gay, lesbian, or bisexual. In many circumstances, physical contact, such as holding hands and kissing, can also be construed as homosexual conduct. However, going to gay bars, marching in gay rights demonstrations in civilian attire, or having gay publications would generally not be considered homosexual conduct. Even though President Clinton may have intended for a new spirit to be reflected in the policy, the policy seems to be more harmful than helpful for gay men and lesbians because it "has broadened the definition of [homosexual] conduct, and, therefore, is ensnaring many more people."[87] The number of people dismissed from the military due to homosexuality is at an all-time high (1,250 in 2001).[88] In 1999, a ruling by a European Court of Human Rights forced Britain to allow those who are openly gay or lesbian to serve in the military.

U.S. courts have not been consistent in their rulings on gays in the military. Some judges believe that the military has a vested interest in keeping gays and lesbians from serving. Others believe that Congress and the president should decide. Another perspective is that sexual orientation is not related to service and using it to exclude qualified individuals constitutes discrimination.[89] The U.S. Supreme Court has not resolved the issue.

The Rights of Gay, Lesbian, Bisexual, and Transgender (GLBT) Youth

Most school personnel receive no training about the needs of gay, lesbian, bisexual, and transgender (GLBT) youth, especially those who confront systemic hostility in their schools and community.[90] GLBT youth are five times more likely than their peers to skip school because they fear for their own safety, and they experience higher rates of school dropout, poor school performance, truancy, isolation, suicidal ideation, and other emotional difficulties than their heterosexual counterparts. Some school districts are sensitive to the needs of GLBT youth and youth unsure of their sexual identity, and some campuses have organizations of GLBT students.

In 1996, the Salt Lake City School Board terminated all student groups on campus rather than allow a gay organization because the federal Equal Access Act of 1984, which arose to support Bible groups, also seemed to support the gay student organization.[91] The Utah legislature came to the school board's aid with a law supporting the board's efforts to outlaw gay student groups. In 1997 "a unanimous federal appeals court struck down an Alabama law that sought to keep lesbian, gay, and bisexual student groups off university campuses, saying the law violated the First Amendment rights of students and is wholly unenforceable."[92] Subsequent law suits have supported GLBT students' rights. For example, in 1998, Alana Flores, a bisexual high school student, complained to her assistant principal after receiving graphic death threats on her school locker.[93] The vice principal's response: "Go back to class, stop complaining, and stop bringing me this trash, this is disgusting." After years of harassment, threats, and physical violence, Alana and several of her classmates sued the school for ignoring and for promoting homophobia that led to harassment and violence. The students' suit sought damages and training for district personnel and students. Six years later, the 9th District Court of Appeals found in favor of the students. In Wyoming, a lesbian couple was escorted out of their school's homecoming dance. After receiving a letter from the ACLU, the school district agreed to allow same-sex couples to attend future dances. And in Kentucky, the court found in favor of students wanting to form a gay-straight alliance club, declaring that the school district must treat all student clubs equally and conduct anti-harassment training for all middle and high school staff and students.

In all, 15 lawsuits have been brought against school districts for failing to protect GLBT youth. Each has been litigated or settled in the plaintiff's favor. Most often lawyers invoke federal protection rights to win their suits (generally Title IX of the Education Amendments Act of 1972, the Equal Protection Clause of the U.S. Constitution, and the Equal Access Act of 1984). States are becoming more aware of their responsibilities in protecting *all* students. Eight states and the District of Columbia have passed laws banning discrimination and harassment of sudents on the basis of sexual orientation, and three states have included gender identity as a protected class. Five other states have implemented protections for gay youth through other policies and regulations. At the other extreme, five states prohibit the discussion of homosexuality in school, or mandate that it be discussed in a negative manner. The Boy Scouts of America's credo requires that members be "morally straight." In 2000, the U.S. Supreme Court ruled 5–4 that the Boy Scouts, a private organization, can exclude gay members and leaders. The Lambda Legal Defense and Education Fund, the Human Rights Campaign, the American Civil Liberties Union, and other organizations are working to end discrimination based on sexual orientation.

RACIAL EQUALITY: HOW FAR HAVE WE COME?

Some people would have us think that race relations have improved tremendously in the United States. Others sway us to believe that the country remains deeply divided along racial lines, pointing to police brutality against people of color, racial profiling, disproportionate arrest and conviction rates, inequity in public education, housing, employment and wages, and infringements on voting rights.[94] Since the September 11th terrorist attacks, more groups have been subjected to the injustices that American Indians, blacks, and Latinos have experienced in the United States.

Perhaps the fairest thing that can be said about the living conditions of people of color, especially blacks and Hispanic Americans, is that they have improved substantially, but not on a par with whites. On the average, blacks are in poorer health than whites, and they do not live as long; they earn less and are more likely to be in poverty, and they are overrepresented in public assistance programs. Poverty and lower earnings also contribute to a less adequate lifestyle for many Americans of Hispanic origin. About 18 percent of black and 11 percent of Hispanic American families earn less than $10,000 annually, compared with 8 percent of white families. White families are twice as likely as black or Hispanic American families to earn over $75,000 annually, and the median income of whites is substantially more than for black or Hispanic American families. Table 11.6 compares the incomes of these three groups.

As described in Chapter 3, poverty rates continue to be about three times higher for black and Hispanic Americans than for whites. Chapter 3 also showed that while educational attainment is closely related to income for all ethnic groups, even after controlling for education, black and Hispanic Americans are more likely to be poor and less likely to earn as much as whites. Blacks comprise nearly 13 percent of the total U.S. population, but they are 39 percent of families receiving public assistance and 30 percent of disabled SSI recipients.[95] Although the General Accounting Office found that blacks were more likely to be rejected for disability benefits than whites (see Chapter 5), the proportion of blacks in public assistance programs reinforces stereotypes that they prefer welfare to work. According to one report, "surveys show that racial attitudes are the most important reason behind white opposition to welfare programs. Political issues, such as crime and welfare, are viewed as 'coded issues' as they stimulate white Americans' anti-black feelings without explicitly raising racial discrimination."[96] Racial discrimination is so firmly entrenched in U.S. society that the term **institutional racism** has been used to refer to these practices.

TABLE 11.6

Total Money Income of Households by Race or Ethnicity, 2001

Income	Percent of Total White	Percent of Total Black	Percent of Total Hispanic[a]
Under $10,000	7.6%[b]	17.7%[b]	10.6%[b]
$10,000 to $24,999	19.7	25.2	25.8
$25,000 to $49,999	27.7	29.2	32.7
$50,000 to $74,999	18.8	15.4	16.5
$75,000 and over	26.2	12.4	14.5
Median Income	$44,517	$29,470	$33,565

Source: U.S. Bureau of the Census, *Money Income in the United States: 2001,* Current Population Reports, Series P60-218 (Washington, DC, 2001), Table 1, p. 4; Table A-1, p. 15.

[a]May be of any race.

[b]Percentages may not add to 100 due to rounding.

Separate but Not Equal

The Fourteenth Amendment to the U.S. Constitution guarantees all citizens equal protection under the law, but this amendment is also an example of how ideas that sound rational can be used to maintain and perpetuate racial discrimination. Until 1954, the Fourteenth Amendment served as legal grounds for *equal* but *separate* protection under the law. Segregation of blacks and whites in public schools, on public buses, and in other public (and private) places was official policy. Although public facilities for blacks were supposed to be equal to facilities for whites (see *Plessy v. Ferguson,* 1896), this was generally not the case. It was not until the middle of the twentieth century that the U.S. Supreme Court overturned the "separate but equal" doctrine set forth in *Plessy v. Ferguson.* The civil rights movement had begun.

In 1954 a growing dissatisfaction among blacks with the separate but equal doctrine resulted in a U.S. Supreme Court ruling that marked the official recognition of racial inequality in America. Schools in Topeka, Kansas, were segregated but essentially equal in terms of physical conditions and quality of education. However, in the case of *Brown v. Board of Education of Topeka, Kansas,* the Supreme Court ruled that separate was *not* equal. In its decision, the Court took the position that "the policy of separating the races is usually interpreted as denoting the inferiority of the Negro Group." The Court also stated that "segregation with the sanction of law, therefore, has a tendency to retard the education and mental development of Negro children." The *Brown* decision remains a landmark case in the history of equal rights.

Nevertheless, *de facto* segregation of schools due to neighborhood segregation continues to exist, and has even been exacerbated.[97] When children from inner-city neighborhoods attend their local schools, the schools are almost totally composed of black students. One solution to *de facto* school segregation is busing. In 1971 in the case of *Swann v. Charlotte-Mecklenburg Board of Education,* the U.S. Supreme Court approved court-ordered busing of children to achieve integration in school districts that had a history of discrimination. But, in 1974, in *Milliken v. Bradley,* the Court ruled that mandatory busing across city–suburban boundaries to achieve integration is not required unless segregation has resulted from an official action, and a 1991 decision permitted use of neighborhood schools rather than busing despite any effect it might have on "resegregation." As a result, *de facto* segregation occurs in many school districts, especially inner-city districts, more than 50 years after the *Brown* decision.

Busing has been one of the most bitter controversies surrounding public school education in the United States. Parents often reject the idea of sending their child to a school several miles away when a neighborhood school is nearby.[98] Parents—generally white parents—who purposely purchased homes in the school districts they prefer, are often angered when their child must be bused to a school that they feel is inferior. Critics point to the irony of forced busing. They believe busing has contributed to "white flight"—white families moving to avoid busing. Furthermore, they point to the trend toward private-school enrollments, which also thwarts efforts to integrate public schools. In describing its 1996 decision in *Sheff v. O'Neill* concerning the Hartford, Connecticut, public school system, that state's high court said, "racial and ethnic segregation has a pervasive and invidious impact on schools, whether segregation results from intentional conduct or from unorchestrated demographic factors."[99] Others believe that the focus should be less on whether schools are racially balanced and more on whether children are receiving an adequate education. Some see the problem as a class rather than as a race issue because of the way public education is financed. The major source of elementary and secondary school funding is the local property tax, which generally provides schools in middle- and upper-class areas with larger financial bases than schools in poor areas. This has led to a call for equal educational expenditures for all schoolchildren, regardless of their communities' economic status.

Students, parents, and civil rights groups continue to take states to court for failing to provide all students with an adequate education. In 1995, a lawsuit was filed against the State of New York for failing to provide a "sound basic education," as required by the state constitution. The case reached the New York Court of Appeals, which required the state to reform its finance system to "ensure that every school in New York City has sufficient resources to provide its students with the opportunity for a meaningful high school education."[100] In California, civil rights groups and attorneys, naming 46 school districts representing one million low-income students, filed a class-action suit against the state for failure to provide a basic education. The complaint stated:

All too many California school children must go to schools that shock the conscience. Those schools lack the bare essentials required of a free and common school education that the majority of students throughout the State enjoy: trained teachers, necessary ed-

ucational supplies, classrooms, even seats in classrooms, and facilities that meet basic health and safety standards. Students must therefore attempt to learn without books and sometimes without any teachers, and in schools that lack functioning heating or air conditioning systems, that lack sufficient numbers of functioning toilets, and that are infested with vermin, including rats, mice, and cockroaches. . . . These appalling conditions in California public schools represent extreme departures from accepted educational standards and yet they have persisted for years and have worsened over time. Students who are forced to attend schools with these conditions are deprived of essential educational opportunities to learn.[101]

The State of California claims that more money for poor schools will not solve the problem because the problems are more deep-seated—in homes and neighborhoods.[102] In Texas, the state's "Robin Hood" law, which takes money from richer school districts to help poorer ones, has been met with continued challenges.

The state of public school education in general is alarming. Media accounts suggest that many school systems are in disarray, infested with drugs and violence, and serving children with many social problems that keep them from learning. Congress passed *Goals 2000,* designed to set national outcome standards for schoolchildren. President George W. Bush made the No Child Left Behind (NCLB) Act to raise educational standards a priority on his domestic agenda early in his presidency. In and of itself, raising standards is a laudable goal. But states struggling under budget crises cannot afford to help school districts meet the requirements of the law, and many oppose the law's approach. States are protesting testing mandates and asking the federal government where the money is to do the job.

There is growing pressure to better prepare young people for employment in a highly competitive, high-technology workforce. But the federal government's official role in school financing and policy setting remains limited despite the NCLB, which many consider an unwelcome and unwarranted intrusion. Educational issues are mostly the responsibility of local and state governments where funding issues remain a concern, and where politics and religion strongly influence curriculums, textbook selection, and policies related to student attendance, suspension, and expulsion. Vouchers that would allow parents, especially low-income parents, greater selection in the schools their children attend have added to the controversy.

The Civil Rights Act

Since the 1954 *Brown* decision, the single most important reform with regard to racial equality has been the Civil Rights Act of 1964. The act states:

1. It is unlawful to apply unequal standards in voter registration procedures, or to deny registration for irrelevant errors or omissions on records or applications.

2. It is unlawful to discriminate or segregate persons on the grounds of race, color, religion, or national origin in any public accommodation, including hotels, motels,

restaurants, movies, theaters, sports arenas, entertainment houses, and other places that offer to serve the public. This prohibition extends to all establishments whose operations affect interstate commerce or whose discriminatory practices are supported by state action.

3. The attorney general shall undertake civil action on behalf of any person denied equal access to a public accommodation to obtain a federal district court order to secure compliance with the act. If the owner or manager of a public accommodation should continue to discriminate, he would be in contempt of court and subject to peremptory fines and imprisonment without trial by jury.

4. The attorney general shall undertake civil actions on behalf of persons attempting orderly desegregation of public schools.

5. The Commission on Civil Rights, established in the Civil Rights Act of 1957, shall be empowered to investigate deprivations of the right to vote, study, and collect information regarding discrimination in America, and make reports to the president and Congress.

6. Each federal department and agency shall take action to end discrimination in all programs or activities receiving federal financial assistance in any form. This action shall include termination of financial assistance.

7. It shall be unlawful for any employer or labor union with twenty-five or more people after 1965 to discriminate against any individual in any fashion in employment, because of his race, color, religion, sex, or national origin, and an Equal Employment Opportunity Commission shall be established to enforce this provision by investigation, conference, conciliation, persuasion, and if need be, civil action in federal court.

Amendments to the act in 1968 prohibit housing discrimination, yet the balance of power has not shifted as dramatically as many people would like. Interestingly, Congress exempted itself from complying with the Civil Rights Act until 1988!

Housing and Racial Discrimination

Housing policy in the United States—public and private, formal and informal—is perhaps the most pervasive remaining tool of racial discrimination. Segregation and discrimination have long been evident in the private housing market and in government housing programs. Section 235 of the 1968 Fair Housing Act became "the largest single subsidized housing program and the most controversial."[103] According to the U.S. Civil Rights Commission, the Federal Housing Administration (FHA) contributed to the sale of inferior homes to blacks and others under section 235 by delegating too much authority to private industry, which had failed to comply with the spirit of the Housing Act and other civil rights legislation.

Redlining has also contributed to inferior living arrangements for blacks and other ethnic groups. This practice occurs when a bank, mortgage company, home insurance company, or other enterprise refuses to finance or insure property in certain areas. Redlined areas are generally those occupied by people who are poor and people of color. Online mortgages and low downpayments have eliminated some of the redlining of the past. Web-based mortgage companies have increased access to mortgage capital for people who had been denied in the past. What has cropped up in its place are higher mortgage rates. Even when income is controlled (accounted for), the difference in mortgage rates seems to be racially biased. A Harvard study on home mortgages found that "relatively low shares of prime conventional loans [are] going to African-American and Hispanic borrowers and neighborhoods, [and] race continues to be an important factor in determining the allocation of prime mortgage credit."[104]

Until fair housing and lending practices are enforced at local, state, and national levels, housing discrimination and segregation, and its associated negative outcomes will persist. Discriminatory housing and lending practices explain much of the large gap in homeownership between whites, blacks, and Hispanics. Over the past ten years homeownership rates among blacks and Hispanics has gradually increased, but whites' homeownership far outpaces them. The housing gap among these groups have remained relatively unchanged over the past ten years at between 24 to 26 percent. In 1994, blacks' and Hispanics' homeownership rates were 42 and 41 percent, respectively, while 68 percent of whites owned their homes. By 2003, homeownership among blacks and Hispanics had grown to 48 and 47 percent, respectively, with whites' homeownership up to 72 percent (see Table 11.7). American Indians and Asian

TABLE 11.7

Homeownership Rates by Race, 1994–2003

| | White | Black | | Hispanic | |
	Ownership Rate	Ownership Rate	Gap	Ownership Rate	Gap
Year					
1994	67.7	42.3	25.4	41.2	26.5
1995	68.7	42.7	26	42.1	26.6
1996	69.1	44.1	25	42.8	26.3
1997	69.3	44.8	24.5	43.3	26.0
1998	70.0	45.6	25.2	44.7	25.3
1999	70.5	46.3	24.2	45.5	25.0
2000	71.1	47.2	23.9	46.3	24.8
2001	71.6	47.7	23.9	47.3	24.3
2002	71.8	47.3	24.5	48.2	23.6
2003	72.1	48.1	24	46.7	25.4

Source: U.S. Census Bureau, Housing Vacancies and Homeownership Annual Statistics: 2003, Table 20, retrieved from http://www.census.gov/hhes/www/housing/hvs/annual03/ann03t20.html

Americans have higher homeownership rates than blacks and Hispanics, at 54 percent and 56 percent, respectively.[105]

Blacks are more likely to live in segregated neighborhoods than other people of color.[106] Trend studies do show that segregation for blacks has declined since 1980, while Hispanics show a slight increase in segregation over the same time period.[107] Real estate agents encourage neighborhood segregation when they "steer" members of particular racial and ethnic groups to housing in already segregated areas. In doing so, agents fail to comply with the Fair Housing Act.

Sociologists have found that "racial residential segregation is the principal structural feature of American society responsible for the perpetuation of urban poverty and represents a primary cause of racial inequality in the United States."[108] The benefits of integrated neighborhoods are well documented. Adults who move from high-poverty to low-poverty neighborhoods have higher employment rates and are less likely to receive welfare long term. Their children do better in school, have higher graduation rates, and are more likely to attend college.[109] In 1970, the U.S. Third Circuit Court and the Court of Appeals ruled that, in keeping with the Fair Housing Act and the Civil Rights Acts of 1964 and 1968, HUD is responsible for assessing the racial impact of its decisions in order to prevent housing discrimination. Housing advocates complain that HUD has utterly failed to meet its fair housing responsibilities, especially in the current era where more public housing is being demolished than is being made available to low-income households. They also say that fair housing regulations have no "teeth" in them; local housing authorities or landlords who fail to meet requirements face few, if any, consequences.[110]

The city of Yonkers, New York, gained national notoriety in 1988 when it refused to implement a housing desegregation order, and Vidor, Texas, earned a similar reputation in 1993 when it failed to integrate a public housing complex. In 2000, HUD took control of public housing in Beaumont, Texas, after years of attempts to encourage integration. The problem extends well beyond public housing. In 1988, Congress toughened the Department of Housing and Urban Development's enforcement provisions under the Fair Housing Act and added protections against discrimination for people with disabilities and for families with children. In 1998, HUD proposed new regulations to strengthen fair housing requirements for all jurisdictions, but HUD retracted the proposed regulations when it met with strong opposition from the League of Cities.[111] Another concern of fair housing advocates is the lack of oversight of local housing authorities and contractors working for HUD to provide affordable housing. They cite four major contributors to this problem:

1. The Office of Fair Housing and Equal Opportunity has suffered a severe loss of personnel and is no longer regarded as a serious oversight body.

2. More power has been transferred to local authorities in recent years, making it difficult to adequately monitor local housing practices. For example, the housing authority of Baltimore City, Maryland, reached a court-approved agreement in 1996 with the ACLU (representing low-income tenants) to stop its practice of building low-income housing in segregated areas. In 2000, the courts found that Baltimore City had made

no effort to comply with the agreement and ordered it to begin locating housing units in integrated neighborhoods.[112]

3. Advocates complain that HUD's data collection practices are inadequate to inform policy and practice, and in some of its housing programs, nearly nonexistent.

4. Housing advocates are frustrated by HUD's reluctance to initiate a dialogue to address housing issues.

Congress established the Millennial Housing Commission in 2000 to explore methods of partnering with private industry to increase affordable housing. The commission concluded that "unless we provide greater access to desegregated housing, we will continue to deny access to equal educational and employment opportunities."[113] The commission failed to provide details about how to accomplish this goal.

Affirmative Action

Another aspect of equal rights is **affirmative action** policies designed to achieve equality in school admissions and employment for women and members of certain racial or ethnic groups. Affirmative action is based on the notion that women and minorities should be admitted, hired, and promoted in proportion to their representation in the population. To what extent should affirmative action policies be pursued? Is it enough to use policies that do not discriminate against people because of gender and racial and ethnic background, or should policies go much further in order to reduce imbalances in admissions and employment? Originally, the federal government chose a policy of nondiscrimination. Examples are President Truman's decision to desegregate the military in 1946 and Titles VI and VII of the 1964 Civil Rights Act. Nondiscrimination simply means that preferential treatment will not be given to selected groups.

Those dissatisfied with nondiscrimination as a method of achieving equality believe that a more aggressive approach is needed. One aspect of this concern spurred a debate as to whether quotas rather than goals should be used to achieve equality. **Quotas** are defined as "imposing a fixed, mandatory number or percentage of persons to be hired or promoted, regardless of the number of potential applicants who meet the qualifications," while a **goal** is a

> *numerical objective, fixed realistically in terms of number of vacancies expected, and the number of qualified applicants available. . . . If . . . the employer . . . has demonstrated every good faith effort to include persons from the group which was the object of discrimination . . . but has been unable to do so in sufficient numbers to meet his goal, he is not subject to sanction.*[114]

In addition, an employer is not obligated to hire an unqualified or less qualified person in preference to a prospective employee with better qualifications.

The Philadelphia Plan of 1967 issued by the U.S. Office of Federal Contract Compliance was one of the first examples of an affirmative action plan. It required that those bidding on federal contracts submit plans to employ specific percentages of minority workers. Another quota-type plan was adopted in 1971 by the Federal Aviation Administration. It essentially placed a freeze on hiring any additional employees if every fifth vacant position was not filled by a member of a minority group.

Opponents of quota setting generally believe that giving preferential treatment to members of particular groups violates the equal protection clause (Fourteenth Amendment) of the U.S. Constitution. In 1974 a federal court upheld this belief in its decision that the University of Washington Law School should admit Marco DeFunis, Jr. DeFunis had protested the university's decision to reject his application while admitting blacks with lower grades and test scores. The courts have heard other cases charging "reverse discrimination." The U.S. Supreme Court ruled on the issue of admitting less-qualified minority applicants over white applicants in the case of Alan Bakke. The Court determined that Bakke had been unfairly denied admission to the University of California Davis Medical School because his qualifications were stronger than those of some people of color admitted to the school. Proponents of the decision hoped the *Bakke* case would help change what they perceived to be a trend of reverse discrimination against whites. Opponents feared that the Bakke decision threatened the future of affirmation action. Other reverse discrimination charges in California arose when the University of California at Berkeley was accused of discriminating against whites by favoring black, Hispanic, and Filipino applicants, and when complaints were leveled against the University of California system for using more stringent admissions requirements for Asian Americans. Asian Americans generally have higher test scores than other groups, and they have been admitted at rates higher than their representation in the population.

Threats to affirmative action mounted during the Reagan administration. Civil right advocates accused the administration of reversing a pattern of improvement in civil rights that began in the 1960s and had been supported under both Democratic and Republican administrations. Reagan's recommendations for appointments to the U.S. Civil Rights Commission and his attempts to get rid of some members raised the ire of civil rights groups. Controversy also brewed in the U.S. Department of Justice. During the Carter presidency, the department was a strong proponent of civil rights. It had, for example, helped to implement a court decree requiring that the police and fire departments of Indianapolis establish quotas for hiring and promoting women and blacks. But in 1984, the U.S. Supreme Court ruled in the case of *Firefighters Local Union No. 1784 v. Stotts* that the jobs of blacks with less seniority cannot be protected at the expense of jobs of whites with more seniority. The Department of Justice used this decision to get Indianapolis and forty-nine other jurisdictions to abandon the use of quotas. The National Association for the Advancement of Colored People (NAACP) and others called the Department of Justice action illegal.

The Reagan administration also challenged the use of **class action suits** to benefit groups of people. During Reagan's terms, the Equal Employment Opportunity Commission expressed its desire to address cases of discrimination against particular individuals rather than assisting classes of people who have been treated unfairly. William Bradford Reynolds, then head of the Department of Justice, declared that what was needed was a color- and sex-blind society rather than a color- and sex-conscious one. He contended that quotas are a form of discrimination.

The U.S. Supreme Court did deal a victory for affirmative action during the Reagan years with two 1986 decisions (one involved Cleveland firefighters, the other a New York sheet metal workers' union). According to these decisions, "federal judges may set goals and timetables requiring employers guilty of past discrimination to hire or promote specific numbers of minorities, even if the jobs go to people who are not themselves the proven victims of bias."[115] But Supreme Court rulings in 1989 again put affirmative action on shaky ground. In *City of Richmond v. J. A. Croson Co.*, it struck down many state and local "set-aside" programs that gave preference to minority-owned firms in awarding contracts, saying that such programs should be used only to remedy discrimination. The high court said, however, that federal set-aside programs were exempt because of the wide latitude that Congress has in determining what is needed to achieve equality nationally.[116] The decision reportedly caused a severe drop in the contracts awarded to minority-owned businesses. In *Wards Cove Packing Co., Inc. v. Atonio* (a case primarily involving Asian American and Alaska Native employees of a salmon cannery in Alaska), the Supreme Court placed the onus of proving that an employer intended to discriminate (rather than unintentionally discriminated) on the employee. This reversed the Court's long-standing 1971 decision in *Griggs v. Duke Power*, in which the burden was placed on the employer to show that hiring criteria have a direct relation to the job. Other 1989 decisions also made it easier to challenge affirmative action programs, and more difficult for employees to bring discrimination suits. Many thought that these decisions were ironic given that higher unemployment rates and lower earnings among women, blacks, and Hispanics do not support the contention of reverse discrimination.

During the Reagan years, the NAACP, NOW, and other groups were outraged by the president's position on civil rights and the reductions in the number of discrimination cases pursued by the federal government in education, employment, and housing.[117] They hoped that President George H. W. Bush's position would indeed be "kinder" and "gentler" to them, but given Bush's lack of action, Congress decided that the real recourse to fair treatment in job bias cases was to pass new civil rights legislation to undo the 1989 Supreme Court rulings. Although expressing strong concern for civil rights, the president used one of his trademark vetoes to overturn Congress's 1990 civil rights restoration effort, saying it would lead employers to use quotas to avoid lawsuits. The American Civil Liberties Union accused Bush of using a "smokescreen of 'quotas' to prevent restoration of critically important civil rights laws that give minorities equal access to education, housing, employment and the ballot box."[118]

In 1991 the House of Representatives hammered out a new bill that strengthened antiquota language. President George H. W. Bush again rejected the bill, but eventually a compromise emerged that helped to restore the decision in the *Griggs* case. The bill also eliminated a practice called "race norming" in which job-related test scores are adjusted for differences across racial or ethnic groups. The bill further allowed punitive and compensatory damages to be collected for the first time in sexual discrimination (including sexual harassment) cases, as well as in cases of discrimination against people with disabilities and members of religious groups. The bill extended provisions to Senate and White House staff for the first time, with the stipulation that senators who violate the law are personally liable for damages.

Another civil rights issue that arose during the first Bush administration was questioning whether college scholarships awarded solely on the basis of race violated Title VI of the Civil Rights Act. Since only a tiny fraction of the nation's scholarships are awarded on race alone (most include other criteria such as financial need and merit), there was concern that animosity among ethnic groups was being aroused over a non-issue.[119] In 1993, President Clinton's Secretary of Education announced that such scholarships are a legal remedy to correct past inequities.

In the late 1990s a number of ballot initiatives and court rulings challenged past gender and racial preference practices in public colleges and universities. In California (Proposition 209) and Washington State (Initiative 200), voters decided to ban gender and racial preferences in higher education, employment, and contracting, effectively abolishing the states' affirmative action programs.[120] Court decisions followed condemning the use of preferences to achieve racial balance as unconstitutional under the 14th Amendment. For example, in 1996, Cheryl Hopwood and three other white students who were denied admission to the University of Texas at Austin Law School sued the State of Texas for discrimination because students of color with lower qualifying scores were admitted. The U.S. Court of Appeals, Fifth Circuit's decision in *Hopwood v. Texas* declared the use of racial preferences in university admissions unconstitutional (see also *Johnson v. Board of Regents of University of Georgia*). Following this decision, admissions of Hispanic and black students to the University of Texas at Austin and Texas A&M University dropped significantly. The concern was that this ruling sent a message that students of color were not welcomed on campuses. In 1998, the Texas legislature adopted the Ten Percent Plan as an alternative approach to achieve racial balance. This plan gives Texas high school students placing in the top 10 percent of their high school graduating class automatic admission to the Texas public university of their choice. This corrected some of the loss of minority students following the *Hopwood* decision, but Texas universities were still admitting a smaller percentage of black and Hispanic applicants than they did before *Hopwood* (for example, in 1996, the University of Texas at Austin admitted 57 percent of black students who applied, but in 1999 only 46 percent were admitted). After Proposition 209 passed, California began guaranteeing all students graduating in the top 12.5 percent of their high school class admission to the state university system (but not necessarily the school of their choice). The University of California at Berkeley is the state's flagship institution. Some civil rights groups have filed suit claiming that Berkeley discriminates, citing figures that Berkeley admitted 48 percent of white applicants with GPAs of 4.0 or higher but only 32 percent of Filipino American, 38 percent of African American, and 40 percent of Hispanic American applicants with the same GPA.

Also unresolved is how to create admission policies and procedures for applicants who do not fall within the "percent plans' " parameters. The U.S. Commission on

Civil Rights assessed the percent plans in use in Texas, California, and Florida and found that people of color are losing ground, even on campuses that have increased outreach efforts. Overall, the commission found fewer people of color applying to these universities and declines in the percentage of applicants accepted. This trend was true of law and medical schools as well. They also noted a marked decrease in minority admissions to states' flagship universities including the University of California at Berkeley, Los Angeles, and San Diego, the University of Texas at Austin, and the University of Florida. The commission's conclusion: "Simply guaranteeing admission to a certain percentage of students is not enough; the [percent] plans must be supplemented with proactive recruitment, financial aid, outreach, and academic support programs."[121]

The Supreme Court's June 2003 decisions in *Grutter v. Bollinger* and *Gratz v. Bollinger*[122] added more food for thought to the affirmative action debate. Both were discrimination cases against the University of Michigan (UM). Gratz was denied admission to the College of Literature, Science, and Arts and sued the university, claiming that minority students with lesser qualifications had been admitted. Grutter filed a similar case against the UM Law School. The Supreme Court heard the cases together but reached different conclusions in each. They agreed that Gratz suffered discrimination because the admission procedure automatically awarded 20 points to minority students. In the Grutter case, the court found in favor of UM, stating that the law school's admission procedures used race in a narrowly tailored way that furthered the schools compelling interest in obtaining the benefits accruing from a diverse student body. Thus, the court ruled against a point system, believing that it reduced race to a deciding factor in admissions. In the Grutter case, among other admission requirements, students wrote an essay describing the diverse contributions they could make to the law school. The law school defined diversity broadly, and had set educational goals dependent on a diverse student body. Race was one of many factors used in making admissions decisions, not the deciding factor. Since the UM decision, universities have gone to great lengths to create new procedures for insuring diverse student populations. UM supported its commitment to diversity by investing an additional $1.8 million in evaluating applications. This helped to ward off decline in enrollments of students of color. In the year after the *Bollinger* decisions, the percentage of undergraduate students of color at UM dropped slightly from 11 percent to 10 percent.

The NAACP strongly supports affirmative action, but a growing group of black conservatives, including some black scholars, feel that affirmative action is no longer helping blacks. For example, businessman Ward Connerly helped spearhead California's Proposition 209. His efforts to get similar initiatives on the ballot in Florida and Michigan failed. More recently, California voters handily defeated Connerly's drive for Proposition 54, which called for a constitutional amendment prohibiting public agencies from collecting data on race, ethnicity, and national origin. The measure would have had disastrous consequences for collecting important information about health, education, public safety, and civil rights.

Some conservative blacks take the position that affirmative action helped blacks in the past but that the future rests on blacks helping themselves.[123] When comedian Bill Cosby, who has an earned doctorate in education, said that blacks in undesirable circumstances needed to take responsibilty for themselves, he found his share of both critics and defenders.[124] Liberals who support policies like affirmative action have been implored to "let race go" and to not make "race the organizing principle of our polity and civic culture."[125] Others believe that racial justice will not occur until there is economic justice and that this requires addressing the country's wealth gap through decent wages, health coverage, and affordable housing.[126]

Voting Rights

One way groups can achieve equity is to exercise their right to vote. The abolition of poll taxes and literacy tests were important steps in extending voting rights. Since the mid-1900s many more steps have been taken to ensure that all groups have the same opportunities to vote. Especially important is the 1965 Voting Rights Act, designed to further ensure, protect, and encourage the right to a voice in the electoral process. Congress periodically reviews the act, and constant improvements have been made to promote and protect voting rights. In recent years the emphasis is on making it even easier to register by doing away with laws requiring people to register in advance of elections and by allowing people to register in many public offices, as well as super-markets and shopping malls. The National Voter Registration Act of 1993 requires states to allow registration by mail.

More blacks and Hispanic Americans can be counted among those holding elected office. The number of blacks holding elected federal, state, and local office increased sixfold from 1,469 in 1970 to 9,061 in 2001, with black women making the most re-cent substantial gains. Hispanics held 5,205 elected offices in 2001, up from 3,147 in 1985.[127] However, very few people of color have ever served in the U.S. Senate. Among members of the 108th Congress in 2004, there were 39 black U.S. represen-tatives (up from 25 in 1991) but no black senators.[128] Black mayors have been elected in some of America's larger cities—Los Angeles, Detroit, Cleveland, New York, and Atlanta. The nation's first black governor, Douglas Wilder, was elected by Virginia voters in 1989. In 2004, there were 25 Hispanic American U.S. representatives and no senators. Florida has had a Hispanic American governor, and several large cities—Miami, San Antonio, and Denver—have had Hispanic American mayors. Hispanics are by far the fastest-growing ethnic group in the country, now comprising 14 per-cent of the population. Groups promoting the political agenda of Hispanic Ameri-cans include the National Council of La Raza, the Mexican American Legal Defense and Education Fund (MALDEF), and the League of United Latin American Citizens (LULAC). The number of U.S. residents of Asian ancestry has also grown rapidly, now nearing 4 percent of the U.S. population. Five Asian American and Pacific Is-lander representatives and two senators served in the 108th Congress. By 2050 the United States will look quite different from the way it does today—non-Hispanic whites may be 50 percent of the U.S. population, rather than the 69 percent they are now. Hispanics are projected to make up 24 percent and blacks 15 percent of the population by 2050.[129] Such major changes will certainly be reflected in the country's politics. For example, Hispanics as a group may favor the Democratic party, but their political leanings also suggest they favor conservative positions with respect to abortion and gay rights.[130]

Many issues of importance are on today's voting rights agenda. Single-member districts, the shape of districts, and cumulative voting (where everyone gets several votes that can all be used for one candidate or spread among candidates) are some methods that have been used to promote representation of all racial and ethnic groups in elected office. Of course, cumulative voting is no more effective than having one vote if people fail to exercise their voting rights. More than once the U.S. Supreme Court has found that some voting districts have been drawn to favor blacks or Hispanics, and it has struck down "gerrymandering" by using race as a predominant factor to create voting districts.

Disturbing events occurred during the 2000 presidential election. That election was certainly the most controversial in recent years, partly because of the numbers turned away from the polls or whose votes were not counted (see Chapter 2). The U.S. Commission on Civil Rights conducted an extensive investigation in Florida, the most troublesome state, and found that the votes of 14.4 percent of blacks were rejected, compared to 1.6 percent of other voters. The commission concluded that the most salient feature of the 2000 election was *not* the close race, but the disenfranchisement of Florida voters. The Commission concluded that the state's highest officials had failed to "ensur[e] efficiency, uniformity, and fairness in the election."[131] Accusations in other elections concerned the Republicans' use of uniformed security guards at Hispanic precincts in Orange County, California, in 1988, and of Republican poll watchers in Arkansas photographing blacks as they voted in 2002.[132] In the 1990 North Carolina Senate race, campaign workers for Senator Jesse Helms were accused of mailing 125,000 postcards to mainly black voting precincts that contained misleading residency requirements for voting and warned that misinformation given to the voting officials could result in five years in prison. Native American voters in South Dakota complained that poll workers harassed them by making fun of their names and threatening them with false voter fraud charges. The minority vote can be a deciding vote. In 2002, Native Americans in South Dakota were credited with the narrow victory of Senator Tim Johnson, who won by just 528 votes.

In recent elections, voting machine malfunctions have disrupted elections and called results into question (see Chapter 2). As states scurry to fix antiquated voting machinery, concerns arise about the possibility of widespread voter disenfranchisement. Many states are opting for direct-recording electronic (DRE) voting machines. Lost ballots have already occurred with DREs, and since many DREs do not have paper trails, a vote recount is impossible. California has mandated that all of its DRE voting machines produce a paper trail by 2006. An independent study of DREs indicated serious flaws in the machines produced by four leading vendors and identified

57 potential security problems that could leave the machines open to hackers and lead to false ballot tallies.[133] DRE voting machine manufacturers have been reluctant to provide information about programming software. In cases where the software must be registered with the state and voting machines certified, some manufacturers have been accused of ignoring the rules.[134]

In the past, voting has been a fairly transparent process documented and open to public scrutiny. High-tech electronic voting systems are owned by private industry that may have special interests. The public does not have access to the kind of information that might reveal built-in biases (unintentional or otherwise) in these systems. Eyebrows have been raised about the close relationships between voting machine manufacturers and politicians. For instance, Walden O'Dell, CEO of Diebold, a leading manufacturer of DRE voting machines, wrote in a Republican fundraising letter that he was "commited to helping Ohio deliver its electoral votes to the president" in the 2004 election.[135]

The Marginalization of Native Americans

In the United States, no group has suffered a longer history of racial discrimination and violence. As a direct result, Native Americans have endured tremendous social, economic, and health problems. Congress members from states with the largest Native American populations may find it difficult to represent these constituents because Indians' needs often conflict with those of larger, more powerful constituent groups.[136] Ben Nighthorse Campbell (R-Colorado), the only Native American serving in the U.S. Senate, is retiring. Two Native Americans are serving in the U.S. House of Representatives—Brad Carson, a Democrat, and Tom Cole, a Republican—both from Oklahoma.

There are 562 federally recognized tribal governments,[137] but many Native communities do not have this recognition. Native groups must be recognized to receive the benefits and services that the government is required to provide to tribes. Today it seems astonishing that American Indians were not accorded citizenship until 1924, that some remained slaves until 1935, and that New Mexico did not allow American Indians to vote until 1940.[138] Many federal policy decisions have wrought great suffering for the Indian tribes in the United States. Native Americans have been robbed of land and minerals rights, thus depriving them of a livelihood. They have also faced displacement from their reservations and have encountered problems in adapting to urban life. Many hardships have been attributed to attempts to force Indians to assimilate into the majority culture, even though their family structures, religions, and communication patterns differ substantially from those of whites.

In acknowledging the abuses experienced by Native Americans, the Indian Self-Determination and Education Assistance Act of 1975 emphasized tribal self-government and the establishment of independent health, education, and welfare services. Thirty years later it is clear that this legislation has not led to many improvements in the lives of Indian people. One of the worst degradations has been the removal of Indian children from their families to be raised by others, a practice ratio-nalized by welfare professionals who viewed Native American childrearing practices as overly harsh.[139] The Indian Child Welfare Act of 1978 was designed to remedy prob-lems in the placement of Native American children by restoring greater control over these decisions to the tribes. Priority for placement is now given to members of the child's own tribe rather than to non-Indian families.

The Bureau of Indian Affairs (BIA), part of the U.S. Department of the Interior, is the primary federal agency responsible for assisting Native Americans in meeting many of their economic and education needs. Almost all BIA employees are Native Americans,[140] but the agency has long been criticized for its paternalistic and au-thoritarian attitude toward its clientele. Critics have said, "The BIA takes care of In-dians' money, land, children, water, roads, etc. with authority [as] complete as that of a prison."[141] Despite long-standing criticisms, it was not until October 1987 that of-ficial action to investigate the bureau began. Senator Daniel Inouye (D-Hawaii), then chairperson of the Senate Select Committee on Indian Affairs, called for full inves-tigative hearings after an astonishing series of articles appeared in the *Arizona Re-public* claiming "widespread fraud, mismanagement and waste in the almost $3 billion-a-year federal Indian programs."[142] Other accusations were that the govern-ment had assisted oil companies in bilking Indians of billions of dollars from oil and gas reserves.[143]

The BIA has called itself an agency that "manages for excellence," fostering coop-eration and coordination in consultation with Native American tribes while support-ing self-determination and tribal sovereignty,[144] but an ongoing lawsuit, *Cobell v. Norton* raises more serious questions about the federal government's assistance to peo-ple in Indian Country. This class-action suit, which has shut down the BIA website, was originally filed in 1996 as *Cobell v. Babbit* (Bruce Babbitt was the former Secretary of the Interior; Gale Norton currently holds that position). Other defendants are the Treasury Secretary and the Assistant Secretary of Indian Affairs. In 1887, the General Allotment Act divided Native American lands into 80- to 160-acre portions and allo-cated them to individual Indians.[145] This was a government attempt to destroy reser-vations and force Native Americans to assimilate. The process created Indian Individual Money Accounts that the Department of the Interior holds in "trust" (manages) be-cause the lands generate revenues from activities such as oil and gas leases. The situ-ation can best be described as a mess because the government apparently cannot provide a decent accounting of what is owed to Native Americans or even how many accounts there are (estimates are 300,000 to 500,000). In 1994 the Indian Trust Act di-rected the Interior Secretary to provide an accounting, but that has not happened. A district court has set a 2007 deadline for the accounting. In the United States, anyone with any kind of trust account has a legal right to a full accounting. Until the matter is resolved, Native Americans cannot receive any money from these accounts. The gov-ernment has spent millions defending itself, with some arguing that the money could have gone to Native Americans instead. Elouise Cobell, a Blackfoot from Montana and a banker as well as the lead plaintiff in the case, warns Native Americans not to make small individual settlements that would rob them of their just deserts and not to believe that a settlement will result in an end to spending on programs for Native Americans.[146] Some people believe that only an act of Congress will bring an end to *Cobell v. Norton*.

The agency responsible for providing healthcare to many Native Americans is the Indian Health Service (IHS), formerly part of the BIA, and now part of the U.S. Department of Health and Human Services. Criticisms of the IHS include inadequate and incompetent treatment of patients.[147]

Edward Carpenter assessed the status of American Indians by stating

> that a part of the problem is related to the Indian's cultural diversification and a history of limited tribal cooperation is probably true. However, the impact of the Indian's legal status, the failure of the Congress, and the concomitant administrative morass created by the BIA appear to be the critical variables.[148]

Carpenter called for a hands-off policy by non-Indians and a return of authority to Native Americans. A special Senate committee recommended abolishing the BIA and replacing it with a program of direct financial grants to Indian tribes. The National Congress of American Indians (NCAI) is an advocacy organization which tracks legislative issues of concern to Indian people and is particularly concerned about maintaining Indian sovereignty.

Racial Profiling

Racial profiling is the practice of stopping, interrogating, searching, and/or arresting people based on some immutable characteristic, such as skin color or gender. This practice is based on stereotypical beliefs that people of certain racial, ethnic, or religious groups are more likely than others to commit crimes.[149] Racial profiling is widely recognized as a problem in communities across the country today. Consider the following examples. In April 2004, the American Civil Liberties Union contacted the police chief of Charlottesville, Virginia, to request that he stop detaining African American men and subjecting them to "practically random" DNA testing. In rape investigations, when the attacker was identified as a black man, the police force began detaining large numbers of black men because they were black. By the time the ACLU requested a halt to the testing, the police force in this town of 45,000 had already collected DNA samples on 197 African American men. The ACLU began a public information campaign to inform black men in Charlottesville of their constitutional rights.[150]

An investigation of traffic stops in New Jersey in 1999 found that three-fourths of the cars searched on state highways were driven by African American or Hispanic individuals. Following the New Jersey investigation, the federal government and the state of New Jersey came to an unprecedented agreement: Highway patrolmen could no longer make traffic stops on the basis of race. In that same year, the Department of Justice (DOJ) reported that African Americans were 20 percent more likely to be stopped than whites, 50 percent more likely to be stopped twice, and twice as likely to have their car searched. Subsequent studies in Colorado, Massachusetts, and Los Angeles in 2002 confirmed that racial profiling is common.[151] In addition to traffic stops, other forms of racial profiling are also common, such as the targeting of Hispanics by the U.S. Immigration and Naturalization Service.[152] A General Accounting

Office (GAO) report on the U.S. Customs Service found that black females were nine times more likely than white females to be X-rayed following a frisk or pat down, but less than half as likely to be found carrying contraband.[153]

In 2000, the DOJ issued voluntary guidelines to police departments for collecting racial profiling data. In recent years, 20 states have enacted laws against racial profiling, but only 12 of them collect some type of data on race.[154]

Racial profiling promotes fear and alienation and uses precious police resources to process "suspects" with no probable cause. It takes time that could be better spent on serious and scientifically based criminal investigations. The End Racial Profiling Act was initially introduced in 2001 in response to the blatant racial profiling of Arabs and South Asians following the September 11th attacks, and reintroduced to the 108th Congress in February 2004. The bill would (1) define racial profiling and make it illegal, (2) provide victims of racial profiling with the right to sue, (3) introduce national data collection for tracking and monitoring bias-based policing and increase police accountability, (4) authorize the attorney general to withhold funds from police departments that do not comply with the law, and (5) provide grants to help police departments implement anti-racial profiling policies and data collection.[155] The bill, introduced by Senator Russell Feingold (Democrat-Wisconsin), has 140 cosponsors.

Civil Rights and the War on Terror

The United States, which prides itself on being a refuge for people escaping persecution, is also guilty of gross maltreatment of people with roots in other countries. During World War I, Attorney General A. Mitchell Palmer ordered the detention and deportation of large numbers of immigrants from Eastern Europe after his house was bombed by extremists. Federal agents were ordered to conduct "Palmer raids" by rounding up thousands of immigrants who were detained or deported solely because of their ethnicity.[156]

The treatment of Japanese Americans after Japan attacked Pearl Harbor in 1941 and World War II erupted is another disturbing example of discrimination against Americans of foreign backgrounds. Following the attack, Japanese Americans were interned in ten relocation camps by President Franklin D. Roosevelt for fear that they might threaten U.S. security and to protect them from potential harm by Americans who were angered by Japan's attack.[157] Japanese Americans believe that this action was neither necessary nor benevolent. They were forced to give up their jobs and their possessions. To prove they were indeed Americans, many volunteered for the armed services. Internment ended in 1943 with the recognition that citizenship and loyalty to one's country, not racial characteristics, make one an American. Not until 1983 did the U.S. government actually acknowledge wrongdoing. The statement came as a result of the work of the Commission on Wartime Relocation and Internment of Civilians. Reparation payments were later approved for the approximately 78,000 remaining survivors of internment.[158]

In February 2001, President George W. Bush called for an end to racial profiling,[159] but those words began to ring hollow. In the wake of the September 11th terrorist attacks, several thousand Arab, South Asian, and Muslim men residing in the United States were interviewed or sought for questioning because of national origin or religion. At least 1,200 were detained. Many lacked access to an attorney and other resources to fight unlawful arrest. Family, friends, and employers of many detainees had no idea where these individuals were. Deportation hearings for Arabs were closed to the public and held in secret.[160] Civil rights, human rights, and immigrant rights organizations were unable to get a list of detainees and the charges against them from the U.S. Attorney General or the FBI. The ACLU filed a lawsuit in October 2001 under the Freedom of Information Act to force the government to release information about the prisoners. A federal judge ordered the government to provide information of detainees, noting that "secret arrests are a concept odious to a democratic society."[161] The federal government refused, and a higher court overturned the judge's ruling. An investigation by the Office of the Inspector General (located within the Department of Justice) found that arrests were indiscriminate and that detainees were denied access to counsel, interrogated about their religion and political views, detained in degrading conditions, and in some instances, verbally and physically abused. Many were detained for months without charges, some in solitary confinement. For those with legal counsel, Attorney General Ashcroft used "emergency authority" to order monitoring of all attorney–client conversations, which many declared a violation of the Sixth Amendment. Most detainees were eventually released, and large numbers were deported. But several hundred were held at the U.S. naval base in Guantanamo Bay, Cuba.[162] President George W. Bush declared these prisoners "enemy combatants." Their treatment has been hotly debated. They were not formally charged with a crime and continued to be denied legal counsel and contact with the outside world. In June 2004, the Supreme Court told the President that the remaining Guantanamo detainees can challenge their detention. Military tribunals will be used to hear the cases, but this gives the detainees only limited legal representation.

In October 2001, Congress hastily passed the USA PATRIOT Act to aid in capturing and detaining terrorists. The law gives enforcement agencies unprecedented power to conduct wiretaps, access computer data, and search property without a court order.[163] The act prohibits "domestic terrorism," which is defined in such broad terms that civil rights groups believe that it infringes upon the First Amendment right of free speech like protests and demonstrations.[164] Some individuals have been questioned and subpoenaed after participating in peaceful protests against the war in Iraq.[165] Both Republicans and Democrats have expressed concerns about the USA PATRIOT Act's far-reaching powers. Some provisions will sunset in 2005. The act still has some staunch defenders, and President Bush and Attorney General John Ashcroft are pushing Congress to make all the act's provisions permanent. With some distance since September 11, 2001, Congress is seriously debating the act's renewal, especially provisions that threaten constitutional rights, while retaining provisions to lawfully enhance the ability to fight terror.[166]

IMMIGRATION AND SOCIAL WELFARE

When white men and women arrived to colonize what is now the United States, they became the first immigrants to set foot on this land. Today, more than one hundred years after the Statue of Liberty—a symbol of freedom for many immigrants—was erected, people from virtually every country and every cultural, ethnic, racial, and religious group inhabit the United States. Most Americans are now the descendants of those who came to this country in search of a better life. The questions that concerns us today are how much immigration should the U.S. allow, and what should immigration policy be in this post–September 11th environment?

Immigration Policy

U.S. laws regulating immigration have existed since the 1800s. The Chinese Exclusion Act of 1833 and the Oriental Exclusion Law of 1924 severely restricted the entrance of Asian groups, as did the Quota System Law of 1921 and the Immigration Act of 1924. Chinese immigrants were brought to this country in 1864 to do the back-breaking work of building the nation's railroads, but as larger numbers of Asians entered the United States and began to prosper, their successes made Americans uneasy. Immigration policies were more favorable to others, such as northern Europeans, perhaps because of the greater similarity of their physical characteristics to those of many Americans.

In 1965 Congress abolished stringent quotas limiting the number of entrants from various countries, but new issues arose. The Vietnam War displaced and impoverished many Vietnamese who later sought refuge in the United States. Of special concern were "Amerasian" children, children born to American servicemen and Vietnamese women. Several thousand of these children lived in poverty in Vietnam because it was difficult to establishing their fathers' identities, a requirement for them to come to the United States. In other cases, fathers were unable to locate their children, or they faced bureaucratic problems in trying to get their children out of Vietnam. Under the Orderly Departure Program and the Amerasian Homecoming Act of 1987, the United States attempted to bring all these Amerasians (many of whom had reached adulthood) and their families to America.

Another immigration issue that emerged in the 1960s was Cubans seeking political asylum from the communistic Castro regime. As a result of the Cold War, U.S. immigration policy was more generous to those seeking asylum for fear of political persecution from communist governments. Freedom flights brought thousands of Cubans to the United States through the early 1970s. Then in 1980 Castro opened the port of Mariel and allowed thousands more Cubans to leave. To accommodate the new influx, President Carter opened several refugee-processing centers in the United States. Many refugees came to join their families in the United States, but the convicted criminals and undesirables that were also sent caused criticism that Castro had used the United States as a dumping ground. Cubans continue to risk their lives to come to the United States. One of the most dramatic escapes occurred when a Cuban pilot flew a small plane from the United States and landed on a highway in Cuba to pick up his wife and sons and bring them to the United States. Others continue to brave shark-infested waters in small boats and make-shift rafts.

Elián Gonzalez captured the hearts of Americans when he survived a harrowing trip at sea but his mother perished. Cuban refugees have been entitled to privileges not afforded other immigrants, such as temporary public assistance on arrival. After one year, most can become permanent residents. But thirty-five years after the first Cuban exodus, a new wave of immigrants and political pressures caused President Clinton to announce that Cuban refugees would be treated more like refugees from other countries. In 1994 many of those trying to flee were intercepted and detained at the U.S. naval base in Guantanamo Bay, Cuba. The Clinton administration reversed its position in 1996 and granted them asylum but said that those caught at sea in the future would be returned to Cuba.

With the fall of many communistic governments, immigration from a variety of other countries has made headlines. Immigration from the tiny island of Haiti was spurred by both the overwhelming poverty on the island and the repressive Duvalier government. The Duvaliers were eventually overthrown and a democratic election was held, but the elected leader, Jean-Bertrand Aristide, was ousted twice, first in 1991, less than a year after being elected, and then again in February 2004.[167] Efforts to establish an acceptable governing structure during the uprising in 1991 resulted in continuing turmoil and violence. Under the Refugee Act of 1980, those seeking asylum are admitted to the United States if they have "a well-founded fear of persecution on account of race, religion, nationality, membership in a particular social group or political opinion"; it does not include those fleeing for "economic" reasons. The George H. W. Bush administration viewed those coming from Haiti as economic rather than political refugees, despite the country's brutal political situation. Many of those fleeing Haiti were sent to Guantanamo Bay (where many Cuban refugees were then being held). As Haitians fled in larger numbers and the camps filled to capacity, George H. W. Bush ordered that Haitians intercepted at sea be immediately sent back to Haiti, without offering them legal counsel. There were court challenges to this policy and rulings pro and con amid concern about the plight of the Haitian people. The Clinton administration continued the policy, also encouraging the Haitians not to risk their lives at sea. In 1993 the U.S. Supreme Court upheld the practice of turning the Haitians back, stating that protections offered by the 1952 Immigration and Nationality Act pertain only to those who reach U.S. soil. During the 2004 uprising, President George W. Bush was adamant about not helping those fleeing the Haitian rebellion. Refugee advocates believe this policy effectively ignores the legal and ethical obligation to refugees put forth by international law.[168]

The debate over political or economic refugee status also applies to those coming from Central America. Many blamed the United States for contributing to the political strife in Central America through foreign policies that increased the desire of Central Americans to immigrate to the United States. In 1990, Salvadorans already in the United States were temporarily granted stays of deportation, and their work permits were extended. This occurred after pleas from the Salvadoran president that his country's economy could not incorporate so many returning citizens.

The "sanctuary" movement is another aspect of immigration concerns. Americans involved in the movement provided food, clothing, shelter, and jobs to immigrants from El Salvador and Guatemala fleeing right-wing political movements. Sanctuary workers felt their actions were justified even if they were helping people who entered the country illegally. They believed that these individuals should have been treated as political refugees because they faced grave political oppression and persecution in their homeland. But immigration officials believe that transporting illegal immigrants and related acts violate the law.

Between 1998 and 2002, following the breakup of the former Yugoslavia, nearly 100,000 Bosnians immigrated to the United States. Similarly, after the U.S. involvement in the uprising in Somalia, the U.S. became a sanctuary for those fleeing poverty and oppression in Somalia.[169]

Immigration in a Post–September 11th Environment

Since the September 11, 2001, terrorist attacks, immigration regulations have changed and enforcement has become more stringent. In the past, many immigrants overstayed their visas with little fear of being caught or of severe punishment if caught. Now, thousands of people are being deported for immigration infractions.

After discovering that some of the September 11th terrorists had been admitted as foreign students, new policies were instituted. Students cannot enter the United States until they confirm that they have been accepted to the school they plan to attend. Foreign nationals already in the United States who wish to attend school in the United States must return to their home country before applying for a student visa. The J-visa program, which allowed foreign students attending medical school in the United States to remain in the country after finishing their training if they agreed to practice in an underserved area, was discontinued. New doctors must now return to their home countries for two years following graduation before they can apply to work in the United States.[170]

Some of the terrorists may have entered the United States from Canada. To tighten controls at the northern and southern U.S. borders, the number of border patrol agents was increased and the National Guard dispatched for support. In a "test" case in Florida, police officers were given the right to detain people for immigration violations, a power usually reserved for immigration agents. Immigration advocates fear that if extended to other states, this practice would undermine the civil rights accorded legally admitted immigrants in the United States.[171]

Soon after September 11th, it became clear that immigration authorities did not have good information on the whereabouts of many foreign nationals—those legally residing in the United States and those whose visas had expired. To correct that problem, the U.S. Attorney General implemented a new program in June 2002 called the National Security Entry Exit Registration System (NSEERS), requiring all males aged 15 and older from 25 countries to register with the U.S. government and be fingerprinted, photographed, and questioned. Except for North Korea, all targeted countries were Arab and Muslim, making the program look like another form of racial profiling. The program has been poorly advertised, so many do not know that they are required to register. Failure to register can result in detention and deportation. In December 2002, immigration authorities sponsored a program in Southern California where immigrants could call a number to register, resulting in 700 males from

Arab and Muslim countries being rounded up on minor immigration violations. Many are now too fearful to register. After one year, the Immigration and Naturalization Service (INS) had registered over 83,000 foreign nationals with nearly 14,000 being placed in deportation proceedings; none were publicly charged with terrorism.[172] In March 2003, the INS, located in the Department of Justice, became the U.S. Citizenship and Immigration Services (USCIS) and was moved to the new Department of Homeland Security. A registration system has been added called US-VISIT, which tracks the entry and exit of visitors to the United States holding nonimmigrant visas, regardless of country of origin. This program uses digital, inkless, biometric fingerscans and digital photographs that will be required for new visas. By 2004's end, US-VISIT entry procedures should be in place at 115 airports and 14 seaports.[173]

How Much Immigration?

In 2002, over 1 million immigrants came to the U.S. through legal channels. Most were approved through family ties, while 175,000 were given employment-based visas, and 126,000 were admitted as refugees or asylees.[174] The Border Patrol of the USCIS apprehended 929,000 individuals trying to enter the country illegally at the expansive Mexican-American border in 2002. Most returned to Mexico voluntarily.[175] Many more entered undetected. The USCIS estimates that there are 7 million unauthorized immigrants in the United States, and that 350,000 enter the country each year.[176] Many initially enter legally, but their visas expire and they become undocumented. Since September 11th, the number of deportations has increased significantly. In September 2001, 11,000 were deported, increasing to 17,000 in May 2003, and leveling off to 13,500 in September 2003.[177]

The National Research Council took a close look at the effects of *legal* immigration on the United States.[178] It found that immigration provided an overall economic benefit for the country but with some negative effect on the income of high school dropouts. In the short run and on the average, immigrants used more public services than they paid for in taxes, though the situation varied depending on the immigrant's country of origin. From a macro perspective and in the longrun, there were gains from immigration at the federal level, but losses for states and localities with large immigrant populations. Country of origin also plays a role in determining whether immigrants present an economic cost, as do immigrants' age and education. Those who entered during their working years and had higher levels of education made the greatest economic contributions. But what about *illegal* immigration? Is it helpful or harmful? Undocumented workers are useful to farmers or others who hire them as cheap labor at crucial times. But some believe that undocumented workers drive down wages and take jobs away from legally admitted immigrants and Americans. They object to providing services such as health care to undocumented immigrants and to a 1982 U.S. Supreme Court ruling that guarantees their children a public school education. Others counter that these costs are offset by income and Social Security taxes paid on the wages of those who work because undocumented workers do not gain most of the direct benefits from these taxes; for example, they are not entitled to Social Security or public assistance payments. A Harvard University economist estimated that "by increasing the supply of labor between 1980 and 2000, immigration reduced the average earnings of native-born men by an estimated $1,700 or roughly 4 percent."[179] Although the effects vary by group, he contends that such effects occur whether immigration is legal or illegal, temporary or permanent. Others raise concerns that groups such as African Americans might be hurt the most. These perspectives throw cold water on President George W. Bush's proposal to give temporary visas to large numbers of foreign workers.[180]

Two types of approaches have been used to stem illegal immigration—internal and external. Internal approaches occur within the United States, such as punishing employers who hire undocumented workers and enforcing provisions such as deportation of those who entered illegally. External solutions focus on enforcement at the border to prevent those coming illegally from entering in the first place.

After years of debate, Congress passed the Immigration Reform and Control Act of 1986, incorporating both internal and external approaches. The law's main features were amnesty for some people who had entered the United States illegally, increased enforcement at the border, employer sanctions, and a temporary worker program. Amnesty was the most controversial provision. Under this provision, those who had illegally resided in the United States before 1982, and could prove this, were allowed to remain and obtain citizenship. The irony was that undocumented entrants previously had to hide their residence and were unlikely to have rent receipts or other records to verify their residence. To qualify for amnesty, applicants could not have received welfare (such as AFDC and food stamps) previously and were prohibited from doing so for five years after legalization. The number of people who initially applied for amnesty fell considerably short of official estimates, perhaps due to fear that family and friends who did not qualify for amnesty might be discovered and deported. There was also a substantial fee to apply for amnesty, which might have served as a deterrent, but nearly 3 million people gained citizenship through this provision.[181] A number of Americans balked at amnesty, contending that it unfairly penalized those who had been waiting to enter the United States through legal channels and that it might encourage even more individuals to enter illegally. Some caught without U.S. documents are able to select "voluntary departure" (which can result in fewer legal consequences, and perhaps gives hope of later returning to the U.S.), but today, they are more likely to be detained and deported.

The 1986 law also requires employers to verify that employees are eligible to work in the United States. Violations can result in fines and prison terms if the employer has a pattern of hiring undocumented workers. Some employers have been prosecuted under the law, but many seem to get off lightly. Employers complain that the law unfairly places the burden of proof on them and may cause them to do without needed workers. As a concession to some employers, primarily farmers, the law permits hiring foreign workers when domestic workers are not available. It also contains more liberal rules for agricultural workers who want to remain in the country. The president of the National Council of La Raza said there is no shortage of agricultural workers in the United States and that guest workers desperate for jobs may be vulnerable to abuses by employers.[182] The debate also includes the "high-tech" industries. Employers who claim that the number of work visas should be upped because they cannot find enough qualified Americans face opposition from those who counter that these employees want to bring in foreign workers because they can pay them less than Americans.

In retrospect, few people think that the 1986 law did much to deter illegal immigration. Many people continue to make their way to the United States without legal sanction. The Immigration Act of 1990 increased the number of people entering the country by making it easier for relatives of new immigrants to join them. The *Congressional Quarterly Almanac* called the law "the most sweeping revision of legal-immigration laws in a quarter century."[184] The law reduced favoritism toward immigrants from certain countries and increased the abilities of employers to bring in immigrants with skills such as in science and engineering. It also made it more difficult to ban individuals from entering the country because of their political beliefs, sexual orientation, or health status. Another program, this one with a April 30, 2001, deadline, allowed about 640,000 undocumented individuals to apply for legal resident status if they were sponsored by an employer or a close relative with U.S. citizenship or legal permanent resident status. The U.S. foreign-born population is now 11.5 percent of the country's inhabitants.[183] Figure 11.2 shows their countries of origin. One

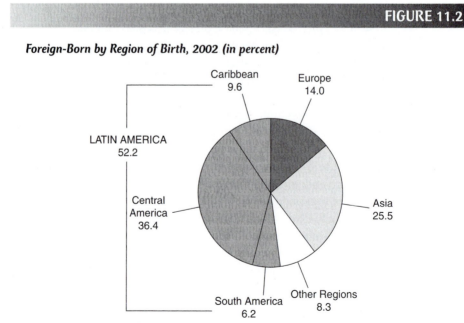

FIGURE 11.2

Foreign-Born by Region of Birth, 2002 (in percent)

Caribbean 9.6

Europe 14.0

LATIN AMERICA 52.2

Central America 36.4

Asia 25.5

South America 6.2

Other Regions 8.3

Source: U.S. Census Bureau, Current Population Survey, March 2002.

FIGURE 11.3

U.S. Citizenship of the Foreign-Born Population by Year of Entry: 2002 (in percent)

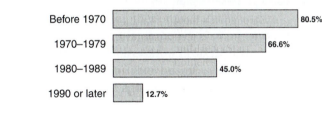

Before 1970	80.5%
1970–1979	66.6%
1980–1989	45.0%
1990 or later	12.7%

Source: U.S. Census Bureau, Current Population Survey, March 2002.

issue that has been raised concerns various aspects of immigrants' assimilation, not only their use of the English language, but also their citizenship rates, which have declined over time (see Figure 11.3).

In 1996, a new Illegal Immigration Act increased border control, and welfare reform legislation made many immigrants ineligible for public assistance benefits. However, the Fourteenth Amendment to the U.S. Constitution adopted in 1868 still entitles anyone born on U.S. soil to citizenship with all the rights and privileges due every American. The Center for Immigration Studies, which recommends less immigration but a "warmer welcome for those admitted," questions whether welfare reform has stemmed immigrants' welfare use.[185] In particular, it reports that Medicaid use has remained substantial, though TANF and food stamp use has declined.

Attempts to count all U.S. residents in the decennial census, including undocumented immigrants, is serious business because seats in the U.S. House of Representatives and the amount of federal funds received by states and communities for various purposes depend on census figures. The census can also affect the very contentious political process of redistricting. Some states with large immigrant populations (California, Florida, Arizona, and Texas) have filed suit against the federal government, claiming that immigrants were undercounted and that state and local budgets are unfairly burdened with providing services to people who enter illegally. During the 2000 census, many appeals were made to Hispanic communities urging people to participate in the census without fear of reprisal and assuring confidentiality for undocumented individuals. Democrats wanted to improve the count of hard-to-reach populations, including immigrants, using statistical sampling for part of the census. The National Academy of Sciences endorsed this approach. Republicans claimed that the method would produce grossly erroneous results and that the Constitution requires a full enumeration, not sampling. In early 1999 the U.S. Supreme Court ruled that an enumeration is necessary for apportioning House seats, the only constitutionally specified purpose of the census. The ruling did not preclude using statistical adjustments for other purposes, but the Census Bureau refused to use the adjustment, citing time constraints. In addition, the Commerce Secretary stripped the Census director and demographers of the power to adjust census estimates.

While the Department of Homeland Security focuses on border security, President George W. Bush's proposal to grant temporary legal status to Mexicans desiring to work in the United States is causing no small groundswell of disapproval. His program would allow immigrants to cross the border legally if a job is waiting for them, and provide a way for undocumented Mexican workers already in the United States to gain legal status. The program would also operate a job website where U.S. jobs would first be made available to U.S. workers, and then to workers in Mexico.[186] In opposition, Representative Tom Tancredo (R-Colorado) has proposed a moratorium on immigration. Tancredo fears that a work program with Mexico would lead to similar programs with other countries, and that such programs would increase competition for American jobs at a time when outsourcing or offshoring of U.S. jobs is on the rise. That is not his only concern. Tancredo contends that too much multiculturalism prevents children from learning American values in the classroom,[187] that minimal immigration should be allowed for work purposes only, and that most immigration visas should be granted to refugees and those seeking asylum (but even those should be limited to 25,000 a year).[188] Immigration policy continues to evolve as Americans adjust in the post–September 11th environment and respond to ever-changing economic conditions.

SUMMARY

Racial and gender inequality continue to manifest themselves in many aspects of American life. Women won the right to vote in 1920, but an Equal Rights Amendment to the U.S. Constitution has eluded them. Only recently have the effects of abuses such as domestic violence and sexual harassment been seriously considered in public policy. Other recent movements to secure equality for women include passage of the Family and Medical Leave Act of 1993. A particularly contentious issue is abortion. The U.S. Supreme Court has upheld the right of women to abortions since its 1973 decision in *Roe v. Wade,* but in recent years abortion rights have been threatened by some court decisions and state and federal legislation that limits access to abortions.

In the last few decades, the rights of gay men and lesbians have made their way to the public policy agenda. Gay men and lesbians have made some progress on the state and local level in gaining equal treatment, and the U.S. Supreme Court finally overturned state sodomy laws. The much watered-down version of a policy allowing gay men and lesbians to serve in the military, and efforts to ban antidiscrimination laws for gay men and lesbians, attest to the deep-seated controversies that remain over the gay rights agenda in this country. Marriage of same-sex couples has not only made its way to the public policy agenda, but Massachusetts began issuing marriage licenses to same-sex couples in May 2004.

Black Americans have faced numerous struggles in their fight for civil rights. Not until 1954 did the Supreme Court strike down the "separate but equal" doctrine by stating that separate public facilities cannot be equal facilities. The Civil Rights Act of 1964 addressed a number of black Americans' concerns, including equal treatment in employment and access to public facilities. Inequality, however, remains an issue, as demonstrated by issues such as racial profiling as well as poverty rates and home-ownership rates.

The vigorous support of civil rights by presidents during the 1960s and 1970s changed during the Reagan and George H. W. Bush administrations. With regard to affirmative action, conservative blacks believe that racial preferences are not war-ranted, and that blacks should focus more on utilizing available educational and economic opportunities. The U.S. Supreme Court has upheld affirmative action as a valid tool for increasing diversity on college campuses but struck down procedures for achieving diversity that relied on point systems.

Hispanic Americans are the fastest-growing ethnic group in the United States. Their political presence at the local and state level is also growing, and they will be an increasingly important political and social force in the years ahead.

Many Native Americans continue to suffer from severe economic and social problems. The Indian Self-Determination and Education Assistance Act of 1975 was an attempt to restore to Native Americans planning power over social welfare issues. The many tribal groups do not speak with one voice, and improvements for them are especially slow in coming. The *Cobell v. Norton* lawsuit is another attempt to return to Native Americans resources that are rightfully theirs.

Conditions in Haiti, Mexico, Russia, China, and other countries add to the number of people who want to live in the United States. The large numbers of people entering this country both legally and illegally has resulted in debate over what appropriate immigration policy should be. Legislation in 1986 granted amnesty to many undocumented immigrants residing in the United States. In 1990 Congress again began permitting an increased number of people to enter the United States. Many immigrants fare quite well, finding jobs and becoming self-sufficient. Those concerned about immigration, however, believe that too many are entering the country to the disadvantage of those already here.

New challenges to civil rights have emerged since the September 11, 2001, terrorist attacks on the World Trade Center and the Pentagon. Civil rights groups continue to file lawsuits and lobby Congress in an effort to reclaim lost civil rights, especially among citizens and noncitizens targeted solely because of national origin or religion. The years to follow will test the U.S. resolve to adhere to the constitutional principles upon which this democracy was built.

NOTES

1. Diana Pearce, "The Feminization of Poverty: Women, Work, and Welfare," *The Urban and Social Change Review* (Special Issue on Women and Work), Vol. 11, pp. 28–36, 1978. Republished in Vol. 4, Women's Studies Yearbook, *Working Women and Families* (Thousand Oaks, CA: Sage, 1979).

2. Social Security Administration (SSA), *SSI Annual Statistical Report, 2002* (Washington, DC: SSA, August 2003), Table 4, p. 20, retrieved February 27, 2004, from http://www.ssa.gov/policy/docs/statcomps/

3. "Fact Sheet: A Statistical Profile of Older Americans Aged 65 +" (Washington, DC: Administration on

Aging, n.d.), retrieved April 6, 2004, from http://www.aoa.gov/press/oam/May_2004/media/factsheets/Statistical%20FS.pdf; see also "Profile of Older Americans" (Jefferson City: Missouri Women's Council, March 2003), retrieved from www.womenscouncil.org

4. Poverty figures are from U.S. Census data, Current Population Survey, March 2001 Supplement, Tables 2 & 22 (Washington, DC, March 2001), retrieved from http://ferret.bls.census.gov/macro/032002/pov/new22_003.htm; http://ferret.bls.census.gov/macro/032002/pov/new02_000.htm

5. See, for example, Barbara J. Nelson, "The Origins of the Two-Channel Welfare State: Workmen's Compensation and Mothers' Aid," in Linda Gordon, Ed., *Women, the State, and Welfare* (Madison: University of Wisconsin Press, 1990), pp. 123–150.

6. U.S. Social Security Administration, *Annual Statistical Supplement, 2003* (Washington, DC, March 2004), Table 6.B3, retrieved April 7, 2004, from http://www.ssa.gov/policy/docs/statcomps/supplement/2003/index.html#toc

7. Social Security Administration, *Women and Social Security* (Washington, DC, October 2003), retrieved April 8, 2004, from http://www.ssa.gov/pressoffice/factsheets/women-alt.htm

8. See U.S. Department of Health, Education and Welfare, *Social Security and the Changing Roles of Men and Women* (Washington, DC: U.S. Government Printing Office, February 1979), Chapters 1 & 2; also see Ekaterina Shirley and Peter Spiegler, *The Benefits of Social Security Privatization for Women,* The Cato Institute, SSP No. 12, July 20, 1998, http://www.cato.org/pubs/ssps/ssp12es.html

9. Social Security Administration, *Income of the Population 55 and Older* (Washington, DC, 2000), retrieved April 8, 2004, from http://www.ssa.gov/policy/docs/statcomps/income_pop55/2000/sect5a.pdf

10. Darcy Ann Olsen, *Women in the So-Called Safety Net* (Washington, DC: Project on Social Security Choice, November 1, 1998), Cato Institute, retrieved April 8, 2004, from http://www.socialsecurity.org/pubs/articles/dao-11-01-98.html

11. Cato Institute/Zogby International, *Polling on Social Security* (Washington, DC, July 7, 2002), retrieved April 8, 2004, from http://www.socialsecurity.org/daily/02-15-01.html

12. *Women Disagree over Private Accounts* (Washington, DC: Cato Institute, April 25, 2002), retrieved April 8, 2004, from http://www.socialsecurity.org/daily/4-25-02.html

13. *Social Security and Women: Some Facts* (Washington, DC: AARP, October 2003), retrieved April 8, 2004, from http://research.aarp.org/econ/fs96_sswom.html

14. Edith U. Fierst, "Privatization of Social Security—A Threat to Women: Part 1," *Womansword,* a newsletter for activists, Vol. 1, Issue 13, February 1997, http://feminist.com/ww9.htm

15. Bureau of Labor Statistics, *Highlights of Women's Earnings in 2002* (Washington, DC: U.S. Department of Labor, September 2003), retrieved April 8, 2004, from http://www.bls.gov/cps/cpswom2002.pdf

16. U.S. Census Bureau, *Statistical Abstracts of the United States, 2003* (Washington, DC, 2003), Table No. 66, retrieved April 9, 2004, from http://www.census.gov/prod/2004pubs/03statab/pop.pdf

17. Information about women in the workforce relies on Marisa DiNatale and Stephanie Boraas, "The Labor Force Experience of Women from 'Generation X,'" *Monthly Labor Review,* March 2002, pp. 3–15; Mahshid Jalilvand, "Married Women, Work and Values," *Monthly Labor Review,* August 2000, pp. 26–31; U.S. Department of Labor, Bureau of Labor Statistics, *Highlights of Women's Earnings in 2002;* U.S. Census Bureau, *Current Population Survey, Annual Demographic Supplements, Historical Income Table—People* (Washington, DC), Tables P-36, P-36a, P-36b, P-36c, P-36d, retrieved from http://www.census.gov/hhes/income/histinc/incperdet.html; and U.S. Bureau of the Census, *Current Population Survey, 2003 Annual Social and Economic Supplement,* retrieved from http://ferret.bls.census.gov/macro/032003/perinc/new06_019.htm

18. Women's Bureau, *What Is Women's Labor Force Participation Rate?* (Washington, DC: U.S. Department of Labor, 2003), retrieved April 9, 2004, from http://www.dol.gov/wb/faq38.htm

19. U.S. Census Bureau, "Women's History Month: March 1–31," February 19, 2002, retrieved September 1, 2002, from http://www.census.gov/press-release/www/2002/cb02ff03.html

20. DiNatale and Boraas, "The Labor Force Experience of Women from 'Generation X.'"

21. See M. Anne Hill and Mark R. Killingsworth, Eds., *Comparable Worth: Analyses and Evidence* (Ithaca, NY: ILR Press, New York State School of Industrial and Labor Relations, Cornell University, 1989); Elaine Sorensen, *Comparable Worth: Is It a Worthy Policy?* (Princeton, NJ: Princeton University Press, 1994).

22. Some of this paragraph relies on Jill Johnson Keeney, "Not a Crazy Proposal," *Louisville Times,* 1984, reprinted in the *Office Professional,* Vol. 5, No. 2, February 15, 1985, p. 7.

23. Information on comparative worth policy trends is from Employment Policy Foundation, *Background on Comparable Worth* (Washington, DC, 2000), retrieved from http://www.epf.org/research/newsletters/2000/compworth.asp; Mackinac Center for Public Policy, *The Fallacy of Comparable Worth* (Midland,

MI, 1989), retrieved from http://www.mackinac.org/article.asp?ID = 213; National Committee on Pay Equity, *Two Progressive Models on Pay Equity: Minnesota and Ontario* (Washington, DC), retrieved from http://www.pay-equity.org/; National Committee on Pay Equity, "Long and Winding Road to Equal Pay: National Summary Table"(Washington, DC: AFL-CIO Public Policy Department, n.d.), retrieved August 3, 2004, from http://www.google.com and www.aflcio.org

24. Americans for a Fair Chance, "The History of Affirmative Action Policies," *In Motion* (Washington, DC: August 7, 2003), retrieved April 13, 2004, from http://www.inmotionmagazine.com

25. Angie Cannon, "Women Are Holding Historically High Rank in New White House," *Austin American-Statesman,* October 2, 1993, p. A8.

26. Information in this section about women in government is from Center for American Women and Politics (CAWP), National Information Bank on Women in Public Office, Eagleton Institute of Politics, Rutgers University, and Susan J. Carroll, "Women in State Government: Historical Overview and Current Trends," in *The Book of the States* (Lexington, KY: Council of State Governments, 2004).

27. Chris Lombardi, "Equal Rights Amendment Introduced in Congress" (Washington, DC: National Organization for Women, April 10, 2001), *eNews,* retrieved April 14, 2004, from http://www.now.org/eNews/april2001/041001era.html

28. National Organization for Women, "ERA Ratification Status Summary," in ERA *Countdown Campaign* (Washington, DC: NOW, 1981), p. A.

29. As quoted in Chris Lombardi, "Equal Rights Amendment Introduced in Congress."

30. Sharon K. Long and Sandra J. Clark, *The New Child Care Block Grant: State Funding Choices and Their Implications* (Washington, DC: The Urban Institute, 1997), quote from p. 4.

31. "Child Care in Trouble," *New York Times,* retrieved April 10, 2004, from http://nytimes.com

32. Robert Rector (The Heritage Foundation), "Give Parents Who Stay at Home an Even Break," *Austin American-Statesman,* January 30, 1998, p. A15.

33. National Organization for Women, *Women's Rights Advocates Decry Bush's Family Leave Decision* (Washington, DC: December 9, 2002), retrieved April 15, 2004, from http://www.now.org/issues/family/120902ui.html

34. Ellen Goodman *(Boston Globe),* "Helping Families, but Just Barely," *Austin American-Statesman,* November 16, 1999, pp. A11, A36.

35. "California Paid Family Leave" (Berkeley, CA: Labor Project for Working Families, 2004), retrieved August 4, 2004, from http://www.paidfamilyleave.org/law.html

36. Bob Keefe, "California OKs Paid Leave for Baby, Sick Care," *Austin American-Statesman,* September 24, 2002, p. A6; see also Steven K. Wisensale, *Family Leave Policy: The Political Economy of Work and Family in America* (Armork, NY: M. E. Sharpe, 2001).

37. International Labour Organization, 1998 Press Releases, "More Than 120 Nations Provide Paid Maternity Leave," February 16, 1998, retrieved from http://www.ilo.org/public/english/235 press/pr/1998/7.htm; see also Kirstin Downey Grimsley *(The Washington Post),* "Report: U.S. Lags on Benefits for Maternity," *Austin American-Statesman,* February 16, 1998, pp. A1, 5; "Social Work in the Public Eye," *NASW News,* newsletter of the National Association of Social Workers, April 1998, p. 13. For a comparison of family leave policies, see Wisensale, *Family Leave Policy.*

38. *Code of Federal Regulations,* Vol. 29, Sec. 1604.11.

39. For more on sexual assault and the military, see Terri Spahr Nelson, *For Love of Country: Confronting Rape and Sexual Assault in the U.S. Military* (Binghamton, NY: Haworth Maltreatment and Trauma Press, 2002).

40. Louis Obdyke, "Small Business Q & A: What Is the Definition of Sexual Harassment?" *Austin American-Statesman,* September 10, 1997, p. D2.

41. Camille Paglia, "A Call for Lustiness: Just Say No to the Sex Police," *Time,* March 23, 1998, p. 54.

42. See Joan Biskupic, "Court Draws Line on Harassment," *Washington Post,* June 27, 1998, p. A1.

43. "Colorado Ex-Kicker Says She Was Raped," CNN.com, February 18, 2004, retrieved from http://www.cnn.com/2004/US/Central/02/17/colorado.kicker.rape.ap/; see also "Football Coach Defends Colorado Program," *Firstcoastnews.com,* retrieved February 18, 2004, from http://www.firstcoastnews.com

44. Karen Tumulty, "White House May Delay Abortion-Funding Order," *Austin American-Statesman,* December 5, 1993, p. A2.

45. Abortion figures are from U.S. Bureau of the Census, *Statistical Abstract of the United States: 1992,* (Washington, DC: U.S. Government Printing Office, 1992), pp. 74–75; "Abortion Surveillance, 2000," Centers for Disease Control and Prevention, December 10, 2003, retrieved from http://www.cdc.gov/reproductive health/surv_abort00.htm

46. "1995 Abortion Rate Hits Lowest Level in 20 Years," *Austin American-Statesman,* December 5, 1997, p. A8; Barbara Vobejda, "Proportion of Unintended Pregnancies Declines Significantly since Late 1980s," *The Washington Post,* January 18, 1998, p. A25.

47. Rene Sanchez *(Washington Post),* "Court: Anti-abortion Web Site Protected by First Amendment," *Austin American-Statesman,* March 29, 2001, p. A7.

48. Frederick Clarkson, "New Version of Nuremberg Files Yanked off Web," *Women's eNews,* December 15, 2003, retrieved May 3, 2004, from http://www/womensenews.org/article/cfm/dyn/aid/1627

49. "Anti-abortion Activists Using Covert Tactics Against Clinics," *Austin American-Statesman,* May 31, 2002, p. A8.

50. Information on the proposed Freedom of Choice Act relies on Library of Congress, "Thomas: Legislative Information on the Internet," retrieved from http://thomas.loc.gov

51. NARAL Pro-Choice America Foundation and NARAL Pro-Choice America, *Who Decides? A State-by-State Report on the Status of Women's Reproductive Rights,* 13th ed., 2004, retrieved from http://www.naral.org/yourstate/whodecides/trends/index.cfm; Americans United for Life, *2003 State Legislative Session Report* (Chicago: August 11, 2003), retrieved from http://www.unitedforlife.org/misc_files/2003_session_update.pdf

52. Sheryl Gay Stolberg *(New York Times),* "3 Lawsuits Seek to Stop Abortion Bill," *Austin American-Statesman,* November 1, 2003, p. A6.

53. Ellen Goodman *(Boston Globe),* "Men Making Abortion Policy Show True Colors in Photo," *Austin American-Statesman,* November 13, 2003, p. A15.

54. NARAL Pro-Choice America Foundation and NARAL Pro-Choice America, *Who Decides? A State-by-State Report on the Status of Women's Reproductive Rights.*

55. Barbara Boxer, *News from U.S. Senator Barbara Boxer* (Washington, DC, January 22, 2004).

56. Joanne Jacobs *(San Jose Mercury News),* "FDA Proposal Will Discourage Use of RU-486," *Austin American-Statesman,* June 14, 2000, p. A15.

57. Patricia Tjaden and Nancy Thoennes, *Findings from the National Violence Against Women Survey* (Washington, DC: National Institute of Justice, July 2000), retrieved April 16, 2004, from http://www.ojp.usdoj.gov/nij/pubs-sum/181867.htm

58. U.S. Commission on Civil Rights, *The Federal Response in Domestic Violence* (Washington, DC: U.S. Government Printing Office, January 1982), pp. iv–v; see also Anne Sparks, "Feminists Negotiate the Executive Branch: The Policing of Male Violence," in Cynthia R. Daniels, Ed., *Feminists Negotiate the State: The Politics of Domestic Violence* (Lanham, MD: University Press of America, 1997), pp. 35–52.

59. Lisa G. Lerman, "Legal Help for Battered Women," in Joseph J. Costa, Ed., *Abuse of Women: Legislation, Reporting, and Prevention* (Lexington, MA: Lexington Books, 1983), p. 29.

60. *Family Violence: The Battered Woman* (Austin: League of Women Voters of Texas Education Fund, 1987), p. 33.

61. Ashley Peterson, "TCFV Prepares for Upcoming Legislative Session," *The River* (newsletter of the Texas Council on Family Violence), Fall/Winter 2000–2001, p. 1.

62. Sarah Kershaw, "Digital Photos Give the Police a New Edge in Abuse Cases," *New York Times,* September 3, 2002, retrieved September 3, 2002, from http://www.nytimes.com

63. Victoria L. Holt, Mary A. Kernic, Thomas Lumley, Marsha E. Wolf, and Frederick R. Rivara, "Civil Protection Orders and Risk of Subsequent Police-Reported Violence," *Journal of the American Medical Association,* Vol. 228, 2002, pp. 589–594.

64. Office on Violence Against Women, *The Violence Against Women Act of 2000 Summary* (Washington, DC, April 3, 2001), retrieved April 17, 2004, from http://www.ojp.usdoj.gov/vawo/regulations.htm

65. U.S. Department of Justice, *Justice Department to Spearhead President's Family Justice Center Initiative to Better Serve Domestic Violence Victims* (Washington, DC, October 8, 2003), retrieved April 17, 2004, from http://www.ojp.usdoj.gov/pressreleases/OVW03164.htm

66. San Diego Family Justice Center, *2003 Annual Report,* retrieved April 17, 2004, from http://genesis.sannet.gov/infospc/templates/attorney/index.jsp

67. National Organization for Women, *Action Alert: Support Survivors of Domestic and Sexual Assault!* (Washington, DC, November 6, 2003), retrieved April 17, 2004, from http://www.capwiz.com/now/mail/oneclick_compose/?alertid=4014006

68. For more information on these and other legal cases, see Arthur S. Leonard, *Sexuality and the Law: An Encyclopedia of Major Legal Cases* (Hamden, CT: Garland, 1993). William N. Eskridge, Jr., and Nan D. Hunter, *Sexuality, Gender and the Law,* 2nd ed. (University Casebook Series ®) (Eagan, MN: West Publishing, 2003).

69. Ruth Harlow, "Kentucky Ruling a Milestone in Struggle for Gay Rights," *Civil Liberties,* Winter 1992–93, pp. 1, 11.

70. See Supreme Court of the United States, *Lawrence v. Texas* (Washington, DC: June 26, 2003), No. 02-102, retrieved April 18, 2004, from http://a257.g.akamaitech.net/7/257/2422/26jun20031200/www.supremecourtus.gov/opinions/02pdf/02-102.pdf; see also *Planned Parenthood of Southeastern Pa. v. Casey,* 505 U.S. 833, 850 (1992) and *Romer v. Evans,* 517 U.S. 620 (1996).

71. "High Court Affirms Gays' Civil Rights" (New York Times), *Austin American-Statesman*, May 21, 1996, pp. A1 & 7.

72. American Civil Liberties Union, "Maine Becomes 10th State with Gay Civil Rights Law, New Hampshire Will Lock Up New England," May 16, 1997, retrieved from http://www.aclu.org/news/n051697a.html

73. *Equality in the States: Gay, Lesbian, Bisexual and Transgender Americans and State Laws and Legislation in 2004* (Washington, DC: Human Rights Campaign, March 2004), retrieved August 3, 2004, from http://www.hrc.org; *States, Counties, Cities, and Towns with Anti-Discrimination Laws Based on Sexual Orientation* (Preble, OH: Gay Rights Info, March 11, 2004), retrieved April 18, 2004, from http://www.actwin.com/eatonohio/gay/GAY.htm; see also Library of Congress, *Legislative Information on the Internet,* H. R. 3285 and S.1705, 108th Congress, retrieved April 18, 2004, from http://thomas.loc.gov

74. *Ibid.*

75. *States, Counties, Cities, and Towns with Some Type of Benefit or Recognition to Domestic Partners for Homosexuals* (Preble, OH: Gay Rights Info, April 10, 2004), retrieved April 18, 2004, from http://www.actwin.com/eatonohio/gay/GAY.htm

76. Human Rights Campaign, *The State of the Workplace, 2002* (July 1, 2003), retrieved April 18, 2004, from http://www.hrc.org/Template.cfm?Section = Search&template = /Search/SearchDisplay.cfm

77. American Civil Liberties Union, *Fact Sheet: Overview of Lesbian and Gay Parenting, Adoption and Foster Care* (New York, April 6, 1999), retrieved April 18, 2004, from http://www.aclu.org/LesbianGayRights/LesbianGayRights.cfm?ID = 9212&c = 104

78. Human Rights Campaign, *Equality in the States: Gay, Lesbian, Bisexual, and Transgender Americans and State Laws and Legislation in 2004;* States that Prohibit Homosexuals from Adopting Children (Preble, OH: Gay Rights Info, March 11, 2004), retrieved April 18, 2004, from http://www.actwin.com/eatonohio/gay/GAY.htm

79. Randy Thomasson, "Questions and Answers: The California Defense of Marriage Act," *Capitol Resource Backgrounder,* July 1998, retrieved from http://www.capitolresource.org/b_doma.htm

80. Information in this section on the Vermont and Massachusetts Supreme Court cases is drawn from the following sources: Joanna Grossman, "How Same-Sex Marriage Became Legal in Massachusetts: The State's Supreme Court Rebukes Its Legislature's Attempt to 'Circumvent' the Court's Decision," *FindLaw's Legal Commentary,* February 6, 2004, retrieved April 17, 2004, from http://writ.findlaw.com/grossman/20040206.html; see also *Goodridge et al. v. Department of Public Health,* Massachusetts Supreme Court (March 9, 2004), retrieved April 19, 2004, from http://www.mass.gov/courts/courtsandjudges/courts/supremejudicialcourt/goodridge.html; *Baker v. State,* Vermont Supreme Court, retrieved August 5, 2004, from http://www.findlaw.om/11Stategov/vt/vta.html

81. Information on California and San Francisco same-sex marriage is from Joanna Grossman, "San Francisco Takes Center Stage by Permitting Gay Couples to Marry: The Legal Questions the City's Actions Raise," *FindLaw's Legal Commentary,* February 24, 2004, retrieved April 17, 2004, from http://writ.news.findlaw.com/scripts/printer_friendly.pl?page = /grossman/20040224.html; California Supreme Court, "San Francisco Marriage Cases," retrieved April 19, 2004, from http://www.courtinfo.ca.gov/courts/supreme/

82. Joanna Grossman, "Are Bans on Same-Sex Marriage Constitutional? New Jersey Says Yes, but Massachusetts, in a Landmark Decision, Says No," *FindLaw's Legal Commentary,* November 20, 2003, retrieved April 17, 2004, from http://writ.news.findlaw.com/scripts/printer_friendly.pl?page = /grossman/20031120.html

83. Anthony J. Sebok, "What Gay Couples Lack—Besides Marriage: The Crucial Rights under Tort Law that Only Spouses Can Assert," *FindLaw's Legal Commentary,* April 9, 2004, retrieved April 17, 2004, from http://writ.news.findlaw.com/scripts/printer_friendly.pl?page = /sebok/20040409.html

84. Human Rights Campaign, *Equality in the States: Gay, Lesbian, Bisexual, and Transgender Americans and State Laws and Legislation in 2004.*

85. "Federal Marriage Amendment—S. J. Res. 30," Library of Congress, *THOMAS: Legislative Information on the Internet* (Washington, DC: March 22, 2004), retrieved August 4, 2004, from http://thomas.loc.gov

86. "Bush Calls for Ban on Same-Sex Marriages" (Washington, DC: CNN.com, February 25, 2004), retrieved April 17, 2004, from http://www.cnn.com/2004/ALLPOLITICS/02/24/elec04.prez.bush.marriage/index.html

87. Michelle M. Benecke, cited in "Challenges to Old Gay Ban Spark Questions on Military's New Policy," *Miami Herald,* December 19, 1993, p. 7A; this paragraph also relies on "Clinton: Let Military Bar Gay Conduct," *Miami Herald,* July 17, 1993, p. 11A; "Pentagon Outlines Revised Conduct Code for Gays in Military," *Miami Herald,* December 23, 1993, p. 4A; Steven Lee Myers *(New York Times),* "More Gays Forced Out of Service Than before 'Don't Ask,' " *Austin American-Statesman,* January 23, 1999, p. A21.

88. "Military Ousters for Homosexuality Hit 14 Year High," *Orange County Register,* March 15, 2002, p. News 15.

89. See American Civil Liberties Union, "Court Upholds 'Don't Ask, Don't Tell,' " retrieved September 8, 1997, from http://www.aclu.org/news/w090897a.html; Neil A. Lewis *(New York Times),* "Court Upholds Military Policy of 'Don't Ask, Don't Tell' for Gays," *Austin American-Statesman,* April 6, 1996, p. 6.

90. Unless otherwise noted, the information in this section on gay, lesbian, bisexual, and transgender youth relies on Jason Cianciotto and Sean Cahill, *Education Policy: Issues Affecting Lesbian, Gay, Bisexual, and*

Transgender Youth (Washington, DC: National Gay and Lesbian Task Force Policy Institute, 2003), retrieved April 19, 2004, from http://www.thetaskforce.org/downloads/EducationPolicy.pdf; "Lesbian, Gay, Bisexual and Transgender Youth Issues," *SIECUS Report,* Vol. 29, No. 4, April/May 2001, retrieved April 19, 2004, from file://C:\DOCUME ~ 1\Owner\LOCALS ~ 1\Temp\EKOBW5X9.htm; "Doing the Math: What the Numbers Say about Harassment of Gay, Lesbian, Bisexual, and Transgendered Students" (Washington, DC: American Civil Liberties Union, April 5, 2001), retrieved April 19, 2004, from http://www.aclu.org/LesbianGayRights/LesbianGayRights.cfm?ID = 10091&c = 106; "LGBT Students Are Five Times More Likely than Their Peers to Skip School out of Fear for Their Own Safety. What Are You Going to Do about It?" (Washington, DC: American Civil Liberties Union, April 5, 2001), retrieved from http://www.aclu.org/LesbianGayRights/LesbianGayRightslist.cfm?c = 106; "Settlement Fact Sheet: *Flores v. Morgan Hill Unified School District*" (Washington, DC: American Civil Liberties Union, January 6, 2004), retrieved April 20, 2004, from http://www.aclu.org/LesbianGayRights/LesbianGayRights.cfm?ID = 14658&c = 106; "District Will Allow Club to Meet and Will Provide Anti-Harassment Training for Students and Staff" (Washington, DC: American Civil Liberties Union, February 3, 2004), retrieved April 20, 2004, from http://www.aclu.org/LesbianGayRights/LesbianGayRights.cfm?ID = 14856&c = 106

91. Jeff Stryker, "The Gay Team," *Austin American-Statesman,* June 8, 1996, p. A13.

92. "Federal Appeals Court Strikes Down Alabama Law Barring Gay Student Groups from Campus," *American Civil Liberties Freedom Network,* April 30, 1997, retrieved from http://www.aclu.org/news/n043097e.html

93. For detailed information on the harassment GLBT students endured for years before suing in this case, see "Case Background: *Flores v. Morgan Hill Unified School District,*" ACLU, January 6, 2004, retrieved from http://www.aclu.org/LesbianGayRights/LesbianGayrights.cfm?ID = 14659&c = 106

94. For a consideration of social policies and people of color, see King E. Davis and Tricia B. Bent-Goodley, Eds., *The Color of Social Policy* (Alexandria, VA: Council on Social Work Education, 2004).

95. U.S. Department of Health and Human Services, Office of Families and Children, *Temporary Assistance to Needy Families, Fifth Annual Report to Congress* (Washington, DC, February, 2003), retrieved April 22, 2004, from http://www.acf.hhs.gov/programs/ofa/annualreport5/index.htm; Committee on Ways and Means, U.S. House of Representatives, *2004 Green Book,* "Supplemental Security Income (SSI)," pp. 3–39, retrieved May 10, 2004, from http://waysandmeans.house.gov/documents.asp?section = 813

96. Martin Giles, "'Race Coding' and White Opposition to Welfare," *American Political Science Review,* Vol. 90, No. 3, 1996, pp. 593–604.

97. Gary Orfield, Susan E. Eaton, and the Harvard Project on School Desegregation, *Dismantling Desegregation: The Quiet Reversal of* Brown v. Board of Education (New York: New Press, 1995); Michael Dobbs *(The Washington Post),* "School Segregation Has Slipped Back to 1969 Levels, Study Finds," *Austin American-Statesman,* January 18, 2004.

98. Attitudes of black and white parents towards desegregation, busing, and related issues are found in *Time to Move on: African American and White Parents Set an Agenda for Schools,* April 1998, Public Agenda Online, retrieved from http://www.public agenda.org/moveon/moveon.html

99. See "With Fairness in Education for All," *Civil Liberties,* November 1997, pp. 1, 2.

100. *"CFE v. State of New York:* Summary of Court Decision" (New York: Campaign for Fiscal Equity, June 2003), retrieved April 22, 2004, from http://www.cfequity.org/

101. American Civil Liberties Union, *Williams v. State of California, Court Brief* (Sacramento, CA: May 17, 2000), retrieved April 22, 2004, from http://www.aclunc.org/students/williams-brief.htm

102. Nanette Asimov, "Bitter Battle over Class Standards: State Spends Millions to Defeat Student Suit," *San Francisco Chronicle,* May 5, 2003, retrieved April 22, 2004, from http://www.sfgate.com/cgi-bin/article.cgi?file = /chronicle/archive/2003/05/05/MN102341.DTL

103. The remainder of this paragraph relies on Chester W. Hartman, *Housing and Social Policy* (Englewood Cliffs, NJ: Prentice Hall, 1975), pp. 136, 139.

104. Joint Center for Housing Studies, *Harvard Study Finds That Unequal Access to Home Mortgages Persist in Rapidly Changing Marketplace* (Cambridge, MA: Harvard University, March 5, 2004), press release, retrieved April 22, 2004, from http://www.jchs.harvard.edu/media/ccc_release_3-5-04.htm

105. U.S. Census Bureau, *Housing Vacancies and Homeownership Annual Statistics: 2003* (Washington, DC, 2003), Table 20, retrieved April 22, 2004, from http://www.census.gov/hhes/www/housing/hvs/annual03/ann03t20.html

106. Douglas S. Massey and Nancy A. Denton, "Suburbanization and Segregation in U.S. Metropolitan Areas," *American Journal of Sociology,* Vol. 94, No. 3, 1988, pp. 592–626.

107. U.S. Census Bureau, *Housing Patterns* (Washington, DC: May 7, 2003), retrieved April 23, 2004, from http://www.census.gov/hhes/www/housing/resseg/ch1.html

108. Douglas S. Massey and Nancy A. Denton, *American Apartheid: Segregation and the Making of the Underclass* (Cambridge, MA: Harvard University Press, 1993).

109. Lawyers' Committee for Better Housing, *Locked Out: Barriers to Choice for Housing Voucher Holders* (Chicago, 2001), retrieved April 23, 2004, from http://www.lcbh.org/images/hdvoucher.pdf; see also Douglas S. Massey and Nancy A. Denton, *American Apartheid: Segregation and the Making of the Underclass.*

110. Testimony of Philip Tegeler, Legal Director Connecticut Civil Liberties Union, on *Fighting Discrimination against the Disabled and Minorities through Fair Housing Enforcement* before the Oversight and Investigations Subcommittee and Housing and Community Opportunity Subcommittee of the House of Representatives Committee on Financial Services (Washington, DC, June 25, 2002), retrieved April 22, 2004, from http://www.aclu.org/news/NewsPrint.cfm?ID = 10472& c = 151; "HUD's Fair Housing Duties and the Loss of Public and Assisted Housing" (National Housing Law Project), *Housing Law Bulletin*, retrieved April 23, 2004, from http://www.nhlp.org/html/hlb/199/199fairhsg.htm

111. This paragraph relies on testimony of Philip Tegeler on *Fighting Discrimination against the Disabled and Minorities.*

112. "ACLU Wins Appeal in Public Housing Desegregation, Suit" (Washington, DC, July 14, 2000), press release, retrieved April 22, 2004, from http://aclu.org/news/NewsPOrint.cfm?ID = 8036&c = 151

113. Millennial Commission on Housing, *Meeting Our Nation's Housing Challenges*, Report to Congress (Washington, DC, May 30, 2002), retrieved April 23, 2004, from http://www.mhc.gov/MHCReport.pdf

114. *Federal Policies on Remedies Concerning Equal Employment Opportunity in State and Local Government Personnel Systems*, March 23, 1973, cited in Felix A. Nigro and Lloyd G. Nigro, *The New Public Personnel Administration* (Itasca, IL: Peacock, 1976), p. 21.

115. See Frank Trippet, "A Solid Yes to Affirmative Action," *Time*, July 14, 1986, p. 22.

116. Michael de Courcy Hinds, "Minority Firms Reeling from Ruling on Set-Aside Programs," *Austin American-Statesman*, December 25, 1991, pp. A27, 31.

117. For a summary of reductions in litigation, see D. Lee Bawden and John L. Palmer, "Social Policy, Challenging the Welfare State," in John L. Palmer and Isabel V. Sawhill, Eds., *The Reagan Record* (Cambridge, MA: Ballinger, 1984), pp. 204–206.

118. From an undated letter to ACLU members from Ira Glasser, executive director of the American Civil Liberties Union, 132 West 43rd St., New York, NY 10036-6599.

119. Bob Dart, "Education Department Unveils New Minority Scholarship Policy," *Austin American-Statesman*, December 15, 1992, p. A2; see also Karen Dewitt, "Education Chief Backs Minority Scholarships," *New York Times*, March 19, 1993, p. A15.

120. Unless otherwise noted, information in the remainder of this section relies on *Hopwood et al. v. State of Texas et al.*, U.S. Court of Appeals for the Fifth Circuit, No. 94-50569, retrieved April 24, 2004, from http://www.ca5.uscourts.gov/opinions/pub/94/94-50569-CV0.htm; U.S. Commission on Civil Rights Papers and Press Releases, *Toward an Understanding of Percentage Plans in Higher Education: Are They Effective Substitutes for Affirmative Action?* (2000); *Beyond Percentage Plans: The Challenge of Equal Opportunity in Higher Education* (2002); *The U.S. Department of Education's Race-Neutral Alternatives in Postsecondary Education: Innovative Approaches to Diversity—Are they Viable Substitutes for Affirmative Action?* (May 2003); *The Supreme Court Revisits Affirmative Action: Will Grutter and Gratz Mean the End of Bakke?* (April 2003); *U.S. Commission on Civil Rights Staff Report Concludes Percentage Plans Fail to Improve Diversity in Higher Ed* (Washington, DC, November 20, 2002), retrieved April 24, 2004, from http://www.usccr.gov; Michael C. Dorf, "The University of Georgia Affirmative Action Ruling Poses a Fundamental Question: What Is Binding Precedent?", *FindLaw's Legal Commentary*, September 5, 2001, retrieved April 13, 2004, from http://writ.news.findlaw.com/scripts/printer_friendly.pl?page = /dorf/20010905.html; Greg Winter, "After Ruling, 3 Universities Maintain Diversity of Admissions," *New York Times*, April 13, 2004, retrieved April 13, 2004, from http://www.nytimes.com; The Center for Individual Rights Papers, *Hopwood v. Texas* (November 25, 2002); *Chronology of the University of Michigan Cases* (April 2003); *Federal Appeals Court Hears Affirmative Action Suit against U. Washington* (February 14, 2004), retrieved April 13, 2004, from http://www.cir-usa.org; "Judge Rules against Affirmative Action Petition," *CNN.com*, March 27, 2004, retrieved April 13, 2004, from www.cnn.com; Melissa Charbonneau, "'One Florida' Aims for Diversity without Discrimination," (Tallahassee: MyFlorida.com, May 24, 2000), retrieved April 13, 2004, from http://www.oneflorida.org/myflorida/government/governorinitiatives/one_florida/articles; Americans for a Fair Chance, "The History of Affirmative Action Policies," *In Motion*, October 12, 2003, retrieved April 13, 2004, from http://www.inmotionmagazine.com/aahist.html

121. *U.S. Commission on Civil Rights Staff Report Concludes Percentage Plans Fail to Improve Diversity in Higher Ed.*

122. See *Grutter v. Bollinger et al.*, No. 02-241 and *Gratz et al. v. Bollinger et al.*, No. 02-516 (June 23, 2003), Supreme Court of the United States, retrieved

April 25, 2004, from http://www.supremecourtus.gov/opinions/02slipopinion.html

123. Glenn C. Loury, "The Moral Quandary of the Black Community," *Public Interest,* No. 79, Spring 1985, pp. 9–22; see also A. Phillips Brooks, "New Black Leaders Shifting from Traditional Civil Rights," *Austin American-Statesman,* November 10, 1993, pp. A10, 12. Loury has since modified his position; see Jenny Attiyeh, "Black Scholar Renounces Conservative 'Crown,' " *Christian Science Monitor,* September 5, 2002; retrieved August 5, 2004, from http://www.csmonitor.com/2002/0905/p18s01-ussc.html

124. Thomas Sowell, "How Dare Liberals Lecture Cosby on Blacks," *Austin America-Statesman,* July 14, 2004, p. A11.

125. Jim Sleeper, *Liberal Racism* (New York: Viking, 1997), p. 182.

126. Peter Dreier, "There's No Racial Justice without Economic Justice," in Chester Hartman, Ed., *Challenges to Equality: Poverty and Race in America* (New York: M. E. Sharpe, 2001), pp. 270–273.

127. David A. Bositis, *Black Elected Officials: A Statistical Summary 2000* (Washington, DC: Joint Center for Political and Economic Studies, 2002); and U.S. Census Bureau, *Statistical Abstracts of the United States, 2003,* Tables No. 417, 418, p. 268, retrieved August 4, 2004, from http://www.census.gov/statab/www/

128. "Minorities and Women in the 108th Congress," Infoplease, retrieved May 5, 2004, from http://www.infoplease.complipa/A0878575.html

129. U.S. Census Bureau, "U.S. Interim Projections by Age, Sex, Race, and Hispanic Origin," Table 1a, retrieved April 25, 2004, from http://www.census.gov/ipc/www/usinterimproj/

130. Adam Nagourney and Janet Elder *(New York Times),* "Hispanics Praise Democrats and Bush," *Austin American-Statesman,* August 3, 2003, p. A6.

131. U.S. Commission on Civil Rights, "Voting Irregularities in Florida during the 2000 Presidential Election" (Washington, DC, June 2001), retrieved April 25, 2004, from http://www.usccr.gov/pubs/vote2000/report/main.htm

132. The remainder of this paragraph relies on "Bad New Days for Voting Rights," *New York Times,* April 18, 2004, retrieved April 18, 2004, from http://www.nytimes.com/2004/04/18/opinions/18sun1.html

133. Election Reform Information Project, *Election Reform 2004: What's Changed, What Hasn't, and Why* (Washington, DC: Electionline.org, October 2001), retrieved April 25, 2004, from http://www.electionline.org/index.jsp?page=Search%20Results

134. "Making Votes Count: A Compromised Voting System," *New York Times,* April 24, 2004, retrieved April 24, 2004, from http://www.nytimes.com/2004/

04/24/opinion/24SAT1.html; Adam Cohen, "The Results Are in and the Winner Is . . . or Maybe Not," *New York Times,* February 29, 2004, retrieved February 20, 2004, from http://www.nytimes.com/2004/02/29/opinion/29SUN3.html

135. Julie Carr Smyth, "Voting Machine Controversy," *Cleveland Plain Dealer,* August 28, 2004, retrieved August 4, 2004, from http://www.commondreams.org/headlines03/0828-08.htm

136. Gerald Thomas Wilkinson, "On Assisting Indian People," *Social Casework,* Vol. 61, No. 8, 1980, pp. 451–454.

137. Michael P. Shea, "Indians Skeptical of Report Urging Program Overhaul," *Congressional Quarterly,* Vol. 48, No. 2, 1990, pp. 98–100.

138. U.S. Department of the Interior, Bureau of Indian Affairs, retrieved April 25, 2004, from http://www.doi.gov/bureaus.html

139. Joseph J. Westermeyer, "Indian Powerlessness in Minnesota," *Society,* Vol. 10, No. 3, March–April 1973, pp. 45–47, 50–52; see also Walz and Gary Askerooth, *The Upside Down Welfare State* (Minneapolis: Elwood, 1973), p. 31.

140. Bureau of Indian Affairs, retrieved April 25, 2004, from http://www.doiu.nbc.gov/orientation/bia2.cfm.

141. Thomas H. Walz and Askerooth, *The Upside Down Welfare State,* p. 25.

142. Chuck Cook, "BIA Ordered to Prepare for Inquiry," *Arizona Republic,* October 16, 1987, pp. A1, 5.

143. Chuck Cook, Mike Masterson, and M. N. Trahant, "Indians Are Sold Out by the U.S.," *Arizona Republic,* October 4, 1987, pp. A1, 18, 20.

144. Bureau of Indian Affairs, "Vision Statement," retrieved April 2, 1997, from http://www.doi.gov/bia/mission.html

145. "The Indian Trust Fund Lawsuit-101," U.S. House of Representatives, Committee on Resources, retrieved May 6, 2004, from http://resourcescommittee.house.gov/issues/naia/trustfund101.htm

146. Elouise Cobell, "The Cobell Lawsuit and Your Individual Trust Accounts," IndianTrust: *Cobell v. Norton,* retrieved May 6, 2004, from http://www.indiantrust.com

147. Chuck Cook, Mike Masterson, and M. N. Trahant, "Child's Suffering Is Cry for Reform," *Arizona Republic,* October 7, 1987, p. A18.

148. Edward M. Carpenter, "Social Services, Policies, and Issues," *Social Casework,* Vol. 61, No. 8, 1980, pp. 455–461.

149. Leadership Conference on Civil Rights Education Fund, *Wrong Then, Wrong Now: Racial Profiling before and after September 11, 2001* (Washington, DC: February 26, 2003), retrieved August 4, 2004, from

http://www.civilrights.org/publications/reports/racial_profiling/

150. This paragraph relies on American Civil Liberties Union, "ACLU of Virginia Asks Charlottesville Police to Halt DNA Collection from African-American Males" (New York, April 12, 2004), retrieved April 22, 2004, from http://www.aclu.org/news/NewsPrint.cfm?ID = 15466&c = 129

151. "Racial Profiling" (Washington, DC: Center for Policy Alternatives, 2003), retrieved March 27, 2004, from http://www.stateaction.org/issues/racial profiling/index.cfm

152. Leadership Conference on Civil Rights Education Fund, *Wrong Then, Wrong Now: Racial Profiling before and after September 11, 2001.*

153. General Accounting Office, *United States Customs Service: Better Targeting of Passengers for Personal Searches Could Produce Better Results* (Washington, DC: March 2000), GAO/GGD-00-38, retrieved April 28, 2004, from http://ntl.bts.gov/data/GAO/0038.pdf

154. "Racial Profiling."

155. Information on the End Racial Profiling Act was obtained from Library of Congress, *THOMAS, Legislative Information on the Internet,* retrieved April 27, 2004, from http://thomas.loc.gov

156. "Crackdown: When Bombs Terrorized America, the Attorney General Launched the 'Palmer Raids,'" *Smithsonian Magazine* (Washington, DC: Smithsonian Institution, 2002), retrieved from http://www.smithsonianmag.si.edu/smithsonian/issues02/feb02/red_scare.html; *Sanctioned Bias: Racial Profiling since 9/11* (New York: American Civil Liberties Union, February 2004), retrieved April 25, 2004, from http://www.aclu.org/SafeandFree/SafeandFree.cfm?ID = 15102&c = 207

157. Donald Brieland, Lela B. Costin, and Charles R. Atherton, *Contemporary Social Work: An Introduction to Social Work and Social Welfare,* 2nd ed. (New York: McGraw-Hill, 1980), p. 404.

158. Neil Skene, ed., *Congressional Quarterly Almanac, 1992,* Vol. XLVIII (Washington, DC: Congressional Quarterly, 1993), pp. 335–336.

159. President George W. Bush, *Address to Joint Session of Congress* (Washington, DC, February 27, 2001), retrieved April 28, 2004, from http://usconservatives.about.com/bln0227bushaddress.htm

160. Testimony of Nadine Strossen, president of the American Civil Liberties Union, before the Senate Judiciary Committee, Department of Justice Oversight: *The Massive, Secretive Detention and Dragnet Questioning of People Based on National Origin in the Wake of September 11* (Washington, DC, December 4, 2001), retrieved April 28, 2004, from http://archive.aclu.org/congress/112040a.html

161. American Civil Liberties Union, *America's Disappeared: Seeking International Justice for Immigrants Detained after September 11* (New York, January 2004), retrieved April 28, 2004, from http://www.aclu.org/SafeandFree/SafeandFree.cfm?ID = 14800&c = 206; see also Muzaffar A. Chishti, Doris Melissner, Demetrios G. Papademetriou, Jay Peterzell, Michael J. Wishnie, and Stephen W. Yale-Loehr, *America's Challenge: Domestic Security, Civil Liberties, and National Unity after September 11* (Washington DC: Migration Policy Institute, 2003), retrieved April 29, 2004, from http://www.migrationpolicy.org/pubs/challenges.html

162. Center for Constitutional Rights, *The State of Civil Liberties: One Year Later . . . Erosion of Civil Liberties in the Post 9/11 Era* (New York, 2002), retrieved April 20, 2004, from http://www.ccr-ny.org/v2/reports/docs/Civil_Liberties.pdf; Neil A. Lewis and Eric Schmitt, "Cuba Detentions May Last Years," *New York Times,* February 13, 2004, retrieved February 15, 2004, from http://www.nytimes.com/2004/02/13/politics/13GITM.html?th; Linda Greenhouse, "Case before Supreme Court Will Test Limits of Presidential Power," *New York Times,* April 18, 2004, retrieved April 19, 2004, from http://www.nytimes.com/2004/04/18/politics/18SCOT.html?th; "The Court and Guantanamo," *New York Times,* retrieved April 19, 2004, from http://www.nytimes.com/2004/04/19/opinions/19MON1.html?th; American Civil Liberties Union, *Constitution at Crossroads: Landmark Post-9/11 Cases before Supreme Court Will Test America's Values of Fairness and Justice for All* (New York, April 12, 2004), retrieved April 19, 2004, from http://www.aclu.org/news

163. Center for Constitutional Rights, *The State of Civil Liberties: One Year Later;* American Civil Liberties Union, "Bush to Promote Patriot Act in New York, Pennsylvania; ACLU Urges Congress to Resist Calls to Make Law's Problems Permanent" (New York, April 19, 2004), retrieved April 19, 2004, from http://www.aclu.org/news

164. Library of Congress, THOMAS, Legislative Information on the Internet, USA PATRIOT ACT, P.L. 107-56, retrieved April 29, 2004, from http://thomas.loc.gov

165. Monica Davey, "An Antiwar Forum in Iowa Brings Federal Subpoenas," *New York Times,* February 10, 2004, retrieved February 10, 2004, from http://www.nytimes.com/2004/02/10/national/10PROT.html?th

166. American Civil Liberties Union, "Bush to Promote Patriot Act in New York, Pennsylvania."

167. "2004 Haiti Rebellion," *Wikipedia,* retrieved April 29, 2004, from http://en.wikipedia.org/wiki/2004_Haiti_rebellion#Controversy_over_Aristide's_departure

168. U.S. Committee for Refugees, "President Bush Finally Speaks the Truth about America's Unlawful Treatment of Haitian Refugees" (Washington, DC, February 26, 2004), retrieved April 29, 2004, from http://www.refugees.org/news/press_releases/2004/022604.cfm

169. U.S. Committee on Refugees, "The Statistical Issue," *Refugee Reports,* Vol. 23, No. 9, December 31, 2002, retrieved April 29, 2004, from http://www.refugees.org/world/articles/RR_December_2002_Admission.cfm#admissionsNat1

170. About, "Immigration Before and After: Putting It in Perspective," *Library Weekly,* April 26, 2002, retrieved April 29, 2004, from http://immigration.about.com/library/weekly/aa042602a.htm

171. Library of Congress, "Clear Law Enforcement for Criminal Alien Removal Act of 2003 (H.R. 2671)," *THOMAS: Legislative Information on the Internet,* retrieved April 29, 2004, from http://thomas.loc.gov

172. American Civil Liberties Union, *Sanctioned Bias: Racial Profiling since 9/11.*

173. U.S. Department of Homeland Security, "Fact Sheet: US-VISIT" (Washington, DC), retrieved April 29, 2004, from http://www.dhs.gov/dhspublic/interapp/press_release/press_release_0385.xml

174. U.S. Department of Homeland Security, *Fiscal Year 2002 Yearbook of Immigration Statistics* (Washington, DC, January 2003), Table 4, retrieved April 29, 2004, from http://uscis.gov/graphics/shared/aboutus/statistics/IMM02yrbk/IMM2002list.htm

175. U.S. Department of Homeland Security, "Southwest Border Apprehensions" (Washington, DC, 2003), retrieved April 29, 2004, from http://uscis.gov/graphics/shared/aboutus/statistics/msrsep03/SWBORD. HTM

176. U.S. Department of Homeland Security, *Estimates of the Unauthorized Immigrant Population Residing in the United States: 1990 to 2000* (Washington, DC, January 31, 2003), retrieved April 29, 2004, from http://uscis.gov/graphics/shared/aboutus/statistics/index.htm

177. U.S. Department of Homeland Security, "Removals" (Washington, DC, 2003), retrieved April 29, 2004, from http://uscis.gov/graphics/shared/aboutus/statistics/msrsep03/removal.htm

178. James P. Smith and Barry Edmonston, Eds., *The New Americans: Economic, Demographic, and Fiscal Effects of Immigration* (Washington, DC: National Academy Press, 1997), p. 51.

179. George J. Borjas, "Increasing the Supply of Labor through Immigration," Center for Immigration Studies, May 2004, retrieved May 9, 2004, from http://www.cis.org/articles/2004/back504.html

180. Julia Malone, "House Panel Pans Bush Immigration Plan," *Austin American-Statesman,* March 25, 2004, p. A12.

181. See Smith and Edmonston, *The New Americans: Economic, Demographic, and Fiscal Effects of Immigration,* p. 29.

182. "NCLR (National Council of La Raza) Opposes Guestworker Legislation," Statement of Raul Yzaguirre, president of NCLR, June 24, 1998; retrieved from http://www.nclr.org/press/063098a.html

183. U.S. Census Bureau, "The Foreign-Born Population in the United States: March 2002" (Washington, DC: U.S. Department of Commerce, February 2003); retrieved March 9, 2004, from http://www.census.gov

184. Neil Skene, Ed., "Sizable Boost in Immigration OK'd," *Congressional Quarterly Almanac,* 1990, Vol. XLVI (Washington, DC: Congressional Quarterly, 1991), pp. 474–485.

185. Steven A. Camarota, "An Examination of Trends in Immigrant Welfare Use since Welfare Reform" (Washington, DC: Center for Immigration Studies, March 2003), retrieved March 9, 2004, from http://www.us.org/articles/2003/back503release.html

186. President George W. Bush, "Fact Sheet: Fair and Secure Immigration Reform" (Washington, DC, January 2004), retrieved April 29, 2004, from http://www.whitehouse.gov/news/releases/2004/01/20040107-1.html; Mike Allen, "Immigration Reform on Bush Agenda," *Washington Post,* December 24, 2003, retrieved April 29, 2004, from http://www.washingtonpost.com

187. Rep. Tom Tancredo, "Immigration Policy," Speech to the House of Representatives (Washington, DC, February 24, 2004), retrieved April 29, 2004, from http://www.limitstogrowth.org/WEB-text/Tancredo.html

188. Federation for American Immigration Reform, "Rep. Tancredo Introduces an Immigration Moratorium Bill, April, 2003," retrieved September 28, 2004, from http://www.fairus.org/news/NewsPrint.cfm?ID=1306&C=54

CHAPTER

12

Implementing and Evaluating Social Welfare Policy: What Happens after a Law Is Passed

A mericans were once confident that if Congress adopted a policy and appropriated money for it, and the executive branch organized a program, hired people, spent money, and carried out the activities designed to implement the policy, then the effects of the policy felt by society would be those that Congress intended. But today, as the following discussion of implementation and evaluation demonstrates, Americans have serious reservations about governments' ability to solve many social problems.

THE POLITICS OF IMPLEMENTATION

Many problems in social welfare policy arise after a law is passed—in the implementation process. Policy implementation includes all the activities designed to carry out the intention of the law: (1) creating, organizing, and staffing agencies to carry out the new policy, or assigning new responsibilities to existing agencies and personnel; (2) issuing directives, rules, regulations, and guidelines to translate policies into specific courses of action; (3) directing and coordinating both personnel and expenditures toward the achievement of policy objectives; and (4) monitoring the activities used to carry out the policy.

There is always a gap—sometimes small, sometimes very large—between a policy decision and its implementation. Over the years scholars of implementation have taken an almost cynical view of the process:

> Our normal expectation should be that new programs will fail to get off the ground and that, at best, they will take considerable time to get started. The cards in this world are stacked against things happening, as so much effort is required to make them move. The remarkable thing is that new programs work at all.[1]

What are the obstacles to implementation? Why isn't implementation a *rational* activity? Why can't policies be directly implemented in decisions about organization, staffing, spending, regulation, direction, and coordination? The obstacles to successful implementation are many, but they can be categorized in terms of (1) communications, (2) resources, (3) attitudes, and (4) bureaucratic structure.[2]

Communications

The first requirement for effective policy implementation is that the people who are running the program must know what they are supposed to do. Directives must not only be received but must also be clear. Vague, inconsistent, and contradictory directives confuse administrators. Directives give meanings to policies, but these meanings may not be consistent with the original intention of the law. Moreover, poor directives enable people who disagree with the policy to read their own biases into programs. The U.S. Department of Health and Human Services, a major federal government agency, is divided into many offices that are responsible for administering hundreds of programs (see Figure 12.1). These programs affect every state, community, and individual in the country. The DHHS constantly struggles with maintaining accurate communications. Similar problems are faced by every other federal, state, and local bureaucracy.

Generally, the more decentralized the administration of a program, and the greater the number of layers of administration through which directives must flow, the less likely it is that policies will be transmitted accurately and consistently. As discussed in Chapter 4, the Social Security retirement program is highly centralized. The Food Stamp Program (see Chapter 7) has uniform eligibility rules but they must be communicated to thousands of state and local eligibility workers. TANF, another public

FIGURE 12.1

Department of Health and Human Services Organizational Chart

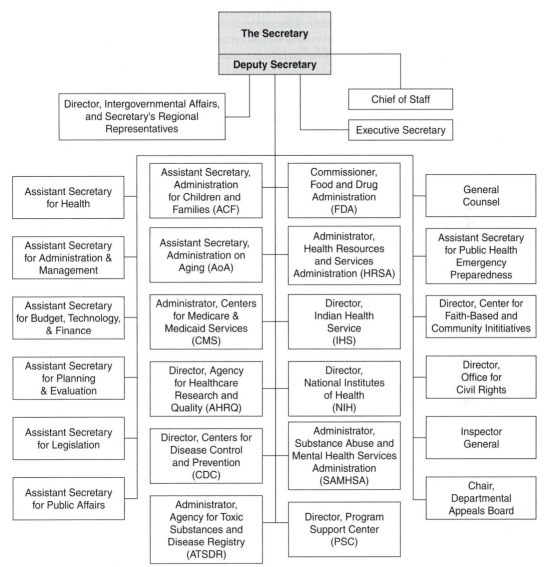

Source: U.S. Department of Health and Human Services (Washington, DC), retrieved July 27, 2003, from http://www.hhs.gov/about/orgchart.html

assistance program (see Chapter 6), is much more decentralized with the federal government establishing broad guidelines, and each state setting many of the rules of the program. Other block grant programs give even more discretion to the states. Whatever the advantages of decentralization may be, prompt, consistent, and uniform policy implementation is *not* usually found in a decentralized structure.

Frequently, Congress (and state legislatures) is deliberately vague about public policy. Congress and the president may pass vague and ambiguous laws largely for symbolic reasons—to reassure people that "something" is being done to help with a problem. In these cases, Congress and the president may not really know exactly what to do about the problem. They therefore delegate wide discretion to administrators who act under the "authority" of broad laws to determine what, if anything, actually will be done. Often Congress and the president want to claim credit for the high-sounding principles enacted into law but do not want to accept responsibility for any unpopular actions that administrators must take to implement these principles. It is much easier for political leaders to blame the "bureaucrats" and pretend that government regulations are a product of an "ungovernable" Washington bureaucracy.

One of the best examples of this problem occurred during the War on Poverty (also see Chapter 9). In the Economic Opportunity Act of 1964, Congress and President Johnson wrote into the law a provision calling for "maximum feasible participation of the poor" in community action agencies and other programs supported by the Office of Economic Opportunity (OEO). But no one knew exactly what that phrase meant. How were the poor to help plan and run the programs? Did this phrase authorize poverty workers to organize the poor politically? Did this phrase mean that social activists paid by the government should help organize the poor to pressure welfare and housing agencies for better services? The policy was not clear, and its implementation was confusing and frustrating. Eventually, of course, the OEO was abolished, in part because of its problems in administering an unclear mandate from Congress.

Policies and related communications can also conflict with one another. As part of the 2002 Farm Bill, Congress authorized states to increase access to the Food Stamp Program by simplifying the food stamp application and recertification processes, but states concerned about keeping error rates low often require more documentation from applicants and recipients than the law requires. Cumbersome application and recertification processes deter rather than increase access.[3]

Resources

Even if policy directives are clear, accurate, and consistent, when administrators lack the resources to carry out these policies, implementation fails. A crucial resource is funds—the money needed to implement new policies. Sometimes new policies require only limited funds to implement, but many new policies and programs seem doomed to fail because insufficient resources are allocated for startup and maintenance functions. An obvious example is the relatively limited amount of funds given to each community to fight the War on Poverty. Another is the lack of child care placements available to ensure that a substantial number of TANF parents are able to obtain and maintain employment (see Chapter 6).

Implementation or **process evaluation studies** can be useful in determining whether modifications in rules, regulations, procedures, or resources are needed as new policies and programs are put into place. For example, an implementation study might help identify communities having difficulty in developing sufficient child care placements to accommodate parents receiving TANF and the obstacles encountered. Some major implementation studies have been conducted of the Job Training Partnership Act[4] and the JOBS programs,[5] but it is generally difficult to acquire the resources needed to conduct these studies. Everyone from policymakers to the public is more interested in **outcome evaluation**—the final results of the program.

Resources also include staff with the proper skills to carry out their assignments and with the authority and facilities necessary to translate a paper proposal into a functioning public service. It is common for government agencies to claim that problems with implementation arise from undersized staffs. And many of these claims are true. Even adequate funds to hire personnel to carry out a policy are not enough. The personnel must have the skills necessary for the job. Consider that convicted sex offenders are often required to get treatment. There may not be enough highly skilled therapists available to provide this treatment, even if treatment programs were adequately funded. Staffing is especially difficult in new programs, especially those few that are highly innovative and experimental. There are frequently no ready-made reserves of people who are trained for new programs and who know what to do. Yet there is always pressure to show results as quickly as possible, to ensure the continuation of the program the next year.

Sometimes agencies lack the authority, even on paper, to implement policy. Agencies may not be authorized to issue checks to citizens, or to purchase goods or services, or to provide funds to other government agencies, or to withdraw funds in the case of noncompliance, or to go to court to force compliance. Even if agencies do have the necessary authority (for example, to withhold federal funds from a local government agency or a nonprofit corporation), they may be reluctant to exercise this authority because of the adverse political repercussions that might ensue. Agencies that do not have the necessary authority to carry out policy (or agencies that fear that exercising that authority may be politically risky) must rely on persuasion and cooperation. Rather than order local agencies, private corporations, or individual citizens to do something, higher-level officials may consult with them, ask for their cooperation, or appeal to their sense of public service. Successful implementation generally requires goodwill on the part of everyone involved. Agencies or administrators who must continually resort to sanctions will probably be unsuccessful in the long run.

Physical facilities may also be crucial in implementation. Programs generally need offices, telephones, computers, and supplies. Yet government agencies (especially new ones) often find it difficult to acquire the necessary facilities to carry out their programs. Once again, most government administrators must rely on persuasion and cooperation to get other government agencies to provide them with offices, equipment, travel approvals, and so on.

The opponents of a particular policy may prefer to see resources reduced. One tactic of opponents, even after they lose the fight over the actual policy in Congress, is to try to reduce the size of the budget and staff that is to implement the policy. The political battle does not end with the passing of a law. It continues each year in fights over resources to implement the law. This has certainly been the case with the Legal Services Corporation (LSC), an agency that provides legal aid to low-income people (see Chapter 9). The Reagan administration wanted to abolish the LSC and appointed members to the LSC's board that shared these sentiments. "When Congress refused to . . . cut the corporation's budget further, . . . the board actually hired lobbyists to press the lawmakers for less . . . money."[6] The LSC has no permanent authorization. Each year it is at the mercy of Congress to renew its funding.

Attitudes

If administrators and program personnel sympathize with a particular policy, it is likely to be carried out as the original policymakers intended. But when the attitudes of agency administrators and staff personnel differ from those of the policymakers, the implementation process can be anything but smooth. Because administrators always have some discretion (and occasionally a great deal) in implementation, their attitudes toward policies have much to do with how a program is implemented. When people are told to do things with which they do not agree, inevitable slippage will occur between a policy and its implementation.

Generally, social service personnel enter the field because they want to "help people"—especially those who are aged, poor, disabled, or otherwise vulnerable. There is seldom any attitudinal problem in social agencies in implementing policies to expand social services. But highly committed social service personnel may find it very difficult to implement policies to cut back or eliminate social services.

Conservative policymakers are aware of the social service orientation of the "welfare bureaucracy." For example, they do not believe that welfare administrators really try to enforce work provisions of welfare laws. These conservatives say that eligibility requirements have been given liberal interpretation by sympathetic administrators, and they believe that the welfare bureaucracy is directly responsible for much of the growth in caseloads over the years. They see welfare administrators as a major obstacle to policies designed to tighten eligibility, reduce overlapping benefits, and encourage work. School lunch administrators, for example, have been criticized for lax certification processes that allow ineligible students to receive free lunches.[7] Conservatives therefore try to impose fiscal sanctions on agencies that fail to keep error rates below a certain level. Even if these sanctions fail to prove effective, opponents of public assistance want to make their point (see Illustration 12.1).

In government agencies, it is generally impossible to remove staff simply because they disagree with a policy. Direct pressures are generally unavailable. Pay increases are primarily across the board, and promotions are infrequent and often based on seniority. "Selling" a policy—winning support through persuasion—remains a more effective strategy to overcoming opposition than threatening sanctions. If those who

ILLUSTRATION 12.1

How Much Fraud, Abuse, and Error in Welfare?

If social welfare programs reached only their intended target groups, there would be no concern about fraud, abuse, and error. Everyone knows that these problems occur in large, bureaucratically administered programs, but there is substantial disagreement over their extent. The United Council on Welfare Fraud's website says it is a group of 2,000 individuals detected to fighting "fraud, waste, and abuse in social service programs." Others study the problem and conclude that most individuals "are simply unaware of how little waste, fraud, and abuse there is in the public welfare system."[a]

The media like to dramatize blatant examples of fraud and abuse. *Reader's Digest* once declared, "federal food stamps are being traded for automobiles, drugs, and automatic weapons." Even Senate hearings carry titles like "Milking Medicaid and Medicare." A *Miami Herald* headline was equally provocative: "Audit: Fraud, Errors, Bleed Medicare by $13.5 Billion" (8 percent of Medicare funds, a lot of money, but better than the 11 percent previously reported[b]). Much of the blame can be placed on vendors—medical facilities, medical supply companies, doctors, and others who provide goods and services to public assistance and social insurance recipients—and those who process claims. They may intentionally or unintentionally overcharge for services or charge for unneeded services or services that were never rendered. A great deal more attention is being to paid to these sources of the problem.

With the change to electronic benefit transfer, paper stamps are no longer being trafficked, but the system is not foolproof. Hackers can still break into EBT systems. Those convicted of food stamp trafficking of $500 or more are permanently barred from the Food Stamp Program and may face legal penalties.

People occasionally apply for duplicate public assistance benefits by using more than one name or applying in different states. Older people may transfer assets to their children in order to obtain long-term care through Medicaid without depleting their savings.

Governments go to great lengths to deter fraud, error, and abuse. Computer-assisted methods are used to audit healthcare vendors' charges to determine if they might be perpetrating fraud. Welfare departments use computer matching to check Internal Revenue Service, Social Security, unemployment insurance, and other agencies' files to see if applicants or recipients are underreporting income. Matching can also indicate if benefits are being issued to deceased individuals as well as probation and parole violators and others who may not qualify.

Finger imaging (electronic fingerprinting) is another fraud detection method. An image is taken when an individual applies for benefits, similar to procedures used when people get a driver's license. Does finger imaging help? Researchers found that 15 percent of welfare program participants expressed concerns about finger imaging, although the vast majority were not deterred from participating.[c] They estimated a 1.3 percent reduction in program participation (reflecting a combination of reduced fraud and deterrence of eligible individuals) and detection of approximately one duplicate case for every 5,000 program cases. Another finger imaging study demonstration project did not find

continued

ILLUSTRATION 12.1 *(continued)*

anyone receiving duplicate benefits, and no savings could be attributed to the system.[d]

Fraud detection efforts are euphemistically called "promoting integrity." Promoting integrity also includes increasing competition to help governments get the best prices for items like prescription drugs. Reducing errors is another aspect. Social welfare program rules, regulations, and eligibility requirements are complex and change often. Clients make about half the errors; caseworkers and administrators make the other half.[e] Clients may misremember information or misunderstand questions. Staff may be inadequately trained, not understand or even know some program rules, and process large number of cases, all contributing to mistakes.

To curb fraud, abuse, and error, the federal government uses quality control (QC) procedures. QC involves taking a sample of cases (scientifically selected to be representative of the entire recipient population) to ensure that recipients are eligible, that they are receiving the correct amount of benefits, and that applicants have not been incorrectly denied benefits. In the Food Stamp Program alone, over 90,000 cases are reviewed each year.

The federal government sets quality control standards and tolerates only a certain amount of error. State welfare agencies review food stamp and Medicaid cases by conducting field investigations, including interviewing clients and verifying records rent receipts and paychecks. (Federal personnel conduct quality control studies in the Supplemental Security Income program.) QC has been a major bone of contention for state governments, which are liable for fines if their error rate exceed limits. By 1987, only three states had kept food stamp error rates to acceptable levels for any period of time. States argued that the

5 percent allowable Food Stamp Program (FSP) error rate was unrealistic. Even a miscalculation of a dollar could add to the error rate. The General Accounting Office urged states to recoup more overpayments from recipients. The states wanted QC modifications and continued to appeal. The federal government has collected only $20 million of the $2 billion in FSP sanctions assessed to the states since the 1980s. Penalties usually have been forgiven, or states have been allowed to invest the money to make improvements. Several changes were made in how penalties are calculated.

In 2002, food stamp overpayment error rates ranged from 10.56 percent in New Hampshire and 10.15 in California to 1.73 percent in South Dakota. Underpayment error rates ranged from 4.69 in California to .23 in South Carolina. The average overpayment error rate was 6.16, the lowest on record, and the average underpayment error rate was 2.10 (this rate has been relatively constant over the years). The combined average error rate was 8.26. The rate of improper denials or terminations was 7.9 percent.

Any state with a combined FSP error rate greater than 6 percent is supposed to take corrective action. Penalties are assessed when a state's combined overpayment and underpayment rate exceeds 105 percent of the national average for two consecutive years. A formula is used to determine the penalty amount. The federal government can require the state to spend half the penalty amount on methods to reduce error. If a state exceeds the error rate in the next consecutive year, the federal government can ask the state to pay the entire penalty amount. Cases most prone to error include larger households with earned income and immigrant households. States may try to limit errors by obtaining more information from par-

continued

ILLUSTRATION 12.1 (continued)

ticipants or requiring more frequent recertification periods. When procedures are too onerous, they may also deter people from applying and eligible individuals from participating.

Since the welfare reform of 1996 (see Chapter 6), the federal government no longer requires the states to calculate TANF error rates. Some states continue to calculate them because they believe it is important in their stewardship role. The Medicaid tolerance rate is 3 percent. The national average has been 2 percent. Rather than the usual quality control study, states with lower rates can utilize their Medicaid quality control funds to help further reduce errors. They may focus on cases where eligibility determination is more complex, like spousal impoverishment cases, in which one spouse is in a nursing home receiving Medicaid and the other spouse remains at home (see Chapter 8).

Even when ineligible individuals or families receive benefits or eligible recipients are overpaid, these households are usually not financially well off. Warnings about misreporting information on public assistance applications and similar notices posted in some welfare offices have been called intimidation tactics designed to keep people from applying at all. The government has also been criticized for paying excessive attention to sniffing out errors in public assistance while practically ignoring problems in other sectors (recall the effects of deregulation and the resulting collapse of many savings and loan institutions, scandals in the securities industry, and cases such as Enron). And it is unlikely that fraud and error in public welfare would ever match the money lost in tax avoidance and evasion by the nonpoor.

NOTES

[a] Edward M. Gramlich, "The Main Themes," in Sheldon H. Danzinger and Daniel H. Weinberg, Eds., *Fighting Poverty: What Works and What Doesn't* (Cambridge, MA: Harvard University Press, 1986), p. 346.

[b] "Audit: Fraud, Errors Bleed Medicare by $13.5 Billion," *Austin American-Statesman*, March 10, 2000, p. A16; "Medicare Audit: Fraud Still Rampant" (AP), *Miami Herald*, April 25, 1998, p. A4.

[c] Paul J. Sticha, David Thomas, Chris Amberlan, and Monica A. Gribben, *Use of Biometric Identification Technology to Reduce Fraud in the Food Stamp Program: Final Report* (Alexandria, VA: U.S. Department of Agriculture, Food and Nutrition Service, 1999).

[d] "UT Austin Researchers Determine Welfare Reform Project Did Not Reduce, Deter Fraud," *On Campus*, November 11, 1997, p. 3.

[e] Much of the remainder of this section relies on Committee on Ways and Means, U.S. House of Representatives, "Section 15, Food Stamps," *2004 Green Book;* retrieved August 10, 2004, from http://waysandmeans.house.gov/Documents.asp?section=813

implement policy cannot be convinced that the policy is good for their clients or themselves, perhaps they can be convinced that it is less offensive than other alternatives that might be imposed by policymakers.

Bureaucracy

Despite widespread distaste for the word "bureaucracy,"[8] nearly all public functions are handled by this type of organization. Previously established organizations and procedures in bureaucracies often hinder implementation of new policies and programs. Bureaucratic "inertia" slows changes in policy. Administrators become accustomed to certain ways of doing things (called *standard operating procedures*), and administrative structures generally remain in place long after their original functions have changed or even disappeared.

Standard operating procedures (SOPs) are routines that enable officials to perform numerous tasks every day; SOPs save time. If every worker had to invent a new way of doing things for every case, there would not be enough time to help very many people. SOPs bring consistency in handling cases; rules can be applied more uniformly.

However, SOPs can also obstruct policy implementation. "Once requirements and practices are instituted, they tend to remain in force long after the conditions that spawned them have disappeared."[9] Routines are not regularly re-examined; they tend to persist even when policies or times change. If SOPs are not revised to reflect policy changes, these changes are not implemented. Many bureaucrats prefer the stability and familiarity of existing routines, and they are reluctant to revise their patterns. Organizations have spent time, effort, and money in developing these routines. These "sunk costs" commit organizations to limit change as much as possible. This is why advocacy organizations like the Food Research and Action Center closely monitor changes in nutrition policy, publicize them, and encourage their constituents to make sure that state and local agencies implement changes that will be beneficial to those eligible to participate.[10]

SOPs can make it difficult to handle nonconforming cases in an individual fashion. Frustrations arise for social service employees when they attempt to help people in need who do not meet specific eligibility criteria. Even though particular cases may not conform to prewritten SOPs, many administrators and staff try to force them into one or another of the established classifications. Over time, these frustrations with bureaucracy may lead to staff "burnout." This occurs frequently among child welfare workers. Their job turnover is high because often they can intervene in only the most serious cases, and even in these cases they may be unable to do what in their professional judgment is necessary.

Bureaucractic organization also affects workers' abilities to implement policy, especially when responsibility for a policy is dispersed among many governmental units. The number of governments has proliferated. There are more than 87,000 governments in the United States: a national government, 50 state governments, about 3,000 county governments, over 19,000 city governments, and nearly 17,000 township governments, as well as nearly 14,000 school districts, and about 35,000 special districts.[11] Even within the national government, many departments have responsibility for social welfare programs. For example, the U.S. Department of Health and Human Services has responsibility for TANF and Medicaid; the U.S. Department of Agriculture administers the Food Stamp and WIC programs; and the U.S. Department of Labor administers job training programs. A similar dispersement of responsibility for social welfare programs may occur at the state level. Descriptions of TANF in Chapter 6 and the Food Stamp Program in Chapter 7 illustrate some of the difficulties clients face in dealing with what are supposed to be rational bureaucracies. All of us have been frustrated by bureaucracies from public agencies such as the IRS to private organizations such as insurance companies. These situations must be even more frustrating for those who are ill, disabled, or have little formal education.

The more governments and agencies involved with a particular policy, and the more independent their decisions, the greater the problems of implementation. Every government and every agency becomes concerned with its own "turf"—areas each considers its exclusive responsibility. The national government and the states frequently struggle over how states will implement federal regulations. State governments often fight with the national government to hold onto their traditional areas of authority, particularly when the federal government imposes regulations on them (such as requirements to expand Medicaid eligibility) but fails to provide sufficient funding for the new mandate, or when the states perceive that federal rules and regulations are unfair. The No Child Left Behind Act discussed in Chapters 2 and 9 is an area where states believe that Congress and the president have overstepped their authority, not only in telling schools what and how to teach, but in failing to provide sufficient funds to meet the new standards for students and teachers that the law imposes.

Proponents of particular programs may insist to Congress that their programs be administered by separate agencies that are largely independent of traditional executive departments or other agencies. These proponents believe their projects are special. They fear that consolidating program responsibilities will downgrade the emphasis that a separate department will give to their particular program. For example, advocates of special programs for alcoholics do not want the National Institute on Alcohol Abuse and Alcoholism to merge with the National Institute on Drug Abuse, despite the number of people who abuse both alcohol and other drugs. They fear that a merger will reduce attention to alcohol problems because the public views illegal drugs as the greater menace to society even though many more people abuse alcohol than abuse other drugs (see Chapter 10).

Some separation of programs among governments is probably desirable. The argument for federalism—the division of responsibilities between the national government and the fifty state governments—is that it allows each state to deal more directly with the particular conditions confronting its residents. Government "closer to home" is sometimes thought to be more flexible, manageable, and personal than a distant bureaucracy in Washington. But some states are more generous to people in need than others, as noted in programs such as TANF and Supplemental Security Income. To see that more people receive adequate services, many social welfare advocates press for centralized programs, such as national health insurance.

When programs and services are fragmented, policy coordination is difficult. This is true whether we are talking about the distribution of responsibilities among different agencies at the national, state, or local government level, or the division of responsibilities between the national government and the 50 states. Uniformity is lost. Consider, for example, that every state in the nation has its own, separate TANF program. These are state-administered programs that operate with federal financial assistance. As we saw in Chapter 6, program rules vary widely among the states.

The federal government does recognize the maze involved in applying for public assistance benefits, and it has considered ways to reduce the red tape. In 1990 the Secretary of the USDA was directed to develop an Advisory Committee on Welfare Simplification and Coordination.[12] The committee was charged with recommending policies that will help program administrators more efficiently serve those who qualify for more than one program. The committee studied differences in eligibility requirements across programs such as Food Stamps, AFDC, Medicaid, and public housing to see how they might impede receiving benefits from multiple programs. In 1993, the committee recommended replacing the country's [public assistance] programs with "one, family-focused, client-oriented comprehensive program" that "should be overseen by only one committee in the House and Senate," rather than "the 24 congressional subcommittees [that] oversee the various welfare programs."[13] It also suggested a single application form and the same means tests for programs. Some states have merged their TANF, Medicaid, and Food Stamp Program applications, but given that different federal (and sometimes state) agencies are responsible for each of these programs, no serious consideration has been given to merging them into anything like one comprehensive program. Such a move would be too drastic for the government bureaucracies already in place.

Making bureaucracy more rational is a challenge to every social welfare administrator. In an effort to follow the rules and respond to so many in need, administrators may forget that they are helping consumers or clients. Administrators rarely ask for clients' input. Congress does hold hearings at which citizens testify about social problems. Senate hearings may be publicized and sometimes televised. Often these occur in the wake of a scandal. They allow senators to show constituents how concerned or outraged they are by the lack of attention to an issue or insensitive treatment received. Presidents sometimes hold summits or forums on particular issues. Hunger forums and education summits are cases in point. From time to time, state and local agencies hold community forums to obtain input on homelessness, mental health services, or other social concerns. Small changes may be made as a result of citizen input, but these meetings are often little more than symbolic gestures. Community officials may be constrained by resources and rules and regulations about what they can do, or they may have their own ideas about what course of action to follow.

Privatization, in which governments utilize not-for-profit and for-profit organizations to deliver services, can add to governments' administrative headaches. On the surface, one can list the pros and cons of private and public services. Government agencies are often thought of as inefficient monopolies, but as salaried employees, public agency personnel are usually not motivated by the thought of putting more money in their pockets. "Better services at lower costs" that result from increased competition might be advantages of privatized services, but in some social service areas, there is not much competition.[14] In many communities, few agencies run shelters for battered women or provide housing to people with serious mental illness.

The public sector has increasingly contracted with the private sector to supply social welfare services, particularly following the welfare reform legislation of 1996. Contractors include large firms like Electronic Data Systems (founded by businessman and former presidential candidate Ross Perot) and weapons industry giant Lockheed Martin. It is becoming more difficult to distinguish between the public and private sectors. As Katz notes, "By moving into public assistance administration, Lockheed furthered its dependence on government funds. It could no more sustain itself without them than could a single mother on welfare."[15]

There are numerous examples of the perils of privatization, or as Barbara Ehrenreich called it, "spinning the poor into gold."[16] In numerous accounts of state governments contracting with private businesses, the picture that emerges is that governments are not yet well equipped to oversee large and sometimes even small contracts with regard to financial or performance auditing.[17] The American Federation of State, County, and Municipal Employees (AFSCME) says that eligibility determination is a public responsibility that should never be contracted out. As might be expected, AFSCME's publication "Safety Net for Sale" would give many people pause about the merits of privatization on cost and quality grounds. If a goal of privatization is to reduce the size of government, that has not happened. When contractors are included, the federal workforce alone has reportedly grown tremendously, to over 12 million with the vast majority working for government contractors.[18] When large private enterprises and large public contracts are involved, they too often end up in disputes over millions of dollars in expenditures. Given that privatization in areas once reserved for the public sector is not likely to go away, it would be useful to have more information about where the private sector can do the best job, though one study found that "the privatization of social services in New York state has transferred public monopoly power and authority to private monopolists, with few increases in performance and accountability."[19]

EVALUATING SOCIAL POLICY

Interest in **policy evaluation**—learning about the consequences of public policy—has grown. Government agencies regularly report how much money they spend, how many people receive various services, and how much these services cost. Congressional committees may receive testimony from influential individuals and groups about how popular or unpopular various programs and services are. But even if programs and policies are well organized, adequately funded, efficiently operated, appropriately used, and politically popular, the questions still arise "So what?" "Do they make a difference?" "Do these programs have any beneficial effects on society?" "What about people not receiving the benefits or services?" "What is the relationship between the costs of the program and the benefits to society?" and "Could we be doing something else of more benefit to society with the money and human resources devoted to these programs?"

Can the federal government answer these questions? Can it say, for example, that TANF and Medicaid, family preservation programs, or community mental health services are accomplishing their objectives? that their benefits to society exceed their costs? that there are no better or less costly means of achieving the same ends? In

1970, one surprisingly candid report by the liberally-oriented think tank, the Urban Institute, argued convincingly that the federal government did *not* know whether most of its social service programs were worthwhile:

> *The most impressive finding about the evaluation of social programs in the federal government is that substantial work in this field has been almost nonexistent.*
>
> *Few significant studies have been undertaken. Most of those carried out have been poorly conceived. Many small studies around the country have been carried out with such lack of uniformity of design and objective that the results rarely are comparable or responsive to the questions facing policy makers. . . .*
>
> *The impact of activities that cost the public millions, sometimes billions, of dollars has not been measured. One cannot point with confidence to the difference, if any, that most social programs cause in the lives of Americans.*[20]

In the 1980s there was still considerable pessimism about social service program evaluation. Take, for example, comments by two social scientists on the state of job creation and training programs:

> *Despite nearly twenty years of continuous federal involvement, . . . we still have to do a good deal of guesswork about what will work and for whom. We have had substantial and on-going difficulties in identifying what works, for whom, and why. This has been, in large part, because of an unwillingness on the part of Congress and policy makers to allow for adequate experimentation in the delivery of employment and training services.*[21]

In the 1990s some people were more optimistic about the future of program evaluation. According to a *New York Times* story lauding evaluations of job training programs,

> *Recent experiments designed and monitored by the Manpower Demonstration Research Corporation, a nonprofit organization spun off from the Ford Foundation in 1974, have had enormous impact on the direction of welfare reform. And with admirers in high places, the experimenters are likely to influence everything from the design of public schools that work to so-called managed competition in health care, in which prepaid health plans such as HMOs would compete for the insurance business of consumers.*[22]

But with people's lives hanging in the balance and with the price tags that accompany programs, we need far more definitive information in this new millennium about what social policies work, for whom they work, and why they work. The need for improved program evaluation is especially great because of the proliferation of social programs and competing demands for scarce social welfare dollars. Large-scale, methodologically rigorous, scientific evaluations of social programs can easily cost hundreds of thousands of dollars or more. The National Institute on Alcohol Abuse and Alcoholism spent at least $25 million to compare the effectiveness of three psychosocial treatments for alcoholism (the three proved equally effective).[23] Now it is conducting another ambitious project to determine whether certain medications in combination with psychosocial treatments can increase the effectiveness of alcoholism treatment. The Urban Institute's Assessing the New Federalism (ANF) project has been analyzing many of the effects of devolution—the transfer of responsibility for social programs from the federal government to the states that has occurred through legislation, primarily the Personal Responsibility and Work Opportunity Reconciliation Act (welfare reform) of 1996. These are but some of the current, major efforts to study social programs.

The titles of ANF studies and reports tracking what has occurred since 1997 are instructive: "Many Families Turn to Food Pantries for Help," "Children of Immigrants Show Slight Reductions in Poverty, Hardship," "Child Support Gains Some Ground," "Fewer Welfare Leavers Employed in Weak Economy," "Childrens' Insurance Coverage and Service Use Improve," "Gains in Public Health Insurance Offset Reductions in Employer Coverage among Adults." Reports from "think tanks" and policy planning groups may serve as calls to action or as the bases for the work of scores of advocacy groups that want action on these issues of concern.

Policy Evaluation as a Rational Activity

From a rational perspective, policy evaluation involves more than just learning about the consequences of public policy. Consider the following definitions by scholars in the field:

> Policy evaluation is the objective, systematic, empirical examination of the effects ongoing policies and programs have on their target in terms of the goals they are meant to achieve.[24]
>
> Evaluation research is viewed by its partisans as a way to increase the rationality of policy making. With objective information on the outcomes of programs, wise decisions can be made on budget allocations and program planning. Programs that yield good results will be expanded; those that make poor showings will be abandoned or drastically modified.[25]
>
> Formal evaluation is an approach which uses scientific methods to produce reliable and valid information about policy outcomes but evaluates such outcomes on the basis of policy-program objectives that have been formally announced by policy makers and program administrators. The major assumption of formal evaluation is that formally announced goals and objectives are appropriate measures of the worth or value of policies and programs.[26]

These definitions of policy evaluation assume that the goals and objectives of programs and policies are clear, that we know how to measure progress toward these goals, that we know how to measure costs, and that we can impartially weigh benefits against costs in evaluating a public program. In short, these definitions view policy evaluation as a rational activity. Contemporary evaluation scholars do understand that policy and program evaluations must be "adapted to their political and organizational environments"[27] but they also want evaluation to be a more rational activity.

If we were to undertake a truly rational evaluation, we would want to address all the questions about program conceptualization and design, monitoring, and utility described in Illustration 12.2, "Rational Evaluation: What Questions to Ask," and we would consider the model of evaluation shown in Figure 12.2. Evaluative research might be directed at any of the linkages in the policy process suggested in this diagram. For example, one might want to inquire about whether the agency's objectives are consistent with the legislated goals, whether the program's administrative structure is effective in meeting program objectives, or whether the program's activities have any impact on society.

Ideally, the evaluation of a program would include all its effects on real-world conditions. Evaluators would want to: (1) identify and rank all the goals of a program; (2) devise measures to describe progress toward these goals; (3) identify the "target" situation or group for which the program was designed; (4) identify nontarget groups who might be affected indirectly by the program ("spillover" effects) and nontarget groups who are similar to the target groups but did not participate in the program or receive its direct benefits ("control group"); (5) measure program effects on target and nontarget groups over as long a period of time as possible; (6) identify and measure the costs of the program in terms of all the resources allocated to it; and (7) identify and measure the indirect costs of the program, including the loss of opportunities to pursue other activities.

Identifying target groups in social welfare programs means defining the segment of the population for whom the program is intended—those who are poor, sick, ill housed, and so on. Then, the desired effect of the program on the target population must be determined. Is it to change their physical or economic conditions—their health, their nutrition, their income? Or is it to change their behavior—encourage them to work or improve their parenting skills? Or perhaps it is to change their knowledge, attitudes, awareness, or interests—to pressure slum landlords into improving housing conditions, to increase voter turnout among poor persons, to discourage unrest, riots, and violence among inner-city residents. If multiple effects are intended, what are the priorities (rankings) among different effects? What are the possible unintended effects (side effects) on target groups—for example, does public housing achieve better physical environments for the urban poor at the cost of increasing their segregation and isolation from the mainstream of the community? Are children from low-income families who receive school lunches and breakfasts to improve their nutrition stigmatized in the process? Are children left unsupervised when their parents are meeting TANF work requirements?

In making these identifications and measurements, the evaluators must not confuse policy **outputs** (what governments do) with policy **impacts** (what consequences these government actions have). Benefits should not be measured in terms of government activity alone. For example, the number of dollars spent per member of a target group (per student educational expenditures, per capita welfare or health expenditures) is not really a measure of the impact of government activity. We cannot be content with

ILLUSTRATION 12.2

Rational Evaluation: What Questions to Ask

Several ideal, rational models of program evaluation have been proposed. Social scientists Peter Rossi, Howard Freeman, and Mark Lipsey suggest that rational evaluation include five types of questions:

1. Questions about the need for program services
   ♦ What are the nature and magnitude of the problem to be addressed?
   ♦ What are the characteristics of the population in need?
   ♦ What are the needs of the population?
   ♦ What services are needed?
   ♦ How much service is needed, over what time period?
   ♦ What service delivery arrangements are needed to provide those services to the population?

2. Questions about program conceptualization or design
   ♦ What clientele should be served?
   ♦ What services should be provided?
   ♦ What are the best delivery systems for the services?
   ♦ How can the program identify, recruit, and sustain the intended clientele?
   ♦ How should the program be organized?
   ♦ What resources are necessary and appropriate for the program?

3. Questions about program operations and service delivery
   ♦ Are administrative and service objectives being met?

♦ Are the intended services being delivered to the intended persons?
♦ Are there needy but unserved persons the program is not reaching?
♦ Once in service, do sufficient numbers of clients complete service?
♦ Are the clients satisfied with services?
♦ Are administrative, organizational, and personnel functions handled well?

4. Questions about program outcomes
   ♦ Are the outcome goals and objectives being achieved?
   ♦ Do the services have beneficial effects on the recipients?
   ♦ Do the services have adverse side effects on the recipients?
   ♦ Are some recipients affected more by the services than others?
   ♦ Is the problem or situation the services are intended to address made better?

5. Questions about program cost and efficiency
   ♦ Are resources used efficiently?
   ♦ Is the cost reasonable in relation to the magnitude of the benefits?
   ♦ Would alternative approaches yield equivalent benefits at less cost?

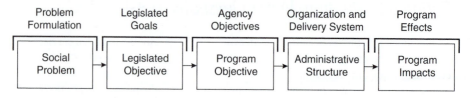

FIGURE 12.2

A Rational Model of Program Evaluation

Problem Formulation	Legislated Goals	Agency Objectives	Organization and Delivery System	Program Effects
Social Problem	Legislated Objective	Program Objective	Administrative Structure	Program Impacts

Source: Adapted from Dennis N. T. Perkins, "Evaluating Social Interventions: A Conceptual Schema," *Evaluation Quarterly,* Vol. 1, No. 4, 1977, P. 642, copyright © 1977 by Sage Publications, Inc. Reprinted by permission of Sage Publications, Inc.

counting how many times a bird flaps its wings; we must learn how far the bird has flown. In assessing the impact of public policy, we cannot simply count the number of dollars spent or clients served; rather, we must identify the changes in individuals, groups, and society brought about by public policies.

Identifying the effects of a program on nontarget groups is equally important. For example, what effects has the change from AFDC to TANF had on social workers, social welfare bureaucracies, working families who are not receiving public assistance, taxpayers, and others? Nontarget effects may turn out to be costs (such as the displacement of poor residents as a result of urban renewal and gentrification), but they can also be benefits (such as the increased income to physicians who see Medicare patients).

Evaluators must also determine whether the program's goals are supposed to be long range or immediate. When will the benefits and costs be felt? Is the program designed for a short-term, emergency situation, or is it a long-term, developmental effort? Many impact studies show that new or innovative programs have short-term positive effects—for example, Head Start, D.A.R.E., and other educational programs. The newness of the program, or the realization by the target group that is being given special treatment and being watched closely, may create measurable changes (the **Hawthorne** or **halo effect**). These positive effects may disappear as the novelty and enthusiasm of the new program wear off. Longitudinal studies that assess the far-reaching impacts of social welfare programs are rarely conducted due to constraints of time and money. This leaves policymakers and the public with insufficient information to assess the positive and negative consequences of many social welfare programs.

Perhaps the most difficult problem confronting evaluators is weighing costs against benefits. Benefits may be measured in terms of bettering human conditions—greater educational attainment, longer life spans, better nutrition, steady employment, and so on. Costs are usually measured in dollars, but many of the values of education, health, or self-esteem cannot be measured in dollars alone. Cost savings are not the only goals that society wants to achieve. It is difficult to pursue rational evaluation when benefits and costs are measured in different ways.

Politics at Work: Evaluating Social Programs

Studies of the effectiveness or outcomes of social welfare programs like Head Start, job training, and TANF have been noted throughout this book. One particularly well-known example of the federal government's attempts to experiment with public policy is the New Jersey Graduated Work Incentive Experiment funded by the Office of Economic Opportunity. The experiment was designed to resolve some serious questions about the effect of welfare payments on the incentives for poor people to work.[28] To learn more about the effects of the welfare system on human behavior and, more important, to learn about the possible effects of guaranteed family income proposals, the OEO funded a three-year social experiment involving 1,350 families in New Jersey and Pennsylvania. The research was conducted by the Institute for Research on Poverty at the University of Wisconsin.

To ascertain the effects of different levels of guaranteed income, some families in the experiment were chosen to receive 50 percent of the federal government's official poverty-level income, others 75 percent, others 100 percent, and still others 125 percent. To ascertain the effects of graduated payments in relation to earnings, some families had their payments reduced by 30 percent of their outside earnings, others by 50 percent, and still others by 70 percent. Finally, a control sample was observed—low-income families who received no payments at all.

The experiment was initiated in August 1968 and continued until September 1972. But political events moved swiftly and soon engulfed the study. In 1969, President Nixon proposed the Family Assistance Plan (FAP), which would have guaranteed all families a minimum income of 50 percent of the poverty level with a payment reduction of 50 percent for outside earnings (also see Chapter 6). The Nixon administration had not waited to learn the results of the OEO experiment before introducing the FAP. Nixon wanted welfare reform to be his priority domestic legislation, and the FAP bill was symbolically numbered HR 1 (House of Representatives Bill 1). After the FAP was introduced, the Nixon administration pressured the OEO to produce favorable evidence—specifically, evidence that a guaranteed income at the levels proposed in the FAP would not reduce incentives to work among the poor. The OEO obliged by hastily publishing a short preliminary report, showing no differences between the outside earnings of families receiving guaranteed incomes (the experimental group) and those not (the control group).[29]

The research director warned that "the evidence from this preliminary and crude analysis of the results is less than ideal," but he concluded that "no evidence has been found in the urban experiment to support the belief that negative-tax type income maintenance programs will produce large disincentives and consequent reductions in earnings."[30] Moreover, the early results indicated that families in all experimental groups, with different guaranteed minimums and different graduated payment schedules, behaved similarly to each other and to the control group receiving no payments. Predictably, later results confirmed the preliminary results, which were used to assist the FAP in Congress.[31]

However, when the RAND Corporation (which was not responsible for designing the original study) later reanalyzed data from the Graduated Work Incentive Experiment, results were markedly different.[32] RAND reported that the original researchers working for OEO had chosen New Jersey because it had no state welfare programs for "intact" families—families with a mother and an able-bodied, working-age father. The guaranteed incomes were offered to these intact families to compare their work behavior with similar intact families who received no such payments. But six months after the experiment began, New Jersey changed its state law and offered all poor families rather substantial welfare benefits. This meant that for most of the period of the experiment, the control group was offered benefits equivalent to those given the experimental group—an obvious confound to the experimental research design. The original researchers failed to consider this factor. The RAND Corporation researchers, in contrast, considered the New Jersey state welfare program in their estimates of work behavior. RAND concluded that recipients of a guaranteed annual income would work six and one-half fewer hours per week than they would work in the absence of such a program. In short, the RAND study suggested that a guaranteed annual income would produce a substantial disincentive to work.

The RAND study was published in 1978 after Congress's enthusiasm for welfare reform via a guaranteed annual income program had already cooled. A similar but larger and longer experiment was later conducted in Denver and Seattle, called the Seattle-Denver Income Maintenance Experiment, or SIME/DIME for short.[33] Job counseling and training were added for some participants. The SIME/DIME study also found substantially lower earnings and hours worked for both husbands and wives across the various payment and earnings deduction groups, even with the additional job services. These studies confirmed many Congress members' intuition that a guaranteed annual income would reduce willingness to work.

A more recent example of how programs flourish even in the face of negative evaluations concerns the popular Drug Abuse Resistance Education (D.A.R.E.) program.[34] The idea that children may use drugs strikes fear in the hearts of most parents. Sources like *Monitoring the Future* and the *National Survey on Drug Use and Health* (formerly the *National Household Survey on Drug Use)*, both ongoing surveys funded by the federal government, provide data that substantial numbers of youth at least experiment with alcohol, and to a lesser extent with other drugs. For example, in 2002, nearly 21 percent of youth reported that they had tried marijuana at least once.[35] This type of information has given rise to a spate of drug prevention programs.

Throughout the 1970s, most drug abuse prevention programs were educational in nature, directed at adolescents, and implemented through the schools. Early programs combined information with scare tactics. These programs were generally so ineffective that the federal government's Special Office for Drug Abuse Prevention (SODAP) denounced them.[36] In fact, SODAP was so disillusioned that it temporarily banned funding for drug information programs. Lacking evidence of effective information approaches, interest grew in *affective* approaches and other alternatives. Affective approaches assume that adolescents will be deterred from using drugs if their self-esteem and interpersonal, decision-making, and problem-solving skills are improved. Recreational activities, community service, and involvement in the arts were stressed as ways of providing meaningful, fulfilling experiences that would deter drug use. These methods also proved ineffective.

Then a new generation of programs began to emerge based on theories of *social and cognitive inoculation* that addressed children's social milieu. These approaches are based on the premise that if adolescents are provided with counterarguments and techniques with which to resist peer pressure to use drugs, as well as factual information about drugs, they are more likely to abstain.

In 1983 D.A.R.E. was established as a joint project of the Los Angeles Police Department and the Los Angeles Unified School District.[37] Combining elements of affective education and social inoculation, it was initially designed to help fifth- and sixth-grade students recognize and resist peer pressure, a major factor in youths' experimenting with alcohol and drugs. Several lessons focused on building self-esteem, others emphasized the consequences of alcohol and drug use and identification of alternative ways to cope with stress, gaining peer acceptance, and having fun. Most important, the program teaches students ways to respond to peers who offer drugs, and it helps them practice these techniques (changing the subject, walking away, saying "no" and repeating it as often as necessary). The curriculum contained 17 classroom sessions conducted by a police officer, coupled with other activities taught by the regular classroom teacher. Curricula were also developed for middle and high school students to reinforce the lessons taught during the fifth and sixth grades. D.A.R.E. reports that its program is used in 80 percent of all school districts in the United States and in 54 foreign countries. Many of you reading this book are probably D.A.R.E. graduates.

A great deal of public funding has gone to support this program, and initial reports suggested that the program was effective. But a later evaluation study funded by the U.S. Department of Justice (DOJ) and conducted in 1994 by the widely respected Research Triangle Institute found the program ineffective in preventing or reducing drug use.[38] The DOJ refused to approve the report, and D.A.R.E. tried to prevent others from publishing criticisms of the program.[39] Subsequent reports of D.A.R.E.'s ineffectiveness also did little to dull enthusiasm for the program. A ten-year follow-up study by researchers at the University of Kentucky found "no reliable short-term, long-term, early adolescent, or young adult positive outcomes associated with receiving the intervention."[40] The Kentucky researchers also noted that even though most children do not use drugs even when they do not participate in a drug prevention program, "teaching children to refrain from drug use is a widely accepted approach with which few individuals would argue. . . . [T]hese 'feel-good' programs are ones that everyone can support, and critical examinations of their effectiveness may not be perceived as necessary."[41]

The Government Accounting Office (GAO) also decided to review the major evaluations of D.A.R.E. In a 2003 report, the GAO stated:

> *In brief, the six long-term evaluations of the DARE elementary school curriculum that we reviewed found no significant differences in illicit drug use between students who received DARE in the fifth and sixth grade (the intervention group) and students who*

did not (the control group). . . . All of the evaluations suggested that DARE had no statistically significant long-term effect on preventing youth illicit drug use. Of the six evaluations we reviewed, five also reported on students' attitudes toward illicit drug use and resistance to peer pressure and found no significant differences between the intervention and control groups over the long term. Two of these evaluations found that the DARE students showed stronger negative attitudes about illicit drug use and improved social skills about illicit drug use about 1 year after receiving the program. These positive effects diminished over time.[42]

Thus, the scientific community came to recognize the approach as ineffective.

Some schools dropped D.A.R.E. Nevertheless, because of the program's already extensive, established network, the prestigious Robert Wood Johnson Foundation, which has a history of funding alcohol and drug research, invested $13.7 million to modify the curriculum, aiming it at older students, relying less on lectures, and including an approach that will have students question their assumptions about drug use.

An evaluation of the new D.A.R.E. Plus program involving 6,000 seventh graders in the Minneapolis–St. Paul area may breathe new life into the program.[43] The study compared D.A.R.E. Plus with the original D.A.R.E. program and with no training. The added components received by the students who got D.A.R.E. Plus included a peer-led parent classroom program, youth-led extracurricular activities, community adult teams to address local drug problems and violence, and postcards mailed to parents. The students who received the original D.A.R.E. did not do better than those who received no intervention, and there were no differences among the girls who received D.A.R.E. and D.A.R.E. Plus, but boys who received D.A.R.E. Plus did better than those who received no training on tobacco, alcohol, and multiple drug use and victimization. D.A.R.E. Plus boys also did better than boys who received the original D.A.R.E. on tobacco use and they were less violent.

The Many Faces of Program Evaluation

Most governments make some attempt to assess the utility of their programs. These efforts usually take one or more of the following forms.

Public Hearings

Public hearings are one type of program review. Legislative committees often ask agency heads to give formal or informal testimony regarding the accomplishments of their programs. This usually occurs near budget time. At the state and local level citizen input may also be requested. In addition, written "program reports" or "annual reports" may be provided to legislators and interested citizens by agencies as a "public information" activity. However, testimonials and reports of program administrators and those served by the program are not very objective means of program evaluation. Unless there has been substantial wrongdoing, public hearings frequently magnify the benefits and minimize the costs of programs.

Site Visits

Occasionally teams of legislators, high-ranking federal or state officials, or expert consultants (or some combination of all of these people) will descend on agencies to conduct investigations "in the field." These teams can interview workers and clients and directly observe the operation of the agency. They can accumulate impressions about how programs are being run, whether they have competent staffs, whether the programs seem to be having beneficial effects, and perhaps even whether or not the clients (target groups) are pleased with the services. But site visits can also provide a biased view of the program. Program staff are usually on their best behavior, and clients that meet with the site visit team are usually hand-picked.

Program Measures

The evaluation data developed by the agencies themselves usually describe program or output measures—for example, the number of people enrolled in work and training programs, the number of hospital beds available, or the number of people treated by mental health programs. Less frequently, these measures also indicate the impact these numbers have on society—for example, reductions in poverty figures, decreases in criminal activity by drug addicts, the success of work trainees in later finding and holding useful employment in the nation's workforce, or improvements in parenting skills that lessen the need for intervention by child protective service programs.

Comparison with Professional Standards

In some areas of social welfare activity, professional associations have developed their own "standards" of benefits and services. These standards may be expressed in terms of the maximum number of cases that a mental health, child welfare, or public assistance worker can handle effectively, or the minimum number of hospital beds required by a population of 100,000 people, or in other ways. Actual governmental outputs can be compared with these "ideal" outputs. Although this kind of study may be helpful, it still focuses on the outputs and not on the impacts that government activities have on the conditions of target and nontarget groups. Though the standards are usually developed by professionals, these individuals may lack concrete data on which to determine the ideal levels of benefits and services. Having too many cases can obviously result in insufficient attention to each client, and too many hospital beds waste resources, but there is very little hard evidence about what optimal caseload sizes are or that these supposedly ideal levels of government outputs have significant impact.

Formal Research Designs

Another rational approach is to conduct formal evaluation studies employing the techniques of scientific research. In many social scientists' opinion,[44] the most highly regarded, though least frequently used, approach is the **classic experimental design.** This design employs two groups—an **experimental group** and a **control group**—that are theoretically equivalent in every way except that the policy has been applied only to the experimental group. In order to ensure that control and experimental groups are comparable, research subjects or participants are assigned randomly to the two groups and the program must be applied only to the experimental group. After the application of the policy for a given length of time, its impact is measured by comparing the status of the experimental group with the status of the control group. The postprogram status of both groups must be carefully measured. Also, every effort must be made to make certain that any observed postprogram differences between the two groups can be attributed to the program and not to some other intervening cause that affected one of the groups as the program was administered. This classic research design (see Figure 12.3) is preferred because it provides the best opportunity for estimating changes that can be directly attributed to policies and programs.

Although revered by many, the classic experimental design presents many challenges in the social sciences. Methodologically, it is difficult to avoid contamination (the introduction of extraneous factors) in social science research. Many studies of new medications use double-blind procedures in which neither the person administering the "medication" nor the research subject taking the "medication" know whether it is the real thing or a placebo. Such studies are nearly impossible to conduct when it comes to social interventions. Generally, both those administering the

FIGURE 12.3

Classic Experimental Research Design

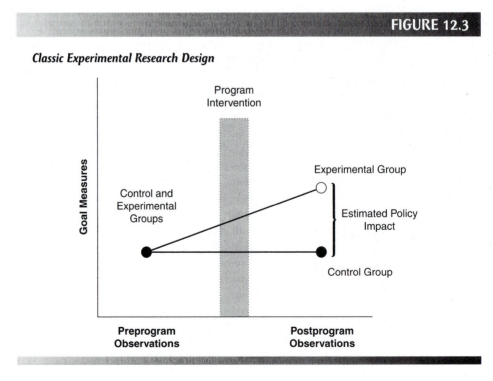

social intervention (for example, a job training program or drug rehabilitation services) and the research subjects or participants know who is is receiving the intervention and who is not. More importantly, controlled experiments are often reductionistic because they focus on narrowly defined interventions and narrowly defined outcomes. As described by Lisbeth Schorr in Illustration 12.3, controlled studies may not be well suited to studying complex interventions offered to individuals who face myriad problems and changing life circumstances. Schorr recognizes the difficulty of "breaking with the dogma of experimental designs," because, as noted evaluation expert Robinson G. Hollister has said, it is "like the nectar of the gods" when it comes to evaluation. But she believes that some evaluation alternatives, though providing less certainty about cause and effect, can offer "both rigor and relevance." If there is hope for bridging the gap between rational evaluation and politics, maybe the model of "theoretical evaluation" Schorr suggests will help. This approach begins with interested parties, like social service personnel, working *together* with evaluators to develop a "conceptual map" that links theoretical assumptions about what works to promote change with interventions that flow from these ideas and with interim measures of progress as well as outcome measures. Schorr offers the example of early childhood education programs. These programs are often based on assumptions that children who are "ready to learn" do better in school than children who are "not ready to learn." Policies and programs would focus on factors that appear to be most useful in helping children become ready to learn, such as good health, proper nutrition, high-quality preschool education, and supportive families. Interim measures might include more children receiving regular health care, more children enrolled in high-quality preschool education programs, and more families receiving supportive services like decent housing, earlier intervention to prevent child abuse or neglect and education to help them read to their children and encourage learning. As program personnel deliver services and review with evaluators interim and outcome measures, the conceptual map is refined, hopefully leading to more effective services and improved outcomes for children and their families, like better school performance.

Another reason to consider methods like theoretical evalution is that even when one wants to conduct controlled experiments in public policy, it is frequently impossible to do so because sometimes the human beings involved cannot be placed arbitrarily in experimental or control groups just for the sake of program evaluation. Indeed, if experimental and control groups are really identical, the application of public policy to one group of citizens and not the other may violate the "equal protection of the laws" clause of the Fourteenth Amendment to the U.S. Constitution. In addition to legal issues, differential treatment of people with the same social problems raises ethical concerns. Social workers and other professionals may find it unacceptable to deny what may be a promising treatment to clients, even if better program evaluation is desired. Frequently, it is only possible to conduct studies that compare individuals and groups that have participated in programs with those that have not, or to compare cities, states, and nations that have programs with those that do not. Comparisons are made of the extent to which the groups that participated in the program achieved the desired goals in relation to those groups that did not participate. Such studies are called **quasiexperimental** because subjects are not randomly assigned to experimental and control groups—researchers cannot be certain that the two groups were alike before the experiment began. They must try to eliminate the possibility that any difference between the two groups in goal achievement was caused by some factor other than experience with the program. For example, the employment records of job program participants may be compared with those who did not participate. Following the quasiexperiment, if the job program group did not have higher employment rates and greater earnings than other groups, it may be because the job program participants were less skilled to begin with. If they were more successful, it may be because the job program officials "creamed off" the local unemployed and gave services only to those who already possessed skills and job experience. Thus, quasiexperimental research designs (see Figure 12.4), like most social science research, still leave room for discussion and disagreement about the utility of social welfare programs.

Another type of research design involves a comparison of conditions before and after a policy or program has been adopted. Usually only the target group is examined. This design may be the only choice in jurisdictions where no control or comparison group can be identified. The simplest before–after or **pretest–posttest** study involves taking one measure before the program is implemented and one after the program is administered, but this is a very weak design. When several observations are made before and several observations are made after, this is generally referred to as a **time series** design (see Figure 12.5). These studies are also intended to show program impacts, but it is still very difficult to know whether any changes that might have occurred were due to the program itself or were a result of other changes occurring in society at the same time. For example, a program evaluator may be faced

FIGURE 12.4

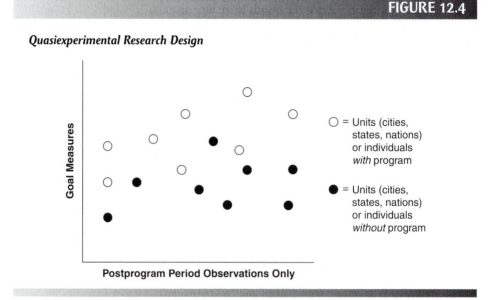

Quasiexperimental Research Design

Goal Measures

○ = Units (cities, states, nations) or individuals *with* program

● = Units (cities, states, nations) or individuals *without* program

Postprogram Period Observations Only

FIGURE 12.5

Time Series Research Design

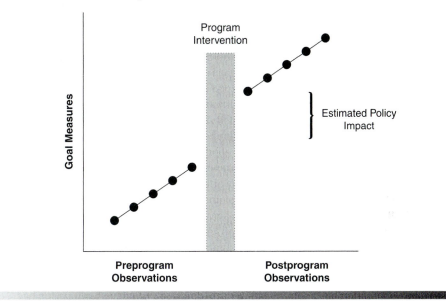

with the problem of determining whether a high school drug education program reduced the frequency of students' drug use or whether a decrease in the supply of drugs that occurred simultaneously in the community was responsible for this effect.

Policy Evaluation as a Political Activity

Policy and program evaluation may resemble rational, scientific inquiry, but it can never really be separated from politics. Let us consider just a few of the political problems that make rational policy evaluation difficult, if not impossible.

Unclear, Ambiguous Program Goals

Evaluators are often told to evaluate a program and yet are not informed of its goals or purposes. Reading the language of the original legislation that established the program may not be very helpful; legislative language is frequently vague—"improve nutrition" or "increase school readiness" are examples. There may be no indication of what improvements or how much improvement is expected or intended. Even interviews with the original legislative sponsors (Congressmembers, state legislators, county commissioners, or city council members) may produce ambiguous, or even contradictory, goals. There is also a "confusion between policy ends and policy means. . . . While federal and state governments are committed to 'doing something' about certain vulnerable populations, the end product of their efforts has not been specified."[46] If the goal of welfare reform is to reduce dependency, does it mean that researchers should be measuring how many people left the public assistance rolls, how many got jobs, or how many are no longer poor, have health insurance, child care, or other resources? When or how will we know if welfare reform has been successful? The answer might be different for different stakeholders. Often the evaluators, at the risk of offending someone, must define the goals or purposes themselves. In this way, evaluation itself becomes a political activity.

Symbolic Goals

Many programs and policies have primarily symbolic value. They are not designed so much to change social conditions as they are to make groups feel that their government "cares." Of course, an agency does not welcome a study that reveals its efforts have no tangible effects. Indeed, such a finding, if widely publicized, is likely to reduce the symbolic impact of the program by telling target groups or other supporters of its uselessness. Drug prevention programs, for example, are popular initiatives, but most have done little to deter drug use. The Defense of Marriage Act might please conservatives, but it is unclear how it will help save the institution of marriage.

Unhappy Findings

Agencies and administrators usually have a heavy investment—organizational, financial, psychological—in current programs and policies. They are predisposed against findings that these programs do not work, involve excessive costs, or have unexpected negative consequences. If a negative report is issued, the agency may adopt a variety of strategies to offset the findings, as suggested in Illustration 12.3, "What to Do If Your Agency's Program Receives a Negative Evaluation."

Program Interference

Most serious evaluation studies involve some burdens on ongoing program activities. Accomplishing an agency's day-to-day business is generally a higher priority in the minds of program administrators and line workers than making special arrangements for evaluation. Evaluation also requires funds, facilities, time, and personnel, all of which administrators may not want to sacrifice from their programs.

Usefulness of Evaluations

Program administrators are clearly dissatisfied with evaluative studies that conclude, "The program is not achieving the desired results." Not only is such a finding a threat to the agency, but standing alone, it fails to tell administrators why the program is failing. Evaluations are better received by agencies when they include some action recommendations that might conceivably rescue the program. But even when studies show programs to be failures, the usual reaction is to patch things up and try again. Few programs are ever abolished.

ILLUSTRATION 12.3

What to Do If Your Agency's Program Receives a Negative Evaluation

What if you are faced with clear evidence that your favorite program is useless, or even counterproductive? Here is a tongue-in-cheek list of last-ditch efforts to save it.

1. Claim that the effects of the program are long range and cannot be adequately measured for many years.
2. Argue that the effects of the program are general and intangible, and that these effects cannot be identified with the crude methodology, including statistical measures, used in the evaluation.
3. If the classic experimental research design was used, claim that withholding services or benefits from the control group was unfair; and claim that there were no differences between the control and experimental groups because both groups had knowledge of the experiment.
4. If a quasiexperimental design was used, claim that initial differences between the

experimental and comparison groups make the results useless.

5. If a time series research design was used, claim that there were no differences between the "before" and "after" observations because of other coinciding variables that hid the program's effects. That is to say, claim that the participants' condition would be even worse without the program.
6. Argue that the lack of differences between the people receiving the program services and those not receiving them only means that the program is not sufficiently intensive and indicates the need to spend more resources on the program.
7. Argue that the failure to identify positive program effects is due to the inadequacy of the evaluation research design or of bias on the part of the evaluators.

Evaluation by Whom?

A central political issue is who will do the evaluation. From the agency's perspective, the evaluation should be done by the agency itself. This type of "in-house" evaluation is most likely to produce favorable results. The next best thing, from the agency's perspective, is to allow the agency to contract with a private firm for an "outside" evaluation. A private firm that wants to win future contracts from the agency, or from any other agency, is very hesitant about producing totally negative evaluations. The worst evaluation arrangement, from the agency's perspective, is to have an outside evaluation conducted by an independent office (for example, the Congressional Budget Office, the General Accountability Office [formerly the General Accounting Office], or a state comptroller's office or auditor general's office). Agency staff fear that outsiders do not understand clearly the nature of their work or the problems faced by the clients they serve and that this will hurt the program.

Threats to Everyone

Political obstacles to evaluation operate at all levels of the social service delivery system. Evaluation is threatening to elected officials because it might imply that they have developed poor policies, passed inadequate laws, provided inadequate funding in relation to need, or funded ineffective programs. Evaluation is threatening to social service administrators because it might suggest that they have done a poor job of implementing and managing the policies and programs developed by legislators. Evaluation is threatening to social service workers because it might indicate that they are not adequately skilled in delivering and providing social services to clients. Finally, evaluation can be threatening to clients because the process may invade their privacy, place additional pressure on them in times of personal crisis, and make them feel even more conspicuous about receiving social services.

SUMMARY

Implementing public policy can be a difficult task for social welfare program administrators. Implementation involves many activities, including organizing and staffing agencies, translating policies into specific courses of action, and spending funds to operate programs. In addition to determining the intent of social policies, which is not always clearly defined in legislation, problems may include obtaining sufficient resources, overcoming negative attitudes toward a program, and seeing that bureaucratic structures do not prevent the program from operating smoothly. These problems are amplified when there is political opposition to a program.

Americans have learned how difficult it is to remedy social problems. As a result, policymakers are increasingly concerned with obtaining evidence about whether social welfare policies and programs are effective. A rational, scientific approach to evaluation includes identifying and ranking program goals and objectives, developing ways to measure these goals, identifying target groups as well as nontarget groups that might be affected, measuring tangible and intangible program effects, and measuring direct and indirect program costs. However, policy evaluation is no less political than other aspects of the policy process. Program goals and objectives are often fuzzy, but evaluators must evaluate something, even if goals are unclear or there is disagreement about program goals. No administrator wants to receive a negative program evaluation. Administrators generally criticize unfavorable evaluations and take steps to counteract negative findings. Evaluations are not useful when they fail to provide information about how to improve the program. The well-known evaluations of the New Jersey Graduated Work Incentive Experiment and the D.A.R.E. program are examples of the politics of policy evaluation.

NOTES

1. Jeffrey Pressman and Aaron Wildavsky, *Implementation* (Berkeley: University of California Press, 1973), p. 109.

2. This discussion relies on George C. Edwards, *Implementing Public Policy* (Washington, DC: Congressional Quarterly, 1980).

3. Robert Kornfeld, *Explaining Recent Trends in Food Stamp Program Caseloads, Final Report* (Cambridge, MA: Abt Associates, March 2002), retrieved July 7, 2003, from http://www.usda.gov

4. Fred Doolittle and Linda Traeger, *Implementing the National JTPA Study* (New York: Manpower Demonstration Research Corporation, 1990).

5. Jan L. Hagen and Irene Lurie, *Implementing JOBS: Initial State Choices* (Albany: Nelson A. Rockefeller College of Public Affairs and Policy, University at Albany, State University of New York, March 1992).

6. Richard Lacayo, "The Sad Fate of Legal Aid," *Time,* June 20, 1988, p. 59.

7. Child Nutrition Program Reauthorization Center, *Overcertification Talking Points* (Washington, DC: Food Research and Action Center, n.d.), retrieved January 28, 2004, from http://www.frac.org/html/federal_food_programs/cnreauthor/overcerttalkingpoints.htm

8. Larry B. Hill, Ed., *The State of Public Bureaucracy* (Armonk, NY: Sharpe, 1992).

9. Herbert Kaufman, *Red Tape* (Washington, DC: Brookings Institution, 1977), p. 13.

10. "Get Ready for Food Stamp Reauthorization Changes in Your State" (Washington, DC: Food Research and Action Center, revised February 2003), retrieved on January 4, 2004, from http://www.frac.org

11. U.S. Bureau of the Census, *Statistical Abstract of the United States: 2002* (Washington, DC: U.S. Government Printing Office, 2002), Table 407, p. 261.

12. *Federal Register,* Vol. 58, No. 38, March 1, 1993, p. 11830.

13. Richard Whitmire, "Study: Single State Agency Should Direct Welfare," *Gannett News Service,* Tuesday, June 29, 1993.

14. David M. Van Slyke, "The Mythology of Privatization in Contracting for Social Services," *Public Administration Review,* Vol. 63, No. 3, 2003, pp. 296–315.

15. Michael B. Katz, *The Price of Citizenship: Redefining the American Welfare State* (New York: Metropolitan Books, 2001), p. 153.

16. Barbara Ehrenreich, "Spinning the Poor into Gold: How Corporations Seek to Profit from Welfare Reform," *Harper's Magazine,* August 1997, pp. 44–52.

17. See American Federation of State County and Municipal Employees, "Safety Net for Sale" (Washington, DC, 2002), retrieved August 11, 2004, from http://www.afscme.org/wrkplace/snettc.htm; Welfare Information Network, "Devolution Tracking Meeting," September 12, 2002, retrieved August 10, 2004, from http://www.financeprojectinfo.org/win/networksummaries/devotrack902.htm; Government Accounting Office, Social Service Privatization: Ethics and Accountability Challenges in State Contracting, GAO/HEHS-99–41 (Washington, DC, April 1999).

18. Paul C. Light, *Fact Sheet on the Continued Thickening of Government* (Washington, DC: Brookings Institution, July 23, 2004).

19. Van Slyke, "The Mythology of Privatization in Contracting for Social Services," pp. 307–308.

20. Joseph S. Wholey, John W. Scanlon, Hugh G. Duffy, James S. Fukumoto, and Leona M. Vogt, *Federal Evaluation Policy* (Washington, DC: Urban Institute, 1970), p. 15.

21. Laurie J. Bassi and Orley Ashenfelter, "The Effect of Direct Job Creation and Training Programs on Low-Skilled Workers," in Sheldon H. Danzinger and Daniel H. Weinberg, Eds., *Fighting Poverty: What Works and What Doesn't* (Cambridge, MA: Harvard University Press, 1986), p. 150.

22. Peter Passell, "Like a New Drug, Social Programs Are Put to the Test," *New York Times,* March 9, 1993, pp. C1, 10.

23. Project MATCH Research Group, "Matching Alcoholism Treatments to Client Heterogeneity: Project MATCH Posttreatment Drinking Outcomes," *Journal of Studies on Alcohol,* Vol. 58, 1997, 7–29.

24. David Nachmias, *Policy Evaluation* (New York: St. Martin's, 1979), p. 4.

25. William N. Dunn, *Public Policy Analysis: An Introduction* (Englewood Cliffs, NJ: Prentice Hall, 1981), p. 345.

26. Peter H. Rossi, Howard E. Freeman, and Mark W. Lipsey, *Evaluation: A Systematic Approach,* 6th ed. (Thousand Oaks, CA: Sage Publications, 1999), pp. 87–88.

27. *Ibid.,* p. 2.

28. See Harold M. Watts, "Graduated Work Incentives: An Experiment in Negative Taxation," *American Economic Review,* Vol. 59, May 1969, pp. 463–472.

29. Office of Economic Opportunity, *Preliminary Results of the New Jersey Graduated Work Incentive Experiment* (Washington, DC: Office of Economic Opportunity, February 18, 1970).

30. Harold M. Watts, *Adjusted and Extended Preliminary Results from the Urban Graduated Work Incentive Experiment* (Madison: Institute for Research on Poverty, University of Wisconsin, rev. June 10, 1970), p. 40.

31. David Kershaw and Jerelyn Fair, Eds., *Final Report of the New Jersey Graduated Work Incentive Experiment*, Vol. 4 (Princeton, NJ: University of Wisconsin, Institute for Research on Poverty and Mathematica, 1974).

32. John F. Cogan, *Negative Income Taxation and Labor Supply: New Evidence from the New Jersey-Pennsylvania Experiment* (Santa Monica, CA: Rand, 1978).

33. Stanford Research Institute, *Final Report of the Seattle-Denver Income Maintenance Experiment* (Washington, DC: U.S. Government Printing Office, 1983), quote from p. 250.

34. Some of this section relies on C. Aaron McNeece and Diana M. DiNitto, *Chemical Dependency: A Systems Approach*, 3rd ed. (Boston: Allyn and Bacon, 2005).

35. "22 Million in U.S. Suffer from Substance Dependence or Abuse" (Rockville, MD: U.S. Department of Health and Human Services, Substance Abuse and Mental Health Services Administration, September 5, 2003), retrieved October 8, 2003, from http://www.dhhs.gov/news/press/2003pres/20030905.html

36. This paragraph relies on Lawrence Wallack and Kitty Corbett, "Illicit Drug, Tobacco, and Alcohol Use among Youth: Trends and Promising Approaches in Prevention," in Hank Resnick, Ed., *Youth and Drugs: Society's Mixed Messages*, Office of Substance Abuse Prevention Monograph No. 6 (Rockville, MD: U.S. Department of Health and Human Services, Alcohol, Drug Abuse, and Mental Health Administration, 1990).

37. D.A.R.E. website, retrieved January 27, 2004, from http://www.dare.org

38. Christopher L. Ringwalt, Jody M. Green, Susan T. Ennett, Ronaldo Iachan, Richard Clayton, and Carl G. Leukfeld, *Past and Future Directions of the D.A.R.E. Program: Draft Final Report* (Research Triangle Park, NC: Research Triangle Institute, June 1994).

39. Stephen Glass, "Don't You D.A.R.E.," *New Republic*, March 3, 1997, pp. 18–20, 22–23, 26–28.

40. Donald R. Lynam, Richard Milich, Rick Zimmerman, Scott P. Novak, T. K. Logan, Catherine Martin, Carl Leukefeld, and Richard Clayton, "Project DARE: No Effects at 10-year Follow-up," *Journal of Consulting and Clinical Psychology*, Vol. 67, No. 4, pp. 590–593, retrieved January 23, 2004, from http://www.apa.org/journals/ccp/ccp674590.html

41. *Ibid.*, p. 592.

42. Marjorie E. Kanof, *Youth Illicit Drug Use Prevention: DARE Long-term Evaluations and Federal Efforts to Identify Effective Programs* (Washington, DC: United States General Accounting Office, 2003), GAO-03-172R, p. 2.

43. Chery L. Perry, Kelli A. Komora, Sara Veblen-Mortenson, Linda M. Bosma, Kian Farbakhsh, Karen A. Munson, Melissa H. Stigler, and Leslie A. Lytle, "A Randomized Controlled Trial of the Middle and Junior High School D.A.R.E. and D.A.R.E. Plus Programs," *Archives of Pediatrics and Adolescent Medicine*, Vol. 157, February 2003, pp. 178–184.

44. For further discussion of classic experimental research in the area of public policy, see Bassie and Ashenfelter, "The Effects of Direct Job Creation and Training Programs on Low-Skilled Workers"; Douglas J. Besharov, Peter Germanis, and Peter H. Rossi, *Evaluating Welfare Reform: A Guide for Scholars and Practitioners* (College Park, MD: School of Public Affairs, University of Maryland, 1997). For an interesting account and critique see also William M. Epstein, *Welfare in America: How Social Science Fails the Poor* (Madison: University of Wisconsin Press, 1997).

45. The remainder of this paragraph relies on Lisbeth B. Schorr, *Common Purpose: Strengthening Families and Neighborhoods to Rebuild America* (New York: Anchor Books/Doubleday, 1997).

46. Robert Morris, *Social Policy of the American Welfare State: An Introduction to Policy Analysis* (New York: Harper & Row, 1979), p. 133.

Name Index

Subject Index

AAFRC. *see* American Association of Fundraising Counsel
AARP (American Association of Retired Persons), 317
AB. *see* Aid to the Blind
able-bodied adults without dependent children (ABAWD), 195
abortion, 14, 25, 26, 71, 458–63
  clinics, harassment of, 461
  laws, 458, 459–60
  and Medicaid, 459
  "medically necessary," 459
  prochoice, 460
  prolife, 460, 461
  rights, 458–63
    eroding, 459–62
Abortion Non-Discrimination Act, 462
absentee voting, 64
abuse, 410–13, 431–32; *see also* alcohol abuse; drug abuse
  child, 410–13
  of the elderly, 431–32
ACLU. *see* American Civil Liberties Union
acquired immune deficiency syndrome (AIDS), 294
  and drug abuse, 397
  Supplemental Security Income (SSI) benefits for people with, 172
ADA. *see* Americans with Disabilities Act
ADAPT (American Disabled for Attendant Programs Today), 181
Adelphia Communications, 68
adoption, of children, 418–19
Adoption and Safe Families Act (1997), 418
Adoption Assistance and Child Welfare Act (1980), 418
adult categorical public assistance programs, 162
Advisory Council on Social Security, 142
AFDC (Aid to Families with Dependent Children) program, 204–46; *see also* Temporary Assistance for Needy Families (TANF) program
  benefits, 215–16
  and child support enforcement, 207–17
  and child welfare, 419
  costs of, 226

  and food stamps, 227, 276
  and the JOBS program, 220
  job training, 218–19
  man-in-the-house rules, 207
  Medicaid and, 304
  recipients of, 225
  vocational rehabilitation, 218
  and vocational rehabilitation, 218
  and workfare, 219–20
  and the Work Incentive Now (WIN) program, 218–19
AFDC-Unemployed Parent (AFDC-UP) program, 206
affirmative action, 19, 481–86
The Affluent Society (Galbraith), 351
affordable housing, 108–12
Afghanistan, 66
AFL-CIO, 27
African Americans
  and child abuse/neglect, 415
  and food stamps, 277
  as homeowners, 111, 479, 480
  infant mortality among, 295
  job training for, 369
  life expectancy, 295
  poor, 360
  and poverty, 88
  and racial equality, 474
  racial profiling of, 490
  and Social Security, 141
  and Supplemental Security Income (SSI) benefits, 172–73
  total household income, 475t
  unemployment rates for, 151
  uninsured, 297
  voting rights of, 486
aged. *see* elderly
agenda setting, policymaking, 14
Agricultural Risk Protection Act (2000), 307
Aid to Dependent Children (ADC) program, 162
Aid to the Blind (AB), 162, 304
Aid to the Permanently and Totally Disabled (APTD), 162, 206, 304
Air Carrier Access Act, 183
Alabama, Temporary Assistance for Needy Families (TANF) program in, 237